Assuring Continuous Compliance with Joint Commission Standards: A Pharmacy Guide

Eighth Edition

John P. Uselton, R.Ph.
Vice President
Quality and Regulatory Affairs
Cardinal Health Pharmacy Solutions

Patricia C. Kienle, R.Ph., MPA, FASHP
Director, Accreditation and Medication Safety
Quality and Regulatory Affairs
Cardinal Health Pharmacy Solutions

Lee B. Murdaugh, R.Ph., Ph.D.
Director, Accreditation and Medication Safety
Quality and Regulatory Affairs
Cardinal Health Pharmacy Solutions

American Society of Health-System Pharmacists®
Bethesda, Maryland

Any correspondence regarding this publication should be sent to the publisher, American Society of Health-System Pharmacists, 7272 Wisconsin Avenue, Bethesda, MD 20814, attention: Special Publishing.

Director, Special Publishing: Jack Bruggeman

Senior Editorial Project Manager: Dana Battaglia

Production Editor: Johnna Hershey

Design and Composition: David Wade

Library of Congress Cataloging-in-Publication Data

Uselton, John P.

Assuring continuous compliance with Joint Commission standards : a pharmacy guide / John P. Uselton, Patricia C. Kienle, Lee B. Murdaugh – 8th ed.

p. ; cm.

Rev. ed. of: Assuring continuous compliance with Joint Commission standards / Charles P. Coe, John P. Uselton. 7th ed. ©2008.

Includes bibliographical references and index.

Includes bibliographical references and index.

ISBN 978-1-58528-242-5

1. Hospital pharmacies--Quality control. 2. Hospital pharmacies--Standards--United States. I. Kienle, Patricia C. II. Murdaugh, Lee B. III. Coe, Charles P. Assuring continuous compliance with Joint Commission standards. IV. Joint Commission. V. American Society of Health-System Pharmacists. VI. Title.

[DNLM: 1. Pharmacy Service, Hospital. 2. Accreditation--standards. 3. Guideline Adherence. 4. Quality Control. WX 179 U84a 2010]

RA975.5.P5C54 2010

362.17'820685--dc22

2010011212

ISBN: 1-58528-242-5

Table of Contents

Appendix

CD of Checklists and Example Forms (in Microsoft® Word format). **Downloadable Gap Analysis application for Chapters 4 and 6.**

Dedications

To Susan, Sarah, and Brian

To Kurt

To Jean and Herbert Brown

About the Authors

The authors have helped hundreds of health-system pharmacies comply with Joint Commission and other standards. This book reflects their experiences in guiding pharmacies through more than 2,000 accreditation and certification surveys since 1980.

About the Contributors

Charles P. Coe, R.Ph.
President
Eagle Rx
Health System Pharmacy Services

Robert Jordin, R.Ph.
Director, Accreditation and Medication Safety
Quality and Regulatory Affairs
Cardinal Health Pharmacy Solutions

The contributors are actively involved in helping health-system pharmacies incorporate Joint Commission standards into their everyday practice. They participated in the planning, writing, review, and critique of this edition and their contributions, experiences, and suggestions are reflected in every chapter.

Acknowledgments

As with past editions, many Cardinal Health Pharmacy Solutions pharmacists provided survey-related information that is reflected in this edition. Their criticisms, comments, and suggestions are reflected in the text, checklists, and examples. We are also grateful to Dana Battaglia and other ASHP staff who reviewed and edited the manuscript and ensured the timely completion of the project.

Reviewers

Chapter 23 – Reviewed by American Osteopathic Association (AOA).

Introduction and How to Use This Book

There have been a number of changes in The Joint Commission's accreditation process since the seventh edition of this book was published in early 2008. Among them are the increased enhancements to standards and requirements (including their relationship to the Centers for Medicare and Medicaid Services' Conditions of Participation), reduced emphasis on preparing for surveys, and a requirement that health care organizations be in continuous compliance with standards. For several years, *preparing* for surveys has been impractical as surveys evolved into unannounced evaluations of how organizations continuously comply with the standards and improve care, treatment, and services.

This book reflects The Joint Commission's decreased emphasis on survey preparation and its increased emphasis on continuous compliance with standards. To that end, it aims to help pharmacies comply with the standards and National Patient Safety Goals (NPSGs) and incorporate them into their everyday practice.

Also, since the seventh edition was published, The Joint Commission has revised medication management standards, numerous other standards, and its NPSGs. As a result of its Standards Improvement Initiative (SII), many redundant standards have been eliminated and others have been consolidated. A primary goal of the SII was to enhance the clarity of standards and NPSGs. A new numbering system for standards and NPSGs was introduced to accommodate the addition of new requirements for many of the standards and goals.

Every chapter of the eighth edition has been completely reviewed, updated, and expanded to reflect current standards and NPSGs, requirements, expectations, and interpretations. Standards and requirements effective from March 2010 are addressed to the extent they are known. New standards, requirements, expectations, and interpretations can be announced at any time. Chapter 1 lists services and resources to help pharmacists stay current. Readers are encouraged to review the literature and monitor The Joint Commission and other Web sites regularly.

Although some of the changes are significant, for most pharmacies, compliance with the current standards and NPSGs are not much more difficult than compliance with previous standards and goals. In some cases, compliance may be even easier if the pharmacy's services have been improved since the last survey.

Improvements to the Eighth Edition

The eighth edition contains a number of changes aimed at improving readability and ease of locating items. The Joint Commission's new numbering system for standards and NPSGs is used throughout this edition. Updated checklists clearly distinguish the authors' notes from the "check-off" items. These changes in format and the expanded index should make it easier for the reader to navigate through the book. However, continuous compliance is not guaranteed. For example, interpretation of standards may change, staff may fail to document, and/or documents may be misplaced.

The current edition contains the most up-to-date medication management (MM) standards and requirements and the medication-related 2010 NPSGs and their requirements. It also contains the most current standards, other than MM standards, that pharmacies must comply with to have a successful survey.

The book contains a chapter that describes the Centers for Medicare and Medicaid Services' Conditions of Participation for hospitals related to medication management. In addition to The Joint Commission-related information, another chapter provides information on the Healthcare Facilities Accreditation Program which is another accreditation organization.

In September 2008, CMS recognized the National Integrated Accreditation for Healthcare Organizations (NIAHO^{SM}) of Det Norske Veritas (DNV) Healthcare as an organization that provides a national accreditation program for hospitals wishing to participate in the Medicare or Medicaid program. A new chapter provides information about the NIAHO accreditation process, the NIAHO standards, and its requirements for medication management.

A companion CD includes many example forms and documents in a Microsoft® Word format. Readers can easily customize the forms and documents for their organization. For the first time, the companion CD also includes a downloadable gap analysis tool for tracking "no" responses to checklist items in Chapter 4, Medication Management Standards Checklist, and Chapter 6, National Patient Safety Goals Checklist. This simple gap analysis tool allows you to collect and print an assessment report of all "no" responses to checklist items.

Overview of This Book

This book provides a guide for achieving continuous compliance with Joint Commission standards relating to pharmacy and medication use. It reflects onsite experiences and survey reports from hundreds of hospitals.

- ***Chapter 1*** is a general discussion of The Joint Commission and the role of accreditation in improving care, treatment, and services.
- ***Chapter 2*** describes The Joint Commission's survey process and includes updated examples of survey agendas.
- ***Chapter 3*** provides an organized approach to achieving continuous compliance with Joint Commission standards.
- ***Chapter 4*** is a checklist for compliance with medication management standards.
- ***Chapter 5*** describes the medication management individual-based system tracer.
- ***Chapter 6*** presents each medication-related 2010 NPSG and its requirements for hospitals in a checklist format.
- ***Chapters 7 through 12*** are checklists that address human resources standards; education and training of patients and family; infection control; safety, security, and storage; policies and procedures; and frequently requested documents.
- ***Chapters 13 through 15*** address pharmacy and therapeutics activities, competence assessment, and performance improvement activities.
- ***Chapters 16 through 19*** provide overviews of The Joint Commission's ORYX® initiative, the Occupational Safety and Health Administration's Hazard Communication Standard, the National Institute for Occupational Safety and Health Recommendations for Handling Hazardous Drugs, and the United States Pharmacopeia Chapter <797>: Pharmaceutical Compounding—Sterile Preparations.
- ***Chapters 20 and 21*** are devoted to medication safety, adverse drug reactions, and an overview of the Food and Drug Administration's MedWatch program.
- ***Chapters 22 through 24*** summarize current medication- and pharmacy-related standards of the Centers for Medicare and Medicaid Services (CMS), the Healthcare Facilities Accreditation Program (HFAP) of the American Osteopathic Association (AOA), and the National Integrated Accreditation for Healthcare Organizations (NIAHO) of Det Norske Veritas (DNV) Healthcare.
- *The* ***Appendix*** contains contact information (e.g., names, addresses, telephone numbers, and Web sites) for the organizations mentioned in the book.
- ***References and Resources*** contains the references grouped by chapter as well as suggested resource materials for selected chapters.
- ***Example Forms and Documents*** are examples that are useful in pharmacy practice and for documenting continuous compliance with the standards. You may use the examples as they are or customize them to meet your needs.

How to Use This Book

Begin by Reading—Begin by reading the first three chapters of this book. Read the other chapters as you address the standards to which they pertain.

Determine Whether Standards in Other Accreditation Manuals Apply—Determine whether standards in other Joint Commission manuals of standards apply to your organization. (*See* Chapter 1.)

Complete the Checklists—Complete the checklists in this book (i.e., Chapter 4 and Chapters 6 through 12).

Identify Current Deficiencies—Use the checklists to identify current deficiencies, and develop an action plan for progressing toward continuous compliance. (*See* Develop an Action Plan in Chapter 3.)

Work with the Organization's Leaders—Work closely with the organization's leaders. Perform a Periodic Performance Review (PPR) as described in Chapter 2 and share information with the organization as described in Chapter 3.

Focus on Problematic Areas—Give special attention to the problematic areas described in Chapter 3.

Follow the Suggestions in Chapter 3—Chapter 3 contains additional suggestions for using this book. These include organizing documents and conducting mock surveys and tracers. Attention to these suggestions provides an organized approach to progressing toward continuous compliance.

John P. Uselton

Patricia C. Kienle

Lee B. Murdaugh

March 2010

CHAPTER 1

The Joint Commission

The Joint Commission (formerly known as The Joint Commission on Accreditation of Healthcare Organizations® or JCAHO®) is a nonprofit, private (i.e., independent, nongovernmental) organization. Its mission "is to continuously improve the safety and quality of care provided to the public through the provision of health care accreditation and related services that support performance improvement in health care organizations." "The Joint Commission's corporate members are the American College of Physicians, the American College of Surgeons, the American Dental Association, the American Hospital Association, and the American Medical Association." The Joint Commission maintains "state-of-the-art standards that focus on improving the quality and safety of care provided by health care organizations."[1]

Surveys—Compliance with Joint Commission standards is voluntary; any health care organization may request a survey (i.e., an evaluation) to determine its level of compliance. (*See* Chapter 2.) Health care organizations request a survey by completing an application for accreditation.

Accreditation

The Joint Commission has accredited hospitals for over 50 years and currently accredits about 4,600 hospitals of different types. Approximately 88% of the nation's hospitals are currently accredited by The Joint Commission.

The Joint Commission accredits acute care hospitals, critical access hospitals, and other health care organizations (e.g., long term, ambulatory, home, and behavioral health care organizations). To be accredited, organizations must provide evidence that they are in continuous compliance with the standards applicable to their organization. They must also comply with The Joint Commission's National Patient Safety Goals (NPSGs). (*See* Chapter 6.) Organizations can provide evidence that they comply with the standards and NPSGs by doing the following:

- Performing self-assessments of compliance
- Providing corrective action plans to The Joint Commission
- Providing data and information for assessment by The Joint Commission
- Undergoing on-site surveys by Joint Commission representatives (i.e., surveyors). (*See* Chapter 2.)

The director of pharmacy must ensure that the pharmacy department complies continuously with relevant standards (e.g., medication management and infection control) and the NPSGs. However, note that The Joint Commission accredits health care organizations—not pharmacies or other individual departments and services. The Joint Commission provides a certificate of accreditation to organizations that comply with its standards and accreditation requirements.

Accreditation Period—Accreditation is valid until the next full survey (which may occur at any time within 18–39 months from the previous survey) and is not renewed automatically. To continue their accreditation beyond this period, organizations must undergo another full survey and comply with the standards, NPSGs, and other requirements in effect at that time.

Accreditation Incentives

Organizations seek accreditation to be assured that they are providing safe, high-quality patient care on a continuous basis. Although Joint Commission accreditation is voluntary, failure to meet Joint Commission standards or the loss of accreditation may signal substandard patient care. Patients may be at risk, organizations may find it difficult to attract qualified practitioners, and the adverse publicity may cause patients to go elsewhere for medical care. Some states may consider Joint Commission accreditation in their state licensure process and/or exempt accredited organizations from some inspections.

Medicare Participation—Organizations must be certified by the Centers for Medicare and Medicaid Services (CMS) to participate in the federal Medicare program. CMS confers "deemed status" on a health care organization when that organization is in compliance with relevant CMS requirements because it has been accredited by an organization whose standards are determined by CMS to be equivalent to those of the Medicare program. Joint Commission-accredited organizations are eligible for reimbursement in the Medicare program. Without accreditation, organizations must undergo a CMS survey and demonstrate compliance with CMS Conditions of Participation. (*See* Chapter 22.) Organizations accredited by the Healthcare Facilities Accreditation Program (HFAP) of the American Osteopathic Association (AOA) and those accredited by the National Integrated Accreditation for Healthcare Organizations (NIAHO) program of Det Norske Veritas (DNV) Healthcare are also eligible for reimbursement in the federal Medicare program. (*See* Chapters 23 and 24.) Note that The Joint Commission, HFAP, and NIAHO accredit; CMS certifies.

Standards versus Legal Requirements

The Joint Commission provides uniform, nationally recognized standards on which many accredited and nonaccredited organizations base their bylaws, rules, regulations, policies, and procedures. Although Joint Commission standards are not legal requirements, they may be used to define the expected standards of care and failure to comply with Joint Commission standards might present legal difficulties for an organization. Furthermore, Joint Commission standards are consistent with guidelines and standards published by other organizations (e.g., the Life Safety Code® of the National Fire Protection Association). Organizations must be aware that legal requirements take precedence when Joint Commission standards conflict with laws, rules, regulations, and the guidelines and standards of other organizations.

Standards Used to Support Improving Services

The Joint Commission may be the pharmacy's best ally in its efforts to improve pharmacy services. Because compliance with Joint Commission standards is important to patients, leaders, and the medical staff, standards can often be used to support proposals for additional personnel and equipment needed to expand and improve services. Proposals should clearly indicate the following:

- Specific standards that will be met
- Quality of care and patient safety improvements that will be made
- Problems that will be avoided
- Legal liability for failure to meet the standards

Accreditation Manual for Acute Care Hospitals

The Joint Commission publishes its standards for acute care hospitals in several formats. Organizations should choose the format or formats that meet their needs. Standards for acute care hospitals are quoted in this book.

Comprehensive Accreditation Manual for Hospitals: The Official Handbook (CAMH)—The Joint Commission provides a current *Comprehensive Accreditation Manual for Hospitals: The Official Handbook (CAMH)* to all accredited acute care organizations and all acute care organizations seeking accreditation.[2] The *CAMH* includes accreditation policies and procedures, accreditation participation requirements, the most current standards and National Patient Safety Goals (NPSGs), compliance information, how to gauge compliance, and a glossary of terms. *CAMH* chapters that contain accreditation standards are listed alphabetically and address each of the organization's important functions. Table 1-1 lists the standards chapters and examples of topics for each.

The *CAMH* is available as a subscription service with twice a year updates published in March and September. The updates ensure that organizations have new standards and current information. Organizations may order additional copies of the *CAMH* from The Joint Commission.

Hospital Accreditation Standards (HAS)—The Joint Commission also publishes its standards in the *Hospital Accreditation Standards (HAS)*. It is smaller and more compact that the *CAMH* and is intended to be a quick reference to the standards. Since the *HAS* is published annually, it may not be as current as an up-to-date *CAMH*.

Accreditation Manager Plus—An annual software product, *Accreditation Manager Plus—An Interactive Tool Kit for Continuous Compliance*, is also available from The Joint Commission. *Accreditation Manager Plus* contains all the information in the *CAMH* and has project management, documentation, and performance tracking capabilities.

Accreditation Manuals for Other Types of Care

In addition to the manual of standards for acute care hospitals, The Joint Commission publishes accreditation manuals for other types of care. A complete list is on The Joint Commission's Web site. (*See* Joint Commission Web site in this chapter and Appendix.) These manuals include the following:

- *Comprehensive Accreditation Manual for Ambulatory Care (CAMAC)*
- *Comprehensive Accreditation Manual for Laboratory and Point of Care Testing (CAMLAB)*
- *Comprehensive Accreditation Manual for Long-Term Care (CAMLTC)*
- *Comprehensive Accreditation Manual for Behavioral Health Care (CAMBHC)*
- *Comprehensive Accreditation Manual for Home Care (CAMHC)*
- *Comprehensive Accreditation Manual for Critical Access Hospitals (CAMCAH)*
- *Comprehensive Accreditation Manual for Office-Based Surgery Practices (CAMOBS)*

Pharmacists should check with their organization's leaders to determine whether any areas or services (e.g., long-term care and behavioral health units) will be surveyed under standards in these manuals. If necessary, they should review the standards for these services and modify the process for assuring compliance accordingly.

Joint Commission Resources

The Joint Commission provides several resources and services to help organizations comply continuously with standards and improve services. Organizations may inquire about services, order Joint Commission publications and periodicals, and subscribe to free Joint Commission e-mail newsletters and information by telephoning Joint Commission Customer Service or through The Joint Commission's Web site. (*See* Joint Commission Web site in this chapter and Appendix.)

Joint Commission Web Site—The Joint Commission's Web site offers information about The Joint Commission and its affiliated organizations. It also provides information about Joint Commission educational programs and services, proposed standards and standards undergoing field reviews, and how to order publications. (*See* Appendix.) Information relating to an organization's accreditation status is available on The Joint Commission's Quality Check® Web site. (*See* Quality Reports in Chapter 2.)

Joint Commission Connect™ Extranet Site—The Joint Commission Connect password-protected extranet site provides organizations with a means to perform selected functions electronically. In addition, The Joint Commission posts organization-specific reports on this site. (*See* Appendix.)

Standards Interpretation Group—The Joint Commission will provide official interpretation of its standards and information on how to comply with standards upon request. Requests must be submitted to The Joint Commission's Standards Interpretation Group. Organizations can also submit requests by using the online question submission form on The Joint Commission's Web site. (*See* Appendix.) Although oral advice may be sufficient, a written response will be provided if requested.

Standards Clarifications—The Joint Commission's Standards Interpretation Group develops standards clarifications when a significant number of organizations have questions about standards that are not clearly addressed in an accreditation manual. Organizations should review these clarifications carefully to determine if they apply to practices within the organization.

Frequently Asked Questions—Frequently asked questions (FAQs) relating to standards are available on The Joint Commission's Web site. (*See* Appendix.) Organizations should be aware that surveyor interpretations of the standards might not be consistent with the FAQs and other Joint Commission clarification and interpretation resources.

Accreditation Process Guide for Hospitals—The Joint Commission's annual publication *Accreditation Process Guide for Hospitals* helps organizations understand The Joint Commission's accreditation process, how to apply for accreditation, and what to expect during a survey. It contains sample survey agendas and other information needed to ensure a smooth survey experience. Although the guide does not focus on the pharmacy, pharmacy managers may find it a useful supplement to the material in this book.

Survey Activity Guide—The Joint Commission's *Survey Activity Guide* is available on each accredited organization's extranet site. The guide contains survey preparation tools and current information about each survey activity. Pharmacy managers may find the guide contains useful information to help them prepare for surveys.

Joint Commission Perspectives®—The Joint Commission's official monthly newsletter, *Joint Commission Perspectives*, is the primary source of information on changes to standards, accreditation requirements (e.g., the survey process), and Joint Commission initiatives. *Joint Commission Perspectives* is available to subscribers on The Joint Commission's Web site. (*See* Appendix.) Pharmacy managers should read the newsletter.

Joint Commission Perspectives on Patient Safety™ — The Joint Commission's monthly newsletter *Joint Commission Perspectives on Patient Safety* provides information on preventing errors and improving patient safety. Topics include strategies for meeting The Joint Commission's NPSGs (*see* Chapter 6), creating a culture of safety, risk management, and specific patient safety issues (e.g., falls and suicide prevention). *Joint Commission Perspectives on Patient Safety* is available to subscribers on The Joint Commission's Web site. (*See* Appendix.) Pharmacy managers should read the newsletter.

Sentinel Event Alert—The Joint Commission's *Sentinel Event Alert* publication provides information for chief executive officers, chief medical officers, chief nursing officers, and other organization leaders (e.g., pharmacy directors) about the occurrence, cause, and management of sentinel events. (*See* Chapter 15.) It includes information relating to sentinel event policies and procedures, describes specific types of sentinel events, and offers suggestions for preventing sentinel events. The newsletter is currently distributed by e-mail and is available on The Joint Commission's Web site. (*See* Appendix.) Organizations are expected to forward the newsletter to appropriate staff. Pharmacy managers should read the newsletter.

Other Patient Safety Publications—The Joint Commission publishes other patient safety publications. A complete list is available on The Joint Commission's Web site. (*See* Appendix.) These publications include the following:

- *Preventing Medication Errors: Strategies for Pharmacists*
- *Medication Reconciliation Handbook*
- *Medication Use: A Systems Approach to Reducing Errors, 2nd Edition*
- *The Nurse's Role in Medication Safety*
- *The Pharmacist's Role in Patient Safety*
- *Understanding & Preventing Sentinel Events in your HCO*
- *Root Cause Analysis: Tools and Techniques, 4th Edition*
- *Failure Mode and Effects Analysis in Health Care: Proactive Risk Reduction, 2nd Edition*
- *Patient Safety Essentials for Healthcare, 5th Edition*

Joint Commission Resources Consulting—The Joint Commission, through Joint Commission Resources (JCR) Consulting, offers consulting and educational services to hospitals, long-term care facilities, and other types of health care organizations. JCR Consulting can provide a thorough assessment of an organization and offer clear suggestions for improving compliance. JCR Consulting is entirely separate from The Joint Commission. Organizations that retain JCR Consulting will not receive special treatment from The Joint Commission. Organizations can obtain information about JCR Consulting on the JCR Web site or by telephoning JCR Customer Service. (*See* Appendix.)

JCR Seminars—JCR offers seminars on standards compliance, performance improvement, and other survey-related topics. However, these programs tend to focus on organizationwide standards and most are not specific to pharmacy. With the national focus on medication safety, JCR offers resources, including consulting, specific to this topic. Organizations can obtain additional information on the JCR Web site or by telephoning JCR Customer Service. (*See* Appendix.)

American Society of Health-System Pharmacists

The American Society of Health-System Pharmacists (ASHP) works closely with The Joint Commission in developing standards relating to the practice of health-system pharmacy and the use of medications. ASHP's involvement has led to significant improvements in pharmacy-related standards and the survey process.

ASHP Resources

ASHP has several resources to help pharmacists keep current and comply continuously with Joint Commission standards. Organizations can obtain information about ASHP resources on ASHP's Web site. (*See* ASHP Web site in this chapter and Appendix.)

ASHP Web Site—ASHP's Web site offers resources that help pharmacists stay current on standards, laws, and how to comply continuously with Joint Commission standards. (*See* Appendix.) These include the following:

- Sections and Forums (e.g., Clinical Specialists and

Scientists; Home, Ambulatory, and Chronic Care Practitioners; Inpatient Care Practitioners; and Pharmacy Practice Managers)

- Resource Centers (e.g., Compounding, Emergency Preparedness, Patient Safety, and Quality Improvement Initiatives)
- Continuing Education (e.g., courses and publications)

American Journal of Health-System Pharmacy—The *American Journal of Health-System Pharmacy (AJHP)* is a source of timely information on standards and laws pertaining to health-system pharmacy practice. Articles in the *AJHP* may include suggestions for compliance and are often accompanied by editorial comment.

ASHP Meetings—Educational programming at ASHP's Summer Meeting and Midyear Clinical Meeting includes topics relevant to Joint Commission standards. Joint Commission representatives often make presentations at these meetings. Expert pharmacy practitioners share their experiences and offer advice on how to ensure continuous compliance. Information about ASHP meetings is available on ASHP's Web site and in the *AJHP*. (*See* ASHP Web site in this chapter and Appendix.)

ASHP Policy Positions, Statements, and Guidelines—ASHP has established best practices for pharmacy services. Since these are often more stringent, more explicit, and less subject to misinterpretation than some Joint Commission standards, they can help an organization meet or exceed Joint Commission requirements. ASHP's best practices are contained in its professional policy positions, statements, and guidelines. (*See Best Practices for Hospital & Health-System Pharmacy* in this chapter.)

Best Practices for Hospital & Health-System Pharmacy—ASHP's *Best Practices for Hospital & Health-System Pharmacy* is a compilation of ASHP's policy positions, statements, and guidelines. These documents are also available on ASHP's Web site. (*See* Appendix.)

Competence Assessment Tools for Health-System Pharmacies—*Competence Assessment Tools for Health-System Pharmacies* contains job descriptions, performance evaluations, study materials, tests, skills assessment checklists, and guidelines for assessing the competence of pharmacists and support staff. It is available by telephoning ASHP Customer Service or through ASHP's Web site. (*See* Appendix.)

Handbook of Institutional Pharmacy Practice—ASHP's *Handbook of Institutional Pharmacy Practice* contains material on investigational drugs, controlled substances management, sterile preparations, medication safety, and many other topics relating to Joint Commission standards. It is available by telephoning ASHP Customer Service or through ASHP's Web site. (*See* Appendix.)

Other Resources

In addition to Joint Commission and ASHP resources, the following may be helpful:

Hospital Pharmacy—*Hospital Pharmacy* focuses on topics of interest to pharmacists in a variety of practice environments. Topics include preventing medication errors, reducing adverse drug reactions, and compliance with Joint Commission standards. Subscription information and issues of *Hospital Pharmacy* are available on the Internet. (*See* Appendix.)

Medication Errors—*Medication Errors* edited by Michael R. Cohen provides a comprehensive, authoritative examination of the causes of medication errors and the means to prevent them. Information in this publication can help organizations meet the intent of The Joint Commission's patient safety standards. The American Pharmacists Association (APhA) publishes *Medication Errors*. It is available by telephoning ASHP's Customer Service or through ASHP's Web site. (*See* Appendix.)

ISMP Medication Safety Alert!—The Acute Care Edition of the *ISMP Medication Safety Alert!* is a biweekly publication of the Institute for Safe Medication Practices (ISMP). Issues contain vital, potentially life-saving information about medication and device errors and adverse drug reactions that can help organizations meet the intent of The Joint Commission's patient safety standards. Similar publications for nurses, community/ambulatory practitioners, and consumers are also available. ISMP sends the Acute Care Edition of the *ISMP Medication Safety Alert!* to subscribers by e-mail. Subscription information about the *ISMP Medication Safety Alert!* is available on ISMP's Web site. (*See* Appendix.)

ISMP Medication Safety Self Assessment®—ISMP also provides a Medication Safety Self Assessment® for hospitals. Subscription information about ISMP's Medication Safety Self Assessment® is available on ISMP's Web site. (*See* Appendix.)

Consultant Publications—Health care organizations often subscribe to independent publications that focus on compliance with Joint Commission standards. Some of them are easily confused with official Joint Commission publications. Although they may be helpful, they are sometimes inaccurate and misleading. Often they focus on impressing surveyors and passing surveys instead of using the standards to improve patient safety and the quality of patient care. The Joint Commission makes it clear that it has no relationship with these publications. The Joint Commission is the best source for accurate information related to standards and surveys.

Consultants—Health care organizations often employ independent consultants to assess their survey readiness and help them prepare for a survey. Many are excellent; some are questionable. JCR Consulting is likely to be more current and reliable than independent consultants. Organizations can obtain information about independent consultants from other organizations, health care journals, and the Internet (e.g., by searching for "joint commission consultants" or "jcaho consultants").

Table 1-1. *CAMH* Standards Chapters and Example Topics

CAMH Standards Chapters	Example Topics
Accreditation Participation Requirements (APR)	Specific requirements for participation in the accreditation process
Environment of Care (EC)	Reducing risks and hazards, preventing accidents and injuries, maintaining safe and secure conditions, managing hazardous materials, managing medical equipment and utilities
Emergency Management (EM)	Developing an Emergency Operations Plan (EOP), managing critical processes (e.g., communications, security, resources, personnel, utilities) during emergencies
Human Resources (HR)	Providing adequate competent staff; orienting, training, and educating staff; and assessing, maintaining, and improving competence
Infection Prevention and Control (IC)	Reducing the risk of acquiring and transmitting infections
Information Management (IM)	Capturing, analyzing, comparing, transmitting, and using data and information
Leadership (LD)	Establishing effective leadership, fulfilling governance and leadership responsibilities, and providing culture of safety and quality
Life Safety (LS)	Following Interim Life Safety Measures, complying with NFPA Life Safety Code
Medication Management (MM)	Selecting and procuring medications, storing medications, ordering medications, transcribing medication orders, preparing and dispensing medications, administering medications, and monitoring the effects of medications
Medical Staff (MS)	Medical staff organization, bylaws, rules, regulations, credentialing, medical education, and role in telemedicine
National Patient Safety Goals (NPSGs)	Promotes specific improvements to problematic areas specific to patient safety with a focus on system-wide solutions when possible
Nursing (NR)	Responsibilities of the nurse executive and nursing leaders, establishing standards of nursing care, treatment, and services
Provision of Care, Treatment, and Services (PC)	Assessing, planning, providing, and coordinating care, treatment, and services that meet patients' needs
Performance Improvement (PI)	Measuring the performance of processes, improving patient outcomes by improving patient-related processes
Record of Care, Treatment, and Services (RC)	Components of a complete medical record, audit processes, and record retention
Rights and Responsibilities of the Individual (RI)	Relationships with patients; providing adequate information to patients; involving patient and family in decisions; research; and informing patients and families about outcomes of care, privacy, and confidentiality
Transplant Safety (TS)	Donating and procuring organs and tissues, transplanting organs and tissues
Waived Testing (WT)	Identification of staff and their competence, quality control checks, and record keeping

CHAPTER 2

Joint Commission Surveys

The Joint Commission's accreditation process includes undergoing an on-site survey by Joint Commission representatives. (*See* Accreditation in Chapter 1.) Joint Commission surveys focus on assessing the quality of care, continuous operational improvement, and continuous compliance with all standards and National Patient Safety Goals (NPSGs). An understanding of the standards and the survey process is essential to demonstrating continuous compliance. This chapter provides an overview of the standards; self-assessments of compliance; types of surveys; and what to expect before, during, and after a survey.

Standards

The Joint Commission assigns a prefix to each standard. The following prefixes are used:

APR	=	Accreditation Participation Requirements
EC	=	Environment of Care
EM	=	Emergency Management
HR	=	Human Resources
IC	=	Infection Prevention and Control
IM	=	Information Management
LD	=	Leadership
LS	=	Life Safety
MM	=	Medication Management
MS	=	Medical Staff
NPSG	=	National Patient Safety Goals
NR	=	Nursing
PC	=	Provision of Care, Treatment, and Services
PI	=	Performance Improvement
RC	=	Record of Care, Treatment, and Services
RI	=	Rights and Responsibilities of the Individual
TS	=	Transplant Safety
WT	=	Waived Testing

Standards Numbering—The Joint Commission assigns a number to each standard. For example, MM.01.01.01 is medication management standard number 01.01.01.

Rationale—A rationale for a standard follows some, but not all, standards.

Element of Performance—At least one element of performance (EP) is provided for each standard, and the EPs for each standard are numbered consecutively, although not all numbers are used in each survey type (e.g., hospital).

Notes and Footnotes—Notes and footnotes clarify some standards and EPs.

Standard Example—An example medication management standard with its rationale, EPs, and a note follows:[1]

"Standard MM.01.01.01

The hospital plans its medication management processes.

Rationale for MM.01.01.01

Medication management is often complicated, involving many people and processes. For this reason, the hospital plans each part of the process with care so that safety and quality are maintained. This planning may involve the coordinated efforts of multiple services and disciplines.

Elements of Performance for MM.01.01.01

1. Ⓓ The organization has a written policy, which describes that the following information is accessible to licensed independent practitioners and staff who participate in the management of the patient's medications:
   - Age
   - Sex
   - Diagnoses
   - Allergies
   - Sensitivities
   - Current medications

- Height and weight (when necessary)
- Pregnancy and lactation information (when necessary)
- Laboratory results (when necessary)
- Any additional information required by the organization

(*See* MM.04.01.01, EP 10; IM.02.01.01, EP 3; RC.01.01.01, EP 13.)

2. The hospital implements its policy to make information about the patient accessible to licensed independent practitioners and staff who participate in the management of the patient's medications.

Note: *This element of performance does not apply in emergency situations.*"

Standard Icons—The Joint Commission includes icons with some EPs for ease of use and clarity. Special attention should be paid to EPs with an icon. The following icons are used in this publication:

The document/page icon (in this publication) before an EP indicates documentation is required. In the *CAMH*, The Joint Commission uses an uppercase letter D within a circle as its icon for documentation required.

The triangle icon (in this publication) before an EP indicates noncompliance is likely to create an immediate risk to patient safety or to the quality of care provided. These EPs may have a direct impact on survey requirements. In the *CAMH*, The Joint Commission uses the numeral 3 within a triangle as its icon for EPs that may have a direct impact on patient care.

The checkmark icon (in this publication) before an EP indicates a Measure of Success (MOS) is required if the EP is scored noncompliant. An MOS is a quantifiable measure used to determine if a corrective action has been effective and has been sustained. (*See* Measure of Success in this chapter.) In the *CAMH*, The Joint Commission uses an uppercase letter M within a circle as its icon if an MOS is required.

Scoring EPs and Judging Compliance with Standards

The Joint Commission's scoring and accreditation decision process is based on the criticality of standards and other requirements that affect the quality and safety of patient care. Accreditation decisions are based on the criticality of findings and, to a lesser degree, the number of requirements for improvement (RFI) that the organization receives. (*See* Requirement for Improvement in this chapter.) The more critical the finding, the higher the risk to patient safety and the quality of care delivered. The Joint Commission uses four levels of criticality to determine the level of risk and, ultimately, the organization's accreditation status. The Joint Commission's *Comprehensive Accreditation Manual for Hospitals: The Official Handbook (CAMH)* contains detailed information on scoring and the accreditation decision process.[1]

Scoring EPs—Scoring each EP determines the organization's compliance within that standard (i.e., standards are not scored; only EPs are scored). Organizations must demonstrate sufficient compliance with each EP or a requirement for improvement (RFI) will be issued. (*See* Requirement for Improvement in this chapter.) Specific measurable requirements for each EP are scored on the following scale:

Score	
0	Insufficient compliance
1	Partial compliance
2	Satisfactory compliance
NA	Not applicable

Scoring Categories—Each EP is assigned to a scoring category (i.e., A or C). Scoring of EPs varies by category. The Joint Commission's *CAMH* contains additional information on scoring categories and scoring of EPs.[1]

Note: Scoring category B was eliminated in January 2009.

Periodic Performance Review (PPR)

A periodic performance review (PPR) is an integral part of the continuous accreditation process. It is designed to assist organizations in their continuing effort to comply with Joint Commission standards. A PPR consists of a mandatory annual self-assessment for compliance with all Accreditation Participation Requirements (APRs), all applicable standards and EPs, and all NPSGs. A Plan of Action (POA) must be developed for all noncompliant APRs, EPs, and NPSGs that are identified. Organizations use The Joint Commission's extranet to obtain an electronic PPR tool and to submit the completed PPR to The Joint Commission.

Plan of Action (POA)— Organizations must complete and submit the PPR, submit corrective POAs for standards that are not in full compliance, and identify how they will evaluate the success of the plans. Although PPR results will not affect the accreditation decision, failure to complete a PPR or develop a POA could affect the decision. More information on completing the PPR and POA is in the *CAMH*.[1]

PPR Options—Alternatives to participating in the full PPR self-assessment are described below. After legal counseling, an organization may choose one of the options described below. More information on PPR options is in the *CAMH*.[1]

> *Option 1*—Complete, but not submit, a PPR, POA, and Measures of Success (MOS) for deficiencies identified during the assessment. (*See* Measures of Success in this chapter.) The organization *may* elect to participate in a conference call with The Joint Commission to discuss issues relating to the standards. During the next full survey, surveyors validate that MOS data show that performance was achieved and sustained.

> *Option 2*—Undergo a limited survey or a full-length PPR survey. The organization must submit a plan of action and MOS for *written* deficiencies cited at the survey. The organization also *may* elect to participate in a conference call with The Joint Commission to discuss the POA and MOS. During the next full survey, surveyors validate that MOS data demonstrates that performance was sustained.

> *Option 3*—Undergo a limited survey or a full-length PPR survey. Thirty days following the survey, the organization must submit the PPR tool, which addresses *oral* deficiencies cited at the survey. The organization *may* elect to participate in a conference call with The Joint Commission to discuss issues relating to the standards.

Survey Types

There are several types of Joint Commission surveys. The *Comprehensive Accreditation Manual for Hospitals: The Official Handbook (CAMH)* provides a full description of each type. (*See CAMH* in Chapter 1.) Brief descriptions of some types of surveys follow:

Unannounced Survey—The Joint Commission conducts unannounced surveys of acute care organizations. In the past these were about every three years. Currently, these surveys can occur at any time 18 to 39 months from the previous full survey. In these full on-site surveys, surveyors look for 12 months of implementation of the standards and continuous compliance. Since regular unannounced surveys are the most common, they are the focus of this book.

Initial Survey—An initial survey is a survey of an organization that has never been accredited by The Joint Commission or a survey performed without reference to any prior survey findings. Organizations that are operating and are seeking an initial accreditation must undergo a full survey.

Early Survey—A new organization may choose to be surveyed before it begins operating. The Joint Commission's Early Survey Policy requires the organization to undergo two onsite surveys. The first survey may be conducted up two months prior to the organization beginning business. It uses limited standards and focuses on physical facilities and plans, polices and procedures, and structural issues. The second survey, conducted approximately six months following the first survey, is a full unannounced survey.

Multiorganization Survey—Systems that include two or more organizations may undergo a multiorganization survey. A multiorganization survey includes a corporate orientation and a survey of each of the organizations within the system. Accreditation is awarded to the individual organizations (i.e., not the system).

Complex Organization Survey—Organizations that provide more than one level or type of care in more than one type of setting may undergo a complex organization survey. These organizations will be surveyed under standards and EPs from two or more accreditation manuals. (*See* Chapter 1.)

For-Cause Survey—An unannounced for-cause survey is usually performed when there is reason to believe that a serious situation is present (e.g., a threat to patient care or safety) or credible reason to believe that an organization has falsified accreditation information. No advance notice is provided for these surveys. These surveys can include all of an organization's services or address only those areas where serious concerns exist. The results may prompt follow-up activities and alter an organization's accreditation status (e.g., from "accredited" to "denial of accreditation").

Random Validation of Evidence of Standards Compliance Survey—Each year, The Joint Commission performs random, unannounced surveys of about 5% of its accredited organizations that were required to submit an Evidence of Standards Compliance (ESC) report, with or without a Measure of Success (MOS). The Joint Commission may perform these surveys at any time.

The purpose of these random, unannounced validation surveys is to maintain the credibility of the ESC process. Surveys are usually conducted for one day by one surveyor. The surveyor assesses compliance with the organization's ESC (with or without an MOS) to determine if stated corrective actions were actually implemented. (*See* Evidence of Standards Compliance Report in this chapter.)

Survey Length

The number of days required for a survey is based on information in the organization's application for accreditation (e.g., size and patient populations). (*See* Chapter 1.) Most surveys last three or four days. However, surveys of very small organizations may be shorter, and those of very large organizations may be longer. Tables 2-1 and 2-2 are examples of survey agendas.

Survey Team

The composition of the survey team is based on information in the organization's application for accreditation. (*See* Chapter 1.) Teams usually consist of two or three members (e.g., a physician and registered nurse, or a physician, registered nurse, and administrator). A single surveyor may conduct some surveys.

Life Safety Code® Specialist Surveyors—Survey teams also include a *Life Safety Code®* Specialist. This surveyor conducts a one- or two-day review of life safety and physical plant requirements (including building construction and fire safety).

Specialist Surveyors—Surveys of large organizations or multiple-site facilities or organizations with specialized services may require additional team members (e.g., long-term care, home health, or behavioral health surveyors). Occasionally, surveyors or inspectors from other agencies (e.g., the state health department or a licensing entity) accompany Joint Commission surveyors.

Laboratory Surveyors—A medical technologist may inspect the laboratory at another time (e.g., three to four weeks before the survey). Laboratory surveyor findings will be integrated with the findings of the other surveyors.

Pre-Survey Activities

The Joint Commission must conduct several activities before surveying an organization. The Joint Commission's pre-survey activities include the following:

Priority Focus Areas (PFAs)—The Joint Commission analyzes pre-survey data and identifies the organization's Priority Focus Areas (PFAs). PFAs are an organization's processes, systems, or structures that have a significant effect on the quality and safety of patient care. Examples of PFAs are medication management, infection control, and patient safety. PFAs help surveyors set their focus for the survey, identify potential processes and relevant standards to assess, and schedule on-site survey activities.

Clinical/Service Groups (CSGs)—The Joint Commission also analyzes pre-survey data to identify the organization's Clinical/Service Groups (CSGs). CSGs are categories of patients or services. CSGs vary by organization. Examples of CSGs are general surgery and pediatrics. CSGs help surveyors determine the tracer activities to be conducted during the survey. As with PFAs, CSGs help surveyors set their focus for the survey, identify potential processes and relevant standards to assess, and schedule on-site survey activities.

Priority Focus Process (PFP)—The Joint Commission uses data from the organization's application for accreditation, previous survey findings, ORYX data (*see* Chapter 16), other data provided by the organization, and data from external sources (e.g., state inspection reports) to prepare a Priority Focus Process (PFP) for the survey. Each accredited organization will receive PFP information for its top priority focus areas (PFAs) and clinical/service groups (CSGs) on its extranet site. (*See* Priority Focus Areas and Clinical/Service Groups in this chapter.) The same PFP information is also available to surveyors before an on-site survey.

Opening Survey Sessions and Activities

Organizations can expect their survey to begin with the following sessions and activities:

Surveyor Preliminary Planning Session—On the first morning of the survey, surveyors hold a Surveyor Preliminary Planning Session immediately after arriving at the organization. Surveyors use this session to look at PFAs, CSGs, MOS from the PPR, and other information about the organization; plan the survey agenda; select the initial individual tracers to use in the survey; and identify representative CSGs. Hospital staff will not participate in this session unless requested. Key staff should be available to answer questions or provide additional information if needed.

Opening Conference—Immediately following the planning session, surveyors will conduct an Opening Conference. During the Opening Conference, surveyors explain how the survey will be conducted and the organization's senior leaders and key staff ask questions about the survey.

Orientation to the Organization—An Orientation to the Organization follows immediately after the Opening Conference. During the Orientation to the Organization, the organization's senior leaders and key staff explain and describe the organization to the surveyors.

Tracers

Much of a survey consists of visits to care and service areas (e.g., patient care units and pharmacy) and the use of tracers to assess continuous compliance with relevant standards (including implementation of NPSGs) and determine how well the organization provides care, treatment, and services. Tracer methodology is used in the building assessment, visits to patient care areas, patient record reviews, and staff and patient interviews. In addition, surveyors use tracers to validate the organization's self-assessment and implementation of its plan of action. (*See* Periodic Performance Review and Plan of Action in this chapter.)

Individual Tracers—Individual tracers follow a specific individual (e.g., patient, resident, or client) from preadmission to post discharge (i.e., all areas associated with the individual's care). Surveyors review output from the PFP to identify individual tracers based on the organization's top CSGs. During the Surveyor Preliminary Planning Session, surveyors and the organization select initial individual tracers from a list of active patients, residents, or clients. Individual tracer activities begin where the selected individual is currently located and track the individual throughout his/her stay. Surveyors may go to where the patient first entered the organization, then to all the areas where the patient received care, treatment, or services. Tracers may lead surveyors to the pharmacy or any other department. Pharmacy personnel must be ready to respond to questions relating to medications.

Individual-Based System Tracers—Individual-based system tracers focus on important organizationwide high-risk processes or functions and are used in visits to departments or areas involved in a process or function. Individual-based system tracers for medication management, infection control, data use, and patient flow are described below.

Medication Management System Tracer—The medication management system tracer includes a review of patient records to identify high-risk patients and/or patients on high-alert and other specified medications. The activity traces the path of medications through the organization and addresses medication processes (i.e., selection and procurement, storage, ordering and transcribing, preparing and dispensing, administering, and monitoring). It includes area visits and an evaluation of the organization's medication management process; processes for reporting errors, system breakdowns, close calls (near misses); other issues relating to safe and effective use of medications; and implementation of NPSGs relating to medication management. (*See* Chapter 5.)

Infection Control System Tracer—The infection control system tracer evaluates the organization's infection control processes. It includes a review of a patient record followed by a review of the patient's progress through the organization to determine how staff complies with infection control processes (including processes that reduce the risk of health care–associated infections). Staff can expect surveyors to observe and discuss processes relating to the NPSGs (e.g., continuous compliance with CDC or WHO hand hygiene guidelines, practices to prevent health care–associated infections due to multidrug-resistant organisms [MDROs], and appropriate and correct use of antimicrobial agents). Infection control system tracer activities may lead surveyors to the pharmacy and other departments. Pharmacy personnel must be ready to respond to questions relating to infection control (e.g., procedures for compounding sterile preparations, risk points in the process for compounding sterile preparations, education and training in compounding sterile preparations, and environmental monitoring of sterile preparation compounding areas). (*See* Chapter 9.)

Data Use System Tracer—The data use system tracer evaluates how the organization uses data to improve patient safety and patient care. Surveyors may review data relating to medication errors, adverse drug events, staffing effectiveness, and infection control. Staff can expect surveyors to discuss and evaluate how the organization uses data associated with the NPSGs (e.g., accurate patient identification, effective communication, safe use of medications, reduced risk of health care–associated infections, the safe use of anticoagulants, reconciliation of medications, and reduced risk of patient falls). Organizations must be able to show how they use data to monitor adherence to CDC or WHO hand hygiene guidelines. (*See* Chapter 6.) Pharmacy personnel must be ready to respond to questions relating to data use (e.g., ensuring data security and integrity, methods for tracking pharmacy interventions, methods for monitoring overrides of automated distribution cabinets, and methods for tracking adverse drug events).

Patient Flow System Tracer—The patient flow system tracer evaluates the potential for treatment delays, medical errors, and unsafe practices due to periods of patient congestion and disruptions in the flow. When a patient flow problem exists, it can affect the entire organization. This can lead to noncompliance with multiple Joint Commission standards, NPSGs, and core measures. The organization must evaluate all areas (e.g., emergency department, laboratory, and diagnostic imaging) where the flow of patients may have a negative effect on the care, treatment, or services provided.

Program-Specific Tracers—Program-specific tracers may be conducted in organizations that have unique characteristics (e.g., suicide prevention and laboratory integration). These tracers aim to identify safety concerns within different levels and types of care. The *CAMH* contains additional information about the applicability of program-specific tracers to specific organizations.[1]

Other Survey Sessions and Activities

Other survey sessions and activities include the following as applicable:

Life Safety Code® Building Assessment—During the *Life Safety Code®* Building Assessment, a specialist surveyor will tour the facilities and determine how the organization complies with fire protection requirements of the National Fire Protection Association (NFPA). The surveyor might visit the pharmacy during this tour. (*See* Survey Team in this chapter.) Pharmacy personnel must be ready to respond to questions pertaining to fire safety (e.g., fire evacuation routes and location of fire extinguishers).

Environment of Care Session—The Environment of Care (EC) Session includes a group discussion of the organization's environment of care management plans and EC issues identified during the survey. A surveyor asks questions pertaining to the organization's EC management process. The surveyor may observe how the organization implements specific EC processes or trace how the organization addresses a specific risk.

Emergency Management Session—The Emergency Management (EM) Session assesses the organization's emergency preparedness processes. The organization's role in the community, county, or region's emergency management program will also be discussed. The surveyor may observe how the organization implements specific EM processes or trace how the organization addresses a specific emergency situation.

Competence Assessment Process Session—The Competence Assessment Process Session focuses on how the organization determines that staff, including contract staff, are qualified and competent. A surveyor uses data from tracer activities to guide the discussion. Topics pertain to determining compliance with policies and procedures, staffing adequacy, and orientation and education.

Medical Staff Credentialing and Privileging Activity—During the Medical Staff Credentialing and Privileging activity, a surveyor facilitates a discussion of the organization's process for credentialing and privileging medical staff members and licensed individual practitioners (LIPs). The organization and surveyors identify issues relating to credentialing and the assignment of clinical responsibilities. The surveyor reviews credentials files of selected medical staff members and LIPs. Activities include determining if practitioners practice within their scope of assigned clinical responsibilities.

Special Issue Resolution—Surveyors reserve about 30 minutes daily in the late afternoon to resolve issues that may have arisen during the day or to devote extra time to some areas.

Surveyor Team Meeting/Planning Session—The survey day ends with a Surveyor Team Meeting/Planning Session. Surveyors use this meeting to share their findings and plan for the remainder of the survey.

Daily Briefings—The second and subsequent survey days (except for the last day) begin with a briefing for the organization's leaders. During the daily briefings, surveyors discuss general observations from the previous day and give staff an opportunity to note important information that may have been missed on previous days. Surveyors also review the agenda for the upcoming day.

Leadership Session—In most surveys, surveyors meet with the organization's leaders on the last day of the survey to discuss issues relating to their findings at the system level and identify opportunities for improving the system. The organization's leaders will discuss their role in organizationwide processes and functions. The session also includes a review of how leaders (including the governing body) communicate, their knowledge of laws and regulations, their understanding of performance improvement approaches and methods, and their understanding of leadership standards relating to its role in the organization.

Closing Survey Sessions and Activities

Surveys close with the following sessions and activities:

Surveyor Report Preparation—On the final day of the survey, surveyors meet to integrate their findings and prepare a report that reflects the organization's compliance with the standards. Surveyors also use this session to prepare for the CEO Exit Briefing and the Organization Exit Conference.

Requirement for Improvement (RFI)—A requirement for improvement (RFI) is assigned to each noncompliant standard. All requirements for improvement must be addressed in the organization's Evidence of Standards Compliance Report. (*See* Evidence of Standards Compliance Report in this chapter.) Failure to adequately address an RFI after two opportunities may result in the organization being placed on Conditional Accreditation. (*See* Conditional Accreditation in this chapter.)

Summary of Survey Findings Report—The Summary of Survey Findings Report is posted on the organization's extranet site shortly after the survey and includes the surveyors' findings, RFIs for any noncompliant standards, and other pertinent information. Reports do not include numerical scores.

Accreditation Decision Process—The accreditation decision process is based on the number of standards judged "not compliant" at the time of the survey. If there are no RFIs, the organization is accredited as of the day after completing the survey. (*See* Requirement for Improvement in this chapter.) If there are RFIs, the organization has 45 or 60 days to submit an Evidence of Standards Compliance (ESC) report to address corrections to the RFIs. (*See* Evidence of Standards Compliance Report in this chapter.) The accreditation decision follows the submission of the ESC and reflects one of the following accreditation decision recommendations: accredited, provisional accreditation, conditional accreditation, preliminary denial of accreditation, denial of accreditation, or preliminary accreditation. (*See* Accreditation Decision in this chapter.)

CEO Exit Briefing—At the conclusion of the survey, the survey team presents its Summary of Survey Findings Report to the organization's chief executive officer (CEO). The surveyors and CEO discuss the report and decide if it will be shared with the organization's staff at the Organization Exit Conference.

Organization Exit Conference—Immediately after the CEO Exit Briefing, surveyors hold an Organization Exit Conference with the organization's leaders and staff. The surveyors present the survey findings if authorized by the CEO. Leaders and staff may ask questions and make comments during this session. They may also question the findings and submit additional evidence of compliance.

Post-Survey Activities

After the Organization Exit Conference, the survey team leaves the Summary of Survey Findings Report with the organization and transmits the results to The Joint Commission's Central Office. Post-survey activities vary with the findings reflected in the report.

Evidence of Standards Compliance (ESC) Report—If the Summary of Survey Findings Report indicates that an organization is accredited *with no RFIs*, no further action is required of the organization. Organizations that receive RFIs must submit a corrective and/or clarifying Evidence of Standards Compliance (ESC) Report within 45 or 60 days of the survey, depending on the criticality of the noncompliant EP. Organizations that receive conditional accreditation or preliminary denial of accreditation must submit an ESC Report and undergo an on-site survey. The complete requirements are in the *CAMH.*[1]

The ESC Report is *not* a plan that describes how the organization *will* meet the RFIs. Rather, it must state how the organization currently complies with the standards or clarify how the organization believes it was compliant at the time of the survey. The ESC Report must include, when applicable, a measure of success (MOS) used to assess sustained compliance with an EP. (*See* Measures of Success Report in this chapter.)

Measures of Success (MOS)—A ☑ (in this publication) in the left margin next to some EPs is a Measure of Success (MOS) icon. Organizations must develop an MOS for these EPs when a standard is judged to be out of compliance through an on-site survey or a PPR. An MOS usually relates to an audit process that demonstrates that the action taken was successful and sustained. When demonstrating achievement with an MOS, The Joint Commission defines specific criteria for sample sizes when conducting audits. (*See* the *CAMH* for more on developing an MOS and sample sizes.)

Measures of Success (MOS) Report—An MOS Report is due to The Joint Commission four months after The Joint Commission approves the organization's ESC Report.

Accreditation Decisions—The Joint Commission bases its accreditation decision on its review of the ESC Report and the findings of any follow-up on-site survey. Accreditation decision categories are described below. They are described more fully in the *CAMH*. There is a process for appealing The Joint Commission's accreditation decision.

Accredited—The organization meets The Joint Commission's accreditation requirements.

Provisional Accreditation—The organization does not address all requirements for improvement in the ESC Report or the organization's Measures of Success Report does not show that actions taken were successful and sustained.

Conditional Accreditation—The organization was previously in Preliminary Denial of Accreditation due to an immediate threat to health or safety, or failed to resolve the requirements of Provisional Accreditation, or is not in compliance with standards that pose a risk to patient care or safety. The organization must correct problems identified in the ESC report and undergo an on-site survey.

Preliminary Denial of Accreditation—The organization poses a threat to patient safety, or failed to resolve requirements of a Conditional Accreditation, or is substantially out of compliance with Joint Commission standards.

Denial of Accreditation—The organization is not compliant with the standards and has no more review and appeal opportunities.

Preliminary Accreditation—The organization is compliant with selected standards in the first of two surveys in an early survey option. (*See* Early Survey in this chapter.)

Quality Reports

The Joint Commission publishes Quality Reports on its Quality Check® Web site. (*See* Appendix.) Quality Reports provide meaningful, comparative performance information about the quality and safety of accredited organizations. Information in Quality Reports pertains to an organization's accreditation status, implementation of The Joint Commission's NPSGs, and other measures and indicators of quality. Quality Reports do not contain scores for the standards.

Table 2-1. Example Three Day/Two Surveyor Agenda

Day 1

Time	Physician	Nurse
8:00–8:30 A.M.	Opening Conference and Orientation to Organization	
8:30–11:00 A.M.	Preliminary Planning Session	
11:00–12:30 P.M.	Individual Tracer Activity	Individual Tracer Activity
12:30–1:00 P.M.	Surveyor Lunch	
1:00–1:30 P.M.	Individual Tracer Activity	Individual Tracer Activity
1:30–3:00 P.M.		*Life Safety Code®* Building Tour[a]
3:00–4:00 P.M.	Special Issue Resolution	
4:00–4:30 P.M.	Surveyor Team Meeting/Planning Meeting	

Day 2

Time	Physician	Nurse
8:00–8:30 A.M.	Daily Briefing	
8:30–9:30 A.M.	Individual Tracer Activity	System Tracer—Data Use
9:30–12:00 P.M.		Individual Tracer Activity
12:00–12:30 P.M.	Surveyor Lunch	
12:30–1:00 P.M.	Surveyor Team Meeting/Planning Meeting	
1:00–1:30 P.M.	Individual Tracer Activity	System Tracer—Infection Control
1:30–2:00 P.M.		
2:00–2:30 P.M.		Individual Tracer Activity
2:30–3:00 P.M.	System Tracer—Medication	
3:00–3:30 P.M.	Management	
3:30–4:00 P.M.	Special Issue Resolution	
4:00–4:30 P.M.	Surveyor Team Meeting/Planning Meeting	

Day 3

Time	Physician	Nurse
8:00–9:00 A.M.	Leadership Session	
9:00–9:30 A.M.	Individual Tracer Activity	Competence Assessment Process
9:30–10:00 A.M.		
10:00–10:30 A.M.		Environment of Care Session[b]
10:30–11:00 A.M.		
11:00–11:30 A.M.	Medical Staff Credentialing	
11:30–12:00 P.M.	and Privileging	Individual Tracer Activity
12:00–1:00 P.M.	Surveyor Lunch	
1:00–3:30 P.M.	Surveyor Report Preparation	
3:30–4:30 P.M.	CEO Exit Briefing and Organization Exit Conference	

[a]Survey teams include a *Life Safety Code®* Specialist who conducts a one- or two-day review of life safety and physical plant requirements.

[b]The Environment of Care (EC) Session includes time focused on Emergency Management.

Table 2-2. Example Three Day/Three Surveyor Agenda

Day 1

Time	Physician	Nurse	Administrator
8:00–9:00 A.M.	Opening Conference and Orientation to Organization		
9:00–11:00 A.M.	Preliminary Planning Session		
11:00–12:30 P.M.	Individual Tracer Activity	Individual Tracer Activity	*Life Safety Code®* Building Tour[a]
12:30–1:00 P.M.	Surveyor Lunch		
1:00–3:30 P.M.	Individual Tracer Activity	Individual Tracer Activity	Individual Tracer Activity
3:30–4:00 P.M.	Special Issue Resolution		
4:00–4:30 P.M.	Surveyor Team Meeting/Planning Meeting		

Day 2

Time	Physician	Nurse	Administrator
8:00–8:30 A.M.	Daily Briefing		
8:30–9:30 P.M.	Individual Tracer Activity		System Tracer—Data Use
9:30–12:00 P.M.			Individual Tracer Activity
12:00–12:30 P.M.	Surveyor Lunch		
12:30–1:00 P.M.	Surveyor Team Meeting/Planning Meeting		
1:00–2:30 P.M.	Individual Tracer Activity	Individual Tracer Activity	Individual Tracer Activity
2:30–3:30 P.M.	System Tracer—Medication Management		
3:30–4:00 P.M.	Special Issue Resolution		
4:00–4:30 P.M.	Surveyor Team Meeting/Planning Meeting		

Day 3

Time	Physician	Nurse	Administrator
8:00–9:00 A.M.	Leadership Session		
9:00–9:30 A.M.	Individual Tracer Activity	Competence Assessment Process	Environment of Care Session[b]
9:30–10:00 A.M.			
10:00–10:30 A.M.		System Tracer—Infection Control	
10:30–11:00 A.M.			Individual Tracer Activity
11:00–11:30 A.M.		Individual Tracer Activity	
11:30–12:00 P.M.			
12:00–12:30 P.M.	Surveyor Lunch		
12:30–1:30 P.M.	Medical Staff Credentialing and Privileging	Individual Tracer Activity	Individual Tracer Activity[c]
1:30–3:30 P.M.	Surveyor Report Preparation		
3:30–4:30 P.M.	CEO Exit Briefing and Organization Exit Conference		

[a]Survey teams include a *Life Safety Code®* Specialist who conducts a one- or two-day review of life safety and physical plant requirements.

[b]The Environment of Care (EC) Session includes time focused on Emergency Management.

[c]Three-day surveys are distinguished from one- or two-day surveys by the increase in the number of Individual Tracer Activities performed.

CHAPTER 3

Achieving Continuous Compliance with Joint Commission Standards

Organizations must comply continuously with Joint Commission standards. Start preparing now. This chapter provides an organized approach to achieving continuous compliance.

Continuous Compliance Steps

The following steps for achieving continuous compliance are suggested:

Begin by Reading—Begin by reading the first three chapters of this book. Read the other chapters as you address the standards to which they pertain.

Determine Whether Standards in Accreditation Manuals for Other Types of Care Apply—Check with the organization's leaders to determine whether any areas or services (e.g., long-term care and behavioral health units) will be surveyed under standards in other Joint Commission accreditation manuals. (*See* Chapter 1.) If necessary, review the standards for these areas and services and modify the process for assuring compliance accordingly.

Complete the Checklists—Complete the checklists in this book (i.e., Chapter 4 and Chapters 6 through 12). If necessary, read the standards in context in the *Comprehensive Accreditation Manual for Hospitals: The Official Handbook (CAMH)*. Also read the medication management (MM) standards and pharmacy-related standards in other Joint Commission manuals that are applicable to the organization. (*See* Chapter 1.) Modify the process for assuring compliance accordingly.

Identify Current Deficiencies—The checklists include the MM standards, other pharmacy-related standards, and notes and suggestions for compliance. Use the checklists to identify current deficiencies, assess the organization's compliance status, and develop an action plan for achieving continuous compliance. (*See* Develop an Action Plan in this chapter.)

Perform a Periodic Performance Review (PPR)—Assist the organization in performing a PPR. (*See* Chapter 2.)

Provide Information to the Organization—The Joint Commission uses information provided by an organization to determine the length of the survey and the numbers and types of surveyors. The pharmacy may need to supply some of this information to the organization's administrative staff for inclusion in the application for accreditation (e.g., provision of pharmacy services to home care and long-term care patients). Be sure the information is accurate. Inaccurate information may result in additional costs to the organization and/or delay The Joint Commission's accreditation decision.

Obtain Information from the Organization—Obtain information about the next survey from the organization. Examples include areas to be surveyed, type of survey, and expected format for the survey (e.g., length and composition of the survey team). The organization should also update the pharmacy on the status of previous deficiencies relating to medications (e.g., the organization's failure to meet National Patient Safety Goals [NPSGs]).

Focus on Problematic Areas—Some standards are problematic in many organizations. Give special attention to the following problematic areas:

- ***Security of Medications.*** Failure to secure and control access to medications in all areas of the organization. (*See* MM.03.01.01, EP 3 and EP 6 in Chapter 4.)
- ***Order Clarity and Accuracy.*** Failure to ensure medication orders are written clearly and transcribed accurately. (*See* MM.04.01.01 in Chapter 4.)
- ***Reconciliation of Medications.*** Failure to accurately and completely reconcile medications across the continuum of care. (*See* NPSG 8 in Chapter 6.)
- ***Medication Order Review.*** Failure of a pharmacist to review medication orders prior to administration of the drug. (*See* MM.05.01.01 in Chapter 4.)
- ***Prohibited Abbreviations.*** Failure to prevent the use of prohibited abbreviations as defined by the organization. (*See* IM.02.02.01, EP 2 and EP 3.) (*See* MM.04.01.01 in Chapter 4.)

- ***Expired Medications.*** Failure to remove all expired medications in the pharmacy and patient-care areas. (*See* MM.03.01.01, EP 8 in Chapter 4.)
- ***Labeling of Medications.*** Failure to label medications correctly in all areas of the organization. (*See* MM.05.01.09 in Chapter 4 and NPSG.03.04.01 in Chapter 6.)
- ***Contrast Media.*** Failure to control the handling of contrast media and other medications in the Imaging department. (*See* MM.03.01.01, MM.05.01.01, MM.05.01.07, and MM.05.01.09 in Chapter 4 and NPSG.03.04.01 in Chapter 6.)
- ***Respiratory Care Medications.*** Failure to control the handling of respiratory care medications throughout the organization. (*See* MM.03.01.01, MM.05.01.01, MM.05.01.07, and MM.05.01.09 in Chapter 4.)
- ***Emergency Medications.*** Failure to ensure that emergency medications are secure and controlled. (*See* MM.03.01.03 in Chapter 4.)
- ***After-Hours Medications.*** Failure to provide medications in a safe manner when the pharmacy is closed. (*See* MM.05.01.13 in Chapter 4.)
- ***Look-Alike/Sound-Alike Medications.*** Failure to identify a list of look-alike/sound-alike medications and consistently implement processes to prevent errors involving the interchange of those medications. (*See* MM.01.02.01, EP 1 through EP 3 in Chapter 4.)
- ***High-Alert Medications.*** Failure to develop and consistently implement processes for managing high-alert medications. (*See* MM.01.01.03 in Chapter 4.)
- ***Controlled Substances.*** Failure to secure and account for controlled substances. (*See* MM.03.01.01, EP 3 and MM.05.01.11, EP 2 in Chapter 4 and Examples 4-9 through 4-12.)
- ***Hand-off Communications.*** Failure to implement a standardized approach to "hand-off" communications relating to medications. (*See* PC.02.02.01, EP 2.) (See Chapter 20.)
- ***Concentrated Electrolytes.*** Failure to remove concentrated electrolytes (e.g., potassium chloride, potassium phosphate, and sodium chloride greater than 0.9%) and other high-alert medications specified by the organization from patient care areas. (*See* MM.01.01.03 and MM.03.01.01, EP 9 in Chapter 4.)
- ***Sterile Preparations.*** Failure to compound sterile preparations properly. (*See* MM.05.01.07, EP 2 and Chapter 19.)
- ***Temperature Checks.*** Failure to completely document medication refrigerator and freezer temperature checks. (*See* MM.03.01.01, EP 2 in Chapter 4 and Examples 4-6 through 4-8.)
- ***Competence Assessment.*** Failure to assess the competence of staff (e.g., age-specific, sterile preparation compounding, and medication safety competencies). (*See* Competence Assessment in Chapters 7 and 14, and Examples 7-5 through 7-6.)

Develop an Action Plan—Although the time needed to prepare an action plan for achieving continuous compliance may be substantial, the benefits of a plan are worth the effort. Make the plan easy to update. The following approach is suggested:

1. Using the checklists in this book, identify deficiencies and list each on a form with four columns labeled *What*, *When*, *Who,* and *Status*:

   What—Break each deficiency down into the steps required for its resolution. Then list the steps in the order that they should be completed. Several drafts may be needed to develop a satisfactory listing.

   When—Assign target dates for the completion of each step. Steps with the highest priorities should have the earliest target dates.

   Who—List the names of the individuals responsible for the completion of each step. Consider their capabilities as well as their experience and interests. Divide responsibilities so that no one is overloaded.

   Status—Track progress in correcting deficiencies.
2. Check off the steps as they are completed.
3. Refer to the checklists in this book and move the check marks from "No" to "Yes" as deficiencies are corrected.

Organize Documents—Improvements in pharmacy services and patient care are fostered and pharmacy management is enhanced if files and records are organized and thinned of unneeded materials. The Joint Commission does not specify a length of time for retaining documents. At a minimum, organizations must retain documents for the period required by law.

The Joint Commission has identified Elements of Performance (EP) that require documentation and tagged each with a Ⓓ icon. EPs that are tagged with a 🗎 icon (in this publication) require special attention to assure documentation is available for surveyors. Surveyors may ask to see specific documents (e.g., policies and procedures). Only documents that surveyors request are necessary. Documents for the previous 12 months should be sufficient in most cases.

Chapter 12 is a checklist of frequently requested documents (including those tagged with a icon). Record the document locations on the checklist (especially if they are kept outside the pharmacy). If necessary, identify (e.g., highlight or underline) statements or areas of the documents that show compliance with standards (e.g., entries in Pharmacy and Therapeutics [P&T] Committee minutes).

Update Policies and Procedures—Ensure that all policies and procedures are updated regularly, reflect current practices, and do not conflict with policies and procedures of other departments. Chapter 11 is a checklist of suggested policies and procedures. Some pharmacies organize their policies and procedures according to the organization's functions. (*See* Pharmacy and Therapeutics Policies in Chapter 13.)

Check with Other Pharmacies—Check with other directors of pharmacies to determine how they ensure continuous compliance. Their experiences may help you understand how they demonstrate continuous compliance. Determine whether their surveyors had special interests. Surveyors who are interested in continuing education (CE) may want to see instructional materials, CE records, and evidence that the pharmacy used CE activities to address its problems. Surveyors who are interested in infection control may want to see records pertaining to sterile preparations (including assurance of competence for persons who prepare those products).

Conduct Mock Surveys and Tracers—Mock surveys and tracers—conducted by the organization's administration, performance improvement (PI) staff, the pharmacy director, another organization, or an outside consultant—help to ensure continuous compliance. (*See* Chapter 2.) Because their own staff may be biased or reluctant to criticize, some organizations look to outside consultants for an objective and unbiased approach. Surprise mock surveys may help increase the likelihood of continuous compliance. Persons who normally staff patient care areas as well as part time and temporary staff should be included in mock surveys. Plan carefully for the survey sessions and be prepared to respond to questions that surveyors might ask. (*See* Chapter 5.)

Prepare Pharmacy Staff—Involve pharmacy staff in preparing for continuous compliance and keep them informed of how the pharmacy and organization are progressing. Keep them informed of any changes in standards or survey procedures. Discuss patient care and safety-related topics (e.g., new or revised policies and procedures) during staff meetings and in-service education presentations.

Cooperate with Other Departments and Services—Meet regularly with other departments and services. Regular meetings with representatives from other departments and services (especially nursing service) can identify mutual problems and help departments work together to resolve them.

Emphasize Continuous Readiness—Surveys may be conducted at any time; there is no advance notice. Keep policies and procedures up-to-date. Keep documentation current and materials well organized. Concentrate on the list of problematic areas in this chapter, but do not neglect other areas. Inspect areas often. Open refrigerators, automated dispensing cabinets, medication carts, and drawers in medication rooms to inspect them as a surveyor would. Examine seals on emergency medication boxes and carts. Look under sinks and behind linen. Be alert for infection control and safety violations and risks. (*See* Chapters 9 and 10.) Keep the pharmacy clean and ensure that areas for compounding sterile preparations meet current requirements. Aim for continuous compliance. Example 3-1 is a list of pharmacy activities with suggested frequencies for performing them.

Interact with Surveyors—Surveyors understand that people are often apprehensive about surveys and they try to make them as painless as possible. Experienced surveyors do not embarrass staff before their peers and superiors. So relax and be courteous and attentive. Answers must be honest and should be complete and concise. Advise staff to be patient and ask questions if they become confused. Surveyors like to explain new standards and offer suggestions. It is not true that surveyors "always find something!" Some organizations finish the survey with no deficiencies.

There is no substitute for documented compliance with the standards. However, the following suggestions may be helpful when interacting with surveyors:

- *Show and Tell*—Convert data to pictures, graphs, tables, and charts that tell a story and lend credibility to your responses. Posters or storyboards displaying PI activities remind staff of projects and showcase improvements.
- *Emphasize Measurements*—Quantify problems in terms of time, numbers, and cost (e.g., how long it took, how many errors were made, and how much it cost).

- *Emphasize Action Taken*—State what has been done to improve patient care (e.g., processes revised, new equipment purchased, forms revised, orientation and education provided, and staffing and organization changes made).
- *Emphasize Improvements*—Describe improvements as a result of actions taken. State how current measurements compare with initial measurements (e.g., faster, more accurate, safer, and less costly).
- *Emphasize Medication Safety*—Give specific examples of actions that resulted in safer medication processes.
- *Emphasize Teamwork*—Stress how the pharmacy works with other departments, patients, and the community to improve safety and patient care.
- *Stress Competence*—Show that individuals demonstrate their competence prior to assuming their duties.
- *Discuss Differences*—Discuss differences in interpretation of a standard or a legal requirement. Surveyors may reverse their opinions if an organization can demonstrate that it meets the standard or legal requirement.
- *Do Not Panic*—If a policy, procedure, or other document cannot be located, continue to look for it. If surveyors see the document before the exit conference, they may change the finding.
- *Relax*—Surveyors' comments and suggestions are not meant to be critical and will not necessarily be reflected in a deficiency.

Provide Truthful and Accurate Information—Information, whether verbal, written, or electronic, provided to The Joint Commission must be truthful and accurate. Never provide surveyors with falsified or misleading information (including redrafted or reformatted documents or documents that have had contents deleted). If The Joint Commission determines that an organization has falsified information, it may deny or remove accreditation and prohibit the organization from being surveyed for a period of one year.

Look Ahead—Continue to emphasize continuous compliance between surveys. Keep up with changes in contemporary pharmacy practice and address new Joint Commission standards and NPSGs promptly. Continuous compliance fosters safe, high-quality care and ensures readiness for an unannounced survey at any time.

CHAPTER 4

Medication Management Standards Checklist

The Joint Commission's medication management (MM) standards[1] address critical MM processes and support compliance with the National Patient Safety Goals (NPSGs) (*See* Chapter 6.) Chapter 5 provides an overview of the MM individual-based system tracer and a strategy for demonstrating compliance with the MM standards. The Joint Commission standards are based on the Pharmaceutical Services section of the Medicare Hospital Conditions of Participation.[2]

> ***Note:*** Organizations surveyed under the *Comprehensive Accreditation Manual for Hospitals: The Official Handbook (CAMH)* must comply with the MM standards that are applicable to them. Organizations surveyed under other Joint Commission accreditation manuals should review the appropriate manual. (*See* Chapter 1.)

Outsourced/Contracted Pharmacy Services—When pharmacy services are outsourced or provided through a contract, the contract should address responsibility for meeting the MM standards. Organizations must ensure that outsourced/contracted pharmacy services comply with the standards, including LD.04.03.01.

Medication Definition

The Joint Commission defines *medication* broadly and includes items that in the past may not have been considered to be medications. In the glossary for the *CAMH*, The Joint Commission defines a **medication** as "any prescription medications, sample medications, herbal remedies, vitamins, nutraceuticals, vaccines, or over-the-counter drugs; diagnostic and contrast agents used on or administered to persons to diagnose, treat, or prevent disease or other abnormal conditions; radioactive medications, respiratory therapy treatments, parenteral nutrition, blood derivatives, and intravenous solutions (plain, with electrolytes and/or drugs); and any product designated by the Food and Drug Administration (FDA) as a drug. This definition of medication does not include enteral nutrition solutions (which are considered food products), oxygen, and other medical gases." The MM standards apply to *all* medications included in the definition.

Checklist Organization

This chapter presents the MM standards, notes, rationales, and elements of performance (EPs) for hospitals in a checklist format. Their sequence follows their arrangement in the *CAMH* (i.e., planning, selection and procurement, storage, ordering and transcribing, preparing and dispensing, administration, monitoring, and evaluation). The checklist quotes the standards, notes, rationales, and EPs.

Checklist Symbols—Special attention should be paid to EPs displaying an icon. The checklist uses a 🗎 icon before an EP if documentation is required and a ⚠ icon before an EP if noncompliance is likely to create an immediate risk to patient safety or to the quality of care provided. A ☑ icon before an EP indicates that a Measure of Success (MOS) is required if the EP is scored non-compliant during a survey.

Authors' Comments, Experiences, and Suggestions—Checklist items reflect the authors' comments, experiences, and suggestions; reports from surveyed organizations; and surveyors' statements. They include suggestions to comply with the EPs requiring specific documentation, metrics, or attention to implementation of specific care. Some items reflect legal requirements, previous Joint Commission standards, or commonly accepted standards of practice. Others note variations in interpretation of the standards.

Checklist Usage Suggestions

To assess compliance, use the checklist and proceed systematically. Mark the element and standard "Yes" if you are currently compliant and are sure you will continue to be compliant. Mark the element and standard "No" if you are currently not compliant (even if you are sure you will be compliant later). If you are not sure of your answer, leave a blank response. A few items may be not applicable (NA). Answer honestly, use a pencil (so you can change your answers), and make notes on the pages (e.g., reasons for noncompliance). It might be helpful to record the locations of the documents on the checklist (especially if they are kept outside the pharmacy). Concentrate your efforts on resolving all "No" and blank responses.

Checklist	Yes	No	NA

PLANNING MEDICATION MANAGEMENT PROCESSES

Standard MM.01.01.01

The hospital plans its medication management processes.

Rationale for MM.01.01.01

Medication management is often complicated, involving many people and processes. For this reason, the hospital plans each part of the process with care so that safety and quality are maintained. This planning may involve the coordinated efforts of multiple services and disciplines.

Elements of Performance for MM.01.01.01

1. The organization has a written policy that describes that the following information about the patient is accessible to licensed independent practitioners and staff who participate in the management of the patient's medications:

	Yes	No	NA
• Age	____	____	____
• Sex	____	____	____
• Diagnoses	____	____	____
• Allergies	____	____	____
• Sensitivities	____	____	____
• Current medications	____	____	____
• Height and weight (when necessary)	____	____	____
• Pregnancy and lactation information (when necessary)	____	____	____
• Laboratory results (when necessary)	____	____	____
• Any additional information required by the organization	____	____	____

(See also MM.04.01.01, EP 10; IM.02.01.01, EP 3; RC.01.01.01, EP 13)

Authors' Comments, Experiences, and Suggestions

Patient Information Access

- *A written policy is required.*
- *The element does not define the term "accessible." Surveyors will determine if care providers can access relevant patient-specific information when they need it, where they need it, and in time to be of value. There should be no undue difficulty or delay in accessing the information.*
- *Information in the pharmacy's patient profiles should be accessible to other care providers (directly or indirectly). Care providers may obtain after-hours access to the pharmacy's patient profiles by contacting an on-call pharmacist who can make the profile information available.*

Yes No NA

- *The pharmacy must make patient-related data and information available for analysis and decision making.*
- *The information may include the date of birth instead of the patient's age.*

Patient Information Security

- *There should be procedures in place to protect patient records and prevent their loss and destruction. (See IM.02.01.03, EP 2.)*
- *Data must be protected from accidental or unauthorized intentional change. (See IM.02.01.03, EP 2.)*
- *Surveyors may ask pharmacy staff how they protect patient information data (e.g., data on billing documents, pharmacy patient profiles, medication and IV labels, copies of physicians' orders, and other documents that can be linked by name or number to a patient).*
- *The pharmacy must maintain the privacy and confidentiality of information. Disclosure of personal information must be limited and access must be restricted to individuals who have need, reason, and permission for such access. (See IM.02.01.01.)*
- *Discussions relating to patients must be out of the hearing range of staff, visitors, other patients, and individuals who do not have a need or reason to know the information. Staff should not discuss patient-care issues in elevators, food service areas, and other public places.*
- *Medication orders, pharmacy patient profiles, labels, meeting minutes, and other patient-related documents (i.e., those that contain patients' names or identifying numbers, or information relating to patients' status, treatment, diagnosis, and medications) must be securely stored and access restricted to those who have a legitimate need or reason to know and use the information. Some hospitals require staff to sign a confidentiality of patient information agreement. (See Example 4-1.)*
- *Disposal of patient-related documents must guarantee confidentiality. These documents must not be placed in regular trash for disposal. Complete destruction (e.g., by shredding) is usually required.*
- *Staff must be aware that communication technology presents additional confidentiality problems. For example, patient information (and other confidential information) contained in e-mail messages can be inadvertently disseminated inside and outside the organization. Also, measures should be taken to prevent unauthorized individuals from viewing fax transmissions, computer screens containing patient information, and screens of automated dispensing cabinets (ADCs).*

Patient Record Retention

- *The organization must retain patient-related data and information for a length of time that complies with laws and regulations. The Centers for Medicare and Medicaid Services (CMS) requires retention for five years. Many organizations require a longer retention period.*

Pharmacy Patient Profile

- *If the pharmacy system is not integrated with the hospital information system, the pharmacy should maintain a profile of important informa-*

	Yes	No	NA

tion for each patient in addition to patient-specific information in the medical record.

- *Pharmacists should verify the accuracy of entries in pharmacy patient profiles (e.g., by initials or a computer code).*

Medication Administration Record

- *Surveyors expect to see a computerized or electronic medication administration record that is provided by the pharmacy and reconciled by nursing staff.*

2. The hospital implements its policy to make information about the patient accessible to licensed independent practitioners and staff who participate in the management of the patient's medications. ___ ___ ___

   Note: This element of performance does not apply in emergency situations.

Authors' Comments, Experiences, and Suggestions

Medication List

- *A current list of medications for each patient must be included in the patient's record in accordance with the organization's medication reconciliation policy.*
- *Current medications should include nonprescription (i.e., over-the-counter) drugs, herbal remedies, blood derivatives, and all other medications included in The Joint Commission's definition of medications. (See Medication Definition in this chapter.)*

Patient Record Information

- *Standard RC.02.01.01, EP 1 requires each patient medical record to contain the patient's name, sex, address, date of birth, the name of any legally authorized representative, legal status if receiving behavioral health care services, and language and communication needs.*
- *Standard RC.02.01.01, EP 2 requires each patient medical record to include the following:*
  - *Initial diagnosis and conditions*
  - *Any allergies to medications*
  - *Any medications ordered or prescribed*
  - *Any medication administered, including the strength, dose, and route*
  - *Any access site for medication, administration device used, and rate of administration*
  - *Any adverse drug reactions*
  - *Any medication dispensed or prescribed on discharge*
- *Known problems should be documented when diagnoses are not known.*

Yes **No** **NA**

- *Weight, height, or both weight and height must be available when one or the other or both are needed to determine the dose for the patient.*
- *Other information required for safe medication management may include the patient's use of illegal drugs; misuse of prescription and nonprescription medications; use of investigational medications; potential medication–food interactions; creatinine clearance (especially for patients 65 years of age and older); serum drug concentrations; hemoglobin; hematocrit; and body surface area.*

Medication Administration

- *Surveyors may look at medical records to ensure that administration is documented for contrast agents, blood derivatives, respiratory therapy treatments, and other medications included in The Joint Commission's definition of medication. (See Medication Definition in this chapter.)*

Ambulatory Care

- *The medical record of patients who receive continuing ambulatory care services must contain the following:*
  - *Any adverse or allergic drug reactions. (See RC.02.01.07, EP 2.)*
  - *Any current medications, over-the-counter medications, and herbal preparations. (See RC.02.01.07, EP 2.)*

Standard MM.01.01.03

The hospital safely manages high-alert and hazardous medications.

Rationale for MM.01.01.03

High-alert medications are those medications involved in a high percentage of errors and/or sentinel events, as well as medications that carry a higher risk for abuse or other adverse outcomes. Lists of high-alert medications are available from such organizations as the Institute for Safe Medication Practices (ISMP). (*See* Appendix.) Examples of high-alert medications include investigational medications, controlled medications, medications not on the approved U.S. Food and Drug Administration (FDA) list, medications with a narrow therapeutic range, psychotherapeutic medications, and look-alike/sound-alike medications.

Hazardous medications are those in which studies in animals or humans indicate that exposure to them have a potential for causing cancer, development or reproductive toxicity, or harm to organs. Lists of hazardous medications are available from organizations such as the National Institute for Occupational Safety and Health (NIOSH). (*See* Appendix.)

For safe management, the hospital needs to develop its own list(s) of high-alert medications and hazardous medications based on its unique utilization patterns of medications and its own internal data about medication errors and sentinel events. It is up to the hospital to determine whether medications that are new to the market or new to the hospital are high alert or hazardous.

	Yes	No	NA

Elements of Performance for MM.01.01.03

1. The hospital identifies, in writing, its high-alert and hazardous medications. (See also EC.02.02.01, EP 8) ___ ___ ___

   Footnote: For a list of high-alert medications, see www.ismp.org. For a list of hazardous medications, see www.cdc.gov/niosh.

   Authors' Comments, Experiences, and Suggestions

   High-Alert Medications

   - *A written list of high-alert medications is required.*
   - *Consider a small number of high-alert medications, so the list is well known to all personnel who store, order, dispense, administer, and monitor medications. Most organizations have 5 to 10 medications on their list.*
   - *Medications often designated as high-alert include concentrated electrolytes (e.g., potassium chloride, potassium phosphate, and sodium chloride greater than 0.9%,), insulin, opiates and narcotics, anticoagulants (e.g., heparin, low molecular weight heparins, and warfarin), antineoplastic medications, neonatal and pediatric medications, epidural medications, patient-controlled analgesia medications, neuromuscular blocking agents, and look-alike/sound-alike medications.*

   Hazardous Medications

   - *A written list of hazardous medications is required.*
   - *Preventing Occupational Exposure to Antineoplastic and Other Hazardous Drugs in Health Care Settings, a NIOSH document, provides a list that can be used either in total, or as the starting point for an organization to develop its own list of hazardous medications.*[3]

2. The hospital has a process for managing high-alert and hazardous medications. (See also EC.02.02.01, EP 8; MM.03.01.01, EP 9) ___ ___ ___

   Authors' Comments, Experiences, and Suggestions

   High-Alert Medications

   - *Staff should be able to discuss the high-alert medications identified by the organization and the safeguards in place to prevent errors with them.*
   - *Many medications have a potential for an error with a serious outcome if staff is not trained adequately, patients are not informed, and information is not readily available.*
   - *All preparations containing high-alert medications should be compounded in the pharmacy.*
   - *High-alert medications that are easily confused (e.g., heparin vials and insulin vials) must be clearly labeled.*
   - *Staff should always double-check doses before administering high-alert medications.*

Yes **No** **NA**

- *Many organizations require documentation of the double check of a few medications. These often include insulin (including injections and the doses on infusion pumps) and heparin.*
- *Organizations should use distinctive packaging and labeling to the extent practical. The use of combinations of upper and lower case (e.g., "Tall Man") letters on medication labels can reduce errors due to look-alike names. For example, labeling medications as hydrOXYzine or hydrALAZINE can help prevent mistaking one medication for the other. Some manufacturers include these combinations on their labels. Organizations may also use these combinations on their internally created labels and on ADC, Computerized Prescriber Order Entry (CPOE), and pharmacy computer screens.*
- *External medications should be stored separately from medications intended for internal use.*
- *High-alert medications (e.g., neuromuscular blocking agents) should be stored only in patient care areas where they are clinically necessary and clearly marked as high-alert medications.*
- *In addition to segregation from other medications, limited access to high-alert medications and conspicuous warning labels also help to reduce the potential for errors.*
- *Organizations should consider using different color medication storage bins in pharmacy, patient care area, and clinic refrigerators to separate and distinguish insulin products with sound-alike and look-alike names (i.e., Humulin® and Humalog®, Novolog® and Novolin®, etc.) and IV solutions that are easily confused (e.g., bags with and without potassium chloride).*
- *High-alert medications should not be stored in open stock drawers or matrix drawers in ADCs. Separate (preferably lidded) bins should be used and the bins and/or lids should be distinctive and labeled as high-alert.*
- *Organizations should consider purchasing medications from different manufacturers to avoid packages that are visually similar.*

Hazardous Medications

- *See Chapters 10, 17, and 18.*
- *Safety materials and equipment include personal protective apparel (e.g., gowns, gloves, hair covers, shoe covers, eyewear, and face protection).*
- *Clearly labeled spill kits must be readily available to staff in areas where hazardous medications and materials are received, stored, compounded, or administered.*
- *There must be provisions for safe disposal of hazardous trash and waste, contaminated apparel, and contaminated work equipment (e.g., vials, ampuls, syringes, and needles) in accordance with laws and regulations.*
- *Antineoplastic and other hazardous medications must be prepared in a biological safety cabinet (BSC) or compounding aseptic containment isolator (CACI) specifically designed for the preparation of hazardous medications. These agents must never be compounded in a laminar air flow workbench (LAFW) or compounding aseptic isolator (CAI).*
- *BSCs or CACIs used for preparing hazardous medications must not be used for preparing non-hazardous medications.*

	Yes	No	NA
3. ☑ ⚠ The hospital implements its process for managing high-alert and hazardous medications. (See also EC.02.02.01, EPs 1 and 8)	___	___	___
5. For hospitals that use Joint Commission accreditation for deemed status purposes: The hospital reports abuses and losses of controlled substances, in accordance with law and regulation, to the individual responsible for the pharmacy department or service and, as appropriate, to the chief executive.	___	___	___

Authors' Comments, Experiences, and Suggestions

Report controlled substances discrepancies to the administrator to whom pharmacy reports and to the CEO of the hospital. Check with the hospital's legal department to identify the appropriate method (i.e. verbal, written, e-mail) of reporting.

Some pharmacies aggregate the information from unresolved controlled substance discrepancies and report it to the appropriate individuals and/or committees. Ensure that information from both automated and non-automated patient care and procedural units are included.

See MM.03.01.01, EP 3 for additional actions required for loss or theft of controlled substances.

Standard MM.01.02.01

The hospital addresses the safe use of look-alike/sound-alike medications.

Elements of Performance for MM.01.02.01

	Yes	No	NA
1. 🗎 The hospital develops a list of look-alike/sound-alike medications it stores, dispenses, or administers.	___	___	___

Note: One source of look-alike/sound-alike medications is The Institute for Safe Medication Practices (www.ismp.org/Tools/confuseddrugnames.pdf).

Authors' Comments, Experiences, and Suggestions

A written list is required.

Prior to 2010, The Joint Commission required a list of ten pairs, taken from a specific list published by The Joint Commission. This standard no longer requires a specific number or source.

Although not required by the standard, a list of approximately ten pairs is a practical number. A smaller number may not be adequate to prevent a significant number of interchanges and a larger number may be impractical for staff to use consistently.

The list should be developed from commonly confused drug pairs, including those reported through the hospital's error reporting system and those reported by safety-related organizations or in the literature. Surveyors may ask how the list was chosen.

	Yes	No	NA
2. The hospital takes action to prevent errors involving the interchange of the medications on its list of look-alike/sound-alike medications.	___	___	___

Authors' Comments, Experiences, and Suggestions

The specific actions are up to the organization and should be based on an analysis of the medication systems, recognized best practices, and specific strategies and general recommendations published in the literature.

Some hospitals consider different concentrations of the same medication as look-alike/sound-alike medications.

This requirement applies to medication storage areas throughout the organization—not just in the pharmacy.

This requirement applies to sample medications.

Some organizations require orders for medications with look-alike and sound-alike names to include an indication for use and/or to contain both brand and generic names.

Some organizations require individuals who give verbal or telephone orders for medications with sound-alike names to spell out the name of the medication.

Some organizations do not store medications in alphabetical order and require look-alike medications to be physically separated.

Organizations should determine if medications have the potential for errors due to look-alike/sound-alike names when adding them to their formulary, and take safety steps to prevent errors.

Organizations should use distinctive packaging and labeling to the extent practical. The use of combinations of upper and lower case (e.g., Tall Man) letters on medication labels can reduce errors due to look-alike names. For example, labeling medications as hydrOXYzine or HydrALAZINE can help prevent mistaking one medication for the other. Some manufacturers include these combinations on their labels. Organizations may also use these combinations on their internally created labels.

Some organizations use distinct displays (e.g., Tall Man letters, warning messages) on MARs, ADC and computer screens, and on bins in the ADCs.

Look-alike/sound-alike medications should not be stored in open stock drawers or matrix drawers in ADCs. Separate (preferably lidded) bins should be used, and the bins and/or lids should be distinctive and labeled as look-alike/sound-alike medications.

	Yes	No	NA
3. ⚠ The hospital annually reviews and, as necessary, revises its list of look-alike/sound-alike medications.	___	___	___

Authors' Comments, Experiences, and Suggestions

Documentation of the annual review and revision of the list should be recorded in the Pharmacy and Therapeutics (P&T) Committee minutes.

Yes **No** **NA**

SELECTION AND PROCUREMENT OF MEDICATIONS

Standard MM.02.01.01

The hospital selects and procures medications.

Elements of Performance for MM.02.01.01

1. Members of the medical staff, licensed independent practitioners, pharmacists, and staff involved in ordering, dispensing, administering, and/or monitoring the effects of medications develop written criteria for determining which medications are available for dispensing or administering to patients. ____ ____ ____

   Authors' Comments, Experiences, and Suggestions

   A written list of criteria is required.

   Organizations should document their criteria and ensure that they address all medication processes (e.g., ordering, dispensing, administering, monitoring).

   In many organizations, the P&T Committee or its equivalent develops and maintains the formulary list. However, any collaborative, multidisciplinary mechanism may be used provided the medical staff approves the medications on the list. (See Formularies in Chapter 13.)

   Staff often include representatives from nursing services, administration, nutrition services, infection control, quality/performance improvement, and laboratory.

   Staff involved in ordering, dispensing, administering, and/or monitoring medications include physicians, pharmacists, nurses, dentists, podiatrists, respiratory therapists, imaging technologists, physical therapists and aides, speech pathologists, paramedics, perfusionists, anesthesiology assistants, and licensed independent practitioners.

2. The hospital develops and approves criteria for selecting medications, which, at a minimum, include the following:
   - Indications for use (See also MM.05.01.01, EP 10) ____ ____ ____
   - Effectiveness ____ ____ ____
   - Drug interactions ____ ____ ____
   - Potential for errors and abuse ____ ____ ____
   - Adverse drug events ____ ____ ____
   - Sentinel event advisories ____ ____ ____
   - Other risks ____ ____ ____
   - Costs ____ ____ ____

	Yes	No	NA

Authors' Comments, Experiences, and Suggestions

A formulary addition request form (see Example 4-2), if used, should include the criteria for selection and an assessment of safety.

The formulary review should include specific approved indications. This may be limited to the FDA-approved indications, or may include other indications. (See MM.05.01.01, EP 10.)

Risks include look-alike/sound-alike medications, packaging and labeling, known incidence of adverse drug reactions, and other factors that affect patient safety.

The organization should review black box warnings to ensure it is prepared to use the medications appropriately and safely (e.g., perform laboratory tests and monitor patients). Black box warnings are listed in the FDA Safety Alerts, which are available on the FDA MedWatch Web site. (See Appendix.)

Other product labeling changes should be monitored and information provided to the P&T Committee.

Organizations should review the ISMP Medication Safety Alerts! *that are available by subscription from ISMP. (See Appendix.)*

Some organizations require a failure mode and effects analysis (FMEA) to identify the risks associated with medications proposed for inclusion on the list. (See Chapter 15.)

Evidence of approval by the medical staff (e.g., documentation in P&T Committee minutes) should show that the criteria were considered when selecting medications for inclusion on the list.

3. Before using a medication new to the hospital, the hospital determines the method to monitor the response of the patient. (See also MM.07.01.01, EP 2) ____ ____ ____

Authors' Comments, Experiences, and Suggestions

The method should be written and approved by the medical staff (e.g., by the P&T Committee).

If the labeling for a newly added medication requires specific monitoring or tests, the organization must ensure that it is prepared to perform them and report the results in a timely manner.

Before a newly added medication is dispensed or administered, pharmacists, nurses, physicians, and other care providers must be educated about the expected side effects of the medication and must know how to monitor patient responses. Information on the medication and monitoring guidelines should be readily available to care providers.

4. 📄 The hospital maintains a formulary, including medication strength and dosage. ____ ____ ____

Note 1: Sample medications are not required to be on the formulary.

Note 2: In some settings, the term "list of medications available for use" is used instead of "formulary." The terms are synonymous.

	Yes	No	NA

Authors' Comments, Experiences, and Suggestions

A simple alphabetical listing meets the standard (because only the medication names, strengths, and dosage forms are required). Organizations may include other information.

The list must include all medications available for dispensing or administration (e.g., herbal remedies, diagnostic and contrast agents, and blood derivatives). (See Medication Definition in this chapter.)

The list must include all medications used in clinics and off-site facilities if those areas are part of the hospital survey.

The Joint Commission does not require sample medications to be on the list. However, many organizations choose to include them. If the organization regularly dispenses and administers samples of medications (e.g., from ambulatory clinics), the medications should be approved and listed on the formulary.

The standard does not explicitly require on-site storage. However, there should never be undue difficulty or delay in patient care because a formulary medication is stored off site.

Sample Medications

- *Most organizations do not allow sample medications to be used in acute or ambulatory care areas of the hospital.*
- *If sample medications are permitted (such as for clinics or hospital-owned physician offices), the Medication Management standards apply, including*
  - *Availability of patient information (See MM.01.01.01.)*
  - *Safe storage (See MM.03.01.01.)*
  - *Safe use of look-alike/sound-alike medications (See MM.01.02.01.)*
  - *Clear and accurate orders or prescriptions (See MM.04.01.01.)*
  - *Safe dispensing practices (See MM.05.01.11.)*
  - *Proper labeling (See MM.05.01.09.)*
  - *Recording doses provided in the patient's medical record (See RC.02.01.01.)*
  - *Ability to retrieve recalled medications (See MM.05.01.17.)*
  - *Monitoring to determine the effects of the medication (See MM.07.01.01.)*
  - *Response to actual or potential adverse drug events, significant ad verse drug reactions, and medication errors (See MM.07.01.03.)*
  - *Patient education based on each patient's needs and abilities (See PC.02.03.01.)*

5. The hospital makes its formulary readily available to those involved in medication management. ___ ___ ___

Yes **No** **NA**

Authors' Comments, Experiences, and Suggestions

A current list must be available to all prescribers, nurses, pharmacists, and other care providers who may need it.

The formulary may be maintained in an electronic format (e.g., on the hospital's computer system). However, the organization must ensure that there is a process for accessing the formulary in case of a power outage or computer failure.

6. ⚠ The hospital standardizes and limits the number of drug concentrations available to meet patient care needs. ____ ____ ____

Authors' Comments, Experiences, and Suggestions

The hospital does not need to limit medications to one concentration, but the number of concentrations should be as limited as possible to fulfill clinical needs.

7. The hospital has a process to select, approve, and procure medications that are not on its formulary. ____ ____ ____

Authors' Comments, Experiences, and Suggestions

The process should be written and approved by the medical staff (e.g., by the P&T Committee).

The process for procuring nonformulary medications should require justification for the procurement.

The process does not require a complete review and approval of a nonformulary medication prior to procuring it. However, there must be written criteria to guide the pharmacy in procuring the nonformulary medication (e.g., review of safety concerns, need to educate staff who will dispense and administer the medication, cost of the medication, and amount to procure).

Organizations often require procurement of nonformulary medications to be approved by one or two designated, qualified individuals (e.g., director of pharmacy and/or chairman of the P&T Ccommittee).

Some organizations require a nonformulary medication request form for ordering nonformulary medications. (See Example 4-3.) The Joint Commission does not require such a form.

Although The Joint Commission does not require documentation, some organizations document approval on a nonformulary medication request form.

Organizations should periodically (e.g., quarterly) aggregate and analyze requests for nonformulary medications and use the findings to improve their formulary review process. (See Example 4-4.)

8. ☑ The hospital implements the process to select, approve, and procure medications that are not on its formulary. ____ ____ ____

	Yes	No	NA

Authors' Comments, Experiences, and Suggestions

Periodic review by the P&T Committee can be used to demonstrate this process.

Calculation of the percent of formulary/non-formulary use can be determined by line items, orders, or doses dispensed or administered.

9. Medications designated as available for dispensing or administration are reviewed at least annually based on emerging safety and efficacy information. ___ ___ ___

Authors' Comments, Experiences, and Suggestions

Formulary review and updating should reflect new knowledge about medications currently on the list, availability of new medications, and cost changes. Although the standards require a review at least annually, many organizations conduct more frequent (e.g., quarterly or continuous) reviews. Whatever the mechanism, each medication on the formulary must be reviewed at least once in a 12-month period.

Annual reviews should determine if medications should be deleted based on the organization's written criteria.

The medical staff's review and revision of the list should be documented (e.g., in P&T Committee minutes). Some organizations require a signed cover page of a master copy.

Physicians and other staff who prescribe medications should be kept informed of additions, deletions, and changes to the formulary (usually through P&T Committee reports, letters, newsletters, memoranda, etc.).

Outdated editions of formularies should be destroyed or archived and labeled so that it is clear that an updated edition replaced them. Outdated editions should not be available to care providers.

10. The hospital has a process to communicate medication shortages and outages to licensed independent practitioners and staff who participate in medication management. ___ ___ ___

Authors' Comments, Experiences, and Suggestions

Processes should be written and approved by the medical staff (e.g., by the P&T Committee).

Processes should address shortages that occur repeatedly or can be anticipated as well as unexpected shortages.

11. ☑ The hospital implements its process to communicate medication shortages and outages to licensed independent practitioners and staff who participate in medication management. ___ ___ ___

	Yes	No	NA

Authors' Comments, Experiences, and Suggestions

The pharmacy should maintain a list of shortages and outages and the communication provided to demonstrate compliance with the EP. (See Example 4-5.)

12. The hospital develops and approves written medication substitution protocols to be used in the event of a medication shortage or outage. ____ ____ ____

Authors' Comments, Experiences, and Suggestions

The pharmacy should maintain documentation of substitution and therapeutic interchange protocols, including the approval date, who or what medical staff committee approved it, the agent being substituted or interchanged and the specific interchange, and the date of the communication.

The organization must ensure the availability of medications for prophylaxis and treatment in the event of a disaster. See information about the organization's Emergency Operations Plan in the Emergency Management (EM) chapter of the CAMH. Because stockpiling of adequate supplies of medications locally may not be practical, there must be a mechanism for obtaining additional supplies from vendors and emergency supply depots (e.g., the Strategic National Stockpile).

13. ☑ The hospital implements its approved medication substitution protocols. ____ ____ ____

14. The hospital has a process to communicate to licensed independent practitioners and staff who participate in medication management about the medication substitution protocols for shortages or outages. ____ ____ ____

Authors' Comments, Experiences, and Suggestions

Education about these protocols may be through P&T Committee reports, letters, newsletters, memoranda, etc.

15. ☑ The hospital implements its process to communicate to licensed independent practitioners and staff who participate in medication management about the medication substitution protocols for shortages and outages. ____ ____ ____

Authors' Comments, Experiences, and Suggestions

The pharmacy should maintain a copy of communications concerning shortages and outages and a record of to whom the information was sent.

STORAGE OF MEDICATIONS

Standard MM.03.01.01

The hospital safely stores medications.

	Yes	No	NA

Rationale for MM.03.01.01

Medication storage is designed to assist in maintaining medication integrity, promote the availability of medications when needed, minimize the risk of medication diversion, and reduce potential dispensing errors. Law and regulation and manufacturers' guidelines further define the hospital's approach to medication storage.

Elements of Performance for MM.03.01.01

2. ☑ The hospital stores medications according to the manufacturers' recommendations or, in the absence of such recommendations, according to a pharmacist's instructions. ___ ___ ___

Authors' Comments, Experiences, and Suggestions

Prepackaging

- *Prepackaged medications should be in light-resistant containers to ensure their stability.*

Temperature Control

- *Temperatures in the pharmacy, sterile preparations area, and any other area used for storage of medications must be monitored to ensure that medications are stored at appropriate temperatures.*
- *Though The Joint Commission does not specifically require organizations to perform temperature checks or maintain a log of temperature checks, most organizations use some type of temperature monitoring to demonstrate compliance with the EP. (See vaccine information below for specific requirements.) If the organization requires temperature checks, the organization must specify the frequency. Many organizations require daily monitoring and recording of temperatures. Other mechanisms may be used (e.g., self-recording temperature devices, electronic temperature monitoring, and temperature alarms). (See Chapter 9 and Examples 4-6 through 4-8.)*
- *Organizations must ensure that medication refrigerators, freezers, and warmers contain an accurate and reliable thermometer. The thermometer should be calibrated at intervals defined by the organization, consistent with any laws or regulations. Standard EC.02.04.01 requires that organizations describe and implement processes to maintain and monitor equipment performance.*
- *In areas that are not open every day, organizations should consider using continuous temperature monitoring or thermometers that show high and low temperatures reached. The thermometer must be checked as soon as the area reopens (e.g., on Monday morning). The staff in that area needs to know how to detect if the temperature was out of range and who to contact for instructions on what to do with the medications.*
- *If a temperature is not within the appropriate range, the temperature log (or other record) must describe the action taken. The organization should have a defined process outlining disposition of medi-*

	Yes	No	NA

cations from a refrigerator, freezer, or warmer which has deviated from the recommended temperature range.

- *If the temperature of a medication storage refrigerator, freezer, or warmer has been out of range, the pharmacy should have a defined process to determine if the integrity of the medication has been compromised. In many cases, this may include contacting the manufacturer for information.*
- *Most surveyors expect medications to be stored in refrigerators and freezers designated solely for medications. Organizations should prohibit storage of medications in refrigerators and freezers that contain food, chemicals, reagents, and patient specimens.*
- *Organizations must ensure temperatures in receiving areas and storerooms are appropriate for the medications stored there. These areas are more likely to be subject to temperature extremes. Medications that are not stored in refrigerators or freezers may require storage at a controlled room temperature (maintained between 68°F and 77°F [20°C and 25°C] with occasional fluctuations to 59°F and 86°F [15°C and 30°C] permitted).*
- *Refrigerator temperatures for medications must be maintained between 36°F and 46°F (2°C and 8°C).*
- *Freezer temperatures for medications must be maintained between -13°F and 14°F (-25°C and -10°C).*
- *Freezers in some small (e.g., dormitory type) refrigerators will not maintain the required temperature range. Some medications must be maintained at temperatures below this range.*
- *Freezers used for drug storage should be separate units, not a section of a combined refrigerator/freezer. If freezers are used for drug storage, ensure that they are defrosted when necessary to maintain the required temperature.*
- *There is no standard temperature range for warmers. Warmer temperatures vary with the product stored. Different warmer temperatures are required for irrigation solutions in surgical areas, contrast media in imaging, and mannitol in pharmacy. Contact product manufacturers to receive written information concerning appropriate warming temperatures and the beyond-use dates to use.*
- *ECRI recommends that temperatures for warmers do not exceed 110°F (43°C). (See Appendix.)*

Vaccines

- *Storage of vaccines must be consistent with product labeling (check the temperature requirements for each product stocked). Temperatures in refrigerators and freezers used for the storage of vaccines should be monitored and recorded twice daily.*[4]
- *Ensure that emergency departments, clinics, physicians' offices, employee health department, and other areas where vaccines may be stored comply with the specific requirements for vaccines.*

Yes **No** **NA**

- *The CDC's National Center for Immunization and Respiratory Diseases (www2a.cdc.gov/vaccines/ed/shtoolkit/pages/temp_monitoring.htm) and the Immunization Action Coalition (www.immunize.org) have various resources available, including checklists that are valuable for clinics and temperature monitoring graphs that can be downloaded.*

Beyond-Use Dates for Refrigerated Medications Stored at Room Temperature

- *Beyond-use dates—not just the date opened—must be assigned to vials (e.g., succinylcholine, atracurium, insulin, lorazepam) taken from the refrigerator and stored at room temperature.*
- *Use the beyond-use dating information provided by manufacturers. Other information or data from the literature may only be used if there are no manufacturers' recommendations.*

IV Solutions

- *The stability of the product is shortened when the overwrap is removed from a parenteral solution bag. If the overwrap is removed, a new beyond-use date must be assigned in accordance with the manufacturers' recommendations.*

Flammable Products

- *Flammable medications must be stored safely. Flexible collodion, tincture of benzoin, acetone, ethyl chloride spray, and other flammable products must be stored in a cabinet designed for the storage of flammable products.*

Internal and External Product Separation

- *Agents for external use should be stored separately from agents for internal use.*

3. The hospital stores all medications and biologicals, including controlled (scheduled) medications, in a secure area to prevent diversion, and locked when necessary, in accordance with law and regulation. ___ ___ ___

Note: Scheduled medications include those listed in Schedules II–V of the Comprehensive Drug Abuse Prevention and Control Act of 1970.

Authors' Comments, Experiences, and Suggestions

The Centers for Medicare and Medicaid Services (CMS) definition of "secured" requires (1) that all drugs and biologicals be kept in a secure area, and locked when appropriate (2) drugs listed in Schedules II, III, IV, and V of the Comprehensive Drug Abuse Prevention and Control Act of 1970 must be kept locked within a secure area (3) only authorized personnel may have access to locked areas. (See Chapter 22.)

Locked storage for controlled substances in the pharmacy and throughout the organization is required. CMS regulations require locked storage in a secure area for all controlled substances. A few states specify double-locked

	Yes	No	NA

storage; a locked pharmacy door is counted as the second lock in many, but not all, of these states.

Keys to medication storage areas must be in the possession of authorized staff. They must not be left unattended in a drawer or other area.

There must be adequate security for lorazepam and other controlled substances in pharmacy and patient care area refrigerators (e.g., locked refrigerators, locked boxes in refrigerators, or locked doors to rooms in which refrigerators are located).

Organizations should be particularly attentive to controlled substances stored in anesthesia areas and procedural units (e.g., Schedule II controlled substances, thiopental, midazolam, ketamine, and testosterone).

Expired, recalled, or otherwise unusable controlled substances must be stored securely in a manner that prevents their distribution and diversion and ensures that they are disposed of safely and properly. Periodic inventories should be performed.

Inventories of controlled substances (including expired items) must be in accordance with state and federal regulations and the organization's policy. (See Examples 4-9 and 4-10.)

Wastage and destruction of controlled substances must be witnessed and properly documented in accordance with state and federal regulations and the organization's policy. Organizations should be particularly attentive to documentation of waste and destruction of controlled substances patches, patient-controlled analgesia (PCA) containers, epidurals, and other controlled substances infusions.

Surrender, loss, and theft of controlled substances must be properly documented in accordance with state and federal regulations and the organization's policy. (See Examples 4-11 and 4-12.)

Surveyors expect all controlled substances (e.g., diazepam, midazolam, and phenobarbital) stocked in emergency carts and containers to be locked. An unsealed cart or container or a cart or container with a breakable seal provides less control and accountability than carts and containers where controlled substances are stored using a "real" lock.

4. The hospital has a written policy addressing the control of medication between receipt by an individual health care provider and administration of the medication, including safe storage, handling, security, disposition, and return to storage. ____ ____ ____

Authors' Comments, Experiences, and Suggestions

Organizations must develop a written policy for how medications are handled from the time the health care provider receives the medication (or removes the medication from stock areas including ADCs) until the time it is administered. The policy should detail processes and metrics (such as times or temperatures that should not be exceeded) that include the elements listed in the EP.

	Yes	No	NA

Measurement of conformity with the times established in the policy can be used to demonstrate compliance with this EP.

Patient care unit bins used for temporary storage for medications sent to and from the pharmacy must be secure.

The organization must have written guidelines for the disposition of the remaining medication if the entire dose of the medication is not administered to a patient during a single medication pass.

The policy must address the disposition of medications at the end of the individual's shift.

The security of these medications must meet or exceed the minimum levels defined by the CMS regulations, Joint Commission standards, federal and state laws and regulations, and the organization's policy.

5. ☑ The hospital implements its policy addressing the control of medication between receipt by an individual health care provider and its administration. ____ ____ ____

Authors' Comments, Experiences, and Suggestions

Individual doses of medications should be removed from floor stock, medication carts, or ADCs and administered immediately to patients.

Medications cannot be stored in a fanny pack or the pocket of a health care provider.

Medications must be properly labeled until administered to a patient.

6. The hospital prevents unauthorized individuals from obtaining medications in accordance with its policy and law and regulation. ____ ____ ____

Authors' Comments, Experiences, and Suggestions

All drugs and biologicals must be stored in a manner to prevent access by nonauthorized individuals.

Persons without legal access to drugs and biologicals should not have unmonitored access to drugs and biologicals.

Persons without legal access to drugs or biologicals should not have access to keys or codes to medication storage rooms, carts, cabinets, or containers.

All Schedule II through V controlled substances must be locked in a secure area wherever they are stored throughout the organization.

Locked storage may be necessary for some medications and some areas. Some states require locked storage for all medications. Constant observation may be sufficient for other medications and other areas. Security must be sufficient to prevent diversion or tampering.

ADCs with security features, such as logon and password or biometric identification, are considered to be locked since they can only be accessed by authorized personnel who are permitted access to the medications. ADCs must be located in a secure area.

Yes	No	NA

Individuals who access ADCs must be able to obtain only the medications they are permitted to access within their scope of practice. For example, respiratory therapists must be able to obtain only respiratory therapy medications and imaging technologists must be able to obtain only medications they are authorized to administer (i.e., contrast agents).

The element does not stipulate that all medications must be stored in the pharmacy. Some medications (e.g., contrast agents and intravenous solutions without added medications) may be stored in other areas (e.g., central supply/materials management) provided they are secure and their integrity and stability ensured.

Keys to medication storage areas must be in the possession of authorized staff. They must not be left in a drawer or other area. Where combination locks are used, only authorized staff members are allowed to have knowledge of the codes. Most surveyors do not consider housekeeping personnel, security personnel, dietary personnel, orderlies, unit clerks, etc., to be authorized staff.

Time-outs set on electronic locking mechanisms of medication carts and ADCs should not allow unauthorized individuals to access medications after authorized staff members have left the device.

If the hospital permits bedside storage of medications for self-administered medications, the medications must be secure. However, if hospital personnel will administer the medications stored at bedside, the medications must be locked.

Anesthesia Medications

- *Security, control, and accountability for controlled substances, inhalation gases, and other medications in anesthetizing areas are often problematic. They must never be left unattended on the tops of anesthesia carts, in unsecured cart drawers, or in anesthesia workrooms. All controlled substances in these areas must be stored in an ADC, or locked in a substantially constructed cabinet or anesthesia cart.*
- *Anesthesia carts and workrooms must be secure (e.g., locked or under constant surveillance) when not in use.*
- *After hours when the OR is not being used, anesthesia carts must be properly locked in an area that prohibits tampering by unauthorized individuals.*
- *Inhalation gases (e.g., desflurane and sevoflurane) should be stored to reduce the potential for diversion and abuse.*

Medication Samples

- *Surveyors expect to see a control system (e.g., a perpetual log) that tracks the receipt and distribution of each medication sample. Although The Joint Commission does not require a log, many organizations find that a log is the best way to demonstrate adequate control. (See Example 4-13.)*
- *Each medical record (e.g., patient chart) must contain all medications ordered or prescribed and every medication dispensed or prescribed on discharge. This includes sample medications. (See RC.02.01.01, EP 2.)*
- *There must be an order for all medication samples dispensed, and all samples dispensed should be properly labeled for patient use*

Yes **No** **NA**

(including patient name, clear instructions for use, and any applicable cautionary statements).

- *Samples must not be repackaged.*
- *Surveyors expect medication samples to be in locked storage or under constant surveillance throughout the organization (including the emergency department, ambulatory clinics, and physicians' offices). If patients, visitors, manufacturers' representatives, and unauthorized staff can remove samples, the storage is not secure.*
- *The Prescription Drug Marketing Act of 1987 and the Prescription Drug Amendments of 1992 prohibit charging patients for medication samples.*

7. ☑ ⚠ All stored medications and the components used in their preparation are labeled with the contents, expiration date, and any applicable warnings. ____ ____ ____

Authors' Comments, Experiences, and Suggestions

Logs for batch preparations should include the components used, name of the manufacturer, the expiration date of the product, and the beyond-use date of the compounded preparation.

Organizations must assign beyond-use dates to chemicals that do not have expiration dates (e.g., one year from date of receipt).

Some chemicals (e.g., Monsel's solution and Lugol's solution) are available in unit-of-use containers that are labeled appropriately (including expiration dates).

8. ☑ The hospital removes all expired, damaged, and/or contaminated medications and stores them separately from medications available for administration. ____ ____ ____

Authors' Comments, Experiences, and Suggestions

Ensure that there is always a current list of all areas where medications are stored. This must include areas where medications are obtained from sources other than the hospital pharmacy. Most organizations require all medications to be obtained from the hospital pharmacy to ensure control and ability to access complete information in case of a recall.

Maintain a log (including those products sent to a reverse distributor for destruction) to demonstrate compliance with this EP.

This element should also apply to damaged and defective devices (e.g., insulin devices, infusion pumps, and IV administration sets).

Periodic inspections of medication storage, administration, and dispensing areas can identify most unusable medications and devices.

Unusable medications include those with broken packages or seals; those that are mislabeled, illegibly labeled, or whose labels are worn or missing; deteriorated medications; defective medications (e.g., improperly packaged medications, discolored medications, and medications whose integrity, effectiveness, and stability are questionable).

Expired controlled substances must be kept in secure, locked storage.

	Yes	No	NA
Containers or cabinets that contain expired and unusable medications should be clearly labeled "Outdated and Unusable. Do Not Dispense, Administer, or Use" or a similar warning. The containers should be segregated from usable medications. *Defective devices should be clearly identified with a distinctive label or tag stating "Defective. Do Not Use" (or a similar warning).* *If expired and unusable medications are stored outside the pharmacy, the storage area must be locked to prevent access by unauthorized individuals.*			
9. ⚠ The hospital keeps concentrated electrolytes present in patient care areas only when patient safety necessitates their immediate use and precautions are used to prevent inadvertent administration. (See also MM.01.01.03, EP2)	____	____	____

Authors' Comments, Experiences, and Suggestions

Concentrated potassium chloride includes strengths of 2 mEq/mL and greater. The Joint Commission does not consider piggyback bags of 20 mEq or 40 mEq per 100 mL to be concentrated solutions.

Sodium chloride greater than 0.9% is considered concentrated. This includes both injections for parenteral use and containers for respiratory use.

Concentrated electrolytes must only be stored in the pharmacy and controlled and monitored by the pharmacy. (Exceptions are noted below.)

Unless clinically necessary, concentrated electrolytes must not be stored in patient care areas. Prior to storage outside the pharmacy, complete a risk assessment and ensure safe practices are implemented to mitigate potential concerns.

When it is necessary for a concentrated electrolyte to be stored in a patient care area, access to the medication must be strictly restricted and controlled and special precautions taken to avoid inadvertent misuse. Precautions should include explicit warning labels, limited quantities and sizes, restricted access, separation (segregation) from all other medications, and education, training, and competence testing of staff.

Replace vials of concentrated magnesium sulfate in obstetrics with premixed solutions.

Staff should monitor patient care areas to ensure that concentrated electrolytes are not inadvertently brought to the areas from areas where their storage may be permitted or from outside services (e.g., a contract dialysis service).

Electrolytes in emergency drug containers (e.g., emergency drug trays or crash carts) should be in a ready-to-use form (i.e., already diluted). If an undiluted form must be stored, there must be special precautions against misuse. Precautions against misuse include limiting the quantity stored, size of vials, separated storage, and the application of warning labels.

	Yes	No	NA
10. ☑ ⚠ Medications in patient care areas are available in the most ready-to-administer forms commercially available or, if feasible, in unit doses that have been repackaged by the pharmacy or a licensed repackager.	____	____	____

	Yes	No	NA

Authors' Comments, Experiences, and Suggestions

Pharmacies should avoid providing medications in bulk containers to patient care areas.

Prepackaging must comply with FDA and United States Pharmacopeia (USP) requirements (e.g., maintaining appropriate records and the use of beyond-use dates that are suitable for the medication and the packaging materials used). (See Example 4-14.)

Prescription vials, counters for loose tablets/capsules, and plastic bags are not acceptable containers for prepackaging medications.

18. ☑ The hospital periodically inspects all medication storage areas. ____ ____ ____

Authors' Comments, Experiences, and Suggestions

Inspections must be documented. Any reasonable form may be used to document inspections. Inspection forms should include the criteria used in the inspections. Most surveyors prefer a separate form for each area (rather than a single form for multiple areas). Deficiencies should be noted and corrective actions should be documented. Many surveyors like inspection forms that provide spaces to document corrective action taken. Surveyors like to see evidence that inspection findings were shared with staff in the area (e.g., signature of the individual in charge of the area). (See Examples 4-15 through 4-17.)

Inspections should focus on safety of storage conditions (e.g., compliance with hospital criteria), security (especially for controlled substances), integrity (e.g., refrigeration and protection from light), removal of expired and other unusable medications and devices, identification and correction of hazardous conditions, and labeling.

Inspections should include all areas where medications are stored, dispensed, or administered (e.g., patient care units, ambulatory clinics, ADCs, emergency medication carts and containers, anesthesia, emergency department, imaging, surgery and post-anesthesia care areas, respiratory care, dialysis, nuclear medicine, laboratory, after-hours stocks, and areas where procedures are performed [e.g., endoscopy, interventional radiology, and cardiac catheterization]). (See Medication Definition in this chapter.)

Some state regulations may require a pharmacist to perform the inspections. However, most surveyors allow inspections by other professionals (e.g., nurses and pharmacy support staff) provided they are qualified. Surveyors often ask for evidence that individuals who perform inspections have competence assessment documentation. There should be evidence that a pharmacist reviews the inspection findings and has overall responsibility for the inspection process.

Current standards do not specify an inspection frequency. The organization must define the frequency. However, many surveyors expect inspections to be performed at least monthly and some state regulations may require monthly inspections. Surveyors expect organizations to comply with their policies and state requirements.

If the organization permits inspections to be less than monthly (e.g., quarterly), medications that are due to expire before the next scheduled inspection must be removed.

	Yes	No	NA
Organizations must show compliance with their inspection policy for 12 continuous months (e.g., every month for the last 12 consecutive months or, if the organization requires quarterly inspections, every quarter for the last four consecutive quarters).			
19. For hospitals that use Joint Commission accreditation for deemed status purposes: The hospital has a pharmacy directed by a registered pharmacist or a supervised drug storage area, in accordance with law and regulation.	___	___	___

Authors' Comments, Experiences, and Suggestions

A similar standard appears in the Human Resources chapter: For hospitals that use Joint Commission accreditation for deemed status purposes: A full-time, part-time, or consulting pharmacist develops, supervises, and coordinates all the activities of the pharmacy department or pharmacy services. (See HR.01.01.01, EP 28.)

Standard MM.03.01.03

The hospital safely manages emergency medications.

Rationale for MM.03.01.03

Patient emergencies occur frequently in health care settings. The hospital, therefore, needs to plan how it will address patient emergencies and what medications and supplies it will need. Although the processes may be different, the hospital treats emergency medications with the same care for safety as it does medications in nonemergency settings.

Elements of Performance for MM.03.01.03

	Yes	No	NA
1. Hospital leaders, in conjunction with members of the medical staff and licensed independent practitioners, decide which emergency medications and their associated supplies will be readily accessible in patient care areas based on the population served.	___	___	___

Authors' Comments, Experiences, and Suggestions

Joint Commission standards do not require specific emergency medications to be available in patient care areas. Although surveyors seldom contest the items stocked, they frequently determine if the kinds and quantities on hand agree with the list of approved emergency medications. The list of emergency medications should be reviewed regularly (e.g., annually) to ensure the needs of patients seen by the organization are continually met and to meet professional practice standards (e.g., Advanced Cardiac Life Support [ACLS] and Pediatric Advanced Life Support [PALS] guidelines).

The organization should limit the strengths and sizes of medications available in emergency carts and containers. Multiple strengths and sizes increase the potential for error. If multiple strengths and sizes are needed, there should be provisions (e.g., distinctive packaging, warning labels, and segregated storage) to decrease the potential for error.

Yes **No** **NA**

Emergency carts and containers should be standardized to the extent practical (e.g., standard concentrations of medications, standard sizes of medications, and standardized arrangement of medications and supplies).

Emergency medications should be stored at nursing and special care units (especially critical care units) and in emergency department or service areas, ambulatory care areas, and other designated areas. Pediatric emergency medications and equipment should be available in areas where they may be needed.

Medications and supplies for the treatment of malignant hyperthermia and neonatal resuscitation should be available in operating suites in labor and delivery units.

Products in emergency carts should be in a ready-to-use formulation and in dosages appropriate for the patient population.

Common antidotes and medications used for the management of poisoned patients should be kept where needed (e.g., the emergency department).

The imaging department should have an emergency medication supply for treating reactions caused by radiographic contrast media.

The Joint Commission does not specify the type of containers in which emergency medications and supplies are to be stored. Emergency medications may be kept in emergency carts and other containers (e.g., cabinets, boxes, and kits) and include all supplies of medications used in emergency situations (e.g., malignant hyperthermia carts, thrombolytic boxes, rapid sequence intubation boxes, and toxemia kits).

Emergency medication carts and containers must be secure (i.e., locked, in a locked room, or stored so that unauthorized individuals [e.g., patients, visitors, and staff] do not have access to them). Emergency medication carts and containers that are not secure must be under constant observation.

Although plastic seals are permitted, they are not as secure as a lock and do not prevent theft or tampering. If seals are used, numbered seals are preferred. A numbered seal may provide a higher degree of control and accountability if personnel record the number each time they inspect the emergency cart or container. The organization must use seals that cannot be removed and reattached without evidence of tampering.

Pharmacy should assume ultimate responsibility for the locking system. Locking mechanism should guarantee the integrity of the entire emergency container. All excess seals must be secured in the pharmacy department. Ensure that the pharmacy seal for the medication drawers in the crash cart is distinctive (e.g., a specific color). No other department should have a similar seal.

Surveyors expect the pharmacy to control the seals. Other mechanisms are permitted providing the security and integrity of the cart or container is assured.

It may not be feasible for the pharmacy to have strict control over seals for emergency medications in remote locations (e.g., off-site clinics). However, surveyors expect to see a process that ensures that emergency medications are readily available and their integrity maintained. Some pharmacists train individuals at remote locations in replacement procedures and how to control the seals. Pharmacy staff should visit the sites periodically (e.g., monthly or quarterly) to verify that the process works and it is being followed.

	Yes	No	NA

All emergency medication carts, kits, etc., throughout the organization must be included in the periodic inspection of medication storage areas. (See MM.03.01.01, EP 18 in this chapter.) The inspection must be documented.

Many surveyors expect periodic inspections of emergency medications and supplies to occur at least monthly. At a minimum, the inspection must ensure that all required medications are present and usable. Tags or stickers on the outside of carts or containers that indicate the expiration dates of the contents are helpful but are not sufficient to ensure that all required medications are present and usable (e.g., unbroken and not deteriorated).

Responsible health care professionals (e.g., nurses, respiratory therapists, and imaging technologists) should observe sealed carts and containers frequently to ensure that the seals are present and unbroken. They must also inspect sealed carts and containers regularly. The inspection frequency and process should be consistent throughout the organization. Most organizations require daily inspections to check the integrity of the seal. Other ways to ensure the integrity of emergency medications are acceptable to The Joint Commission provided they ensure that when emergency medications, supplies, and equipment are needed for a patient's care, all are present and in usable condition. (See Example 4-18.)

Departmental staffs must not establish and maintain their own (independent) emergency drug supply outside of the organization's emergency system.

2. ⚠ Emergency medications and their associated supplies are readily accessible in patient care areas. (See also PC.03.01.01, EP 8) ____ ____ ____

Authors' Comments, Experiences, and Suggestions

Medications must be secure, but accessible in an emergency.

Crash carts and other emergency medication containers must not be obstructed by equipment, furnishings, cartons, etc.

3. ☑ Whenever possible, emergency medications are available in unit-dose, age-specific, and ready-to-administer forms. ____ ____ ____

Authors' Comments, Experiences, and Suggestions

Dobutamine, dopamine, heparin, magnesium sulfate, nitroglycerin, and lidocaine should be in commercially available, ready-to-administer forms provided by the manufacturer.

If Broselow® tapes are used with carts or containers for pediatric emergencies, they should be the most current edition available and the same edition must be used throughout the organization. The required medication strengths listed on the tapes must be available in the carts or containers. If commercial preparations are not available, there must be clear directions for dilution.

6. ⚠ When emergency medications or supplies are used, the hospital replaces them as soon as possible to maintain a full stock. ____ ____ ____

Yes No NA

Authors' Comments, Experiences, and Suggestions

The replacement process must ensure that emergency medication carts or containers are restocked in a timely manner. The organization should define the time period for replacing medications and supplies and monitor the process to ensure compliance with the policies and procedures. A complete emergency medication container must be available in the department before removing the used container. At no time should an area with designated emergency medications be without them.

Most organizations require a complete cart replacement (i.e., after the cart is used, the entire cart is replaced).

Emergency medication carts or containers that have been used and are waiting restocking must be secure (e.g., removed from the patient care area and stored in central supply, pharmacy, or other secure area until they are restocked). Many organizations provide a different color seal that can be used to secure the used cart and indicate that the cart is incomplete.

Although current standards do not prohibit nurses or others from restocking, checking, and sealing emergency medication carts or containers, many surveyors insist that pharmacy personnel perform these functions. Some states regard restocking as dispensing and restrict restocking to pharmacists or pharmacy personnel under the supervision of a pharmacist.

Standard MM.03.01.05

The hospital safely controls medications brought into the hospital by patients, their families, or licensed independent practitioners.

Rationale for MM.03.01.05

A number of valid reasons exist for allowing the patient to use his or her own medications in an organization. The hospital needs to control the use of these medications in order to protect the safety of the patient and the quality of care provided. Therefore, the hospital needs to define its responsibilities for the safe use of these medications.

Elements of Performance for MM.03.01.05

1. The hospital defines when medications brought into the hospital by patients, their families, or licensed independent practitioners can be administered. ____ ____ ____

Authors' Comments, Experiences, and Suggestions

Patient's Own Medications

- *Each organization must determine if patients' own medications may be used and how they are stored, controlled, and administered.*
- *Some organizations prohibit the use of medications brought into the organization by patients or their families if the medications are on the organization's formulary and are available for use.*

	Yes	No	NA

- *Medications brought into the organization by patients or their families must be administered only in response to orders that permit their administration.*
- *The organization's policies must address the administration of investigational medications brought into the organization by patients or their families. (See Orders for Investigational Medications under MM.04.01.01, EP 1 in this chapter.)*

Prescribers' Medications

- *Most organizations prohibit prescribers from bringing medications into the hospital for patient use.*
- *Organizations should develop written policies that discourage physicians and other prescribers from using medications that are acquired from sources other than the organization.*
- *Organizations should develop written policies that define the procedure that a physician must follow to acquire and use medications from sources that have been approved by the organization.*
- *A committee that includes representatives from the medical staff and hospital leaders should approve each instance where medications from unapproved sources are requested for use in the organization.*
- *The process should comply with the formulary process requirements. (See MM.02.01.01.)*
- *If practitioners are allowed to bring in medications from other sources, the process to evaluate their integrity must include verification of identity, appropriate labeling, evidence that they have been stored under appropriate conditions (e.g., proper temperature), and are procured from a reputable source (i.e., they are not counterfeit or adulterated).*

2. ☑ ⚠ Before use or administration of a medication brought into the hospital by a patient, his or her family, or a licensed independent practitioner, the hospital identifies the medication and visually evaluates the medication's integrity. (See also MM.05.01.07, EP 3; MM.06.01.01, EP 4) ___ ___ ___

Authors' Comments, Experiences, and Suggestions

Medications brought into the organization by patients or their families must not be administered until identified. Although not required by The Joint Commission, a pharmacist should identify the medications. If physicians, nurses, or others identify medications that belong to patients, there should be a process to ensure the accuracy of the identification (including the availability of current references to aid in identification). The competence of individuals who identify medications should be documented.

Because of the difficulty in identifying and evaluating the integrity of liquid medications (including oral liquids, ophthalmics, and compounded preparations) in unsealed containers, many hospitals do not permit such items to be administered during the patient's stay.

Yes **No** **NA**

There should be a mechanism to alert nursing staff that patients' own medications have been identified and are suitable for administration. Some organizations attach a sticker that indicates the pharmacy identified the medication and the initials of the pharmacist who identified it.

If the medications are not to be used during the patient's stay in the facility, they should be packaged and sealed and either given to the patient's family or stored and returned to the patient or patient's family at discharge.

Storage of medications not to be used may be at the nursing unit, in the pharmacy, or at a central location (e.g., a valuables vault). Storage must be secure. Organizations often require the medications to be counted and sealed in the presence of the patient or the patient's family. They also document the process (e.g., record the kind and quantity of the medications on a log or other record). (See Examples 4-19 and 4-20.)

If the medication is a controlled substance, it must be counted, recorded, and held in locked storage in a secure area to prevent diversion. A representative of the organization (e.g., a nurse) should witness the counting and sealing of controlled substances.

Patients' own medications that are not claimed by the patient should be disposed of according to policy. Disposal after 30 days is suggested.

3. ☑ The hospital informs the prescriber and patient if the medications brought into the hospital by patients, their families, or licensed independent practitioners are not permitted. ___ ___ ___

ORDERING AND TRANSCRIBING MEDICATIONS

Standard MM.04.01.01

Medication orders are clear and accurate.

Elements of Performance for MM.04.01.01

1. 📄 The hospital has a written policy that identifies the specific types of medication orders that it deems acceptable for use. ___ ___ ___

   Note: There are several different types of medication orders. Medication orders commonly used include the following:

   - As needed (PRN) orders: Orders acted upon based on the occurrence of a specific indication or symptom
   - Standing orders: A pre-written medication order and specific instructions from the licensed independent practitioner to administer a medication to a person in clearly defined circumstances

Yes **No** **NA**

- Automatic stop orders: Orders that include a date or time to discontinue a medication
- Titrating orders: Orders in which the dose is either progressively increased or decreased in response to the patient's status
- Taper orders: Orders in which the dose is decreased by a particular amount with each dosing interval
- Range orders: Orders in which the dose or dosing interval varies over a prescribed range, depending on the situation or patient's status
- Orders for compounded drugs or drug mixtures not commercially available
- Orders for medication-related devices (e.g., nebulizers, catheters)
- Orders for investigational medications
- Orders for herbal products
- Orders for medications at discharge or transfer

Authors' Comments, Experiences, and Suggestions

A written policy is required for each type of order accepted in the organization.

As Needed (PRN) Orders

- *PRN orders for medications must be qualified to include the symptom or indication for use. There should be no question as to the prescriber's intent. For example, prn for nausea for 3 days, prn at bedtime for sleep, every 4 hours prn for pain scale of 5–7, and prn for temperature over 100°F.*

Standing Orders

- *Some organizations refer to "standing" orders as "standard" orders, "protocols," or other names.*
- *Organizations may limit standing orders to specific indications, specific medications, specific prescribers, or specific settings.*
- *Standing orders should be reviewed and approved periodically (e.g., annually) by the appropriate committee (e.g., the P&T Committee), printed or electronically accessible, and be available to physicians, nurses, pharmacists, and other staff who need them.*
- *Versions of standing orders that are no longer current should be destroyed or not available for use. An archived file with dates each standing order set was used should be maintained for the time period required by hospital record retention policy.*
- *When standing orders are prescribed, a copy of the standing order must be placed in the patient's medical record and authenticated by the prescriber.*

Automatic Stop Orders

- *The Joint Commission does not require organizations to have an automatic stop order policy. However, some state regulations do. Organizations that adopt an automatic stop order policy should consider the following:*

Yes **No** **NA**

- *Automatic stop orders should define when all or some of a patient's medication orders must be canceled. There should also be a mechanism for notifying the prescriber when these orders are about to expire (e.g., an electronic or printed notification or a stamp or sticker on the patient's chart).*
- *Blanket reinstatement of previous orders (including automatic stop orders) is not acceptable. (See MM.04.01.01, EP 8 in this chapter.)*

- *The Joint Commission does not specify medications that must be included in an automatic stop order policy. However, some states specify the medications. Medications frequently included in automatic stop order policies include antibiotics, anticoagulants, controlled substances, corticosteroid medications, antineoplastic medications, hypnotic and sedative medications, and oxytocic medications.*
- *The Joint Commission does not specify time limits for automatic stop orders. However, some states do. Time limits vary with the medication and type of organization. Policies often specify time limits ranging from 24 hours to 10 days. The trend is toward shorter time limits (e.g., 48–72 hours). Long-term care facilities and units often assign up to 30-day limits for medications.*
- *The CMS hospital Conditions of Participation stipulate that unless a specific time or number of doses is indicated, medication orders must be automatically stopped after a reasonable time that is predetermined by the medical staff. (See Chapter 22.)*

Titrating Orders

- *Titrating orders should include the amount of dose increase or decrease for each step in response to the patient's status, the titrating interval or frequency, and the maximum allowable dose.*
- *The order must include an objective parameter (e.g., a specific blood pressure, level on a pain scale, or level on a sedation scale) used to titrate the medication, including the endpoint.*
- *Some organizations establish titrating protocols for specific medications and require orders to state that the medications be given according to the protocol.*

Taper Orders

- *Taper orders should address the tapering steps, the amount of dose decrease for each step, and the tapering interval or frequency.*
- *Some organizations establish taper protocols for specific medications and require orders to state that the medication be given according to the protocol.*

Range Orders

- *Range orders contain doses or dosing time intervals (i.e., time between doses) that vary over a prescribed range, depending on the situation or the patient's status.*
- *Range orders should be limited and avoided entirely when possible.*

Yes No NA

- *The organization should specify how ranges should be expressed and how nurses should interpret the order.*
- *Organizations may use their pain measurement scale to manage pain medications if this process is permitted and described in their policies.*
- *Some organizations place a limit on the upper range of the order. For example, the American Pain Society's consensus statement on The Use of 'As Needed' Range Orders for Opioid Analgesics in the Management of Acute Pain (see Appendix) states that the maximum dose within the range for pain medications should not be greater than four times the minimum dose.*
- *Range order policies should guide health care personnel in selecting the appropriate dose and time for administering medications.*
- *The organization should identify how health care providers should select the starting dose and starting time interval between doses. For example, orders for 1 or 2 tablets will start at 1 tablet and, if needed, increase to 2 tablets. Orders for every 4 to 6 hours will start as every 6 hours and, if needed, decrease the time interval between doses to every 4 hours. Surveyors look for consistent interpretation of range orders among staff.*

Orders for Compounded Drugs Not Commercially Available

- *The organization should require the order to include the formula or refer to a standardized, approved formula that is on file in the pharmacy. The formula must be available to prescribers and care providers.*
- *Formulas for commonly used compounded medications or medication mixtures should be reviewed and approved by the medical staff (e.g., P&T Committee).*
- *If compounding is performed by an outside entity (e.g., a nuclear pharmacy or a pharmacy that compounds sterile preparations), the hospital leaders must approve the entity and the medical staff must be aware that the compounding is performed by an outside entity. See standard LD.04.03.09, EP 3 concerning leaders approving contractual agreements.*

Orders for Medication-Related Devices

- *Orders for medication-related devices should specify the devices and include all the information needed to ensure they are used appropriately and safely.*
- *Hospitals should adopt an organizational policy concerning patients' use of their own devices, such as infusion pumps. Risk Management should be involved in the discussion and the development of policies and consent forms.*

Orders for Investigational Medications

- *Standard RI.01.03.05 states that the hospital protects the patient and respects his or her rights during research, investigation, and clinical trials. See the* CAMH *for additional requirements relating to this topic.*
- *Orders for an investigational medication must be limited to prescribers authorized to order the investigational medication.*

Yes **No** **NA**

- *Orders for investigational medications shall be subject to the provisions of the investigational medication protocol.*
- *See MM.06.01.05 in this chapter.*

Orders for Herbal Products

- *The organization must control the use of herbal products (remedies) and other alternative therapies. They are medications and are subject to all of the provisions of the MM standards. (See Medication Definition in this chapter.)*
- *There must be a documented indication or reason for use for orders for herbal products.*

Orders for Medications at Discharge

- *Medications ordered for discharged patients must be included on the medication reconciliation form. The complete current list must be provided to the patient or the patient's family at discharge.*
- *Discharged patients should not be permitted to take the remainder of their inpatient medications home unless permitted by state regulations and organization policy and they are dispensed in an appropriate container and labeled appropriately for outpatient use.*
- *Medications may be dispensed to discharged patients only on written order of an authorized prescribing practitioner.*

Other Types of Orders

- *Hold orders must include the time, situation, or circumstance for initiating the hold and the time, situation, or circumstance for ending the hold.*
- *Some organizations consider hold orders to be discontinued orders unless a specific parameter is indicated (e.g., hold digoxin for one dose).*

2. The hospital has a written policy that defines the following: The required elements of a complete medication order. ___ ___ ___

Authors' Comments, Experiences, and Suggestions

A written policy is required.

Organizations as well as some laws and regulations often require medication orders to include the patient's name, medication, strength, route, rate, and frequency. They may require an indication for use, a limit on the number of doses, or a specific duration of administration for some medications.

Medication orders should clearly state administration times or time intervals between doses.

Terms such as "prn" and "on call" must be qualified so that there is no question as to the prescriber's intent (e.g., "q4h prn pain scale of 5-7" and "on call to OR").

The metric system should be used for ordering medications (as well as labeling and recording administration of medications).

	Yes	No	NA
3. The hospital has a written policy that defines the following: When indication for use is required on a medication order.	___	___	___

Authors' Comments, Experiences, and Suggestions

A written policy is required.

The element does not require the diagnosis, condition, or indication for use to be on a medication order. However, this information must be contained in the patient's medical record.

The organization must determine when the diagnosis, condition, or indication for use must be on a medication order.

Some organizations require an indication for use on all as needed (prn) medication orders and for specified high-alert medications (e.g., medications with look-alike/sound-alike). (See MM.04.01.01, EP 4 in this chapter.)

Although not required by the element, some organizations provide a place on the medication order to record the diagnosis, condition, or indication for use for each medication ordered.

	Yes	No	NA
4. The hospital has a written policy that defines the following: The precautions for ordering medications with look-alike or sound-alike names.	___	___	___

Authors' Comments, Experiences, and Suggestions

A written policy is required.

Some organizations include a warning in the pharmacy information system, alerting the pharmacy to double check orders for look-alike or sound-alike medications.

Some organizations require an indication or the use of both the generic and trade names in orders for look-alike/sound-alike medication orders.

	Yes	No	NA
5. The hospital has a written policy that defines the following: Actions to take when medication orders are incomplete, illegible, or unclear.	___	___	___

Authors' Comments, Experiences, and Suggestions

A written policy is required, which should include the actions to be taken if medication orders must be clarified.

To be considered complete, medication orders must contain all elements required by the organization's written policy (e.g., drug, strength, dosage form, and route). All missing elements must be clarified.

Pharmacists, nurses, and other qualified individuals must contact the prescriber to clarify medication orders that are incomplete, illegible, or unclear.

Medication orders that are incomplete, illegible, or unclear cannot be carried out until clarified by the prescriber.

Yes **No** **NA**

Organizations should not permit orders for multiple medications with the same indication without guidelines for which medication to use and when to use it.

The clarification should be entered in the patient's medical record as a new order.

Staff members who make entries (e.g., clarifications of orders) in patients' medical records must be authorized by the organization to do so. (See RC.01.02.01, EP 1.)

The organization must define which entries require countersigning and/or authentication. (See RC.01.02.01, EP 2 and EP 4.)

Medical record entries must be dated (see RC.01.01.01, EP 11) and the author identified. (See RC.01.02.01, EP 3.)

Abbreviations

A list of approved and prohibited abbreviations, symbols, acronyms, and dose designations must be established by the hospital. (See IM.02.02.01, EP 2 and 3.) ____ ____ ____

Prohibited abbreviations, symbols, acronyms, and dose designation units must not be used. (See IM.02.02.01, EP 2 and 3.) The Joint Commission specifically prohibits the following abbreviations and dose designations: ____ ____ ____

- U, u
- Q.D., QD. q.d., qd
- Q.O.D., QOD, q.o.d., qod
- MS
- MSO_4
- $MgSO_4$
- Trailing zero (e.g., X.0 mg)
- Lack of leading zero (e.g., .X mg)

Authors' Comments, Experiences, and Suggestions

A trailing zero may be used only when required to demonstrate the level of precision of the value being reported, such as for laboratory results, imaging studies that report the size of lesions, or catheter/tube sizes. It may not be used in medication orders or other medication-related documentation. (See note in IM.02.02.01, EP 2.)

If a surveyor finds prohibited abbreviations, Requirements for Improvement (RFIs) can be cited under medical staff standards MS.03.01.01 and MS.05.01.01, EP 2.

The organization's prohibited abbreviation list may include additional items of the organization's own choosing. The development of the expanded list should be interdisciplinary (i.e., have participation of pharmacists, nurses, physicians, and other health care providers). An interdisciplinary effort fosters greater acceptance of the items on the list. If an organization chooses to add additional prohibited items beyond those listed on The Joint Commission's core list, all items (including those added by the organization) will be surveyed as prohibited.

	Yes	No	NA

The prohibited list must be consistent throughout the organization.

The prohibited list applies to all orders, preprinted forms, and all medication-related documentation including free-text entry in electronic systems. This includes medication administration records (MARs), medication reconciliation documents, patient history and progress notes, consultation reports, and discharge summaries that contain medication-related documents.

The Joint Commission states that it is not the responsibility of nurses and pharmacists to manage the behavior of prescribers. The Joint Commission standards assign that responsibility to the medical staff.[5]

Contracted services must not use the terms on the organization's prohibited abbreviation list.

Pharmacists, nurses, and others who receive orders containing abbreviations not listed on the organization's approved abbreviation list or items on the prohibited abbreviation list must contact the prescriber for clarification and confirmation of the item if the order is unclear.

6. The hospital minimizes the use of verbal and telephone medication orders. ____ ____ ____

Authors' Comments, Experiences, and Suggestions

Verbal, as used in this element, refers to spoken (orally transmitted) orders rather than written orders. A telephone order is a specific type of orally transmitted order.

Some organizations differentiate between verbal and telephone orders. They will not allow verbal orders (except in emergencies, such as codes, or perioperatively from the surgeon) because the prescriber is present and could write the order.

The organization's policies and procedures should discourage the use of verbal and telephone orders. The process applies to all verbal and telephone orders. The requirement is not limited to orders for medications.

Staff must be prepared to discuss the steps the organization takes to minimize the use of verbal and telephone orders.

Some organizations prohibit telephone orders for non-urgent, high-alert medications (e.g., antineoplastic medications) or high-risk patients (e.g., neonatal and pediatric patients).

Medical staff rules and regulations or hospital policy should identify, by title or category, personnel who are qualified and authorized to accept (receive) and transcribe (record) verbal orders (e.g., nurses and pharmacists). This process must be in accordance with state and federal law. (See RC.02.03.07, EP 1 and EP 2.)

Organizations should designate the locations where verbal orders should be recorded.

The record on which the verbal or telephone order is written should be the final document (e.g., an order form or computer entry). The organization's process must require the person who receives the order or test result to read it back verbatim (i.e., exactly as written) to the person who gave it to verify that the order or test result was received and written correctly. (See PC.02.01.03, EP20.)

	Yes	No	NA

Verbal orders must reflect authentication as specified in the organization's policy and state or federal law or regulation (e.g., dated, timed, and authenticated with the names and signatures of the individuals who gave and received the orders). The records must indicate the individuals who gave, received, recorded, and implemented the orders. (See RC.02.03.07, EP 3.) The organization's policies must set the time period for verifying the order. The time period must be consistent with state and other regulations.

Verbal orders must be authenticated within the specified time frame and in accordance with state and federal law. (See RC.02.07.07, EP 4.)

Organizations can improve the accuracy of verbal and telephone orders and help ensure their accuracy and clarity by following the recommendations of the National Coordinating Council for Medication Error Reporting and Prevention (NCCMERP). (See Appendix.)

If necessary, words should be spelled out using a phonetic alphabet (e.g., alpha for a, bravo for b, charlie for c). A number of phonetic alphabets are available on the Internet by searching for "Phonetic Alphabet."

Numbers should be pronounced individually (e.g., one five for fifteen).

Read Back of Orders

☑ ⚠ Before taking action on a verbal order or verbal report of a test result, staff uses a record and "read back" process to verify the information. (PC.02.01.03, EP 20) ____ ____ ____

Authors' Comments, Experiences, and Suggestions

A repeat back is not the same as a read back. To read back an order or test result, it must first be written on paper or entered into a computer. Reading the order back while it is being written is a repeat back and does not meet the requirement of a read back.

Some organizations require documentation that verbal orders were read back to the prescriber (e.g., writing "read back" or "RBV" [if approved as an abbreviation for "read back verbal"] on patients' medical records). Not all organizations require documentation of the read back. Individuals who receive verbal orders must comply with their organization's policy.

Most voice mail systems do not meet the intent of the standard. When orders or test results are left on a voice mail message, the person who receives it must:

- *Call the person who gave it*
- *Receive the order directly*
- *Read it back to the person who gave it*
- *Receive verbal confirmation that the order or test result was written correctly.*

If the voice mail system incorporates all the steps in the read back process (including confirmation of correctness) in a timely manner that meets patient care needs, it will be acceptable. Organizations should contact The Joint Commission to confirm that their voice mail system meets the read back requirements.[6]

	Yes	No	NA

If electronic messaging (e.g., text messaging, email) is acceptable to the organization to communicate orders and test results, the individual receiving the order or test results must confirm receipt of the results (i.e., electronically or verbally). An electronic confirmation should contain identification of the confirming individual (e.g., electronic signature). A record of the confirmation should be entered in the medication record. The organization's policies and procedures should reflect the processes for the use of electronic formats in communication of orders and test results.[6]

Organizations should eliminate transcription of orders and test results to the extent possible. Order forms (or electronic entry) should be available to pharmacists and pharmacists should enter orders directly on the order forms. After reading back an order to the prescriber, the pharmacist should take the order form to the patient care area (or comparable electronic process), place it in the patient's medical record, and ensure that the appropriate patient care staff in the area is aware of the new order.

Writing orders or test results on paper or entering them in electronic medical records may not be practical in emergency situations where time is of essence (e.g., during a code or when performing sterile procedures). Nevertheless, accuracy is essential in these situations. If a read back is not practical or is impossible, persons who receive orders or test results may repeat them back instead of reading them back to the person who gave the order. When possible, the person who gave the order or test result should verbally confirm the repeat back. These orders must be written as soon as practical.[6]

7. The hospital reviews and updates preprinted order sheets, within time frames it identifies or sooner if necessary, based on current evidence and practice. ____ ____ ____

Authors' Comments, Experiences, and Suggestions

The P&T Committee often reviews preprinted orders. Other mechanisms for review and updating are permitted. A formal review and approval process should be in place.

There should be an initial review and periodic (e.g., annual) reviews thereafter. Reviews should ensure that preprinted orders are clear, contain all required elements, and reflect appropriate and safe medication usage. For example, terms on the organization's prohibited abbreviation list must not appear on preprinted orders.

Preprinted orders must comply with all medication management standards (e.g., not specify blanket reinstatement of orders). (See MM.04.01.01, EP 8 in this chapter.)

When using preprinted or electronic orders, the prescriber must sign the order or authorize its use before the order is initiated.

8. ⚠ The hospital prohibits summary (blanket) orders to resume previous medications. ____ ____ ____

Authors' Comments, Experiences, and Suggestions

This element applies to "continue pre-operative medications" orders, "continue home medications" orders, automatic stop orders, and all other or-

Yes **No** **NA**

ders. The organization can not exempt specific medications or types of orders from this element.

Organizations must require clarification of a "resume medications" order to list the previous orders (including medication name, strength, dose, route, frequency, and other elements of a medication order). Prescribers may write the orders or sign orders that are prepared for their signature. (See MM.04.01.01, EP 2 in this chapter.)

The reinstated orders must include all of the required elements of a medication order (including medication name, strength, dose, route, and frequency). That is, the order must be rewritten.

Some organizations use a function of their information system to create a list of current medications for the physician to continue or discontinue after invasive procedures or change in level of care.

9. ☑ A diagnosis, condition, or indication for use exists for each medication ordered. ___ ___ ___

Note: This information can be anywhere in the medical record, and need not be on the order itself. For example, it might be part of the medical history.

Authors' Comments, Experiences, and Suggestions

The organization should review patients' records to determine compliance with this element. Medical records' personnel often perform this function when they review patients' medical records.

Though the diagnosis, condition, or indication for each medication could be in admission notes, care plan, progress notes, or other area of the patient's record, the clearest method is to include it with the medication order. (See MM.04.01.01, EP 3 in this chapter.)

When the organization reviews and revises its preprinted or electronic orders, it should consider adding an indication or condition for each medication listed. Note, however, that adding the indication or condition is not required and might not be feasible for all medications.

Having this information only in the records of other departments (e.g., pharmacy patient profiles or imaging film jackets) does not comply with the element. The information must be contained in the patient's medical record.

This element applies to all medications (including herbal remedies, vitamins, and over-the-counter drugs) ordered in any setting in the organization. There must be an indication (or reason) for each medication ordered. (See Medication Definition in this chapter.)

10. The hospital defines, in writing, the circumstances for which weight-based dosing is required for pediatric populations. (See also MM.01.01.01, EP 1) ___ ___ ___

Yes No NA

Authors' Comments, Experiences, and Suggestions

A written policy is required.

Organizations often require weight-based dosing for aminoglycosides, other antibiotics, specific high-alert medications, and for children less than a specific age or weight. The decision is up to the organization.

13. ☑ ⚠ The hospital implements its policies for medication orders. ___ ___ ___

14. The hospital requires an order from a doctor of medicine or osteopathy, or, as permitted by law and regulation, a hospital-specific protocol(s) approved by a doctor of medicine or osteopathy, to administer influenza and pneumococcal polysaccharide vaccines. ___ ___ ___

Authors' Comments, Experiences, and Suggestions

The element corresponds with CMS requirements and allows for appropriate staff, other than physicians, to administer these vaccines without an individual physician order.

PREPARING AND DISPENSING MEDICATIONS

Standard MM.05.01.01

A pharmacist reviews the appropriateness of all medication orders for medications to be dispensed in the hospital.

Elements of Performance for MM.05.01.01

1. Before dispensing or removing medications from floor stock or from an automated storage and distribution device, a pharmacist reviews all medication orders or prescriptions unless a licensed independent practitioner controls the ordering, preparation, and administration of the medication or when a delay would harm the patient in an urgent situation (including sudden changes in a patient's clinical status), in accordance with law and regulation. ___ ___ ___

Authors' Comments, Experiences, and Suggestions

The Joint Commission defines a licensed independent practitioner (LIP) as any individual permitted by law and by the organization to provide care, treatment, and services, without direction or supervision, within the scope of the individual's license and consistent with individually granted clinical privileges.[1]

This element applies to all medications and all patient care areas. No medication or patient care area is specifically exempt from this requirement. For

Yes	No	NA

example, the element applies to preprinted labor and delivery orders, orders for respiratory therapy medications, orders for emergency department patients who are waiting for transfer to an inpatient room, orders for preoperative patients in an ambulatory surgery unit, post anesthesia care unit (PACU), dialysis units, and orders for patients in a 23-hour observation unit.

Nurses are not permitted to administer medications they obtain from floor stock or ADCs if a pharmacist has not reviewed the order. (See EP 1 of this standard for exceptions.)

Cardiopulmonary arrest is an example of a situation in which the resulting delay would harm the patient.

The Joint Commission does not define a time for "when delay would harm the patient." The organization must determine this.

The name of the pharmacist who reviewed and entered the medication order should be recorded.

Interim Measure for Emergency Department[7]

An interim measure is in effect (as of March 2010) that allows organizations to implement two exceptions for orders written for patients in the emergency department (ED).

Implementation of the two exceptions to this standard will be permitted as follows:

EXCEPTION 1: ...unless a licensed independent practitioner controls the ordering, preparation, and administration of the medication. ___ ___ ___

IMPLEMENTATION: When using this exception, medications ordered by a licensed independent practitioner (LIP) in the ED can be processed, including administration of the medication, by an RN or other licensed staff with medication administration responsibilities (e.g., respiratory therapist) in accordance with law and regulation. An LIP will not be required to remain at the bedside when the medication is administered. However, the LIP must remain available to provide immediate intervention should a patient experience an adverse medication event.

EXCEPTION 2: ...in urgent situations when the resulting delay would harm the patient, including situations in which the patient experiences a sudden change in clinical status. ___ ___ ___

IMPLEMENTATION: When using this exception, urgent care situations will be defined by the LIP who is providing care to the patient.

Authors' Comments, Experiences, and Suggestions

Though not required, many organizations review emergency department orders as they do in the rest of the organization.

Some organizations have specific medications that require a pharmacist review prior to administration.

Since patients in the emergency department awaiting inpatient beds are considered inpatients, this exemption does not apply.

	Yes	No	NA
Ensure that policy defines the proximity of the LIP in the ED needed to provide immediate intervention should a patient experience an adverse medication event.			

Interim Measure for Radiology Department

An interim measure is in effect (as of March 2010) for contrast media orders in the radiology department.

A hospital's radiology services (including hospital-associated ambulatory radiology) will be allowed to define, through protocol or policy, the role of the LIP in the direct supervision of a patient during and after IV contrast media is administered. The protocol/policy is to be approved by the medical staff and the role of the LIP is to be defined so that there can be timely intervention by the LIP in the event of a patient emergency. The Joint Commission recommends that organizations refer to the American College of Radiology Practice Guidelines for the Use of Intravascular Contrast Media during development of the protocol/policy.[8] ____ ____ ____

Oral/Rectal contrast media may be administered in imaging areas without prior pharmacy review as long as the following standards and safeguards are followed:

- The organization adopts clinical practice guidelines or approved screening tools to address the safe administration of contrast media that are approved by the medical staff and pharmacy (See LD.04.04.07.) ____ ____ ____
- Only trained, designated individuals retrieve medications from a limited set of medications ____ ____ ____
- The appropriateness of the medication is reviewed by a health care professional determined to be qualified by the organization ____ ____ ____
- The organization implements quality control procedures to prevent retrieval errors (e.g., a double check, bar-coding) ____ ____ ____
- A pharmacist is available on-call if needed ____ ____ ____
- Retrospectively, the organization evaluates its system by sampling records where contrast media were administered without prior pharmacy review to determine if the system as designed is working or if there are opportunities for improvement (See MM.08.01.01.)[9] ____ ____ ____

Authors' Comments, Experiences, and Suggestions

The American College of Radiology's Practice Guidelines are available at www.acr.org/SecondaryMainMenuCategories/quality_safety/guidelines/dx/iv_contrast.aspx.[10]

Pharmacy must review all radiology non-contrast medication orders unless a licensed independent practitioner, such as a radiologist or an anesthesiologist, is physically present at the patient's side when the medication is given and has done the review himself or herself. (Note: In urgent situations when the risk of delay exceeds the risk of a medication error due to lack of a pre-administration review, this review may be deferred.)

IV contrast may be administered in imaging areas without prior pharmacy review if medical staff-approved protocols or policies define the role of the LIP in the direct supervision of a patient during and after IV contrast media

Yes **No** **NA**

is administered. The protocols/policies must ensure that there can be timely intervention by the LIP in the event of a patient emergency (i.e., proximity defined).

Pharmacy must review orders for contrast media that will be administered on inpatient units.

Sample forms, policies, etc. for contrast agents are available at www.ashp.org/Import/PRACTICEANDPOLICY/PracticeResourceCenters/ContrastMedia.aspx.

2. ☑ When an on-site pharmacy is not open 24 hours a day, 7 days a week, a health care professional determined to be qualified by the hospital reviews the medication order in the pharmacist's absence. ___ ___ ___

Authors' Comments, Experiences, and Suggestions

Qualified health care professionals include nurses and physicians. Other health care professionals may be designated provided they are qualified. The organization should assess the competence of all health care professionals who review medication orders in the absence of a pharmacist, and maintain a current list.

Organizations should develop a policy and procedure specifying when nurses and other care providers are allowed to obtain medications (e.g., from floor stock or an ADC prior to a pharmacist review of the medication order). (See MM.05.01.13 in this chapter.)

3. ☑ When an on-site pharmacy is not open 24 hours a day, 7 days a week, a pharmacist conducts a retrospective review of all medication orders during this period as soon as a pharmacist is available or the pharmacy opens. ___ ___ ___

Authors' Comments, Experiences, and Suggestions

A pharmacist should conduct the retrospective review as soon as possible, and at a minimum within 24 hours. The review must be documented (e.g., in a night log).

The record should include the time the medication was obtained, the patient's name and other required hospital identifier, and the medication name, strength, and dosage form.

4. ☑ ⚠ All medication orders are reviewed for the following: Patient allergies or potential sensitivities. ___ ___ ___

Authors' Comments, Experiences, and Suggestions

A method to demonstrate that allergy information is available for all patients should be developed.

5. ☑ ⚠ All medication orders are reviewed for the following: Existing or potential interactions between the medication ordered and food and medications the patient is currently taking. ___ ___ ___

	Yes	No	NA
6. ☑ ⚠ All medication orders are reviewed for the following: The appropriateness of the medication, dose, frequency, and route of administration.	____	____	____
7. ☑ ⚠ All medication orders are reviewed for the following: Current or potential impact as indicated by laboratory values.	____	____	____
8. ☑ ⚠ All medication orders are reviewed for the following: Therapeutic duplication.	____	____	____
9. ☑ ⚠ All medication orders are reviewed for the following: Other contraindications.	____	____	____
10. ☑ ⚠ All medication orders are reviewed for the following: Variation from the hospital's indications for use. (See also MM.02.01.01, EP 2)	____	____	____

Authors' Comments, Experiences, and Suggestions

Although orders for the use of approved medications for unlabeled indications (i.e., off-label use) may be legal and commonplace, it may, in some cases, be inappropriate and potentially dangerous. The organization's rules, regulations, or policies should provide guidelines for controlling the off-label use of medications and the organization should obtain legal advice if the safe use of these medications is in doubt.

"Pharmacists' role in facilitating evidence-based prescribing for unlabeled use of medications" from the American Journal of Health-System Pharmacy may be helpful in developing policies.[11]

There should be a mechanism to ensure that medications are ordered for indications approved by the hospital.

	Yes	No	NA
11. ☑ ⚠ After the medication order has been reviewed, all concerns, issues, or questions are clarified with the individual prescriber before dispensing.	____	____	____

Authors' Comments, Experiences, and Suggestions

The clarification of concerns, issues, or questions with the individual prescriber should be documented. (See Example 4-21.)

Standard MM.05.01.07

The hospital safely prepares medications.

Elements of Performance for MM.05.01.07

	Yes	No	NA
1. ⚠ A pharmacist, or pharmacy staff under the supervision of a pharmacist, compounds or admixes all compounded sterile preparations except in urgent situations in which a delay could harm the patient or when the product's stability is short.	____	____	____

Yes **No** **NA**

Authors' Comments, Experiences, and Suggestions

All areas where sterile preparations are compounded should be in compliance with USP Chapter <797>.[12] *(See Chapter 19 for information about USP Chapter <797>.) If sterile preparations are mixed outside of USP Chapter <797> compliant facilities, they should be limited to the immediate use definition in USP Chapter <797>.*

The use of commercially available, premixed sterile medications as well as commercially available, point-of-care activated parenteral solution bag and medication vial combinations may eliminate the need for preparing many sterile preparations outside the pharmacy.

The pharmacy should provide premixed oxytocin and epidural infusions for obstetrics, heparin for cardiac catheterization laboratory and interventional radiology suites, dipyridamole and dobutamine infusions for cardiac stress testing, and other compounded sterile preparations for procedural areas (e.g., sincalide for nuclear medicine).

When parenteral nutrition services are provided, there must be mechanisms to assure safe preparation and dispensing of parenteral nutrition preparations (e.g., calibration of automatic compounders, verification of fluids and additives attached to automatic compounders, and testing of the final product at the end of the process).

Routine preparation of epidural medications by anesthesia providers should be discouraged.

The organization must ensure the quality and integrity of medications obtained from outside sources and provide for their appropriate storage and safe use.

If the organization uses an outside pharmacy for any sterile compounding, the organization should obtain a written statement that the compounding pharmacy meets or exceeds the requirements of USP Chapter <797>.

2. ☑ ⚠ Staff use clean or sterile techniques and maintain clean, uncluttered, and functionally separate areas for product preparation to avoid contamination of medications. ___ ___ ___

Authors' Comments, Experiences, and Suggestions

See Chapter 9 and NPSG Goal 7 in Chapter 6.

Compliance with the requirements of USP Chapter <797> will help ensure the sterility of parenteral medications and thus reduce the risk of health care–acquired infections.

Nursing and other personnel who mix compounded sterile preparations for immediate use must comply with the Immediate Use requirements listed in USP Chapter <797>. (See Chapter 19.)

Staff who compound or prepare sterile preparations (e.g., pharmacy personnel, nursing, respiratory therapists, and radiology and nuclear medicine technologists) must be educated, trained, and competent to do so.

There must be evidence that primary engineering controls (laminar airflow workbenches, biological safety cabinets, compounding aseptic isolators, and

Yes **No** **NA**

compounding aseptic containment isolators) are maintained according to the organization's policy (e.g., through certification records).

Intravenous admixtures and other sterile preparations addressed in this element must not be prepared on a medication cart in a patient care area as these are not functionally separate.

When appropriate, filter needles/straws should be used to withdraw medications from glass ampuls.

There are specific requirements for preparation of radiopharmaceuticals in USP Chapter <797>.

There are specific requirements for preparation of allergy extracts in USP Chapter <797>.

3. ⚠ During preparation, staff visually inspect the medication for particulates, discoloration, or other loss of integrity. (See also MM.03.01.05, EP 2; MM.06.01.01, EP 4) ___ ___ ___

4. ⚠ The hospital uses a laminar airflow hood or other ISO Class 5 environment in the pharmacy for preparing intravenous (IV) admixture or any sterile product that will not be used within 24 hours. ___ ___ ___

Authors' Comments, Experiences, and Suggestions

A class 100 environment is equivalent to an ISO 5 environment.

USP Chapter <797> establishes a 1-hour limit for the use of immediate use sterile preparations.

5. ⚠ For hospitals that use Joint Commission accreditation for deemed status purposes: Medications are prepared and administered in accordance with the orders of a licensed independent practitioner responsible for the patient's care, and in accordance with law and regulation. ___ ___ ___

   Footnote: For law and regulation guidance pertaining to those responsible for the care of patients, refer to 42 CFR 482.12(c).

Authors' Comments, Experiences, and Suggestions

See Appendix for a link to the Code of Federal Regulation (CFR).

6. ⚠ For hospitals that use Joint Commission accreditation for deemed status purposes: In-house preparation of radiopharmaceuticals is done by, or under the supervision of, an appropriately trained registered pharmacist or doctor of medicine or osteopathy. ___ ___ ___

Yes No NA

Authors' Comments, Experiences, and Suggestions

The hospital's nuclear medicine department should obtain unit-dose preparations from their contracted nuclear pharmacy.

"Procedure Guideline for the Use of Radiopharmaceuticals 4.0" from the Journal of Nuclear Medicine Technology may be helpful in developing a hospital policy.[13]

Standard MM.05.01.09

Medications are labeled.

Rationale for MM.05.01.09

A label on every medication and medication container has long been a standard of practice by the pharmacy profession and is required by law and regulation. A standardized method to label medications and containers promotes medication safety.

Elements of Performance for MM.05.01.09

1. ⚠ Medication containers are labeled whenever medications are prepared but not immediately administered. ___ ___ ___

   Note: An immediately administered medication is one that an authorized staff member prepares or obtains, takes directly to a patient, and administers to that patient without any break in the process.

Authors' Comments, Experiences, and Suggestions

All reconstituted and mixed medications (including oral liquid antibiotics, oral contrast media, and diagnostic agents) must be labeled with the reconstitution or dilution date and/or date beyond which the medication should not be used. The concentrations of reconstituted and diluted medications must be noted on labels.

Labels for medications and medication containers are also covered by NPSG.03.04.01. (See Chapter 6.)

The organization must not allow unlabeled containers of medications in any area of the organization (e.g., unlabeled medication cups and unlabeled syringes that are prefilled for later use).

The organization must not allow empty medication containers that are prelabeled for future use (e.g., pre-labeled empty syringes) to be stored in any area of the organization.

The Association of periOperative Registered Nurses (AORN) practice guidelines includes information on appropriate labeling of medications on and off the sterile field. (See Appendix.)

	Yes	No	NA
2. Information on medication labels is displayed in a standardized format, in accordance with law and regulation and standards of practice.	____	____	____

Authors' Comments, Experiences, and Suggestions

There should be evidence that medications are labeled in a standardized manner.

All medications (including inpatient medications, metered dose inhalers, parenteral nutrition products, diagnostic and contrast agents, floor stock, sample medications, medications obtained from other pharmacies, and medications dispensed to ambulatory care and home care patients) must be labeled appropriately and safely and include accessory or cautionary statements and beyond-use dates.

Check FDA, USP, and state regulations for assigning beyond-use dates to prepackaged medications (e.g., unit-dose packages). (See Appendix.)

Medications dispensed to discharged and ambulatory care patients must be labeled for outpatient use and in an appropriate child-resistant container. Instructions for storage and administration of the medication must be clear. Some states require a separate pharmacy permit for this activity.

Although not included in The Joint Commission's definition of medication, disinfectants and cleaning products should be labeled appropriately and safely and include accessory and cautionary statements. (See Medication Definition in this chapter.)

	Yes	No	NA
3. ⚠ All medications prepared in the hospital are correctly labeled with the following: Medication name, strength, and amount (if not apparent from the container).	____	____	____
4. ⚠ All medications prepared in the hospital are correctly labeled with the following: Expiration date when not used within 24 hours.	____	____	____

Authors' Comments, Experiences, and Suggestions

Organizations should check manufacturers' recommendations, USP, FDA, and state requirements for assigning beyond-use dates to prepackaged and compounded preparations.

	Yes	No	NA
5. ⚠ All medications prepared in the hospital are correctly labeled with the following: Expiration time when expiration occurs in less than 24 hours.	____	____	____
6. ⚠ All medications prepared in the hospital are correctly labeled with the following: The date prepared and the diluent for all compounded intravenous admixtures and parenteral nutrition formulas.	____	____	____

Authors' Comments, Experiences, and Suggestions

EPs 2 through 6 apply to medications prepared and dispensed by the pharmacy, as well as all other medications and sterile preparations prepared or admixed outside of a USP Chapter <797> compliant area (e.g., anesthesia

	Yes	No	NA

medication syringes in anesthesia areas, oral contrast agents in the imaging department).

7. ⚠ When preparing individualized medications for multiple patients, the label also includes the following: The patient's name. ___ ___ ___

Authors' Comments, Experiences, and Suggestions

The Joint Commission does not provide complete guidelines for labeling medications. The following is typical in many organizations:

- *Patient's name and other approved identifiers*
- *Patient location, if applicable*
- *Medication name, strength, and dosage form*
- *Appropriate accessory or cautionary statements (e.g., shake well)*
- *Beyond-use date, when applicable*
- *Manufacturer (if not clearly apparent from the brand name)*
- *Manufacturer's lot number or pharmacy control number*

The Joint Commission does not provide complete guidelines for labeling parenteral and sterile preparations. The following is typical in many organizations:

- *Patient's name and other approved identifiers*
- *Patient location, if applicable*
- *Name and volume of the parenteral solution (i.e., the base solution or diluent)*
- *Generic medication name (and trade name or manufacturer, if applicable) and amount added*
- *Name or identifying code (e.g., initials) of the individual who prepared the solution*
- *Name or identifying code (e.g., initials) of the individual who checked the final preparation*
- *Rate of administration*
- *Date and time prepared*
- *Date and time to be administered*
- *Beyond-use date and time*
- *Supplemental instructions (e.g., storage information)*

8. When preparing individualized medications for multiple patients, the label also includes the following: The location where the medication is to be delivered. (See also NPSG.01.01.01, EP 1) ___ ___ ___

	Yes	No	NA
Note: The location is not to be used as a patient identifier during administration of a medication, as indicated by NPSG.01.01.01, EP 1.			
9. ⚠ When preparing individualized medications for multiple patients, the label also includes the following: Directions for use and applicable accessory and cautionary instructions.	___	___	___
10. ⚠ When an individualized medication(s) is prepared by someone other than the person administering the medication, the label includes the following: The patient's name.	___	___	___
11. When an individualized medication(s) is prepared by someone other than the person administering the medication, the label includes the following: The location where the medication is to be delivered. (See also NPSG.01.01.01, EP 1)	___	___	___
Note: The location is not to be used as a patient identifier during administration of a medication, as indicated by NPSG.01.01.01, EP 1.			
12. ⚠ When an individualized medication(s) is prepared by someone other than the person administering the medication, the label includes the following: Directions for use and applicable accessory and cautionary instructions.	___	___	___

Standard MM.05.01.11

The hospital safely dispenses medications.

Elements of Performance for MM.05.01.11

	Yes	No	NA
1. ☑ The hospital dispenses quantities of medications that are consistent with patient needs.	___	___	___

Authors' Comments, Experiences, and Suggestions

The pharmacy should not dispense bulk quantities of medications.

The organization should determine the quantities of medications to dispense. Many organizations limit quantities to a 24-hour supply.

	Yes	No	NA
2. ☑ The hospital dispenses medications and maintains records in accordance with law and regulation, licensure, and professional standards of practice.	___	___	___

Note: Dispensing practices and record keeping include antidiversion strategies.

Yes **No** **NA**

Authors' Comments, Experiences, and Suggestions

A licensed pharmacist must prepare and dispense all medications and monitor all medication preparation and dispensing performed by nonpharmacists.

The Joint Commission expects pharmacies to meet state requirements for the use of nonpharmacists.

Medications must be dispensed only on the order of a legally authorized prescriber who has been granted clinical privileges to write such orders. (See MM.04.01.01, EP 14 for an exception to this.)

The pharmacy should have a mechanism to determine whether medication orders are written by individuals who are currently privileged to prescribe (e.g., a written or electronic list of authorized prescribers).

Pharmacy staff should be aware of state laws and regulations and organizational policies concerning practitioners other than physicians who can order medications (e.g., dentists, podiatrists, optometrists, advanced practice registered nurses, certified nurse midwives, and physician assistants).

Pharmacy staff should be able to describe how they verify that individuals are permitted to prescribe medications and their prescribing restrictions, if any.

Pharmacy staff should have a mechanism to verify that individuals who prescribe controlled substances are legally permitted to do so (i.e., have a valid DEA number).

Electronic data analysis tools and proactive diversion assessments should be routinely incorporated into practice to identify concerns as soon as possible.

Medications dispensed to a discharged patient must be recorded in the patient's medical record.

Medication Containers

- *Medications must be dispensed in clean containers that are appropriate for the contents and do not interact physically with the medication or otherwise absorb, adsorb, or deleteriously affect their contents. Containers must protect the contents from light, moisture, temperature, air, and handling, as required.*
- *Medications dispensed to outpatients must be in child-resistant containers.*
- *Medications dispensed from the emergency department (if such dispensing is permitted) must be in appropriate containers that comply with the state's dispensing regulations.*

3. ☑ ⚠ The hospital dispenses medications within time frames it defines to meet patient needs. ___ ___ ___

Authors' Comments, Experiences, and Suggestions

Organizations should define specific time expectations for stat, as soon as possible (ASAP), and routine orders. Some organizations use 30 minutes for stat, 60 minutes for ASAP, and 120 minutes for routine. Those organizations with document management systems and ADCs may be able to reduce or shorten times.

	Yes	No	NA
4. ☑ Medications are dispensed in the most ready-to-administer forms commercially available, and, if feasible, in unit doses that have been repackaged by the pharmacy or licensed repackager.	___	___	___

Authors' Comments, Experiences, and Suggestions

The organization should purchase all medications (including liquid oral medications and topical medications) in unit-dose and ready-to-use forms to the extent practical. The organization should avoid dispensing or providing medications in bulk containers.

The pharmacy should prepackage bulk medications in appropriate, tamper-evident, unit-dose packages when unit-dose forms are not available from the manufacturer or licensed repackager.

The organization should purchase premixed IV medications when available (e.g., premixed dobutamine, dopamine, heparin, magnesium sulfate, nitroglycerin, and lidocaine infusions).

Standard MM.05.01.13

The hospital safely obtains medications when the pharmacy is closed.

Rationale for MM.05.01.13

In today's health care settings, many organizations that provide 24-hour care do not provide 24-hour pharmacy services. However, patients in these settings may require medications during the times the pharmacy is not in operation. For safe, quality care, the hospital provides for the patient's urgent or emergent medication needs when the pharmacy is closed.

Elements of Performance for MM.05.01.13

	Yes	No	NA
1. The hospital has a process for providing medications to meet patient needs when the pharmacy is closed.	___	___	___

Authors' Comments, Experiences, and Suggestions

The process should be described in writing.

Physicians, nurses, and pharmacists should participate in developing the process.

The process must be in accordance with state laws and regulations and cannot permit entry into the pharmacy by non-pharmacy personnel, even if allowed by state law or regulation.

	Yes	No	NA
2. ☑ When non-pharmacist health care professionals are allowed by law or regulation to obtain medications after the pharmacy is closed, the following occurs: Medications available are limited to those approved by the hospital.	___	___	___

Authors' Comments, Experiences, and Suggestions

The P&T Committee or its equivalent should approve the limited list of medications. This list should be reviewed periodically (e.g., quarterly).

The list must be limited to medications that are likely to be urgently needed when the pharmacy is closed and should not include any medications that are not safe for storage outside of the pharmacy (e.g., concentrated electrolytes and medications in bulk containers).

	Yes	No	NA
3. ☑ When non-pharmacist health care professionals are allowed by law or regulation to obtain medications after the pharmacy is closed, the following occurs: The hospital stores and secures the medications approved for use outside of the pharmacy.	___	___	___

Authors' Comments, Experiences, and Suggestions

These medications must be stored outside the pharmacy (e.g., in a night cabinet/closet or ADC).

	Yes	No	NA
4. ☑ When non-pharmacist health care professionals are allowed by law or regulation to obtain medications after the pharmacy is closed, the following occurs: Only trained, designated prescribers and nurses are permitted access to approved medications.	___	___	___

Authors' Comments, Experiences, and Suggestions

Individuals who are permitted access to the medications should be oriented initially and, if needed, periodically (e.g., annually) thereafter. Surveyors may request evidence that these individuals are competent to make removals (e.g., a record that their competence was assessed). (See Example 4-22.)

	Yes	No	NA
5. ☑ When non-pharmacist health care professionals are allowed by law or regulation to obtain medications after the pharmacy is closed, the following occurs: Quality control procedures (such as an independent second check by another individual or a secondary verification built into the system such as bar coding) are in place to prevent medication retrieval errors.	___	___	___

Authors' Comments, Experiences, and Suggestions

The organization should have a mechanism to ensure that staff complies with second checks or other quality control requirements (e.g., signature or initials of the individual who performs the second check and/or observation of the process).

The second check is often performed by the staff nurse who requested the medication from a nursing supervisor.

	Yes	No	NA
6. ☑ When non-pharmacist health care professionals are allowed by law or regulation to obtain medications after the pharmacy is closed, the following occurs: The hospital arranges for a qualified pharmacist to be available either on-call or at another location (for example, at another organization that has 24-hour pharmacy service) to answer questions or provide medications beyond those accessible to non-pharmacy staff.	___	___	___

Authors' Comments, Experiences, and Suggestions

A log should be maintained for documentation of after-hours consultations and returns to the hospital.

	Yes	No	NA
7. ☑ ⚠ The hospital implements its process for providing medications to meet patient needs when the pharmacy is closed.	___	___	___

Authors' Comments, Experiences, and Suggestions

Most surveyors examine entries in removal records to determine that removals are made by individuals who are permitted access to the medications. (See Example 4-23.) There must be a record of medications removed from after-hours stocks. (See Example 4-24.)

Pharmacists should document their review of medications removed from after-hours stock (e.g., by initialing the removal record). Their review should include determining the appropriateness of the removal (e.g., a clinically urgent situation), if there was an order for the medication, and that the right medication, right dosage form, right strength, and right amount of medication were obtained. (See MM.05.01.01, EP 1 in this chapter.)

Ongoing monitoring and analysis should compare medication errors made when a pharmacist is not available to those made when a pharmacist is available.

Removals from after-hours stocks must be minimized. Non-pharmacists are not permitted to remove medications from the pharmacy when the pharmacy is closed.

Medications that repeatedly require dispensing by an on-call pharmacist should be made available in after-hours stocks outside the pharmacy with the exception of those not considered safe for storage outside the pharmacy (e.g., concentrated electrolytes).

Standard MM.05.01.17

The hospital follows a process to retrieve recalled or discontinued medications.

Elements of Performance for MM.05.01.17

	Yes	No	NA
1. 📄 The hospital has a written policy describing how it will retrieve and handle medications within the hospital that are recalled or discontinued for safety reasons by the manufacturer or the U.S. Food and Drug Administration. (See also EC.02.01.01, EP 11)	___	___	___

Yes **No** **NA**

Authors' Comments, Experiences, and Suggestions

A written policy is required.

There should be a record of the response to the recall (including recalls for medications and devices that are not stocked). (See Example 4-25.) Organizations should keep a file of initialed and dated notices with the response to the recall noted.

This policy should also apply to recalled medication-related devices.

Policies and procedures should describe a process that addresses recalled medications and devices, including medication samples, and devices stored in the pharmacy and throughout the organization. In addition, the pharmacy's periodic inspection routine should include a check of these areas for recalled medications and devices. (See MM.03.01.01, EP 18 in this chapter.)

All medications in stock, including those obtained from other pharmacies, and dispensed to patients must be labeled so that recalls can be performed (e.g., labeled with manufacturer's lot number or pharmacy control number).

2. ☑ The hospital implements its policy on retrieving and handling medications when they are recalled or discontinued for safety reasons. (See also EC.02.01.01, EP 11) ___ ___ ___

Authors' Comments, Experiences, and Suggestions

Many organizations report recalls and actions taken to an internal safety committee and/or the P&T Committee.

3. ☑ When a medication is recalled or discontinued for safety reasons by the manufacturer or the U.S. Food and Drug Administration, the hospital notifies the prescribers and those who dispense or administer the medication. (See also EC.02.01.01, EP 11) ___ ___ ___

Authors' Comments, Experiences, and Suggestions

Notification may be by memorandum, letter, newsletter, e-mail, copies of committee minutes, or any mechanism that ensures the appropriate individuals are informed of the recall.

4. ☑ When required by law and regulation or hospital policy, the hospital informs patients that their medication has been recalled or discontinued for safety reasons by the manufacturer or the U.S. Food and Drug Administration. (See also EC.02.01.01, EP 11) ___ ___ ___

Authors' Comments, Experiences, and Suggestions

The process should be documented if implemented.

Patients currently receiving a medication that is recalled for safety reasons must be notified.

The process should be in writing and staff should be able to describe the process.

Yes **No** **NA**

Standard MM.05.01.19

The hospital safely manages returned medications.

Rationale for MM.05.01.19

Medications may be returned to the hospital when allowed by law or regulation and organization policy. Previously dispensed but unused, expired, or returned medications in the hospital must be accounted for, controlled, and disposed of in order to keep patients safe and prevent diversion.

Elements of Performance for MM.05.01.19

1. The hospital determines under what circumstances unused, expired, or returned medications will be managed by the pharmacy or the hospital. ____ ____ ____

   Authors' Comments, Experiences, and Suggestions

   See MM.03.01.01, EP 8 in this chapter.

   The process should be described in writing, address accountability, and ensure that the medications are not diverted.

   If only a month and year of expiration are provided, the medication may be used until the last day of the month.

   Unused intact medications should be returned to a return bin in ADCs. Returning unused medications to a regular storage pocket used for distribution is unsafe because they could be placed in the wrong pocket.

   Unused portions of medications removed from unit-dose containers (e.g., partial tablets and remaining liquid medication) should be disposed of properly and not retained for later use.

   There must be a procedure for making external reports of defective medications (e.g., to the manufacturer and the FDA).

2. When the hospital accepts unused, expired, or returned medications, it has a process for returning medications to the pharmacy's control, which includes procedures for preventing diversion. ____ ____ ____

   Authors' Comments, Experiences, and Suggestions

   The process should be described in writing.

   The process must provide for security of medications while awaiting return to the pharmacy and return to the supplier or reverse distributor.

   The process must describe secure storage for medications after returned to pharmacy control.

   Returned unused medications dispensed in non-tamper evident containers should not be redispensed.

Yes No NA

USP Chapter <797> discusses redispensing compounded sterile preparations. See Chapter 19.

The process should be consistent with infection control guidelines. Most organizations prohibit partially used medications, or medications exposed in patient rooms, from being returned to the pharmacy.

3. The hospital determines if and when outside sources are used for destruction of medications. ___ ___ ___

Authors' Comments, Experiences, and Suggestions

The process should be described in writing.

The process should describe how outside sources are notified, how medications are stored securely while waiting for destruction, and what destruction records shall be maintained.

4. ☑ The hospital implements its process for managing unused, expired, or returned medications. ___ ___ ___

Authors' Comments, Experiences, and Suggestions

There should be evidence that medications returned to the pharmacy are controlled and accounted for according to policy.

Some surveyors inspect patient care areas for the presence of unused medications for discharged patients.

ADMINISTRATION OF MEDICATIONS

Standard MM.06.01.01

The hospital safely administers medications.

Elements of Performance for MM.06.01.01

1. The hospital defines, in writing, licensed independent practitioners and the clinical staff disciplines that are authorized to administer medication, with or without supervision, in accordance with law and regulation. (See also MM.06.01.03, EP 1) ___ ___ ___

Authors' Comments, Experiences, and Suggestions

Pharmacy should have access to the roster and/or policy of licensed independent practitioners and clinical staff who are authorized to administer medications.

	Yes	No	NA

Standard PC.03.01.01, EP 1 specifies that individuals who administer moderate or deep sedation and anesthesia have credentials to manage and rescue patients at whatever level of sedation or anesthesia is achieved, either intentionally or unintentionally.

Standard PC.02.01.01, EP 15 specifies that intravenous medications are administered in accordance with state law and approved medical staff policies and procedures.

2. ⚠ Only authorized licensed independent practitioners and clinical staff administer medications. ___ ___ ___

Note: This does not prohibit self-administration of medications by patients when indicated. (See also MM.06.01.03, EP 1)

3. ☑ ⚠ Before administration, the individual administering the medication does the following: Verifies that the medication selected matches the medication order and product label. ___ ___ ___

Authors' Comments, Experiences, and Suggestions

Medications should be removed from storage areas (e.g., medication carts, general stock, or ADCs) for only one patient and one medication pass at a time.

The patient's medication administration record should be taken to the patient's bedside to verify that the correct medication is administered to the correct patient, by verifying the two hospital-approved patient identifiers with the patient and on the medication.

Patients must be identified before medications are administered. (See NPSG.01.01.01 in Chapter 6.)

To the extent possible, a medication should be administered by the individual who prepared the dose (unless the medication was prepared by the pharmacy).

Medications should be removed from the packaging only at the patient's bedside and immediately before administration.

4. ☑ ⚠ Before administration, the individual administering the medication does the following: Visually inspects the medication for particulates, discoloration, or other loss of integrity. (See also MM.03.01.05, EP 2; MM.05.01.07, EP 3) ___ ___ ___

Authors' Comments, Experiences, and Suggestions

Medications should be administered as soon as possible after preparation (i.e., within the shorter of the stability range or beyond-use date).

Medications that appear to be deteriorated or otherwise unusable must not be administered.

	Yes	No	NA
5. ☑ ⚠ Before administration, the individual administering the medication does the following: Verifies that the medication has not expired.	___	___	___

Authors' Comments, Experiences, and Suggestions

Multiple-dose vials must be marked with the beyond-use date after opening or moving to a temperature different from the product labeling. Labeling with only the date opened is not sufficient.

Some pharmacies place the beyond-use date on an unpunctured multiple-dose vial when dispensed to ensure that the beyond-use date is not exceeded.

	Yes	No	NA
6. ☑ ⚠ Before administration, the individual administering the medication does the following: Verifies that no contraindications exist.	___	___	___

Authors' Comments, Experiences, and Suggestions

Current and appropriate references should be available to those who administer medications. (See IM.03.01.01.)

Those who administer medications should review the patient's medical record for contraindications.

	Yes	No	NA
7. ☑ ⚠ Before administration, the individual administering the medication does the following: Verifies that the medication is being administered at the proper time, in the prescribed dose, and by the correct route.	___	___	___

Authors' Comments, Experiences, and Suggestions

Individuals who administer medications must review the medication orders and the medications to ensure that medications are administered as ordered.

Each dose administered must be recorded properly in the patient's medical record. This requirement applies to all medications as defined by The Joint Commission's definition of medication (including diagnostic and contrast agents, blood derivatives, and herbal remedies). (See Medication Definition in this chapter.)

Though not specified in the CMS standards or Interpretive Guidelines, the CMS surveyor procedures suggest that an indicator for assessing appropriate administration of drugs should include administration within 30 minutes of the scheduled time.

MARs should be checked against the patient's medical record according to the organization's defined interval (generally each shift but no less frequently than every 24 hours).

	Yes	No	NA
8. ☑ ⚠ Before administration, the individual administering the medication does the following: Discusses any unresolved concerns about the medication with the patient's licensed independent practitioner, prescriber (if different from the licensed independent practitioner), and/or staff involved with the patient's care, treatment, and services.	___	___	___

	Yes	No	NA

Authors' Comments, Experiences, and Suggestions

Medications must not be administered until all significant concerns are resolved.

Staff members should be able to describe how they report medication errors and ADRs to the organization's reporting system.

9. ☑ ⚠ Before administering a new medication, the patient or family is informed about any potential clinically significant adverse drug reactions or other concerns regarding administration of a new medication. (See also MM.06.01.03, EPs 3-6; PC.02.03.01, EP 10) ____ ____ ____

Authors' Comments, Experiences, and Suggestions

Individuals who administer medications must ensure compliance with the organization's policy regarding who is allowed to advise the patient and how the advice is given.

Standard MM.06.01.03

Self-administered medications are administered safely and accurately.

Note: The term "self-administered medication(s)" may refer to medications administered by a family member.

Elements of Performance for MM.06.01.03

1. 📄 If self-administration of medications is allowed, written processes that address training, supervision, and documentation guide the safe and accurate self-administration of medications or the administration of medications by a family member. (See also MM.06.01.01, EPs 1 and 2) ____ ____ ____

Authors' Comments, Experiences, and Suggestions

A written policy is required.

Patients may self-administer medications only if there is a specific order in accordance with the organization's policy.

Organizations often limit the medications that may be self-administered.

Policies should address storage, security, and labeling for medications that are self-administered.

Medications stored at the patient's bedside must be stored securely so that unauthorized individuals do not have access to them. If self-administration is permitted by hospital policy, the medication may be unlocked (if allowed by hospital policy), but must be secure.

A method to accurately record the administration of self-administered medications in the patient's medical record must be developed.

	Yes	No	NA
2. ☑ The hospital implements its written processes for medication self-administration or medication administration.	___	___	___
3. ☑ The hospital educates patients and families involved in self-administration about the following: Medication name, type, and reason for use. (See also MM.06.01.01, EP 9; PC.02.03.01, EP 10)	___	___	___

Authors' Comments, Experiences, and Suggestions

See Chapter 8 concerning education of patients and family members.

	Yes	No	NA
4. ☑ The hospital educates patients and families involved in self-administration about the following: How to administer medication, including process, time, frequency, route, and dose. (See also MM.06.01.01, EP 9; PC.02.03.01, EP 10)	___	___	___

Authors' Comments, Experiences, and Suggestions

The training and information to be provided to patients and families should be defined.

Staff members who provide the training (including pharmacy staff) must be competent to do so.

All patients and their caregivers (e.g., parents, guardians, relatives, friends, home care nurses, and home care aides) should be educated about all medications administered during the patients' hospitalization as well as medications to be taken after discharge. Emphasis should be on educating high-risk patients (e.g., geriatric patients, pediatric patients), patients with specific diseases (e.g., diabetes, hypertension), and patients receiving specific medications (e.g., anticoagulants, insulin).

	Yes	No	NA
5. ☑ The hospital educates patients and families involved in self-administration about the following: Anticipated actions and potential side effects of the medication administered. (See also MM.06.01.01, EP 9; PC.02.03.01, EP 10)	___	___	___
6. ☑ The hospital educates patients and families involved in self-administration about the following: Monitoring the effects of the medication. (See also MM.06.01.01, EP 9; PC.02.03.01, EP 10)	___	___	___

Authors' Comments, Experiences, and Suggestions

Patient education should include information on the safe and effective use of medications, medical equipment, and supplies. (See PC.02.03.01, EP 10.)

	Yes	No	NA
7. ☑ ⚠ The hospital determines that the patient or the family member who administers the medication is competent at medication administration before allowing him or her to administer medications.	___	___	___

Authors' Comments, Experiences, and Suggestions

There should be evidence that these persons are competent (e.g., a determination that they possess the knowledge, their performance has been observed,

Yes No NA

and they successfully demonstrate their skills). Documentation should be in the patient's medical record.

Pharmacy staff who administer medications must be competent to do so and their activities must be within the scope of practice defined by the state regulations and the organization's policy.

Standard MM.06.01.05

The hospital safely manages investigational medications.

Rationale for MM.06.01.05

Investigational medications can be of great help to the patient. In some cases, investigational medications may represent one of a few options in the patient's care plan. The hospital contributes to the safety of patients participating in investigational or clinical medication studies by controlling and monitoring the use of these medications.

Note: For a discussion of patient rights regarding the use of investigational medications, see Standard RI.01.03.05.

Elements of Performance for MM.06.01.05

1. 📄 The hospital has a written process addressing the use of investigational medications that includes review, approval, supervision, and monitoring. ____ ____ ____

   Authors' Comments, Experiences, and Suggestions

   A written policy that details the institutional review board's (IRB) process is required.

2. The hospital's written process for the use of investigational medications specifies that the pharmacy controls the storage, dispensing, labeling, and distribution of investigational medications. ____ ____ ____

3. The written process for the use of investigational medications specifies that when a patient is involved in an investigational protocol that is independent of the hospital, the hospital evaluates and, if no contraindication exists, accommodates the patient's continued participation in the protocol. ____ ____ ____

4. ☑ ⚠ The hospital implements its processes for the use of investigational medications. ____ ____ ____

Yes No NA

Authors' Comments, Experiences, and Suggestions

Handling of investigational medications must comply with all applicable Medication Management standards.

See Orders for Investigational Medications under MM.04.01.01, EP 1 in this chapter.

Protocols for investigational medications must be approved by the appropriate group (i.e., the institutional review board).

The pharmacy may dispense investigational medications only pursuant to the prescription of an authorized investigator or prescriber.

Administration of investigational medications may only be by those approved to do so, and only after they have been educated regarding the actions and possible adverse effects of these medications.

An accurate record of doses received, dispensed, administered, and destroyed must be maintained.

Standard RI.01.03.05 in the Rights and Responsibilities of the Individual chapter of the CAMH provides information on the rights of patients who participate or refuse to participate in research, investigations, and clinical trials.

MONITORING OF MEDICATIONS

Standard MM.07.01.01

The hospital monitors patients to determine the effects of their medication(s).

Elements of Performance for MM.07.01.01

1. ☑ The hospital monitors the patient's perception of side effects and the effectiveness of his or her medication(s). ___ ___ ___

Authors' Comments, Experiences, and Suggestions

Ongoing patient medication monitoring is a collaborative assessment by physicians, nurses, pharmacists, and other individuals responsible for providing care to the patient.

The patient's response to medications administered must be recorded in the patient's medical record.

Nurses and other care providers who monitor patients must alert the prescriber to adverse effects of medications (e.g., adverse reactions).

Nurses and other care providers should suggest medication therapy modifications when appropriate.

	Yes	No	NA

Modifications include changing the medication, modifying the dose, and changing the timing or rate of administration. Suggestions must be documented (e.g., in the medical record).

2. ☑ The hospital monitors patient response to medication(s) by taking into account clinical information from the medical record, relevant lab values, clinical response, and medication profile. (See also MM.02.01.01, EP 3) ____ ____ ____

   Note: Monitoring the patient's response to medications is an important assessment activity for nurses, physicians, and pharmacists. In particular, monitoring the patient's response to the first dose to a new medication is essential to the safety of the patient because any adverse reactions, including serious ones, are more unpredictable if the drug has never been used before with the patient.

   Authors' Comments, Experiences, and Suggestions

   NPSG.03.05.01 details specific medication-related monitoring for anticoagulants.

   Standard PC.03.01.05 details specific medication-related monitoring for moderate or deep sedation or anesthesia.

Standard MM.07.01.03

The hospital responds to actual or potential adverse drug events, significant adverse drug reactions, and medication errors.

Rationale for MM.07.01.03

Adverse drug reactions and medication errors place patients at considerable risk. For safe, quality care, hospitals must have systems in place to respond to and monitor a patient in the event of an adverse drug reaction or medication error.

Elements of Performance for MM.07.01.03

1. 🗎 The hospital has a written process to respond to actual or potential adverse events, significant adverse drug reactions, and medication errors. ____ ____ ____

   Authors' Comments, Experiences, and Suggestions

   A written policy is required.

   The process should include clinics and other ambulatory patient care areas.

   Staff should be able to describe how they respond to an actual or potential adverse medication event.

Yes **No** **NA**

Example 4-26 is a form for reporting medication errors internally.

Examples 4-27 and 4-28 are forms for reporting adverse drug reactions internally.

2. The hospital has a written process addressing prescriber notification in the event of an adverse drug event, significant adverse drug reaction, or medication error. ___ ___ ___

Authors' Comments, Experiences, and Suggestions

A written policy is required.

Staff should be able to describe how they notify the prescriber if there is an adverse drug reaction or medication error.

3. ☑ The hospital complies with internal and external reporting requirements for actual or potential adverse drug events, significant adverse drug reactions, and medication errors. ___ ___ ___

Authors' Comments, Experiences, and Suggestions

Evidence of the organization's reporting process should be maintained, such as in P&T or Quality Committee minutes.

Organizations, at their discretion, may report medication errors to an external agency (i.e., ISMP Medication Errors Reporting Program at www.ismp.org). (See Chapter 20.)

Serious adverse events should be reported to the FDA's MedWatch Program at www.fda.gov/medwatch/how.htm. (See Chapter 21.) (See Example 4-29.)

Vaccine-related adverse events must be reported to the Vaccine Adverse Event Reporting System at www.vaers.org. (See Chapter 21.) (See Example 4-30.)

Device-related adverse events must be reported to the FDA MedWatch program (See Chapter 21.) (See Example 4-31.)

5. ☑ ⚠ The hospital implements its process for responding to adverse drug events, significant adverse drug reactions, and medication errors. ___ ___ ___

Authors' Comments, Experiences, and Suggestions

The action taken should be documented.

The appropriateness of the action taken and the outcome should be evaluated.

Data should be aggregated and analyzed and information reported to the appropriate committee. (See Examples 4-32 and 4-33.)

	Yes	No	NA
6. ⚠ For hospitals that use Joint Commission accreditation for deemed status purposes: Medication administration errors, adverse drug reactions, and medication incompatibilities as defined by the hospital are reported to the attending physician or clinical psychologist, immediately when possible, and as appropriate, to the organization-wide performance improvement program.	___	___	___

Note: The definition of *physician* is the same as that used by the Centers for Medicare & Medicaid Services (CMS).

Authors' Comments, Experiences, and Suggestions

CMS defines a physician as: "(1) a doctor of medicine or doctor of osteopathy who, by virtue of education, training, and demonstrated competence, is granted clinical privileges by the hospital to perform a specific diagnostic or therapeutic procedure(s) and who is fully licensed to practice medicine. (2) As defined by the Centers for Medicare & Medicaid Services in 42 CFR Ch.IV 482.12 Condition of participation: Governing body – In accordance with the hospital policy, the governing body must ensure that the following requirements are met: (1) Every Medicare patient is under the care of:

(i) A doctor of medicine or osteopathy (This provision is not to be construed to limit the authority of a doctor of medicine or osteopathy to delegate tasks to other qualified health care personnel to the extent recognized under State law or a State's regulatory mechanism.);

(ii) A doctor of dental surgery or dental medicine who is legally authorized to practice dentistry by the State and who is acting within the scope of his or her license;

(iii) A doctor of podiatric medicine, but only with respect to functions which he or she is legally authorized by the State to perform;

(iv) A doctor of optometry who is legally authorized to practice optometry by the State in which he or she practices;

(v) A chiropractor who is licensed by the State or legally authorized to perform the services of a chiropractor, but only with respect to treatment by means of manual manipulation of the spine to correct a subluxation demonstrated by x-ray to exist; and

(vi) A clinical psychologist as defined in §410.71 of this chapter, but only with respect to clinical psychologist services as defined in §410.71 of this chapter and only to the extent permitted by State law."[14] (See Chapter 22.)

Medication incompatibilities include situations such as a solution that precipitates after dispensing. This should be a part of the medication error reporting process.

Data should be aggregated and analyzed and information provided to the appropriate committee.

Yes No NA

EVALUATION OF THE MEDICATION MANAGEMENT PROCESS

Standard MM.08.01.01

The hospital evaluates the effectiveness of its medication management system.

Elements of Performance for MM.08.01.01

1. The hospital collects data on the performance of its medication management system. (See also PI.01.01.01, EPs 14 and 15) ___ ___ ___

   Authors' Comments, Experiences, and Suggestions

   See Failure Mode and Effects Analysis in Chapter 15.

   This is often a Medication Safety Committee function.

2. The hospital analyzes data on its medication management system. ___ ___ ___

   Authors' Comments, Experiences, and Suggestions

   Data include reports of medication errors and adverse drug events, performance monitors, medication use evaluations, failure mode and effects analysis (FMEA) findings and recommendations, reports of hazardous conditions, and sentinel event review findings.

   Information from the organization's review of data should be used to improve medication management processes.

   Examples of external data include data from ISMP, Core Measure data, ORYX® data, and MEDMARX. (See Chapters 1, 16, and 20.)

3. The hospital compares data over time to identify risk points, levels of performance, patterns, trends, and variations of its medication management system. ___ ___ ___

   Authors' Comments, Experiences, and Suggestions

   The organization may ask the pharmacy to collect and aggregate data related to pharmacy services (e.g., clarifications of medication orders, requests for non-formulary medications, and numbers of dispensing errors that were caught before the medication left the control of the pharmacy).

   Analyzing MAR correction forms to assess the reason listed (e.g. order entry errors or convenience requests) can provide documentation of variation.

4. The hospital reviews the literature and other external sources for new technologies and best practices. ___ ___ ___

	Yes	No	NA

Authors' Comments, Experiences, and Suggestions

Literature evaluations may be P&T Committee and/or Medication Safety Committee topics.

There should be evidence that the organization evaluates the literature (e.g., documentation in P&T Committee minutes).

5. Based on analysis of its data as well as review of the literature for new technologies and best practices, the hospital identifies opportunities for improvement in its medication management system. ___ ___ ___

6. The hospital takes action on improvement opportunities identified as priorities for its medication management system. ___ ___ ___

Authors' Comments, Experiences, and Suggestions

New technologies (e.g., automated delivery systems, bar coding, infusion devices, robotics) should be reviewed and, if deemed appropriate for the organization, implemented.

Best practices that have proved successful in other organizations (including American Society of Health-System Pharmacists [ASHP], ISMP, and those from other health care facilities) should be considered and, if deemed appropriate for the organization, implemented.

7. The hospital evaluates its actions to confirm that they resulted in improvements for its medication management system. ___ ___ ___

Authors' Comments, Experiences, and Suggestions

When new medication processes are implemented, the organization must develop a method to measure the success of the process.

The organization may choose to conduct a FMEA to identify potential problems with new medication processes.

The organization should establish a baseline and develop metrics that can be used to document improvement. Examples of metrics include performance indicators and observation of processes.

8. The hospital takes additional action when planed improvements for its medication management processes are either not achieved or not sustained. ___ ___ ___

Authors' Comments, Experiences, and Suggestions

Data gathered through adverse event reporting processes (e.g., adverse drug reaction and medication error reporting) must be used to identify opportunities for improvement within the organization.

Information gathered through the organization's root cause analysis (RCA) or FMEA may be useful in identifying opportunities for improvement.

Yes **No** **NA**

The organization should apply process improvement techniques to drive and sustain improvements. (See Chapter 15.)

CHAPTER 5

Individual-Based System Tracer: Medication Management

Joint Commission surveys include visits to patient care and service areas where surveyors use tracers to assess compliance with relevant standards and how well the organization provides care, treatment, and services. This chapter provides an overview of the individual-based system tracer: medication management (MM) system tracer. (*See* Tracer Activities in Chapter 2.) It focuses on survey specifics (i.e., what to expect during the MM system tracer), strategy (i.e., how to prepare for and participate in the MM system tracer), and example surveyors' questions (i.e., questions that surveyors have asked during the MM system tracer).

Medication Management System Tracer Description

The organization should ensure that staff members understand what to expect during the MM system tracer. The descriptions that follow may be helpful.

Surveyors—One or more

Session Length—60 minutes

Participants—Participants include personnel who have a role in managing medications for the individual patient chosen for the MM system tracer. In addition to the director of pharmacy and other pharmacists involved with patient care, participants often include physicians, nurses, therapists, dietitians, personnel responsible for educating staff and patients about medications, clinical personnel with a special knowledge or perspective on medication use (e.g., pediatrics or geriatrics), performance improvement personnel who focus on improving the MM system, laboratory clinicians, and biomedical engineers involved in managing medications (e.g., maintaining infusion pumps).

Purpose—The purpose of this activity is to review the organization's MM system, determine if the organization complies with MM standards, identify MM issues that require further review, assess competence of staff, discuss relevant standards related to the United States Pharmacopeia (USP) Chapter <797> (*see* Chapter 19), and assess how the organization complies with National Patient Safety Goals (NPSGs) relating to medications. (*See* Chapter 6.)

Location—Organizations may choose the location for the group discussion. Although many organizations designate a conference room, surveyors often expand the discussion to other areas of the organization that play a role in the individual patient's medication care (e.g., pharmacy, nursing units, diagnostic and procedural areas, laboratory, dietary department, and materials management).

When—This activity occurs during individual tracers, for example, when a surveyor identifies a patient who is receiving a high-alert medication.

Materials/Documents—The following materials and documents may be helpful:

- MM system description/flowchart (*See* Medication Management System Description in this chapter.)
- List of high-alert medications
- List of look-alike/sound-alike combinations of medications
- List of hazardous medications
- List of prohibited abbreviations
- List of medication use improvement activities
- List of actions taken in response to medication errors and other adverse drug events (ADEs)
- List of medication safety education activities

Format—The MM system tracer often includes a review of medication records to identify a patient on a high-alert medication. A focused tracer activity traces the path of medications through the organization and addresses medication management processes (i.e., selection and procurement, storage, ordering and transcribing, preparing and dispensing, administering, and monitoring). It includes area visits, staff interviews, and an evaluation of the organization's MM process; processes for reporting medication errors and other adverse drug events, system breakdowns, and close calls (near misses); other issues related to safe and effective use of medications; and implementation of NPSGs related to MM. In surveys of small facilities, the MM system tracer may be combined with other tracers (e.g., data use and infection control).

Medication Management System Tracer Strategy

The organization should ensure that staff are educated and understand how it complies continuously with the standards. The suggestions that follow may help staff prepare for and participate in the MM system tracer.

Medication Management System Description

- Prepare a description and/or flowchart of the MM system. (*See* Table 5-1.)
- Include all MM system processes in the description (i.e., planning, selection and procurement, storage, ordering and transcribing, preparing and dispensing, administering, monitoring, and evaluating).
- Ensure that all medications from all sources are included. For example, parenteral solutions; surgical kits with medications; other medications that are purchased, stored, or distributed by the materials management department; contrast agents; albumin and other blood derivatives; radiopharmaceuticals; and medications from compounding pharmacies and other outside sources.
- Be able to discuss all components of the MM system description and/or flowchart.
- Be able to discuss how the organization ensures that medications from sources other than the pharmacy (e.g., materials management, laboratory, and imaging) meet the same standards of quality and integrity as those from the pharmacy. For example, medications from other sources must be evaluated for inclusion in the formulary, stored and labeled properly, and included in adverse drug event reporting. Areas where these medications are stored must be inspected periodically (e.g., monthly).
- Be able to discuss how medications brought into the organization by patients and, if allowed, by practitioners are handled. The process should include a visual check for integrity of the medications.
- Be able to discuss how departments (including pharmacy) communicate with each other.

Medication Use Improvement Activities

- Prepare a summary of medication use improvement activities for the past 12 months.
- Prepare a medication management plan that lists future medication use improvement activities.
- Prepare a list of improvements made in each of the MM processes (i.e., planning, selection and procurement, storage, ordering and transcribing, preparing and dispensing, administering, monitoring, and evaluating).

High-Alert Medications

- List the high-alert medications identified by the organization.
- For each high-alert medication, list the safeguards in place to reduce the potential for errors in each of the MM processes.
- Ensure that staff who use high-alert medications can discuss these medications and safeguards in place to prevent errors.

Look-Alike/Sound-Alike Medications

- List the look-alike/sound-alike medication combinations chosen by the organization. Ensure that the list includes several relevant combinations chosen from authoritative sources such as The Institute for Safe Medication Practices. (*See* Appendix.)
- Be able to discuss the process for identifying and reviewing the list of look-alike/sound-alike medications used in your organization.
- For each look-alike/sound-alike combination, list the safeguards in place throughout the organization (e.g., Tall-Man letters, separate storage areas, and spell-out requirements) to reduce the potential for errors for the MM processes.
- Ensure that appropriate staff can discuss the look-alike/sound-alike medication combinations and safeguards in place to prevent errors throughout the organization.

Hazardous Medications

- List the hazardous medications identified by the organization.
- For each hazardous medication, list the safeguards in place to reduce the potential for errors in each of the MM processes.
- Ensure that staff who use hazardous medications can discuss these medications and safeguards in place to prevent errors.

Medication Errors

- Be able to discuss how medication errors are detected, reported, and assessed.

- Be able to give examples of how medication error data are used to improve patient care (i.e., actions taken).
- Be able to describe how ongoing medication safety education relating to medication errors is provided for medical staff (including licensed independent practitioners), nursing staff, pharmacy staff, and other personnel who provide patient care.
- Be able to discuss how nationally-reported errors are assessed to minimize risk in the organization.

Adverse Drug Events (ADEs)

- Be able to discuss how adverse drug events (ADEs) are detected, reported, and assessed.
- Be able to give examples of how ADE data are used to improve patient care (i.e., actions taken).
- Be able to describe how ongoing medication safety education relating to ADEs is provided for medical staff (including licensed independent practitioners), nursing staff, pharmacy staff, and other personnel who provide patient care.

Sentinel Events

- Be able to provide a root cause analysis (RCA) for each sentinel event or serious incident. (*See* Chapter 15.)
- If conducted, be able to provide a failure mode and effects analysis (FMEA) for each sentinel event or serious incident. (*See* Chapter 15.)

Formulary

- Be able to discuss how medications are evaluated for addition to the formulary (including specific evaluation criteria used).
- Be able to discuss the process for procurement and use of nonformulary medications.
- Be able to discuss the processes used to address medication shortages/outages and recalls.

Medication Management System Evaluation

- Be prepared to discuss how the MM system is evaluated to identify risk points and areas that need improvement (e.g., the ISMP Medication Safety Self-Assessment®, FMEA of medication use processes, and performance improvement indicators).

Medication Management System Tracer Questions

The following questions are examples that surveyors have asked during the MM system tracer. Discussing the questions with participants is educational and should foster an understanding of how the organization complies continuously with the standards.

Surveyors may ask participants to introduce themselves and identify their positions or roles. Surveyors may direct some questions to specific individuals and other questions to the group. Questions often focus on potential problems identified during the survey, other areas of concern, medication safety, NPSGs, and the MM processes. Participants should be prepared to respond to questions and describe processes that are in place to provide a safe medication management system.

National Patient Safety Goals

Patient Identifiers

- What are the organization's patient identifiers used when administering medications?
- How do you ensure that patient identifiers are checked?

Anticoagulant Therapy

- Has an anticoagulant management program been implemented throughout the organization?
- Is all intravenous heparin administered using a programmable infusion pump?
- What strengths of heparin are stored outside the pharmacy?
- What safeguards are in place for patients using oral anticoagulants (i.e., warfarin)?
- How does dietary receive information regarding patients on oral anticoagulants?
- What is the organization's procedure for monitoring patients on warfarin therapy?
- How does the organization educate patients who receive anticoagulants?

Health Care–Associated Infections

- How do you monitor compliance with guidelines for hand hygiene?

- How are health care–associated infections identified in the organization?
- How does the organization treat infections involving multidrug-resistant organisms?
- Does the organization have a written policy for preventing surgical site infections?
- What is the role of antimicrobial prophylaxis in preventing surgical site infections?
- How is hair removed from patients prior to surgical procedures?

Reconciliation of Medications

- How do you obtain and document a complete list of a patient's current medications upon admission to the organization?
- When and how is the patient involved in the medication reconciliation process?
- How are medication reconciliation discrepancies handled?
- How do you communicate a complete list of a patient's medications to the next provider when a patient is referred or transferred?
- How is the communication to the next provider documented?
- How do you provide a current list of medications to patients upon discharge from the organization?

Patient-Specific Information

Patient Information Availability

- What information about the patient is available to the pharmacy?
- How do you obtain laboratory results?
- How are you notified about critical test results that are outside normal ranges?

Allergies

- How does the pharmacy obtain information about patient allergies?
- What is the order entry process if patient allergy information is missing?
- Who enters allergy information into the system?
- If allergy information is unavailable to the pharmacy, are there instances when medications can be dispensed to the patient?

Patient Record Maintenance

- How do you document the administration of respiratory care medications in patients' medical records?
- How do you document the administration of contrast agents in patients' medical records?
- How do you reconcile patients' medication administration records?
- How is the pharmacy informed of medications administered in the emergency department?

Selection and Procurement

Formulary

- What is the process for adding medications to the formulary?
- What criteria do you use to evaluate medications for inclusion in the formulary?
- Are Black Box Warnings considered when you evaluate medications for inclusion in the formulary?
- How do you evaluate medications for their safety?
- Are contrast agents included in the formulary?
- What medications were removed from the formulary in the last 12 months and why were they removed?

Medication Shortages/Outages

- How do you manage shortages of medications?
- How do you communicate shortages to the medical staff?
- If your organization uses bar code medication administration, what is your process when barcoded medications are unavailable?
- How do you address outages of medications?
- How do you communicate outages to the medical staff?

Storage

Medication Stability

- How do you ensure that medications are stored to maintain their stability (inside the pharmacy and outside the pharmacy)?
- What do you do when the temperature of a medication refrigerator is outside the acceptable range?
- What process is followed when refrigerated medications are stored outside the refrigerator?
- How you ensure the stability of vaccines?

Security

- How do you prevent unauthorized individuals from having access to medications?
- How do you ensure the security of contrast agents?
- What security measures are in place for automated dispensing cabinets (ADCs)?
- How often are you notified to remove someone's access from ADCs?
- How do you ensure the security of anesthesia medications?

Controlled Substances

- Are all controlled substances throughout the organization locked?
- What do you do if there is an unexplained loss of a controlled substance?
- What procedures are in place to prevent the loss or diversion of controlled substances?

Emergency Medications

- In the event of a terrorist attack, what emergency medications are stocked in your organization?
- How do you decide what emergency medications will be available on crash carts?
- What do you do when an emergency medication must be replaced?

Personal Medications (Patients')

- What do you do with patients' personal medications (i.e., medications brought into the organization by patients or their families)?
- How does the pharmacy indicate that it has visually examined a patient's personal medications?
- When is it acceptable for patients to use their personal medications?
- How are a patient's personal medications stored?

Personal Medications (Practitioners')

- Do you allow the use of practitioners' personal medications (i.e., medications brought into the organization by practitioners to be used on patients)?
- How does the pharmacy indicate that it has visually examined practitioners' personal medications?

Ordering and Transcribing

Ordering

- Who enters medication orders into the system?
- How do you ensure that medication orders are entered into the system correctly?
- What medication orders require an indication for use?
- What orders or types of orders are restricted to specific prescribers?

Look-Alike/Sound-Alike Medications

- What look-alike/sound-alike medications are problematic in this organization?
- How do you prevent errors with look-alike/sound-alike medications?
- What preventive measures to decrease the potential for errors have been implemented throughout the organization, including offsite clinics?

Illegible Orders

- Are there prescribers whose orders are often illegible?
- How do you address illegibility issues with prescribers?
- What processes are in place to improve legibility?

Unclear Orders

- What do you do if a medication order is unclear?
- How do you ensure that unclear orders are clarified?
- How do you document the clarification of medication orders?
- What is the organization's most problematic type of unclear order?

Abbreviations

- What abbreviations are prohibited in your organization?
- Has the use of prohibited abbreviations decreased during the previous year?
- What do you do when a prescriber uses a prohibited abbreviation?
- Do you have a list of abbreviations that has been approved for use within the organization?

Verbal Orders

- What departments read back verbal orders?
- What process do you follow when you receive a verbal order?
- What has been done to minimize the use of verbal orders?
- What limitations are placed on verbal orders?
- What improvements have been made for reading back verbal orders?

Telephone Orders

- Who is authorized to accept/transcribe telephone orders?
- How are telephone orders processed?
- What limits are placed on telephone orders?

Preprinted Orders

- How do you review, approve, and update preprinted orders?
- What roles do prescribers have in developing preprinted orders?
- How do you ensure that all preprinted orders have been reviewed?
- Do you use protocols for oral contrast agents?
- How do you choose samples of preprinted orders for retrospective review?

Standing Orders

- What is your process for ensuring that standing orders are current?
- Where do you keep master copies of standing orders?

Weight-Based Dosing

- When is weight-based dosing for pediatric patients required?

As Needed (PRN) Orders

- How do you qualify as needed (prn) orders?
- Must *all* as needed orders be qualified?

Hold Orders

- Are hold orders allowed in your organization?
- What must be included in a hold order in your organization?
- How do you know when a hold order ends?

Automatic Stop Orders

- How do you notify a prescriber when a medication order is to be cancelled?
- What medications are subject to your automatic stop order policy?

Resume Orders

- What must a prescriber do to order the resumption of previous medications?

Titrating Orders

- What must be included in a titrating order in your organization?
- How do you know when to end a titration order?

Taper Orders

- How do you express taper orders in your organization?
- How do you know when to end a taper order?

Range Orders

- Does the organization allow range orders?
- How do you express range orders in your organization?
- What limits are placed on range orders?

Compounded Medications Orders

- Where do you keep formulas for compounded medications or medication mixtures?
- What is your process for reviewing and approving formulas for compounded medications or medication mixtures?
- What process is followed when an order is received for a medication from an outside compounding pharmacy?

Medication-Related Device Orders

- What must be included in an order for a medication-related device?

Investigational Medications Orders

- What prescribers are permitted to order investigational medications?
- What do you do if a patient who is taking an investigational medication is admitted to the organization?

Off-Label Use of Medications

- How do you monitor medications used for non-FDA approved indications (i.e., off-label use)?

Herbal Medications Orders

- Are herbal medications included in your formulary?
- Must orders for herbal medications include an indication or reason for use?
- If permitted, how are patients' own herbal medications identified/verified prior to administration to the patient?

Discharge Medication Orders

- What is your process for ordering medications at discharge?
- Under what circumstances, if any, are patients permitted to take the remainder of their inpatient medications home?

Preparing and Dispensing

Review of Orders for Appropriateness

- How do you review medication orders for appropriateness?
- What is the review process for medication orders written in the emergency department?
- Are medication orders reviewed for appropriateness in the organization's off-site clinics?

Review of Orders in the Absence of a Pharmacist

- How do you ensure that medication orders are reviewed by a qualified health care professional in the absence of a pharmacist?
- What qualified health care professionals are permitted to review medication orders in the absence of a pharmacist?

After-Hours Pharmacy Services

- How are medications obtained when the pharmacy is closed (e.g., after-hours)?
- Can nursing supervisors enter the pharmacy after-hours to obtain medications?
- What do nurses do at night if a medication is not available in the automated dispensing cabinet (ADC)?
- How often does this occur?
- How are medication orders reviewed when the pharmacy is closed?
- How do you ensure that personnel who are authorized to review medication orders after-hours are trained and competent?

Preparing Medications Safely

- What safeguards are in place to ensure that medications are prepared safely?
- After preparation, which medications are double checked?
- Are high-alert medications checked prior to dispensing to nursing staff?

Hazardous Medication Preparation

- How do you ensure that the preparation of hazardous medications presents no risk of harm to staff?
- How is the waste from preparing hazardous medications handled?
- Where do you store spill kits?
- How is staff trained to clean up a hazardous spill?

Preparing Medications Accurately

- What techniques do you use to ensure that medications are prepared accurately?

Sterile Preparation Compounding

- When do nonpharmacy personnel (e.g., nurses) prepare intravenous solutions?
- What sterile preparations do nonpharmacy personnel prepare and where do they prepare them?
- How is staff trained on USP Chapter <797> requirements?
- How do you handle USP Chapter <797> quality control issues?
- What progress have you made toward compliance with USP Chapter <797> requirements?
- What are the USP risk levels for the sterile preparations that are compounded in your organization?

Dispensing Medications in a Timely Manner

- What is the time period between when an order is written and when the medication is administered?
- How do you know if medications are delivered to patient care areas in a timely manner?
- How many nursing complaints concerning delivery time are received monthly?
- Do you have specific time expectations for "stat" or "now" medication orders?

Ready-to-Administer Medications

- Are all medications dispensed in a ready-to-administer form?
- What medications are not dispensed in a ready-to-administer form or unit-dose package?
- How are doses that require a partial tablet (e.g., ½ tablet) dispensed?

Medication Labels

- What information is included on a label on a sterile preparation?
- Do all labels include an expiration date for the medication?
- How do you ensure that medications are labeled in a standardized manner?
- How does the anesthesia department label medication syringes?
- How are medications labeled on the sterile field?

Recalled Medications

- How do you receive notification of medication recalls?
- What do you do when a medication is recalled or discontinued by the manufacturer?
- How do you ensure that all recalled medication is removed from stock and sequestered?
- How do you communicate medication recalls or discontinuations to prescribers and staff?

Returned Medications

- How do you handle medications that are returned to the pharmacy?
- Are controlled substances allowed to be returned to the pharmacy?
- On what occasions can medications that are returned to the pharmacy be reused?
- Where do you store medications that are returned to the pharmacy?
- Do you use an outside firm for disposal of your outdated medications?

Administering

Safe Administration

- How do you ensure that medications are safely and accurately administered?
- How do you ensure the competence of staff who administer medications?

Infusion Pumps

- What types of infusion pumps are used in the organization?
- Are "smart pumps" used?
- How do you know that your infusion pumps are protected against free-flow?
- Can infusion pump alarms be heard from the nurses' stations?
- How does pharmacy collaborate with nursing to ensure that infusion pumps are used in a safe manner?
- How does the organization plan to provide safer infusion devices?
- Does the organization use infusion pumps for all intravenous anticoagulant medications?
- Do infusion pumps have a mechanism (e.g., software) that provides minimum/maximum dosing levels for high-alert medications?

Self-Administration of Medications

- Do patients self-administer medications?
- How do you assess the patient's competence to self-administer medications?
- How do you document the patient's competence to self-administer medications?
- Where are self-administered medications stored?

Personal Medications (Patients')

- Are patients allowed to use their personal medications?
- Where do you store patients' personal medications?

Education

- What education have you provided relating to high-alert medications?
- What education have you provided relating to new medications?
- What role does the dietary department have in providing medication education to patients?
- What education have you provided relating to new medication-related devices?
- How do you provide medication information to patients?

Reference Materials

- What reference materials are available to pharmacy personnel?
- What reference materials are available to nursing personnel?
- How do you ensure that reference materials are current?

Monitoring

Monitoring Medication Therapy

- How do you monitor the effects of new medications on patients?
- How are medication effects documented in patients' medical records?
- How does pharmacy receive International Normalized Ratio (INR) results for warfarin?
- What role does the laboratory have in monitoring the effects of medications?

Medication Errors

- How do you detect, report, and assess medication errors?
- What is your process for reporting errors, close calls (near misses), and system failures?
- How do you notify the prescriber if there is a medication error?
- How do you document that you have notified the prescriber of a medication error?
- How do you collect, aggregate, and analyze medication error data?
- What steps are in place to prevent medication errors?

Adverse Drug Events (ADEs)

- How do you detect, report, and assess adverse drug events (e.g., adverse drug reactions)?
- How do you notify the prescriber if there is an adverse drug event?
- How do you document that you notified the prescriber?

High-Alert Medications

- What high-alert medications have you identified in your organization?
- What safety measures are in place to prevent errors with high-alert medications?

Evaluation

Medication Management (MM) System Evaluation

- What risk points have you identified in your MM system?
- How often do you evaluate the effectiveness and safety of your medication processes?
- Have you conducted any medication-related FMEAs?
- What methods do you use to identify MM system problems?
- What improvements did you make when you identified problems?

Literature Evaluation

- How do you evaluate the literature for new technologies or successful practices that can be used to improve your MM system?
- What new technologies or successful practices have you implemented?

Table 5-1. Medication Management System Processes

Selection and Procurement			
P&T or Equivalent	**Purchasers**	**Vendors/Sources**	**Products**
Set formulary criteria Develop formulary Provide for nonformulary drugs Develop policies & procedures Review drug literature Review & revise formulary Address shortages & outages Address recalls/discontinuations Communicate/educate	Pharmacy Ambulatory Care Materials Management Imaging Other departments & services	Wholesalers Manufacturers Investigational drug prescribers Compounding pharmacies Other suppliers & sources	Medications—Joint Commission definition: • Medication samples • IVs (plain & with additives) • Respiratory therapy • Anesthesia gases • Blood derivatives • Contrast media • Investigational drugs • Other medications Drug-related devices/ supplies

Storage—All Department/Areas
Securely: Locked/accountable Safely: High risk/hazardous Properly: Temperature/light
Emergency: Available & controlled Patient & Family: Identified & controlled Outdated/Recalled: Removed & disposed of

Ordering & Transcribing—All Prescribers	
Before Ordering: • Obtain patient information • Record patient information • Assess patient • Choose appropriate medication **Ordering:** • Order accurately, clearly, & legibly (written, verbal, or telephone)	**After Ordering:** • Verify order • Transcribe order to MAR properly • Verify transcription • Send/deliver/transmit order

Preparing & Dispensing—Pharmacy		
Pharmacist Review, evaluate, & clarify/change order	**Pharmacist or Staff** Prepare or compound safely, properly, & accurately	**Pharmacist** Perform final check & dispense medication
Maintain patient profile	Package/label properly	Deliver to patient area

Distributing—Pharmacy
Distribute floor stock drugs & supplies to the following: • Patient care & other storage areas • Automated dispensing cabinets Provide for after-hours pharmacy services

Table 5-1. Medication Management System Processes (cont'd)

Administering Prescribers, Nurses, Respiratory Therapists, Radiology Technologists, Patients, & Others			
Obtain & prepare right drug for right patient	Identify patient correctly Verify no contraindication Advise patient about medication	Administer right drug & right dose to right patient at right time	Document completely, accurately, & correctly
Perform double checks & take other precautions	Perform double checks & take other precautions	Perform double checks & take other precautions	Comply with policy

Monitoring—All Services
Observe/assess. Monitor effect/response. Intervene as needed. Document effect/response. Document action. Report internally/externally.

MEDICATION MANAGEMENT SYSTEM SUPPORT PROCESSES

Patient & Family Education—All Services
Provide verbal teaching. Provide printed instructions. Evaluate comprehension & competence. Follow-up. Document education.

Surveillance & Process/Performance Improvement Activities—All Services				
Evaluate staff education Evaluate patient education	Evaluate medication use Review literature Review NPSG compliance	Review and analyze adverse drug reactions (ADRs)	Review and analyze medication errors	Conduct FMEA & RCA Perform inspections Do ISMP Self-Assessment Evaluate the medication management system
Outcome: Improve education	Outcome: Improve medication use	Outcome: Reduce ADRs	Outcome: Reduce errors	Outcome: Reduce risks

CHAPTER 6

National Patient Safety Goals Checklist

The Joint Commission has an ongoing commitment to improving patient safety. To support its commitment, The Joint Commission develops National Patient Safety Goals (NPSGs) and integrates them into the accreditation process. This chapter reviews the development of the NPSGs, provides a general discussion of The Joint Commission's expectations for the goals, and describes how organizations can pursue alternative approaches to meeting the requirements. The 2010 medication-related NPSGs for hospitals are included in this chapter in a checklist format and provides suggestions on how to implement them.

NPSG Development

The Joint Commission's Patient Safety Advisory Group recommends potential NPSGs to The Joint Commission's Board of Commissioners. The Board of Commissioners reviews the group's recommendations and announces a final set of approved NPSGs during the year before they become effective.[1] Some NPSGs may be carried over from year to year; others may be retired or modified. The 2010 NPSGs were published in October of 2009 and are effective from January 1, 2010.[2]

Joint Commission Perspectives®—NPSGs for each accreditation program are published in *Joint Commission Perspectives®* and the accreditation manual for each accreditation program. (*See* Chapter 1.) They are also available at The Joint Commission's Web site. (*See* Appendix.)

Sentinel Event Alert—Many of the NPSGs stem from The Joint Commission's publication *Sentinel Event Alert.* (*See* Chapter 1.) *Sentinel Event Alert* identifies high-risk patient safety concerns and offers recommendations for minimizing risks to patients. The first *Sentinel Event Alert*, published in 1998, addressed dangers associated with concentrated potassium chloride injection. Subsequent issues addressed medication errors, blood transfusions, high-alert medications, wrong-site surgery, dangerous abbreviations, infection control, infusion pumps, medication reconciliation, and other patient safety concerns. (*See* Table 6-1 for a list of *Sentinel Event Alerts.*)

NPSG Format—The NPSGs are formatted to be similar to formatting of the standards in the accreditation manuals. Rationales follow some of the NPSGs. Each NPSG has one or more elements of performance (EPs). The elements of performance are numbered consecutively for each NPSG. Notes and footnotes clarify some of the NPSGs and EPs.

NPSG Frequently Asked Questions—Organizations can direct specific questions about NPSGs to The Joint Commission at its Web site. (*See* Appendix.) The Joint Commission publishes frequently asked questions (FAQs) about the NPSGs and their requirements on the site.

Evaluating Compliance with the NPSGs

The Joint Commission evaluates compliance with the NPSGs during all types of surveys (e.g., full surveys and for cause surveys). (*See* Chapter 2.) Organizations must evaluate their compliance with the goals during their annual self-assessments (i.e., Periodic Performance Reviews). (*See* Chapter 2.) All accredited health care organizations that provide care relevant to the goals must show continuous compliance with carry over NPSGs *for at least 12 months.* They must show continuous compliance with new NPSGs from the date they became effective. Some requirements may have a phase-in period after the NPSGs become effective.

NPSG Documentation and Evidence of Compliance—Surveyors evaluate compliance with NPSGs throughout the survey (e.g., through tracer methodology). (*See* Chapter 2.) Organizations do not need extra documentation, new processes, and additional evidence of compliance. Nevertheless, some organizations might find it difficult to demonstrate compliance unless they modify their current documentation to reflect evidence of compliance.

Surveyors are instructed to look at current processes and relevant documentation, observe performance, and discuss with leaders and caregivers how the organization implemented the EPs. Surveyors state that a policy and procedure that describes how the organization will comply with a NPSG is not, by itself, sufficient.

Alternative Approaches to a NPSG

The Joint Commission must approve alternative approaches to a NPSG.[3] Organizations may request The Joint Commission to consider an alternative approach to a NPSG by submitting a form, Request for Review of an Alternative Approach to a National Patient Safety Goal (NPSG) Requirement. (*See* Example 6-1.) The most current version of the form is available on The Joint Commission's Web site. (*See* Appendix.) Complete instructions for completing and submitting the form are on the Web site and on the form itself. Organizations are not required to submit a Request for Review form if they implement an approved acceptable alternative (i.e., one that The Joint Commission has approved and published).[3]

Submitting the Form—Organizations may submit the form electronically, by fax, or by mail. However, The Joint Commission prefers forms to be filled out and transmitted electronically as an e-mail attachment. A separate form must be submitted for each proposed alternative approach. Organizations must submit the form to their account representatives, if known; The Joint Commission will not consider forms submitted by consultants.[3]

Joint Commission Review of the Request—The Joint Commission's Patient Safety Advisory Group reviews each request and advises The Joint Commission on whether the alternative is acceptable (i.e., meets or exceeds the published requirements) or unacceptable. The Joint Commission advises organizations if their alternative is acceptable or unacceptable.[3]

If Requests Are Not Accepted—If a request is not accepted, The Joint Commission provides the rationale for nonacceptance to the organization. The organization must implement The Joint Commission's published NPSG or revise the proposed alternative until approved by The Joint Commission.[3]

If Requests Are Accepted—The Joint Commission publishes acceptable alternatives to NPSGs in *Joint Commission Perspectives* and on its Web site. (*See* Appendix.) Organizations should determine if The Joint Commission has published acceptable alternatives to the NPSGs. If an organization implements an acceptable alternative, surveyors will evaluate the organization's implementation of the alternative.[3]

If the Organization Implements an Alternative That Has Not Been Reviewed and Accepted—If a surveyed organization implements an alternative approach that has not been reviewed and accepted, surveyors will score the EP as noncompliant. Surveyors will describe the organization's alternative in their report and note that it must be reviewed. The Joint Commission will review the alternative and either accept or reject it. If, after review, The Joint Commission rejects the alternative, it will issue a special Requirement for Improvement for the goal. The organization must address the Requirement for Improvement and submit evidence of compliance with the published EPs for the goal.[3]

Leadership Standards Relating to Patient Safety

The Joint Commission clearly places the responsibility for patient safety on the organization's leaders. The complete requirements are addressed in the Leadership (LD) standards in the *Comprehensive Accreditation Manual for Hospitals: The Official Handbook (CAMH).*

National Patient Safety Goals Checklists in This Chapter

Health care professionals who understand The Joint Commission's NPSGs and the accreditation process should be able to achieve continuous compliance with the goals if they use a well organized approach. The checklists in this chapter present the 2010 medication-related NPSGs and EPs for hospitals in a format that promotes understanding, provides an organized approach to implementing the goals, and helps foster continuous compliance. This chapter contains the following checklists:

2010 NPSG 1	Improve the accuracy of patient identification
2010 NPSG 2	Improve the effectiveness of communication among caregivers
2010 NPSG 3	Improve the safety of using medications
2010 NPSG 7	Reduce the risk of health care–associated infections
2010 NPSG 8	Accurately and completely reconcile medications across the continuum of care

The checklists address only the medication-related NPSGs and EPs that are applicable to hospitals. They do not address goals that have been retired and those that are only applicable to other accreditation programs. NPSGs for other accreditation programs are available in the accreditation manual for each program and on The Joint Commission's Web site. (*See* Appendix.)

> ***Note:*** Organizations should determine if The Joint Commission has published acceptable alternatives to the NPSGs. (*See* Alternative Approaches to a NPSG section above.)

> ***Note:*** Organizations should refer to The Joint Commission's Web site for answers to frequently asked questions (FAQs) about the NPSGs. (*See* Appendix.)

Checklist Updates—Because the NPSGs and survey expectations may change, organizations should check regularly for updates. NPSGs for 2011 and subsequent years are expected to be announced during the year before they become effective. (*See* NPSG Development *section above.*) The Joint Commission's Web site (*see* Appendix), *Joint Commission Perspectives*, and *Joint Commission Perspectives on Patient Safety*™ are the best sources for updates on NPSGs and survey expectations.

Checklist Organization

This chapter presents the medication-related NPSGs, rationales, elements of performance (EPs), and notes in a checklist format. Their sequence follows their arrangement in the *CAMH*. The checklist quotes the standards, notes, rationales, and EPs.

Checklist Symbols— Special attention should be paid to EPs displaying an icon. The checklist uses a 🗎 icon before an EP if documentation is required and a ⚠ icon before an EP if noncompliance is likely to create an immediate risk to patient safety or to the quality of care provided. A ☑ icon before an EP indicates that a Measure of Success (MOS) is required if the EP is scored non-compliant during a survey.

Authors' Comments, Experiences, and Suggestions—Checklist items reflect the authors' comments, experiences, and suggestions; reports from surveyed organizations; and surveyors' statements. They include suggestions to comply with the EPs requiring specific documentation, metrics, or attention to implementation of specific care. Some items reflect legal requirements, clarifying statements from Joint Commission standards, previous Joint Commission standards, or commonly accepted standards of practice. Others note variations in interpretation of the standards.

Checklist Usage Suggestions

To assess compliance, use the checklist and proceed systematically. Mark the item "Yes" if you are currently compliant and are sure you will continue to be compliant. Mark the item "No" if you are currently not compliant (even if you are sure you will be compliant later). If you are not sure of your answer, leave a blank response. A few items may be not applicable (NA). Answer honestly, use a pencil (so you can change your answers), and make notes on the pages (e.g., reasons for noncompliance). It might be helpful to record the locations of the documents on the checklist (especially if they are kept outside the pharmacy). Concentrate your efforts on resolving all "No" and blank responses.

Checklist

Yes No NA

Goal 1. Improve the Accuracy of Patient Identification

NPSG.01.01.01

Use at least two patient identifiers when providing care, treatment, and services.

Rationale for NPSG.01.01.01

Wrong-patient errors occur in virtually all stages of diagnosis and treatment. The intent for this goal is two-fold: first, to reliably identify the individual as the person for whom the service or treatment is intended; second, to match the service or treatment to that individual. Acceptable identifiers may be the individual's name, an assigned identification number, telephone number, or other person-specific identifier.

Elements of Performance for NPSG.01.01.01

1. ☑ ⚠ Use at least two patient identifiers when administering medications, blood, or blood components; when collecting blood samples and other specimens for clinical testing; and when providing treatments or procedures. The patient's room number or physical location is not used as an identifier. ___ ___ ___

Authors' Comments, Experiences, and Suggestions

For the purpose of its standards, The Joint Commission states that the term ***medication*** *is "any prescription medications, sample medications, herbal remedies, vitamins, nutraceuticals, vaccines, or over-the-counter drugs; diagnostic and contrast agents used on or administered to persons to diagnose, treat, or prevent disease or other abnormal conditions; radioactive medications, respiratory therapy treatments, parenteral nutrition, blood derivatives, and intravenous solutions (plain, with electrolytes and/or drugs); and any product designated by the Food and Drug Administration (FDA) as a drug. This definition of medication does not include enteral nutrition solutions (which are considered food products), oxygen, and other medical gases."*[4]

The two identifier requirement also applies to delivering special diets and snacks associated with special diets including nutritional supplements.[5]

The two identifier requirement also applies to reporting critical test results.[5]

The two identifier requirement also applies to writing orders for treatment (including computerized prescriber order entry).[5]

The organization should (as much as possible) actively involve the patient and, as needed, the family in the identification process.

The two patient identifiers must be patient specific (i.e., directly associated with the patient).[5]

If the organization uses more than two identifiers, at least two of the identifiers are patient specific.

Organizations frequently use the patient's name, an identification number that is specific to the patient (e.g., billing or medical record number), and the patient's date of birth. Surveyors have suggested that other acceptable patient-specific identifiers might include the patient's social security number,

Yes **No** **NA**

driver's license number, telephone number, and home address (although the latter two are not always specific to the patient). Organizations should consider using biometric recognition techniques (e.g., fingerprint and retinal scans) as technology develops, reliability improves, and the cost of equipment and implementation becomes affordable.

Surveyors also point out that identifiers may be in the same place (e.g., printed on the patient's wristband and/or contained in a bar code on the patient's wristband). For example, a single bar code that contains two or more patient-specific identifiers (e.g., name, identification number, and date of birth) meets the requirement.[5]

The Joint Commission does not require the use of wristbands for identification. If wristbands are used, they must be attached to the patient at all times. Wristbands must not be attached to the bed or lie at the bedside.[5]

The two patient identifiers must be directly associated with the medication, blood product, blood sample, specimen, treatment, or procedure (e.g., on the medication administration record or on an attached label).[5]

The requirement states that the ***patient*** *must be identified using two patient-specific identifiers. The Joint Commission does not require* ***medications*** *to be labeled with two patient identifiers. However, the authors suggest that all patient-specific medications (e.g., compounded IVs, inhalers, insulin pens, other non-unit dose items) contain the two patient identifiers. Medication bin/drawer labels should include the two identifiers to the extent practical. However, labeling unit-dose packaged medications and medications in automated dispensing cabinets with two identifiers might not be possible.*

Many organizations enter the two patient identifiers on the medication administration record (MAR). Some surveyors expect this. Before administering the medication, nurses (1) match the two identifiers on the MAR with the two identifiers on the patient's wristband and then (2) match the order on the MAR with the medication to be administered. Surveyors expect staff to take MARs to the bedside to verify the patient's identity and the medication to be administered.

The ***same*** *two patient identifiers must be used throughout the* ***same*** *setting (i.e., not necessarily throughout the organization).*[5] *Staff cannot select the identifiers that they choose to use; this must be defined in policy.*

If ***different*** *patient identifiers are used in* ***different*** *settings within the organization,*

- *The identifiers are consistent in each setting.*[5]
- *Use of the identifiers meets the intent of the requirement.*[5]

If ***different*** *patient identifiers are used for* ***different*** *processes (e.g., name and birth date for the laboratory and name and patient number for medication administration), all of the following are to be in place:*[6]

- *Their use is specified in the organization's policy.*
- *Their use is followed consistently for each process.*
- *Identifiers are not switched on a patient-by-patient basis for the same process.*

Yes **No** **NA**

- *Different individuals do not use different identifiers for the same process.*
- *Patients display all of the identifiers used for all processes (e.g., name, birth date, and patient identification number).*

Home care surveyors state that visual identification of the patient may be allowed in some home care settings. However, the surveyors insist that two patient-specific identifiers be used when caregivers first meet the patient. After the patient is well known to the caregivers, they may use visual identification in place of ***one*** *of the patient-specific identifiers. Caregivers in home care settings should contact The Joint Commission to confirm that visual identification, as described here, is permitted in their practice.*[5]

Behavioral health surveyors state that visual identification of the patient may be allowed in some behavioral health care settings (e.g., those with low turnover of patients and staff). Surveyors caution that two patient-specific identifiers must be used when administering high-alert medications (i.e., visual identification cannot be one of the identifiers). Organizations should contact The Joint Commission to confirm that visual identification, as described here, is permitted in their organization.[5] *Some surveyors recommend that the patient's photo be readily available to help staff recognize the patient. The organization should specify which medications are high alert and state in their policies that high-alert medications require the use of two patient-specific identifiers.*

In emergencies and other situations when patients are not able to communicate with their caregivers, some organizations assign emergency patient-specific identifiers. One or both of the identifiers may be temporary (e.g., a temporary name if the patient is unknown and a temporary number if there is no medical record or emergency department number).[5]

Staff should be able to state the organization's two patient-specific identifiers.

Suggested Measurement Indicators (Performance Trackers):

- *Number of patients with appropriate identifiers on wristbands* ***divided by*** *number of patients audited during the period*
- *Number of patients who confirm that staff checked their wristbands and asked them to state their name and date of birth (or other organization-approved patient identifiers) before administering medications or blood products, taking blood samples or other specimens for clinical testing, or providing any other treatment or procedures* ***divided by*** *number of patients audited during the period*

Goal 2. Improve the Effectiveness of Communication Among Caregivers

NPSG.02.03.01

Report critical results of tests and diagnostic procedures on a timely basis.

Rationale for NPSG.02.03.01

Critical results of tests and diagnostic procedures fall significantly outside the nor-

Yes No NA

mal range and may indicate a life-threatening situation. The objective is to provide the responsible licensed caregiver these results within an established time frame so that the patient can be promptly treated.

Elements of Performance for NPSG.02.03.01

1. Develop written procedures for managing the critical results of tests and diagnostic procedures that addresses the following:
   - The definition of critical results of tests and diagnostic procedures ____ ____ ____
   - By whom and to whom critical results of tests and diagnostic procedures are reported ____ ____ ____
   - The acceptable length of time between the availability and reporting of critical results of tests and diagnostic procedures ____ ____ ____

Authors' Comments, Experiences, and Suggestions

Written procedures are required (e.g., in a written policy).

Critical results are findings for which rapid communication is warranted.[5]

The term "critical results" applies to all diagnostic tests and diagnostic procedures including imaging studies, electrocardiograms, laboratory tests, and other diagnostic tests defined by the organization as "critical."[5]

The organization must establish by policy the expected turn-around time from the time critical results are available until the time they are reported.[5]

2. Implement the procedures for managing the critical results of tests and diagnostic procedures. ____ ____ ____

Authors' Comments, Experiences, and Suggestions

Time of reporting of critical results of tests and diagnostic procedures should be documented in the patient record.

3. Evaluate the timeliness of reporting the critical results of tests and diagnostic procedures. ____ ____ ____

Authors' Comments, Experiences, and Suggestions

The evaluation should include

- *Collecting data on the timeliness of reporting critical results of tests and diagnostic procedures that can be compared with the defined turn-around times.*
- *Comparing the collected data with the defined turn-around times and determine if there is a need for improvement.*
- *Taking appropriate action to improve timeliness of reporting and measure the effectiveness of those actions.*

Yes **No** **NA**

The organization does not need to collect data, measure, assess, and improve the reporting of all critical results at all times. The organization may focus on selected tests and diagnostic procedures and then shift its focus to other tests and diagnostic procedures.[6-5]

Suggested Measurement Indicators (Performance Trackers):

- *Number of records documenting compliance with the requirements for reporting critical results of tests and diagnostic procedures* ***divided by*** *number of records audited during the period*

Goal 3. Improve the Safety of Using Medications

NPSG.03.04.01

Label all medications, medication containers, and other solutions on and off the sterile field in perioperative and other procedural settings.

Note: Medication containers include syringes, medicine cups, and basins.

Rationale for NPSG.03.04.01

Medications or other solutions in unlabeled containers are unidentifiable. Errors, sometimes tragic, have resulted from medications and other solutions removed from their original containers and placed into unlabeled containers. This unsafe practice neglects basic principles of safe medication management, yet is routine in many organizations.

The labeling of all medications, medication containers, and other solutions is a risk-reduction activity consistent with safe medication management. This practice addresses a recognized risk point in the administration of medications in perioperative and other procedural settings. Labels for medications and medication containers are also addressed at MM.05.01.09.

Elements of Performance for NPSG.03.04.01

1. ⚠ In perioperative and other procedural settings both on and off the sterile field, label medications and solutions that are not immediately administered. This applies even if there is only one medication being used. ___ ___ ___

   Note: An immediately administered medication is one that an authorized staff member prepares or obtains, takes directly to a patient, and administers to that patient without any break in the process. Refer to NPSG.03.04.01, EP 5, for information on timing of labeling.

Authors' Comments, Experiences, and Suggestions

"Other solutions" referred to in the requirement include, but are not limited to, sterile water, formalin, povidine iodine, chlorhexidine, tincture of benzoin, ferric subsulfate (Monsel's) solution, and Lugol's solution.

	Yes	No	NA

The Joint Commission states that this requirement "applies to any surgical or other procedural setting and includes pre-, intra-, and post-operative/ procedural components. Consequently, it applies not only to the surgical suite but also to prep areas, pre-op holding, and Post Anesthesia Care Unit (PACU). It also applies to medications used by anesthesia providers." Other settings to which the requirement applies include "all procedural areas that use medications or solutions including, but not limited to, radiology and other imaging services, endoscopy units, dental services, and patient care units where 'bedside' procedures are done."[5]

*For the purpose of its standards, The Joint Commission states that the term **medication** is "any prescription medications, sample medications, herbal remedies, vitamins, nutraceuticals, vaccines, or over-the-counter drugs; diagnostic and contrast agents used on or administered to persons to diagnose, treat, or prevent disease or other abnormal conditions; radioactive medications, respiratory therapy treatments, parenteral nutrition, blood derivatives, and intravenous solutions (plain, with electrolytes and/or drugs); and any product designated by the Food and Drug Administration (FDA) as a drug. This definition of medication does not include enteral nutrition solutions (which are considered food products), oxygen, and other medical gases."*[4]

	Yes	No	NA
2. ⚠ In perioperative and other procedural settings both on and off the sterile field, labeling occurs when any medication or solution is transferred from the original packaging to another container.	____	____	____

Authors' Comments, Experiences, and Suggestions

This requirement includes containers such as syringes, medicine cups, basins, vials, irrigations, and IV bags/bottles.

Medications, medication containers, or other solutions must be labeled even if there is only one medication, medication container, or solution.

The only exception to this is when one solution or medication is removed from its original container and immediately administered by the person who prepared it or disposed of in some fashion, labeling is not required. This also applies to anesthesia services. (See NPSG.03.04.01, EP 5.)

	Yes	No	NA
3. ⚠ In perioperative and other procedural settings both on and off the sterile field, medication or solution labels include the following:			
• Medication name	____	____	____
• Strength	____	____	____
• Quantity	____	____	____
• Diluent and volume (if not apparent from the container)	____	____	____
• Expiration date when not used within 24 hours	____	____	____
• Expiration time when expiration occurs in less than 24 hours	____	____	____

Note: The date and time are not necessary for short procedures, as defined by the hospital.

Yes No NA

Authors' Comments, Experiences, and Suggestions

It is not acceptable to "label" a syringe by taping the vial from which the medication was removed to the syringe.[5]

The label must be affixed to the container. It is not acceptable to place the label beside or under the container.

The hospital should define in writing "short procedures" for which the date and time are not required on the label.

Suggested Measurement Indicator (Performance Tracker):

- *Number of properly and correctly labeled medications, medication containers, or other solutions* ***divided by*** *number of medications, medication containers, or other solutions inspected during the period*

4. ☑ ⚠ Verify all medication or solution labels both verbally and visually. Verification is done by two individuals qualified to participate in the procedure whenever the person preparing the medication or solution is not the person who will be administering it. ___ ___ ___

Authors' Comments, Experiences, and Suggestions

If the same person prepares and administers a medication, or pours and uses a solution, a two-person verification is not required.

Medications prepared and labeled by a pharmacist (e.g., a pharmacist assigned to surgery) do not require a two-person verification.[5]

5. ⚠ Label each medication or solution as soon as it is prepared, unless it is immediately administered. ___ ___ ___

Note: An immediately administered medication is one that an authorized staff member prepares or obtains, takes directly to a patient, and administers to that patient without any break in the process.

Authors' Comments, Experiences, and Suggestions

If the medication or solution is prepared and slowly used over the course of a procedure, is prepared by a staff member other than the administering provider, is prepared in bulk for the day's cases, or if the provider preparing the medication or solution participates in another function prior to use, the container must be labeled.[5]

If an individual draws up two medications into two separate syringes and then administers both medications, both syringes need to be labeled.[5]

Labeling expectations for contrast media that are loaded into power injectors are the same as for other medications. If the contrast media is administered immediately, the injector does not need to be labeled. If the contrast media is not administered immediately, the injector must be labeled.

Although presterilized, prelabeled empty syringes are commercially available, prelabeling medication and solution containers is not acceptable. However, commercially available or pharmacy-prepared prefilled, prelabeled syringes are acceptable.[5]

	Yes	No	NA

Prelabeling syringes for anesthesia medications for the anesthesia cart as a means of reducing the time it takes to prepare needed medications in an emergency situation is not acceptable.[5]

Prelabeled or pre-engraved basins for use only with sterile saline, sterile water, or other routine solutions are not acceptable.[5]

Preprinted adhesive labels for application to syringes when medications are drawn up are acceptable. Labels can be prepared by the organization or purchased commercially. Sterile labels are available from commercial sources.

6. ⚠ Immediately discard any medication or solution found unlabeled. ____ ____ ____

Authors' Comments, Experiences, and Suggestions

The Joint Commission does not specify a procedure for discarding unlabeled medications or solutions.

7. ⚠ Remove all labeled containers on the sterile field and discard their contents at the conclusion of the procedure. ____ ____ ____

   Note: This does not apply to multiuse vials that are handled according to infection control practices.

Authors' Comments, Experiences, and Suggestions

The Joint Commission does not specify a procedure for discarding containers at the conclusion of a procedure.

8. ☑ ⚠ All medications and solutions both on and off the sterile field and their labels are reviewed by entering and exiting staff responsible for the management of medications. ____ ____ ____

Authors' Comments, Experiences, and Suggestions

The Joint Commission does not specify a procedure for reviewing medications, solutions, and their labels.

NPSG.03.05.01

Reduce the likelihood of patient harm associated with the use of anticoagulant therapy.

Note: This requirement applies only to hospitals that provide anticoagulant therapy and/or long-term anticoagulation prophylaxis (for example, atrial fibrillation) where the clinical expectation is that the patient's laboratory values for coagulation will remain outside normal values. This requirement does not apply to routine situations in which short-term prophylactic anticoagulation is used for venous thromboembolism prevention (for example, related to procedures or hospitalization); the clinical expectation is that the patient's laboratory values for coagulation will remain within, or close to, normal values.

Yes No NA

Authors' Comments, Experiences, and Suggestions

This requirement does not apply to organizations that are only providing monitoring or education on anticoagulant therapy.[5]

The anticoagulants included under this requirement are unfractionated heparin, low molecular weight heparins, and warfarin. The organization may choose to include other anticoagulants.[5]

This requirement does not apply to heparin flush solutions.

Rationale for NPSG.03.05.01

Anticoagulation therapy can be used as therapeutic treatment for a number of conditions, the most common of which are atrial fibrillation, deep vein thrombosis, pulmonary embolism, and mechanical heart valve implant. However, it is important to note that anticoagulation medications are more likely than others to cause harm due to complex dosing, insufficient monitoring, and inconsistent patient compliance. This National Patient Safety Goal has great potential to positively impact the safety of patients on this class of medications and result in better outcomes.

To achieve better patient outcomes, patient education is a vital component of an anticoagulation therapy program. Effective anticoagulation patient education includes face-to-face interaction with a trained professional who works closely with patients to be sure that they understand the risks involved with anticoagulation therapy, the precautions they need to take, and the need for regular International Normalized Ratio (INR) monitoring. The use of standardized practices for anticoagulation therapy that include patient involvement can reduce the risk of adverse drug events associated with the use of heparin (unfractionated), low molecular weight heparin, and warfarin.

Elements of Performance for NPSG.03.05.01

1. ⚠ Use only oral unit-dose products, prefilled syringes, or premixed infusion bags when these types of products are available. ___ ___ ___

   Note: For pediatric patients, prefilled syringe products should be used only if they are specifically designed for children.

Authors' Comments, Experiences, and Suggestions

Only heparin infusions that are commercially available or that are prepared by the pharmacy should be used throughout the organization. (See MM.05.01.07, EP 1.)

All warfarin doses, including half-tablets, must be dispensed in unit-dose packages that are commercially available or repackaged by the pharmacy.

2. ☑ ⚠ Use approved protocols for the initiation and maintenance of anticoagulant therapy. ___ ___ ___

	Yes	No	NA

Authors' Comments, Experiences, and Suggestions

Protocols must be used for all anticoagulants covered by this goal (i.e., unfractionated heparin, low molecular weight heparin, and warfarin).

Protocols can be in the form of standing orders, written protocols, critical pathways, or clinical guidelines.

Protocols must be medication- and indication-specific and address ordering, dosing, administering, monitoring (including laboratory tests), identification and treatment of adverse drug events, and medication interactions.

Protocols should address any age-specific therapy considerations (e.g., adjusted dosing).

Protocols must be approved by the Pharmacy and Therapeutics (P&T) Committee or other comparable medical staff committee.

Protocols must standardize care (including dosing) across all patients and prescribers unless there is a clinical justification. The clinical justification should be documented in the patient's medical record. Use of different protocols for different physician preferences for the same anticoagulant and indication is not acceptable.

3. ⚠ Before starting a patient on warfarin, assess the patient's baseline coagulation status; for all patients receiving warfarin therapy, use a current International Normalized Ratio (INR) to adjust this therapy. The baseline status and current INR are documented in the medical record. ____ ____ ____

Authors' Comments, Experiences, and Suggestions

Warfarin must not be dispensed until the baseline coagulation status or the current INR is available. The results of the test must be available for use in adjusting therapy, if needed, before dispensing warfarin.

Warfarin should not be accessible via override in automated dispensing cabinets or in non-profiled floor stock (manual and automated systems).

Critical results of laboratory tests must be reported to the appropriate caregiver(s) within the time frame specified by the organization. (See NPSG.02.03.01.)

4. ⚠ Use authoritative resources to manage potential food and drug interactions for patients receiving warfarin. ____ ____ ____

Authors' Comments, Experiences, and Suggestions

Pharmacy should be involved in the evaluation and selection of resources used to manage warfarin food and drug interactions (e.g., patient educational materials, information resources for clinical staff).

Dietary services should be notified of all patients receiving warfarin and respond according to the organization's food/medication interaction policies and procedures.

Yes **No** **NA**

Dietary services and interventions for patients receiving warfarin must be documented in the patient record.

Staff should be aware that many common medications (e.g., lipid-lowering agents, erythromycin, metronidazole, and trimethoprim–sulfamethoxazole) will enhance the anticoagulant effect of warfarin.

5. ⚠ When heparin is administered intravenously and continuously, use programmable pumps in order to provide consistent and accurate dosing. ___ ___ ___

Authors' Comments, Experiences, and Suggestions

Staff must receive training and have their competence assessed on the use of programmable infusion pumps to administer heparin. Training and competence must be documented.

6. ⚠ A written policy addresses baseline and ongoing laboratory tests that are required for heparin and low molecular weight heparin therapies. ___ ___ ___

Authors' Comments, Experiences, and Suggestions

A written policy is required.

Results of all laboratory tests must be documented in the patient record.

Critical results of laboratory tests must be reported to the appropriate caregiver(s) within the time frame specified by the organization. (See NPSG.02.03.01.)

7. ☑ ⚠ Provide education regarding anticoagulant therapy to prescribers, staff, patients, and families. Patient/family education includes the following:
   - The importance of follow-up monitoring ___ ___ ___
   - Compliance ___ ___ ___
   - Drug–food interactions ___ ___ ___
   - The potential for adverse drug reactions and interactions ___ ___ ___

Authors' Comments, Experiences, and Suggestions

Staff Education

- *Staff who should be educated include pharmacists, pharmacy technicians, nurses, and dietary and laboratory personnel. Education should be appropriate to their roles in anticoagulant therapy management.*
- *The organization must assess the competence of staff who participate in anticoagulant therapy management. (See Chapter 7.)*
- *Education and competence of staff must be documented. (See Chapter 7.)*

Patient and Family Education

- *Anticoagulant therapy education must be provided while anticoagulants are administered during the patient's stay as well as upon discharge.*

	Yes	No	NA

- *Anticoagulant therapy education must be provided to patients receiving anticoagulants from hospital-owned outpatient pharmacies. Offering to counsel or provide education is not sufficient.*
- *Anticoagulant therapy education must be provided to employees of the organization who receive prescription services from the organization's pharmacy. Offering to counsel or provide education is not sufficient.*
- *Patient and family education must be provided in an understandable manner and appropriate to the patient's needs. (See Chapter 8.)*
- *The organization must assess patients' and families' comprehension of anticoagulant therapy education provided by the organization. (See PC.02.03.01, EP 25.)*
- *Patient and family education must be documented in the patient record.*

8. Evaluate anticoagulation safety practices, take action to improve practices, and measure the effectiveness of those actions in a time frame determined by the organization. ___ ___ ___

Authors' Comments, Experiences, and Suggestions

See MM.08.01.01 in Chapter 4.

Examples of evaluation methods include failure mode and effects analysis, medication use evaluation, analysis of adverse drug reaction and medication error reports, and tracking the percentage of patients who reach specific clinical goals (e.g., therapeutic laboratory values).

To demonstrate improvement, organizations should determine their baseline parameters and compare them with subsequent measurements.

The organization should review reports from programmable pumps (e.g., overrides of set limits) and aggregate data to determine trends in timing of doses, variances in practices in patient-care areas, etc.

When using high-alert medications such as anticoagulants, safeguards for safe use should be implemented. (See MM.01.01.03.) The safe use of anticoagulants involves all medication use processes. For example:

- *Selection and procurement (e.g., reducing the number of concentrations of heparin available)*
- *Storage (e.g., separating anticoagulants from other medications)*
- *Ordering and transcribing (e.g., eliminating the use of the abbreviation "U" or "u" and writing the word "unit")*
- *Dispensing (e.g., dispensing anticoagulants in unit-of-use, ready-to-administer forms)*
- *Administering (e.g., implementing double-checks)*
- *Monitoring (e.g., using a current INR when adjusting warfarin therapy)*

Yes **No** **NA**

Suggested Measurement Indicators (Performance Trackers):

- *Orders for anticoagulants that are weight based compared with orders that should be weight based*
- *Percentage of patients receiving anticoagulants under approved protocols*
- *Percentage of patients with required labs and other monitoring*
- *Percentage of patients receiving dietary education*
- *Percentage of patients receiving anticoagulant therapy education*
- *Percentage of staff receiving anticoagulant therapy education*

Goal 7. Reduce the Risk of Health Care–Associated Infections

NPSG.07.01.01

Comply with either the current Centers for Disease Control and Prevention (CDC) hand hygiene guidelines or the current World Health Organization (WHO) hand hygiene guidelines.

Rationale for NPSG.07.01.01

According to the Centers for Disease Control and Prevention, each year millions of people acquire an infection while receiving care, treatment, and services in a health care organization. Consequently, health care–associated infections (HAIs) are a patient safety issue affecting all types of health care organizations. One of the most important ways to address HAIs is by improving the hand hygiene of health care staff. Compliance with the World Health Organization (WHO) or Centers for Disease Control and Prevention (CDC) hand hygiene guidelines will reduce the transmission of infectious agents by staff to patients, thereby decreasing the incidence of HAIs. To ensure compliance with this National Patient Safety Goal, an organization should assess its compliance with the CDC and/or WHO guidelines through a comprehensive program that provides a hand hygiene policy, fosters a culture of hand hygiene, and monitors compliance and provides feedback.

Elements of Performance for NPSG.07.01.01

1. ⚠ Implement a program that follows categories 1A, 1B, and 1C of either the current Centers for Disease Control and Prevention (CDC) or the current World Health Organization (WHO) hand hygiene guidelines. (See also IC.01.04.01, EP 5) ___ ___ ___

Authors' Comments, Experiences, and Suggestions

Table 6-2 lists all Category I CDC recommendations (i.e., IA, IB, and IC).

Full CDC guidelines are available on the CDC Web site. (See Appendix.)

	Yes	No	NA

Full WHO guidelines are available on the WHO Web site. (See Appendix.)

The Joint Commission requires organizations to implement all Category IA, IB, and IC recommendations. The organization should consider implementing Category II recommendations.[5]

The organization's policies and procedures must reflect current CDC or WHO hand hygiene guidelines.

Hand hygiene processes for compounding sterile preparations in the pharmacy should also incorporate the requirements of United States Pharmacopeia (USP) Chapter <797>: Pharmaceutical Compounding—Sterile Preparations. (See Chapter 19.)

Surveyors often observe staff to determine compliance with policies and procedures relating to CDC or WHO hand hygiene guidelines.

Staff must use approved cleaning agents and alcohol-based hand rubs according to the organization's policies and procedures and CDC or WHO hand hygiene guidelines. Surveyors may look for the presence of non-approved hand hygiene products and lotions.

Staff members are not required to use alcohol-based hand rubs unless mandated by hospital policy. Staff may use soap and water instead of alcohol-based hand rubs.[5] *The hand hygiene guidelines specify conditions in which alcohol-based gel hand rubs may be used instead of an organization-approved cleaning agent.*

Alcohol-based hand rubs must be conveniently located in safe areas and are readily available to staff. Check local fire codes and the organization's infection control policies for guidance in locating alcohol-based hand rubs. Some codes specify that alcohol-based hand rub dispensers must be in egress corridors outside the patients' rooms. There may be other requirements for foam hand rubs. Some organizations provide staff with pocket-sized containers of the alcohol-based hand rubs.[5]

Staff use sterile gloves as specified in the organization's policies and procedures. (Some procedures require sterile gloves; others do not.)

Staff members who are in direct contact with patients must comply with hand hygiene guidelines (e.g., the use of alcohol-based hand rubs). This includes food service personnel and telemedicine providers who are in direct contact with patients.[5]

Staff members who provide direct care to high-risk patients must not wear artificial nails.[5]

2. Set goals for improving compliance with hand hygiene guidelines. (See also IC.03.01.01, EP 3) ____ ____ ____

Authors' Comments, Experiences, and Suggestions

Pharmacy should participate on the hospital's Infection Control Committee to provide input on hand hygiene compliance goals and other infection control issues.

3. Improve compliance with hand hygiene guidelines based on established goals. ____ ____ ____

Yes **No** **NA**

Authors' Comments, Experiences, and Suggestions

The organization must have an active program for monitoring and promoting compliance with CDC or WHO hand hygiene guidelines.

The organization must provide education and training to staff regarding current CDC or WHO hand hygiene guidelines and universal precautions for preventing infection. (See HR.01.04.01, EP 4 and HR.01.05.03, EP 1.)

The organization must assess the competence of staff to use current CDC or WHO hand hygiene guidelines and infection control and prevention procedures. (See HR.01.06.01.)

Education, training, and competence assessment of staff regarding appropriate hand hygiene must be documented in employee records. (See HR.01.04.01, EP 4 and HR.01.05.03, EP 1.)

The organization must monitor compliance with policies and procedures relating to using CDC or WHO hand hygiene guidelines, identify areas for improvement, and take action as necessary to improve compliance.

Suggested Measurement Indicators (Performance Trackers):

- *Number of staff and physicians observed in compliance with the hand hygiene guidelines after patient contact **divided by** number of staff and physicians observed*
- *Number of staff observed in compliance with policies dealing with length of natural nails **divided by** number of staff observed*

The CDC recommends the following performance indicators (See Table 6-2, Part III. Performance Indicators):

- *Periodically monitor and record adherence as the number of hand hygiene episodes performed by personnel **divided by** number of hand hygiene opportunities, by ward or by service. Provide feedback to personnel regarding their performance.*
- *Monitor the volume of alcohol-based hand rub (or detergent used for handwashing or hand antisepsis) used per 1000 patient days.*

Note: *Only the first method (direct observation) will meet Joint Commission criteria for corrective action or clarification. Details about the corrective action and clarification processes can be found in the Accreditation Process chapter of the CAMH.*[5]

- *Monitor adherence to policies dealing with wearing of artificial nails.*
- *When outbreaks of infection occur, assess the adequacy of health care worker hand hygiene.*

Hand hygiene educational aids, posters, monitoring tools, slide presentations, and other materials are available on the CDC and Hand Hygiene Resource Center Web sites. (See Appendix.)

Surveyors may review evidence of improved compliance with hand hygiene guidelines (e.g., improvement in hand hygiene performance measures).

Yes No NA

NPSG.07.03.01

Implement evidence-based practices to prevent health care–associated infections due to multidrug-resistant organisms in acute care hospitals.

Note: This requirement applies to, but is not limited to, epidemiologically important organisms such as methicillin-resistant staphylococcus aureus (MSRA), clostridium difficile (CDI), vancomycin-resistant enterococci (VRE), and multidrug-resistant gram-negative bacteria.

Rationale for NPSG.07.03.01

Patients continue to acquire health care–associated infections at an alarming rate. Risks and patient populations, however, differ among hospitals. Therefore, prevention and control strategies must be tailored to the specific needs of each hospital based on its risk assessment. The elements of performance for this requirement are designed to help reduce or prevent health care–associated infections from epidemiologically important multidrug-resistant organisms (MDROs).

Note: Hand hygiene and contact precautions as well as cleaning and disinfecting patient care equipment and the patient's environment are essential strategies for preventing the spread of health care–associated infections. Hand hygiene is addressed in NPSG.07.01.01. Contact precautions for patients with epidemiologically significant multidrug-resistant organisms (MDROs) are covered in IC.02.01.01, EP 3. Cleaning and disinfecting patient care equipment are addressed in IC.02.02.01.

Elements of Performance for NPSG.07.03.01

1. Conduct periodic risk assessments (in time frames defined by the hospital) for multidrug-resistant organism acquisition and transmission. (See also IC.01.03.01, EPs 1–5) ____ ____ ____

Authors' Comments, Experiences, and Suggestions

Monitoring of antimicrobial susceptibility reports may provide information on the risk of multidrug-resistant organisms (MDRO) acquisition and transmission in the organization.

2. ☑ Based on the results of the risk assessment, educate staff and licensed independent practitioners about health care–associated infections, multidrug-resistant organisms, and prevention strategies at hire and annually thereafter. ____ ____ ____

   Note: The education provided recognizes the diverse roles of staff and licensed independent practitioners and is consistent with their roles within the hospital.

Authors' Comments, Experiences, and Suggestions

Education on the appropriate use of antimicrobial agents should be provided to prescribers, pharmacists, and other appropriate clinicians.

	Yes	No	NA

The pharmacy should assist in the preparation of an organization-specific antibiogram that is distributed to the medical staff and other appropriate clinicians at least annually to guide antimicrobial prescribing practices.

The organization must provide education and training to staff regarding CDC or WHO hand hygiene guidelines and universal precautions for preventing infection. (See HR.01.04.01, EP 4 and HR.01.05.03, EP 1.)

Education and training of staff regarding hand hygiene and other infection prevention measures must be documented in employee records. (See HR.01.04.01, EP 4 and HR.01.05.03, EP 1.)

4. Implement a surveillance program for multidrug-resistant organisms based on the risk assessment. ___ ___ ___

Note: Surveillance may be targeted rather than hospital-wide.

Authors' Comments, Experiences, and Suggestions

Monitoring of antimicrobial susceptibility reports may be useful for identifying changes in antimicrobial resistance that may indicate the emergence or transmission of MDROs.

5. Measure and monitor multidrug-resistant organism prevention processes and outcomes, including the following:
   - Multidrug-resistant organism infection rates using evidence-based metrics ___ ___ ___
   - Compliance with evidence-based guidelines or best practices ___ ___ ___
   - Evaluation of the education program provided to staff and licensed independent practitioners ___ ___ ___

Note: Surveillance may be targeted rather than hospital-wide.

Authors' Comments, Experiences, and Suggestions

The appropriate utilization of antimicrobial agents should be monitored using medication use evaluations and clinical intervention programs such as antibiotic streamlining (assuring appropriate antibiotic use), IV to PO conversion, and renal dose adjustment.

An organization-specific antibiogram should be monitored and updated at least annually to track patterns and trends in antimicrobial susceptibility.

6. Provide multidrug-resistant organism process and outcome data to key stakeholders, including leaders, licensed independent practitioners, nursing staff, and other clinicians. ___ ___ ___

Authors' Comments, Experiences, and Suggestions

Antimicrobial utilization and resistance patterns and trends should be presented to the medical staff and other appropriate clinicians at least annually.

	Yes	No	NA
7. ⚠ Implement policies and practices aimed at reducing the risk of transmitting multidrug-resistant organisms. These policies and practices meet regulatory requirements and are aligned with evidence-based standards (for example, the Centers for Disease Control and Prevention [CDC] and/or professional organization guidelines).	___	___	___

Authors' Comments, Experiences, and Suggestions

The CDC provides recommendations on preventing MDROs in health care settings, including education, surveillance, antimicrobial use, and infection control precautions.[7]

The Infectious Disease Society of America (IDSA) provides guidelines for developing an antimicrobial stewardship program.[8]

NPSG.07.05.01

Implement best practices for preventing surgical site infections.

Elements of Performance for NPSG.07.05.01

	Yes	No	NA
7. ☑ ⚠ Administer antimicrobial agents for prophylaxis for a particular procedure or disease according to evidence-based best practices.	___	___	___

- Administer intravenous antimicrobial prophylaxis one hour before incision (two hours are allowed for the administration of vancomycin and fluoroquinolones).
- Discontinue the prophylactic antimicrobial agent within 24 hours after surgery (within 48 hours is allowed for cardiothoracic procedures).

Authors' Comments, Experiences, and Suggestions

See Joint Commission core measures at www.jointcommission.org/PerformanceMeasurement.

The organization should develop medical staff–approved protocols for surgical antimicrobial prophylaxis based upon evidence-based standards and guidelines.

A toolkit of resources is available from the Institute for Healthcare Improvement (IHI).[9]

Suggested Measurement Indicators (Performance Trackers):

- *The Surgical Care Improvement Project (SCIP) National Hospital Quality Measures (NHQM) are available on The Joint Commission's Web site.*[10]

Yes No NA

Goal 8. Accurately and Completely Reconcile Medications Across the Continuum of Care

> **Authors' Note:** At the time of this publication, The Joint Commission had suspended the scoring of this goal during surveys. The Joint Commission continues to evaluate this goal during surveys, but findings are not included in accreditation decisions and Requirements for Improvement are not issued. The Joint Commission expects a revised version of the goal to be approved by mid-2010 with implementation of the revised goal in January 2011.

NPSG.08.01.01

A process exists for comparing the patient's current medications with those ordered for the patient while under the care of the hospital.

Authors' Comments, Experiences, and Suggestions

Different processes may be used for different care settings (e.g., inpatient, outpatient, and emergency department). However, the process should be consistent within a specific care setting.

Rationale for NPSG.08.01.01

Patients are at high risk for harm from adverse drug events when communication about medications is not clear. The chance for communication errors increases whenever individuals are involved in a patient's care change. Communicating about the medication list, making sure it is accurate, and reconciling any discrepancies whenever new medications are ordered or current medications are adjusted are essential to reducing the risk of transition-related adverse drug events.

Elements of Performance for NPSG.08.01.01

1. At the time the patient enters the hospital or is admitted, a complete list of the medications the patient is taking at home (including dose, route, and frequency) is created and documented. The patient and, as needed, the family are involved in creating this list. ___ ___ ___

Authors' Comments, Experiences, and Suggestions

The list must include all medications the patient is currently taking. For the purpose of its standards, The Joint Commission states that the term ***medication*** *is "any prescription medications, sample medications, herbal remedies, vitamins, nutraceuticals, vaccines, or over-the-counter drugs; diagnostic and contrast agents used on or administered to persons to diagnose, treat, or prevent disease or other abnormal conditions; radioactive medications, respiratory therapy treatments, parenteral nutrition, blood derivatives, and intravenous solutions (plain, with electrolytes and/or drugs); and any product designated by the Food and Drug Administration (FDA) as a drug. This definition of medication does not include enteral nutrition solutions (which are considered food products), oxygen, and other medical gases."*[4]

Yes No NA

The Joint Commission does not specify who is to create the medication list. Physicians, nurses, and pharmacists are often involved in the reconciliation process. The organization must determine the qualifications and competency of those who create the list of medications, consistent with laws and regulations.[5]

There must be a single, complete list that is updated as needed and is provided to the patient and all of the patient's care providers.[5]

The medication list may be in a written or electronic format. Regardless of the format used, access to the list must be provided to all providers who participate in the medication management process. (See MM.01.01.01, EP 1 and EP 2.)

Only a list of current medications is required. A complete medication history is not required.

To ensure that prescribers have the information they need when ordering medications, every effort should be made to obtain a list of the patient's current medications as soon as possible.

The organization is expected to define a time frame for obtaining and documenting the list. Ideally the information should be available prior to ordering new medications. Some surveyors expect the list to be completed within 24 hours for inpatients.

In emergency or urgent situations, immediate care of the patient takes precedence. However, the organization must take steps as soon as possible thereafter to obtain this information.

If the patient is unable to provide information on medications or clarification is needed, the organization should contact other potential sources of the information such as the patient's family, pharmacy(ies), and physician(s).

If a complete list of current medications is not obtained, the organization must provide a reasonable patient-related explanation.[5]

This requirement is not just for inpatients. Across the continuum of care includes admission, discharge, emergency department, ambulatory clinic, home care, and all other settings or services where medications are used.[11]

Surveyors evaluate compliance by reviewing patient records for a list of current medications on admission.

Suggested Measurement Indicator (Performance Tracker):

- *Number of patients for whom a list of current medications was obtained and documented upon admission* ***divided by*** *number of patients audited during the period*

2. ☑ ⚠ The medications ordered for the patient while under the care of the hospital are compared to those on the list created at the time of entry to the hospital or admission. ____ ____ ____

Authors' Comments, Experiences, and Suggestions

The Joint Commission does not specify who is to do the comparison. Physicians, nurses, and pharmacists are often involved in the reconciliation process. The organization must determine the qualifications and competency of those who reconcile medications, consistent with laws and regulations.[5]

	Yes	No	NA
3. ☑ ⚠ Any discrepancies (that is, omissions, duplications, adjustments, deletions, additions) are reconciled and documented while the patient is under the care of the hospital.	___	___	___

Authors' Comments, Experiences, and Suggestions

Reconcile means to compare and reach agreement. The purpose is "to avoid errors of transcription, omission, duplication of therapy, drug–drug and drug–disease interactions, etc."[5]

The Joint Commission does not specify who is to do the reconciliation. Physicians, nurses, and pharmacists are often involved in the reconciliation process. The organization must determine the qualifications and competency of those who reconcile medications, consistent with laws and regulations.[5]

Although The Joint Commission does not require organizations to have a medication reconciliation form, a standardized form can foster accuracy and prevent errors. Example forms are available at the Massachusetts Coalition for the Prevention of Medical Errors Web site. (See Appendix.)

If a medication list or reconciliation form is used as an order form, all required elements of a complete medication order must be present. (See MM.04.01.01, EP 2 and EP 13.)

	Yes	No	NA
4. ☑ ⚠ When the patient's care is transferred within the hospital (for example, from the ICU to a floor), the current provider(s) inform the receiving provider(s) about the up-to-date reconciled medication list and document the communication.	___	___	___

Note: Updating the status of a patient's medications is also an important component of all patient hand-offs.

Authors' Comments, Experiences, and Suggestions

This requirement applies to all transfers within the organization, including short term transfers to areas such as imaging and other diagnostic services, dialysis, and surgery.

The patient's current medication list should be communicated as part of patient hand-off communications. (See PC.02.02.01, EP 2.)

The list may be a paper document or in an electronic format. If an electronic format is used, access must be provided to all providers receiving transferred patients and within a time frame that corresponds with the patient's transfer to the area.

The current medication administration record (MAR) for inpatients may be used to communicate the medication list to the receiving provider.

Surveyors evaluate compliance by reviewing patient records for documentation of communication of the current medication list to the receiving care provider upon transfer to another practitioner, setting, service, or level of care within the hospital.

	Yes	No	NA

NPSG.08.02.01

When a patient is referred to or transferred from one hospital to another, the complete and reconciled list of medications is communicated to the next provider of service, and the communication is documented. Alternatively, when a patient leaves the hospital's care to go directly to his or her home, the complete and reconciled list of medications is provided to the patient's known primary care provider, the original referring provider, or a known next provider of service.

Note: When the next provider of service is unknown or when no known formal relationship is planned with a next provider, giving the patient and, as needed, the family the list of reconciled medications is sufficient.

Rationale for NPSG.08.02.01

The accurate communication of a patient's reconciled medication list to the next provider of service reduces the risk of transition-related adverse drug events. The communication enables the next provider of service to receive thorough knowledge of the patient's medications and to safely order/prescribe other medications that may be needed. This communication is especially important at transitions in care when a patient is referred or transferred from one organization to another.

Elements of Performance for NPSG.08.02.01

1. ☑ ⚠ The patient's most current reconciled medication list is communicated to the next provider of service, either within or outside the hospital. The communication between providers is documented. ____ ____ ____

Authors' Comments, Experiences, and Suggestions

The next provider of service is "that individual (or individuals) with whom the patient has an established relationship for receiving health care services or if there is not yet an established relationship, has accepted a scheduled appointment for follow-up care."[5]

For the purpose of its standards, The Joint Commission states that the term ***medication*** *is "any prescription medications, sample medications, herbal remedies, vitamins, nutraceuticals, vaccines, or over-the-counter drugs; diagnostic and contrast agents used on or administered to persons to diagnose, treat, or prevent disease or other abnormal conditions; radioactive medications, respiratory therapy treatments, parenteral nutrition, blood derivatives, and intravenous solutions (plain, with electrolytes and/or drugs); and any product designated by the Food and Drug Administration (FDA) as a drug. This definition of medication does not include enteral nutrition solutions (which are considered food products), oxygen, and other medical gases."*[4]

A complete reconciled list of the patient's medications must be communicated to the next provider of service when a patient is referred or transferred to another hospital or health care organization (e.g., nursing home, clinic, home health service).

A complete reconciled list of the patient's medications must be communicated to the patient's known primary care provider, the original transferring provider, or a known next provider of service when the patient is discharged to home.

Yes **No** **NA**

The list must contain all medications to be continued, including those home medications that were discontinued or held during the patient's stay, but are to be resumed after leaving the organization. The list should be reconciled against the current inpatient medication list and the home medication list.[5] It is not acceptable to provide a list containing only the medications that have been added and/or changed.

The list may be written or electronic. If the complete discharge medication list is available electronically (e.g., an electronic medical record) and the next provider of care can access the list, this process will meet the goal requirement.[5]

The medication list can be part of the discharge summary sent to the next provider of care.[5]

The medication list must be communicated directly to the next provider of care. The only exception is when the next provider is unknown. In this case, it is permissible to make the patient responsible for communicating the information. The list must always be communicated to the patient.

The reconciled medication list must be sent to the practitioner providing follow-up care even if he/she is the attending practitioner caring for the patient while in the organization.[5]

The reconciled medication list must be communicated to the next provider of care in a timely manner that facilitates follow-up care.[5]

The patient can refuse to allow information to be sent to the next provider of care. However, the organization is obligated to inform the patient of the reason for sending the list and the potential risks of not sharing the information with the next provider of care.[5]

Surveyors evaluate compliance by reviewing patient records for documentation of communication of the current reconciled medication list to the next provider of service when the patient leaves the organization's care.

Suggested Measurement Indicator (Performance Tracker):

- *Number of patients with a complete list of medications communicated to the next provider of service* ***divided by*** *number of patients audited during the period*

2. ☑ At the time of transfer, the transferring hospital informs the next provider of service how to obtain clarification on the list of reconciled medications. ___ ___ ___

Authors' Comments, Experiences, and Suggestions

This information can be provided on the medication list or in the patient discharge summary to the next provider.

NPSG.08.03.01

When a patient leaves the hospital's care, a complete and reconciled list of the patient's medications is provided directly to the patient and, as needed, the patient's family, and the list is explained to the patient and/or family.

	Yes	No	NA

Rationale for NPSG.08.03.01

The accurate communication of the patient's medication list to the patient and to the patient's family, if needed, reduces the risk of transition-related adverse drug events. A thorough knowledge of the patient's medications is essential for the patient's primary care provider or next provider of service to manage the subsequent stages of care for the patient.

Element of Performance for NPSG.08.03.01

1. ☑ When the patient leaves the hospital's care, the current list of reconciled medications is provided and explained to the patient and, as needed, their family. This interaction is documented. ___ ___ ___

   Note: Patients and families are reminded to discard old lists and to update any records with all medication providers or retail pharmacies.

Authors' Comments, Experiences, and Suggestions

The discharge list must include all medications (e.g., prescription, over-the-counter, and herbal) that the patient will be taking after discharge. The list should be reconciled against the current inpatient medication list and the home medication list.[5] It is not acceptable to provide a list containing only the medications that have been added and/or changed.

For the purpose of its standards, The Joint Commission states that the term ***medication*** *is "any prescription medications, sample medications, herbal remedies, vitamins, nutraceuticals, vaccines, or over-the-counter drugs; diagnostic and contrast agents used on or administered to persons to diagnose, treat, or prevent disease or other abnormal conditions; radioactive medications, respiratory therapy treatments, parenteral nutrition, blood derivatives, and intravenous solutions (plain, with electrolytes and/or drugs); and any product designated by the Food and Drug Administration (FDA) as a drug. This definition of medication does not include enteral nutrition solutions (which are considered food products), oxygen, and other medical gases."[4]*

The list of discharge medications is an excellent place to include information about the dose, route, frequency, duration of therapy, indications for the drug, and other relevant information about each medication.[5]

The discharge list must be provided in a format that is understandable to the patient. The use of medical abbreviations and terms should be avoided.[5]

The discharge medication list is not a physician's order. It is considered as part of the discharge instructions to the patient and used to provide patient medication education.[5]

Patients should be advised about home medications taken before admission that should not be resumed after leaving the organization.

Surveyors evaluate compliance by reviewing patient records for documentation that a complete list of medications was communicated and explained to the patient on discharge.

Suggested Measurement Indicator (Performance Tracker):

- *Number of patients with a complete list of medications communicated on discharge* ***divided by*** *number of patients audited during the period*

	Yes	No	NA

NPSG.08.04.01

In settings where medications are used minimally or prescribed for a short duration, modified medication reconciliation processes are performed.

Note: This requirement does not apply to hospitals that do not administer medications. It may be important for health care organizations to know which types of medications their patients are taking because these medications could affect the care, treatment, and services provided.

Rationale for NPSG.08.04.01

A number of patient care settings exist in which medications are not used, are used minimally, or prescribed for only a short duration. This includes areas such as the emergency department, urgent and emergent care, convenient care, office-based surgery, outpatient radiology, ambulatory care, and behavioral health care. In these settings, obtaining a list of the patient's original, known, and current medications that he or she is taking at home is still important; however, obtaining information on the dose, route, and frequency of use is not required.

Elements of Performance for NPSG.08.04.01

1. ☑ ⚠ The hospital obtains and documents an accurate list of the patient's current medications and known allergies in order to safely prescribe any setting-specific medications (for example, intravenous contrast media, local anesthesia, antibiotics) and to assess for potential allergic or adverse drug reactions. ____ ____ ____

   #### *Authors' Comments, Experiences, and Suggestions*

   *For the purpose of its standards, The Joint Commission states that the term **medication** is "any prescription medications, sample medications, herbal remedies, vitamins, nutraceuticals, vaccines, or over-the-counter drugs; diagnostic and contrast agents used on or administered to persons to diagnose, treat, or prevent disease or other abnormal conditions; radioactive medications, respiratory therapy treatments, parenteral nutrition, blood derivatives, and intravenous solutions (plain, with electrolytes and/or drugs); and any product designated by the Food and Drug Administration (FDA) as a drug. This definition of medication does not include enteral nutrition solutions (which are considered food products), oxygen, and other medical gases."*[4]

2. 📄 ☑ ⚠ When only short-term medications (for example, a preprocedure medication or a short-term course of an antibiotic) will be prescribed and no changes are made to the patient's current medication list, the patient and, as needed, their family is provided with a list containing the short-term medication additions that the patient will continue after leaving the hospital. ____ ____ ____

   Note: This list of new short-term medications is not considered to be part of the original, known, and current medication list. When patients leave these settings, a list of the original, known, and current medications does not need to be provided, unless the patient is assessed to be confused or unable to comprehend adequately. In this case, the patient's family is provided both medication lists and the circumstances are documented.

	Yes	No	NA
Authors' Comments, Experiences, and Suggestions			
Organizations should determine which areas or settings qualify as minimal medication use settings and develop modified medication reconciliation processes for those areas or settings.			
3. ☑ ⚠ In these settings, a complete, documented medication reconciliation process is used when: Any new long-term (chronic) medications are prescribed.	___	___	___
4. ☑ ⚠ In these settings, a complete, documented medication reconciliation process is used when: There is a prescription change for any of the patient's current, known long-term medications.	___	___	___
5. ☑ ⚠ In these settings, a complete, documented medication reconciliation process is used when: The patient is required to be subsequently admitted to an organization from these settings for ongoing care.	___	___	___
6. ☑ ⚠ When a complete, documented, medication reconciliation is required in any of these settings, the complete list of reconciled medications is provided to the patient and, as needed, their family, and to the patient's known primary care provider or original referring provider or a known next provider of service.	___	___	___

Table 6-1. Sentinel Event Alerts

Issue	Date	Topic
1	Feb 27, 1998	Medication Error Prevention—Potassium Chloride
2	Mar 20, 1998	Board to Review Modifications to Sentinel Event Procedures
3	May 1, 1998	Board Approves Changes to Sentinel Event Policy and Procedures
4	May 11, 1998	Accreditation Committee Approves Examples of Voluntarily Reportable Sentinel Events
5	Jul 24, 1998	Board Approves Changes to Sentinel Event Policy and Procedures
6	Aug 28, 1998	Lessons Learned: Wrong Site Surgery
7	Nov 6, 1998	Inpatient Suicides: Recommendations for Prevention
8	Nov 18, 1998	Preventing Restraint Deaths
9	Apr 9, 1999	Infant Abductions: Preventing Future Occurrences
10	Aug 30, 1999	Blood Transfusion Errors: Preventing Future Occurrences
11	Nov 19, 1999	High-Alert Medications and Patient Safety
12	Feb 4, 2000	Operative and Post-Operative Complications: Lessons for the Future
13	Apr 21, 2000	Making an Impact on Health Care
14	Jul 12, 2000	Fatal Falls: Lessons for the Future
15	Nov 30, 2000	Infusion Pumps: Preventing Future Adverse Events
16	Feb 27, 2001	Mix-up Leads to a Medication Error
17	Mar 20, 2001	Lessons Learned: Fires in the Home Care Setting
18	Apr 2001	Kernicterus Threatens Healthy Newborns
19	May 2001	Look-alike, Sound-alike Drug Names
20	Jun 2001	Exposure to Creutzfeldt-Jakob Disease
21	Jul 2001	Medical Gas Mix-ups
22	Aug 2001	Preventing Needlestick and Sharps Injuries
23	Sep 2001	Medication Errors Related to Potentially Dangerous Abbreviations
24	Dec 5, 2001	A Follow-up Review of Wrong Site Surgery
25	Feb 26, 2002	Preventing Ventilator-Related Deaths and Injuries
26	Jun 17, 2002	Delays in Treatment
27	Sep 6, 2002	Bed Rail-Related Entrapment Deaths
28	Jan 22, 2003	Infection Control Related Sentinel Events
29	Jun 24, 2003	Preventing Surgical Fires
30	Jul 21, 2004	Preventing Infant Death and Injury During Delivery
31	Aug 31, 2004	Revised Guidance to Help Prevent Kernicterus
32	Oct 6, 2004	Preventing, and Managing the Impact of, Anesthesia Awareness
33	Dec 20, 2004	Patient-Controlled Analgesia by Proxy
34	Jul 14, 2005	Preventing Vincristine Administration Errors
35	Jan 15, 2006	Using Medication Reconciliation to Prevent Errors
36	Apr 3, 2006	Tubing Misconnections—A Persistent and Potentially Dangerous Occurrence
37	Sep 6, 2006	Preventing Adverse Events Caused by Emergency Electrical Power Failures
38	Feb 14, 2008	Preventing Accidents and Injuries in the MRI Suite
39	Apr 11, 2008	Preventing Pediatric Medication Errors
40	Jul 9, 2008	Behaviors that Undermine a Culture of Safety

Table 6-1. Sentinel Event Alerts (cont'd)

Issue	Date	Topic
41	Sep 24, 2008	Preventing Errors Relating to Commonly Used Anticoagulants
42	Dec 11, 2008	Safely Implementing Health Information and Converging Technologies
43	Aug 27, 2009	Leadership Committed to Safety
44	Jan 26, 2010	Preventing Maternal Death

Source: Adapted from www.jointcommission.org/SentinelEvents/SentinelEventAlert/. Accessed February 24, 2010.

Table 6-2. CDC Hand-Hygiene Guidelines

Centers for Disease Control and Prevention. Guideline for Hand Hygiene in Health-Care Settings. *Morbidity and Mortality Weekly Report.* 2002; 51(No. RR-16):31–4.

PART II. RECOMMENDATIONS

Categories

These recommendations are designed to improve hand-hygiene practices of HCWs and to reduce transmission of pathogenic microorganisms to patients and personnel in health care settings. This guideline and its recommendations are not intended for use in food processing or food-service establishments, and are not meant to replace guidance provided by FDA's Model Food Code.

As in previous CDC/HICPAC guidelines, each recommendation is categorized on the basis of existing scientific data, theoretical rationale, applicability, and economic impact. The CDC/HICPAC system for categorizing recommendations is as follows:

Category IA. Strongly recommended for implementation and strongly supported by well designed experimental, clinical, or epidemiologic studies.

Category IB. Strongly recommended for implementation and supported by certain experimental, clinical, or epidemiologic studies and a strong theoretical rationale.

Category IC. Required for implementation, as mandated by federal or state regulation or standard.

Category II. Suggested for implementation and supported by suggestive clinical or epidemiologic studies or a theoretical rationale.

No recommendation. Unresolved issue. Practices for which insufficient evidence or no consensus regarding efficacy exist.

Recommendations

1. **Indications for handwashing and hand antisepsis**

A. When hands are visibly dirty or contaminated with proteinaceous material or are visibly soiled with blood or other body fluids, wash hands with either a nonantimicrobial soap and water or an antimicrobial soap and water (IA) (*66*).

B. If hands are not visibly soiled, use an alcohol-based hand rub for routinely decontaminating hands in all other clinical situations described in items 1C–J (IA) (*74, 93, 166, 169, 283, 294, 312, 398*). Alternatively, wash hands with an antimicrobial soap and water in all clinical situations described in items 1C–J (IB) (*69–71, 74*).

C. Decontaminate hands before having direct contact with patients (IB) (*68, 400*).

D. Decontaminate hands before donning sterile gloves when inserting a central intravascular catheter (IB) (*401, 402*).

E. Decontaminate hands before inserting indwelling urinary catheters, peripheral vascular catheters, or other invasive devices that do not require a surgical procedure (IB) (*25, 403*).

F. Decontaminate hands after contact with a patient's intact skin (e.g., when taking a pulse or blood pressure, and lifting a patient) (IB) (*25, 45, 48, 68*).

G. Decontaminate hands after contact with body fluids or excretions, mucous membranes, nonintact skin, and wound dressings if hands are not visibly soiled (IA) (*400*).

H. Decontaminate hands if moving from a contaminated-body site to a clean-body site during patient care (II) (*25, 53*).

I. Decontaminate hands after contact with inanimate objects (including medical equipment) in the immediate vicinity of the patient (II) (*46, 53, 54*).

J. Decontaminate hands after removing gloves (IB) (*50, 58, 321*).

K. Before eating and after using a restroom, wash hands with a nonantimicrobial soap and water or with an antimicrobial soap and water (IB) (*404–9*).

L. Antimicrobial-impregnated wipes (i.e., towelettes) may be considered as an alternative to washing hands with nonantimicrobial soap and water. Because they are not as effective as alcohol-based hand rubs or washing hands with an antimicrobial soap and

Table 6-2. CDC Hand-Hygiene Guidelines (cont'd)

water for reducing bacterial counts on the hands of health care workers (HCWs), they are not a substitute for using an alcohol-based hand rub or antimicrobial soap (IB) (*160, 161*).

M. Wash hands with nonantimicrobial soap and water or with antimicrobial soap and water if exposure to *Bacillus anthracis* is suspected or proven. The physical action of washing and rinsing hands under such circumstances is recommended because alcohols, chlorhexidine, iodophors, and other antiseptic agents have poor activity against spores (II) (*120, 172, 224, 225*).

N. No recommendation can be made regarding the routine use of nonalcohol-based hand rubs for hand hygiene in health care settings. Unresolved issue.

2. Hand-hygiene technique

A. When decontaminating hands with an alcohol-based hand rub, apply product to palm of one hand and rub hands together, covering all surfaces of hands and fingers, until hands are dry (IB) (*288, 410*). Follow the manufacturer's recommendations regarding the volume of product to use.

B. When washing hands with soap and water, wet hands first with water, apply an amount of product recommended by the manufacturer to hands, and rub hands together vigorously for at least 15 seconds, covering all surfaces of the hands and fingers. Rinse hands with water and dry thoroughly with a disposable towel. Use towel to turn off the faucet (IB) (*90–2, 94, 411*). Avoid using hot water, because repeated exposure to hot water may increase the risk of dermatitis (IB) *(254, 255).*

C. Liquid, bar, leaflet, or powdered forms of plain soap are acceptable when washing hands with a nonantimicrobial soap and water. When bar soap is used, soap racks that facilitate drainage and small bars of soap should be used (II) (*412–415*).

D. Multiple-use cloth towels of the hanging or roll type are not recommended for use in health care settings (II) (*137, 300*).

3. Surgical hand antisepsis

A. Remove rings, watches, and bracelets before beginning the surgical hand scrub (II) (*375, 378, 416*).

B. Remove debris from underneath fingernails using a nail cleaner under running water (II) (*14, 417*).

C. Surgical hand antisepsis using either an antimicrobial soap or an alcohol-based hand rub with persistent activity is recommended before donning sterile gloves when performing surgical procedures (IB) (*115, 159, 232, 234, 237, 418*).

D. When performing surgical hand antisepsis using an antimicrobial soap, scrub hands and forearms for the length of time recommended by the manufacturer, usually 2–6 minutes. Long scrub times (e.g., 10 minutes) are not necessary (IB) (*117, 156, 205, 207, 238–41*).

E. When using an alcohol-based surgical hand-scrub product with persistent activity, follow the manufacturer's instructions. Before applying the alcohol solution, prewash hands and forearms with a nonantimicrobial soap and dry hands and forearms completely. After application of the alcohol-based product as recommended, allow hands and forearms to dry thoroughly before donning sterile gloves (IB) (*159, 237*).

4. Selection of hand-hygiene agents

A. Provide personnel with efficacious hand-hygiene products that have low irritancy potential, particularly when these products are used multiple times per shift (IB) (*90, 92, 98, 166, 249*). This recommendation applies to products used for hand antisepsis before and after patient care in clinical areas and to products used for surgical hand antisepsis by surgical personnel.

B. To maximize acceptance of hand-hygiene products by HCWs, solicit input from these employees regarding the feel, fragrance, and skin tolerance of any products under consideration. The cost of hand-hygiene products should not be the primary factor influencing product selection (IB) (*92, 93, 166, 274, 276–8*).

C. When selecting nonantimicrobial soaps, antimicrobial soaps, or alcohol-based hand

Table 6-2. CDC Hand-Hygiene Guidelines (cont'd)

rubs, solicit information from manufacturers regarding any known interactions between products used to clean hands, skin care products, and the types of gloves used in the institution (II) (*174, 372*).

D. Before making purchasing decisions, evaluate the dispenser systems of various product manufacturers or distributors to ensure that dispensers function adequately and deliver an appropriate volume of product (II) (*286*).

E. Do not add soap to a partially empty soap dispenser. This practice of "topping off" dispensers can lead to bacterial contamination of soap (IA) (*187, 419*).

5. Skin care

A. Provide HCWs with hand lotions or creams to minimize the occurrence of irritant contact dermatitis associated with hand antisepsis or handwashing (IA) (*272, 273*).

B. Solicit information from manufacturers regarding any effects that hand lotions, creams, or alcohol-based hand antiseptics may have on the persistent effects of antimicrobial soaps being used in the institution (IB) (*174, 420, 421*).

6. Other aspects of hand hygiene

A. Do not wear artificial fingernails or extenders when having direct contact with patients at high risk (e.g., those in intensive-care units or operating rooms) (IA) (*350–3*).

B. Keep natural nails tips less than 1/4-inch long (II) (*350*).

C. Wear gloves when contact with blood or other potentially infectious materials, mucous membranes, and nonintact skin could occur (IC) (*356*).

D. Remove gloves after caring for a patient. Do not wear the same pair of gloves for the care of more than one patient, and do not wash gloves between uses with different patients (IB) (*50, 58, 321, 373*).

E. Change gloves during patient care if moving from a contaminated body site to a clean body site (II) (*50, 51, 58*).

F. No recommendation can be made regarding wearing rings in health care settings. Unresolved issue.

7. Health care worker educational and motivational programs

A. As part of an overall program to improve hand-hygiene practices of HCWs, educate personnel regarding the types of patient care activities that can result in hand contamination and the advantages and disadvantages of various methods used to clean their hands (II) (*74, 292, 295, 299*).

B. Monitor HCWs' adherence with recommended hand-hygiene practices and provide personnel with information regarding their performance (IA) (*74, 276, 292, 295, 299, 306, 310*).

C. Encourage patients and their families to remind HCWs to decontaminate their hands (II) (*394, 422*).

8. Administrative measures

A. Make improved hand-hygiene adherence an institutional priority and provide appropriate administrative support and financial resources (IB) (*74–5*).

B. Implement a multidisciplinary program designed to improve adherence of health personnel to recommended hand-hygiene practices (IB) (*74–5*).

C. As part of a multidisciplinary program to improve hand-hygiene adherence, provide HCWs with a readily accessible alcohol-based, hand-rub product (IA) (*74, 166, 283, 294, 312*).

D. To improve hand-hygiene adherence among personnel who work in areas in which high workloads and high intensity of patient care are anticipated, make an alcohol-based hand rub available at the entrance to the patient's room or at the bedside, in other convenient locations, and in individual pocket-sized containers to be carried by HCWs (IA) (*11, 74, 166, 283, 284, 312, 318, 423*).

E. Store supplies of alcohol-based hand rubs in cabinets or areas approved for flammable materials (IC).

Table 6-2. CDC Hand-Hygiene Guidelines (cont'd)

PART III. PERFORMANCE INDICATORS

1. **The following performance indicators are recommended for measuring improvements in HCWs' hand-hygiene adherence:**

A. Periodically monitor and record adherence as the number of hand-hygiene episodes are performed by personnel/number of hand-hygiene opportunities, by ward or by service. Provide feedback to personnel regarding their performance.

B. Monitor the volume of alcohol-based hand rub (or detergent used for handwashing or hand antisepsis) used per 1000 patient-days.

C. Monitor adherence to policies dealing with wearing of artificial nails.

D. When outbreaks of infection occur, assess the adequacy of health care worker hand hygiene.

CHAPTER 7

Human Resources Standards Checklist

The Joint Commission, in its management of human resources (HR) standards, addresses planning (including licensure and staffing), qualifications relating to job responsibilities, roles in minimizing risks, performance evaluations, job descriptions, and competence assessment. The HR standards also address orientation, education, and training; personnel records; and other topics relating to personnel who provide services in the organization.

> ***Note:*** Organizations surveyed under the *Comprehensive Accreditation Manual for Hospitals: The Official Handbook (CAMH)* must comply with the HR standards that are applicable to them. Organizations surveyed under other Joint Commission accreditation manuals should review the appropriate manual. (*See* Chapter 1.)

> ***Note:*** The Provision of Care, Treatment, and Services (PC) chapter of the *CAMH* (*see* PC.02.03.01) addresses patient and family education and training relating to the care, treatment, and services provided. (*See* Chapter 8.)

Checklist Organization

This chapter presents selected Joint Commission HR standards, rationales, and elements of performance (EPs) for hospitals in a checklist format.[1] Their sequence in the checklist may sometimes differ from the *CAMH.* Requirements that are quoted or paraphrased are clearly indicated (e.g., HR.01.02.05 or HR.01.02.05, EP 3).

> ***Note:*** This checklist also includes standards from other chapters in the *CAMH* that relate to staff qualifications and competence.

> ***Note:*** Although this checklist does not address the HR standards completely, it should be sufficient to ensure compliance with most HR standards pertaining to pharmacy personnel. Health care organizations should check for new and updated requirements on the The Joint Commission's Web site. (*See* Appendix.)

A few items are not explicit in the HR standards but are consistent with Joint Commission expectations and/or professional practice standards. These items are not referenced to Joint Commission standards.

The notes are compliance expectations and suggestions that are based on the authors' personal experiences, reports from surveyed organizations, and surveyors' statements. Some notes reflect legal requirements, clarifying statements from Joint Commission standards, previous Joint Commission standards, or commonly accepted standards of practice. Others note variations in interpretation of the standards.

Checklist Symbols— Special attention should be paid to EPs preceded by an icon. The checklist uses a 🗎 icon before an EP if documentation is required, and a ⚠ icon before an EP if noncompliance is likely to create an immediate risk to patient safety or to the quality of care provided. A ☑ icon before an EP indicates that a Measure of Success (MOS) is required if the EP is scored non-compliant during a survey.

Checklist Usage Suggestions

To assess compliance, use the checklist and proceed systematically. Mark the item "Yes" if you are currently compliant and are sure you will continue to be compliant. Mark the item "No" if you are currently not compliant (even if you are sure you will be compliant later). If you are not sure of your answer, leave a blank response. A few items may be not applicable (NA). Answer honestly, use a pencil (so you can change your answers), and make notes on the pages (e.g., reasons for noncompliance and location of documents). It might be helpful to record the locations of the documents on the checklist (especially if they are kept outside the pharmacy). Concentrate your efforts on resolving all "No" and blank responses.

Checklist — **Yes** **No** **NA**

Staffing

⚠ The numbers and types of qualified staff are sufficient to support the care, treatment, and services provided by the organization. (*See* LD.03.06.01, EP 3.) ___ ___ ___

> ***Note:*** In the glossary to the *CAMH*, Joint Commission defines staff as follows: "as appropriate to their roles and responsibilities, all people who provide care, treatment, and services in the organization, including those receiving pay (e.g., permanent, temporary, and part-time personnel, as well as contract employees), volunteers and health profession students. The definition of staff does not include licensed independent practitioners who are not paid staff or who are not contract employees."

⚠ The number and mix of qualified and competent pharmacists and support staff are appropriate to the scope and complexity of services offered. (*See* the note for LD.03.06.01, EP 3.) ___ ___ ___

> ***Note:*** Staffing to provide sufficient pharmacy services in a 600-bed, tertiary care, urban medical center might require several pharmacists and support personnel on duty 24 hours a day. However, a rural facility with 30 beds or fewer might fully meet the requirements with only one pharmacist and part-time support personnel on duty 8 hours a day. An on-call or consultant pharmacist might adequately staff other facilities that provide less acute care and have a low patient census.

Staffing Plan

There is a staffing plan/schedule for the pharmacy. ___ ___ ___

> ***Note:*** Surveyors may ask to see a staffing schedule for the pharmacy. The pharmacy should be able to show that there is adequate staff on duty during peak hours and that staffing is sufficient to handle increases in patient census and intensity of care, and changes in types of patients.

> ***Note:*** During a survey, surveyors may compare the organization's staffing plan with actual staffing patterns. Although the organization's leaders must meet these standards, the pharmacy may be called upon to supply pharmacy staffing data for analysis.

Staff Qualifications

The director of pharmacy defines the qualifications of pharmacy staff that are specific to their job responsibilities. (*See* HR.01.02.01, EP 1.) ___ ___ ___

	Yes	No	NA

License Verification

Pharmacy staff members for whom law or regulation require current licensure, certification, or registration to practice a profession, have had their credentials verified with the primary source. Verification is performed and documented at time of hire and when credentials are renewed. (*See* HR.01.02.05, EP 1.) ____ ____ ____

> ***Note:*** The verification of credentials should be done as soon as possible upon the date of renewal of licensure, certification, or registration.

> ***Note:*** Verification of credentials can be performed via a secure electronic communication or by telephone, if the verification is documented. (*See* Notes for HR.01.02.05, EP 1.)

> ***Note:*** The primary source may delegate authority to verify credentials to another agency. An electronic or telephone verification is acceptable if it is documented. (*See* Notes for HR.01.02.05, EP 1.) (*See* HR.01.02.05 for more on verification requirements.)

☑ Pharmacy staff members for whom the organization (but not law or regulation) requires licensure, registration, or certification, have had their credentials verified at time of hire and when credentials are renewed. The verification is documented. (*See* HR.01.02.05, EP 2.) ____ ____ ____

Volunteer practitioners assigned responsibilities during a disaster who are not licensed independent practitioners, but are required by law and regulation to have a license, certification, or registration must also have their credentials verified with the primary source. (*See* EM.02.02.15, EP 8 and EP 9 for more on verification requirements for volunteers during a disaster.) ____ ____ ____

Education (Pharmacy)

☑ Pharmacy verifies that job applicants have the education and experience required by the job responsibilities. The verification is documented. (*See* HR.01.02.05, EP 3.) ____ ____ ____

Continuing Education

Pharmacy staff members have met the mandatory continuing education (CE) requirements to maintain their licenses and permits. ____ ____ ____

> ***Note:*** Some pharmacies keep a log of staff CE credits or keep copies of CE certificates in personnel files. You may need to require staff to provide evidence that they have met their CE requirements.

	Yes	No	NA
Background Checks			
☑ The pharmacy ensures that a criminal background check is obtained and documented on job applicants if required by law and regulation or the organization's policies. (*See* HR.01.02.05, EP 4.)	___	___	___
Staff Health Screening			
☑ The pharmacy verifies and documents staff compliance with applicable health screening requirements if required by law and regulation or the organization's policies. (*See* HR.01.02.05, EP 5.)	___	___	___
Staff Responsibilities			
The following information is used in making decisions regarding staff job responsibilities (*See* HR.01.02.05, EP 6.):			
• Required licensure, certification, or registration verification	___	___	___
• Required credentials' verification	___	___	___
• Education and experience verification	___	___	___
• Criminal background check	___	___	___
• Applicable health screenings	___	___	___
Licenses			
Pharmacy staff who provide patient care, treatment, and services possess a license, certification, or registration as required by law and regulation. (*See* HR.01.02.07, EP 1.)	___	___	___
Pharmacy staff who provide patient care, treatment, and services practice within the scope of their license, certification, or registration and as required by law and regulation. (*See* HR.01.02.07, EP 2.)	___	___	___
Students			
☑ Pharmacy staff oversee the supervision of students when they provide patient care, treatment, and services as part of their training. (*See* HR.01.02.07, EP 5.)	___	___	___
Screening Indicators			
Adequacy of staffing is included in the analysis of possible causes of undesirable patterns, trends, or variations in performance related to safety or patient care identified by the organization. (See PI.02.01.01, EP 12.)	___	___	___

Note: The organization may require the director of pharmacy to assist in this activity.

Yes No NA

Note: When problems with adequacy of staffing are identified, leaders responsible for the organization's patient safety program must be notified including actions taken to resolve the problem(s). (See PI.02.01.01, EP 13.)

Note: At least once a year, leaders responsible for the organization's patient safety program must review a written report of any results of analysis related to adequacy of staffing and any actions taken to resolve identified problems. (See PI.02.01.01, EP 14.)

Orientation (Pharmacy)

New pharmacy staff receive orientation to the organization and the pharmacy. (*See* HR.01.04.01.) ___ ___ ___

Note: Orientation to the organization and the pharmacy should start as soon after employment as practical to ensure that personnel are provided with essential information before they perform their activities. Orientation may take only a few hours or may extend over several weeks or months.

Note: Individuals new to the organization must be oriented to inform them of their responsibilities and how to fulfill them. The pharmacy should ensure that all pharmacy staff members receive this orientation.

Note: Individuals new to the pharmacy (including contract and temporary personnel) must be oriented to inform them of their responsibilities and how to fulfill them. Individuals new to the pharmacy but not the organization must be oriented to the pharmacy and their role within it. Individuals who frequently work in more than one department must be appropriately oriented to each department and their corresponding responsibilities. Surveyors sometimes ask to see the orientation record of a recently hired employee.

Orientation to the organization includes, at a minimum, the following:

- 📄 ☑ Key elements determined by the organization that are to occur before providing care, treatment, and services. (*See* HR.01.04.01, EP 1 and EP 2.) ___ ___ ___

  Note: Key elements of organization orientation programs often include topics relating to infection control, environment of care, emergency management, and life safety.

- 📄 ☑ Organization-wide policies and procedures (including safety and infection control). (*See* HR.01.04.01, EP 3.) ___ ___ ___

  Note: Organization-wide policies and procedures also include work schedules, holidays, vacations, sick leave, and related topics.

	Yes	No	NA
Note: Many organizations provide a general orientation to employee health.			
Orientation to the pharmacy includes, at a minimum, the following:			
• 📄 ☑ Pharmacy policies and procedures. (*See* HR.01.04.01, EP 3.)	___	___	___
• 📄 ☑ Specific job duties and responsibilities. (*See* HR.01.04.01, EP 4.)	___	___	___
Note: Specific job duties and responsibilities include individual performance expectations (e.g., performance and competence standards), educational expectations (e.g., attendance at in-service education programs), and applicable pharmacy law and professional standards of pharmacy practice.			
• 📄 ☑ Specific job duties and responsibilities related to infection prevention and control. (*See* HR.01.04.01, EP 4.)	___	___	___
Note: Infection control duties and responsibilities should include prevention of infection (e.g., adherence to standard precautions, hand washing techniques, and appropriate techniques for preparing sterile medications).			
• Specific job duties and responsibilities related to safety.	___	___	___
Note: Safety duties and responsibilities include fire safety, emergency management, management of hazardous materials and wastes, appropriate precautions for handling hazardous medications, and emergency procedures. Orientation should include pharmacy safety plans, Material Safety Data Sheets (MSDSs), location of fire alarms and fire extinguishers, emergency exit routes, and precautions for safe storage, lifting, and transport of materials.			
• Processes for minimizing security risks (including emergency procedures to follow during a security incident).	___	___	___
• Processes for reporting accidents, injuries, safety hazards, and security risks.	___	___	___
• 📄 ☑ Cultural diversity and sensitivity. (*See* HR.01.04.01, EP 5.)	___	___	___
• 📄 ☑ Patient rights, including ethical aspects of care, treatment, and services and the process used to address ethical issues. (*See* HR.01.04.01, EP 6.)	___	___	___
📄 ☑ Orientation is documented. (*See* HR.01.04.01, EP 2 through EP 6.)	___	___	___
Note: Orientation records should include, at a minimum, the name of the individual undergoing orientation, topics covered, date orientation was completed, and signature of the individual who confirmed the completion of orientation. (*See* Example 7-1.)			
The pharmacy assesses the effectiveness of orientation (e.g., gives pre- and post-tests, observes performance, and assesses competence in critical areas).	___	___	___

	Yes	No	NA

Education (Pharmacy)

☑ Pharmacy staff are provided ongoing education and training to maintain and improve their competency (i.e., their knowledge, skills, and ability to do a job). (*See* HR.01.05.03, EP 1.) ____ ____ ____

> ***Note:*** Staff education and training can be accomplished through any method (e.g., off-site seminars and conferences, in-service education programs, self-study materials, correspondence courses, newsletters, and audio and video recordings). On-the-job training may be sufficient. The standards do not require the pharmacy to provide all of the education and training programs for pharmacy staff (i.e., the organization and/or other departments might provide some of them).

> ***Note:*** Some surveyors expect pharmacy staff to receive education and training at least once a month. The time required for education and training sessions can vary from a few minutes to several hours.

> ***Note:*** Although not specifically required by the standards, some surveyors state that the pharmacy and other departments should hold staff meetings regularly (e.g., monthly). Either combined or separate meetings of pharmacists and support personnel should satisfy most surveyors. Many pharmacies combine educational programs and staff meetings. Minutes of meetings or similar records are adequate documentation.

> ***Note:*** Appropriate education and training should be developed as new types of therapies emerge (e.g., gene therapy).

☑ Staff is provided education and training when job responsibilities or duties change. (*See* HR.01.05.03, EP 4.) ____ ____ ____

Education and training address individual staff member needs. ____ ____ ____

> ***Note:*** Sources of information relating to learning needs include findings from individual competence assessments, performance evaluations, and peer review activities and findings from quality and performance improvement activities.

> ***Note:*** Staff member needs may include dispensing procedures; controlled substance handling; prepackaging; compounding of sterile preparations; laws, rules and regulations pertaining to medications and the practice of pharmacy; professional standards; equipment (including computers); bar coding of medications; automated dispensing cabinets; and performing medication area inspections.

> ***Note:*** Educational topics should ensure the professional competence of pharmacists and the technical expertise of support personnel. However, you need not limit their education to topics that are related to their work. Any educational topic that increases staff effectiveness is acceptable (e.g., planning, time man-

Yes **No** **NA**

agement, and personnel relations). Also, staff should be encouraged to participate in professional activities that are educational in nature (e.g., writing professional articles and joining professional societies).

Education includes cardiopulmonary resuscitation (CPR) and other lifesaving interventions (as required by the organization). ___ ___ ___

Note: The Joint Commission does not require pharmacy staff to receive CPR training. However, if the organization requires CPR training for pharmacy staff, some surveyors may look for documented evidence that they have been trained.

☑ Education and training of staff are specific to the needs of the patient population served. (*See* HR.01.05.03, EP 5.) ___ ___ ___

Education and training address care of patient age groups served by the organization (e.g., neonatal, pediatric, adolescent, adult, and geriatric populations). (Implied by HR.01.05.03, EP 5.) ___ ___ ___

Education and training address the type and nature of care provided by the organization and the department (e.g., skilled nursing, psychiatric, substance abuse, and rehabilitation care). (Implied by HR.01.05.03, EP 5.) ___ ___ ___

Ongoing education, training, or other staff activities emphasize specific job-related aspects of safety and infection prevention and control. (Implied by HR.01.05.03, EP 1.) ___ ___ ___

Note: Job-related aspects of safety include basic approaches to patient safety; medication safety; security measures; response to aggressive behavior and hostile situations (e.g., robbery, riot, or hostage situations); reporting of accidents, injuries, damages, and safety and security incidents involving patients, staff, visitors, and property; and processes for minimizing security risks.

Note: Job-related aspects of infection prevention and control include techniques for controlling infection (e.g., hand hygiene and aseptic technique) and findings from the organization's infection control activities.

Note: Pharmacy staff meetings and educational programs should address safety and infection control-related topics (e.g., findings from the safety management program and the infection control program, general safety measures and measures for preventing infection, fire prevention, methods of containing smoke and fires, hazardous materials, hazards associated with specific jobs [e.g., preparation of antineoplastic agents], and emergency preparedness). Staff members who are involved in safety and infection control incidents should be given additional training.

	Yes	No	NA
☑ Staff participate in education and training that incorporate the skills of team communication, collaboration, and coordination of care. (*See* HR.01.05.03, EP 6.)	___	___	___
☑ Ongoing education and training include information about the need to report unanticipated adverse events and how to report these events. (*See* HR.01.05.03, EP 7.)	___	___	___

> ***Note:*** Education and training should include the need to report and the means available to report adverse drug reactions and medication errors.

The pharmacy assesses the effectiveness of staff education and training activities. (e.g., give pre- and post-tests and observe performance).	___	___	___
☑ Ongoing staff education and training are documented. (*See* HR.01.05.03, EP 1 and EP 4 through EP 7.)	___	___	___

> ***Note:*** Education and training records include at least a summary of the topic; date of education and training session, program, or meeting; provider (e.g., instructor or lecturer); names of attendees; and CE credit (number of hours), if any.

> ***Note:*** Records should show that all shifts were included. Surveyors sometimes ask for lesson plans, training manuals, outlines, handouts, and audiovisual materials. These materials give credence to the documentation. Examples 7-2 and 7-3 are forms for recording attendance at education programs and meetings. Example 7-4 is an individual record of education completed.

Orientation (Professional Staff)

The pharmacy participates in the orientation of medical staff, nursing service, and other professional staff.	___	___	___

> ***Note:*** An orientation program for medical staff, nursing service, and other professional staff (e.g., respiratory therapists, emergency medical service personnel, radiology technologists, and nutrition service personnel) can improve medication use, prevent problems, avoid misunderstandings, and provide for safer medication processes. The Joint Commission has no specific requirements relating to pharmacy participation in this program.

> ***Note:*** Examples of orientation topics include recommendations for the safe prescribing and administration of medications, formulary (e.g., generic and therapeutic medication interchange policies), adverse drug event monitoring and reporting, and use of automated dispensing cabinets.

	Yes	No	NA

Education (Professional Staff)

	Yes	No	NA
The pharmacy participates in the education and training of medical staff, nursing service, and other professional staff.	___	___	___

> *Note:* Education and training may consist of presentations at medical and nursing staff meetings and at pharmacy-sponsored programs. Pharmacists should make sure that their presentations are consistent with the organization's medication use and cost-containment goals.

> *Note:* Examples of education and training topics include information on medication incompatibilities, interactions, contraindications, and adverse reactions; compounding of sterile preparations; automated dispensing cabinets; media fill testing; processes that improve the safe use of medications (i.e., ensure legibility, eliminate trailing zeros); medication error reporting and prevention; and findings relating to adverse drug reactions.

Competence (Safety)

	Yes	No	NA
The pharmacy staff has participated in assessing safety risks.	___	___	___
The pharmacy staff has made suggestions on how to improve safety within the organization.	___	___	___

Pharmacy staff members can describe or demonstrate the following:

	Yes	No	NA
• ☑ Methods for eliminating and minimizing physical risks in the environment of care. (*See* EC.03.01.01, EP 1.)	___	___	___
• ☑ Actions to take in the event of an environment of care incident. (*See* EC.03.01.01, EP 2.)	___	___	___
• ☑ How to report environment of care risks. (*See* EC.03.01.01, EP 3.)	___	___	___

Competence Assessment

	Yes	No	NA
Pharmacy staff are competent to perform their job responsibilities. (*See* HR.01.06.01 and LD.03.06.01, EP 4.)	___	___	___

> *Note:* Competence assessments determine if the individual has the knowledge, skills, and ability to do a job and actually performs the job according to defined expectations. (*See* Chapter 14.)

> *Note:* The Joint Commission requires organizations to assess the competence of staff members who assess, treat, and otherwise work directly with patients. Many organizations extend this requirement to all staff, including staff whose duties are not directly related to patient care (e.g., secretaries or administrative assistants).

	Yes	No	NA
Note: Pharmacy staff must have access to current and authoritative knowledge-based information resources to help them acquire, maintain, and improve their competence.			
Note: The pharmacy must define the specific tasks needed to perform a job and identify competence requirements for the job (e.g., in a job description or other document). Competence requirements must be updated periodically (e.g., annually).			

Competence assessment of staff includes the following:

- Defined competencies required to perform job duties and responsibilities (e.g., knowledge, skills, and ability needed to perform jobs; dispense medications; compound sterile preparations; and provide pharmacokinetic consultations). (*See* HR.01.06.01, EP 1.) ____ ____ ____

  Note: For example, assessing the competence of pharmacists who provide pharmacokinetic consultations should be based on the completion of education and training and by demonstration of their ability to make appropriate dosing recommendations (e.g., by written tests). In addition, there should be a period during which an experienced pharmacist reviews all of the pharmacist's work prior to making dosing recommendations. Thereafter, the pharmacist's competence should be reassessed periodically.

  Note: Competence assessment should be included in ongoing education and training, introduction of new procedures, assignment of new duties, and training associated with new or updated equipment. Continued competence can be ensured through periodic (e.g., quarterly) testing and frequent (e.g., daily or weekly) observation of work techniques.

- Populations served by the organization (e.g., skilled nursing, psychiatric, substance abuse, and rehabilitation). (*See* Introduction to HR.01.06.01 and HR.01.07.01.) ____ ____ ____
- Special needs and behaviors of patient age groups served by the organization (e.g., neonatal, pediatric, adolescent, adult, and geriatric patients). (*See* Introduction to HR.01.06.01 and HR.01.07.01.) ____ ____ ____

  Note: Staff members who prepare medications must be familiar with dosages and dosage forms for these age groups and demonstrate their competence before they prepare medications for these patients. Furthermore, staff members who assess, treat, or care for these age groups must be able to understand and react effectively to their unique needs. For example, individuals who educate patients must be aware that pediatric patients might not have the ability to understand the material, adolescent patients may resent an authoritative educational style, and geriatric patients may be hearing impaired. They can gain this awareness through education, training, and/or experience. However, competence assessments must determine if they address these limitations effectively when working with patients in these age groups.

Yes No NA

- Security and safety (including ability to use equipment safely and effectively). (*See* Introduction to HR.01.06.01 and HR.01.07.01.)

  Note: Equipment includes primary engineering controls for compounding sterile preparations, medication prepackaging equipment, automated dispensing cabinets, automated compounding devices and computers. Equipment management procedures must address operator competence. Individuals must be trained to operate the equipment effectively and safely (i.e., without harm to patient or operator) and detect malfunctions (e.g., inaccurate measurements) and signs of impending malfunction (e.g., damage due to dropping or abuse). If necessary, training should be repeated periodically to ensure continued competence of the operator.

- Prevention of contamination and transfer of infection (infection control) (e.g., appropriate hand hygiene and appropriate techniques in preparing sterile medications).
- CPR and other lifesaving interventions (as required by the organization).

  Note: The Joint Commission does not require pharmacy staff to be competent in CPR. However, if the organization requires CPR competence for pharmacy staff, surveyors may look for documented evidence that they are competent.

Staff competence is initially assessed and documented as part of orientation. (*See* HR.01.06.03, EP 5.)

Note: Competence must be assessed before individuals are allowed to perform their duties.

Assessment methods are used to determine staff competence. (*See* HR.01.06.01, EP 2.)

Note: Competence can be assessed through written or verbal tests, skills checklists, random direct observations, or any combination of these. Reviewing pharmacy and patient records may reveal information relating to an individual's competence. Actual, on-the-job assessments of daily work are preferred. However, simulated competence assessment situations may be necessary. Example 7-5 is a skills test, and Example 7-6 is a skills checklist.

Qualified individuals assess competence. (*See* HR.01.06.01, EP 3.)

Note: Qualified individuals are those who are familiar with the organization's competence assessment process and have the educational background, knowledge, training, and experience related to the skills being reviewed. (*See* HR.01.06.01, EP 3.)

Note: HR.01.06.01, EP 3 notes that if no individual within the organization is qualified to assess competence:

Yes No NA

- Qualified outside individuals may assist with the assessment of competence, or
- Appropriate professional organization guidelines relating to competence expectations may be used to assess competence.

There is documented evidence (e.g., competence assessment and certification of competence) that pharmacy personnel (including students, volunteers, contract service personnel and temporary agency staff) are competent.

Note: The organization may ask the pharmacy, contract service, and/or temporary agency to provide an annual summary of the pharmacy staff's competence to the organization's administration and/or governing body (e.g., a letter, memo, or completed certifications of competence). The organization should specify how this should be reported.

☑ Staff competence is assessed and documented once every three years or more frequently as required by organization policy or in accordance with law and regulation. (*See* HR.01.06.01, EP 6.)

⚠ Appropriate action is taken when a staff member's competence does not meet expectations. (*See* HR.01.06.01, EP 15.)

Note: Appropriate action may include additional education or retraining followed by reassessment of competence or modifying the person's job assignment.

Performance Evaluations

☑ The pharmacy evaluates staff performance based on the performance expectations that reflect their job responsibilities. (*See* HR.01.07.01, EP 1.)

☑ The pharmacy evaluates staff performance once every three years or more frequently as required by organization policy or in accordance with law and regulation. (*See* HR.01.07.01, EP 2.)

Note: Performance evaluations relate to how well the individual performs a job according to defined expectations. Performance evaluations may also relate to punctuality, attitude, compliance with policies and procedures, completion of education requirements, attendance at meetings, participation in required activities, maintenance of licensure, etc.

Note: Some laws, regulations, or other requirements (e.g., USP Chapter <797>) may specify more frequent performance evaluations and describe the performance expectations that must be met. (*See* Chapter 19.)

Yes **No** **NA**

Note: Performance evaluations can be combined with competence assessments or can be completed separately. If they are combined, performance evaluations must contain the specific competencies required. (*See* Introduction to HR.01.06.01 and HR.01.07.01.)

☑ The pharmacy documents performance evaluations. (*See* HR.01.07.01, EP 2.) ___ ___ ___

Job Descriptions

There is a written job description for each employee. (Implied by HR.01.06.01, EP 1 and HR.01.07.01, EP 1.) ___ ___ ___

Note: Managers must provide job descriptions that clearly and accurately define the minimum qualifications for the position, reporting relationships, authority (e.g., right to purchase equipment), and representative responsibilities and duties (tasks, services, and functions associated with the position). Job descriptions such as those described in this section should satisfy most surveyors.

Note: Job descriptions should be prepared for the director of pharmacy, staff pharmacists, and support staff. (*See* Example 7-7.) For some positions, such as pharmacy secretary or administrative assistant, a general job description will suffice. In other cases, job descriptions must be tailored to the individual (e.g., describe the special training and responsibilities in oncology pharmacy or pediatric pharmacy).

Note: Job descriptions should be provided at the time of hire. Thereafter, individuals should participate in developing their job descriptions.

The qualifications and performance expectations for positions are defined in the job descriptions and stated in measurable terms. ___ ___ ___

Note: Qualifications include education, training, experience, skills, and licensure. Performance expectations relate to the tasks, duties, services, and functions associated with the position and are often stated as performance or competence standards.

Performance and/or competence standards are employee-specific and job related. ___ ___ ___

Note: Performance and/or competence standards must be realistic, relevant, achievable, and measurable, and must be used in evaluating performance. They should be agreed on by both the manager and the employee.

Job descriptions (or other documents) address the special needs and behaviors of the patient age groups served (e.g., neonatal, pediatric, adolescent, adult, and geriatric patients). ___ ___ ___

	Yes	No	NA

Note: There must be evidence that the organization has considered age-specific needs when defining the qualifications of individuals who deal directly with patients of various age groups. Although including statements in individual job descriptions is a common way to meet this requirement, other evidence is acceptable (e.g., an organization policy or other document that defines age-related competencies required for all positions).

Note: If the staff deals directly with infants, children, adolescents, adults, or geriatric patients, the requirements for dealing effectively with these patients must be defined. Many surveyors, with good reason, extend this requirement to staff who do not deal directly with patients. For example, they expect job descriptions of staff that fill orders for pediatric patients to reflect that these individuals must be able to meet the needs of these patients (e.g., be familiar with pediatric dosages). Job descriptions for individuals who deal with patients of all ages must indicate that these individuals must be able to meet the needs of patients of all ages.

Job descriptions are reviewed and updated periodically (e.g., annually) to reflect current requirements. ____ ____ ____

Note: Job descriptions should be reviewed, revised, signed, and dated by employees and their supervisors as provided for in the organization's policies.

Personnel Records

There is a personnel record for each pharmacy staff member (e.g., pharmacists, technicians, and clerks). ____ ____ ____

Personnel records are stored in the pharmacy and/or centrally in the organization's files. ____ ____ ____

Each personnel record includes, at a minimum, the following:

- Employment application. ____ ____ ____
- Evidence that references were checked. ____ ____ ____

Note: Although The Joint Commission does not explicitly require personnel records to include employment applications and evidence that references were checked, these are good hiring practices and are consistent with The Joint Commission's HR requirements.

- Licensure information. ____ ____ ____

Note: There should be evidence that licensure was verified with the primary source when the person was hired and upon renewal thereafter. (*See* Licensure Verification in this chapter.)

	Yes	No	NA
• Evidence of orientation to the organization and the department (signed and dated by the staff member).	___	___	___
• Records of education and training provided by the organization and the department.	___	___	___
• Job description.	___	___	___
• Performance evaluations.	___	___	___
• Evidence of competence assessments.	___	___	___
• Records of counseling and disciplinary action.	___	___	___
• Health records (e.g., physical examinations, blood tests, chest X-rays, immunizations, and tuberculosis skin tests) required by the organization (including follow-ups as required).	___	___	___

Note: Pharmacy staff (including contract services staff) must comply with the organization's health record requirements. Copies of test results should satisfy the organization. Complete health records for the pharmacy staff need not be maintained in the pharmacy. Many organizations store health records in a central location.

CHAPTER 8

Education of Patients and Family Checklist

The Joint Commission, in its provision of care, treatment, and services (PC) standards, requires organizations to provide patient education and training based on each patient's needs and abilities. (*See* PC.02.03.01.) Patients and their caregivers (e.g., parents, guardians, relatives, friends, home care nurses, and home care aides) should be educated about medications administered during the patient's hospitalization as well as medications to be taken after discharge.

> ***Note:*** Organizations surveyed under the *Comprehensive Accreditation Manual for Hospitals: The Official Handbook (CAMH)* must comply with the patient education standards that are applicable to them. Organizations surveyed under other Joint Commission accreditation manuals should review the appropriate manual. (*See* Chapter 1.)

> ***Note:*** The Management of Human Resources (HR) chapter of the *CAMH* addresses staff orientation, education, and training. (*See* Chapter 7.)

Checklist Organization

This chapter presents selected Joint Commission patient education standards and elements of performance (EPs) for hospitals in a checklist format.[1] Their sequence in the checklist may sometimes differ from the *CAMH.* Requirements that are quoted or paraphrased are clearly indicated (e.g., PC.02.03.01 or PC.02.03.01, EP 4).

> ***Note:*** Although this checklist does not address the patient education requirements completely, it should be sufficient to ensure compliance with most requirements pertaining to pharmacy. Health care organizations should check for new and updated requirements on The Joint Commission's Web site. (*See* Appendix.)

A few items are not explicit in the patient education standards but are consistent with Joint Commission expectations and/or professional practice standards. These items are not referenced to Joint Commission standards.

The notes are compliance expectations and suggestions that are based on the authors' personal experiences, reports from surveyed organizations, and surveyors' statements. Some notes reflect legal requirements, clarifying statements from Joint Commission standards, previous Joint Commission standards, or commonly accepted standards of practice. Others note variations in interpretation of the standards.

Checklist Symbols—Special attention should be paid to EPs preceded by an icon. The checklist uses a 📄 icon before an EP if documentation is required and a ⚠ icon before an EP if noncompliance is likely to create an immediate risk to patient safety or to the quality of care provided. A ☑ icon before an EP indicates that a Measure of Success (MOS) is required if the EP is scored noncompliant during a survey.

Checklist Usage Suggestions

To assess compliance, use the checklist and proceed systematically. Mark the item "Yes" if you are currently compliant and are sure you will continue to be compliant. Mark the item "No" if you are currently not compliant (even if you are sure you will be compliant later). If you are not sure of your answer, leave a blank response. A few items may be not applicable (NA). Answer honestly, use a pencil (so you can change your answers), and make notes on the pages (e.g., reasons for noncompliance and location of documents). It might be helpful to record the locations of the documents on the checklist (especially if they are kept outside the pharmacy). Concentrate your efforts on resolving all "No" and blank responses.

Checklist	Yes	No	NA
Education Appropriateness			
☑ The pharmacy provides education that is appropriate to the patient's needs. (*See* PC.02.03.01, EP 4.)	___	___	___
Note: Providing education that is appropriate to the patient's needs may include an assessment of patients' knowledge and skills relating to their medications. Organizations must also ensure that patient education is appropriate to the needs of high-risk patients (e.g., geriatric and pediatric patients), patients with specific diseases (e.g., diabetes and asthma), and patients receiving specific medications (e.g., anticoagulants and insulin). Pharmacy staff must have access to current and authoritative knowledge-based information resources to help them provide appropriate information and education.			
☑ Providing education that is appropriate to the patient's needs includes an assessment of the patient's cultural and religious beliefs, emotional barriers, desire and motivation to learn, physical or cognitive limitations, and barriers to communication. (*See* PC.02.03.01, EP 1.)	___	___	___
The pharmacy provides patient education in an understandable manner. (*See* RI.01.01.03.)	___	___	___
☑ ⚠ Education and instructions are appropriate to the patient's age, language, and ability to understand. (*See* RI.01.01.03, EP 1.)	___	___	___
☑ ⚠ Interpreters and translation services are provided as needed. (*See* RI.01.01.03, EP 2.)	___	___	___
☑ ⚠ The needs of patients who have vision, speech, hearing, or cognitive impairments are met. (*See* RI.01.01.03, EP 3.)	___	___	___
Note: There must be a mechanism to ensure that education is understood and effective. Multilingual instructions should be available in those areas that have a significant number of patients who speak languages other than English. Instructions that use pictures rather than words can be used to educate patients who cannot read or have low literacy and patients who speak languages in which written instructions are unavailable. Instructions for visually impaired and blind patients can be in Braille or recorded.			

	Yes	No	NA

Education Topics

☑ The pharmacy provides patient education that addresses the safe and effective use of medications. (*See* PC.02.03.01, EP 10.) ___ ___ ___

Note: Education relating to the safe and effective use of medications might include the name and use of the medication; dosage, administration route, and frequency of administration; expected actions; special directions and precautions; what to do if a wrong dose is taken or a dose is missed; potential interactions with foods and other medications; expected side effects and what to do if a side effect is serious; contraindications; prevention of contamination; proper storage; proper disposal of unused or expired medications; and how to obtain prescription refills.

☑ ⚠ Patients and families are provided education about anticoagulant therapy that includes follow-up monitoring, compliance issues, food–drug interactions, and potential for adverse drug reactions and interactions. (*See* NPSG.03.05.01, EP 7 in Chapter 6.) ___ ___ ___

☑ Patients and families are provided education about medications that are self-administered during the patient's stay. (*See* MM.06.01.03, EP 3 through EP 6 in Chapter 4.) ___ ___ ___

OBRA-90

The pharmacy complies with OBRA-90 patient education requirements. ___ ___ ___

Note: The Omnibus Budget Reconciliation Act of 1990 (OBRA-90) requires pharmacists in a retail setting to offer to provide patient counseling to Medicaid patients. Many states extend these requirements to all patients. Some states apply the act to employee prescriptions, discharge prescriptions, and furlough (or pass) medications (i.e., medications supplied to patients who are not discharged but are temporarily on leave from the organization). Health-system pharmacists should ensure that they comply with federal OBRA-90 requirements, their state requirements, and their organization's policies.

Note: Some pharmacists contend that health-system organizations do not have to educate patients about medications to be taken after discharge because OBRA-90 requires a retail pharmacist to offer to educate patients when they fill their prescriptions. The Joint Commission's position is that an organization cannot be certain that retail pharmacists will provide the education nor can the organization be certain that the education will be adequate. Therefore, the fact that pharmacists in retail settings may educate patients when they fill their prescriptions does not relieve organizations from their responsibility to educate patients about their medications prior to discharge.

	Yes	No	NA
Note: OBRA-90 specifies patient education requirements that organizations might consider when developing their education program for patients to be discharged. These include name and description of the medication; dose and dosage form, route of administration, and duration of therapy; special directions and precautions for preparation, administration, and use of the medication; techniques for self-administering medications and action to be taken in the case of a missed dose; common and serious side effects, adverse effects, as well as interactions and therapeutic contraindications that may be encountered including their avoidance and the action required if they occur; proper storage; and prescription refill information.			

Medication–Food Interactions Education

	Yes	No	NA
Patients are educated about potential medication–food interactions.	___	___	___

Note: At a minimum, The Joint Commission expects organizations to educate patients about medication–food interactions associated with medications to be taken after discharge. Organizations may limit education to the prevention of well-documented, clinically significant interactions that pose a risk of discomfort or harm to the patient. Medication–food interaction education should emphasize foods to avoid, effect of dietary supplements, effect of alcohol consumption, timing of medication administration (e.g., before meals), importance of adequate fluid consumption, and signs of interactions and adverse reactions.

Vaccine Education

	Yes	No	NA
The organization provides relevant information to patients who receive specific vaccines. (*See* Chapter 21.)	___	___	___

Equipment Education

	Yes	No	NA
☑ As appropriate, the pharmacy provides education that addresses the safe and effective use of medical equipment or supplies when provided by the organization. (*See* PC.02.03.01, EP 10.)	___	___	___

Note: Medical equipment and supplies include inhalation devices (e.g., spacers and nebulizers), glucose meters, patient-controlled analgesia devices, and infusion pumps. Pharmacies that provide or support these devices should educate patients on their safe and effective use (including how to detect defects and problems and what to do if there are defects and problems).

Education Methods

	Yes	No	NA
The pharmacy uses education and teaching methods that address the patient's learning needs and are matched to the patient's level of understanding. (*See* Introduction to PC.02.03.01.)	___	___	___

	Yes	No	NA

Note: Patient education may be oral or written. The teaching format may be by individual instruction and/or in a group setting. For consistency (and because oral instructions may be forgotten or remembered incorrectly), printed instructions should be provided when possible. Providing instructional cards and leaflets is a popular way to educate patients. These materials may be prepared by the organization or obtained from pharmaceutical companies, government agencies, specialty professional groups (e.g., the American Heart Association and American Diabetes Association), and other outside sources. A copy of printed materials or summary of instructions should be placed in the patient's medical record.

AHFS Patient Medication Information

The pharmacy uses ASHP's *AHFS MedMaster Consumer Medication Information* (CMI) or similar written medication monographs such as Lexi-Comp's *Patient Advisory Leaflets* (Lexi-PALS™). ___ ___ ___

Note: ASHP's *AHFS MedMaster Consumer Medication Information* is an electronic database that contains easy-to-read patient medication information in nontechnical language.[2] The monographs include medication–food interaction information when applicable. The information may be printed and distributed to patients.

Education Comprehension

☑ The pharmacy evaluates patients' comprehension of education provided. (*See* PC.02.03.01, EP 25.) ___ ___ ___

Note: Techniques for evaluating comprehension include asking specific questions, having patients repeat instructions and demonstrate administration techniques, giving post-tests, and contacting patients after discharge to see if they are having difficulties with their medications.

Education Documentation

☑ ⚠ The pharmacy documents patient and family education (e.g., in the patient's medical record). (Implied by RC.01.01.01, EP 7 through EP 9.) ___ ___ ___

Note: Surveyors encourage the use of a multidisciplinary patient education record in the patient's medical record.

Education Coordination

☑ The pharmacy, as appropriate, coordinates its patient education with other disciplines. (*See* PC.02.03.01, EP 5.) ___ ___ ___

	Yes	No	NA

Note: Patient education is the mutual responsibility of physicians, nurses, pharmacists, dieticians, discharge counselors, and other health care practitioners. Physicians and nurses are in close contact with patients and are in an ideal position to educate patients and families on most aspects of care (e.g., care for a surgical wound). Qualified discharge counselors can do an excellent job of preparing patients for their departure from the facility. However, pharmacists are most knowledgeable about medications and should play a major role in medication-related patient education. Furthermore, some patients may prefer to talk to pharmacists about their medications. When it is not possible for pharmacists to provide medication-related education, they should ensure that current information and appropriate instructional materials are available to health care practitioners who educate patients.

Note: The pharmacy should be able to describe how it collaborates with nursing service, nutrition services, and other services in the education of patients and families. The pharmacy may suggest medications for inclusion in the program, suggest significant medication–food interactions for inclusion in the program, assist in preparing guidelines for patient education, and, when appropriate, provide education and instruction (e.g., diabetic teaching, anticoagulant therapy, and patient-controlled analgesia pump training). The pharmacy should be able to show examples of handouts and other materials that it provides to patients and their families.

Competence Assessment

Pharmacy staff members who educate patients and families are competent to do so. ____ ____ ____

Note: ASHP's *Competence Assessment Tools for Health-System Pharmacies* contains guidelines for assessing the competence of pharmacists and support staff.[3] (*See* Chapters 7 and 14.)

CHAPTER 9

Infection Control Checklist

The Joint Commission, in its prevention and control of infection (IC) standards, requires organizations to take precautions to reduce the risk of acquiring and transmitting infections. Organizations must have effective, organization-wide IC programs. All departments and services must participate in the organization's IC efforts.

> ***Note:*** Organizations surveyed under the *Comprehensive Accreditation Manual for Hospitals: The Official Handbook (CAMH)* must comply with the IC standards that are applicable to them. Organizations surveyed under other Joint Commission accreditation manual(s) should review the appropriate manual. (*See* Chapter 1.)

Checklist Organization

This chapter presents infection control precautions for health care personnel in a checklist format. They are consistent with The Joint Commission's IC standards,[1] current Centers for Disease Control and Prevention (CDC) hand hygiene guidelines[2] (*see* NPSG 7 in Chapter 6), and the provisions of the United States Pharmacopeia (USP) Chapter <797>.[3] (*See* Chapter 19.)

> ***Note:*** Although this checklist does not address these precautions completely, it should help to reduce the risk of acquiring and transmitting infections. Health care organizations should check for new and updated standards on The Joint Commission's Web site, and for new and updated hand hygiene guidelines on the CDC's Web site. (*See* Appendix.) Pharmacies should contact their board of pharmacy and other state agencies to determine how their state integrates USP <797> provisions into its regulations.

The notes are compliance expectations and suggestions that are based on the authors' personal experiences, reports from surveyed organizations, and surveyors' statements. Some notes reflect legal requirements, previous Joint Commission standards, or commonly accepted standards of practice. Others note variations in interpretation of the standards. Some notes are referenced to the standards.

Checklist Symbols—Special attention should be paid to EPs preceded by an icon. The checklist uses a 🗎 icon before an EP if documentation is required, and a ⚠ icon before an EP if noncompliance is likely to create an immediate risk to patient safety or to the quality of care provided. A ☑ icon before an EP indicates that a Measure of Success (MOS) is required if the EP is scored non-compliant during a survey.

Checklist Usage Suggestions

To assess compliance, use the checklist and proceed systematically. Mark the item "Yes" if you are currently compliant and are sure you will continue to be compliant. Mark the item "No" if you are currently not compliant (even if you are sure you will be compliant later). If you are not sure of your answer, leave a blank response. A few items may be not applicable (NA). Answer honestly, use a pencil (so you can change your answers), and make notes on the pages (e.g., reasons for noncompliance and location of documents). Concentrate your efforts on resolving all "No" and blank responses.

Checklist	Yes	No	NA

Infection Risk Identification

Accidents, incidents, unsafe practices, and unsanitary conditions that pose a risk of infection for patients, visitors, and staff are identified.	___	___	___

Infection Risk Reporting

Accidents, incidents, unsafe practices, and unsanitary conditions that pose a risk of infection for patients, visitors, and staff are reported.	___	___	___

Note: Infection control–related incidents are usually reported to the Infection Control Committee or a designated individual. The organization's infection control plan should contain specific information on how to submit these reports.

Infection Control Surveillance

Each department or service participates in infection control surveillance activities as required by the organization.	___	___	___

Cleaning and Disinfecting

The pharmacy and areas where medications are stored, compounded, dispensed, prepared, and administered are clean.	___	___	___
Staff uses organization–approved cleaning procedures and cleaning and disinfecting agents.	___	___	___
There are an adequate number of sinks and sufficient space and materials for cleaning equipment and washing hands.	___	___	___

Note: Cleaning should be coordinated with housekeeping personnel, and cleaning agents and procedures approved by the Infection Control Committee must be used. Particular attention must be given to prepackaging, compounding, and sterile preparation areas as well as areas likely to harbor microorganisms that could contaminate medications or transmit disease to staff.

Alcohol-based hand rub containers are appropriately located.	___	___	___
Cleaning agents and supplies are available to staff.	___	___	___
Cleaning and disinfecting agents are appropriately diluted.	___	___	___
Cleaning and disinfecting agents are appropriately labeled.	___	___	___
Equipment is kept clean and stored in a clean area.	___	___	___

Note: Areas under sinks are not clean areas. Mortars, pestles, glassware, and other equipment that must be kept clean must be stored in a clean area.

	Yes	No	NA
Medication preparation, packaging, and dispensing devices (e.g., mortars, pestles, pill crushers, pill splitters, counting trays, graduated cylinders, unit-dose packaging devices, and balances) are cleaned after each use and disinfected if necessary.	___	___	___
Devices used for crushing or splitting tablets are cleaned immediately after use according to manufacturers' recommendations and instructions.	___	___	___
Medication carts, drawers, and bins containing individual patient's medications are kept clean.	___	___	___
Automated dispensing cabinets and bins are cleaned according to the manufacturer's recommendations and instructions.	___	___	___

Note: Many organizations develop a schedule for cleaning equipment and devices.

Boxes

Cardboard boxes are stored off the floor. ___ ___ ___

Note: This is not specifically required by the standards. However, some organizations and surveyors insist that they be stored off the floor.

Shipping containers are not stored or opened (i.e., torn or cut) in any area reserved for prepackaging medications or compounding sterile preparations. ___ ___ ___

Note: Handling and storing shipping containers (e.g., cardboard boxes) must be done with minimal air disturbances and dissemination of dust particles. Intravenous (IV) bags and bottles and related supplies must be removed from cartons and wiped with an approved disinfecting agent prior to placing them in the sterile preparation area.

Waste

Staff disposes of waste in accordance with the organization's infection control policies and procedures. ___ ___ ___

Waste does not create a nuisance or a breeding place for insects, rodents, and vermin or otherwise permit the transmission of disease. ___ ___ ___

Waste disposal containers are close to the area of use. ___ ___ ___

Noninfectious waste is not mixed with infectious waste. ___ ___ ___

Note: Check the organization's policies on disposal of noninfectious waste and infectious waste.

Infectious Waste

Staff disposes of infectious waste in accordance with the organization's infection control policies and procedures. ___ ___ ___

Infectious waste does not create a nuisance or a breeding place for insects, rodents, and vermin or otherwise permit the transmission of disease. ___ ___ ___

	Yes	No	NA
Infectious waste disposal containers are close to the area of use.	___	___	___
Infectious waste is placed in specially marked containers (e.g., red bags) and disposed of separately from routine trash.	___	___	___

Note: Check the organization's policies on disposal of trash and infectious waste.

	Yes	No	NA
Items used in patient rooms are not returned to the pharmacy.	___	___	___

Attire

	Yes	No	NA
Personnel wear appropriate attire in non-sterile areas.	___	___	___
Attire worn in the sterile compounding area is clean and minimizes the potential for shedding and contamination, and meets the organization's policy and state regulations.	___	___	___

Note: Many organizations require personnel who compound sterile preparations to wear hospital-laundered scrubs in the buffer area.

Note: USP <797> has specific requirements for garb (e.g., attire). (*See* Chapter 19.)

	Yes	No	NA
Personnel remove jewelry and cosmetics prior to compounding sterile preparations.	___	___	___

Hygiene

	Yes	No	NA
Personnel are attentive to personal cleanliness and hygienic practices.	___	___	___
Personnel with rashes, sunburn, weeping sores, conjunctivitis, or active respiratory infection do not prepare sterile preparations.	___	___	___
Fingernail length complies with the organization's policies and procedures.	___	___	___
The use of artificial fingernails complies with the organization's policies and procedures.	___	___	___

Note: Artificial nails or extenders may not be worn by personnel who compound sterile preparations. Organizations often prohibit the wearing of artificial fingernails by individuals who have contact with patients.

Immunizations

	Yes	No	NA
Pharmacy staff participate in the organization's annual influenza vaccination program. (*See* IC.02.04.01, EP 1.)	___	___	___

Note: The organization must offer immunization against influenza to staff and licensed independent practitioners. (*See* IC.02.04.01.) The organization must provide access to influenza vaccination at an accessible site. (*See* IC.02.04.01, EP 3.)

	Yes	No	NA
Education about the following is provided to pharmacy staff:			
• Influenza vaccination	___	___	___
• Non-vaccine control and prevention measures (i.e., the use of appropriate precautions)	___	___	___
• ☑ The diagnosis, transmission, and impact of influenza. (*See* IC.02.04.01, EP 2.)	___	___	___

Note: The organization must annually evaluate vaccination rates and reasons for nonparticipation in the immunization program. The organization must implement enhancements to the program to increase participation. (*See* IC.02.04.01, EP 4 and EP 5.)

Employee Health Program

Staff participate in the organization's employee health program as required (e.g., tuberculin skin testing).	___	___	___

Note: Most organizations provide an employee health program. This program often includes pre-employment physical examinations, blood tests, chest x-rays, and tuberculin skin tests (and annual follow-ups as required) as a condition of employment to ensure that employees are free from communicable diseases.

Note: The employee health program may restrict the activities of employees and visitors. For example, persons with communicable diseases may be prohibited from contact with patients.

Note: All staff must participate in the organization's employee health program and comply with the organization's employee health policies and procedures. Furthermore, staff must be examined, treated, and immunized as required by the organization.

Hand Hygiene (Routine)

Hand washing is the single most important procedure for preventing health care-associated infections. The organization's infection control policies and procedures must address hand washing and require staff to comply with hand hygiene guidelines.[2,4,5]	___	___	___

Note: The Joint Commission requires organizations to comply with either current World Health Organization (WHO) hand hygiene guidelines or CDC hand hygiene guidelines. Most organizations follow the CDC guidelines. (*See* NPSG.07.01.01 in Chapter 6.)

Routine hand washing is performed at the beginning of the shift, after visiting the restroom, before and after eating, and when the hands are obviously soiled. (The areas under the fingernails must be kept clean.)	___	___	___

Yes **No** **NA**

Personnel who have contact with infected or potentially infected patients, body fluids, and contaminated or potentially contaminated objects wash their hands promptly after such contact. ____ ____ ____

Staff uses a hand washing technique and cleaning agent that are approved by the organization. ____ ____ ____

Note: The following routine hand washing technique is typical of most organization-approved techniques:

- Use liquid soap and cool or lukewarm (not hot) water. (Cool or lukewarm water removes less oil from the skin and is less drying.) ____ ____ ____
- Rub all surfaces of lathered hands together vigorously for at least 15 seconds. ____ ____ ____
- Rinse hands thoroughly under a stream of water. ____ ____ ____
- Dry the hands with a disposable (e.g., paper) towel or air dryer. ____ ____ ____
- Use a towel to turn off the water. ____ ____ ____

Staff use alcohol-based hand rubs as permitted by CDC hand hygiene guidelines, organization policy, and manufacturers' recommendations.[2] ____ ____ ____

Hand Hygiene (Sterile Preparation Compounding)

Personnel wash their hands thoroughly prior to compounding sterile preparations. ____ ____ ____

Personnel who leave the sterile preparations compounding area rewash their hands prior to resuming compounding. ____ ____ ____

Note: Staff must use a hand washing technique and cleaning agent that meet USP <797> requirements and are approved by the organization. The following technique for washing hands prior to compounding sterile preparations is typical of most organization-approved techniques:

- Remove debris from under fingernails using running warm water and a nail cleaner ____ ____ ____
- Moisten hands with water and apply a lather of a cleaning agent approved by the organization. The lather must extend to the wrists and forearms (i.e., up to the elbow). ____ ____ ____
- Wash hands under running water for at least 30 seconds. ____ ____ ____
- Rinse hands thoroughly under running water. Hold hands so that the direction of water flow is from the fingertips to the wrists. ____ ____ ____
- Dry the hands with a lint-free disposable towel or electric hand dryer. ____ ____ ____
- Apply a waterless alcohol-based hand rub with persistent activity following the manufacturer's recommendations. Allow hands to dry. ____ ____ ____
- After donning sterile powder-free gloves, apply a waterless alcohol-based hand rub with persistent activity to the gloves. Allow the gloves to dry. ____ ____ ____

	Yes	No	NA

Standard Precautions

	Yes	No	NA
Staff observe standard precautions to reduce the risk of transmission of infection.[4]	____	____	____

Note: Standard (formerly known as universal) precautions apply to all patients receiving care in hospitals, regardless of their diagnosis or presumed infection status. Standard precautions apply to 1) blood; 2) all body fluids, secretions, and excretions except sweat, regardless of whether or not they contain visible blood; 3) nonintact skin; and 4) mucous membranes. Standard precautions are designed to reduce the risk of transmission of microorganisms from both recognized and unrecognized sources of infection in hospitals.

Note: Occupational Safety and Health Administration (OSHA) rules and regulations (Title 29 CFR §1910.1030)[6] require employers to implement plans to dispose of blood and contaminated waste, provide warnings on such waste, and keep records that account for the disposal of the waste. Employers must ensure that health care workers take special precautions to reduce the risk of contracting and transmitting AIDS, hepatitis, and other diseases from exposure to blood and other body fluids.

Note: Standard precautions must be included in the employer's Exposure Control Plan. Health care organizations must regularly educate employees about their Exposure Control Plan and standard precautions. Organizations must offer medical attention, evaluation, testing, and treatment in accordance with their Exposure Control Plan.

Isolation

	Yes	No	NA
Staff understand the organization's isolation policies and procedures.	____	____	____
Only medications needed for the patient's immediate use are taken into an isolation room.	____	____	____
Gowning, masking, and gloving are done as specified in the organization's isolation policies.	____	____	____
All items taken into an isolation room are placed in a designated receptacle after use.	____	____	____
Hand hygiene procedures are performed as specified in the organization's isolation policies after leaving the isolation room.	____	____	____

Sterile Preparation Compounding Area

	Yes	No	NA
Areas for compounding sterile preparations minimize opportunities for particulate and microbial contamination of the preparations.	____	____	____

Note: Areas for compounding sterile preparations must meet the requirements of USP <797> and state regulations. (*See* Chapter 18.)

Yes **No** **NA**

Primary Engineering Controls (PECs)

Sterile preparations are compounded in a properly maintained laminar airflow workbench (LAFW), biological safety cabinet (BSC), compounding aseptic isolator (CAI), or compounding aseptic containment isolator (CACI). ____ ____ ____

> *Note:* Staff must be aware that primary engineering controls ("hoods") do not create a sterile area, but provide a clean area that is suitable for compounding sterile preparations that will not be used immediately.

> *Note:* Ideally, all sterile preparations are compounded in the pharmacy in a USP <797> compliant facility. However, USP <797> has provisions for the preparation of low-risk sterile compounds (e.g., IVs) that will be used immediately. If permitted by hospital policy, preparing medications with a short stability or for immediate use is acceptable if done in a clean, well-lighted, functionally separate area by competent personnel. There must be no intervening steps between the compounding and administration of the sterile preparations. (*See* Chapter 19.)

Compounding of medium- and high-risk preparations, parenteral nutrition, antineoplastic and other hazardous agents, cardioplegia, and other preparations that require specialized knowledge or equipment usually found only in the pharmacy are compounded in the pharmacy by specially trained staff. ____ ____ ____

Cleaning the Sterile Preparation Areas

Floors, walls, and ceilings in the ante and buffer areas are cleaned in accordance with USP <797> requirements. ____ ____ ____

> *Note:* USP <797> contains requirements for cleaning floors, walls, and ceilings in the ante and buffer areas. The housekeeping department must be familiar with these requirements.

Cleaning and Disinfecting Primary Engineering Controls

Primary engineering control surfaces are cleaned and disinfected frequently, including

- at the beginning of each work shift, ____ ____ ____
- before each batch preparation is started, ____ ____ ____
- every 30 minutes during continuous compounding activity, ____ ____ ____
- when spills occur, and ____ ____ ____
- whenever surface contamination is known or suspected. ____ ____ ____

Sterile water for irrigation is used to remove water-soluble residues, and then the same surfaces are disinfected with a non-residue generating agent using a lint-free wipe. ____ ____ ____

	Yes	No	NA
Note: Use sterile 70% isopropyl alcohol as the disinfectant. Other agents may be used if approved by the organization.			
All items (including syringes, vials, and other extraneous items) are removed from the PEC before cleaning it.	____	____	____
Note: Infection control policies and procedures should include a schedule and technique (including cleaning agent) for cleaning primary engineering controls (LAFWs, BSCs, CAIs, and CACIs). Clean the work surface, side panels, and other accessible surfaces, starting at the top and rear and working downward and toward the front, unless the manufacturer recommends a different procedure. Be careful to avoid getting the cleaning agent on the high-efficiency particulate arrestor (HEPA) filter. Document the cleaning. Surveyors frequently look at documentation of cleaning (e.g., a monthly hood cleaning log). (*See* Example 9-1.)			

Primary Engineering Control Maintenance

Routine maintenance, such as cleaning or replacing prefilters, is performed regularly and according to manufacturers' specifications (e.g., monthly or quarterly). ____ ____ ____

Note: These activities must be documented.

HEPA filters are replaced or repaired when recommended by a qualified certifier. ____ ____ ____

Environmental Monitoring of Sterile Preparation Area

Both non-viable (e.g., particles) and viable (e.g., microbial or fungal contamination) environmental monitoring is performed as required (e.g., by USP <797> and/or state regulations). (*See* Chapter 19.) ____ ____ ____

Results of environmental monitoring are reported to the organization. ____ ____ ____

Note: Most organizations report this to the Infection Control Committee.

Certification of Sterile Preparation Areas

Primary engineering controls are checked and certified when they are first placed in service, at least every 6 months, when maintenance is completed, or they are moved to a new location. ____ ____ ____

Note: Certification of primary engineering controls is usually documented by placing a sticker on the device and keeping inspection records on file. Surveyors frequently check these stickers.

Checks of operational efficiency of all primary engineering controls, ante areas, and buffer areas are performed at least every 6 months by a qualified certifier. ____ ____ ____

Yes No NA

Primary Engineering Control Techniques

Proper techniques and precautions are observed when using primary engineering controls.

Note: When using LAFWs, the following precautions are suggested:

- Ensure that the LAFW runs continuously or for the period required by policy (e.g., 30 minutes) prior to compounding sterile preparations. The manufacturers' recommendations must be followed.
- Assemble and organize all necessary materials in or near the LAFW before beginning work, and keep unnecessary items (e.g., labels, worksheets, notepads, and pencils) out of the PEC.
- Work at least 15 centimeters (6 inches) within the hood.
- Keep a clear path between the HEPA filter and sterile objects (i.e., avoid blocking airflow with vials and equipment).
- Do not allow objects (especially sharp or pointed objects) or liquids to contact the HEPA filter.
- Avoid unnecessary talking.

Aseptic Technique

Proper aseptic technique is used in compounding sterile preparations.

Note: Touch is the primary source of contamination.

Note: Individuals with open lesions or communicable diseases must not prepare sterile preparations.

Note: The following aspects of aseptic technique are emphasized:

- Compounding in the pharmacy must comply with USP <797>.
- Perform hand hygiene procedures before handling medications and as needed during the procedure.
- Don proper garb.
- Work with moderate speed to minimize errors.
- Inspect containers for cracks, holes, leaks, and evidence of contamination before and after preparation.
- Do not touch sterile areas of containers or allow nonsterile objects to come in contact with sterile areas.

Note: The exteriors of all containers should be wiped with 70% isopropyl alcohol prior to placement in the ante area or buffer area.

Yes No NA

- Clean diaphragms, injection ports, ampul necks, and vial tops with sterile 70% isopropyl alcohol and allow to dry. ___ ___ ___
- Cover ampul necks with a sterile pad and break ampuls by snapping toward the side of the primary engineering control. Use a filter straw to withdraw contents of the ampule. ___ ___ ___
- Ensure that seals on syringe and needle packages are intact. Do not use items if the sterility is questionable. ___ ___ ___
- Ensure that touch contamination does not occur when attaching needles to syringes and when mixing medications and diluents. ___ ___ ___
- Dispose of used syringes, needles, and other waste in accordance with the organization's policies and procedures. ___ ___ ___

Beyond-Use Dates for Compounded Sterile Preparations

All compounded sterile preparations are labeled with beyond-use dates. ___ ___ ___

Beyond-use dates for compounded sterile preparations do not exceed the periods specified in USP <797>. (*See* Chapter 19.) ___ ___ ___

Sterile Preparations Inspections

Compounded sterile preparations are quarantined and inspected by a pharmacist prior to release from the pharmacy. ___ ___ ___

> ***Note:*** The inspection must include checking for defective containers, cloudiness, turbidity, leaks, precipitates, particulate matter, evidence of contamination, and evidence of incompatibility. Labels must be checked for completeness and accuracy. When possible, the individual who performs the inspection should not be the individual who compounded the preparation. Defective and doubtful preparations must be destroyed.

> ***Note:*** The individual who checks the final preparation must verify that the preparation has passed a final examination and is suitable for administration (i.e., compounded accurately and free from incompatibilities and particulate matter). An individual's written signature or initials on the label is a common means of indicating that the preparation has been checked.

Sterile Preparations Storage

Compounded sterile preparations are properly stored. ___ ___ ___

> ***Note:*** Compounded sterile preparations should be administered as soon after preparation as possible. Storage time limits and storage conditions must maximize stability, minimize microbial growth, and be consistent with the requirements of USP <797>. (*See* Chapter 19.)

Yes **No** **NA**

Note: Protection from light may be necessary if the preparation is light-sensitive. Check manufacturer and other literature carefully for stability data and storage guidelines.

Automated Compounding Devices

Automated compounding devices are cleaned regularly and checked to verify accurate delivery. ____ ____ ____

Note: Personnel must be knowledgeable about the safe and proper operation of these devices. USP <797> provides information relating to the use of these devices. In addition, personnel should consult the manufacturer's information for specific instructions. (*See* Chapter 19.)

Syringes

A sterile syringe is used for each medication withdrawn. ____ ____ ____

Syringes are used on one patient only and then disposed of properly. ____ ____ ____

Note: Organizations must be especially attentive to syringes used in anesthetizing areas and other areas where special procedures are performed.

Needles

A sterile needle is used for each medication withdrawn. ____ ____ ____

Containers for disposal of used needles and other sharp objects are available, used properly, and not overfilled. ____ ____ ____

Single-Use Containers

Single-use containers are not reused. ____ ____ ____

Note: Single-use containers should be used whenever feasible. The organization's infection control policies should prohibit the reuse of single-use containers.

Single-use containers are discarded immediately after use in accordance with the organization's policies. ____ ____ ____

Multiple-Dose Vials

Multiple-dose vials that will be reused after the first puncture are labeled with an appropriate beyond-use date. ____ ____ ____

	Yes	No	NA
Note: All multiple-dose vials intended for reuse must be labeled with a beyond-use date whether they are labeled with the date of the first entry or not.			
Multiple-dose vials are not used beyond the time specified by the organization's policies.	___	___	___
Note: Some organizations require dating containers when first entered and discarding them after a short time period (e.g., end of the shift or 24 hours). Other organizations specify a longer time period. The time period must not exceed 28 days unless a different time period is specifically referenced by the manufacturer.[7] Whatever the policy, the period must not conflict with the manufacturer's recommendations nor extend beyond the manufacturer's expiration date.			
Note: A pharmacy bulk package (PBP) is a container of a sterile preparation for parenteral use that contains many single doses. The contents are intended for use in a pharmacy admixture program and are restricted to the preparation of admixtures for infusion or, through a sterile transfer device, for the filling of empty sterile syringes.[8]			
PBPs of electrolytes and other products are used in the pharmacy for no more than 4 hours after the initial entry into the container unless the manufacturers' product information provides a different time period. Any unused portions are discarded.	___	___	___
Note: This requirement is stated in the package insert of many bulk containers of electrolytes, other products intended for dilution in intravenous infusions (i.e., not for direct infusion), and PBPs of IV contrast media.			

CHAPTER 10

Safety, Security, and Storage Checklist

The Joint Commission, in its management of the environment of care (EC), emergency management (EM), and life safety (LS) standards, requires organizations to provide an environment that minimizes hazardous conditions; prevents accidents; reduces the risk of injury; and provides for the safety and security of patients, visitors, and staff. The Joint Commission's medication management (MM) standards require organizations to ensure that medications are stored properly and safely (*see* MM.03.01.01 in Chapter 4), and that risks associated with managing hazardous medications are minimized. (*See* MM.01.01.03 in Chapter 4.)

> ***Note:*** Organizations surveyed under the *Comprehensive Accreditation Manual for Hospitals: The Official Handbook (CAMH)* must comply with the EC, EM, and LS standards that are applicable to them. Organizations surveyed under other Joint Commission accreditation manuals should review the appropriate manual. (*See* Chapter 1.)

Safety Management Coordination (or Safety Committee)—The Joint Commission requires organizations to identify one or more individuals to coordinate safety management activities. (*See* EC.01.01.01, EP 1 and EP 2.) Many organizations designate a safety officer and appoint a Safety Committee. A pharmacist is often a member of the Safety Committee.

Safety Codes—Buildings must comply with federal, state, and local safety codes which specify the construction requirements and the types of materials permitted. Safety codes may differ because of the types of patients in the area (e.g., codes for long-term care areas are more stringent than codes for ambulatory care areas). Also, some equivalencies (i.e., equivalent ways to meet the intent of the codes) are permitted. The pharmacy should check with the safety officer or Safety Committee to ascertain the organization's safety and security policies and procedures, applicable codes, and permitted equivalencies.

Safety Inspections—The director of pharmacy should ensure that the pharmacy and medication storage areas are inspected regularly (e.g., monthly or quarterly) for safety, security, and storage violations. (*See* MM.03.01.01, EP 18 in Chapter 4.) This checklist and the medication area inspection form may be used as a guide. (*See* Examples 4-15 and 4-16.)

Checklist Organization

This chapter presents safety, security, and storage precautions for health care personnel in a checklist format. They are consistent with current Joint Commission standards relating to these topics.

> ***Note:*** Although this checklist does not address safety, security, and storage completely, it should be sufficient to ensure compliance with most requirements pertaining to pharmacy. Health care organizations should check for new and updated requirements on The Joint Commission's Web site. (*See* Appendix.)

The notes are compliance expectations and suggestions that are based on the authors' personal experiences, reports from surveyed organizations, and surveyors' statements. Some notes reflect legal requirements, clarifying statements from Joint Commission standards, previous Joint Commission standards, or commonly accepted standards of practice. Others note variations in interpretation of the standards.

Checklist Symbols—Special attention should be paid to EPs displaying an icon. The checklist uses a 📄 icon before an EP if documentation is required, and a ⚠ icon before an EP if noncompliance is likely to create an immediate risk to patient safety or to the quality of care provided. A ☑ icon before an EP indicates that a Measure of Success (MOS) is required if the EP is scored non-compliant during a survey.

Checklist Usage Suggestions

To assess compliance, use the checklist and proceed systematically. Mark the item "Yes" if you are currently compliant and are sure you will continue to be compliant. Mark the item "No" if you are currently not compliant (even if you are sure you will be compliant later). If you are not sure of your answer, leave a blank response. A few items may be not applicable (NA). Answer honestly, use a pencil (so you can change your answers), and make notes on the pages (e.g., reasons for noncompliance). It might be helpful to record the locations of the documents on the checklist (especially if they are kept outside the pharmacy). Concentrate your efforts on resolving all "No" and blank responses.

Checklist	Yes	No	NA

Environmental Tours

The pharmacy conducts environmental tours to identify environmental deficiencies, hazards, and unsafe practices. (*See* EC.04.01.01, EP 14.) ___ ___ ___

Note: EC.04.01.01, EP 12 states environmental tours are conducted at least every 6 months in patient care areas.

Note: EC.04.01.01, EP 13 states that environmental tours are conducted at least annually in non-patient care areas.

Safety-Related Incidents Reporting

☑ Pharmacy personnel identify and report accidents, injuries, conditions, and practices that pose a safety hazard to patients, visitors, and staff. (*See* EC.04.01.01, EP 3 through EP 11.) ___ ___ ___

Note: Safety-related incidents are usually reported to the Safety Committee or safety officer. The organization's safety plan should contain specific information on how to make these reports.

Recalls (Products and Equipment)

☑ The pharmacy responds to product notices and recalls in compliance with organizational policy and law and regulation. (*See* EC.02.01.01, EP 11 and MM.05.01.17, EP 1 through EP 4.) ___ ___ ___

Note: Although recalls of primary concern to the pharmacy involve medications, recalls and other safety notices may address equipment (e.g., laminar airflow workbenches and infusion pumps).

SECURITY

The organization identifies and manages its security risks. (*See* EC.02.01.01.) ___ ___ ___

Note: The organization should communicate its security risks to the pharmacy.

Security of Staff

🗎 The organization has a written plan for managing the security of staff. (*See* EC.01.01.01, EP 4.) ___ ___ ___

Yes No NA

Pharmacy personnel are clearly identified (e.g., by visible name badges or other means of identification).

⚠ Unauthorized and unidentified individuals are not allowed in the pharmacy or medication preparation and storage areas. (Intent of EC.02.01.01, EP 8.) (*See* MM.03.01.01, EP 6 in Chapter 4.)

Security of Medication Areas

All pharmacy entrances are locked.

> *Note:* Although not specifically required by the standards, surveyors insist that the pharmacy door be locked (even if not required by law). Surveyors often issue a citation if the pharmacy door is unlocked or a Dutch door is locked but the inside locking mechanism can be accessed from the outside. Surveyors determine if security is adequate to keep unauthorized personnel from entering the pharmacy.

Keys are controlled, and knowledge of access codes is limited.

> *Note:* Surveyors expect locks and access codes to keypad, combination, and similar locks to be changed periodically, especially when personnel leave the employment of the organization.

Pharmacy windows are locked.

Other security measures are provided as necessary (e.g., alarms, bulletproof glass, peepholes, video cameras, and security guards).

> *Note:* Many organizations do not post directions to the pharmacy or identify the pharmacy with a sign.

Prescription pads and prescription computer paper are in locked storage or stored so only authorized personnel have access to them.

Security alarms and equipment, if used, are tested regularly.

☑ Pharmacy personnel can describe or demonstrate actions to be taken if there is a security incident (e.g., robbery or hostile situation). (Intent of EC.03.01.01, EP 2.)

Security of Medications

☑ Medications are secured in accordance with legal requirements and the organization's written policies. (*See* MM.03.01.01, EP 3, EP 5, and EP 6 in Chapter 4.)

Transport Systems

All mechanical transport devices (e.g., robots, dumbwaiters, and pneumatic tubes) are secure and deliver medications to secure areas.

	Yes	No	NA
Robots, dumbwaiters, and pneumatic tubes used to deliver medications pose no risk of harm to patients, visitors, and staff.	___	___	___
There are provisions for delivery of medications if mechanical systems become unsafe or fail.	___	___	___

> *Note:* The pharmacy should have a policy that limits the types of medications that will be transported through a mechanical system. For example, hazardous agents should not be delivered by a mechanical transport system.

Medication Loss or Theft

	Yes	No	NA
There is a process for detecting loss or theft of medications kept in floor stock and automated dispensing cabinets. (*See* Controlled Substances in this chapter.)	___	___	___

> *Note:* This process often includes establishing stock levels and making periodic comparisons of quantity of floor stocks with medication administration and dispensing records.

> *Note:* Surveyors often look for lists of the kind and quantity of medications kept in each area, along with evidence that these medications are monitored regularly to detect tampering and theft.

Anesthesia Medications

	Yes	No	NA
Anesthesia medications are stored securely and access to them is limited. (*See* MM.03.01.01, EP 6 in Chapter 4.)	___	___	___

> *Note:* Special attention should be given to paralytics, inhalation gases, propofol, and other medications considered dangerous.

	Yes	No	NA
⚠ Anesthesia syringes are labeled appropriately. (*See* NPSG.03.04.01, EP 1 through EP 3 in Chapter 6.)	___	___	___

> *Note:* Empty syringes must not have a pre-attached label. Syringes containing medications are for immediate use and are discarded after each case.[1]

Controlled Substances

See MM.03.01.01, EP 3 in Chapter 4.

	Yes	No	NA
Controlled substances are stored securely and locked to prevent diversion.	___	___	___
Controlled substances are stored according to legal requirements and the organization's policies.	___	___	___

	Yes	No	NA
The organization reports abuses and losses of controlled substances, in accordance with law and regulation, to the Pharmacist-in-Charge and, as appropriate, to the chief executive. (*See* MM.01.01.03, EP 5 in Chapter 4.)	___	___	___

EMERGENCY MANAGEMENT

Emergency Operations Plan

🗎 The organization has a written emergency operations plan. (*See* EM.02.01.01, EP 2.)	___	___	___

> ***Note:*** Organizations must have an emergency operations plan (EOP) that addresses internal and external disasters and other emergencies in the organization and the community. Emergency management plans must address the types of emergencies that the organization might reasonably expect to encounter (e.g., catastrophic accidents, fires, explosions, hurricanes, tornadoes, and earthquakes).

> ***Note:*** Acts of terrorism (e.g., biological, chemical, or radiological) may also create conditions in which an organization will implement its EOP.

> ***Note:*** Some organizations (e.g., drug abuse and behavioral health facilities) do not need to be prepared to treat victims of accidents, natural disasters, or acts of terrorism.

> ***Note:*** Organizations must test their EOP at least semiannually, either in an actual emergency or a drill. (*See* EM.03.01.03, EP 1.) At a minimum, the pharmacy can expect to participate in emergency drills about twice a year. However, fire drills are conducted at least quarterly. (*See* EC.02.03.03, EP 1.)

The organization's written EOP is available to pharmacy staff.	___	___	___
The pharmacy's written plan for preparing for and reacting to severe weather situations (e.g., hurricanes, floods, earthquakes, and tornadoes) is available to pharmacy staff.	___	___	___

> ***Note:*** Some severe weather situations (e.g., hurricanes) may be predictable and provide an opportunity for staff to prepare for them. Other situations may be unpredictable and occur suddenly (e.g., earthquakes, tornadoes, and floods). A severe weather plan should address both situations, be proactive, anticipate the worst scenario, and prepare staff to expect the unexpected.

> ***Note:*** The pharmacy's severe weather plan should address providing emergency telephone service, dealing with prolonged loss of electric power (including the use of battery backups), ensuring adequate supplies of routine medications when deliveries are delayed, obtaining additional stocks of emergency medications, and moving the pharmacy to another location.

> ***Note:*** The pharmacy's plan should also address using manual systems when computers and automated systems are inoperative, operating with reduced and tired

Yes No NA

staff, providing sleeping and eating accommodations for staff (and their families and pets if needed), and dealing with personal issues (e.g., sick or injured family members).

The pharmacy's written plan for preparing for and reacting to other emergencies (e.g., fires, catastrophic accidents, and acts of terrorism) is available to pharmacy staff. ___ ___ ___

Note: This plan will include most of the topics addressed in the pharmacy's severe weather plan.

The organization maintains a documented inventory of medication-related resources and assets on site that may be needed during an emergency. (*See* EM.01.01.01, EP 8.) This inventory is reviewed at least annually and updated as necessary. (*See* EM.03.01.01, EP 3.) ___ ___ ___

Note: The Joint Commission expects the hospital to maintain a documented inventory of the medications on hand in the facility that would be needed in an emergency. The medications and amounts to be kept on site for emergencies are determined by the organization but should be appropriate for the types of potential emergencies identified by the organization.

The organization identifies outside sources where additional supplies of medications can be obtained in an emergency, including local, state, and federal pharmaceutical stockpiles. (Intent of EM.02.02.01, EP 7 and EP 10 and EM.02.02.03, EP 1.) ___ ___ ___

Note: Outside sources of medications for emergency situations include wholesale suppliers; pharmaceutical manufacturers; other health care organizations in the geographic area; and local, regional, and federal agencies.

Note: Most pharmacies maintain a list of contact information for outside sources of medications.

☑ Pharmacy personnel are oriented, educated, and trained in their assigned emergency response duties (including assistance in moving and evacuating patients). (*See* EM.02.02.07, EP 7.) ___ ___ ___

Pharmacy personnel understand how to notify other staff members if there is an emergency. ___ ___ ___

Note: Many pharmacies maintain and post a list of staff and their telephone numbers and other contact information.

Pharmacy personnel participate in emergency drills. ___ ___ ___

Emergency Codes

Pharmacy personnel know the organization's emergency codes. ___ ___ ___

	Yes	No	NA
Note: Organizations often have emergency codes for internal and external disasters, security, chemical and hazardous materials spills, cardiac/respiratory arrest, bomb threat, infant or child abduction, and severe weather.			

Emergency Power

⚠ Pharmacy equipment that is designated to be connected to the emergency power system is connected to the system. (*See* EC.02.05.03.)	____	____	____

Note: Organizations may designate some pharmacy equipment to be connected to the emergency power system. Many organizations connect medication refrigerators, freezers, pharmacy computers, automated dispensing cabinets, and devices for compounding sterile preparations (e.g., laminar airflow workbench [LAFW]) to the system. Emergency lighting is often supplied to the pharmacy and medication preparation areas.

SPACE

Sufficient space is provided for storing, preparing (compounding, packaging, and labeling), and dispensing medications (including, if appropriate, parenteral products and radiopharmaceuticals). (Intent of EC.02.06.01, EP 1.)	____	____	____

Note: The standards do not specify minimum requirements for pharmacy space. However, The Joint Commission requires health care organization pharmacies to meet state board of pharmacy requirements. Because state requirements are sometimes nonexistent or vague, surveyors seldom check for compliance. Some surveyors look at state board of pharmacy inspection reports to determine if the pharmacy has failed to meet space requirements.

Medication storage and preparation areas are well lighted. (Intent of EC.02.06.01, EP 11.)	____	____	____
Medication storage areas are clean, organized, and uncluttered.	____	____	____
Medication preparation areas are located where personnel are not interrupted. (Traffic in the pharmacy and other medication preparation areas should be minimized.)	____	____	____
☑ ⚠ Medication preparation areas are neat; clean; uncluttered; and free of equipment, supplies, records, and labels unrelated to the preparation of medications. (*See* MM.05.01.07, EP 2 in Chapter 4.)	____	____	____
Facilities are available for cleaning and hand washing. (*See* IC.01.02.01, EP 3.)	____	____	____

Shelves

Shelves are sealed to the floor or have sufficient space underneath to permit cleaning and the removal of materials that might present a fire or infection control hazard.	____	____	____

	Yes	No	NA
Note: Organizations that are located in earthquake prone areas may be required to meet more stringent regulations (e.g., provide each shelf with a lip so that bottles will not slide off and attach shelving to a wall so that it will not topple).			

Store Rooms

Store rooms located near the pharmacy and medication storage areas (e.g., linen rooms, utility rooms, closets, and attics) contain no safety policy violations.	___	___	___

Equipment (Pharmacy)

Sufficient equipment is provided for preparing (compounding, packaging, and labeling) and dispensing medications (including, if appropriate, sterile preparations and radiopharmaceuticals).	___	___	___
Note: The standards do not specify minimum requirements for pharmacy equipment and supplies. However, The Joint Commission requires health care organization pharmacies to meet state board of pharmacy requirements. Because state requirements are sometimes nonexistent or vague, surveyors seldom check for compliance. Some surveyors look at state board of pharmacy inspection reports to determine if the pharmacy meets space, equipment, and supply requirements.			
Pharmacy equipment is inspected and/or tested periodically for operational effectiveness and to assure safety for patients, visitors, and staff.	___	___	___
Cleaning and preventive maintenance of equipment is performed if required and as scheduled.	___	___	___
Operation and maintenance instructions are kept with individual pieces of equipment or in a designated, readily accessible place.	___	___	___
Exit devices on walk-in refrigerators and freezers work properly.	___	___	___
There are no sharp projections or moving parts on equipment that pose a risk to patients, visitors, and staff.	___	___	___
Insulation or other protection is provided to prevent contact with hot and cold water pipes, water heaters, refrigerator compressors, condensing units, and heat-producing equipment.	___	___	___
Defective equipment is marked and stored so that it cannot be used.	___	___	___

Equipment (Patient Care)

Patient care equipment functions properly and safely.	___	___	___

Note: More stringent electrical safety codes apply to patient care equipment. The Joint Commission defines medical equipment as equipment used in diagnosing, treating, and monitoring patients (e.g., infusion control devices, mechanical ventilators, and electrocardiograph monitors). However, some organizations broadly interpret medical (i.e., patient care) equipment to include

	Yes	No	NA
LAFWs, prescription balances, and equipment used in repackaging and reconstituting medications.			

Note: Organizations must maintain written lists of all patient care equipment and require an initial inspection prior to use as well as periodic (often semiannual or annual) safety and performance testing thereafter. In addition, some equipment may require preventive maintenance. (*See* EC.02.04.01, EP 2 through EP 4 and EC.02.04.03, EP 1 and EP 3.)

Equipment Records

Testing and preventive maintenance records are kept for the period specified by law. ____ ____ ____

Note: Testing and preventive maintenance records are often kept by the safety officer or in the biomedical engineering department.

Biological Safety Cabinets

See Chapters 12, 18, and 19.

Hazardous medications are prepared in a Class II Type B (Type B2 total exhaust is preferred) or Class III biological safety cabinet (BSC) designed for asepsis and containment of hazardous materials to minimize the exposure of workers to the medications.[2] (*See* Containment Isolators in this chapter.) ____ ____ ____

Note: Cytotoxic and other hazardous medications must not be prepared in a LAFW or CAI designed for preparing nonhazardous sterile preparations since they protect products but not the environment and personnel. Cytotoxic and hazardous materials must be prepared in a vertical airflow BSC or a compounding aseptic containment isolator (CACI).

Exhaust from the BSC is HEPA filtered (if applicable) and vented to the outside environment away from air intake locations. ____ ____ ____

The BSC is located in an area separate from the laminar airflow devices used to compound nonhazardous sterile preparations. ____ ____ ____

Containment Isolators

See Chapters 12, 18, and 19.

If hazardous medications are prepared in a containment isolator, it must be designed for asepsis and containment of hazardous materials to minimize the exposure of workers to the medications.[2] (*See* Biological Safety Cabinet in this chapter.) ____ ____ ____

Note: Cytotoxic and other hazardous medications must not be prepared in a LAFW or CAI designed for preparing nonhazardous sterile preparations since they protect products but not the environment and personnel. Cytotoxic and hazardous materials must be prepared in a vertical airflow BSC or a compounding aseptic containment isolator (CACI).

	Yes	No	NA
Exhaust from the CACI is HEPA filtered and vented to the outside environment away from air intake locations.	___	___	___
The CACI is located in an area separate from the laminar airflow devices used to compound nonhazardous sterile preparations.	___	___	___

ELECTRICAL SAFETY

Electrical Equipment Safety Checks

Electrical equipment has been tested for safety. ___ ___ ___

> *Note:* A safety plan must identify types of equipment that may pose an electrical hazard. At a minimum, the plan must include high-risk equipment. Faulty electrical systems are a leading cause of fire and injuries in organizations. Some organizations consider all electrical equipment an electrical hazard and apply this requirement to printers, computers, etc.

> *Note:* In developing the safety plan, staff must consider the environment of use, maintenance, safety features, and the type of service the equipment provides.

> *Note:* Equipment identified by the policy must be inspected prior to initial use and at defined intervals thereafter. Only qualified persons should inspect, repair, or alter electrical equipment and electrical power distribution systems. The organization's inspectors may require periodic access to pharmacy equipment to perform inspections. Inspectors often label equipment that meets the inspection requirements.

Electrical Extension Cords and Adapters

Extension cords and adapters meet safety requirements, are authorized by the organization, and are not overloaded. ___ ___ ___

> *Note:* Most organizations have policies on the use of extension cords and adapters. Some organizations prohibit their use completely. Others permit extension cords and adapters that are approved by the Safety Committee.

Extension cords and adapters are checked regularly as part of the organization's hazard surveillance program. ___ ___ ___

Electrical Panels

Electrical panels are properly labeled and free from lint and grease. ___ ___ ___

Yes **No** **NA**

Electrical Equipment (Personal)

Personal electrical equipment is used in accordance with the organization's safety plans or policies. ____ ____ ____

Note: The organization's safety plans or policies must address the use of personal electrical equipment. For the pharmacy, this often applies to coffee makers, radios, and similar equipment. Some organizations authorize the use of this equipment by policy, but others require an inspection of each item prior to authorizing its use.

HAZARDOUS MATERIALS AND WASTES

Hazardous Materials and Wastes Plan

A written plan for preventing and dealing with exposures to hazardous materials and waste is available to all individuals who handle them. (*See* EC.01.01.01, EP 5.) ____ ____ ____

Note: Organizations must have a plan for safe management of hazardous materials and wastes such as toxic materials, chemicals, hazardous medications, radioactive materials, infectious and regulated medical wastes, and sharp items (e.g., needles, razor blades, and broken ampuls). The plan must cover the safe management of hazardous materials and wastes from receipt or generation at the organization through the final disposition at the organization or other site.

Note: Persons who handle hazardous materials and wastes must be informed of the risks and properly oriented, educated, and trained.

Note: The Joint Commission does not provide explicit guidelines for handling hazardous materials and waste. However, surveyors look for compliance with the Occupational Safety and Health Administration (OSHA) Hazard Communication Standard and National Institute for Occupational Safety and Health (NIOSH) recommendations. (*See* Chapters 17 and 18.) Compliance with this section of this checklist should be sufficient to demonstrate compliance.

Note: Pharmacy personnel must know the location of the hazard communication plan.

Hazardous Materials Storage

The pharmacy has identified all areas where hazardous materials are stored or handled. ____ ____ ____

Hazardous Materials Identification

Hazardous materials and waste are labeled with contents and hazard warnings so that personnel are not unknowingly and unnecessarily exposed or harmed. (*See* EC.02.02.01, EP 12.) ____ ____ ____

	Yes	No	NA
Note: Hazardous materials can be identified by posting lists of the materials and/or by affixing special warning labels to the materials, storage bins, and shelves.			
A list of hazardous materials stored or used routinely in the pharmacy and other areas is maintained and readily available to personnel who work in those areas. (*See* EC.02.02.01, EP 1.) (*See* MM.01.01.03, EP 3 in Chapter 4.)	___	___	___
Note: Pharmacy personnel must know the location of the list. Many organizations post the lists in the appropriate areas. Pharmacy personnel must also know the location of the organization's master list of hazardous materials. The master list is often in the emergency department or office of the safety officer.			

Material Safety Data Sheets (MSDSs)

	Yes	No	NA
Material Safety Data Sheets (MSDSs) for all hazardous materials on the list are readily available to personnel in the pharmacy and other areas where hazardous materials are stored or handled. (*See* EC.02.02.01, EP 11.)	___	___	___
Note: Pharmacy personnel must know the location of MSDSs. MSDSs may be made available electronically. There should be a paper backup up for electronic MSDSs. (*See* Chapter 17.)			

Personal Protective Equipment (PPE)

	Yes	No	NA
Personal protective equipment (e.g., gowns, gloves, eyewear, and face protection) is readily available to personnel who handle and prepare hazardous materials. (*See* Chapters 17 and 18.)	___	___	___
Note: Pharmacy personnel must know the location of PPE.			

Eyewash Fountains

	Yes	No	NA
An eyewash fountain is readily available to personnel in the pharmacy and other areas where chemicals, cytotoxic medications, and medications that pose a similar risk to the eyes are stored or handled.	___	___	___
Note: Manually operated bottles of eye flush solutions are not adequate. The eyewash fountain must operate with a continuous flow (e.g., from a faucet or fountain).			
Note: Guidelines for emergency eyewashes can be found in the American National Standards Institute (ANSI) standard Z358.1. (*See* Appendix.)			

	Yes	No	NA

Spill Kits

Clearly labeled spill kits are readily available to personnel in the pharmacy and other areas where hazardous materials are stored or handled. ___ ___ ___

Note: Pharmacy personnel must know the location of spill kits.

Hazardous Materials and Waste Disposal

☑ ⚠ The pharmacy minimizes risks associated with disposing of hazardous medications. (*See* EC.02.02.01, EP 8.) (*See* Chapter 18 and MM.01.01.03, EP 1 through EP 3 in Chapter 4.) ___ ___ ___

☑ The pharmacy minimizes the risks associated with the disposal of hazardous chemicals. (*See* EC.02.02.01, EP 5.) ___ ___ ___

Pharmacy personnel collect and dispose of needles, sharps, and other hazardous materials and waste in accordance with the organization's plan. ___ ___ ___

Hazardous materials and waste are placed in specially marked containers (e.g., yellow chemotherapy waste containers and black hazardous waste containers) and disposed of separately from routine trash. ___ ___ ___

Appropriate containers for the disposal of hazardous materials and waste, contaminated apparel, and contaminated work equipment (e.g., vials, ampuls, syringes, and needles) are close to the area of use and readily available to personnel. ___ ___ ___

Note: Some states have stringent disposal regulations. Check state regulations and the organization's plan for specific disposal requirements.

Hazardous Materials and Waste Spills and Exposures

📄 The pharmacy has written procedures for responding to hazardous material and waste spills or exposures. Procedures include the use of precautions and personal protective equipment. (*See* EC.02.02.01, EP 3.) ___ ___ ___

☑ Pharmacy personnel report hazardous materials and waste spills and exposures. (*See* EC.04.01.01, EP 8.) ___ ___ ___

Note: OSHA requires organizations to keep records of personnel who are exposed to hazardous materials. The organization should have a mechanism for meeting this requirement.

FIRE SAFETY

Fire Safety Plan

📄 The organization has a written plan for managing its fire safety risks. (*See* EC.01.01.01, EP 6.) ___ ___ ___

Yes No NA

The organization has a written plan for responding to fires that includes the roles of staff, the use of fire alarms, means of containing fire and smoke, use of fire extinguishers, and evacuation procedures. (*See* EC.02.03.01, EP 9 and EP 10.) ____ ____ ____

> ***Note:*** Fires in health care facilities can be more dangerous than fires in other types of facilities because patients are often not able to provide for their own safety. The organization must have a fire plan that minimizes the risk of fires and maximizes detecting and extinguishing of fires.

Combustible Materials

Combustible materials (i.e., cardboard, paper, and other materials capable of burning) are not stored near sources of ignition (e.g., heat, sparks, and flames). ____ ____ ____

Flammable Substances

Flammable substances (i.e., easily set on fire) are not stored with combustible materials (i.e., cardboard, paper, and other materials capable of burning). (Check with the safety officer or safety department.) ____ ____ ____

Flammable substances are stored in a room, vault, cabinet, or container specially designed for such storage, or away from sources of ignition (e.g., heat, sparks, and flames). ____ ____ ____

> ***Note:*** Most surveyors allow small quantities of some flammable substances (e.g., a 1- or 2-day working supply of isopropyl alcohol) in the pharmacy. Fans, lights, alarms, and other electrical equipment in the vicinity of flammable substances must be spark and explosion proof. (Check with the safety officer or safety department.)

> ***Note:*** There is seldom a reason to keep acetone in the pharmacy or patient care or procedural unit. Individual acetone wipes can replace liquid acetone. If the pharmacy needs liquid acetone, it can often be obtained from the laboratory (which usually has special containers or facilities for acetone storage).

> ***Note:*** Flexible collodion contains about 67% ether. It is extremely flammable and should be stored only in a cabinet designed for the storage of flammable substances.

> ***Note:*** Ethyl chloride is extremely flammable and serious burns have been reported from the ignition of this product from sources of sparks and static discharge such as electrical cautery equipment. If needed, it must be stored only in a cabinet designed for the storage of flammable substances.

> ***Note:*** Compound benzoin tincture contains 74–80% ethyl alcohol. Large containers should be stored in a cabinet designed for the storage of flammable substances. Individual tincture of benzoin swabs can replace liquid tincture of benzoin.

Alcohol

Bulk containers of alcohol are stored upright (not on their sides) in a location suitable for storage of flammable substances (e.g., a flammables storage vault). ____ ____ ____

Only an approved hand-operated pump (not a power-driven pump) is used for withdrawal of alcohol from bulk containers. ____ ____ ____

	Yes	No	NA
Alcohol (including bottles of rubbing alcohol) is not stored with combustible materials.	___	___	___
Alcohol-based hand rubs are stored according to the manufacturers' recommendations.	___	___	___

Ether

Ether is not stored in the organization.	___	___	___

Note: Ether is extremely flammable, and upon exposure to oxygen it may form peroxides and become highly explosive. If ether is found, the pharmacy should contact appropriate personnel (as specified in the organization's safety plan), a local fire department, or the Environmental Protection Agency (EPA). The EPA may require disposal by a licensed hazardous waste disposal contractor.

Flammable Liquids Refrigeration

Flammable liquids are not stored in a refrigerator (unless it is a specially constructed, explosion-proof refrigerator).	___	___	___
A notice "NOT FOR THE STORAGE OF FLAMMABLE LIQUIDS" is on refrigerators that are not specially constructed and vented for the storage of flammable liquids.	___	___	___

Flammable Liquids Disposal

Flammable liquids are disposed of properly (i.e., not poured into the sewage system, poured or placed in the trash, or incinerated).	___	___	___

Note: Flammable liquids must be disposed of properly. If disposal of flammable liquids is required, the pharmacy should contact appropriate personnel (as specified in the organization's safety plan), a local fire department, or the Environmental Protection Agency (EPA). The EPA may require disposal by a licensed hazardous waste disposal contractor.

Flammable Gases

Flammable gases are not stored in a refrigerator (unless it is a specially constructed, explosion-proof refrigerator).	___	___	___
Refrigerators are labeled as safe or unsafe for the storage of flammable gases.	___	___	___
Tanks of oxygen and flammable gases are stored in an appropriate location (which usually means storage outside the building or in special rooms). (Check with the safety officer.)	___	___	___
Oxygen and flammable gases are not stored with combustible materials.	___	___	___

	Yes	No	NA
Note: More stringent electrical safety codes apply to anesthetizing areas.			

Aerosol Containers

Aerosol containers (including medication inhalers) are not punctured nor stored or used near a fire or open flame.	____	____	____
Aerosol containers are not incinerated.	____	____	____

Smoking

There is no evidence of smoking in areas where smoking is prohibited. (*See* EC.02.01.03.)	____	____	____

Note: Although health care organizations are smoke-free facilities, the organization may make exceptions for specific patients (e.g., a terminally ill patient). However, fire safety precautions for these patients must be observed (e.g., smoking is allowed only in designated, properly ventilated smoking areas). (*See* EC.02.01.03, EP 4 and EC.02.03.01, EP 2.) The types of patients excepted and fire safety precautions must be in writing. (*See* EC.02.01.03, EP 1.)

Note: Hospital personnel should know the locations of smoking areas outside the building.

Space Heaters

The use of portable space heaters is in accordance with the organization's policies.	____	____	____

Note: Organizations must control the use of portable space heating devices. Some organizations permit portable space heaters in nonsleeping areas for staff and employees. Others prohibit the use of both fuel-burning and portable electric space heaters completely.

Waste Containers

Waste containers are made of noncombustible materials approved by the organization.	____	____	____

Note: Cardboard boxes and other combustible containers must not be used for trash containers.

Fire Walls

There are no holes in smoke and fire walls, ceilings, and floors (including around pipes, wires, and cables).	____	____	____

	Yes	No	NA
Note: Openings for pipes, wires, and cables must be sealed to prevent passage of smoke and fire. Do not cut holes in walls unless approved by the organization.			

Floor Coverings

	Yes	No	NA
Floor coverings (e.g., carpet) comply with fire safety codes.	____	____	____

Note: The pharmacy should ensure there is Safety Committee and Infection Control Committee approval prior to replacing or installing floor coverings in pharmacy areas. The types of floor coverings used must promote cleanliness (e.g., no carpet in dispensing areas), must not present unusual problems for the handicapped, and must have flame-spread and smoke-development ratings appropriate to the area's use (e.g., patient room or exit corridor).

Window Coverings

	Yes	No	NA
Window coverings (e.g., draperies) comply with fire safety codes.	____	____	____

Note: The pharmacy should ensure there is Safety Committee and Infection Control Committee approval prior to replacing or installing window coverings in pharmacy areas.

Doors

	Yes	No	NA
Fire resistance ratings of doors meet current codes. (Check with the safety officer or Safety Committee.)	____	____	____

Note: There are specific construction requirements for doors, door frames, and latches (including type of material, thickness, and windows or peepholes). Check with the safety officer before altering or removing doors.

	Yes	No	NA
Fire resistance ratings of Dutch doors meet current codes. (Check with the safety officer.)	____	____	____
Undercuts of doors (i.e., the area between the bottom of the door and the floor) do not exceed current codes. (Check with the safety officer.)	____	____	____
The gap between fire doors does not exceed current codes. (Check with the safety officer.)	____	____	____
Self-closing fire doors are not blocked from closing.	____	____	____
Doors that must be kept closed are closed.	____	____	____
Door stops are prohibited by the organization and are not available.	____	____	____
Latches on doors meet current codes. (Check with the safety officer.)	____	____	____

	Yes	No	NA

Stairwells

Stairwell doors are closed and equipped with positive latching devices (i.e., the doors do not open when pressure is applied to the doors).	___	___	___
Nothing is stored in stairwells.	___	___	___

Fire Alarms

Fire alarms are unobstructed, visible, accessible, and tested regularly.	___	___	___

> *Note:* Shelving, equipment, and cartons must not be placed where they will obstruct fire alarms.

Pharmacy personnel know the location of the nearest fire alarm.	___	___	___
Pharmacy personnel know how to use a fire alarm.	___	___	___
Pharmacy personnel know how to report a fire.	___	___	___

Fire Responsibilities

Pharmacy personnel know how to respond to a fire alarm.	___	___	___

> *Note:* The acronym RACE (Rescue, Alarm, Control/Contain, and Extinguish/Evacuate) is often used to describe an individual's duties in case of a fire. The exact meaning of the acronym varies from organization to organization.

Fire Extinguishers

Fire extinguishers are unobstructed, visible, accessible, and kept in their designated places.	___	___	___

> *Note:* Shelving, equipment, and cartons must not be placed where they will obstruct fire extinguishers.

> *Note:* There must be a sufficient number of fire extinguishers, appropriate for the type of fire likely to occur in the area, for the contents of the area. Fire extinguishers must be readily available (e.g., no more than 75 feet away) and must not be removed from their designated location except during a drill or actual fire.

Tags on fire extinguishers reflect up-to-date maintenance (usually monthly).	___	___	___
Fire extinguishers are appropriate for the type of fire likely to occur in the area.	___	___	___
Pharmacy personnel know the location of the nearest fire extinguisher.	___	___	___
Pharmacy personnel know how to use fire extinguishers.	___	___	___

> *Note:* The acronym PASS is often used to describe how to use a fire extinguisher (Pull the pin, Aim the nozzle, Squeeze the handle, and Sweep from side to side at the base of the fire).

	Yes	No	NA
Fire Detectors			
Fire, heat, and smoke detectors, where required, are unobstructed and tested regularly (e.g., semiannually).	___	___	___
Fire Sprinklers			
Fire sprinkler heads have at least an 18-inch clearance in all directions (to avoid obstruction of the sprinklers). (*See* LS.02.01.35, EP 6.)	___	___	___
Note: Follow local fire codes, generally, there should be at least 18 inches from items on top of the shelves to the ceiling. A 36-inch clearance is recommended.			
Shutoff Valves and Switches			
Pharmacy personnel can identify the location of shutoff valves and switches for oxygen, water, natural gas, electricity, and other utilities.	___	___	___
Note: Policies in most hospitals identify specific individuals allowed to shut off oxygen.			
Exit Signs			
Exit signs are illuminated (if applicable) and are not combustible (e.g., made of paper).	___	___	___
A "No Exit" sign is posted on courtyard doors and other doors that might be confused with exits. (*See* LS.02.01.20, EP 30.)	___	___	___
Evacuation Routes			
Pharmacy personnel know the evacuation route from the pharmacy or work area and the evacuation procedures to follow.	___	___	___
Pharmacy personnel know they must not use an elevator in case of a fire.	___	___	___
Evacuation routes are posted.	___	___	___
⚠ Exit and evacuation route doors are neither locked nor blocked. (*See* EC.02.03.01, EP 4.)	___	___	___
Evacuation routes and corridors are free from obstructions (i.e., boxes, carts, equipment, and other traffic obstacles). (*See* LS.02.01.20, EP 13.)	___	___	___
Storage of medications and supplies does not interfere with evacuation routes and access by fire-fighting and other emergency equipment.	___	___	___

Yes No NA

STORAGE

Storage of Medications

Medications are stored in accordance with current standards (e.g., United States Pharmacopeia/National Formulary, manufacturer recommendations) so that their integrity, stability, and effectiveness are maintained. ___ ___ ___

Medications requiring special storage conditions are stored properly (e.g., protected from light or at proper temperature). ___ ___ ___

If required, medications are protected from freezing, moisture, light (amber and opaque containers and light-resistant coverings should be available), and excessive heat (above 104°F). ___ ___ ___

Only authorized medications and supplies are present. ___ ___ ___

There are no medications and supplies stored in unauthorized places (e.g., closets, cabinets, drawers, and under sinks). ___ ___ ___

Discontinued medications and medications dispensed to patients who have been discharged are returned to the pharmacy. ___ ___ ___

Storage of Medications with Food

Food or other non-medication items are stored in separate refrigerators and freezers from medications, or stored in a separate compartment from refrigerated medications. ___ ___ ___

> ***Note:*** Joint Commission standards do not prohibit the storage of food and other non-medication items in the same refrigerator as medications. Nevertheless, surveyors often issue a citation if they find food, reagents, and laboratory specimens in medication storage refrigerators.

> ***Note:*** The Joint Commission considers enteral nutrition solutions as food products. (*See* The Joint Commission's definition of a medication in the glossary of the *CAMH*.)

Storage of External and Internal Agents

Agents for external use (e.g., antiseptics and disinfectants) and agents for internal use (e.g., injectable medications and oral formulations) are stored separately. ___ ___ ___

> ***Note:*** Joint Commission standards do not explicitly require separation of external and internal medications. Ideally, however, medications for external use and those intended for internal use should be stored separately and external use products should be clearly labeled as such (e.g., For External Use Only).

> ***Note:*** In practice, most creams and ointments are not likely to be mistaken for internal medications, and there is little risk if they are stored with internal medications. Most surveyors permit the storage of creams, ointments, and similar topical medications (e.g., eye and ear preparations) with internal medications if the risk of an administration error is minimal. However, opened rectal, vaginal,

	Yes	No	NA
and topical medications that might contaminate internal medications should be isolated from other medications.			

Storage of Hazardous Pharmaceutical Chemicals

	Yes	No	NA
☑ The pharmacy minimizes the risks associated with the handling, storing, transporting, and using of hazardous chemicals. (*See* EC.02.02.01, EP 5).	____	____	____
Note: Hazardous chemicals that may be found in hospital pharmacies and other areas in hospitals include liquified phenol, podophyllin, and concentrated mineral acids such as glacial acetic acid and concentrated hydrochloric, nitric, and sulfuric acids.			
Note: There is no medical use for mineral acids and bases in their concentrated forms and storage in the pharmacy is discouraged. Dilute solutions are commercially available if needed for compounding or other purposes.			
Note: Information on the safe handling and storage of hazardous chemicals is found in the MSDS for each chemical.			
Hazardous chemicals are stored separately from medications.	____	____	____
Bulk containers of concentrated acids and caustic substances are stored on lower shelves near floor level (to minimize the risk of breakage by falling from shelves).	____	____	____
Note: These containers must be stored in an upright position. They must not be stored on their side.			

Storage of Large or Heavy Containers

	Yes	No	NA
Large or heavy containers are stored on lower shelves.	____	____	____

Storage of Unusable Medications

	Yes	No	NA
There are no expired, recalled, deteriorated, broken, contaminated, unlabeled, or mislabeled medications.	____	____	____
Medications that cannot be returned for credit are stored properly while awaiting disposition.	____	____	____

Storage of Respiratory Care Medications

	Yes	No	NA
Vials and ampuls of respiratory care medications are separate from injectable medications (to minimize the possibility of accidental injection).	____	____	____

Yes **No** **NA**

Storage of Irrigation Solutions

Containers of irrigation solutions are stored separately from containers of parenteral solutions (to minimize the possibility of accidental parenteral administration). ___ ___ ___

Vials and ampuls of medications used to prepare irrigation solutions are separate from injectable medications (to minimize the possibility of accidental injection). ___ ___ ___

Storage of Poisons and Lethal Concentrations of Medications

Poisons and lethal concentrations of medications (e.g., concentrated potassium chloride) are clearly designated as such and stored securely. ___ ___ ___

Concentrated electrolytes (potassium chloride, potassium phosphate, sodium chloride greater than 0.9%, and others defined by the organization) are not stored in patient care areas unless clinically necessary, and safeguards to prevent accidental administration are in place. (*See* MM.01.01.03, EP 2 and EP 3 and MM.03.01.01, EP 9 in Chapter 4.) ___ ___ ___

Storage of Look-Alike/Sound-Alike Medications

Medications with look-alike/sound-alike (i.e., similar) names and packaging are stored throughout the organization to minimize confusion. (*See* MM.01.02.01 in Chapter 4.) ___ ___ ___

> ***Note:*** Surveyors expect physical separation (e.g., separate bins or trays) in the refrigerator for different insulins, antibiotics, and other similarly packaged medications.

Ventilation

Ventilation in the work area ensures the integrity of medications and the comfort of personnel. (Intent of EC.02.06.01, EP 13.) ___ ___ ___

⚠ Ventilation in areas where sterile preparations are prepared provides appropriate pressure relationships, air-exchange rates, and filtration efficiencies. (Intent of EC.02.05.01, EP 6.) (*See* Chapter 19.) ___ ___ ___

⚠ Ventilation in areas where hazardous medications (e.g., antineoplastics) are stored provides appropriate pressure relationships, air-exchange rates, and filtration efficiencies. (Intent of EC.02.05.01, EP 6.) ___ ___ ___

> ***Note:*** Ventilation requirements for areas where sterile preparations are prepared (including hazardous medications) and hazardous medications are stored are specified in Chapter <797> of the United States Pharmacopeia (USP).[3]

Temperatures

☑ Medications are stored at the appropriate temperatures. (*See* MM.03.01.01, EP 2 in Chapter 4.) ___ ___ ___

	Yes	No	NA
Temperature and humidity levels in the work area ensure the integrity of medications and the comfort of personnel. (Intent of EC.02.06.01, EP 13.)	___	___	___

Thermometers

Thermometers are accurate and reliable.	___	___	___

> *Note:* An accurate and functional thermometer should be kept in refrigerators, freezers, warmers, sterile preparation areas (e.g., IV rooms), and areas subject to temperature extremes (e.g., indoor bulk storage areas and outside receiving areas). Mechanical dial-type thermometers and temperature indicator strips may not give an accurate temperature measurement when damaged, and damage to mechanical thermometers and temperature strips is difficult to detect. Digital and liquid-filled thermometers are more reliable than mechanical dial-type thermometers and temperature indicator strips. Damage to a liquid-filled thermometer is usually apparent.

> *Note:* Some surveyors suggest comparing pharmacy thermometers with a known standard thermometer (e.g., a reference thermometer in the laboratory) periodically. If the pharmacy must refrigerate high-cost medications or medications with narrow temperature requirements (e.g., Factor VIII), consider refrigerators and freezers that sound an alarm when temperatures are outside the required range.

Refrigerators

Medications requiring refrigeration are stored in a refrigerator that maintains the appropriate range. (*See* Examples 4-6 and 4-7.)	___	___	___

Refrigerator Temperature Checks

Refrigerators have thermometers that work properly.	___	___	___
Refrigerators located in areas that are not open every day (e.g., a weekend) have a thermometer that can record temperature fluctuations.	___	___	___

> *Note:* Staff must check the thermometer to ensure that the temperature did not exceed the limits. Some surveyors suggest alarms and other mechanisms that will indicate if refrigerators failed or that temperatures exceeded the limits.

Refrigerator temperatures are in the acceptable range.	___	___	___

> *Note:* Refrigerator temperatures should be checked regularly. Daily refrigerator temperature checks in the pharmacy and patient care areas are reasonable and should be sufficient.

	Yes	No	NA
All medications requiring refrigeration are stored in a refrigerator that maintains the temperature within the acceptable range.	____	____	____
Refrigerator temperature logs are maintained unless a central monitoring system (e.g., automated system with an alarm) is in place and the system is observed constantly.	____	____	____

> ***Note:*** Although the standards do not require temperature logs, most surveyors indicate that daily logs or equivalents are needed. (*See* Examples 4-6 and 4-7.)

> ***Note:*** The CDC recommends recording temperature monitoring of vaccines stored in refrigerators on a temperature log at least twice a day, even if continuous graphing, recording, or digital temperature monitoring devices, or alarm systems are used.[4,5]

	Yes	No	NA
Actions are documented if refrigerator temperatures are out of range.	____	____	____

> ***Note:*** Actions include notifying the pharmacy to check the integrity of the medications and, if necessary, to move the medications to a refrigerator that functions properly.

	Yes	No	NA
Refrigerators are clean and free of excessive frost.	____	____	____

Freezers

	Yes	No	NA
Medications that must be frozen are stored in a freezer that maintains the appropriate range. (*See* Examples 4-6 and 4-8.)	____	____	____

> ***Note:*** Some medications require freezing at lower temperatures; always consult the manufacturers' product literature or specific United States Pharmacopeia/National Formulary monographs. For example, commercially available Prostin E2® (dinoprostone) vaginal suppositories should be stored at temperatures not exceeding -4°F (-20°C). A separate freezer is needed, as some refrigerator freezers do not reach these temperatures.

Freezer Temperature Checks

	Yes	No	NA
Freezers have thermometers that work properly.	____	____	____
Freezers located in areas that are not open every day (e.g., a weekend) have a thermometer that can record temperature fluctuations.	____	____	____

> ***Note:*** Staff must check the thermometer to ensure that the temperature did not exceed the limits. Some surveyors suggest alarms and other mechanisms that will indicate if freezers failed or that temperatures exceeded the limits.

	Yes	No	NA
Freezer temperatures are in the acceptable range.	____	____	____

> ***Note:*** Freezer temperatures should be checked regularly. Daily checks in the pharmacy and patient care areas are reasonable and should be sufficient.

Yes No NA

Note: The CDC recommends temperature monitoring of vaccines stored in freezers at least twice a day.[4,5]

Freezer temperature logs are maintained unless a central monitoring system (e.g., automated system with alarm that is under constant observation) is in place. ____ ____ ____

Note: Although temperature logs are not required by the standards, most surveyors indicate that daily logs or equivalents are needed. (*See* Examples 4-6 and 4-8.)

Note: The CDC recommends recording temperature monitoring of vaccines stored in freezers on a temperature log at least twice a day, even if continuous graphing, recording, or digital temperature monitoring devices, or alarm systems are used.[4,5]

Actions are documented if freezer temperatures are out of range. ____ ____ ____

Note: Actions include notifying the pharmacy to check the integrity of the medications and, if necessary, to move the medications to a freezer that functions properly.

Freezers are clean and free of excessive frost. ____ ____ ____

Warmers

Medications (e.g., intravenous solutions, irrigation solutions, contrast media, and mannitol) stored in warmers are stored at appropriate temperatures. ____ ____ ____

Note: Warmer temperatures should be checked regularly. Daily warmer temperature checks in the pharmacy and patient care areas are reasonable and should be sufficient.

Note: ECRI recommends that the maximum temperature for warmers containing solutions be limied to 110°F (43°C).

Warmer Temperature Checks

Warmers have thermometers that work properly. ____ ____ ____

Warmers located in areas that are not open every day (e.g., weekend) have a thermometer that can record temperature fluctuations. ____ ____ ____

Note: Staff must check the thermometer to ensure that the temperature did not exceed the limits. Some surveyors suggest alarms and other mechanisms that will indicate if warmers failed or that temperatures exceeded the limits.

Warmer temperature logs are maintained unless a central monitoring system (e.g., automated system with alarm that is under constant observation) is in place. ____ ____ ____

Note: Although temperature logs are not required by the standards, most surveyors indicate that daily logs or equivalents are needed.

Actions are documented if warmer temperatures are out of range. ____ ____ ____

Yes	No	NA

Note: Actions include notifying the pharmacy to check the integrity of the medications and, if necessary, to move the medications to a warmer that functions properly.

CHAPTER 11

Policies and Procedures Checklist

The Joint Commission, in its leadership (LD) standards, requires leaders to establish policies and procedures that guide and support patient care, treatment, and services. (*See* LD.04.01.07.) These include policies and procedures that support safe medication management. The pharmacy must ensure that its medication management and other policies and procedures do not conflict with each other or with policies and procedures of other departments; with bylaws, rules, regulations, and policies of the medical staff; with bylaws of the governing body; and with local, state, and federal laws, rules, and regulations.

Policies and Procedures Format—The Joint Commission does not specify a format for policies and procedures, and there is no standard or legally required layout. Although many organizations have adopted a uniform format, other organizations use a variety of formats within the same facility. Example 11-1 is a sample policy and procedure for processing requests for non-formulary medications. The example provides a format that should meet the requirements of most organizations.

Document Management—Only current policies and procedures should be routinely available. Follow organizational processes if they exist or, if such a process is not used, establish a prudent system within the pharmacy. Each policy and procedure should include a descriptive title, number, effective date, revision date (if applicable), and the date by which the document will be reviewed (e.g., annually). Many organizations also include the owner (e.g., pharmacy department or nursing department) of the document.

Policies and Procedures Disposition—The Joint Commission does not address the disposition of outdated policies and procedures. However, good management practices call for their retention. For legal or other reasons, you may need to refer to them to establish the policies and procedures in effect on a specific date. A separate manual or file of outdated policies and procedures, including those with seemingly minor changes, is suggested. Check with your organization for the number of years that discontinued policies should be accessible.

Checklist Organization

This chapter presents suggested policies and procedures in a checklist format. Most of the items in the checklist reflect Joint Commission standards and elements of performance (EPs). The numbers of the standards and EPs follow many of the items. Although the relationships are not always explicit, the items are consistent with the standards and EPs. Some laws and regulations may require policies and procedures for topics not in this checklist.

The Joint Commission requires some specific policies. *See* Table 11-1 for a list of these requirements for medication management.

> ***Note:*** Although this checklist cannot address all pharmacy policies and procedures, it addresses most policy and procedure topics pertaining to the pharmacy.

The notes are compliance expectations and suggestions that are based on the authors' personal experiences, reports from surveyed organizations, and surveyors' statements. Some notes reflect legal requirements, previous Joint Commission standards, or commonly accepted standards of practice. Others note variations in interpretation of the standards. Some notes are referenced to Joint Commission standards.

Checklist Symbols— Special attention should be paid to EPs preceded by an icon. The checklist uses a 🗎 icon before an EP if documentation is required, and a ⚠ icon before an EP if noncompliance is likely to create an immediate risk to patient safety or to the quality of care provided. A ☑ icon before an EP indicates that a Measure of Success (MOS) is required if the EP is scored non-compliant during a survey.

Checklist Usage Suggestions

Pharmacy policies and procedures should clearly address the suggested topics and contain the suggested statements in the checklist. It might be helpful to paraphrase or quote standards and underline key words and statements.

To assess compliance, use the checklist and proceed systematically. Mark the item "Yes" if you are currently compliant and are sure you will continue to be compliant. Mark the item "No" if you are currently not compliant (even if you are sure you will be compliant later). If you are not sure of your answer, leave a blank response. A few items may be not applicable (NA). Answer honestly, use a pencil (so you can change your answers), and make notes on the pages (e.g., reasons for noncompliance and location of documents). It might be helpful to place the page number, policy and procedure number, or other key to locating the policy or procedure beside the item. Concentrate your efforts on resolving all "No" and blank responses.

Checklist

	Yes	No	NA

DEVELOPMENT, ORGANIZATION, REVIEW, REVISION, AND APPROVAL OF POLICIES AND PROCEDURES

Policies and Procedures Development

The pharmacy collaborates with other departments and services in developing policies and procedures for patient care, treatment, and services. (*See* LD.04.01.07.) ____ ____ ____

> ***Note:*** Some organizations have moved from departmental policies and procedures to interdepartmental or organization-wide policies and procedures developed by interdisciplinary groups.

Physicians, nurses, pharmacists, and other appropriate staff have developed written policies and procedures that support effective and safe medication management. (*See* MM.01.01.01 through MM.08.01.01.) ____ ____ ____

Policies and Procedures Organization

Pharmacy policies and procedures are organized in a manner that assures their ready availability to pharmacy staff. ____ ____ ____

> ***Note:*** Many organizations use an electronic format to help ensure only current documents are accessible. There is no requirement for policies and procedures to be kept in a manual. However, a master copy is recommended because it allows personnel to review policies and procedures easily and is readily available if the documents cannot be accessed electronically.

Policies and Procedures Review

The director of pharmacy has reviewed and, if necessary, revised all pharmacy policies and procedures within the last year to ensure consistency with the organization's current practices. ____ ____ ____

> ***Note:*** The Joint Commission does not specify a review frequency. Some state or federal entities and some health care organizations may require annual reviews. An annual frequency should ensure that policies and procedures are current and ready for unannounced surveys. Although all policies and procedures need not be reviewed and revised at the same time, each one should be reviewed and revised as necessary at least once during the year.

	Yes	No	NA
To document the pharmacy's review and revision, the director of pharmacy has signed and dated a master copy of each policy and procedure or a single page that documents review and revision of all policies and procedures. In many organizations, this is an electronic process.	___	___	___

> *Note:* The Joint Commission does not specify how to document the pharmacy's review and revision.

Policies and Procedures Approval (Medical Staff)

The medical staff has approved all medication-related policies and procedures within the last year.	___	___	___

> *Note:* The Joint Commission does not specify an approval frequency. Some state or federal regulations or expectations may specify annual approvals. An annual frequency should ensure that policies and procedures are current and ready for unannounced surveys. Although all policies and procedures need not be approved at the same time, each one should be approved at least once during the year.

To document the medical staff's review and approval, a medical staff representative (e.g., chair of the Pharmacy and Therapeutics [P&T] Committee, chief of the medical staff, or other authorized individual) has signed and dated a master copy of each policy and procedure or a single page that documents review and revision of all policies and procedures. In many organizations, this is an electronic process.	___	___	___

> *Note:* The Joint Commission does not specify how to document medical staff approval.

Policies and Procedures Approval (Infection Control)

The organization's Infection Control Committee has approved the pharmacy's infection control policies within the last year.	___	___	___

Policies and Procedures Approval (Safety Committee)

The organization's Safety Committee has approved the pharmacy's safety policies and procedures within the last year.	___	___	___

Policies and Procedures Approval (Leadership)

If required by the organization, the chief executive officer and/or other persons or committees have reviewed and approved pharmacy and medication-related policies and procedures.	___	___	___

Yes No NA

POLICIES AND PROCEDURES SUGGESTIONS

Pharmacy Services (Scope)

A policy describing the scope of patient care services provided by the pharmacy. ____ ____ ____

> *Note:* The scope of services typically includes maintaining an adequate stock of medications; preparing, labeling, dispensing, and distributing medications, chemicals, sterile products, and parenteral solutions; supervising all medication storage and preparation areas within the pharmacy and throughout the organization; orienting, educating, and training staff; and monitoring medication therapy. Other services typically include medication safety improvement, adverse event reduction, investigational medication studies, patient and family education, home health care services, and drug information services.

> *Note:* The scope of pharmacy services varies with the type and size of the organization and the acuity of care. For example, a large teaching hospital might have a fully staffed drug information center. Smaller hospitals, however, might have only basic reference materials available.

A policy stating the age groups and other populations that the pharmacy serves. ____ ____ ____

A policy stating goals for the pharmacy's patient care services. ____ ____ ____

> *Note:* At a minimum, the goals should reflect the scope of the pharmacy's patient care services and how the pharmacy assesses and meets the needs of all age groups and other populations that the pharmacy serves.

After-Hours Pharmacy Services

☑ ⚠ Policies and procedures for obtaining medications from after-hours supplies when the pharmacy is closed. (*See* MM.05.01.13.) ____ ____ ____

☑ A policy designating individuals who are permitted to remove medications from after-hours supplies when the pharmacy is closed. (*See* MM.05.01.13, EP 4.) ____ ____ ____

☑ A policy requiring a licensed pharmacist, within a specified time period, to review all orders for medications obtained from after-hours supplies when the pharmacy is closed. (*See* MM.05.01.01, EP 3.) ____ ____ ____

☑ ⚠ Policies and procedures for obtaining medications when the pharmacy is closed and medications are not available from after-hours supplies. (*See* MM.05.01.13.) ____ ____ ____

Policies and procedures for evaluating medications obtained from after-hours supplies, assessing why they were obtained, minimizing the need for nonpharmacists to obtain them, and determining how to improve the process for obtaining them. (*See* MM.08.01.01.) ____ ____ ____

Yes **No** **NA**

Obtaining Medications from Other Organizations

Policies and procedures for obtaining medications from hospitals, community pharmacies, and other organizations in routine or emergency situations. ___ ___ ___

Outsourced Pharmacy Services

Policies and procedures for procuring, storing, controlling, and distributing medications from an outside source when the organization does not have a pharmacy. (*See* LD.04.03.09.) ___ ___ ___

Policies and procedures detailing the nature and scope of pharmacy services provided through contractual agreements. (*See* LD.04.03.09.) ___ ___ ___

> ***Note*:** This includes provision of services from external pharmacies (e.g., remote order-entry, other hospitals) and preparations provided by compounding pharmacies (e.g., sterile preparations, nuclear radiopharmaceuticals).

Emergency Pharmacy Services

Policies and procedures for providing medications and pharmacy services when the hospital's emergency plan is instituted. (*See* EM.02.02.01, EP 7 and EP 10 and EM.02.02.03, EP 1.) ___ ___ ___

Job Descriptions

Policies and procedures relating to job descriptions. (*See* HR.01.02.01.) ___ ___ ___

Orientation (Pharmacy)

Policies and procedures relating to orientation of pharmacy staff. (*See* HR.01.04.01.) ___ ___ ___

Policies and procedures relating to the pharmacy's role in orientation of other health care personnel. (*See* HR.01.04.01.) ___ ___ ___

Education (Pharmacy)

Policies and procedures relating to educating and training pharmacy staff. (*See* HR.01.05.03.) ___ ___ ___

Policies and procedures relating to the pharmacy's role in educating other health care personnel. (*See* HR.01.04.01.) ___ ___ ___

Competence Assessment

Policies and procedures relating to verification of staff qualifications. (*See* HR.01.02.05 and HR.01.02.07.) ___ ___ ___

	Yes	No	NA
🗎 ☑ ⚠ Policies and procedures relating to assessing competence of pharmacy staff (*see* HR.01.06.01), including those from staffing services.	___	___	___

Performance Evaluations

🗎 ☑ Policies and procedures relating to performance evaluations. (*See* HR.01.07.01.)	___	___	___

Education (Patient)

☑ ⚠ Policies and procedures relating to the roles of the pharmacy and pharmacists in developing and/or providing patient and family education for the safe and effective use of medications. (*See* MM.06.01.01, EP 9; MM.06.01.03, EP 3 to EP 7; and PC.02.03.01, EP 10.)	___	___	___

Information Management

🗎 ⚠ Policies and procedures to provide for continuity of care in case of interruptions in information management, including a written plan for managing interruptions (*see* IM.01.01.03, EP 1) and backup of electronic systems. (*See* IM.01.01.03, EP 4 and EP 6.)	___	___	___

Patient Information

🗎 A policy stating the minimum amount of patient information to be available to those involved in medication management. (*See* MM.01.01.01, EP 1.)	___	___	___

> ***Note:*** Patient information must include at least the patient's age; sex; current medications; diagnosis, comorbidities, and currently occurring conditions; relevant laboratory values; and past allergies and sensitivities. The patient's height, weight, pregnancy or lactation status, and other elements defined by the organization must be available if appropriate. (*See* MM.01.01.01, EP 1.)

> ***Note:*** The organization must define who has access to the information (*see* IM.02.01.01 and IM.02.01.03), and the information must be available when and where needed. (*See* MM.01.01.01, EP 1.)

🗎 Policies and procedures for maintaining the confidentiality of patient and medical staff information. (*See* IM.02.01.01.)	___	___	___

Formulary

🗎 Policies and procedures for developing and maintaining the formulary. (*See* MM.02.01.01, EP 1 through EP 4.)	___	___	___

	Yes	No	NA
Note: The policy must include the criteria for determining what medications are available for dispensing or administration. (*See* MM.02.01.01, EP 1.) At a minimum, the criteria must include the indication for use, effectiveness, drug interactions, risks (including propensity for medication errors, abuse potential, adverse drug events, and sentinel events), and costs. (*See* MM.02.01.01, EP 2.)			
Policies and procedures for reviewing medications on the formulary at least annually based on emerging safety and efficacy information. (*See* MM.02.01.01, EP 9.)	___	___	___
⚠ A policy stating the standardized medication concentrations available in the organization. (*See* MM.02.01.01, EP 6.)	___	___	___
🗎 Policies and procedures for using herbal products and other alternative medications. (*See* MM.04.01.01, EP 1.)	___	___	___
Policies and procedures for monitoring patients' responses to medications newly added to the formulary before they are available for dispensing or administering. (*See* MM.02.01.01, EP 3.)	___	___	___
Policies and procedures for procuring medications that are not on the formulary. (*See* MM.02.01.01, EP 7.)	___	___	___

Medication Quality

	Yes	No	NA
🗎 A policy stating the quality specifications for all medications, chemicals, and biologicals relating to the practice of pharmacy. (*See* MM.02.01.01, EP 1 and EP 2.)	___	___	___
🗎 Policies and procedures for procuring all medications, chemicals, and biologicals relating to the practice of pharmacy. (*See* MM.02.01.01, EP 1 and EP 2.)	___	___	___

Generic Equivalents

	Yes	No	NA
Policies and procedures for dispensing generic equivalents, if permitted by the organization and law and regulation.	___	___	___

Therapeutic Interchanges

	Yes	No	NA
Policies and procedures for dispensing therapeutic interchanges, if permitted by the organization and law and regulation.	___	___	___

Recalled Medications

	Yes	No	NA
🗎 ☑ Policies and procedures for handling recalled medications. (*See* EC.02.01.01, EP 11 and MM.05.01.17.)	___	___	___

Defective Medications

	Yes	No	NA
☑ A policy requiring defective medications to be reported to the proper authorities (e.g., the Food and Drug Administration). (*See* EC.02.01.01, EP 11 and MM.05.01.17.)	___	___	___

Yes No NA

☑ Policies and procedures for reporting defective medications to the proper authorities (e.g., the Food and Drug Administration [FDA]). (*See* EC.02.01.01, EP 11 and MM.05.01.17.) ___ ___ ___

Defective Devices

Policies and procedures for reporting defective devices to the proper authorities (e.g., the FDA). (*See* EC.02.04.01, EP 5.) ___ ___ ___

Unusable Medications

☑ A policy stating that unusable medications (e.g., expired, defective, damaged, contaminated, recalled, or with worn or missing labels) shall not be distributed or administered. The policy should specify when medications should be returned to the pharmacy. Medications exposed in patient rooms (e.g., inhalers, ointments/creams, partially administered intravenous fluids) should not be accepted back in the pharmacy due to infection control precautions. (*See* MM.05.01.19.) ___ ___ ___

☑ Policies and procedures for removing all unusable medications from stock and segregating them until their proper disposition. (*See* MM.03.01.01, EP 8.) ___ ___ ___

Policies and procedures for ensuring the proper disposition of unusable medications. ___ ___ ___

Emergency Medications

📄 ☑ ⚠ Policies and procedures for ensuring the integrity, ready availability, control, and security of emergency medications. (*See* MM.03.01.03.) ___ ___ ___

Policies and procedures for ensuring the security of mobile or readily portable medication containers. ___ ___ ___

> ***Note:*** The Centers for Medicaid and Medicare Services (CMS) Interpretive Guidelines state: due to their mobility, mobile nursing medication carts, anesthesia carts, epidural carts and other medication carts containing drugs or biologicals must be locked in a secure area when not in use. Hospital policies and procedures are expected to address the security and monitoring of carts, locked or unlocked, containing drugs and biologicals in all patient care areas to ensure their safe storage and to ensure patient safety.[1] (*See* Chapter 22.)

Policies and procedures for controlling seals for emergency medication containers. ___ ___ ___

⚠ Policies and procedures for replacing emergency medications after use. (*See* MM.03.01.03, EP 6.) ___ ___ ___

Controlled Substances

Policies and procedures for distributing, administering, accounting, and securing controlled substances. (*See* MM.03.01.01, EP 3.) ___ ___ ___

	Yes	No	NA
Policies and procedures for storing and distributing controlled substances from automated dispensing cabinets (ADCs). (*See* MM.03.01.01, EP 3.)	___	___	___
Policies and procedures for disposal of (i.e., wasting) unused portions of controlled substances. (*See* MM.03.01.01, EP 3.)	___	___	___
Policies and procedures for using controlled substances in parenteral infusions and in patient-controlled analgesia devices. (*See* MM.03.01.01, EP 3.)	___	___	___
Policies and procedures for epidural administration of controlled substances. (*See* MM.03.01.01, EP 3.)	___	___	___
Policies and procedures for maintaining controlled substances records (e.g., ordering from suppliers, taking inventories, reporting theft and loss, receiving and adding medications to the inventory, distributing to floor stock, reconciling, and prepackaging). (*See* MM.03.01.01, EP 3 and MM.05.01.11, EP 2.)	___	___	___

Investigational Medications

	Yes	No	NA
A policy requiring investigational medications to be used only after approval by the group authorized to grant approval (e.g., institutional review board). (*See* MM.06.01.05, EP 1.)	___	___	___
Policies and procedures for developing and approving protocols for the use of investigational medications. (*See* MM.06.01.05, EP 1.)	___	___	___
Policies and procedures for maintaining essential information on investigational medications in the pharmacy (or other designated area if there is no organized pharmacy service). (*See* MM.06.01.05, EP 1.)	___	___	___
A policy stating that investigational medications shall be prescribed only by those individuals authorized to do so. (*See* MM.06.01.05, EP 1.)	___	___	___
Policies and procedures for ensuring proper labeling, storage, distribution, and control of investigational medications. (*See* MM.04.01.01, EP 1 and MM.06.01.05, EP 2.)	___	___	___
A policy stating that investigational medications shall be dispensed only pursuant to the prescription of an authorized investigator or prescriber. (*See* MM.06.01.05, EP 1.)	___	___	___
A policy specifying the labeling requirements for investigational medications. (*See* MM.05.01.09 and MM.06.01.05, EP 2.)	___	___	___

Note: Investigational medication labels must clearly indicate that the contents are for investigational use. The identity of an investigational medication must be obtainable if needed (e.g., in the case of a double-blind study).

	Yes	No	NA
A policy requiring investigational medications to be administered only in accordance with approved policies and procedures or protocols. (*See* MM.06.01.05, EP 1.)	___	___	___
A policy designating individuals who are approved to administer investigational medications. (*See* MM.06.01.05, EP 1.)	___	___	___

	Yes	No	NA
A policy stating that investigational medications shall be administered only by those approved to do so, and only after they have demonstrated an understanding of the medication's action, possible adverse effects, and appropriate response. (*See* MM.06.01.05, EP 1.)			
Policies and procedures for orienting, educating, and training nurses and others who administer investigational medications. (*See* MM.06.01.05, EP 1.)			
Policies and procedures for requesting and obtaining informed consent from the patient prior to administering investigational medications. (*See* RI.01.03.05.)			
A policy requiring the documentation of any investigational medications ordered, prescribed, or administered, including the strength, dose, route, and, if applicable, the access site, administration device used, and the rate of administration. (*See* RC.02.01.01, EP 2.)			
A policy requiring the documentation of any investigational controlled substance doses destroyed.			
Policies and procedures for returning and disposing of investigational medications. (*See* MM.06.01.05, EP 1.)			
Policies and procedures for auditing investigational medication use to ensure that storage, dispensing, administration, and disposal meet federal and state regulations. (*See* MM.06.01.05, EP 1 and EP 2.)			
Policies and procedures for ensuring appropriate care for patients admitted to the organization who are participating in investigational medication studies or clinical trials. (*See* MM.06.01.05, EP 3 and RI.01.03.05.)			

High-Alert Medications

	Yes	No	NA
Policies and procedures for controlling and ensuring the safe use of high-alert medications (e.g., insulin, anticoagulants, opiates, and potassium chloride and other concentrated electrolytes). (*See* MM.01.01.03 and MM.03.01.01, EP 9.)			

Look-Alike and Sound-Alike Medications

	Yes	No	NA
Policies and procedures for controlling and ensuring the safe use of look-alike and sound-alike medication as defined by the organization. (*See* MM.01.02.01.)			

Radiopharmaceuticals

	Yes	No	NA
Policies and procedures for procuring, storing, controlling, distributing, and administering radiopharmaceuticals whether managed by the pharmacy or by another department.			
If radiopharmaceuticals are prepared in the hospital, policies and procedures to define their preparation and supervision by an appropriately trained pharmacist or physician. (*See* MM.05.01.07, EP 6.)			

Yes **No** **NA**

Contrast Media

Policies and procedures for procuring, storing, controlling, distributing, administering, and monitoring contrast media whether managed by the pharmacy or by another department.

Blood Derivatives

Policies and procedures for procuring, storing, controlling, distributing, administering, and monitoring blood derivatives (e.g., albumin, immune globulins, and clotting factors) whether managed by the pharmacy or by another department.

Personal Medications (Patients')

Policies and procedures for handling and storing medications brought into the organization by patients. (*See* MM.03.01.05, EP 1.)

A policy prohibiting administration of a patient's personal medications without a written order from the responsible practitioner. (*See* MM.03.01.05, EP 1.)

☑ ⚠ A policy prohibiting administration of a patient's personal medications until the medications are properly identified by a pharmacist (preferably the organization's pharmacist) or other qualified staff. (*See* MM.03.01.05, EP 2.)

> ***Note:*** ☑ ⚠ The identification process must include a visual determination of the integrity of the medications. (*See* MM.03.01.05, EP 2.)
>
> ***Note:*** ☑ The prescriber and the patient must be notified if use of the patient's personal medications is not permitted. (*See* MM.03.01.05, EP 3.)
>
> ***Note:*** There must be evidence that these policies and procedures are implemented.

Personal Medications (Practitioners')

Policies and procedures that address the safety and use of medications acquired by a practitioner from sources other than the organization for use in patient care in the organization.

At a minimum, these policies and procedures address the following:

- Whether such medications are allowed to be used. (*See* MM.03.01.05, EP 1.)
- ☑ ⚠ If allowed, a process to evaluate the integrity of the medications brought in by a practitioner prior to use in patient care. (*See* MM.03.01.05, EP 2.)

> ***Note:*** There must be evidence that these policies and procedures are implemented.

Yes No NA

Sample Medications

Policies and procedures for storing and securing medication samples to prevent access by unauthorized individuals (e.g., staff, visitors, and patients). (*See* MM.03.01.01.) ____ ____ ____

Policies and procedures for controlling and documenting the distribution and use of medication samples. (*See* MM.03.01.01.) ____ ____ ____

> ***Note:*** Control of medications must extend to medication samples throughout the organization (including the emergency department, ambulatory clinics, and physician's offices in or associated with the organization). The pharmacy must include medication samples, including those in clinics and off-site locations, in its process for responding to medication recalls and in its monthly inspection routine.

Sales Representatives

Policies and procedures relating to the activities of medical sales representatives. ____ ____ ____

> ***Note:*** Although Joint Commission standards do not explicitly restrict the activities of medical sales representatives, many organizations do so.

Storage of Medications

Policies and procedures for storing medications in a manner that maintains their integrity, stability, and effectiveness. (*See* MM.03.01.01, EP 2.) ____ ____ ____

Policies and procedures for storing medications between receipt of a medication by an individual health care provider and medication administration. At a minimum, the policy addresses the following:

- Safe storage ____ ____ ____
- Safe handling ____ ____ ____
- Security ____ ____ ____
- Disposition of these medications ____ ____ ____
- Return to storage (*See* MM.03.01.01, EP 4.) ____ ____ ____

Policies and procedures for storing medications in accordance with laws, regulations, and the organization's requirements so that unauthorized persons cannot obtain access to them. (*See* MM.03.01.01, EP 6.) ____ ____ ____

> ***Note:*** The CMS definition of "secured" requires (1) that all drugs and biologicals be kept in a secure area, and locked when appropriate; (2) drugs listed in Schedules II, III, IV, and V of the Comprehensive Drug Abuse Prevention and Control Act of 1970 must be kept locked within a secure area; and (3) only authorized personnel may have access to locked areas.[1] (*See* Chapter 22.)

	Yes	No	NA
☑ Policies and procedures describing the actions to be taken if the temperatures of medication refrigerators, freezers, and warmers are not within the normal range. (*See* MM.03.01.01, EP 2.)	___	___	___
🗎 Policies and procedures for segregating easy-to-confuse (e.g., look-alike or sound-alike) medications. (*See* MM.01.02.01.)	___	___	___
⚠ A policy requiring concentrated electrolytes to be stored in the pharmacy or in patient care areas only when patient safety requires their immediate use and precautions are implemented to prevent inadvertent administration. (*See* MM.01.01.03, EP 2 and MM.03.01.01, EP 9.)	___	___	___

Automated Dispensing Cabinets

	Yes	No	NA
Policies and procedures for stocking and using automated dispensing cabinets.	___	___	___

Inspections of Medication Areas

	Yes	No	NA
☑ Policies and procedures for the periodic (e.g., monthly) inspection of medication areas (e.g., patient care units and other areas where medications are dispensed, administered, or stored). (*See* MM.03.01.01, EP 18.)	___	___	___

> ***Note:*** Inspections should be performed by the director of pharmacy or the director's qualified designee.
>
> ***Note:*** Some state boards of pharmacy require specific time intervals and/or specific personnel to perform the inspections.

Medication Orders

	Yes	No	NA
☑ Policies and procedures reflecting medical staff rules and regulations specifying who may write patient care orders. (*See* RC.01.02.01, EP 1.)	___	___	___
🗎 A policy stating the required elements of medication orders. (*See* MM.04.01.01, EP 2.)	___	___	___
Policies and procedures reflecting medical staff rules and regulations regarding verbal (e.g., telephone) orders for medications. (*See* MM.04.01.01, EP 6.)	___	___	___
☑ A policy designating individuals authorized to accept verbal orders for medications. (*See* MM.04.01.01, EP 6 and RC.01.02.01.)	___	___	___
☑ Policies and procedures reflecting medical staff rules and regulations regarding authentication of verbal orders for medications. (*See* RC.01.02.01, EP 4.)	___	___	___
🗎 ☑ A policy requiring a documented diagnosis, condition, or indication for use to be available in the patient's medical record (*see* MM.04.01.01, EP 9) and whether or when indications for use are required on an order. (*See* MM.04.01.01, EP 3.)	___	___	___
Policies and procedures specifying when generic or brand names are acceptable or required.	___	___	___
🗎 Policies and procedures specifying the special precautions needed for ordering look-alike or sound-alike medications. (*See* MM.04.01.01, EP 4.)	___	___	___

	Yes	No	NA
A policy listing the approved abbreviations, acronyms, symbols, and dose designations acceptable to the organization. (*See* IM.02.02.01, EP 2.)	___	___	___
A policy prohibiting the use of dangerous abbreviations, acronyms, symbols, and dose designations (including U, u, IU, QD, Q.D., qd, q.d., QOD, Q.O.D., qod, q.o.d., MS, MSO_4, $MgSO_4$, a trailing zero after a decimal point, and lack of a leading zero before a decimal point for numbers less than 1). (*See* IM.02.02.01, EP 2.)	___	___	___
Policies and procedures defining the use of dosage ranges (if allowed by the organization). (*See* MM.04.01.01, EP 1.)	___	___	___
A policy prohibiting the use of "blanket" or "resume" medication orders (e.g., "resume home medications" and "resume medications after surgery") and other vague medication orders. (*See* MM.04.01.01, EP 1 and EP 8.)	___	___	___
A policy requiring "as needed" (PRN) orders to be qualified (e.g., include the symptom or indication for use) so there is no question about the prescriber's intent. (*See* MM.04.01.01, EP 1.)	___	___	___
Policy and procedures for handling "hold" orders.	___	___	___
Policies and procedures defining the parameters needed for "titrate" orders. (*See* MM.04.01.01, EP 1.)	___	___	___
Note: Parameters must include objective measurements (e.g., specific blood pressure reading, sedation level, or analgesia level) for measurement.			
Policies and procedures defining the parameters needed for "taper" orders. (*See* MM.04.01.01, EP 1.)	___	___	___
Note: Parameters must include objective measurements (e.g., specific blood pressure reading, sedation level, or analgesia level) for measurement.			
Policies and procedures for compounding special formulas in the pharmacy. (*See* MM.04.01.01, EP 1.)	___	___	___
Policies and procedures reflecting specifications for preparations compounded by outside pharmacies and leadership's approval for obtaining preparations from those pharmacies. (*See* LD.04.03.09 and MM.04.01.01, EP 1.)	___	___	___
Policies and procedures for ordering medication-related devices. (*See* MM.04.01.01, EP 1.)	___	___	___
A policy stating the organization's standard times for administering medications.	___	___	___
Policies and procedures for reviewing and approving preprinted orders. (*See* MM.04.01.01, EP 7.)	___	___	___
Policies and procedures for handling standing orders. (*See* MM.04.01.01, EP 7.)	___	___	___
A policy stating when weight-based dosing for pediatric patients is required. (*See* MM.04.01.01, EP 10.)	___	___	___
Policies and procedures stating the actions to be taken when medication orders are illegible, incomplete, or unclear. (*See* MM.04.01.01, EP 5.)	___	___	___

Yes **No** **NA**

Automatic Stop Orders

🗎 Policies and procedures defining situations in which all or some medication orders for a patient will be discontinued. (*See* MM.04.01.01, EP 1.) ___ ___ ___

Note: Some state regulations require automatic stop orders for specific medications.

Medication Dispensing

☑ Policies and procedures for preparing and dispensing medications consistent with applicable laws or regulations. (*See* MM.05.01.11, EP 2.) ___ ___ ___

☑ ⚠ Policies and procedures for dispensing medications safely and accurately. (*See* MM.05.01.11.) ___ ___ ___

☑ Policies and procedures for assuring that medications are dispensed in a timely manner to meet the needs of patients. (*See* MM.05.01.11, EP 3.) ___ ___ ___

Note: Some surveyors expect a policy that defines specific time frames for dispensing stat and routine medications.

☑ Policies and procedures for assuring that the quantities of medications dispensed minimize diversion but are sufficient to meet the needs of patients. (*See* MM.05.01.11, EP 1.) ___ ___ ___

Preparation or Supervision by a Pharmacist

A policy requiring a licensed pharmacist to prepare and dispense all medications or monitor medication preparation and dispensing performed by nonpharmacists. ___ ___ ___

A policy requiring nonpharmacists to work under the direct supervision of a licensed pharmacist who is fully aware of all medication preparation and dispensing activities. ___ ___ ___

A policy defining the limitations on the duties and responsibilities of nonpharmacists. ___ ___ ___

Review of Orders

Policies and procedures for ensuring that all orders are reviewed prior to dispensing. ___ ___ ___

Note: ☑ ⚠ Reviews must include appropriateness of the medication, dose, frequency, and route of administration; therapeutic duplication; real or potential allergies or sensitivities; real or potential interactions between the prescription and other medications, food, and laboratory values; other contraindications; variation from organizational criteria for use; and other relevant medication-related issues or concerns. (*See* MM.05.01.01.)

☑ A requirement that, when not immediately available, a pharmacist reviews medication orders as soon as possible. (*See* MM.05.01.01, EP 1 and EP 3.) ___ ___ ___

Verification of Orders

☑ ⚠ Policies and procedures for verifying prescriber's orders when questions arise. (*See* MM.05.01.01, EP 11.) ___ ___ ___

	Yes	No	NA

Unit-Dose Medications

Policies and procedures relating to a unit-dose medication distribution system. ___ ___ ___

Ready-to-Use Medications

☑ ⚠ A policy requiring medications supplied to care areas or dispensed to be in the most ready-to-use forms available. (*See* NPSG.03.05.01, EP 2; MM.03.01.01, EP 10; MM.03.01.03, EP 3 and MM.05.01.11, EP 4.) ___ ___ ___

Sterile Preparations

Policies and procedures for the safe admixture of sterile preparations (including those prepared outside the pharmacy). ___ ___ ___

> ***Note:*** ☑ ⚠ These should include aseptic technique, compounding procedures, and labeling requirements. (*See* MM.05.01.07.)

⚠ A policy specifying that sterile preparations must be compounded by the pharmacy when the pharmacy is open (except for emergencies or for medications with short stability). (*See* MM.05.01.07, EP 1.) ___ ___ ___

A policy designating the approved individuals (by discipline) who may prepare immediate use compounded sterile preparations, and any limitations. ___ ___ ___

⚠ Policies and procedures for labeling compounded sterile preparations. (*See* MM.05.01.09, EP 3 through EP 12.) ___ ___ ___

Policies and procedures for avoiding incompatibilities in sterile preparations (e.g., consulting compatibility references). ___ ___ ___

☑ ⚠ Policies and procedures for processing orders for sterile products and preparations (e.g., profiling, labeling, and record keeping). (*See* MM.05.01.01, MM.05.01.07, MM.05.01.09, and MM.05.01.11.) ___ ___ ___

⚠ Policies and procedures for establishing and assigning beyond-use dates to compounded sterile preparations. (*See* MM.05.01.09, EP 4 through EP 6.) ___ ___ ___

Parenteral Nutrition

☑ ⚠ Policies and procedures for preparing and dispensing parenteral nutrition products. (*See* MM.05.01.07.) ___ ___ ___

Labeling of Medications

⚠ Policies and procedures defining a standard method for appropriately and safely labeling medications that meet applicable laws and regulations and standards of practice. (*See* MM.05.01.09.) ___ ___ ___

Ambulatory Care Medications

	Yes	No	NA
Policies and procedures for dispensing medications to ambulatory care patients. (*See* MM.05.01.01, EP 1.)	___	___	___

> ***Note:*** Medications may be dispensed to ambulatory care patients only on the order of an authorized prescriber.

	Yes	No	NA
☑ ⚠ A policy stating that medications administered or dispensed to ambulatory care patients shall be recorded in their medical records. (*See* RC.02.01.01, EP 2.)	___	___	___
Policies and procedures ensuring that medications dispensed to ambulatory care patients are labeled for outpatient use. (*See* MM.05.01.09, EP 2.)	___	___	___

Discharge Medications

	Yes	No	NA
Policies and procedures for dispensing medications to discharged patients. (*See* MM.05.01.01, EP 1.)	___	___	___

> ***Note:*** Medications may be dispensed to discharged patients only on the order of an authorized prescriber, and only if permitted by state regulations and organizational policy.

	Yes	No	NA
☑ ⚠ A policy stating that medications administered or dispensed to discharged patients shall be recorded in their medical records. (*See* RC.02.01.01, EP 2.)	___	___	___
Policies and procedures ensuring that medications dispensed to discharged patients are labeled for outpatient use. (*See* MM.05.01.09, EP 2.)	___	___	___

Medication Administration

	Yes	No	NA
🗎 ☑ ⚠ Policies and procedures for administering medications. (*See* MM.06.01.01.)	___	___	___
⚠ A policy defining that intravenous medications are administered in accordance with state law and approved medical staff policies and procedures. (*See* PC.02.01.01, EP 15.)	___	___	___
☑ A policy stating that medications shall be administered only on the order of an individual with clinical privileges and legal authorization to write such orders. (*See* RC.01.02.01.)	___	___	___
🗎 A policy stating that medications shall be administered only by or under the supervision of individuals who are licensed, competent, and permitted by law or regulation to administer medications. (*See* MM.06.01.01, EP 1.)	___	___	___
🗎 ⚠ A policy listing personnel, by title and category, who are permitted to administer medications. (*See* MM.06.01.01, EP 1 and EP 2.)	___	___	___
☑ ⚠ A policy requiring medications to be prepared properly for administration. (*See* MM.06.01.01, EP 3 through EP 7.)	___	___	___
☑ ⚠ A policy requiring medication orders to be verified before administering the medication. (*See* MM.06.01.01, EP 3.)	___	___	___
A policy requiring medications, to the extent possible, to be administered by the person who prepared the dose.	___	___	___

	Yes	No	NA
Note: Unit-dose or patient-specific medications prepared by the pharmacy are excluded from the requirement.			
☑ ⚠ A policy requiring a patient to be identified before administering the medication. (*See* NPSG.01.01.01.)	___	___	___
☑ ⚠ Policies and procedures for advising patients about clinically significant adverse events (e.g., adverse drug reactions) or other concerns. (*See* MM.06.01.01, EP 9.)	___	___	___
☑ ⚠ Policies and procedures for discussing any unresolved significant concerns with the prescriber and other appropriate staff. (*See* MM.06.01.01, EP 8.)	___	___	___
📄 Policies and procedures for notifying the prescriber if there is an adverse drug event (e.g., adverse drug reaction, medication error). (*See* MM.07.01.03, EP 2.)	___	___	___
☑ ⚠ A policy requiring each administered dose to be recorded properly in the patient's medical record. (*See* RC.02.01.01, EP 2.)	___	___	___

Self-Administered Medications

	Yes	No	NA
📄 Policies and procedures for self-administration of medications or administration by a patient or family member, including documenting in the medical record. (*See* MM.06.01.03, EP 1.)	___	___	___
📄 ☑ ⚠ A policy stating that self-administration of medications is allowed only on the written order of the responsible practitioner and in accordance with the organization's policy. (*See* MM.06.01.03.)	___	___	___
If permitted, a policy defining the process by which a patient's own infusion pump may be used.	___	___	___
☑ ⚠ A policy requiring patients or family members who administer medications to receive training and appropriate information and determined to be competent in medication administration. (*See* MM.06.01.03, EP 3 through EP 7.)	___	___	___

Medication Errors

	Yes	No	NA
A policy reflecting the organization's definition of a medication error. (*See* PI.01.01.01, EP 14.)	___	___	___
📄 ☑ ⚠ Policies and procedures for identifying, reporting, and reviewing medication errors. (*See* MM.07.01.03 and PI.01.01.01, EP 14.)	___	___	___
☑ ⚠ A policy requiring medication errors to be reported immediately in accordance with written procedures. (*See* MM.07.01.03, EP 3 and EP 6.)	___	___	___
☑ ⚠ A policy requiring the medication administered (or omitted) in error to be properly recorded in the patient's medical record. (*See* RC.02.01.01, EP 2.)	___	___	___

Adverse Drug Reactions (ADRs)

	Yes	No	NA
A policy reflecting the organization's definition of a significant adverse drug reaction (ADR). (*See* PI.01.01.01, EP 15.)	___	___	___
📄 ☑ ⚠ Policies and procedures for identifying, reporting, and reviewing significant ADRs. (*See* MM.07.01.03 and PI 01.01.01, EP 15.)	___	___	___

	Yes	No	NA
☑ ⚠ A policy requiring ADRs to be reported immediately in accordance with written procedures. (*See* MM.07.01.03, EP 3 and EP 6.)	___	___	___
☑ ⚠ A policy requiring the ADR to be properly recorded in the patient's medical record. (*See* RC.02.01.01, EP 2.)	___	___	___
☑ Policies and procedures for reporting significant ADRs to the FDA. (*See* MM.07.01.03, EP 3.)	___	___	___

Monitoring Medication Therapy

☑ Policies and procedures for monitoring each patient for the effectiveness of medication use, adverse effects, and toxicity. (*See* MM.07.01.01.)	___	___	___
☑ ⚠ Policies and procedures for contacting the prescriber when the pharmacy identifies the potential for an adverse event (e.g., an adverse reaction or a medication–food interaction). (*See* MM.05.01.01, EP 11.)	___	___	___
☑ ⚠ Policies and procedures for contacting prescribers to suggest modifications of orders. (*See* MM.05.01.01, EP 11.)	___	___	___

Medication Management System Evaluation

Policies and procedures for evaluating the medication management system to identify risk points, trends, and methods to improve safety. (*See* MM.08.01.01.)	___	___	___
Policies and procedures for reviewing, considering, and acting on a Joint Commission *Sentinel Event Alert* relating to medication safety. (*See* Table 6-1 in Chapter 6.)	___	___	___

Performance Improvement

☑ Policies and procedures on collecting and analyzing data and using the results of the analysis to identify improvement activities. (*See* LD.03.02.01, EP 5; PI.02.01.01 and PI.03.01.01.)	___	___	___

Infection Control

🗎 Policies and procedures for infection surveillance, prevention, and control for the pharmacy. (*See* IC.01.05.01, EP2 and EP 3.)	___	___	___
Policies and procedures relating to staff participation in the organization's employee health program.	___	___	___
Policies and procedures relating to use of evidence-based national guidelines concerning infection control and prevention. (*See* IC.01.05.01, EP 1.)	___	___	___
☑ Policies and procedures relating to the shelf life of all sterile products, preparations, and items in storage. (*See* IC.02.02.01, EP 4.)	___	___	___
🗎 ⚠ Policies and procedures relating to hand hygiene requirements. (*See* IC.01.04.01, EP 5 and NPSG.07.01.01.)	___	___	___

	Yes	No	NA
Policies and procedures relating to garb worn in sterile compounding areas.	____	____	____
Policies and procedures for using single-use and multiple-dose vials of sterile medications in the pharmacy and throughout the facility.	____	____	____
Policies and procedures relating to standard precautions to reduce the risk of contracting and transmitting AIDS, hepatitis B, and other diseases from exposure to blood and other body fluids.	____	____	____
Policies and procedures for personnel monitoring required in sterile compounding areas and the frequency of assessment. (*See* Chapter 19.)	____	____	____
Policies and procedures for environmental monitoring required in sterile compounding areas and the frequency of assessment. (*See* Chapter 19.)	____	____	____
☑ Policies and procedures for storing sterile products, preparations, and items. (*See* IC.02.02.01, EP 4.)	____	____	____
Policies and procedures for limiting access to sterile preparation compounding areas.	____	____	____
🗎 ☑ ⚠ Policies and procedures for ensuring the proper use of primary engineering controls to include cleaning, maintenance, and checking for operational efficiency. (*See* IC.02.02.01, EP 1 and EC.02.04.03, EP 1, EP 3, and EP 4.)	____	____	____
Policies and procedures for routine cleaning of pharmacy facilities (e.g., cleaning responsibilities, procedures, schedules, and agents approved by the Infection Control Committee).	____	____	____
Policies and procedures for reporting unsanitary conditions and practices.	____	____	____
⚠ Policies and procedures for containing and disposing of trash and infectious waste. (*See* IC.02.01.01, EP 6.)	____	____	____

Safety

	Yes	No	NA
🗎 ☑ ⚠ Policies and procedures relating to a hazard communication program for identifying, managing, packaging, transporting, cleaning up, and disposing of hazardous materials and wastes (e.g., needles, broken ampuls, antineoplastic medications, chemicals, flammable products, and radiopharmaceuticals). (*See* EC.02.02.01.)	____	____	____
🗎 ☑ ⚠ Policies and procedures for ensuring the safe storage of medications and supplies. (*See* MM.03.01.01.)	____	____	____
🗎 Policies and procedures for managing hazardous materials and waste. (*See* EC.01.01.01, EP 5 and MM.01.01.03.)	____	____	____
🗎 Policies and procedures for managing medical equipment. (*See* EC.01.01.01, EP 7.)	____	____	____
🗎 ☑ ⚠ Policies and procedures for ensuring the safe storage and handling of hazardous substances. (*See* EC.02.02.01.)	____	____	____
🗎 ☑ ⚠ Policies and procedures for ensuring proper procedures for hazardous waste. (*See* EC.02.02.01, EP 8 and EM.02.02.05, EP 4.)	____	____	____
🗎 ☑ ⚠ Policies and procedures relating to fire safety precautions (e.g., alarms, reporting processes, fire extinguishers, sprinklers, and evacuation routes). (*See* EC.02.03.01.)	____	____	____

	Yes	No	NA
Policies and procedures relating to utility system safety precautions (e.g., ventilation systems in sterile compounding areas). (*See* EC.02.05.01.)			
Policies and procedures for ensuring adequate control of environmental risks, including adequate ventilation, pressure relationships, air exchange rates, and filtration efficiencies. (*See* EC.02.05.01, EP 6.)			
Policies and procedures for handling of medical device recalls and hazard notices from governmental agencies and manufacturers. (*See* EC.02.01.01, EP 11.)			
Policies and procedures for reporting accidents, injuries, and safety hazards. (*See* EC.02.01.01, EP 1.)			
Policies and procedures relating to emergency preparedness (including disaster drills). (*See* EM.02.01.01 and EM.02.02.03.)			
Policies and procedures relating to latex allergies and sensitivities.			
Policies and procedures for ensuring the safe and proper use of patient care equipment, if applicable. (*See* EC.02.04.03.)			
Policies and procedures for backup when power systems fail. (*See* EC.02.05.03.)			
Policies and procedures for providing backup delivery service when mechanical transport systems (e.g., pneumatic tubes) fail.			
Policies and procedures relating to the pharmacy safety plans and specific hazards (e.g., hazardous materials and Material Safety Data Sheets).			
Policies and procedures for disposing of hazardous materials (*see* EC.02.02.01, EP 4), hazardous chemicals (*see* EC.02.02.01, EP 5), and hazardous medications. (*See* EC.02.02.01, EP 8.)			

Security

	Yes	No	NA
Policies and procedures for ensuring secure storage of medications. (*See* MM.03.01.01, EP 3, EP 4, and EP 6.)			
Policies and procedures for ensuring secure access and egress from the pharmacy. (*See* EC.02.01.01, EP 8.)			
Policies and procedures for ensuring the security of staff. (*See* EC.02.01.01, EP 3.)			
Policies and procedures for controlling visitors and unauthorized personnel. (*See* EC.02.01.01, EP 7.)			
Policies and procedures relating to actions to take if there is a security incident (e.g., robbery or hostile situation). (*See* EC.02.01.01, EP 9.)			

Table 11-1. Documentation Specifically Required in Medication Management Standards

Standard	EP	Written Policy Required
MM.01.01.01	1	The availability of patient information
MM.01.01.03	1	A list of high-alert and hazardous medications
MM.01.02.01	1	A list of look-alike and sound-alike medications
MM.02.01.01	1	Written criteria for formulary agents
MM.02.01.01	4	A formulary, including medication strength and dosage
MM.02.01.01	12	Written medication substitution protocols in event of medication shortage or outage
MM.03.01.01	4	The control of medication between receipt by a health care provider and administration of the medication
MM.04.01.01	1	The types of medication orders deemed acceptable by the organization
MM.04.01.01	2	Required elements of a complete medication order
MM.04.01.01	3	Occasions when the indication for use is required on a medication order
MM.04.01.01	4	Precautions for ordering medications with look-alike or sound-alike names
MM.04.01.01	5	Actions to take when medication orders are incomplete, illegible, or unclear
MM.04.01.01	10	The circumstances for which weight-based dosing is required for pediatrics
MM.05.01.17	1	How medications, recalled or discontinued for safety reasons by the manufacturer or FDA, will be retrieved and handled
MM.06.01.01	1	LIPs and clinical staff disciplines who can administer medications
MM.06.01.03	1	The organization's process for self-administration of medications
MM.06.01.05	1	The organization's process for investigational medications
MM.07.01.03	1	Response to actual or potential adverse drug events, significant adverse drug reactions, and medication errors
MM.07.01.03	2	Notification of the prescriber in the event of an adverse drug event, significant adverse drug reaction, or medication error

CHAPTER 12

Frequently Requested Documents Checklist

The Joint Commission expects organizations to maintain adequate documentation to demonstrate continuous compliance with standards and legal requirements. Well organized and well maintained documentation fosters high-quality patient care and enhances pharmacy management. This checklist should help pharmacies improve their documentation and ensure that most documents and records are readily available.

Checklist Organization

This chapter presents frequently requested documents in a checklist format. Many of the items in the checklist reflect Joint Commission standards and elements of performance (EPs). The numbers of the standards and EPs follow these items. Some laws and regulations may require documents that are not in this checklist.

> ***Note:*** Although the checklist cannot address all documents that might be requested, it should ensure that the pharmacy will have most of the documents needed to demonstrate continuous compliance with Joint Commission and legal requirements pertaining to the medication use process. Unless otherwise requested, the most current 12 months of documentation should be adequate.

The notes are compliance expectations and suggestions that are based on the authors' personal experiences, reports from surveyed organizations, and surveyors' statements. Some notes reflect legal requirements, previous Joint Commission standards, or commonly accepted standards of practice. Others note variations in interpretation of the standards. The notes are not referenced to the standards.

Checklist Symbols—Special attention should be paid to EPs preceded by an icon. A ★ icon preceding an item on the checklist indicates that it is one of the most frequently requested documents during surveys. The checklist uses a 🗎 icon before an EP if documentation is required. A ⚠ icon is used before an EP if noncompliance is likely to create an immediate risk to patient safety or to the quality of care provided. A ☑ icon before an EP indicates that a Measure of Success (MOS) is required if the EP is scored non-compliant during a survey.

Checklist Usage Suggestions

To assess compliance, use the checklist and proceed systematically. Mark the item "Yes" if you are currently compliant and are sure you will continue to be compliant. Mark the item "No" if you are currently not compliant (even if you are sure you will be compliant later). If you are not sure of your answer, leave a blank response. A few items may be not applicable (NA). Answer honestly, use a pencil (so you can change your answers), and make notes on the pages (e.g., reasons for noncompliance and location of documents). It might be particularly helpful if the documents are kept outside the pharmacy. Concentrate your efforts on resolving all "No" and blank responses.

Checklist

Yes No NA

Licenses (Pharmacy)

★ License for the organization's inpatient pharmacy. (*See* LD.04.01.01, EP 1.) ___ ___ ___

Note: The pharmacy must be appropriately licensed.

Note: Surveyors usually determine whether pharmacy licenses, registrations, and permits are current. Sometimes current licenses are not available (e.g., when the board of pharmacy is delayed in furnishing renewal certificates). Copies of renewal applications, letters from the board acknowledging current licensure, or documented evidence of checking the board's Web site will satisfy surveyors.

Retail pharmacy license or dispensing permit, if required. (*See* LD.04.01.01, EP 1.) ___ ___ ___

Licenses (Pharmacist)

★ ☑ License and renewal evidence for each pharmacist, including evidence of current licensure for pharmacists who practice primarily at another site or for a staffing agency. (*See* HR.01.02.05, EP 2.) ___ ___ ___

Note: Pharmacy staff must be appropriately licensed.

Note: Surveyors usually determine whether all pharmacist licenses, registrations, and permits are current. Sometimes current licenses are not available (e.g., for newly licensed pharmacists or when the board of pharmacy is delayed in furnishing renewal certificates). Copies of renewal applications, dated letters from the board acknowledging current licensure, or documented evidence of checking the board's Web site will satisfy surveyors.

Note: Surveyors determine whether pharmacists are currently licensed by the state in which the organization is located. Military pharmacists and pharmacists with the Veterans Administration and U.S. Public Health Service must be currently licensed, but licensure need not be in the state where they practice.

Licenses, registrations, and permits are displayed appropriately or filed in the pharmacy. ___ ___ ___

Note: Some states require licenses and other permits to be displayed in public view. The Joint Commission expects state requirements to be followed.

License Verification

★ ☑ Evidence that pharmacists' licenses have been verified. (*See* HR.01.02.05, EP 2.) ___ ___ ___

Yes **No** **NA**

Note: Joint Commission standards require organizations to verify that staff (including contract services employees) are currently licensed, certified, or registered. The director of pharmacy must verify the licenses of pharmacists and other pharmacy personnel who must be licensed, certified, or registered. Verification should confirm that they can legally practice and that there is nothing in their records that adversely affects their capability to perform their duties.

Note: Pharmacy staff for whom a license, certification, or registration is required by the organization and/or law and regulation must have the currency of their licenses, certifications, or registrations verified by a primary source when *hired.*

Note: Pharmacy staff for whom a license, certification, or registration is required by the organization and/or law and regulation must have the renewal of their licenses, certifications, or registrations verified by a primary source *upon expiration*. Some organizations require annual verification.

Note: The primary source may delegate authority to verify licensure to an agency. An electronic or telephone verification is acceptable if it is documented. Making a telephone inquiry to the state board of pharmacy or checking the board's Web site are acceptable ways to verify current licensure, previous suspension or revocation, and pending challenges. (*See* Chapter 7.)

Note: Pharmacists who are board certified should have their board certification verified, especially if certification is required in their job description.

Note: Verification of licensure, certification, or registration must be documented (e.g., in the individual's personnel record). (*See* Example 12-1.) Some pharmacies keep a master list of names, license numbers, expiration dates, and documentation (signed and dated by the director of pharmacy) indicating that renewal certificates have been checked and are current. Many pharmacies also track completion of continuing education (CE) requirements for employees whose licensure renewal requires it.

Licenses (Other)

📄 ☑ A license, registration, or equivalent for each pharmacy student, technician, intern, extern, and others, if applicable. (*See* HR.01.02.05, EP 2.) ____ ____ ____

📄 ☑ Certification evidence (e.g., a certificate) for each certified pharmacy technician. (*See* HR.01.02.05, EP 2.) ____ ____ ____

★ 📄 Federal Drug Enforcement Administration (DEA) controlled substances registration certificate. (*See* LD.04.01.01, EP 1.) ____ ____ ____

📄 State controlled substances permit, if required. (*See* LD.04.01.01, EP 1.) ____ ____ ____

📄 Other required licenses and permits (e.g., tax-free alcohol permit). (*See* LD.04.01.01, EP 1.) ____ ____ ____

	Yes	No	NA

Note: If separate licensing for retail pharmacies, outpatient pharmacies, home care pharmacies, etc., is required, surveyors expect to see evidence of such licensure. If the pharmacy provides services to out-of-state patients (e.g., home health care), it might need a pharmacy license for each state in which it provides services. Some states require retail sales licenses. These documents should be current and displayed or filed as appropriate.

Organization

An organization chart showing pharmacy's relationship to the organization and other departments and services. ___ ___ ___

Note: Most facilities periodically update their organizational chart. The pharmacy should have the most recent chart.

Pharmacy organization plan. ___ ___ ___

Note: The pharmacy's organization plan should delegate responsibility (e.g., for supervising, interviewing, hiring, orienting, teaching, counseling, and terminating). It should clearly indicate to whom the director of pharmacy reports as well as the person who is responsible in the absence of the director.

Note: Some plans list the routine reports required (e.g., staffing reports), the persons responsible for preparing them, and the persons to whom they are submitted.

Pharmacy organization chart. ___ ___ ___

Note: The pharmacy's organization chart should be consistent with the pharmacy's organization plan and show the lines of authority within the pharmacy and between the pharmacy and the organization's administration. If the pharmacy has standing committees, include them in the plan and on the chart. The policies and procedures manual is a good place to keep the plan and chart.

Pharmacy Services Description

Medication distribution system flowchart or description showing (at a minimum) how the pharmacy processes medication orders, dispenses medications, and distributes medications to patients and floor stocks. (*See* Table 5-1 in Chapter 5.) ___ ___ ___

Note: Some pharmacies include all of the components of the medication management system in their flowchart or description (i.e., selection and procurement, storage, ordering and transcribing, preparing and dispensing, administering, and monitoring). (*See* Chapter 4 and Table 5-1 in Chapter 5.)

	Yes	No	NA

Outsourced/Contracted Pharmacy Services

	Yes	No	NA
🗎 Evidence that medical staff and leadership have approved the use of a contracted or outsourced pharmacy service. (*See* LD.04.03.09, EP 3.)	____	____	____
A statement in the contract for pharmacy services that specifies the provider will ensure that pharmacy services meet Joint Commission standards. (*See* LD.04.03.09, EP 4.)	____	____	____
🗎 Evidence that hospital leadership monitors contracted services by communicating expectations in writing to providers of contracted services. (*See* LD.04.03.09, EP 5.)	____	____	____

Staffing Plan

	Yes	No	NA
⚠ Description of pharmacy staffing (e.g., a staffing plan and a current staffing schedule) that shows that the pharmacy has an adequate number and mix of staff to meet the care, treatment, and service needs of patients. (*See* LD.03.06.01, EP 3.)	____	____	____
Data used to determine that pharmacy staffing meets the care, treatment, and service needs of patients.	____	____	____

After-Hours Pharmacy Services

	Yes	No	NA
★ ☑ ⚠ Records of after-hours removal of medications from after-hours stocks and evidence that a pharmacist reviews the records. (*See* MM.05.01.13.)	____	____	____
Information relating to emergency pharmacy services (e.g., pharmacists' telephone numbers or a procedure for contacting an on-call pharmacist). (Implied by MM.05.01.13, EP 6.)	____	____	____

Emergency Pharmacy Services

	Yes	No	NA
Emergency telephone numbers for hospitals, community pharmacies, wholesale suppliers, and other emergency sources of medications (e.g., state and federal stockpiles). (Implied by EM.02.02.01, EP 7 and EP 10 and EM.02.02.03, EP 1.)	____	____	____
Telephone number of a poison control information center.	____	____	____

> ***Note:*** Many pharmacists affix the telephone number to the telephone. Some also indicate the locations of poison treatment information and medications and antidotes used to treat poisonings.

Policies and Procedures

	Yes	No	NA
★ Policies and procedures for managing the pharmacy. (*See* Chapter 11.)	____	____	____
★ Policies and procedures for medication management. (*See* Chapter 11.)	____	____	____

Yes **No** **NA**

Reference Materials

Up-to-date pharmacy reference materials. (*See* IM.03.01.01.) ____ ____ ____

> ***Note:*** The pharmacy should be able to provide answers to most routine drug information questions. References should be readily available to all pharmacy personnel and to medical, nursing, and other professional staff, as appropriate. Staff should be familiar with the references and know which are the best sources of information for specific needs. Surveyors seldom cite the pharmacy for failure to have the most recent editions. However, references more than 3 years old are questionable, especially when new editions are available.

> ***Note:*** Electronic data-retrieval systems provide ready access to information that can be printed and edited to meet the pharmacy's needs. This information may be more up-to-date than printed materials. Manufacturers may be the best source of product-specific information. However, although manufacturers' information is free and readily available, it may be biased and incomplete.

Forms

Examples of current forms and records. ____ ____ ____

Pharmacy & Therapeutics Activities

Committee minutes or other records of pharmacy and therapeutics activities for the last 12 months. (*See* Chapter 13.) ____ ____ ____

Formulary

★ 🗎 Current formulary or list of medications accepted for use in the organization with dated evidence of approval. (*See* MM.02.01.01, EP 4.) ____ ____ ____

> ***Note:*** At a minimum, the formulary must include medication names, strengths, and dosage forms.

Evidence that the formulary was reviewed at least annually based on emerging safety and efficacy information. (*See* MM.02.01.01, EP 9.) ____ ____ ____

Record of special pharmaceutical formulas for extemporaneous compounding used in the organization. ____ ____ ____

Medication Orders

★ 🗎 ☑ ⚠ List of standardized abbreviations, acronyms, symbols, and dose designations *approved* for use in the hospital. (*See* IM.02.02.01, EP 2 and EP 3.) ____ ____ ____

Yes No NA

★ 🗎 ☑ ⚠ List of *prohibited* abbreviations, acronyms, and symbols. (*See* IM.02.02.01, EPs 2 and 3.) ____ ____ ____

Signatures of practitioners currently authorized to prescribe medications. ____ ____ ____

> ***Note:*** This record must be readily available to pharmacy staff. Surveyors expect the records to be accessible in the pharmacy to ensure immediate access if there is a question about a prescriber's credentials. The record must be up to date and include only current prescribers. If former prescribers are in the record, their status must be clearly noted (e.g., by a notation on the record or by listing them separately from current prescribers). Surveyors sometimes ask to see the record of a newly added and/or a former member of the medical staff.

Copies of routine, standard, or preprinted orders for medications. (*See* MM.04.01.01, EP 7.) ____ ____ ____

Copies of protocols (including the use of medications) with evidence of medical staff approval. ____ ____ ____

Patient Profile (Pharmacy)

★ 🗎 Pharmacy patient profiles (manual or computerized) with patient information (e.g., age; sex; current medications; diagnoses, comorbidities, and currently occurring conditions; and allergies and past sensitivities). (*See* MM.01.01.01, EP 1 and EP 2.) ____ ____ ____

> ***Note:*** Other pertinent information may be included (e.g., height and weight if needed to calculate body surface area; pregnancy and lactation information; relevant laboratory values).

Reconciliation of Medications

🗎 ☑ ⚠ Records of medication reconciliation (e.g., medication reconciliation forms) across the continuum of care. (*See* NPSG.08.01.01 in Chapter 6.) ____ ____ ____

Medication Dispensing

Schedule for filling medication carts and/or automated dispensing cabinets (ADCs). ____ ____ ____

Override and reconciliation records for ADCs. ____ ____ ____

Policy for timely dispensing of medications. ____ ____ ____

> ***Note:*** Organizations should define the time that stat and routine medications will be dispensed after the order is received.

Medication Administration

List of standard medication administration times (e.g., 9 a.m. and 5 p.m. for medications administered twice a day). ____ ____ ____

	Yes	No	NA
A written process addressing self-administration of medications. (*See* MM.06.01.03, EP 1 in Chapter 4.)	____	____	____
Written documentation defining personnel that are authorized to administer medications. (*See* MM.06.01.01, EP 1 in Chapter 4.)	____	____	____

Investigational Medications

	Yes	No	NA
Minutes or other records of the group that approves the use of investigational medications (e.g., Institutional Review Board). (*See* RI.01.03.05.)	____	____	____
A written process addressing the use of investigational medications. (*See* MM.06.01.05 in Chapter 4.)	____	____	____
Records of acquiring, dispensing, administering, and disposing of investigational medications. (*See* MM.06.01.05, EP 1 and EP 2.)	____	____	____

Adverse Drug Events (ADEs)

	Yes	No	NA
★ ☑ ⚠ Reports of actual and suspected adverse drug events (ADEs) (e.g., adverse drug reactions) if available to the pharmacy. (*See* MM.07.01.03, EP 3 and EP 5.)	____	____	____
★ ☑ ⚠ Evidence of tracking and trending of actual and suspected adverse drug events (ADEs) (e.g., adverse drug reactions). (*See* MM.07.01.03, EP 3 and EP 5.)	____	____	____
Copies of reports of ADEs submitted to the Food and Drug Administration (FDA) and manufacturers.	____	____	____

Medication Errors

	Yes	No	NA
☑ ⚠ Reports of actual or suspected medication errors. (*See* MM.07.01.03, EP 1 and EP 5.)	____	____	____
★ Evidence of tracking and trending medication use processes (e.g., errors and variations of performance) to improve safety.	____	____	____
Evidence of performance of failure mode and effects analysis of pharmacy processes. (*See* Chapter 15.)	____	____	____

Defective Medications

	Yes	No	NA
Copies of reports of medication problems or defects submitted to the FDA or manufacturer.	____	____	____

	Yes	No	NA

Recalled Medications

★ 🗎 ☑ Medication recall notices with records of pharmacy action taken. (*See* MM.05.01.17, EP 1 and EP 2.) ____ ____ ____

Inspections

★ ☑ Inspection records for the pharmacy and all medication areas (including offsite clinics and physician offices owned by the organization) for each of the last 12 months. (*See* MM.03.01.01, EP 18.) ____ ____ ____

> ***Note:*** The records should include evidence that action was taken to correct deficiencies.

State board of pharmacy, department of health, DEA, and other inspection reports and evidence that deficiencies were corrected. ____ ____ ____

> ***Note:*** Surveyors may check for correction of deficiencies and may cite the pharmacy if deficiencies have not been corrected.

Performance Improvement

The organization's performance improvement (PI) plan. (*See* Chapter 15.) ____ ____ ____

A description of the pharmacy's role in the organization's PI program (e.g., a policy and procedure or plan). (*See* MM.08.01.01, EP 1 and PI.01.01.01, EP 14 and EP 15.) ____ ____ ____

Evidence that the pharmacy participates in the organization's PI activities (e.g., on PI teams). ____ ____ ____

> ***Note:*** Pharmacy participation need not be limited to medication use improvement teams. The pharmacy should summarize its PI activities for the 12–18 months before the survey and identify examples of improved patient care (or improved pharmacy services). Graphs that show measurable improvements are suggested.

Medication Use Improvement

★ Evidence that the pharmacy participates in medication use improvement activities. (*See* MM.08.01.01.) (*See* Chapter 15.) ____ ____ ____

> ***Note:*** Examples include determining medication use patterns, participating on medication use improvement teams, participating on medication safety teams, monitoring medication use and reporting variations and problems to the medical staff, participating in developing the medication formulary, and identifying and reporting ADEs and medication errors.

Emergencies

List of emergency medications (including crash cart lists) and antidotes approved by the medical staff. (*See* MM.03.01.03, EP 1.) ____ ____ ____

	Yes	No	NA
Current toxicology reference materials and poison treatment medications (in the emergency department/service and poison treatment areas).			
Current edition(s) of the organization's approved Emergency Operations Plan. (*See* EM.02.01.01, EP 2.)			

Note: The plan should address internal emergencies (e.g., fire, bomb threat or explosion, flood, and civil disturbance) and external emergencies (e.g., hurricanes, tornadoes, accidents, and terrorist attacks).

Hazardous Materials and Wastes

	Yes	No	NA
Written plan for handling hazardous materials and wastes, medications, and chemicals located in pharmacy areas. (*See* Chapters 10 and 17.)			
★ List of hazardous medications and materials stored or used routinely in the pharmacy and other areas where hazardous medications are handled. (*See* MM.01.01.03, EP 1 and EC.02.02.01, EP 1.)			
Material safety data sheets (MSDSs). (*See* EC.02.02.01, EP 11.)			

Note: Access to MSDSs must be readily available in the pharmacy and other areas where hazardous medications and materials are stored or handled.

Note: Access may be by a printed copy in the areas or electronically. Some surveyors may question whether electronic access is readily available or if the information is available when electronic systems are unavailable (e.g., during power outage, computer downtime).

Infection Control

	Yes	No	NA
Records of testing for microbial contamination of high-risk sterile preparations and those preparations that exceed USP <797> beyond-use dates. (*See* Chapter 19.)			
Records of non-viable environmental monitoring in the area(s) used for compounding sterile preparations. (*See* Chapter 19.)			
Records of viable environmental monitoring (e.g., electronic air sampling, microbial contamination of the primary engineering control [PEC]) in the area(s) used for compounding sterile preparations. (*See* Chapter 19.)			
Records of media-fill and gloved fingertip challenge testing. (*See* Chapter 19.)			
Records of surface sampling of designated sites within the sterile preparation area.			

Laminar Airflow Workbenches (LAFWs)

	Yes	No	NA
★ Inspection and/or certification records. (*See* Chapters 9 and 19.)			
Cleaning records.			
Maintenance records (e.g., pre-filter changing or cleaning).			

	Yes	No	NA

Biological Safety Cabinets (BSCs)

	Yes	No	NA
★ Inspection and/or certification records. (*See* Chapters 9 and 19.)	____	____	____
Cleaning records.	____	____	____
Maintenance records (e.g., cleaning).	____	____	____

Compounding Aseptic Isolators (CAIs) and Compounding Aseptic Containment Isolators (CACIs)

	Yes	No	NA
★ Inspection and/or certification records. (*See* Chapters 9 and 19.)	____	____	____
Cleaning records.	____	____	____
Maintenance records (e.g., cleaning).	____	____	____

Equipment (Pharmacy)

	Yes	No	NA
Preventive maintenance program/schedule and quality assurance records for pharmacy equipment (e.g., automated compounding devices, robotic devices, repeater pumps, packaging devices). (*See* Chapter 10.)	____	____	____

Prepackaging

	Yes	No	NA
Quality control records for medications that are prepackaged by the pharmacy.	____	____	____

Temperatures

	Yes	No	NA
★ ☑ Records of refrigerator, freezer, and warmer temperature monitoring (including actions taken if temperatures were out of range). (*See* MM.03.01.01, EP 2.)	____	____	____

Floor Stock

	Yes	No	NA
List of the kinds and quantities of all medications in floor stocks (including medications in automated dispensing cabinets).	____	____	____

Controlled Substances

> ***Note:*** The DEA requires all controlled substances records to be readily available. The DEA provides additional information on accountability for controlled substances in its DEA Pharmacist's Manual.[1]

	Yes	No	NA
Power of attorney, if granted, giving authority to obtain and execute official order forms (DEA Form 222) for controlled substances. (*See* Example 12-2.)	____	____	____

	Yes	No	NA
Note: DEA Form 222 must be signed by an individual authorized to sign the form. Surveyors sometimes check to see if individuals who sign these forms have a power of attorney to do so. The receipt of controlled substances must be entered on the form.			
Invoices showing the receipt of controlled substances.	___	___	___
Note: The DEA requires Schedule I and II records be separate from all other records. Some surveyors check this.			
★ Evidence of a current perpetual inventory of Schedule II controlled substances.	___	___	___
Note: Many states require a perpetual inventory for all Schedule II substances; some states also require it for Schedules III–V substances. Expired, recalled, and other unusable controlled substances must be included on the perpetual inventory. Surveyors sometimes spot-check to determine if the amounts on hand agree with the perpetual inventory.			
An annual or biennial inventory of all controlled substances (whichever is required by the state). (*See* Examples 4-9 and 4-10.)	___	___	___
Note: The inventory must include expired, recalled, and other unusable controlled substances.			
★ Records of dispensing and administering controlled substances.	___	___	___
Note: Proof-of-use records must document the administration and use of all controlled substances. Surveyors sometimes spot-check to determine if the amounts on hand agree with the proof-of-use records.			
Records documenting the administration of controlled substances in anesthetizing areas.	___	___	___
Note: Surveyors focus on controlled substances used in anesthetizing areas. They understand that accounting for the use of controlled substances in these areas is difficult. They insist that controlled substances in anesthetizing areas be locked and that the amounts on hand be checked regularly. Surveyors often determine if staff comply with state and federal requirements as well as the organization's policies and procedures for handling controlled substances in anesthetizing areas.			
Note: Anesthesia personnel should be able to account for each dose of a controlled substance at all times. Single-dose ampuls must not be used on more than one patient. Surveyors like to see control systems that have a high degree of accountability (e.g., a tray exchange system or ADC).			
Note: The amounts of controlled substances administered must be recorded accurately (e.g., on a proof-of-use record) and must agree with the amounts recorded in patients' medical records. Many surveyors ask to see evidence of reconciling anesthesia controlled substances proof-of-use records with patients'			

	Yes	No	NA
anesthesia records. The reconciliation process must ensure that records are correct and complete. Wastage must be recorded and witnessed by another authorized individual.			
Records of dispensing controlled substances to out-patients and employees.	____	____	____
Note: Outpatient prescriptions for controlled substances must have prescribers' DEA numbers and, if applicable, be marked with a red "C."			
Records of withdrawals from automated dispensing cabinets.	____	____	____
Note: These records must show that an authorized individual withdrew the medications.			
Evidence of inactivation of employees' ADC access once they leave the employ of the organization.	____	____	____
Records of periodic inventories (e.g., per shift, daily, weekly, or monthly) as required by the organization or legal requirements.	____	____	____
★ Records of controlled substance reconciliation processes.	____	____	____
★ Records documenting controlled substance wastage.	____	____	____
Note: A single-use ampul or vial of medication must be administered to only one patient. If the patient does not receive the entire contents of the ampul, the medication remaining in the ampul must be wasted and the wastage documented appropriately. Proof-of-use records must account for the wastage of unused portions of unit-dose injections and of spilled, contaminated, and refused doses.			
Note: The DEA interprets federal regulations to require a witness to the wastage of all controlled substances. The wastage must be authenticated by an authorized individual.			
Records of theft or loss of controlled substances.	____	____	____
Note: The organization reports abuses and losses of controlled substances, in accordance with law and regulation, to the Pharmacist-in-Charge and, as appropriate, to the chief executive. (*See* MM.01.01.03, EP 5.) (*See* Example 4-12.)			
Signatures and DEA numbers of practitioners currently authorized to prescribe controlled substances.	____	____	____
Note: This record must be readily available to pharmacy staff. Surveyors expect the records to be accessible in the pharmacy to ensure immediate access if there is a question about a prescriber's credentials. The record must be up-to-date and include only current prescribers. If former prescribers are in the record, their status must be clearly noted (e.g., by a notation on the record or by listing them separately from current prescribers). Surveyors sometimes ask to see the record of a newly added and/or a former member of the medical staff. (*See* Example 12-3.)			
Records of the disposal of controlled substances.	____	____	____

	Yes	No	NA
Note: Disposal procedures vary from state to state. Some states permit appropriately witnessed, onsite disposal of unusable or unneeded controlled substances. (*See* Example 4-11.) The area DEA office or the board of pharmacy can provide advice on how to comply with the disposal requirements.			

Personnel Records

	Yes	No	NA
★ 📄 ☑ Evidence that a license check (with the primary source) and criminal background check was performed on each employee (as required by law and regulation or hospital policy) prior to hiring. (*See* HR.01.02.05, EP 2 and EP 4.)	___	___	___
★ Personnel records or files (including job descriptions, performance evaluations, and competence assessments) for each employee. (*See* Chapter 7.)	___	___	___
Note: These may be stored centrally in the organization instead of in the pharmacy.			
☑ Evidence that performance evaluations are based on standards of performance in job descriptions. (*See* HR.01.07.01, EP 1.) (*See* Chapter 7.)	___	___	___
★ 📄 ☑ Evidence that performance evaluations were conducted once every 3 years or more frequently, consistent with hospital policies or law and regulation. (*See* HR.01.07.01, EP 2.)	___	___	___

Orientation (Pharmacy)

	Yes	No	NA
★ 📄 ☑ Evidence that pharmacy personnel have been oriented to the organization and to the pharmacy. (*See* HR.01.04.01, EP 2 through EP 6.) (*See* Chapter 7.)	___	___	___
Evidence that the pharmacy orientation includes medication safety, environmental safety, security, and infection control.	___	___	___

Education (Pharmacy)

	Yes	No	NA
Records (e.g., minutes) of pharmacy staff meetings.	___	___	___
📄 ☑ Evidence of ongoing education and training for pharmacy personnel. (*See* HR.01.05.03, EP 1.)	___	___	___
Evidence of annual education and training on medication safety, environmental safety, security, and infection control.	___	___	___
Records of completion of mandatory continuing education for all personnel.	___	___	___
📄 ☑ Evidence that pharmacy personnel have received education and training specific to relevant patient populations. (*See* HR.01.05.03, EP 5 in Chapter 7.)	___	___	___
★ Evidence of education, training, and competence for individuals who compound sterile preparations.	___	___	___
Written guidelines for compounding parenteral medications (e.g., information relating to compatibility, contraindications, dilution, stability, and flow rates).	___	___	___

	Yes	No	NA
Evidence of education and training for individuals who compound antineoplastic agent preparations.	____	____	____
☑ Evidence of ADE-related education and training. (*See* HR.01.05.03, EP 7.)	____	____	____

Education (Professional Staff)

	Yes	No	NA
☑ Evidence that the pharmacy provides or participates in educational programs (especially for relevant medication safety topics) for medical staff and nursing service. (*See* HR.01.05.03, EP 1 through EP 7.)	____	____	____
Evidence of education, training, and competence for nurses and others (e.g., respiratory therapists, radiologic technologists, nuclear medicine technologists) who prepare sterile medications.	____	____	____
★ Evidence that nurses who obtain medications from after-hours stocks have been adequately oriented and trained.	____	____	____
☑ Evidence of ADE-related education and training for nurses and others who monitor, detect, and report ADEs. (*See* HR. 01.05.03, EP 7.)	____	____	____

CHAPTER 13

Pharmacy and Therapeutics Activities

The Joint Commission's medication management (MM) standards require organizations to develop policies and procedures for planning, selecting and procuring, storing, ordering and transcribing, preparing and dispensing, administering, monitoring, and evaluating medications. Organizations must develop a formulary or list of medications for dispensing or administration (*see* MM.02.01.01), respond to actual or potential adverse drug events and medication errors (*see* MM.07.01.03), and evaluate their medication management system for risk points and identify areas to improve safety. (*See* MM.08.01.01.)

Pharmacy and Therapeutics Committee—Although The Joint Commission does not require organizations to have a Pharmacy & Therapeutics (P&T) Committee, most organizations use a medical staff P&T Committee to perform many medication-related activities. The Centers for Medicare and Medicaid Services (CMS) Conditions of Participation no longer require a P&T Committee. (*See* Chapter 22.) The Healthcare Facilities Accreditation Program (HFAP) standards for pharmaceutical services refer to a P&T Committee. (*See* Chapter 23.) The National Integrated Accreditation for Healthcare Organizations (NIAHO) standards for medication management refer to a medical staff oversight group for certain medication management topics; however, there is no specific reference to a P&T Committee. (*See* Chapter 24.)

This chapter discusses how to organize an effective P&T Committee and provides guidelines for developing policies and procedures and a formulary. (*See* Chapters 4 and 11.) Evaluating the medication management system, responding to medication errors, and responding to adverse drug events are addressed in Chapters 15, 20, and 21, respectively. The approach and suggestions in this chapter can be applied to a P&T Committee or other mechanisms for performing the required activities.

The P&T Committee also provides a forum for educating and advising the medical staff. Pharmacies should use the committee to their advantage; it may be their best opportunity to meet with the medical staff to discuss matters pertaining to medication management.

P&T Committee Organization

The *ASHP Statement on the Pharmacy and Therapeutics Committee and the Formulary System* recommends that organizations have a P&T Committee, or its equivalent.[1] The organization's mechanism for performing the P&T function should be described in the medical staff's bylaws, rules, and regulations. This description should include the composition of the committee, assignment of responsibilities, meeting frequency, reporting requirements, and topics to be addressed. In small organizations, the entire medical staff may participate in P&T activities (sometimes called a "committee of the whole"). In other organizations, the medical staff assigns P&T responsibilities to individuals or divides them among existing committees.

P&T Committee Composition—There should be sufficient medical staff representation on the committee to develop policies and procedures, develop a formulary, evaluate and improve the medication management system, and participate in other P&T activities. In small organizations, one physician member might be adequate. Larger organizations might need representation from each medical staff department/service. The *ASHP Statement on the Pharmacy and Therapeutics Committee and the Formulary System* recommends that the committee consist of at least the following members: physicians, pharmacists, nurses, administrators, quality improvement coordinators, and others as appropriate.[1] It is advisable to have physician members from at least three different services, if possible. Representatives from leadership, dietary, respiratory, imaging, and laboratory often complete the committee.

Many organizations appoint a physician member as the chairperson, and a pharmacist may be designated as secretary. Some organizations also furnish a medical staff secretary, medical records representative, or other individual to help the secretary record minutes.

Persons within or outside the organization with specialized or unique knowledge, skills, and judgments should be invited to meetings. Performance improvement personnel, infection control personnel, and dietary personnel as well as other pharmacists and nurses are often invited. The

P&T Committee should establish and maintain liaison with other committees in the organization concerned with medication use (e.g., the Infection Control Committee).

P&T Committee Meeting Frequency—The Joint Commission does not specify a frequency requirement, however, some state regulations may. Most organizations require the committee to meet regularly. Quarterly meetings are often considered to be the minimum. Some organizations meet at least six times per year, and more often when necessary.

P&T Committee Meeting Agendas—To facilitate an effective meeting, an agenda and supplementary materials (including minutes of the previous meeting) should be prepared by the secretary and submitted to committee members before each meeting in time for them to review the material properly.

Meeting agendas often include the following:

- Routine topics:
    - Status of previous P&T Committee issues (e.g., approval by the medical staff Executive Committee)
    - Formulary additions, deletions, changes, and indications approved for use in the organization.
    - Nonformulary medication usage
    - Marketplace status (e.g., medication recalls, shortages, and FDA updates)
    - Review of newsletters and other communications
    - Policies and procedures update
    - Medication safety issues (e.g., Black Box warnings, recalls, shortages or outages of formulary medications, and problems that are reported nationally)
    - Medication use evaluations
- Quarterly topics:
    - Adverse drug reactions reported
    - Medication error summary and analysis
    - Review of failure mode and effects analyses
    - Summary of pharmacists' interventions
- Annual topics:
    - Review of the entire formulary (including an assessment of emerging safety information)
    - Review, discussion, and approval of the organization's microbial resistance and sensitivity data
    - Review and approval of medication-related policies and procedures

P&T Committee Documentation (Minutes)—Minutes of committee meetings should be prepared by the secretary and maintained in the permanent records of the organization. P&T Committee minutes should include the following:

- Location of meeting
- Date and time of meeting
- Persons present and absent
- Acceptance of minutes of previous meeting
- Old (unresolved) business
- New business
- Problems identified
- Actions taken
- Follow-up activities
- Time of adjournment
- Signature of committee chairperson

Some committees format their minutes in columns that summarize their findings/discussion, conclusions/recommendations, and actions/follow-up. Others use a traditional format for their minutes. Whatever the format, the minutes should summarize the discussion of the various topics in sufficient detail to determine the findings and the actions taken. Supporting data and documents should be attached to the minutes and filed in the permanent records of the organization. Copies of P&T minutes should also be filed in the pharmacy (if permitted by the organization). Example 13-1 contains guidelines for preparing P&T minutes.

The medical staff must review the P&T Committee's findings, recommendations, and actions. A medical staff Executive Committee often performs the review. Acceptance or rejection of the P&T Committee's activities must be noted in medical staff records (e.g., minutes of the medical staff Executive Committee).

P&T Committee Success Suggestions—Although most organizations view the P&T Committee as a medical staff responsibility, the medical staff and the organization's leadership usually expect the pharmacy to ensure the success of the committee. The following suggestions may help to ensure a successful and effective P&T Committee meeting:

- Contact the chairperson, key committee members, and essential guests and speakers to determine a suitable date and time. Choose dates that have minimal conflict with other events.
- Reserve a room for the meeting and arrange for meals or other special needs, if necessary.
- Arrange for visual aids, projectors, flip charts, and other necessary equipment.
- Prepare the agenda and confirm it with the committee chairperson.
- Notify all committee members and attendees in writing or by e-mail of the date, time, and location of the meeting. Include the meeting agenda.
- Discuss any controversial topics with the chairperson and key committee members before the meeting.
- Remind the attendees by e-mail or telephone the day before the meeting. Send additional copies of the agenda and minutes, if necessary. Determine if speakers will need additional equipment or materials.
- Prepare any handouts needed to support agenda topics.
- Follow-up to ensure that the meeting room, meals, and equipment will be ready.

Policies and Procedures

Adherence to comprehensive, explicit policies and procedures is an important factor in managing medications and assuring quality pharmacy services. ASHP's professional policy positions, statements, and guidelines as well as their best practices provide a wealth of information on which to base policies and procedures. (*See* Chapter 1.) This section provides guidelines for developing policies and procedures. (*See* Chapter 11.)

Policies and Procedures Conformance Requirements—Pharmacy policies and procedures should not conflict with each other or with policies and procedures of other departments; with bylaws, rules, regulations, and policies of the medical staff; with bylaws of the governing body; or with local, state, and federal laws and regulations. The organization's medical records department, medical staff, and leadership can supply current documents. Examine them carefully and ensure that pharmacy policies and procedures do not conflict with them.

Policies and Procedures Models—"Generic," "template," or "model" policies and procedures and policies and procedures from other organizations can be excellent examples. However, they should be reviewed carefully. Many of them may not apply to your processes, and they may need numerous revisions to ensure that they reflect the organization's actual practices. Furthermore, poorly written examples may perpetuate unacceptable practices.

Policies and Procedures Disposition—The Joint Commission does not address the disposition of outdated policies and procedures. However, good management practices call for their retention. For legal or other reasons, you may need to refer to them to establish the policies and procedures in effect on a specific date. A separate manual or file of outdated policies and procedures, including those with seemingly minor changes, is suggested.

Policies and Procedures Formats—The Joint Commission does not specify a format for policies and procedures, and there is no standard or legally required format. Furthermore, surveyors seldom question formats. Although many organizations have adopted a uniform format, other organizations use a variety of formats within the same facility. Example 11-1 is a sample policy and procedure for processing requests for nonformulary medications. The example provides a format that should meet the requirements of most organizations.

Many organizations require every document to begin with a policy statement. When applicable, the policy must be followed by a procedure for ensuring compliance with the policy. In addition, they may require any or all of the following to be included in the document:

- Name of the organization and department
- Number of the policy and procedure
- Page number (e.g., 1 of 3)
- Date of original approval
- Dates of subsequent review and revision
- Director of pharmacy's signature or initials confirming review and revision
- Signature(s) indicating approval by the medical staff and others required by the organization's policy
- Title or subject of the policy and procedure
- Background information
- Rationale/purpose of the policy and procedure
- References

Policies and Procedures Manual—Policies and procedures must be accessible to all personnel who require them. Many organizations use an electronic format to improve accessibility and help ensure that only current documents are available. There is no specific requirement for how policies and procedures are made available to users. A (hardcopy) manual may be useful in some settings because it allows personnel to review policies and procedures easily, and it is readily available if they cannot be accessed electronically.

The following sections and topics are often addressed in a pharmacy policy and procedure manual:

- Table of Contents and/or Index
- Introduction or Organization of the Manual
- Patient Rights and Organization Ethics
- Performance Improvement
- Leadership or Administrative
- Medication Use System Plan
- Emergency Preparedness
- Human Resources or Personnel
- Education of Staff
- Education of Patients and Family
- Information Management
- Safety
- Hazardous Materials
- Storage
- Security
- Controlled Substances
- Selection and Procurement of Medications
- Formulary
- Prepackaging
- Patient Care Areas
- Automated Dispensing Cabinets
- Assessment of Patients
- Ordering and Prescribing
- Order Entry, including Computerized Prescriber Order Entry
- Dispensing
- Medication Administration
- Bar-Coding and Scanning
- Monitoring the Effects of Medications
- Evaluating Medication Use System
- Continuum of Care
- Infection Control
- Compounding Sterile Preparations
- Emergency Services
- Ambulatory Care
- Other Services
- Forms
- Resources

Policies and Procedures Review—The director of pharmacy must review and revise all pharmacy policies and procedures regularly (e.g., at least annually). Although not all policies and procedures need to be reviewed and revised at the same time, each one should be reviewed and revised as necessary at least once during the period. In large pharmacies, a pharmacy committee sometimes performs the review. In other organizations, an interdepartmental committee coordinates the review and revision of policies and procedures that cross departmental lines (e.g., nursing and pharmacy policies and procedures on medication distribution). The director of pharmacy's signature and date on each policy and procedure, as well as on a page that documents a review of all policies and procedures, is suggested.

Policies and Procedures Approval (Medical Staff)—The medical staff must review and approve policies and procedures relating to medication management. As with pharmacy's review and revision, approval of all policies and procedures need not be done at the same time.

Ideally, medical staff review and approval would be conducted and documented in a manner similar to pharmacy review and revision (i.e., on each policy and procedure as well as on each page). However, in practice, it is difficult to get a medical staff representative to sign each document. The signature of a medical staff representative (e.g., chief of staff or chairperson of the P&T Committee) on a page that documents approval of all policies and procedures should be sufficient. Medical staff approval should also be documented in P&T and/or medical staff minutes.

Formulary

According to the *ASHP Statement on the Pharmacy and Therapeutics Committee and the Formulary System,* "The P&T committee develops an evidence-based formulary of medications and medication-associated products accepted for use in the organization."[1] Furthermore, the committee "is responsible for administering the formulary system."[1] This section provides guidelines for developing and maintaining a formulary.

Formulary Requirements (Joint Commission)—The Joint Commission's medication management standards require organizations to use criteria to develop and maintain a formulary of medications to be available for dispensing and administration. The formulary must list all medications used in the organization, including those that may not be handled by the pharmacy (e.g., contrast media, anesthetic gases, radiopharmaceuticals, and blood derivatives). (*See* The Joint Commission's definition of medication in Chapter 4.) Medication samples need not be included in the list.

There must be a mechanism for obtaining medications that are not on the formulary. The formulary must be readily available (in electronic or print format) and include the medication's name, strength, and dosage form. A print version should be available when staff members do not have access to an electronic version. The organization must review the formulary at least annually. (*See* Chapter 4.)

Formulary Principles (ASHP)—The *ASHP Statement on the Pharmacy and Therapeutics Committee and the Formulary System* provides broad principles to be considered in the development of an effective formulary.[1] The following principles are especially important:

- Policies and procedures governing the formulary system and developed by the P&T Committee should provide guidelines for the objective evaluation, selection, procurement, storage, distribution, and safe use of medications.
- Medications should be included in the formulary by generic (nonproprietary) names, even though brand (proprietary) names may be used commonly in the organization. Prescribers should be encouraged to prescribe medications by their generic names.
- The number of medication entities and products routinely available from the pharmacy are limited.
- The formulary system should provide for the use of generic equivalents and therapeutic interchanges in accordance with policies and procedures developed by the P&T Committee.

Formulary Development Assistance (ASHP)—The *ASHP Guidelines on the Pharmacy and Therapeutics Committee and the Formulary System* provides detailed assistance in developing a formulary.[2] The following ASHP recommendations are especially important:

- Medications should be listed alphabetically within therapeutic class or by generic name, or a combination of the two systems.
- There should be a provision for "between revision" additions and deletions and other changes to the current formulary.
- Formularies should be reviewed and revised at regularly established intervals (e.g., annually).

Formulary Content—To facilitate ready access to information, the formulary should include a generic name/brand name cross-index. The cross index should not be limited to brand names stocked by the pharmacy.

Other useful information often found in formularies includes the following:

- Dosage forms and strengths
- Formulation (active ingredients) of combination products
- Packaging and sizes available
- Dosage guidelines
- Culture and sensitivity patterns of microbes (reported by the organization's laboratory)
- Policies on the use of investigational medications
- Policies and procedures relating to maintaining and revising the formulary
- Special information (e.g., sodium content of medications)
- List of sugar-free medications
- List of medications that should not be crushed
- Special formulas used in the organization (e.g., active ingredients, compounding information, and ordering information)
- Poison control information
- Electrolyte content of large volume parenterals
- List of *approved* abbreviations, acronyms, and symbols
- List of *prohibited* abbreviations, acronyms, and symbols
- List of look-alike and sound-alike medications
- List of high-alert medications with safeguards for their use
- List of hazardous medications and safeguards for their use
- Standard concentrations of IV infusions
- Upper and lower limits of dosages listed in drug libraries

Formulary Format—The optimal format and size for a printed formulary should be considered carefully. Pocket-sized editions are far more practical than large versions that are limited to use in areas with sufficient storage space. Using a different color paper for each section and boldface type of headings may improve the ease of use.

Formulary Additions, Deletions, and Changes—Additions to the formulary are best handled by the P&T Committee through a formal written request system. This system usually requires the submission of a Request for Formulary Addition. (*See* Example 4-2.) The P&T Committee should compare the proposed addition with other medications currently in the formulary for therapeutic equivalency and delete any therapeutic duplication that offers no advantages in efficacy, safety, convenience, or cost. The P&T Committee should also handle other deletions from the formulary.

Formulary Additions Support—Requests for formulary additions should be supported by the literature. As the formulary system is intended to ensure the appropriate use of medications, consideration of requests for additions to the formulary should include evidence-based reviews. Manufacturer's promotional material should be clearly indicated as such. The P&T Committee should not be swayed by in vitro test results, misleading advertising, and anecdotal reports. For further information on formulary additions and deletions, see the *ASHP Guidelines on the Pharmacy and Therapeutics Committee and the Formulary System*.[2]

Nonformulary Medications—Formularies must provide for the use of nonformulary medications. There should be a process for ensuring that nonformulary medications are obtained expeditiously. Some organizations require a nonformulary medication request form for ordering nonformulary medications. (*See* Example 4-3.) There should be a process for reviewing the use of nonformulary medications to determine if they should be added to the formulary. Example 4-4 is a form for listing nonformulary medications in stock that are awaiting evaluation and approval by the medical staff.

CHAPTER 14

Competence Assessment

The Joint Commission considers a competent individual to be one who has the essential knowledge and skills necessary to perform a job and actually performs the job according to defined expectations. It is important to note that competence is the ability to use *essential* rather than *advanced* knowledge and skills. Assessing competence does not necessarily determine if an individual has a high level of knowledge and proficiency.

Competence Assessment and Quality of Patient Care

In the past, organizations have hired staff and assigned tasks on the basis of education, experience, and, if applicable, licensure. However, these criteria do not assure organizations that the individual is competent. Therefore, many organizations, including health care organizations, assess competence before hiring staff and assigning responsibilities. Health care organizations realize that good competence assessment programs increase the likelihood that staff will provide effective, appropriate, and safe patient care.

Requiring pharmacy staff to be competent is in the best interest of patients, visitors, and staff. For example, competent personnel can be expected to do the following:

- Prepare medications accurately and safely
- Counsel patients and their families on medications effectively
- Understand the unique needs of various patient types and age groups
- Operate equipment properly and safely
- Handle hazardous materials safely
- Minimize opportunities for contamination and transfer of infection
- Respond promptly and properly to medical emergencies and disasters
- Monitor medication therapy for inappropriate prescribing, allergies, interactions, contraindications, and when necessary, act accordingly
- Be attentive to patient safety and meet management and public expectations

Competence Components

For the health care professional, competence can be thought of as encompassing three components:

1. Skill (i.e., either psychomotor or intellectual problem-solving). Compounding sterile preparations requires psychomotor skills. Determining the correct dosage of medication for a pediatric patient requires knowledge (e.g., medication distribution, metabolism, and excretion) and intellectual problem-solving (e.g., calculation) skills.
2. Professional socialization (i.e., the attitudes and values of the profession). Maintaining an appropriate relationship with patients, accepting responsibility, and resolving ethical issues require professional socialization.
3. Judgment (i.e., the capacity to successfully apply context to decisions). Applying clinical knowledge and experience to a situation with several solutions requires judgment to select the best choice (e.g., dosage adjustments for anticoagulant or aminoglycoside therapy).

Competence Assessment Methods

Competence assessment is a measurement of an individual's capability to use the three components to perform up to defined expectations. There are three methods for assessing competence: cognitive tests, simulations, and direct observation of a process or product. Each method has strengths and weaknesses when compared with accepted standards for measuring clinical competence.[1]

Cognitive Tests—Cognitive tests are often multiple-choice, paper-and-pencil tests. Their strengths are accuracy of measurement and generalization to similar tasks, provided enough questions are asked. However, cognitive tests do not indicate what the individual will do in practice, because multiple-choice questions rarely test beyond the recall of facts, understanding of concepts, or straightforward application of rules.

Simulations—Simulations generally take the form of a patient case. The simulations may provide a good indication of how an individual would handle similar cases. However, accuracy of measurement is variable because there may be more than one solution and the best solution may not be clear. Furthermore, extrapolation to what the individual will do in practice is weak because simulations are rarely as complete and complex as real practice.

Direct Observation—The third assessment option, direct observation, involves evaluating the process or product in real practice against a set of objective criteria. Process observations include watching a patient counseling session to assess the individual's patient education skills or monitoring renal dosing adjustments and pharmacokinetic dosing recommendations to assure accuracy and appropriateness. Product observations include reviewing a pharmacist's care plan documentation and examining media-fill tests of compounded sterile preparations. Extrapolation to routine practice is the strength of this method. However, as with simulations, accuracy of measurement is a problem because there may be several solutions. In addition, the time required for direct observation limits the number of observations that can be performed.

Combined Methods—Because no one method provides a valid and reliable assessment of clinical competence, the best approach is a combination of two or three methods, with careful attention to choice of assessment measures. For example, for an initial assessment of basic competence, any combination of the methods (i.e., cognitive tests, simulations, and direct observations) may be used to test the individual on the essential knowledge and skills expected for the position. After evaluating the completed assessments, the manager will have a good idea of the individual's strengths and weaknesses and can design education and training programs to address the weaknesses.

Competence Assessment versus Performance Evaluation

The distinction between competence assessment and performance evaluation is not always clear. Competence assessments determine if the individual has the knowledge, skills, and ability to do a job and actually performs the job according to defined expectations. Performance evaluations determine *how well* the individual performs according to defined expectations. Performance evaluations may also relate to punctuality, attitude, compliance with policies and procedures, management skills, completion of education requirements, attendance at meetings, participation in required activities, maintenance of licensure, etc.

Competence Documentation

Competence should be documented on an ongoing basis beginning with the pre-employment period (if possible) and continuing throughout the duration of employment. Competence should be documented for new employees following orientation as well as for all employees when they are oriented to new patient care areas and new services, procedures, or equipment. Documentation of competence should include, at a minimum, the following information:

- Date
- Reason for assessment
- Method(s) of assessment (e.g., tests, demonstrations, and observations)
- Outcome of assessment
- Recommendations based on assessment (e.g., areas for improvement)
- Date of re-evaluation or next assessment

Pharmacies may use any method to maintain records related to an individual staff member's competence. Some maintain separate records (e.g., in a file or binder). Others keep the records in the individual's human resource file. Still others use combined job descriptions and competence assessment summaries.

Competence Assessment Standards

The Joint Commission's management of human resources (HR) standards require individuals to be competent to perform job responsibilities. (*See* HR.01.06.01.) The elements of the standard include requirements for the organization to define the competencies required, the frequency of assessments, and how assessments will be performed. The Joint Commission's standards relating to competence assessment are in Chapter 7.

Competence Assessment Frequency

The Joint Commission expects competence to be assessed during orientation and at intervals defined in the organization's policies. Standard HR.01.06.01, EP 6 requires competence assessments to be performed "once every 3 years or more frequently as required by hospital policy or in accordance with law and regulation." Many organizations perform assessments at least annually. Some may require more frequent (e.g., semiannual) assessments of competence relating to high-risk processes.

Competence Assessment Tools for Health-System Pharmacies

The American Society of Health-System Pharmacists' (ASHP) *Competence Assessment Tools for Health-System Pharmacies*[2] provides practical tools for assessing, maintaining, and improving the competence of pharmacy staff and complying with Joint Commission standards. The book contains five types of tools:

- Job description templates (to develop customized job descriptions)
- Pre-employment/initial skills assessments (to assess the initial level of competence of pharmacists and support staff)
- Competence assessment checklists (to document the assessment of the specific elements of competence through tests, simulation, and direct observation)
- Written tests (to assess the basic knowledge that is expected of the individual)
- Study guides (to provide a general overview of topics)

CHAPTER 15

Performance Improvement Activities

This chapter describes activities relating to improving performance. It includes an overview of The Joint Commission's performance improvement (PI) requirements, basic process improvement tools, The Joint Commission's sentinel event policy, proactive assessment of high-risk processes, and benchmarking.

Performance Improvement Standards

The Joint Commission's improving organization performance (PI) standards require an organization-wide program for improving performance. The program should be described in a separate plan or within other planning documents. All departments and services (e.g., pharmacy and nursing) must participate in the program.

The Joint Commission does not indicate a specific name for the program; organizations may call their program PI (for either Performance Improvement or Process Improvement), quality improvement (QI), quality management (QM), continuous quality improvement (CQI), or other descriptive terms. Whatever the term, the organization must show that its program meets the intent of the standards (i.e., improves performance).

The Joint Commission does not require organizations to follow a specific PI approach nor adhere to a specific step-wise process for improving performance. Nevertheless, organizations must collect data to measure current performance, assess current performance, and improve performance. The PI standards, as they relate to pharmacy, require organizations to do the following:

- Collect data to monitor its performance of medication management and other processes. (*See* PI.01.01.01 and MM.08.01.01.)
- Systematically aggregate and analyze data in usable formats, at an appropriate frequency, and use statistical tools and techniques. (*See* PI.02.01.01, EP 1 through EP 3.) (*See* Process Improvement Tools in this chapter.)
- Analyze undesirable patterns and trends relating to serious adverse drug reactions and significant medication errors. (*See* PI.01.01.01, EP 14 and EP 15.) (*See* Process Improvement Tools in this chapter.)
- Compare data internally and with external information sources to determine if the data vary excessively or performance is at an unacceptable level. (*See* PI.02.01.01, EP 4.) (*See* Benchmarking in this chapter.)
- Identify and manage sentinel events. (*See* Sentinel Events in this chapter.)
- Use information from data analysis to identify improvement opportunities. (*See* PI.02.01.01, EP 8.)
- Improve performance by taking action on improvement priorities, evaluating those actions, and making changes when the planned action does not achieve or sustain planned improvements. (*See* PI.03.01.01.)
- At least once a year, provide hospital leaders and governance with written reports on the following:
  - All system or process failures
  - The number and types of sentinel events
  - Whether the patients and the families were informed of the event
  - All actions taken to improve safety, both proactively and in response to actual occurrence
  - The determined number of distinct improvement projects to be conducted annually (*See* LD.04.04.05, EP 13.)
- Results of the analysis related to adequacy of staffing (*See* PI.02.01.01, EP 14.)

PI Focus—PI programs must focus on improving processes. Over time, organizations must evaluate the processes that compose their medication management system (i.e., how they select and procure, store, order and prescribe, prepare and dispense, administer, and monitor medications). The Joint Commission's medication management (MM) standards require organizations to do the following related to evaluating their medication management system:

- Evaluate their medication management system to identify risk points and areas to improve patient safety. (*See* MM.08.01.01, EP 3.)
- Review their internal reports to identify trends or issues in their own medication management system. (*See* MM.08.01.01, EP 2 and EP 3.)
- Evaluate literature for new technologies or successful practices that have been shown to enhance safety in other organizations and determine if they can improve their own medication management system. (*See* MM.08.01.01, EP 4.)
- Identify opportunities for improvements in the medication management system. (*See* MM.08.01.01, EP 5.)
- Act to implement improvements in the medication management system based on the following: (*See* MM.08.01.01, EP 6.)
  - Evaluation of the system
  - Review of new technologies
  - External data
  - Successful practices that have enhanced safety in other organizations.
- Measure and evaluate the performance of the new and modified processes. (*See* MM.08.01.01, EP 1 and EP 7.)
- Take action when planned improvements for medication management processes are not achieved or sustained. (*See* MM.08.01.01, EP 8.)

PI Methods—All processes can and must be improved to reduce the likelihood of undesirable outcomes (e.g., sentinel events) and increase the likelihood of desirable outcomes. Process improvements may be achieved by better training, acquiring better equipment, changing or simplifying procedures, and other actions. Although some actions may produce only small improvements, numerous small improvements can add up to significant overall improvements.

PI Priorities—The Joint Commission understands that lack of resources may prevent organizations from addressing all of their processes at the same time. Therefore, organizations must set priorities for addressing processes and concentrate their efforts on improving processes having the highest priority. Organizations should be able to explain the reasoning behind their priorities and have a plan for addressing other processes.

PI Expectations—The Joint Commission does not expect every improvement effort to be successful. However, over a period of time, a well-planned PI program should result in well-designed processes and measurable improvements in one or more of the key dimensions of performance. (*See* PI Team Focus in this chapter.)

PI Committee—Organizations must have a mechanism for coordinating PI activities. Most organizations have a coordinating group (e.g., a PI Committee). The coordinating group is responsible for designing, measuring, assessing, and improving the organization's overall PI approach, allocating resources to the PI effort, setting PI priorities, and assessing the effectiveness of PI activities. There should be a mechanism for the group to oversee or coordinate other groups involved in PI activities.

PI Teams—The Joint Commission does not require PI teams. However, it does require staff (including the medical staff) to participate in multidisciplinary activities to assess and improve performance. Many organizations meet this requirement by forming teams of the organization's leaders, department directors and managers, physicians, other clinicians, trustees, and support staff. In this book, the term "PI team" refers to any multidisciplinary group that uses a planned approach to improve performance.

PI Team Focus—PI teams should focus on processes that make up a function. Emphasis should be given to processes that are high risk, high volume, or problem prone. The team should look at the function from a global perspective and identify key processes of that function.

Some accrediting organizations require evaluation of specific processes. For example, The Joint Commission requires evaluation of anticoagulation management processes and DNV's National Integrated Accreditation of Healthcare Organizations (NIAHO) (*see* Chapter 24) requires evaluation of the medication reconciliation processes. The Joint Commission and NIAHO also require analysis of sentinel events. (*See* Sentinel Events in this chapter.)

Once key processes have been identified, the team should identify processes that are weak, set priorities, and develop a plan to improve one or more of the following key dimensions of performance:

- *Efficacy* Achieves the desired patient outcome
- *Appropriateness* Is relevant to a patient's needs
- *Availability* Can be provided if necessary

• *Timeliness*	Is provided at the optimal time
• *Effectiveness*	Is provided correctly to achieve the desired outcome
• *Continuity*	Is coordinated among services, practitioners, and locations over time
• *Safety*	Reduces risks to the patient and employees
• *Efficiency*	Makes good use of resources
• *Respect and caring*	Is sensitive to a patient's needs and expectations

After identifying the performance measures for the process under evaluation, a data collection system must be developed. The types of data needed will be determined by the measures chosen. For example, if the measure is the percentage of patients receiving warfarin who receive pharmacist counseling on warfarin therapy, data will be needed on the number of patients receiving warfarin and the number of patients receiving warfarin who receive pharmacist counseling.

Data Collection—Two important aspects of data collection are sample size and time frame of data collection.

Sample size depends upon various factors: in particular, the size of the population for the performance measures. For small populations, it may be appropriate to include the entire population as the sample size. For large populations, a portion of the population would be appropriate. Joint Commission suggests the following sample sizes:[1]

Population Size	***Sample Size***
< 30 cases	100%
30–100 cases	30 cases
101–500 cases	50 cases
> 500 cases	70 cases

In general, at least 18 to 24 data points are needed to identify trends that are statistically relevant. Time intervals and length of time of data collection will depend on how often the particular data being collected occurs. For example, if data are being collected on the use of systemic corticosteroids in pediatric patients with asthma, an urban pediatric hospital will be able to collect data more quickly than a rural acute care hospital that admits a small number of pediatric patients.

The Centers for Medicare and Medicaid Services (CMS) and accrediting organizations also require hospital leadership to determine the frequency of data collection for performance measures.

Process Improvement Tools

When possible, PI teams should use tools to help them assess processes, set priorities, determine patterns and trends, and monitor performance. Some of these tools are listed below.[2] It is important that tools be used properly; poorly designed studies, bad data, and decisions based on worthless analysis can be misleading and are a waste of time and resources. Some organizations use consultants to help design sophisticated studies, provide training in using the tools, and assist in the analysis of data.

Flow Chart—A flow chart (or diagram) shows all of the steps and stages of a process (e.g., dispensing process) and sometimes includes the equipment needed and the individuals or departments responsible for each step. Flow charts use standard symbols that represent a start and finish, intermediate steps, decision points, and the direction of workflow. A flow chart is an essential first step in process analysis and can be used to identify areas of a process that might be sources of problems and candidates for improvement.

Check Sheet—A check sheet is a form for gathering data. For example, a check sheet can be used to record the numbers of each kind of dispensing error made (e.g., wrong drug and wrong dose). Data from check sheets are used in Pareto diagrams. (*See* Pareto Diagram in this chapter.)

Cause-and-Effect Diagram—A cause-and-effect diagram (sometimes called a fishbone or Ishikawa diagram) organizes findings from brainstorming sessions (i.e., facts, opinions, ideas, and guesses from a group [e.g., pharmacists, technicians, nurses, and physicians]). Brainstorming data can be used to identify possible causes of problems in processes (e.g., causes of dispensing errors).

Pareto Diagram—A Pareto diagram is a bar graph representing the types of problems (e.g., causes of dispensing errors) and the total number of occurrences (e.g., number of dispensing errors) for each type of problem. Pareto diagrams are based on the Pareto principle or 80:20 rule: only a few causes (about 20% or less) account for 80% or more of an effect. For example, about 20% of the causes of dispensing errors may account for 80% of the errors. A Pareto diagram helps to establish priorities for resolution of problems (e.g., causes of dispensing errors that merit the most attention) and helps to keep the costs of improving processes affordable.

Scatter Plot—A scatter plot is a tool for plotting two variables to show whether and how they relate (e.g., number of dispensing errors and number of orders filled).

Histogram—A histogram is a bar graph that shows how many times each of various events (e.g., different kinds of dispensing errors) occurred.

Run Chart—A run chart tracks patterns and trends over a period of time. For example, a run chart may be used to track the number of dispensing errors made per day during a quarter, year, etc.

Control Chart—A control chart sets upper and lower limits expected in a process (e.g., the expected highs and lows of dispensing errors). Performance that is above or below these limits warrants further study.

Sentinel Events

The Joint Commission's sentinel event policy encourages organizations to respond to serious adverse events, focus on the underlying causes of the events, and take actions that will reduce the frequency of their occurrence. This section describes some elements of the sentinel event policy. The policy is described fully in the Sentinel Events (SE) section of the *Comprehensive Accreditation Manual for Hospitals: The Official Handbook (CAMH).*[1]

Sentinel Event Definition (Joint Commission)—The Joint Commission defines a sentinel event as an unexpected occurrence involving death or serious physical or psychological injury, or the risk thereof. Serious injury specifically includes loss of limb or function. The phrase "or the risk thereof" includes any process variation for which a recurrence would carry a significant chance of a serious adverse outcome.[1]

Sentinel Event Definition (Organization-Specific)—The Joint Commission requires every organization to establish an organization-specific definition of a sentinel event. Although The Joint Commission allows some latitude, the organization's definition must be consistent with The Joint Commission's definition and must include occurrences that The Joint Commission defines as reviewable sentinel events.

Some organizations use the National Quality Forum's list of Serious Reportable Events to establish their sentinel events processes.[3] Many of the events on this list—frequently referred to as the Never Events list—are medication related.

Sentinel Events (Reviewable)—Reviewable sentinel events include those that meet the following criteria:

- The event has resulted in an unanticipated death or major permanent loss of function, not related to the natural course of the patient's illness or underlying condition, or

- The event is one of the following (even if the outcome was not death or major permanent loss of function, unrelated to the natural course of the patient's illness or underlying condition):
    - Suicide of any patient receiving care, treatment, and services in a staffed around-the-clock care setting or within 72 hours of discharge
    - Unanticipated death of a full-term infant
    - Abduction of any patient receiving care, treatment, and services
    - Discharge of an infant to the wrong family
    - Rape
    - Hemolytic transfusion reaction involving administration of blood or blood products having major blood group incompatibilities
    - Surgery on the wrong patient or wrong body part
    - Unintended retention of a foreign object in a patient after surgery or other procedure
    - Severe neonatal hyperbilirubinemia (bilirubin >30 milligrams/deciliter)
    - Prolonged fluoroscopy with cumulative dose >1500 rads to a single field or any delivery of radiotherapy to the wrong body region or >25% above the planned radiotherapy dose.[1]

The Joint Commission may revise the definition of a reviewable sentinel event. Revisions will be published in *Joint Commission Perspectives* and included in updates to the *CAMH*.

Sentinel Event Responses (Organization)—The Joint Commission requires organizations to identify and respond to *all* sentinel events *as defined by the organization*. These include significant "near misses" (e.g., potentially lethal medication errors), even though there was no harm to the patient.

Root Cause Analysis (RCA)—Completion of an acceptable (i.e., thorough and credible) root cause analysis (RCA) after the event or after becoming aware of the event is a mandatory component of the organization's response. An RCA is a process for identifying the underlying causes or reasons why an event (e.g., a sentinel event) occurred. Identifying the underlying causes is more than simply determining who or what caused the event or noting a failure to follow policies and procedures. The underlying causes may include lack of leadership, misplaced priorities, and failure to provide adequate equipment, funding, education, and resources. The elements of the RCA process include the following:

- Identifying causes and analyzing processes and systems related to the causes.
- Identifying ways to improve processes and systems and reduce the likelihood of a recurrence of the event.
- Creating an action plan for implementing the improvements to the processes and systems.
- Implementing the improvements and evaluating the effectiveness of the improvements (i.e., measuring the results of the action).

RCA Assistance—The Joint Commission provides organizations with written guidelines, templates, and forms to help them conduct an RCA of a sentinel event as well as on-site technical help. Although these materials are not required and do not need to be followed strictly, they provide a good framework for conducting an acceptable RCA. Organizations that need to conduct an RCA should obtain up-to-date materials and publications from The Joint Commission. The *CAMH* describes the minimum scope of an RCA for specific types of sentinel events.[1]

Sentinel Event Reporting to The Joint Commission—Organizations are encouraged, *but not required*, to voluntarily self-report to The Joint Commission *actual* occurrences that meet The Joint Commission's reviewable sentinel event definition. "Near misses" (e.g., medication errors that almost occurred and other events that could have resulted in serious consequences) and actual medication errors that do not result in death or major permanent loss of function are examples of events that should *not* be reported to The Joint Commission.

Organizations that do not voluntarily self-report a sentinel event must nevertheless complete an acceptable RCA. Organizations do not have to send their RCA to The Joint Commission or allow it to review it. Organizations must, however, permit The Joint Commission to review relevant documents (e.g., policies, procedures, and action plans) related to the RCA. Although organizations must perform an RCA on sentinel events that are *not* reviewable by The Joint Commission, they are not required to make the RCA-related documents available to The Joint Commission.

Sentinel Event Response (Joint Commission)—The Joint Commission's options in response to a sentinel event include accepting the organization's RCA and action plan, consulting and additional time to resubmit a response, placing an organization on accreditation watch, visiting on site, and issuing an accreditation decision (e.g., preliminary denial of accreditation). These are described in greater detail in the *CAMH*. The *CAMH* also contains information relating to follow-up activity and handling sentinel event-related documents.

Sentinel Event Compliance Assessment—Surveyors expect organizations to have processes in place that relate to identifying and managing sentinel events. During a survey, surveyors will do the following:

- Review minutes and other documents that describe how the organization responds to a sentinel event.
- Conduct interviews relating to identifying, reporting, and responding to sentinel events.
- Review at least one example of an RCA that demonstrates the organization's process for responding to a sentinel event.

Proactive Assessment of High-Risk Processes

Joint Commission standard LD.03.05.01 requires that leaders implement change in existing processes to improve performance of the hospital. Joint Commission standard LD.03.06.01 requires that those who work in the hospital are focused on improving safety and quality. Organizations can help meet these standards by performing a failure mode and effects analysis (FMEA) of processes that are likely to be associated with sentinel events.

FMEA Description—FMEA is the systematic analysis of a process to identify the possible ways it might fail, the effects of failures, and the possible causes of failures. This technique has been used extensively in the aerospace and automobile industries. FMEA aims to proactively identify how and where systems might fail. If the potential effects of a failure are intolerable, actions are taken to eliminate or minimize the possibility of the error occurring, or minimize the consequences of the error when the potential for error cannot be eliminated.

FMEA versus Root Cause Analysis—FMEA is a proactive technique that is used to identify and address problems *before* they occur. In comparison, RCA is used retrospectively to address problems *after* they occur. FMEA is also an ongoing process of quality improvement. Even when improvement is made, efforts to improve processes should continue.

FMEA Steps—Organizations may use the following steps to conduct a FMEA:

1. *Choose a Process*

When utilized as a tool in a medication error prevention program, FMEA should be used to analyze specific medications or drug classes, medication use procedures, medication-related equipment, and other aspects of the medication use system.[4] Good items for analysis include the following:

- *High-Alert Medications*—Examples include heparin, insulin, neuromuscular blockers, concentrated injectable electrolytes, opiates, and narcotics.
- *Error-Prone Procedures*—Examples include dose calculations and measurements, telephone and oral transmission of orders, handwritten and pre-printed or electronic orders, and the use of infusion control and patient-controlled analgesia devices.
- *Errors or Incidents Reported in the Medical Literature*—Examples of publications that regularly publish information about medication errors include ISMP *Medication Safety Alert*, *Hospital Pharmacy*, and *American Journal of Health-System Pharmacy*.
- *Errors or Incidents Reported by Regulatory Agencies, Accreditation Organizations, and Health Care Organizations*—Example organizations and agencies include The Joint Commission (in *Sentinel Event Alerts*) (*see* Chapter 1), American Society of Health-System Pharmacists (ASHP), the United States Pharmacopeia (USP), and the Food and Drug Administration (FDA). (*See* Appendix.)
- *Errors or Incidents Reported within the Facility*—Items for analysis may be identified through the medication error reporting program or other quality improvement processes.

2. *Form a Team*

FMEA is most effective when conducted by a multidisciplinary team. When forming the team, include representatives of all disciplines involved in the process being analyzed. Members should include pharmacists, nurses, physicians, and risk managers. Other potential members include pharmacy technicians, dieticians, nursing and procedural unit secretaries, and materials management personnel.

3. *Analyze the Process*

All team members should understand the process. The following steps should be useful in analyzing the process:

- Prepare a flow chart or diagram that tracks the process from the point of initiation until completion.
- Evaluate each step in the flow chart to determine what could go wrong with the process (i.e., potential failure modes).
- List the effects of the identified failures.
- List the root causes that can produce the failure mode or error.
- Estimate the probability of each failure occurring by using a ranking scale.
- Estimate the severity of the effects of each failure by using a ranking scale.
- Estimate the probability of each failure being detected by using a ranking scale.
- Calculate the Criticality Index (CI) for each failure mode by multiplying the scores for frequency of occurrence, severity of effects, and probability of detection for each failure mode.
- Assign a priority ranking for each failure mode by listing them in decreasing order of CI value (i.e., highest to lowest).

4. *Identify Strategies for Improvement*

Begin with the failure modes that have the highest CI values and identify actions or strategies that could reduce the CI. Include actions that decrease the likelihood of occurrence, decrease the severity of effects, and increase the probability of detection of failures. Example strategies include warning signs and labels, special packaging, limiting access to medications, implementing protocols for high-risk medications or procedures, double checking calculations, and using technology (e.g., bar coding).

5. *Implement Strategies for Improvement*

Develop an action plan to implement the improvement strategies. Implement the action plan.

6. *Evaluate the Effectiveness of Actions Taken*

Evaluate the effectiveness of each action taken. Recalculate the CI of the failure modes to determine if the actions have had an effect. If the CI is not reduced, continue with the FMEA process to identify and implement new improvement strategies. The team should continuously improve the process.

Benchmarks

A benchmark is a standard by which something can be measured or judged. Benchmark standards are commonly considered to be the best performance achievable. To benchmark is to compare performance with benchmark standards. By comparing performance with benchmark standards, organizations can do the following:

- Identify deficiencies in their performance or opportunities to dramatically improve their performance.
- Determine how the best performance was achieved (i.e., learn from others).
- Determine what they can do to improve their performance (i.e., adopt better methods or practices).

Benchmark Focus—Organizations should benchmark key processes that are essential to serving patients (e.g., clinical practice guidelines, patient assessment, transferring patients to other organizations, and medication management). Key medication management processes include selection and procurement, storage, ordering and transcribing, preparing and dispensing, administering, and monitoring. (*See* Chapter 4.)

Benchmarks (National)—There are currently few, if any, nationally recognized medication-use benchmarks. For example, there are no nationally recognized medication error and adverse drug reaction rates.

Benchmark Comparisons—Health care organizations should, over a period of time, compare their current performance with their best historical performance (internal benchmarking) and, if available, with the best performance of other health care organizations that have similar processes (external benchmarking). When possible, they should compare their performance with organizations that rank among the best in their class.

Health care organizations can also compare their performance with organizations outside the health care industry that have similar processes. For example, many organizations have outstanding processes for maintaining records (similar to patient profiles), training staff (similar to pharmacy orientation and education), educating customers (similar to patient education), and assuring accuracy in filling orders for products (similar to medication dispensing).

Benchmark Requirements (Joint Commission)—The Joint Commission does not explicitly require organizations to compare their performance with the best performance achievable. However, benchmarking is consistent with Joint Commission requirements that organizations compare data internally and with external information sources. (*See* PI.02.01.01, EP 4 and EP 5.)

CHAPTER 16

Overview of Quality and Performance Measures

Regulatory agencies (e.g., the Centers for Medicare and Medicaid Services [CMS]) and accreditation organizations (e.g., The Joint Commission, the Healthcare Facilities Accreditation Program [HFAP], the National Integrated Accreditation of Healthcare Organization [NIAHO]) have expectations of safety and quality for patients. Medication safety is generally demonstrated by organizational safety strategies, a robust medication error reporting system, and analysis of improvements. (*See* Chapter 20.) Quality measurement has evolved into structured performance measure sets and consistent reporting.

Development of National Quality Initiatives

The Joint Commission's performance measurement and improvement initiative is known as ORYX®. It began in 1997, and by 2002, Joint Commission required that accredited hospitals collect data on standardized—or core—performance measures. In 2004, The Joint Commission and CMS began working together to align measures common to both organizations. These standardized common measures, called National Hospital Quality Measures, are integral to improving the quality of care provided to hospital patients and bringing value to stakeholders by focusing on the actual results of care. Standardized performance measurement benefits hospitals by making it easier and less costly to collect and report data because the same data set can be used to satisfy CMS initiatives and Joint Commission requirements.[1]

All of the National Hospital Quality Measures common to CMS and The Joint Commission are endorsed by the National Quality Forum (NQF). It is The Joint Commission's intention to remain in alignment with CMS so that the data collection efforts for hospitals can continue to be consolidated and minimized.

Core Measures

The Joint Commission has identified standardized core measures for measuring the performance of hospitals in critical focus areas. Each of the core measures contains data elements, calculation algorithms, and standardized protocols for collecting data.

Core Measure Sets—Core measures are organized into groups called core measure sets. These include:

- Acute myocardial infarction (AMI)
- Heart failure (HF)
- Pneumonia (PN)
- Pregnancy and related conditions (PR)
- Hospital-based inpatient psychiatric services (HBIPS)
- Children's asthma care (CAC)
- Surgical care improvement project (SCIP)
- Hospital outpatient measures (HOP)
- Venous thromboembolism (VTE)
- Stroke (STK)

Details (e.g., data elements) for the core measure sets are available on The Joint Commission's Web site. (*See* Appendix.)

Pharmacy Participation Relating to Core Measures—Pharmacists are well positioned to assist the health care system in improving quality of care, and they are already established as experts in medication management processes. Since many of the elements within most of the core measure sets are medication related, pharmacy's expertise in clinical and operational aspects of quality of care are valuable to the organization.

The pharmacy often participates in performance improvement, medication use evaluation, and other activities relating to the core measures (e.g., collecting and evaluating data on the use of medications associated with the core measures or participating in advice/counseling activities). Table 16-1 lists medication-related core measure elements.

Non-Core Measures and Performance Measures—Some hospitals may not be able to use the core measure sets. (*See* ORYX Requirements in this chapter.) These hospitals may need to use non-core measures or performance measures to satisfy ORYX requirements.

Many performance measurement systems can help hospitals identify and select suitable non-core measures or performance measures. If non-core measures or performance measures focus on medication use, pharmacy services involvement may be significant. (*See* Performance Measurement Systems in this chapter.)

ORYX Requirements—The Joint Commission's ORYX initiative integrates performance measures into the accreditation process and aims to provide health care organizations with an ongoing evaluation of their performance. Organizations can use their findings from the ORYX initiative to focus their performance improvement activities. Standard PI.02.01.01, EP 6 requires that the hospital analyze data from ORYX core measures.

Hospitals must comply with the ORYX requirements in the *Comprehensive Accreditation Manual for Hospitals: The Official Handbook (CAMH).*[2] ORYX requirements for long-term care, behavioral health care, and home care organizations are similar but not the same as for hospitals. These organizations should consult the accreditation manual applicable to their organization for specific ORYX requirements.

Performance Measurement Systems

Organizations must contract with an acceptable performance measurement system to submit ORYX data. They cannot submit ORYX data directly to The Joint Commission. A list of performance measurement systems that The Joint Commission considers acceptable is available on The Joint Commission's Web site. (*See* Appendix.) Many performance measurement systems can accept data related to both core measures and non-core measures.

Initial Accreditation—Organizations seeking their initial accreditation must contract with a performance measurement system and participate in the ORYX initiative. The *CAMH* contains additional information relating to initial surveys. Organizations seeking initial accreditation should contact The Joint Commission for current requirements.

ORYX Requirements for Hospitals

The Joint Commission's ORYX requirements for hospitals surveyed under the *CAMH* follow:

- If four applicable core measure sets can be identified, then no non-core measures are required.
- If three applicable core measure sets can be identified, then three non-core measures are required.
- If only two applicable core measure sets can be identified, then six non-core measures must also be collected.
- If only one applicable core measure set can be identified, then nine non-core measures must also be collected.
- If no core measure sets are applicable, then nine non-core measures must be collected.

Organizations should check The Joint Commission's Web site for changes to the core measure sets and any modified requirements (e.g., for smaller organizations or psychiatric organizations). (*See* Appendix.)

The Role of Performance Measures in Surveys

Organizations receive an ORYX Performance Measure Report based on the data submitted. The ORYX core measures are one of the Priority Focus Processes that surveyors review prior to an organization's survey. (*See* Chapter 2.) The *CAMH* contains additional information on the contents of the Performance Measure Report, sample reports, and sample charts. The Joint Commission uses this information to plan for a survey. (*See* Chapter 2.) During the survey, surveyors assess an organization's use of its selected core measure sets in its performance improvement activities (including the organization's processes for collecting and analyzing data and disseminating the findings).

ORYX Information

Health care organizations can obtain current information about the ORYX initiative through The Joint Commission's ORYX information line, by e-mail, or by accessing The Joint Commission's Web site and selecting "Performance Measurement." (*See* Appendix.)

Quality Measures Reported

Reports of compliance with core measures are nationally reported and publicly available. Hospital Compare[3] and The Joint Commission's Quality Check[4] report the compliance with the nationally developed performance measures.

Other Quality Measure Resources

The Agency for Healthcare Research and Quality (AHRQ) of the United States Department of Health and Human Services maintains the National Quality Measures Clearinghouse (NQMC). Numerous quality measures are available at www.qualitymeasures.ahrq.gov.

The National Quality Forum (NQF) (www.qualityforum.org) is the organization that harmonizes performance measures from various sources, and endorses the measures. NQF serves as the final common pathway for review and approval of performance measures.

The American Society of Health-System Pharmacists' (ASHP) Quality Improvement Initiatives Resource Center is available at www.ashp.org. It contains resources to support pharmacist leadership and engagement in health care quality initiatives that improve patient outcomes and reward performance excellence.

Table 16-1. Core Measures Associated with Medications and Advice/Counseling

Acute Myocardial Infarction (AMI)

- Aspirin at arrival
- Aspirin prescribed at discharge
- Angiotensin converting enzyme inhibitor (ACEI) or angiotensin receptor blocker (ARB) for left ventricular systolic dysfunction (LVSD)
- Adult smoking cessation advice and counseling
- Beta blocker prescribed at discharge
- Fibrinolytic therapy received within 30 minutes of hospital arrival
- Lipid-lowering therapy at discharge (optional test measure)

Heart Failure (HF)

- Discharge instructions
- ACEI or ARB for LVSD
- Adult smoking cessation advice and counseling

Pneumonia (PN)

- Pneumococcal vaccination status
- Blood cultures performed before first antibiotic received in the hospital
- Adult smoking cessation advice and counseling
- Antibiotic timing
- Timing of receipt of initial antibiotic following hospital arrival
- Appropriate initial antibiotic selection
- Influenza vaccination status

Surgical Care Improvement Project (SCIP)

- Prophylactic antibiotic received within 1 hour prior to surgical incision (some situations allow 2 hours)
- Appropriate prophylactic antibiotic selection for surgical patients
- Prophylactic antibiotic discontinued within 24 hours after surgery end time (some situations allow 48 hours)
- Cardiovascular procedures
    - Cardiovascular surgery patients with controlled 6 am postoperative serum glucose
    - Cardiovascular surgery patients on a beta blocker prior to arrival who received a beta blocker during the perioperative period
- Venous thromboembolism (VTE)
    - VTE prophylaxis ordered for surgery patients
    - VTE prophylaxis within 24 hours pre- and post-surgery

Children's Asthma Care (CAC)

- Relievers for inpatient asthma (age 2 years through 17 years)
- Systemic corticosteroid for inpatient asthma

Venous Thromboembolism (VTE)

- VTE prophylaxis
- VTE patients receiving unfractionated heparin with monitoring by protocol or nomogram
- VTE discharge instructions
- Incidence of potentially preventable VTE

Stroke (STK)

- VTE prophylaxis
- Discharged on antithrombotic therapy
- Patients with atrial fibrillation or flutter receiving anticoagulation therapy
- Thrombotic therapy administered
- Antithrombotic therapy by end of hospital day 2
- Discharged on statin medication

CHAPTER 17

Overview of the Occupational Safety and Health Administration (OSHA) Hazard Communication Standards

The Joint Commission requires health care organizations to manage their hazardous materials and wastes' risks, including hazardous medications. (*See* EC.02.02.01, EP 1 through EP 12 and MM.01.01.03, EP 2 and EP 3.) They must also comply with the Hazard Communication Standard (HCS) of the Occupational Safety and Health Administration (OSHA).[1]

This chapter summarizes the application of the HCS to pharmacies in health care organizations. More information about the HCS (including the standard, frequently asked questions, interpretation letters, compliance directives, and compliance guides) is available on OSHA's Web site. (*See* Appendix.) OSHA's eTool pharmacy module provides information specific to pharmacies in health care organizations.[2] (*See* Chapters 10 and 18.)

Hazardous Materials—The HCS covers the following materials:

- Materials that the manufacturer has determined to be hazardous and are known to be present in the workplace in such a manner that employees are exposed under normal conditions of use or in a foreseeable emergency
- Chemicals that are carcinogens, corrosive, toxic or highly toxic, irritating, sensitizing, or target organ effecting
- Liquid medications that contain hazardous chemicals (e.g., antineoplastic medications) and other medications (e.g., powdered medications) that contain hazardous chemicals and are *intended* to be mixed before administration
- Tablets, capsules, pills, and other solid medications that contain hazardous chemicals and are *intended* to be dissolved or crushed before administration. Products that are *on occasion* dissolved or crushed to facilitate administration are exempt.

Note: There is no complete list of hazardous materials (including medications). Manufacturers must determine if a material is hazardous. OSHA provides an incomplete list of common medications that are considered to be hazardous.[3]

Note: The National Institute for Occupational Safety and Health (NIOSH) provides a sample list of medications that should be handled as hazardous. The NIOSH list is on its Web site. (*See* Appendix.) (*See* Table 18-1 in Chapter 18.)[4]

Hazardous Materials Exemptions—The following materials are exempt from the HCS:

- Chemicals and medications that do not contain hazardous materials (including solids and liquids)
- Chemicals and medications in a retail establishment (e.g., in an outpatient pharmacy) that are packaged for sale to consumers
- Personal food, medications, and cosmetics intended for use or consumption while in the workplace
- Hazardous medication-containing products in a solid, final form for direct administration to a patient (e.g., tablets, pills, suppositories, and pellet-, powder-, and liquid-filled capsules)
- Hazardous medication-containing products in a solid, final form that are *on occasion* dissolved or crushed to facilitate administration

HCS Responsibilities (Manufacturers)—The HCS requires manufacturers to do the following:

- Determine if a material is hazardous.
- Label hazardous materials with the chemical identity, appropriate hazard warnings, and name and address of the manufacturer, importer, or responsible party.

  Note: Pharmaceuticals labeled to meet FDA requirements are exempt from the hazard warning label requirements.

- Provide Material Safety Data Sheets (MSDSs) for hazardous materials to distributors, wholesalers, and pharmacies.

Note: MSDSs must inform workers of the hazards, protective measures, and actions to take if exposed to hazardous materials. Package inserts and publications such as the *Physician's Desk Reference* cannot be used instead of MSDSs.

HCS Responsibilities (Distributors and Wholesalers)—The HCS requires distributors and wholesalers to do the following:

- Provide MSDSs for hazardous materials to pharmacies.

HCS Responsibilities (Organizations)—The health care organization must comply with the HCS requirements. Pharmacies may need to help the organization do the following:

- Post a notice of employee rights under the act.
- Have a written hazard communication program that includes policies and procedures for preventing and responding to exposure to hazardous materials.
- Identify areas in which hazardous materials are stored or handled.
- Provide (e.g., post) a list of hazardous materials stored and handled in those areas.
- Provide personal protective equipment (PPE) (e.g., gowns, gloves, eyewear, and face protection) and supplies for cleanup and disposal of hazardous materials (e.g., spill kits and hazardous waste containers).
- Maintain a file (e.g., electronically or in a distinctly labeled binder) of MSDSs that is readily accessible to all personnel in areas where hazardous materials are stored or handled.
- Document an attempt to obtain an MSDS for a hazardous material if the manufacturer, distributor, or wholesaler will not or cannot provide it.
- Keep records of personnel who are exposed to hazardous materials.

HCS Education—The organization must orient, educate, and train staff on handling hazardous materials and procedures to follow if exposed to hazardous materials. Staff must be reeducated as necessary and when a new hazard is introduced into the work area. Orienting, educating, and training staff should include the following topics:

- Selection, storage, handling, use, and disposal of hazardous materials
- Prevention of exposure to hazardous materials
- Health risks associated with mishandling hazardous materials
- Emergency spill and exposure procedures (e.g., what to do if a hazardous material splashes in the eyes or contacts the skin)
- How to report spills, exposures, and other incidents with hazardous materials and wastes

Hazardous materials' orientation, education, and training records should include the following information:

- Dates of orientation, education, or training
- Summary of orientation, education, or training
- Name(s) of instructor(s)
- Names and titles of attendees

Note: The American Society of Health-System Pharmacists' (ASHP) *Competence Assessment Tools for Health-System Pharmacies* contains materials that will help document pharmacy staff competence in handling hazardous materials.[5]

HCS Responsibilities (Pharmacy)—Pharmacy staff must comply with the HCS requirements. The HCS requires health care organizations to ensure that pharmacy staff members know the following:

- The location of
  - the pharmacy's hazard communication program
  - a list of hazardous materials in pharmacy areas
  - a master list of all hazardous materials in the organization
  - MSDSs in pharmacy work areas
  - PPE
  - spill kits (for cleanup and disposal of hazardous materials)
- How to use the information on labels and MSDSs
- How to use PPE and spill kits
- How to report a spill of a hazardous material
- What to do if a hazardous material splashes in the eyes or contacts the skin
- How to report an exposure to hazardous materials

CHAPTER 18

Overview of the National Institute for Occupational Safety and Health (NIOSH) Recommendations for Handling Hazardous Medications

The National Institute for Occupational Safety and Health (NIOSH) in its *NIOSH Alert* "Preventing Occupational Exposure to Antineoplastic and Other Hazardous Drugs in Health Care Settings" warns that "working with or near hazardous drugs in health care settings may cause skin rashes, infertility, miscarriage, birth defects, and possible leukemia or other cancers."[1] The *NIOSH Alert* recommends methods and equipment for protecting worker's health. This chapter provides an overview of selected NIOSH recommendations. The overview is not complete and must not be relied on solely. The complete, detailed recommendations are in the *NIOSH Alert*.[1] They must be read carefully.

NIOSH Regulations and Other Guidelines for Handling Hazardous Medications—The NIOSH recommendations are consistent with practice guidelines of the American Society of Health-System Pharmacists (ASHP)[2] and the United States Pharmacopeia (USP) Chapter <797> requirements for compounded sterile hazardous medication preparations.[3] They are also consistent with Occupational Safety and Health Administration (OSHA) guidelines for the handling of hazardous medications in the workplace. (*See* Chapter 17.) Some of the medications are covered under the Hazard Communication Standard in the Code of Federal Regulations. Individual state and local entities may have regulations that must be followed by pharmacies within that state or locality.

NIOSH Recommendations Applicability—The NIOSH recommendations apply to all personnel in health care settings who may be involved in any phase of hazardous medication handling including receipt, storage, preparation, dispensing, transporting, administering, housekeeping, and clean-up and disposal of unused medications, spills, and patient wastes.

NIOSH Recommendations Enforcement—NIOSH does *not* have regulatory authority. Its recommendations are advisory. NIOSH requests that employers (e.g., health care organizations) bring the recommendations to the attention of all workers who are at risk.

NIOSH Recommendations and Joint Commission Expectations—Joint Commission standards require organizations to safely manage hazardous medications. (*See* MM.01.01.03, EP 1 through EP 3.) The Joint Commission also requires organizations to manage their hazardous materials and waste risks, including those associated with hazardous medication disposal. (*See* EC.02.02.01, EP 8.) The Joint Commission expects an organization's practices for preparing and managing hazardous medications to be consistent with NIOSH recommendations.

NIOSH List of Hazardous Medications—The *NIOSH Alert* provides guidance and criteria for determining whether a medication is hazardous. If a medication meets one or more of the criteria or is known or suspected to be associated with carcinogenicity, genotoxicity, teratogenicity, or reproductive or developmental toxicity, it should be handled as hazardous.

The *NIOSH Alert* includes a sample list of hazardous medications.[4] (*See* Table 18-1.) The list was compiled from several sources. However, it is not complete. This list is available on the NIOSH Web site. (*See* Appendix.) Organizations should check the NIOSH Web site periodically for an updated list. NIOSH encourages organizations to develop their own list of hazardous medications that workers might encounter within the organization. Organizations may want to use the NIOSH list as the basis for creating their own list.

Summary of NIOSH Worker and Employer Recommendations

The NIOSH Web site provides the following summary of worker and employer recommendations for preventing exposures to antineoplastic and other hazardous medications in health care settings. (*See* Appendix.) The summary is not complete. The complete, detailed recommendations are in the *NIOSH Alert*.[1]

Health care workers should take the following steps to protect themselves from hazardous medications:

- Read all information and material safety data sheets (MSDSs) your employer provides to you for the hazardous medications you handle.
- Participate in any training your employer provides on the hazards of the medications you handle and the equipment and procedures you should use to prevent exposure.
- Be familiar with and able to recognize sources of exposure to hazardous medications. Sources of exposure include
  - all procedures involving hazardous medications (including preparation, administration, and cleaning), and
  - all materials that come into contact with hazardous medications (including work surfaces, equipment, personal protective equipment [PPE], intravenous [IV] bags and tubing, patient waste, and soiled linens).
- Prepare hazardous medications in an area that is devoted to that purpose alone and is restricted to authorized personnel.
- Prepare hazardous medications (oral as well as parenteral) inside a ventilated cabinet designed to protect workers and others from exposure and to protect all medications that require sterile handling (i.e., biological safety cabinet [BSC], compounding aseptic containment isolator [CACI]).
- Avoid skin contact by using a disposable gown made of polyethylene-coated polypropylene material (which is nonlinting and nonabsorbent). Make sure the gown has a closed front, long sleeves, and elastic or knit closed cuffs. Do not reuse gowns.
- Use two pairs of powder-free, disposable chemotherapy gloves, with the outer one covering the gown cuff whenever there is risk of exposure to hazardous medications.
- Wear a face shield when splashes to the eyes, nose, or mouth may occur and when adequate engineering controls (such as the sash or window on a ventilated cabinet) are not available.
- Wash hands with soap and water immediately *before* using PPE (such as disposable gloves and gowns) and *after* removing it.
- Use syringes and IV sets with Luer-Lok™ fittings for preparing and administering hazardous medications.
- Place medication-contaminated syringes and needles in chemotherapy sharps containers for disposal.
- When supplemental protection is needed, use closed-system transfer devices (CSTDs), glove bags, and needleless systems inside the ventilated cabinet.
- Handle hazardous wastes and contaminated materials separately from other trash.
- Clean and decontaminate work areas before and after each activity involving hazardous medications and at the end of each shift.
- Clean up small spills of hazardous medications immediately, using proper safety precautions and PPE.
- Clean up large spills of hazardous medications with the help of an environmental services specialist.

Employers of health care workers should take the following steps to protect their workers from exposure to hazardous medications:

- Make sure you have written policies about the medical surveillance of health care workers and all phases of hazardous medication handling—including receipt and storage, preparation, administration, housekeeping, decontamination and cleanup, and disposal of unused medications, contaminated spills, and patient wastes.

  Note: Recommendations for medical surveillance are available from NIOSH.[5]

- Seek input from workers who handle hazardous medications when developing these policies and other programs to prevent exposure.
- Prepare a written inventory of all hazardous medications used in the workplace, and establish a procedure for regular review and updating of this inventory.
- Train workers to recognize and evaluate hazardous medications and to control exposure to them.
- Provide workers who handle or work near hazardous medications with appropriate information and MSDSs.
- Provide a work area that is devoted solely to preparing hazardous medications and is limited to authorized personnel.

- Do not permit workers to prepare hazardous medications using laminar airflow workbenches (LAFWs) that move air from the medication toward the worker.
- Provide and maintain ventilated cabinets designed to protect workers and others from exposure to hazardous medications and to protect all medications that require sterile handling. Examples of ventilated cabinets include BSCs and CACIs designed to prevent hazardous medications from escaping into the work environment.
- Filter the exhaust from ventilated cabinets with high-efficiency particulate air (HEPA) filters. Make sure these cabinets are exhausted to the outdoors whenever feasible—well away from windows, doors, and other air-intake locations.
- Provide supplemental equipment to protect workers further—for example, needleless systems and CSTDs.
- Establish and oversee appropriate work practices for handling hazardous medications, patient wastes, and contaminated materials.
- Provide workers with proper PPE on the basis of a risk assessment and train workers how to use it—as required by the Occupational Safety and Health Administration (OSHA) PPE standard [29 CFR* 1910.132]. PPE may include chemotherapy gloves, nonlinting and nonabsorbent disposable gowns and sleeve covers, and eye and face protections. (*Code of Federal Regulations.)
- Ensure the proper use of PPE by workers.
- Use NIOSH-certified respirators [42 CFR 84].

  Note: Surgical masks do not provide adequate respiratory protection.
- Provide syringes and IV sets with Luer-Lok™ fittings for preparing and administering hazardous medications. Also provide containers for their disposal.
- Consider using CSTDs and needleless systems to protect nursing personnel during medication administration.
- Periodically evaluate hazardous medications, equipment, training effectiveness, policies, and procedures in your workplace to reduce exposures as much as possible.
- Comply with all relevant U.S. Environmental Protection Agency/Resource Conservation and Recovery Act (EPA/RCRA) regulations related to the handling, storage, and transportation of hazardous waste.

Table 18-1. Sample list of drugs that should be handled as hazardous*

Drug	Source	AHFS Pharmacologic-Therapeutic Classification
Aldesleukin	4,5	10:00 Antineoplastic agents
Alemtuzumab	1,3,4,5	10:00 Antineoplastic agents
Alitretinoin	3,4,5	84:36 Miscellaneous skin and mucous membrane agents (Retinoid)
Altretamine	1,2,3,4,5	Not in AHFS (antineoplastic agent)
Amsacrine	3,5	Not in AHFS (antineoplastic agent)
Anastrozole	1,5	10:00 Antineoplastic agents
Arsenic trioxide	1,2,3,4,5	10:00 Antineoplastic agents
Asparaginase	1,2,3,4,5	10:00 Antineoplastic agents
Azacitidine	3,5	Not in AHFS (antineoplastic agent)
Azathioprine	2,3,5	92:00 Unclassified therapeutic agents (immunosuppressant)
Bacillus Calmette-Guérin	1,2,4	80:12 Vaccines
Bexarotene	2,3,4,5	10:00 Antineoplastic agents
Bicalutamide	1,5	10:00 Antineoplastic agents
Bleomycin	1,2,3,4,5	10:00 Antineoplastic agents
Busulfan	1,2,3,4,5	10:00 Antineoplastic agents
Capecitabine	1,2,3,4,5	10:00 Antineoplastic agents
Carboplatin	1,2,3,4,5	10:00 Antineoplastic agents
Carmustine	1,2,3,4,5	10:00 Antineoplastic agents
Cetrorelix acetate	5	92:00 Unclassified therapeutic agents (GnRH antagonist)
Chlorambucil	1,2,3,4,5	10:00 Antineoplastic agents
Chloramphenicol	1,5	8:12 Antibiotics
Choriogonadotropin alfa	5	68:18 Gonadotropins
Cidofovir	3,5	8:18 Antivirals
Cisplatin	1,2,3,4,5	10:00 Antineoplastic agents
Cladribine	1,2,3,4,5	10:00 Antineoplastic agents
Colchicine	5	92:00 Unclassified therapeutic agents (mitotic inhibitor)
Cyclophosphamide	1,2,3,4,5	10:00 Antineoplastic agents
Cyclosporin	1	92:00 Immunosuppressive agents
Cytarabine	1,2,3,4,5	10:00 Antineoplastic agents
Dacarbazine	1,2,3,4,5	10:00 Antineoplastic agents
Dactinomycin	1,2,3,4,5	10:00 Antineoplastic agents
Daunorubicin HCl	1,2,3,4,5	10:00 Antineoplastic agents
Denileukin	3,4,5	10:00 Antineoplastic agents
Dienestrol	5	68:16.04 Estrogens
Diethylstilbestrol	5	Not in AHFS (nonsteroidal synthetic estrogen)
Dinoprostone	5	76:00 Oxytocics
Docetaxel	1,2,3,4,5	10:00 Antineoplastic agents
Doxorubicin	1,2,3,4,5	10:00 Antineoplastic agents
Dutasteride	5	92:00 Unclassified therapeutic agents (5-alpha reductase inhibitor)

Table 18-1. Sample list of drugs that should be handled as hazardous* (cont'd)

Drug	Source	AHFS Pharmacologic-Therapeutic Classification
Epirubicin	1,2,3,4,5	10:00 Antineoplastic agents
Ergonovine/ methylergonovine	5	76:00 Oxytocics
Estradiol	1,5	68:16.04 Estrogens
Estramustine phosphate sodium	1,2,3,4,5	10:00 Antineoplastic agents
Estrogen–progestin	5	68:12 Contraceptives combinations
Estrogens, conjugated	5	68:16.04 Estrogens
Estrogens, esterified	5	68:16.04 Estrogens
Estrone	5	68:16.04 Estrogens
Estropipate	5	68:16.04 Estrogens
Etoposide	1,2,3,4,5	10:00 Antineoplastic agents
Exemestane	1,5	10:00 Antineoplastic agents
Finasteride	1,3,5	92:00 Unclassified therapeutic agents (5-alpha reductase inhibitor)
Floxuridine	1,2,3,4,5	10:00 Antineoplastic agents
Fludarabine	1,2,3,4,5	10:00 Antineoplastic agents
Fluorouracil	1,2,3,4,5	10:00 Antineoplastic agents
Fluoxymesterone	5	68:08 Androgens
Flutamide	1,2,5	10:00 Antineoplastic agents
Fulvestrant	5	10:00 Antineoplastic agents
Ganciclovir	1,2,3,4,5	8:18 Antiviral
Ganirelix acetate	5	92:00 Unclassified therapeutic agents (GnRH antagonist)
Gemcitabine	1,2,3,4,5	10:00 Antineoplastic agents
Gemtuzumab ozogamicin	1,3,4,5	10:00 Antineoplastic agents
Gonadotropin, chorionic	5	68:18 Gonadotropins
Goserelin	1,2,5	10:00 Antineoplastic agents
Hydroxyurea	1,2,3,4,5	10:00 Antineoplastic agents
Ibritumomab tiuxetan	3	10:00 Antineoplastic agents
Idarubicin	1,2,3,4,5	Not in AHFS (antineoplastic agent)
Ifosfamide	1,2,3,4,5	10:00 Antineoplastic agents
Imatinib mesylate	1,3,4,5	10:00 Antineoplastic agents
Interferon alfa-2a	1,2,4,5	10:00 Antineoplastic agents
Interferon alfa-2b	1,2,4,5	10:00 Antineoplastic agents
Interferon alfa-n1	1,5	10:00 Antineoplastic agents
Interferon alfa-n3	1,5	10:00 Antineoplastic agents
Irinotecan HCl	1,2,3,4,5	10:00 Antineoplastic agents
Leflunomide	3,5	92:00 Unclassified therapeutic agents (antineoplastic agent)
Letrozole	1,5	10:00 Antineoplastic agents

Table 18-1. Sample list of drugs that should be handled as hazardous* (cont'd)

Drug	Source	AHFS Pharmacologic-Therapeutic Classification
Leuprolide acetate	1,2,5	10:00 Antineoplastic agents
Lomustine	1,2,3,4,5	10:00 Antineoplastic agents
Mechlorethamine	1,2,3,4,5	10:00 Antineoplastic agents
Megestrol	1,5	10:00 Antineoplastic agents
Melphalan	1,2,3,4,5	10:00 Antineoplastic agents
Menotropins	5	68:18 Gonadotropins
Mercaptopurine	1,2,3,4,5	10:00 Antineoplastic agents
Methotrexate	1,2,3,4,5	10:00 Antineoplastic agents
Methyltestosterone	5	68:08 Androgens
Mifepristone	5	76:00 Oxytocics
Mitomycin	1,2,3,4,5	10:00 Antineoplastic agents
Mitotane	1,4,5	10:00 Antineoplastic agents
Mitoxantrone HCl	1,2,3,4,5	10:00 Antineoplastic agents
Mycophenolate mofetil	1,3,5	92:00 Immunosuppressive agents
Nafarelin	5	68:18 Gonadotropins
Nilutamide	1,5	10:00 Antineoplastic agents
Oxaliplatin	1,3,4,5	10:00 Antineoplastic agents
Oxytocin	5	76:00 Oxytocics
Paclitaxel	1,2,3,4,5	10:00 Antineoplastic agents
Pegaspargase	1,2,3,4,5	10:00 Antineoplastic agents
Pentamidine isethionate	1,2,3,5	8:40 Miscellaneous anti-infectives
Pentostatin	1,2,3,4,5	10:00 Antineoplastic agents
Perphosphamide	3,5	Not in AHFS (antineoplastic agent)
Pipobroman	3,5	Not in AHFS (antineoplastic agent)
Piritrexim isethionate	3,5	Not in AHFS (antineoplastic agent)
Plicamycin	1,2,3,5	Not in AHFS (antineoplastic agent)
Podofilox	5	84:36 Miscellaneous skin and mucous membrane agents (mitotic inhibitor)
Podophyllum resin	5	84:36 Miscellaneous skin and mucous membrane agents (mitotic inhibitor)
Prednimustine	3,5	Not in AHFS (antineoplastic agent)
Procarbazine	1,2,3,4,5	10:00 Antineoplastic agents
Progesterone	5	68:32 Progestins
Progestins	5	68:12 Contraceptives
Raloxifene	5	68:16.12 Estrogen agonists-antagonists
Raltitrexed	5	Not in AHFS (antineoplastic agent)
Ribavirin	1,2,5	8:18 Antiviral
Streptozocin	1,2,3,4,5	10:00 Antineoplastic agents
Tacrolimus	1,5	92:00 Unclassified therapeutic agents (immunosuppressant)
Tamoxifen	1,2,5	10:00 Antineoplastic agents
Temozolomide	3,4,5	10:00 Antineoplastic agents

Table 18-1. Sample list of drugs that should be handled as hazardous* (cont'd)

Drug	Source	AHFS Pharmacologic-Therapeutic Classification
Teniposide	1,2,3,4,5	10:00 Antineoplastic agents
Testolactone	1,2,3,4,5	10:00 Antineoplastic agents
Testosterone	5	68:08 Androgens
Thalidomide	1,3,5	92:00 Unclassified therapeutic agents (immunomodulator)
Thioguanine	1,2,3,4,5	10:00 Antineoplastic agents
Thiotepa	1,2,3,4,5	10:00 Antineoplastic agents
Topotecan	1,2,3,4,5	10:00 Antineoplastic agents
Toremifene citrate	1,5	10:00 Antineoplastic agents
Tositumomab	3,5	Not in AHFS (antineoplastic agent)
Tretinoin	1,2,3,5	84:16 Cell stimulants and proliferants (retinoid)
Trifluridine	1,2,5	52:04.06 Antivirals
Trimetrexate glucuronate	5	8:40 Miscellaneous anti-infectives (folate antagonist)
Triptorelin	5	10:00 Antineoplastic agents
Uracil mustard	3,5	Not in AHFS (antineoplastic agent)
Valganciclovir	1,3,5	8:18 Antiviral
Valrubicin	1,2,3,5	10:00 Antineoplastic agents
Vidarabine	1,2,5	52:04.06 Antivirals
Vinblastine sulfate	1,2,3,4,5	10:00 Antineoplastic agents
Vincristine sulfate	1,2,3,4,5	10:00 Antineoplastic agents
Vindesine	1,5	Not in AHFS (antineoplastic agent)
Vinorelbine tartrate	1,2,3,4,5	10:00 Antineoplastic agents
Zidovudine	1,2,5	8:18:08 Antiretroviral agents

Source: www.cdc.gov/niosh/docs/2004-165/2004-165d.html#o (Accessed March 6, 2010)

*These lists of hazardous drugs were used with the permission of the institutions that provided them and were adapted for use by NIOSH. The sample lists are intended to guide health care providers in diverse practice settings and should not be construed as complete representations of all of the hazardous drugs used at the referenced institutions. Some drugs defined as hazardous may not pose a significant risk of direct occupational exposure because of their dosage formulation (for example, intact medications such as coated tablets or capsules that are administered to patients without modifying the formulation). However, they may pose a risk if solid drug formulations are altered outside a ventilated cabinet (for example, if tablets are crushed or dissolved, or if capsules are pierced or opened).

[1]The NIH Clinical Center, Bethesda, MD (revised 8/2002).

The NIH Health Clinical Center Hazardous Drug (HD) List is part of the NIH Clinical Center's hazard communication program. It was developed in compliance with the OSHA hazard communication standard [29 CFR 1910.1200] as it applies to hazardous drugs used in the workplace. The list is continually revised and represents the diversity of medical practice at the NIH Clinical Center; however, its content does not reflect an exhaustive review of all FDA-approved medications that may be considered hazardous, and it is not intended for use outside the NIH.

[2]The Johns Hopkins Hospital, Baltimore, MD (revised 9/2002).

[3] The Northside Hospital, Atlanta, GA (revised 8/2002).

[4]The University of Michigan Hospitals and Health Centers, Ann Arbor, MI (revised 2/2003).

[5]This sample listing of hazardous drugs was compiled by the Pharmaceutical Research and Manufacturers of America (PhRMA) using information from the AHFS DI monographs published by ASHP in selected AHFS Pharmacologic-Therapeutic Classification categories [ASHP/AHFS DI 2003] and applying the definition for hazardous drugs. The list also includes drugs from other sources that satisfy the definition for hazardous drugs [PDR 2004; Sweetman 2002; Shepard 2001; Schardein 2000; REPROTOX 2003]. Newly approved drugs that have structures or toxicological profiles that mimic the drugs on this list should also be included. This list was revised in June 2004.

CHAPTER 19

Overview of United States Pharmacopeia (USP) Chapter <797>: Pharmaceutical Compounding—Sterile Preparations

Chapter <797> of the United States Pharmacopeia (USP) provides procedures and requirements for the safe preparation of compounded sterile preparations (CSPs).[1] The overview in this chapter addresses Chapter <797> requirements and where they overlap with Joint Commission standards. It is not complete and must not be relied on solely. The complete, detailed procedures and requirements in Chapter <797> must be read carefully and thoroughly. (*See* Chapters 17 and 18 in this book.)

Chapter <797> Revisions—USP Chapters are subject to revisions, based on practice changes. Proposed changes are published in *Pharmacopeial Forum*, a public comment period is announced, and the revision becomes official on the stated date. This overview is based on information that was effective at the time it was written. The USP will publish information relating to revisions and frequently asked questions (FAQs) on its Web site. (*See* Appendix.) The most recent revision of the chapter must be used.

Chapter <797> Application—Chapter <797> applies to all persons who prepare, store, and transport compounded sterile preparations and all places where CSPs are prepared, including hospitals and other health care institutions, pharmacies, clinics, and physicians' office practices. The Food and Drug Administration (FDA) and other federal agencies can cite Chapter <797> in their visits to facilities.

Chapter <797> Enforcement—State boards of pharmacy can enforce all or parts of Chapter <797> if they stipulate so in their regulations. Pharmacies in these states must comply with Chapter <797> provisions as well as other state requirements relating to CSPs. The ASHP Compounding Resource Center (www.ashp.org/compounding) contains links to state-related issues, including sterile compounding laws, regulations, and continuing education requirements.

Chapter <797> and Joint Commission Expectations—The Joint Commission expects organizations to comply with Chapter <797>. The Joint Commission will survey for compliance with provisions of Chapter <797> that overlap with their standards, including those in the following chapters: Medication Management; Infection Control; Environment of Care; Human Resources; Provision of Care, Treatment and Services; Leadership; and Performance Improvement. (*See* Table 19-1.)

Chapter <797> and Medication Management Standards

The Joint Commission's standard MM.05.01.07 deals with safely preparing medications. One of the elements of performance (EP) requires the pharmacy staff to compound all CSPs except for urgent situations or when the product's stability is short. The Joint Commission requires admixtures that will not be used within 24 hours to be prepared in the pharmacy in a laminar airflow workbench (LAFW), or similar device that meets an air quality standard designated ISO 5 by the International Organization for Standardization (ISO). MM.05.01.07, EP 4 requires CSPs prepared outside of a LAFW in the pharmacy to be used immediately or within 24 hours.

> ***Note:*** Chapter <797> requires CSPs prepared outside of an ISO 5 environment (e.g., outside a LAFW) to be used immediately or within 1 hour.

Other EPs incorporated in standards include use of clean or sterile techniques; maintenance of clean, uncluttered, and functionally separate areas for CSP preparation; visual inspection of CSPs for integrity; and direct supervision by appropriately trained pharmacists or physicians if radiopharmaceuticals are prepared in the hospital.

Other medication management standards that relate to compounding sterile preparations include requirements for policies and procedures, processes for high-alert medications, beyond-use dates of preparations, labeling, packaging and transport, patient monitoring (including adverse drug and medication error reporting), and evaluating the effectiveness of the system.

Chapter <797> Risk Levels for Contamination

Chapter <797> defines USP risk levels as low-, medium-, and high-risk according to the probability of contamination. Requirements differ for each level and must be read carefully. There are specific requirements for some CSPs (e.g., those mixed in segregated compounding areas, allergy extracts, hazardous drugs, and radiopharmaceuticals). Additional information about risk levels are in Chapter <797>.

Chapter <797> Beyond-Use Dates and Times

Manufacturers determine the expiration date of their products, which must include the conditions (e.g., temperature) under which the product must be stored. This differs from the beyond-use date of compounded preparations, which is defined in Chapter <797>. (*See* Beyond-Use Times of Single-Dose Containers in this chapter.) (*See* Beyond-Use Times of Multiple-Dose Vials in this chapter.)

Beyond-use dates and times must reflect manufacturers' product labeling or sources in the literature. Otherwise, beyond-use times and dates must be assigned according to USP guidelines, which are dependent on risk level of the preparation and the temperature at which the CSP is stored. (*See* Table 19-2.) The *shorter* of stability time (such as from manufacturers' information or the *Handbook on Injectable Drugs*)[2] or USP limits of microbial sterility must be used. Chapter <797> contains complete and detailed guidelines for assigning beyond-use times and dates. These guidelines must be read completely and thoroughly.

Chapter <797> requires CSPs to be stored under conditions that will assure their stability. CSPs that have not been stored properly must be discarded. The chapter contains complete and detailed storage requirements that must be read completely and thoroughly.

Beyond-Use Times for Preparations for Immediate Use—Preparations of low-risk non-hazardous drugs that need to be compounded outside of a primary engineering control for immediate patient use may be used if the following conditions are met:

- The preparation contains no more than three sterile products (including the IV solution, drug, and diluent),
- There is no direct contact contamination when preparing the solution, and
- Administration begins within 1 hour of preparation.

Chapter <797 provides additional information.

Chapter <797> Compounding Personnel Responsibilities

Chapter <797> requires personnel who compound sterile preparations to possess the skills, education, and training needed to compound sterile preparations. They must clean and disinfect compounding surfaces, use devices to control contamination, use aseptic technique to prepare CSPs, sterilize high-risk level CSPs, and ensure that CSPs are labeled properly. In-process quality control checks, and post-compounding inspections and testing must ensure that final preparations meet specifications of quality. The pharmacy and pharmacy compounding personnel are clearly responsible for the entire sterile compounding process and meeting the requirements contained in Chapter <797>.

> ***Note:*** Personnel compound sterile *preparations*. Manufacturers produce sterile *products*.

Education of Personnel Who Compound Sterile Preparations—Chapter <797> requires personnel who compound sterile preparations to be adequately skilled and educated and trained in appropriate techniques and procedures. All compounding personnel must receive didactic instruction and pass written tests and practical demonstration in aseptic technique, proper garbing, and cleaning and disinfecting the sterile preparation work areas. Several resources that are available from the American Society of Health-System Pharmacists (ASHP) help personnel to comply with the education and training requirements of Chapter <797>. These resources include *Basics of Aseptic Compounding Technique, Getting Started in Aseptic Compounding, Safe Handling of Hazardous Drugs,* and *Compounding Sterile Preparations: ASHP's Video Guide to Chapter <797>.*[3–6]

Competence of Personnel Who Compound Sterile Preparations—Initial and annual assessment of the competence of personnel who compound sterile preparations is required. Personnel who prepare high-risk level CSPs must complete assessments every 6 months. Competence must be documented. ASHP's *Competence Assessment Tools for Health-System Pharmacies* includes documents to help comply with this requirement.[7]

Chapter <797> Cleansing and Garb Requirements

Chapter <797> specifies requirements for personnel cleansing and garb. The chapter addresses outerwear, makeup, jewelry, hand hygiene, hair and shoe covers, masks, gloves, and other issues pertaining to cleansing and garb. The requirements should be read completely and thoroughly.

Chapter <797> Facilities and Equipment

Chapter <797> provides guidelines for facilities and equipment for compounding sterile preparations. Organizations should review the USP guidelines when they plan to design or renovate their sterile compounding area or obtain new equipment.

Buffer Area—A buffer area contains specific design elements (e.g., ISO 7 air quality and high efficiency particulate arrestor [HEPA] filtered air). The primary engineering controls are located in the buffer area.

Ante Area—An ante area adjacent to the buffer area provides an area for locating sinks, donning garb, and storing small amounts of supplies. The buffer area must meet ISO 8 or ISO 7 air quality, depending on the pressure of the buffer area into which it opens. A separate ante area is required for preparing high-risk preparations. For low- and medium-risk preparations, either a separate ante area or delineated area within the combined buffer and ante area can be used.

Storage Area—A storage area should be adjacent to the ante area. This area is used for storing supplies, preparing supplies for transfer into the ante and buffer areas, and other activities that require minimizing particles in the ante and buffer areas.

Segregated Compounding Area—A segregated compounding area used for the preparation of CSPs is a functionally separate area that does not meet the requirements of a buffer and ante area, and contains a primary engineering control. CSPs admixed in a segregated compounding area can only be non-hazardous low-risk agents. Administration of the CSP must be started within 12 hours of preparation.

Primary Engineering Controls (PECs)—Primary engineering controls are informally referred to as *hoods*, and include laminar airflow workbenches (LAFWs), biological safety cabinets (BSCs), compounding aseptic isolators (CAIs), and compounding aseptic containment isolators (CACIs). All PECs must meet ISO 5 air quality. CAIs and CACIs may be located outside of a buffer area if the manufacturer certifies that placement within a buffer area is not required. CACIs placed outside a buffer area must meet additional requirements noted in Chapter <797>. PECs must be inspected and certified initially, every 6 months, and when moved.

Secondary Engineering Control—The secondary engineering controls are the buffer and ante area.

Temperature, Humidity, Light, and Noise—The temperature of the secondary engineering controls should be 19°C ± 1° (66°F ± 2°). Appropriate relative humidity (e.g., between 30 and 65%), lighting, and sound control should be considered.

Pressure and Velocity Gradients—Chapter <797> defines specific pressure differential requirements between rooms (i.e. between the buffer and ante areas, and between the ante and general areas) or, if a single room is used for both the buffer and ante areas, air displacement velocity across the line of demarcation between the buffer and ante areas.

Certification of Sterile Compounding Facilities—Primary engineering controls, buffer areas, and ante areas should be certified by an independent organization. The Controlled Environment Testing Association (CETA) provides guidelines for testing primary engineering controls and sterile compounding facilities.[8–12]

Equipment—Automated compounding devices, robotic devices, repeater pumps, and other equipment must be maintained as recommended by the manufacturers. The biomedical engineering department (or equivalent) should be aware of these devices and include them in its preventive maintenance plan. Backup plans, in case of power or other utility interruptions, should be developed.

Chapter <797> Environmental Monitoring Requirements

Chapter <797> requires organizations to monitor and evaluate the quality of the environment in the compounding area (i.e., for particulate matter and microbes). Required non-viable monitoring includes daily monitoring and recording by compounding personnel of temperature and pressure or velocity between buffer and ante areas, and semiannual monitoring of air quality by qualified certification personnel. Required viable (i.e., microbial and fungal) monitoring includes semiannual electronic air monitoring. A plan for microbial sampling of surfaces in all compounding areas must be developed and implemented. Details are provided in Chapter <797>.

Chapter <797> Infection Control

Chapter <797> specifies requirements for cleaning and disinfecting workspaces. Selected, abbreviated requirements are listed below. Complete, detailed requirements are in the chapter.

- Select cleaning and disinfecting agents that have been approved by the Infection Control Committee.

  Note: Chapter <797> requires use of sterile 70% isopropyl alcohol. Other agents can be used if within Chapter <797> requirements and approved by the organization.

- Ensure that there are no extraneous items (e.g., syringes, vials, and paper) inside the hoods.
- Clean and disinfect the PECs at the beginning of each shift and throughout the compounding processes.
- Use non-shedding cleaning tools.
- Clean and disinfect all easily cleanable surfaces at the beginning of each shift.
- Mop floors at least once daily.
- Remove trash when sterile compounding is not occurring.
- Clean and disinfect storage shelving, walls, and ceilings at least monthly.

Beyond-Use Times of Single-Dose Containers—Single-dose containers are intended to be used immediately after opening. Beyond-use times vary depending on the type of container and air quality in which it is opened. Unless the manufacturer states differently, the maximum beyond-use times for open or needle-punctured containers are the following:

- Single-dose ampules cannot be stored for any time period.
- Single-dose bags, bottles, syringes, and vials opened in worse than ISO 5 air quality can be stored no longer than 1 hour.
- Single-dose bags, bottles, syringes, and vials opened in ISO 5 or better air quality can be stored no longer than 6 hours.

Chapter <797> provides additional information. (*See* Chapter <797> Beyond-Use Dates and Times in this chapter.)

Beyond-Use Times of Multiple-Dose Vials—Multiple-dose vials intended for multiple entries have a beyond-use time of 28 days once opened, unless otherwise specified by the manufacturer or the literature.[2,13] Chapter <797> provides additional information. (*See* Chapter <797> Beyond-Use Dates and Times in this chapter.)

Chapter <797> Quality Assurance and Performance Improvement

Chapter <797> clearly indicates that the pharmacy is responsible for the quality and the control of CSPs in the pharmacy and throughout the organization. The pharmacy must educate and train non-pharmacy personnel in maintaining the quality and control of CSPs. Chapter <797> also provides guidelines that address how CSPs should be packaged, handled, and transported; used and stored in patient care areas; administered; and re-dispensed if not used on the patient for whom it was originally intended. These guidelines must be read completely and thoroughly.

Chapter <797> requires organizations to have written quality assurance (QA) policies and procedures. QA procedures must be in place and followed. QA activities should include monitoring and evaluating all components of the sterile compounding process. Organizations should review USP's QA requirements and include them in their QA program. (*See* Table 19-3.)

Since compounding sterile preparations is a high-risk, high-volume, and problem-prone activity, elements of quality assurance and performance improvement (PI) should be included in the organization's PI activities.

Standard Operating Procedures

Chapter <797> states that organizations must have standard operating procedures (SOPs) to ensure the quality of the environment in the compounding area. USP's recommendations for SOPs address access to compounding areas, handling of cartons, storage and handling of supplies, use of transportation carts, traffic flow, and procedures for compounding sterile preparations.

CSP Processing

Chapter <797> states that compounding personnel must ensure that ingredients and components used for CSPs are sterile as well as defect free. The chapter specifies that if non-sterile ingredients and components are used, compounding must meet high-risk level requirements. Equipment used in preparing CSPs must operate properly, and personnel must be trained to operate the equipment.

Automated Compounding Device Verification—Pharmacies that use automated compounding devices should review USP <797> in its entirety. Specific requirements for accuracy and precision of these devices are in the chapter.

CSP Compounding Accuracy Verification—Chapter <797> requires every CSP to be double-checked for compounding accuracy. Double-checks must verify the accuracy of the ingredients and the label. If necessary, CSP samples must be assayed to determine if the identities and concentrations of ingredients are correct and accurate. Chapter <797> suggests procedures for checking and verifying compounding accuracy.

CSP Identity and Strength Verification—Chapter <797> requires organizations to have procedures for verifying the identity and strength of ingredients. The correct names and amounts or concentrations of the ingredients must be listed on the label. Other labeling requirements include a beyond-use date (and time, if applicable), route of administration, appropriate storage conditions, and information that assures the preparation is used safely.

CSP Sterility Testing—Chapter <797> requires sterility testing for specified high-risk CSPs. The chapter provides guidelines for selecting appropriate sterilization methods and describes methods for sterilization by filtration and by steam. If high-risk preparations are compounded, other USP chapters that should be read in detail include the following:

- Chapter <71> Sterility Tests
- Chapter <85> Bacterial Endotoxin Tests
- Chapter <788> Particulate Matter in Injections
- Chapter <1075> Good Compounding Practices
- Chapter <1116> Microbiological Evaluation of Cleanrooms and Other Controlled Environments
- Chapter <1191> Stability Considerations

CSP Inspections—Chapter <797> requires that each finished CSP be inspected after compounding. Inspection must include observation for visible particulates, other foreign matter, and other evidence of defects. The chapter contains complete and detailed requirements that must be read completely and thoroughly.

Storage of CSPs

Chapter <797> requires CSPs to be stored under conditions that will assure their stability. CSPs that have not been stored properly must be discarded. The chapter contains complete and detailed storage requirements that must be read completely and thoroughly.

Monitoring Controlled Storage Area Temperatures—Chapter <797> requires temperatures in storage areas for sterile products and compounded sterile preparations to be monitored at least daily. The results must be documented. The chapter includes additional guidelines for monitoring temperatures in these storage areas.

Table 19-1. Chapter <797> Crosswalk with Joint Commission 2010 Standards

USP Chapter <797> Requirement	Joint Commission 2010 Hospital Standards and National Patient Safety Goals
Adequate training of personnel	HR.01.04.01 and HR.01.05.03
ADR and error reporting	MM.07.01.03
Air quality testing and environmental monitoring of sterile compounding area	EC.02.04.01 and EC.02.04.03
Beyond-use dating	MM.05.01.09
Cleaning and disinfecting of sterile compounding area	IC.02.02.01
Competence assessment	HR.01.06.01 and HR.01.07.01
Compounder and repeater pump accuracy and testing	EC.02.04.01 and EC.02.04.03
Contaminants	EC.02.05.01 and MM.05.01.07
Environmental design of the sterile compounding area	MM.05.01.07
Facilities	
• Space and equipment	LD.04.01.11 and EC.02.05.01
• ISO 5	MM.05.01.07
Hand hygiene	IC.01.04.01 and NPSG.07.01.01
Hazardous drugs	EC.02.02.01 and MM.01.01.03
High-alert medications	MM.01.01.03
Infection prevention and control	IC.01.05.01
Look-alike and sound-alike medications	MM.01.02.01
Labels	MM.05.01.09 and NPSG.03.04.01
Patient education	PC.02.03.01
Patient monitoring	MM.07.01.01
Patient's own medications	MM.03.01.05
Procedures	MM.05.01.07
Quality assurance	
• Responsibility for safe and quality care	LD.01.03.01
• Evaluates effectiveness of system	MM.08.01.01
• Monitors performance	PI.01.01.01
• Compiles and analyzes data	PI.02.01.01
• Improves performance	PI.03.01.01
Radiopharmaceuticals	MM.05.01.07
Recalls	MM.05.01.17
Redispensing preparations	MM.05.01.19
Regulation and compliance with laws	LD.04.01.01 and MM.05.01.11
Supplies (garb, disposables, etc.)	IC.01.02.01
Temperature testing and documentation	EC.02.06.01 and MM.03.01.01

Table 19-2. Beyond-Use Dates

Unless sterility is tested for the CSP, the beyond-use date of the CSP cannot exceed the dates or times listed.

Risk Level	Controlled Room Temperature 20° to 25° C (68° to 77° F)	Refrigerated 2° to 8° C (36° to 46° F)	Frozen -25° C to -10° C (-13° to 14° F)
Immediate use	1 hour	N/A	N/A
Low with 12 hr or less beyond-use time	12 hours	12 hours	N/A
Low	48 hours	14 days	45 days
Medium	30 hours	9 days	45 days
High	24 hours	3 days	45 days

Table 19-3. Elements of a Quality Assurance Plan for Sterile Compounding

	Competency	Suggested Documentation
Training and Personnel Monitoring	Theoretical and practical skills	Record of didactic and audio-visual training and written tests assessing knowledge
	Hand hygiene	Chapter <797> Appendix III
	Garbing	Chapter <797> Appendix III
	Glove fingertip test	Results of test
	Aseptic technique	Chapter <797> Appendix IV
	Media-fill test	Results of media-fill test
	Cleaning and disinfecting the sterile compounding area	Chapter <797> Appendix V
	Surface sampling	Results of surface samples
	Use of equipment	Training records

	Parameter	Suggested Documentation
Non-Viable Environmental Monitoring	Temperature	Daily log
	Air pressure – between the buffer area and ante area	Daily log
	Air pressure – between the ante area and general area	Daily log
	Air velocity	Daily log
	Each PEC – certification	Semiannual report
	Buffer area certification	Semiannual report
	Ante area certification	Semiannual report
	Air changes per hour – buffer area	Semiannual report
	Air changes per hour – ante area	Semiannual report
	Air changes per hour – hazardous drug storage	Semiannual report
Viable Environmental Monitoring	Electronic air sampling	Semiannual report

CHAPTER 20

Medication Safety Improvement

Improving medication safety is a significant challenge to health care practitioners. There are no simple answers or quick fixes to this complex problem. To be effective, medication safety improvement programs must be comprehensive and include all of the following elements:

- Support of leadership
- Management by an interdisciplinary group
- A supportive culture that emphasizes cooperation and minimizes discipline
- Analysis to determine the causes of reported errors
- Proactive assessments of the medication system to identify risks
- Medication safety education and competence assessment of staff and patients
- Management of patient and drug information to ensure that it is accurate and readily available
- Safe use of appropriate technology
- Improvement of medication use processes

A review of some of these elements (e.g., the use of technology) is beyond the scope of this chapter, and the review of other elements is not covered in detail. However, this chapter will help organizations improve processes for selecting and procuring, storing, ordering and transcribing, preparing and dispensing, administering, and monitoring medications. It emphasizes practices that foster accuracy and reduce the potential for errors. It also provides guidance for detecting, reporting, reviewing, and analyzing medication errors. Chapter 6 addresses The Joint Commission's National Patient Safety Goals (NPSGs). Chapter 15 provides an overview of The Joint Commission's Sentinel Event policy. Chapter 21 addresses adverse drug reactions.

Medication Error Definitions

Definitions of medication errors vary, and in the past tended to include only errors that reached a patient (i.e., with the exception of errors of omission, a patient had to receive the medication for the incident to be classified as a medication error).

National Coordinating Council for Medication Error Reporting and Prevention—The National Coordinating Council for Medication Error Reporting and Prevention (NCC MERP) defines a medication error as "any preventable event that may cause or lead to inappropriate medication use or patient harm while the medication is in the control of the health care professional, patient, or consumer. Such events may be related to professional practice, health care products, procedures, and systems, including prescribing; order communication; product labeling, packaging, and nomenclature; compounding; dispensing; distribution; administration; education; monitoring; and use."[1]

The American Society of Health-System Pharmacists (ASHP) and The Joint Commission are member organizations of NCC MERP. Both organizations endorse the NCC MERP definition.

The Joint Commission—In the glossary to the *Comprehensive Accreditation Manual for Hospitals: The Official Handbook (CAMH)*, The Joint Commission defines sentinel events and near misses:

- A *sentinel event* is an "unexpected occurrence involving death or serious physical or psychological injury, or the risk thereof. The phrase 'or the risk thereof' includes any process variation for which a recurrence would carry a significant chance of a serious adverse outcome."
- A *near miss* is "any variation during the provision of care, treatment, or services that did not affect an outcome, but for which a recurrence carries a significant risk of an adverse outcome. A near miss is a sentinel event, by definition, but near misses are not subject to review by The Joint Commission under its Sentinel Event Policy."[2]

Chapter 15 provides an overview of The Joint Commission's Sentinel Event Policy and guidelines for responding to a sentinel event.

ASHP—ASHP categorizes 12 specific types of medication errors, which are described in Table 20-1.[3]

Organization Definitions—The Joint Commission expects organizations to develop and approve a medication error definition that includes near misses that cause no harm as well as sentinel events that result in serious adverse outcomes. The NCC MERP definition provides an excellent foundation for an organization's medication error definition. (*See* Medication Error Review and Analysis.)

Medication Error Causes

Although human error is often associated with medication errors, most medication errors are caused by problems in the medication use system (i.e., the processes for selecting and procuring, ordering and transcribing, preparing and dispensing, administering, and monitoring the effects of medications on patients). Since human errors cannot be eliminated, organizations should focus on identifying and eliminating root causes related to faulty processes.

Many errors may be due to multiple problems with the system. For example, failure to administer a medication on time may occur because the medication was not available for administration. Reasons for nonavailability of the medication could include the following:

- Order was not written legibly or clearly (e.g., unclear abbreviations used), and filling was delayed until clarified
- Order was not sent to the pharmacy promptly
- Order was written for a nonformulary agent
- Order was not entered correctly in the pharmacy patient profiles
- Medication was not available from the supplier
- Order was not filled promptly
- Organization does not have standardized administration times
- Filled order was not delivered to the patient care unit or was misplaced at the patient care unit

The Institute for Safe Medication Practices (ISMP) has identified several common causes of medication errors. Some of them are listed in Table 20-2.[4]

High-Alert Medications

Some medications pose a high risk for serious errors that may lead to sentinel events. Medications often designated as high-alert include concentrated electrolytes (e.g., potassium chloride, potassium phosphate, and sodium chloride greater than 0.9%), insulin, opiates and narcotics, anticoagulants (e.g., heparin, low molecular weight heparins, warfarin), antineoplastic agents, neonatal and pediatric medications, epidural medications, patient-controlled analgesia medications, neuromuscular blocking agents, and medications with look-alike or sound-alike names. ISMP has identified the high-alert medications listed in Table 20-3. (*See* MM.01.01.03 in Chapter 4.) (Example 20-1 is a list of selected high-alert medications and precautions for administering them.)

There are other medications that pose a risk for errors with serious outcomes. Furthermore, other factors that are unrelated to specific medications may increase the potential for errors with any medication. These factors relate to the environment (e.g., poor lighting), patient education (e.g., failure to educate patients about their medications adequately), and information management (e.g., failure to communicate patient and drug information clearly).

Medication Use System Assessment

Organizations should assess their medication use system proactively to identify risk points in the processes. At a minimum, organizations should assess high-risk processes that are often associated with sentinel events (e.g., processes relating to the use of the high-alert medications listed in Table 20-3).

Data Analysis—Pharmacies should aggregate and analyze data and report the findings through their performance improvement process. Examples of such data include the following:

- Clarifications of questionable medication orders
- Usage patterns of after-hours access to medications
- Administering first doses of medications prior to review by a pharmacist
- Unusual removals of controlled substances from stock

Organizations should review the data and act as necessary (e.g., by using process improvement tools) to improve their medication use processes. (*See* Chapter 15.)

Failure Mode and Effects Analysis—Failure mode and effects analysis (FMEA) (sometimes called failure mode, effects, and criticality analysis) is a proactive method for identifying possible ways that a process might fail (failure modes), the likelihood of the failure, the capability of detecting a failure, and the criticality of the effect. Although FMEA has been traditionally used by engineers, health care organizations have adapted it to identify failure modes in their medication use processes that occur frequently and/or pose a high risk of serious adverse outcomes. They then focus on redesigning the processes to minimize the probability of failure or to protect patients from the effects of the failure. (*See* Chapter 15.)

Performance Improvement (Proactive)

Measures for preventing medication errors should focus on improving processes. Processes for planning, selecting and procuring, storing, ordering, transcribing, preparing and dispensing, administering, monitoring, and evaluating the effects of medications on patients should be reviewed continuously to identify ways to improve them and reduce the potential for medication errors. To improve processes, organizations should do the following:

Develop Policies and Procedures—All departments involved in the process (e.g., medical staff, nursing service, respiratory therapy, imaging, emergency department, ambulatory surgery, clinics, and pharmacy services) should cooperate in developing policies and procedures that will prevent medication errors. Policies and procedures should describe the medication distribution process in detail and should promote consistency and accuracy. There should be an emphasis on points in the process that are most prone to cause errors. For example:

- Transcription of orders
- Calculations
- Labeling

Policies and procedures for compounding medications should emphasize the following:

- Double-checks of critical steps prone to error (e.g., calculations)
- Order (sequence) of preparation
- Compounding technique (e.g., sterile or nonsterile)

Policies and procedures for selecting and procuring, storing, ordering and transcribing, preparing and dispensing, administering, and monitoring the effects of medications on patients should be reviewed and updated regularly. Adherence to policies and procedures must be emphasized.

Standardize—Standardization can greatly reduce the potential for medication errors. Standard dosage charts and standard concentrations of medications can minimize the need for calculations, which are a major source of errors. Standard medication administration times can reduce confusion.

Avoid Dangerous and Confusing Abbreviations and Expressions—All abbreviations pose a risk of misinterpretation, and the use of abbreviations should be minimized throughout the medication use process (e.g., ordering, labeling, and maintaining pharmacy patient profiles). However some abbreviations and expressions are especially dangerous, and a list of standard abbreviations can reduce confusion. The Joint Commission requires organizations to have a list of prohibited abbreviations. The NCC MERP has identified the abbreviations and expressions in Table 20-4 that are commonly misinterpreted and should not be used.[1]

Other examples of dangerous and confusing abbreviations and expressions include the following:

- *Roman Numerals*—Use Arabic numerals (e.g., 6) instead of Roman numerals (e.g., VI or vi).
- *Apothecaries' System and Symbols*—Express quantities in the metric system. The apothecaries' system and symbols are confusing and should be avoided. For example:
  - The dram symbol (ʒ) is easily confused with the number "3."
  - The minim symbol (♍) is sometimes confused with the abbreviations for milliliter (mL).
  - The grain abbreviation (gr) is sometimes confused with the abbreviation for gram (g).
  - The microgram symbol (μ) is sometimes confused with the abbreviation for milligram (mg).
- *Latin*—Limit the use of Latin to common expressions and abbreviations whose meanings are clear and universally understood (e.g., *stat* and *prn*).
- *Decimal Points*—Avoid the use of decimals when possible (e.g., write 500 mg instead of 0.5 g). Decimal points may not reproduce on a copy of the order or may be hidden by lines or imperfections in the copy.
- *Leading and Trailing Zeros*—Place a zero in front of a leading decimal point (e.g., use 0.5 mg rather than .5 mg), and do not use unnecessary decimal points or zeros after a decimal point (e.g., use 25 mg rather than 25.0 mg).

- *Dosage Units*—Express dosage in strengths (e.g., 50 mg) rather than dosage units (e.g., 2 tablets), volume (e.g., 15 mL), or package size (e.g., 1 ampule).
- *Spaces Between the Number and Strength*—Leave a space between the number and strength (e.g., use 10 units instead of 10units).
- *Upper and Lower Case*—Use both upper and lower case letters.
- *Vague Directions*—Do not use vague directions for use (e.g., "take as directed").
- *Chemical Symbols*—Avoid using chemical symbols to abbreviate drug names. For example: $MgSO_4$ (magnesium sulfate) has been misinterpreted as morphine sulfate.
- *Acronyms and Other Coined or Abbreviated Names*—Avoid using acronyms and other coined or abbreviated names. As the numbers of drugs with similar names increase, the risks associated with the use of acronyms and other coined or abbreviated drug names increase. For example:
  - AZT could stand for zidovudine, azathioprine, or aztreonam.
  - HCTZ (for hydrochlorothiazide) has been misinterpreted as hydrocortisone.
  - DPT could stand for Diptheria, Pertussis, and Tetanus or Demerol, Phenergan, and Thorazine.
  - A-pen (for ampicillin) may be quite clear to the prescriber's staff but can be confusing to those who are unfamiliar with the prescriber's personal abbreviations.
  - Coined names (e.g., clafagyl) for a combination of Claforan™ and Flagyl™ are unlikely to be found in drug information sources and could be confusing to those who are not familiar with them.
  - Non-standard names (e.g., "half and half," "banana bag," "GI cocktail," and "magic mouthwash") are nonspecific, and the drug ingredients and strengths may vary from organization to organization. Furthermore, half and half could refer to combinations of medications (e.g., laxatives) or a combination of milk and cream. Nonstandard names are confusing when practitioners move from organization to organization.
- *Computer Mnemonics*—Computer mnemonics can sometimes result in the wrong drug being displayed on the computer screen. Increasing the number of characters can minimize the opportunity for entering a drug with a similarly spelled name. Mnemonics should never be used for high-alert medications (e.g., antineoplastic agents).

Ensure that Personnel Are Qualified—Care should be taken to ensure that personnel are qualified to dispense and administer medications. You should select personnel who demonstrate their ability to give attention to detail, perform accurate work, and follow procedures.

Educate Staff—Ensuring that personnel are qualified also includes orientation, education, and training for prescribers, staff who dispense medications (pharmacists and pharmacy technicians), and persons who administer medications (e.g., nurses, respiratory therapists, and imaging technologists). These individuals must stay informed with current knowledge on the appropriate and safe use of medications (e.g., through reading the literature, participating in educational programs, or by consulting with other health care professionals). Pharmacists should provide educational programs for prescribers and staff who administer medications (e.g., programs on medication actions, indications, precautions, appropriate dosages, and administration techniques). Education for personnel who dispense medications should include the following:

- Weights, measures, and calculations
- Nomenclature and abbreviations
- Incompatibilities
- Compounding procedures (including procedures to promote compounding accuracy)
- Labeling
- Maintaining dispensing records
- Administration routes, devices, and techniques

Standardize Hand-Off Communications—A standardized approach is one that is defined, communicated to staff, and implemented to ensure that information about a patient is communicated in a consistent manner. The hospital's process must be interactive and include the opportunity for discussion between the giver and receiver of patient information. (*See* PC.02.02.01, EP 2.) The information may include the patient's condition, care, treatment, medications, services, and any recent or anticipated changes to any of these. The same processes can be used for discussions involving issues other than patient information.

The standardized approach should be defined in writing and include what to communicate and how to communicate effectively, accurately, and adequately. The organization's approach applies to all individuals, including hospital employees and medical staff.

Hand-off communication may apply to patient information or to general discussion. Information may need to be transmitted among:

- Prescribers, when they are consulting on a patient
- Prescribers and other staff, such as during patient procedures
- Health care providers of different disciplines, such as when a patient is being moved from an inpatient unit to a diagnostic area
- Other health care providers, such as nurses and pharmacists, pharmacies to remote order entry facilities when pharmacies close, and remote order entry facilities to pharmacies when pharmacies reopen

Interruptions during hand-offs should be limited to minimize the possibility that information would fail to be conveyed or would be forgotten.

Assess Staff Competence—Personnel, especially new personnel, must demonstrate their competence through competence assessment before preparing, dispensing, and administering medications. Competence assessment will ensure that the person's education has been successful and should emphasize correct interpretation of orders and accurate calculations. Competence testing for persons who administer medications should include an assessment of administration technique. Testing for persons who prepare medications should include compounding procedures. Continued competence can be assured through periodic (e.g., quarterly or annual) testing and frequent (e.g., daily or weekly) observation of techniques. Records should document education, training, and competence assessment of personnel.

Educate Patients and Involve Them in Their Care—Education should extend to patients and their caregivers (i.e., those who provide postdischarge care for patients). Patients who are knowledgeable about medication use (including drug–drug and drug–food interactions) may be more aware of the need for communicating their medication allergies, sensitivities, and adverse drug reactions. In addition, knowledgeable patients can prevent medication errors by questioning unusual dosages and routes of administration and unfamiliar medications. Education efforts should encourage patients and caregivers to communicate their questions and concerns to physicians, nurses, and pharmacists responsible for the patient's care.

Assess Patient Competence—Assessing patient competence may not be easy. Techniques for assessing patient competence include the following:

- Stop frequently during education and ask questions to see if the patient understands instructions up to that point.
- Ask the patients to repeat instructions or demonstrate a technique.
- Ask questions that test the patient's understanding of signs of events that pose a risk of harm (e.g., signs of toxicity and adverse reactions) and actions to be taken.

Minimize Discipline—Some organizations require explicit educational actions when specified types or numbers of errors occur. For example, an excessive number of omitted doses in a period may result in mandatory attendance at error-prevention educational programs. Punitive actions are likely to be counter-productive (e.g., deter error reporting and delaying process improvements).

When process problems have been ruled out and personnel continue to make errors consistently, they should be reassigned to duties that do not require them to dispense or administer medications. Discipline, such as probation, demotion, suspension, and termination, should be the last resort and reserved for specified, serious errors (e.g., overdose of a medication due to gross negligence and a disregard for established policies and procedures).

Preventing Selecting, Storing, Securing, and Procuring Medication Errors

Measures to prevent errors should start before orders are written or medications are dispensed and administered. Error prevention measures should be in place in all medication storage areas (including pharmacy storerooms and dispensing areas, automated dispensing cabinets, and nonautomated storage areas). Organizations with automated dispensing cabinets should review the ISMP Guidance on the Interdisciplinary Safe Use of Automated Dispensing Cabinets.[5] Organizations that have both automated and nonautomated storage should ensure that error prevention measures are equally effective (although the process may be different). Adherence to the following practices can prevent errors related to selecting, storing, securing, and procuring medications:

- Organize medication storage and work areas to minimize the potential for dispensing errors (i.e., uncluttered and free from distractions and interruptions).
- Review floor stock and night stock lists to ensure that they are limited to urgently needed medications.
- Ensure that a pharmacist is available when the pharmacy is closed and is readily accessible to nursing and medical personnel.
- Ensure that medications are available in the most ready-to-use forms.
- Ensure that medications are clearly and completely labeled (including name, strength, dosage form, and expiration or beyond-use date) and that the information is displayed prominently.
- Ensure that medications with look-alike and sound-alike names are stored to minimize the potential for confusion.
- Label high-alert medications distinctly (e.g., with Tall Man letters, different colors, or bright stickers).
- Store dangerous medications in isolated areas or segregate them from other medications.
- Do not store injections of concentrated potassium chloride, potassium phosphate, or sodium chloride greater than 0.9% in patient care areas.
- Ensure that other concentrated electrolytes (e.g., magnesium sulfate and calcium chloride) are stored only in areas where the concentrated forms are needed.
- Eliminate multiple-dose vials of medications when possible.
- Provide cautionary warnings for medications with a narrow margin of safety.
- Inspect areas regularly to ensure that medications are labeled properly and stored to minimize the likelihood of a medication error. Remove deteriorated, expired, and otherwise unusable medications immediately.
- Adhere to the following precautions for automated dispensing cabinets:
    - Place medications in the devices carefully with particular attention to look-alike and sound-alike medications.
    - Store all high-alert medications in single-access compartments.
    - Arrange medications to minimize errors in retrieving them (e.g., by storing ampuls and vials of medications intended for irrigation and respiratory therapy separately from ampuls and vials for parenteral use, by storing ophthalmic and otic medications separately, and by storing medications and products intended for external use separately from injectable medications and medications intended for internal use).
- Adhere to the following precautions for non-automated medication storage:
    - Assess the storage of all items that are not distributed by the pharmacy (e.g., bulk items, IV products distributed by the materials management department, contrast media, and patients' personal medications).
    - Deliver filled orders promptly to pre-designated, secure points in patient care areas.

Preventing Ordering/Prescribing Errors

Measures for preventing errors in the ordering/prescribing process must focus on standardization of prescribing practices, clarity, and accuracy. Policies and procedures should address these issues. Adherence to the following practices can prevent errors relating to ordering/prescribing medications:

- Review the patient's status, current medication regimen, and laboratory reports prior to ordering medications.
- Order medications that are listed in the organization's formulary. Personnel are probably more familiar with formulary than nonformulary medications and are, therefore, less likely to make medication errors if formulary medications are prescribed.
- Avoid verbal orders except in emergency situations. Organizations should adopt policies that prohibit verbal orders when the prescriber is present and able to provide written orders.
- When a verbal order is received, write the order on the order sheet and read back the written order to the prescriber. Many organizations require the "read back" of the order to be documented.
- Authenticate verbal orders promptly.
- Ensure that the order includes the patient's name, location, required identifiers, age, and, if appropriate, weight and height.

- Write complete orders (i.e., medication name, dosage form, dose, strength, route, frequency, rate, method, and site of administration).
- Do not use vague expressions (e.g., "resume orders" or "continue medications").
- Indicate the reason for ordering the medication (e.g., prochlorperazine 5 mg IM every 4 hours as needed for nausea).
- Prescribe medications to be administered orally (rather than parenterally) when possible.
- Double-check orders to ensure that they are clear and complete.

Preventing Transcription Errors

- Eliminate the need for transcription of orders (and the possibility of transcription errors) by using computerized prescriber order entry or approved preprinted order forms.
- Use scanning technology or fax systems to expedite transmissions to pharmacy without the need to transcribe orders.

Preventing Dispensing Errors

Measures for preventing errors in the dispensing process must focus on accuracy. Examples of dispensing errors include the following:

- Dispensing the wrong medication
- Dispensing the wrong dosage form
- Dispensing the wrong dose
- Dispensing the wrong quantity
- Dispensing a medication that is contraindicated because of the patient's diagnosis or physical condition (unless the prescriber authorizes the administration on the basis that the benefits outweigh the risks)
- Dispensing a medication that interacts with another medication the patient is taking (unless the prescriber authorizes the administration on the basis that the benefits outweigh the risks)
- Dispensing a medication to which the patient has a known or stated allergy (unless the prescriber authorizes the administration on the basis that the benefits outweigh the risks)
- Errors in labeling medications (e.g., wrong medication, wrong strength, and wrong concentration)
- Errors in preparing medications (e.g., compounding errors, wrong ingredients, and wrong amounts or ratios of ingredients)
- Unavailability of doses for administration at the scheduled time (e.g., orders not filled or orders filled but not delivered to the patient care or procedural unit)

Most dispensing errors are caused by problems in the dispensing process. Simply "trying" for zero dispensing errors is rarely sufficient to reduce errors significantly over the long term. Therefore, managers must improve the dispensing process and educate staff continuously. Adherence to the following practices can prevent dispensing errors:

- Provide all doses in a ready-to-use format. Solid oral medications, including partial tablet doses, should be in unit-dose packages. Liquid medications should be in unit-dose packages (e.g., oral syringes or cups), if possible. IV medications should be in ready to administer forms (e.g., manufacturers' premixed solutions, manufacturers' vial/bag point-of-care systems, and pharmacy-prepared IV solutions with additives).
- Ensure that a pharmacist reviews all medication orders before administering the first dose. Possible reasons to make exceptions may include the following situations:
  - The urgency of the patient's condition requires administration before the review.
  - A physician is present to oversee the review, administration of the medication, and monitoring of the patient.
- Ensure that a pharmacist's review includes comparing orders with patient medication profiles (e.g., for allergies, potential interactions, laboratory results, and duplicate therapies).
- Ensure that the pharmacy computer system is enabled to check for interactions, duplicate therapy, and dose ranges.
- Question all orders that call for an unusual number of dosage units (e.g., orders for more than two tablets, or more than one ampul or vial).
- If technicians enter orders, ensure that a pharmacist checks the entries and reviews all warnings (including warnings that the technicians may have bypassed).
- Identify medications, therapies, patient types (e.g., pediatric), and patient conditions (e.g., oncology) that require a second person to check the order.

Ensure that the second checks are performed and documented.

- Ensure that the organization's policies address how pharmacists are to retrospectively review orders when a prospective review is not possible. Ensure that the policies include the time frame for the review. The organization should monitor compliance with the policies, gather data (e.g., types and numbers of errors) relating to compliance, and target processes for improvement. The organization should review and communicate the results of its performance improvement efforts.
- Ensure that policies clearly define when a nurse, respiratory therapist, or radiologic technologist is permitted to administer the first dose of a medication before a pharmacist reviews the order. The policies should address removing medications from automated dispensing cabinets and from non-automated floor stock. A limited list of medications for which this "override" is permitted should be defined by policy. In all cases, administering medications without a pharmacist's review of the order must be warranted by the urgency of the patient's condition or the availability of a physician to oversee the process.
- Review orders carefully. Clarify ambiguous and incomplete orders and inappropriate doses with the prescriber prior to dispensing. Document efforts to resolve questionable medication orders (e.g., by telephone communication with the prescriber).
- Keep the process simple to minimize the chance for errors.
- Ensure that all personnel are familiar with policies and procedures and understand the importance of following them.
- Use standardized concentrations of medications to minimize the need for calculations and the necessity to compound medications.
- Require an independent double-check of all calculations by another qualified individual (especially for compounded medications and for pediatric, oncology, and other high-risk dosage calculations). Incorrect calculations may result in significant underdosing or serious overdosing of patients. All calculations should be documented in writing.
- Triple-check labels on medication containers (i.e., when removing from shelf, before dispensing, and when returning to the shelf).
- Prepare one order at a time.
- Compound medications carefully and correctly. The compounding process must ensure the following:
  - All entries in compounding records are correct.
  - Products (medications, excipients, etc.) are used as ordered.
  - Amounts used are correct.
  - Compounding equipment is used correctly.
  - In-process checks (e.g., inspection of products and checks of calculations) are performed.
- Label medications clearly and accurately. All medications must be labeled with a minimum of the following:
  - Medication name, strength, and amount
  - Patient name, location, and other identifiers, if applicable
  - Expiration date (and time, if applicable)
  - Lot number and manufacturer (if applicable)
  - Ancillary precaution labels that will decrease the risk of medication administration errors (e.g., "For the Ear" and "Not for Injection")
  - Initials of preparer
  - For compounded sterile preparations, the diluent, date prepared, and beyond-use date and time.
- Dispense outpatient prescriptions in containers that meet the requirements of the Poison Prevention Packaging Act of 1970. Label outpatient prescriptions in accordance with state boards of pharmacy and federal regulations.
- Require a final check for accuracy on every order filled. Review the order if there are apparent discrepancies. Compounding errors may be difficult to detect, so compounded preparations should be discarded if errors are suspected. The final check should include the following:
  - Appearance and labeling of the finished preparation
  - Inspection of containers of ingredients used in preparing the medication
  - Accuracy of written calculations relating to the preparation

- Ensure that technicians have their work checked by a pharmacist. Pharmacists *should* have their work checked by another person (preferably a pharmacist), but if a nonpharmacist checks a pharmacist's work (e.g., in organizations with only one pharmacist on duty), the pharmacist retains legal responsibility for the accuracy of the orders filled.
- Provide current drug information references (including standard dosage charts and standard flow rate charts) to personnel who dispense and administer medications.

Preventing Sterile Preparation Errors—Adherence to the following can prevent errors in compounding sterile preparations:

- Avoid compounding sterile preparations when premixed products are available. This also eliminates the risk of contamination during compounding.
- Use premixed solutions with standardized concentrations (e.g., Heparin 25,000 units in 500 mL 5% Dextrose) when possible. The use of standardized concentrations can also minimize the risk of administration errors if flow rate charts are used to eliminate the need for flow rate calculations.
- Inspect stock regularly for expiration dates and package integrity. Remove all expired or damaged stock from the preparation area.
- Avoid stocking concentrated injectable medications that can be lethal if administered without dilution.
- Minimize the use of multiple-dose containers.
- Store potentially lethal additives (e.g., concentrated potassium chloride) only in the pharmacy (not in floor stock or crash carts). Prepare all solutions containing concentrated additives in the pharmacy.
- Eliminate after-hours access to concentrated potassium chloride, potassium phosphate, and sodium chloride greater than 0.9% throughout the organization.
- Prepare only one sterile preparation or a single batch at a time.
- Leave containers of all additives and diluents in the work area (to facilitate checking by a second party). Use a different syringe for each additive and diluent, and leave syringes with their respective containers. Leave the plungers of syringes at the position marking the volume of solution withdrawn.
- Label preparations immediately after they are prepared.
- Ensure that another individual checks the labeled final preparation prior to dispensing.

Preventing Incompatibilities and Particulate Matter in Sterile Preparations—Care must be taken to prevent incompatibilities and particulate matter in sterile preparations. The following measures should be observed:

- Consult compatibility references (e.g., the American Society of Health-System Pharmacists' [ASHP] *Handbook on Injectable Drugs*[6]) to establish the compatibility of compounded sterile preparations.
- Avoid adding more than one drug to a solution unless the compatibility of the mixture is established.
- Use a separate syringe and needle for each additive.
- Reconstitute powdered ingredients thoroughly with diluents and ensure that they dissolve completely.
- To avoid coring (cutting of rubber pieces as a needle is inserted into a vial), make entries into vials with the bevel of the needle (slanted portion of needle tip) facing up and use a slight downward and lateral (toward the bevel) pressure.
- Use a filter needle or filter straw to reduce the number of glass particles from ampuls.
- Inspect solutions for turbidity, discoloration, evidence of incompatibilities, and particulate matter before and after preparation. A haze or a precipitate may be evidence of a physical incompatibility, although some incompatibilities may be chemical or therapeutic and may not be visible. Viewing solutions against both light and dark backgrounds can help to identify particulate matter.

Preventing Medication Administration Errors

Medications should be administered only by persons within their scope of practice who are qualified and authorized to administer them. Policies and procedures often restrict the persons who are authorized to administer specific medications or types of medications, and they usually list those persons by position or title (such as registered nurse, licensed practical nurse, and critical care registered nurse) as well as by the routes by which they are authorized to administer medications. If special training is required (e.g., for oncology agents or moderate sedation), it should be indicated in the organization's policies and procedures. Adherence to the following practices can prevent medication administration errors:

- Ensure that verbal orders are written in the patient's medical record promptly and authenticated by the prescriber.
- Ensure that orders are communicated promptly to the pharmacy.
- Double-check the accuracy of orders transcribed onto medication administration records (MARs) by comparing transcriptions with original orders. Have a second individual make the comparison when possible.
- Check that the pharmacy has interpreted and filled the order correctly. Check the label and appearance of the product provided by the pharmacy. Contact the pharmacy if there are apparent discrepancies.
- Ensure that nurses reconcile MARs with patient medical records within the hospital-defined time frame. Electronic MARs should be reconciled with each new entry; printed or manual MARs should be reconciled at least each shift. Ensure that the reconciliation is documented.
- Clarify ambiguous medication orders or questionable administration routes with the prescriber before administering the medication. Document the clarification and all changes made on the order.
- Question all orders that call for an unusual number of dosage units (e.g., more than two tablets or more than one ampul or vial).
- Consult current drug information and administration references as needed.
- Contact the pharmacy when medications are unavailable for administration. The order may have been discontinued without the discontinuation being noted on nursing records.
- Do not permit borrowing medication from one patient to administer to another patient.
- Prepare medications for administration in an area that is free from distractions and interruptions.
- Prepare doses for one patient for one medication pass at a time.
- Mathematical calculations (e.g., dosage and flow rates) should be independently calculated by two qualified individuals (e.g., a pharmacist or a nurse), and the calculations compared. Reconcile any differences prior to the administration of the medication. Using standard concentrations of medications and standard flow rate charts can reduce the need for mathematical calculations.
- Ensure that patients are identified accurately (using the organization's two selected patient identifiers) immediately prior to medication administration.
- Double-check the name of the medication and strength on the label with the medication and dose prescribed.
- Check the medication, original order, and MAR if the patient questions the administration of the medication. This reduces the likelihood of administering a wrong medication or administering a duplicate dose of a medication.
- Use bedside scanning technology if provided. Do not bypass safety steps in this process.
- Use the proper administration equipment (e.g., infusion pumps) and technique.
- Use infusion pumps properly and safely. Use only devices that protect against allowing uncontrolled flow into a patient. Ensure that those who use these devices understand how to use them. Require two individuals to compare the settings with the order and verify that the drug, concentration, and flow rate are correct.
- Minimize the types of devices used. A single type of device reduces the potential for confusion associated with multiple types of devices.
- Ensure devices that are rented or leased are configured consistently with the organization's own devices and are protected from free flow.
- Organizations should develop a single dosing standard for medications (e.g., heparin either weight-based or not; critical care infusions in mcg/kg/min or mg/hr, but not both).
- Observe the patient after administering oral medications to ensure that he or she swallows the medications.
- Record the administration of medications immediately after their administration. Prompt recording fosters complete and accurate documentation and reduces the likelihood of omitted and duplicate doses.

- If self-administered medications are stored at bedside, they must be secure per hospital policy.
- Return all discontinued and unneeded medications and medications for discharged patients to the pharmacy.

Preventing Self-Administration Errors—Self-administration of medications should be minimized because it decreases accountability (since accurate administration records are difficult to maintain with this process), creates the potential for medication errors, may lead to misuse of medications, and increases the organization's potential liability. However, in some organizations and drug rehabilitation facilities, self-administration of medications is part of the patient's therapy (e.g., for cardiac and transplant patients).

Organizations should have a process to ensure that patients who self-medicate do so correctly. Policies and procedures should emphasize the following:

- Only patients deemed competent are permitted to self-administer medications.
- A member of the professional staff must supervise self-administration.
- Amounts of medications supplied to the patient must be limited.
- Types of medications supplied must be limited to those that can be self-administered with little risk of harm.
- The patient must be instructed in the proper use of the medications. When possible, pharmacists should instruct patients who self-administer medications.

Preventing Patient Monitoring-Related Errors

A complete medication use system includes processes for monitoring the effects of medications on patients. Adherence to the following practices can prevent errors related to monitoring patients:

- Monitor patients for the desired therapeutic effect, including eliciting the patient's perception of medication activity and potential adverse effects. Failure to monitor can lead to prescribing errors.
- Monitor patients for signs and symptoms of adverse drug reactions, toxic doses, and change in status. Failure to respond appropriately can lead to overdoses or inappropriate medication selection.
- Ensure that laboratory tests are performed and the results provided promptly to physicians, nurses, pharmacists, and others who need the information. Failure to monitor laboratory results can result in inappropriate medication use or medication dosing.

Medication Error Detection

Some medication errors are detected by the persons who make the errors, whereas others are detected by chance observation (e.g., observation of administration by the wrong route). However, many errors are undetected because there is no reliable mechanism for detecting them. Methods for improving detection of actual and potential errors include direct observation of persons who prepare and administer medications, evaluation of missing doses, and evaluation of excess doses.

Direct Observation of Persons Who Prepare and Administer Medications—Direct observation of staff who prepare and administer medications may be the most effective method to detect medication errors and may be the only method to detect certain types of errors (e.g., incorrect preparation and administration techniques). Although direct observation may require additional personnel, time, and funds, the potential for improvement outweighs these disadvantages. To reduce costs and the demands on personnel, observation may be conducted randomly.

Review of Patient Medical Records—A review of patient medical records may reveal indications that a medication error occurred. For example, bleeding problems might signal an overdose of an anticoagulant, and the administration of drugs used to treat adverse drug reactions might indicate the misuse of a drug to which a patient has a known allergy.

Evaluation of Missing Doses—Evaluation of the reasons for doses missing from the patient's medication supply may reveal medication errors (e.g., administration of duplicate doses). However, some missing doses may be justified. For example, a missing dose may be justified because the first dose was administered earlier than expected. Missing doses should be recorded as they are identified. Unjustified and unexplained missing doses should be brought to the attention of the clinician in charge of the patient.

Evaluation of Excess Doses—Frequent (e.g., daily) reconciliation of pharmacy dispensing records with MARs and the patient's medication supply (e.g., automated dispensing cabinet reports or unit-dose cassette drawers) can help identify excess doses. Excess doses may be caused by omissions or partial administration of medications or by administration of another patient's medication. However, accountability for excess doses is difficult if clinicians fail to record administration of doses accurately or if pharmacists dispense extra doses routinely (a practice that is strongly discouraged). Unjustified and unexplained excess doses should be brought to the attention of the clinician in charge of the patient.

Some excess doses may be justified. Justified reasons for excess doses include the following:

- Pharmacy dispensed extra doses (e.g., prn medications).
- Pharmacy dispensed enough doses to start administration at once, while nursing waited until the next scheduled administration time before administering the first dose.
- Doses were contraindicated.
- Patient was not to take anything (including medications) by mouth.
- Patient was temporarily absent from the patient care area or organization (e.g., off the floor for a scheduled procedure or on pass).
- Order was discontinued after delivery of the medication.
- Patient refused doses.

Organizations should have a policy and procedure to address administration of medication doses when patients are away from the patient care area. Refused doses are not necessarily justified reasons for omission and should be evaluated carefully. Another equally effective medication or the same medication by a different route or in a different vehicle may be acceptable to the patient.

Medication Error Reports

Prompt attention to the patient and providing appropriate supportive treatment are paramount when medication errors are made. After attending to the patient's immediate needs, medication errors must be reported.

Individuals who have the greatest knowledge of the errors should report them. This is usually the person who discovers the error and may not be the person who made the error. Organizations often rely on voluntary reporting of errors, but individuals who make errors may be unaware that they made them or reluctant to report them because of the stigma associated with errors and fear of disciplinary action. Reporting by individuals who make errors may be improved if the organization does not require them to identify themselves. To further minimize the reluctance to report errors, the beneficial rather than punitive aspects of an error-prevention program should be stressed.

Medication Error Reports to the Physician Responsible for the Patient—Medication errors should be reported immediately to the physician responsible for the patient. Reports may be oral, although oral reports must be supplemented with written reports. The physician responsible for the patient should assess the patient for evidence of harm and document the findings in the patient's medical record.

Medication Error Entries in the Patient's Medical Record—The medication administered in error should be noted in the patient's medical record. The organization's risk management department should determine how this information is to be recorded. Often entries are limited to the same information recorded for doses administered correctly (e.g., name of medication administered, dose administered, site, route, date, and time). Patient medical records (e.g., MARs and nurses' notes) should *not* refer to "wrong" doses of medications or "errors," and should not indicate that a medication error report was filed.

Medication Error Reports to the Organization—In addition to prompt notification of the physician responsible for the patient and documentation in the patient's medical record, written reports of medication errors should be prepared as soon as the error is recognized. Some organizations report medication errors on an incident report form (sometimes called a variance or occurrence report form). ("Incidents" are occurrences that result or could result in harm to patients, staff, or visitors.) Other organizations provide a special form for reporting medication errors. (*See* Example 4-26.) Medication error reports should be reviewed by individuals or committees as defined by the organization's policy. Furthermore, they should be kept confidential and not be filed in the medical record. The organization uses the reports to evaluate errors, minimize further occurrences, report to outside agencies, and assist with risk management.

Medication Error Reports to the ISMP— The ISMP Medication Errors Reporting Program (MERP) is a confidential national voluntary reporting program that provides expert analysis of the system causes of medication errors and disseminates recommendations for prevention. Regulatory agencies and manufacturers are notified of needed changes in products when safety is of concern. Organizations may voluntarily report actual or potential medication errors to MERP. ISMP uses the information in the reports to reduce occurrence of similar errors (e.g., by recommending changes in packaging and labeling and by promoting safe medication practices). Organizations may request that their identity not be released. Information is available on the ISMP Web site. (*See* Appendix.)

Medication Error Reports to the MEDMARX Program—The MEDMARX program is an Internet-based, confidential, subscription service that can be used for both internal and external reporting. MEDMARX enables a health care facility to anonymously report, track, and compare medication error data in a nationally standardized format. More information on subscribing to the MEDMARX program is available from Quantros, Inc. (*See* Appendix.)

Medication Error Reports to The Joint Commission—Organizations are not required to report medication errors (including sentinel events) to The Joint Commission. However, voluntarily submitting reports of sentinel events to The Joint Commission adds to their database. Organizations that do not voluntarily submit a report of a sentinel event must nevertheless complete an acceptable root cause analysis. (*See* Chapter 15.)

Medication Error Review and Analysis

Organization policy should define the types of medication errors that must be reviewed and analyzed. The organization's procedures should provide for prompt review of medication errors by physicians, nurses, pharmacists, risk managers, performance improvement personnel, and other qualified individuals who can act to improve processes and minimize their recurrence. The review should include meeting with persons associated with the errors (e.g., persons who reported the errors, persons who made the errors, and witnesses). The analysis should focus on determining the causes of errors and how the errors could have been prevented. The following can be helpful in reviewing medication errors:

- Use forms for tabulating, summarizing, tracking, and evaluating medication errors. Display the data graphically, if possible. Some organizations use Pareto diagrams and other statistical analysis tools described in Chapter 15. Errors may be summarized by one or more of the following:
    - Name and type of medication
    - Type of error
    - Cause of error
    - Type of patient (e.g., geriatric)
    - Area where error occurred (e.g., nursing unit or emergency department)
    - Shift
    - Time
    - Service (e.g., infectious disease)
    - Department (e.g., anesthesia)
    - Categories of personnel involved (e.g., registered nurses, licensed practical nurses, agency or temporary staff, prescribers, and pharmacists)
- Review and evaluate medication error data monthly or quarterly to identify patterns and trends (e.g., changes in frequency, types of incidents, causes of errors, and personnel involved). Reviews for patterns and trends should cover at least the past 12 months.

Determining the Seriousness of Errors—The clinical effects of many medication errors are minimal. However, other medication errors are disabling or life threatening, and some result in patient mortality. Some organizations evaluate errors for seriousness (one or two serious errors may be worse than numerous minor errors) and focus their efforts on preventing the most serious ones. The NCC MERP adopted the index in Table 20-5 to categorize the severity of medication errors based on patient outcome.[1]

Evaluating Action Taken and Patient Care Provided—It is often not possible to determine if an error caused a change in the patient's condition or an increased length of stay in the organization. However, reviews of medication errors should include an evaluation of the appropriateness of action taken by staff, emergency preparedness, and quality of care provided to patients. Pharmacists should participate in this evaluation, which should include the following:

- Action taken by a physician when notified;
- Observation of the patient for signs of adverse effects;
- Appropriateness and timeliness of supportive treatment, if needed;
- Availability of emergency medications and antidotes; and
- Observation of the patient after treatment.

Conducting a Root Cause Analysis (RCA)—Organizations should conduct a root cause analysis (RCA) when such an analysis is indicated. (*See* Chapter 15 for a description of the RCA process and where to obtain help in conducting an RCA.)

Performance Improvement (Reactive)

Medication use processes should be reviewed when medication errors are made. If necessary, processes must be improved and education relating to the improved processes must be provided. The measures for preventing medication errors listed in this chapter may be helpful in redesigning and improving processes. Leadership support, cultural changes, and the use of appropriate technology may be needed to significantly improve some processes.

Medication Error Rates

Organizations often determine their medication error rates and use their findings to judge the safety of their medication use system or measure their progress in reducing medication errors. However, such measurements and comparisons are of questionable value. High rates can mean that many medication errors occurred—or that the organization has an excellent process for detecting and reporting errors; low rates can mean that only a few medication errors occurred—or that medication errors were not detected and reported. If limited to internal use, determined accurately and used responsibly in conjunction with other measurements, error rates may be a helpful tool in a medication safety improvement program.

Medication Error Rate Calculation—Medication error rates can be calculated a number of ways. Two examples follow:

1. Divide the number of errors by the number of doses administered during a specified period and multiply by 100 to express the error rate as a percentage.
2. Divide the number of errors by the number of admissions or patient days for the period (e.g., monthly or quarterly). It may be necessary to multiply the quotient by 100 or 1000 to yield a rate that can be easily compared with previous or subsequent periods.

"Standard" Medication Error Rates—There are no "national," "standard," or "acceptable" medication error rates against which an organization can compare its error rate. Comparison of error rates between organizations is meaningless because there are too many variables. The NCC MERP notes that "the use of medication error rates to compare health care organizations is not recommended, due to differences in organizational culture, definitions used, patient population served, and types of reporting and detecting systems."[1] An organization's rate may be significantly higher or lower than rates reported by other organizations.

As there are no standard error rates, an organization should establish its own benchmark rate. This can best be done after a 1- or 2-year trend analysis (i.e., an evaluation of the type and seriousness of the errors). The error rate in an organization should reflect its patient characteristics, types of medications used, and the organization's definition of medication errors that must be reported. Organizations should periodically review their error detection process to ensure effective detection and reliable reporting (e.g., by determining if low rates are due to failure to report errors).

Thresholds for Evaluation—An organization can use its benchmark rates as thresholds for evaluating medication errors. (*See* Benchmarking in Chapter 15.) When errors exceed the thresholds, the medication distribution process should be evaluated. Thresholds for medications for which accurate administration is critical should be set at zero (i.e., all occurrences with these medications will be evaluated to determine if problems are present in the process).

Table 20-1. Types of Medication Errors[a]

Type	Definition
Prescribing error	Incorrect drug selection (based on indications, contraindications, known allergies, existing drug therapy, and other factors), dose, dosage form, quantity, route, concentration, rate of administration, or instructions for use of a drug product ordered or authorized by physician (or other legitimate prescriber); illegible prescriptions or medication orders that lead to errors that reach the patient
Omission error[b]	The failure to administer an ordered dose to a patient before the next scheduled dose, if any
Wrong time error	Administration of medication outside a predefined time interval from its scheduled administration time (this interval should be established by each individual health care facility)
Unauthorized drug error[c]	Administration to the patient of medication not authorized by a legitimate prescriber for the patient
Improper dose error[d]	Administration to the patient of a dose that is greater than or less than the amount ordered by the prescriber or administration of duplicate doses to the patient, i.e., one or more dosage units in addition to those that were ordered
Wrong dosage-form error[e]	Administration to the patient of a drug product in a different dosage form than ordered by the prescriber
Wrong drug-preparation error[f]	Drug product incorrectly formulated or manipulated before administration
Wrong administration-technique error[g]	Inappropriate procedure or improper technique in the administration of a drug
Deteriorated drug error[h]	Administration of a drug that has expired or for which the physical or chemical dosage-form integrity has been compromised
Monitoring error	Failure to review a prescribed regimen for appropriateness and detection of problems, or failure to use appropriate clinical or laboratory data for adequate assessment of patient response to prescribed therapy
Compliance error	Inappropriate patient behavior regarding adherence to a prescribed medication regimen
Other medication error	Any medication error that does not fall into one of the above predefined categories

[a]The categories may not be mutually exclusive because of the multidisciplinary and multifactorial nature of medication errors.

[b]Assumes no prescribing error. Excluded would be (1) a patient's refusal to take the medication or (2) a decision not to administer the dose because of recognized contraindications. If an explanation for the omission is apparent (e.g., patient was away from nursing unit for tests or medication was not available), the reason should be documented in the appropriate records.

[c]This would include, for example, a wrong drug, a dose given to the wrong patient, unordered drugs, and doses given outside a stated set of clinical guidelines or protocols.

[d]Excluded would be (1) allowable deviations based on preset ranges established by individual health care organizations in consideration of measuring devices routinely provided to those who administer drugs to patients (e.g., not administering a dose based on a patient's measured temperature or blood glucose level) or other factors such as conversion of doses expressed in the apothecary system to the metric system and (2) topical dosage forms for which medication orders are not expressed quantitatively.

[e]Excluded would be accepted protocols (established by the Pharmacy and Therapeutics Committee or its equivalent) that authorize pharmacists to dispense alternate dosage forms for patients with special needs (e.g., liquid formulations for patients with nasogastric tubes or those who have difficulty swallowing), as allowed by state regulations.

[f]This would include, for example, incorrect dilution or reconstitution, mixing drugs that are physically or chemically incompatible, and inadequate product packaging.

[g]This would include doses administered (1) via the wrong route (different from the route prescribed), (2) via the correct route but at the wrong site (e.g., left eye instead of right), and (3) at the wrong rate of administration.

[h]This would include, for example, administration of expired drugs and improperly stored drugs.

Source: ASHP Guidelines on Preventing Medication Errors in Hospitals[3]

Table 20-2. Common Causes of Medication Errors

Common Causes of Errors	Examples
Failed communication	Poor handwriting Inaccurate transcription of orders Drugs with similar names Inappropriate use of zeroes and decimal points Use of metric and apothecary systems Use of inappropriate abbreviations Ambiguous or incomplete orders
Poor drug distribution practices	Unlabeled and mislabeled drugs Improper storage practices Unlimited access to drugs and pharmacy Improper use of dispensing equipment
Dose miscalculations	Failure to stock standardized concentrations and commercially pre-mixed products
Problems related to drugs and drug devices	Labeling and packaging problems Device design issues
Incorrect administration of drug	Failure to check or improper patient identification Wrong route administration
Lack of patient education	Patients not involved Patients do not understand their medications
Little or no knowledge about the drug	Nursing and/or pharmacy staff are unaware of common dose Staff unaware of side effects or drug interactions Staff unaware of the need for special monitoring or warnings for the drug
Little or no knowledge of the patient's identity, physical state, past or current drug therapy	Staff unaware of liver or kidney function No patient allergy information Little of no physical data on patient (e.g., height, weight, pregnancy or lactation status)

Source: MR Cohen, *Medication Errors*[4]

Table 20-3. ISMP's List of *High-Alert Medications*

Classes/Categories of Medications
adrenergic agonists, IV (e.g., epinephrine, phenylephrine, norepinephrine)
adrenergic antagonists, IV (e.g., propranolol, metoprolol, labetalol)
anesthetic agents, general, inhaled and IV (e.g., propofol, ketamine)
antiarrhythmics, IV (e.g., lidocaine, amiodarone)
antithrombotic agents (anticoagulants), including warfarin, low-molecular-weight heparin, IV unfractionated heparin, Factor Xa inhibitors (fondaparinux), direct thrombin inhibitors (e.g., argatroban, lepirudin, bivalirudin), thrombolytics (e.g., alteplase, reteplase, tenecteplase), and glycoprotein IIb/IIIa inhibitors (e.g., eptifibatide)
cardioplegic solutions
chemotherapeutic agents, parenteral and oral
dextrose, hypertonic, 20% or greater
dialysis solutions, peritoneal and hemodialysis
epidural or intrathecal medications
hypoglycemics, oral
inotropic medications, IV (e.g., digoxin, milrinone)
liposomal forms of drugs (e.g., liposomal amphotericin B)
moderate sedation agents, IV (e.g., midazolam)
moderate sedation agents, oral, for children (e.g., chloral hydrate)
narcotics/opiates, IV, transdermal, and oral (including liquid concentrates, immediate and sustained-release formulations)
neuromuscular blocking agents (e.g., succinylcholine, rocuronium, vecuronium)
radiocontrast agents, IV
total parenteral nutrition solutions

Specific Medications
epoprostenol (Flolan), IV
insulin, subcutaneous and IV
magnesium sulfate injection
methotrexate, oral, non-oncologic use
opium tincture
oxytocin, IV
nitroprusside sodium for injection
potassium chloride for injection concentrate
potassium phosphates injection
promethazine, IV
sodium chloride for injection, hypertonic (greater than 0.9% concentration)
sterile water for injection, inhalation, and irrigation (excluding pour bottles) in containers of 100 mL or more

Source: ISMP website www.ismp.org/Tools/highalertmedications.pdf, Accessed March 6, 2010

Table 20-4. Dangerous and Confusing Abbreviations

Abbreviation	Intended Meaning	Common Error	Recommendations
U	Units	Mistaken as a zero or a four (4) or six (6), resulting in overdose. Also mistaken for "cc" (cubic centimeters) when poorly written.	Write out "units."
ug	Micrograms	Mistaken for "mg" (milligrams) resulting in overdose.	Use "mcg" or write out in an "micrograms."
Q.D.	Latin abbreviation for every day	The period after the "Q" has sometimes been mistaken for an "I," and the drug has been given "QID" (four times daily) rather than daily. Also, QD can be misinterpreted to mean OD (right eye).	Write out "daily."
Q.O.D.	Latin abbreviation for every other day	Misinterpreted as "QD" (daily) or "QID" (four times daily). If the "O" is poorly written, it looks like a period or an "I."	Use "q other day" or write out "every other day."
SC or SQ	Subcutaneous	Mistaken as "SL" (sublingual) when poorly written.	Write out "subcutaneous."
TIW	Three times a week	Misinterpreted as "three times a day" or "twice a week."	Write out "three times a week."
D/C	Discharge; also discontinue	Patient's medications have been prematurely discontinued when D/C (intended to mean "discharge") was misinterpreted as "discontinue," because it was followed by a list of drugs.	Write out "discontinue" and "discharge."
HS	Half strength	Misinterpreted as the Latin abbreviation "HS" (hour of sleep).	Write out the strength of the medication. Writing out "at bedtime" is preferred over using "hs."
cc	Cubic centimeters	Mistaken as "U" (units) when written poorly. Also, can be read as two zeros.	Use "mL" or write out "milliliters."
AU, AS, AD	Latin abbreviation for both ears; left ear; right ear	Misinterpreted as the Latin abbreviation "OU" (both eyes); "OS" (left eye); "OD" (right eye).	Write out the intended meaning in full (i.e., both eyes, both ears, left eye, and right eye).
IU	International Unit	Mistaken as IV (intravenous) or 10 (ten)	Write out "international units."
MS, MSO_4, $MgSO_4$	Confused for one another	Can mean morphine sulfate or magnesium sulfate	Write out "morphine," "morphine sulfate," or "magnesium sulfate."

Adapted from the National Coordinating Council for Medication Error Reporting and Prevention. Rockville, MD.[1]

Table 20-5. NCC MERP Index for Categorizing Medication Errors

Type of Error	Result
No Error	
Category A	Circumstances or events that have the capacity to cause error.
Error, No Harm	
Category B	An error occurred, but the medication did not reach the patient. (An "error of omission" *does* reach the patient.)
Category C	An error occurred that reached the patient but did not cause patient harm.
Category D	An error occurred that reached the patient and required monitoring to confirm that it resulted in no harm to the patient and/or required intervention to preclude harm.
Error, Harm	
Category E	An error occurred that may have contributed to or resulted in temporary harm to the patient and required intervention.
Category F	An error occurred that may have contributed to or resulted in temporary harm to the patient and required initial or prolonged hospitalization.
Category G	An error occurred that may have contributed to or resulted in permanent patient harm.
Category H	An error occurred that required intervention necessary to sustain life.
Error, Death	
Category I	An error occurred that may have contributed to or resulted in the patient's death.

Definitions:

Harm—Temporary or permanent impairment of the physical, emotional, or psychological function or structure of the body and/or pain resulting therefrom requiring intervention.

Monitoring—To observe or record relevant physiological or psychological signs.

Intervention—May include change in therapy or active medical/surgical treatment.

Intervention Necessary to Sustain Life—Includes cardiovascular and respiratory support (e.g., CPR, defibrillation, intubation, etc.).

Source: National Coordinating Council for Medication Error Reporting and Prevention. Rockville, MD.[1]

CHAPTER 21

Adverse Drug Reactions

Improving medication safety includes preventing and reducing adverse drug events (ADEs). ADEs include medication errors and adverse drug reactions (ADRs). Chapter 20 focuses on medication errors. This chapter focuses on ADRs.

The Joint Commission requires organizations to respond to actual or potential ADRs. (*See* MM.07.01.03 in Chapter 4.) Responding to ADRs improves medication safety by:

- Preventing or minimizing the occurrence of ADRs
- Improving the understanding of side effects associated with the use of specific medications
- Identifying previously unreported side effects of newly-approved medications
- Reducing the severity of ADRs
- Improving the detection and reporting of ADRs
- Providing for appropriate care when ADRs occur

ADR Definitions

Definitions of ADRs vary. Examples of current definitions follow:

Food and Drug Administration (FDA)—The FDA MedWatch program (*see* MedWatch Program in this chapter) defines a serious adverse event as any event when the patient outcome is any of the following:

- Death
- Life threatening (i.e., presents a real risk of dying)
- Results in initial hospitalization or prolongs hospitalization
- A disability or causes permanent damage
- Results in a congenital anomaly or birth defect
- Requires medical or surgical intervention to prevent permanent impairment or damage
- Other serious important medical events[1]

American Society of Health-System Pharmacists (ASHP)—*ASHP Guidelines on Adverse Drug Reaction Monitoring and Reporting* defines a significant ADR as "any unexpected, unintended, undesired, or excessive response to a drug that

1. requires discontinuing the drug,
2. requires changing the drug therapy,
3. requires modifying the dose (except for minor dosage adjustments),
4. necessitates admission to a hospital,
5. prolongs stay in a health care facility,
6. necessitates supportive treatment,
7. significantly complicates diagnosis,
8. negatively affects prognosis,
9. results in temporary or permanent harm, disability, or death."[2]

The Joint Commission—In the glossary to the *Comprehensive Accreditation Manual for Hospitals: The Official Handbook (CAMH)*, The Joint Commission defines an ADR as:

"A response to a medicinal product that is noxious and unintended, and that occurs at doses normally used in humans for the prophylaxis, diagnosis, or treatment of disease or for the restoration, correction, or modification of physiological or psychological function."[3]

Organization-Approved—The Joint Commission expects organizations to develop and approve an ADR definition to use in their ADR programs. To clarify their definition, organizations might consider the following effects:

- Life threatening (e.g., anaphylaxis, arrhythmias, and gastrointestinal hemorrhage)
- Temporarily or permanently disables the patient (e.g., renal failure, ototoxicity, shortness of breath, nausea, vomiting, or diarrhea)

- Otherwise poses a risk of harm to the patient (e.g., convulsions)
- Complicates treatment (e.g., hallucinations)
- Results in readmission or prolonged stay in the organization (e.g., severe rashes)
- Necessitates supportive treatment (e.g., treatment with medications or assisted respiration)
- Requires reducing the dose (except for small reductions to improve tolerance)
- Requires stopping or changing the medication (except when the medication is stopped because of minor discomfort and an equally effective alternative medication is ordered)
- Allergic or hypersensitivity reactions (fever, rash, etc.)
- Reactions that are not listed in the manufacturer's product information
- Reactions that occur when medications are not used in accordance with the manufacturer's product information
- Reactions that have not been reported in the literature

ADRs versus Side Effects

Some ADRs (e.g., nausea, vomiting, diarrhea, headache, and rashes) are expected side effects of therapy and are often accepted because the benefits of therapy outweigh the risk. These anticipated ADRs have been reported in the literature, occur with a predictable frequency, and may be related to the size of the dose. Some organization ADR definitions exclude specific side effects associated with specific medications that occur repeatedly and require little or no change in patient management (e.g., drowsiness or dry mouth due to an antihistamine). Although side effects may be excluded from ADR reporting, they should be documented in the patient's record and care should be taken to minimize the patient's distress.

ADR Definition Approval

In many organizations, the medical staff, in collaboration with other departments through the Pharmacy and Therapeutics (P&T) Committee, approves the organization's ADR definition. However, other options that retain the collaborative nature of this function can also be used. A periodic review and confirmation of the definition is suggested. Initial approval and periodic reviews and confirmations of the definition should be documented.

ADR Incidence

Estimates of the incidence of adverse reactions to medications administered in organizations vary greatly. Early studies showed incidences ranging up to 20% of hospitalized patients. However, rates of this magnitude may reflect the reporting of intentional overdoses, overdoses due to drug administration errors, or side effects that require no treatment or change in therapy. Unfortunately, some individuals (including surveyors) cite these rates as typical of the rates that should be identified in institutional ADR reporting programs. Although the true incidence of adverse reactions is in question, many ADRs require treatment or discontinuation of the medication, and some contribute to patient mortality.

ADR Prevention

ADRs occur frequently in susceptible patients (e.g., patients with a history of allergies) and may be dose related. Geriatric patients have more reactions and more severe reactions than younger adults. Therefore, it is possible to predict and prevent some ADRs or minimize their severity by:

- Interviewing patients for a past history of allergies, ADRs, and intolerance to medications
- Administering test doses and conducting skin testing to identify patients at risk for allergic reactions to selected medications
- Identifying high-risk patients (e.g., with a symbol on the patient's chart, bed, or name band)
- Clearly indicating sensitivities or known allergies on the medical record and the pharmacy patient profile
- Administering medications within recommended dosage ranges
- Administering medications by an appropriate technique (e.g., at the appropriate infusion rate)
- Reducing doses of medications known to be associated with ADRs in susceptible patients
- Reducing doses in geriatric patients, underweight patients, patients with impaired renal or hepatic function, and patients with congestive heart failure, as appropriate

- Monitoring to ensure that serum drug concentrations remain within an acceptable therapeutic (yet nontoxic) range

ADR Detection

Because ADRs can be associated with any medication and any patient, some cannot be predicted or prevented. All medications should be suspect; early detection can minimize the effects of ADRs.

ADR Signs and Symptoms—Signs and symptoms of reactions that may be due to a medication include the following:

- Changes in a patient's physical and mental condition (e.g., elevated temperature, confusion, depression, loss of appetite, or other unexplained discomfort)
- Bleeding problems
- Blood dyscrasias (e.g., leukopenia)
- Liver enzyme elevations
- Cardiac arrhythmias
- Skin rashes and hives
- Anaphylactic type reactions
- Convulsions
- Hallucinations
- Renal failure

ADR Detection Programs (Passive)—Nurses, physicians, respiratory therapists, imaging technologists, and nuclear medicine personnel are in the best position to observe ADRs. However, passive programs that rely only on nonpharmacists to detect ADRs and complete ADR reports are minimally effective. Nonpharmacists are often unaware that ADRs must be reported and do not know the procedures for reporting them. Some may find the completion of ADR reports too time consuming.

Another problem with passive detection programs is that nurses and physicians may consider ADRs to be medication administration errors and be reluctant to report them. Furthermore, physicians sometimes believe that ADRs make them look bad and increase their liability. Pharmacists should emphasize that ADRs are not necessarily errors and do not necessarily reflect poor patient care: No one is at fault. In addition, pharmacists should point out that litigation is more likely to result if ADRs go undetected or unreported and patient care suffers.

Patient Medical Record Reviews (Retrospective)—Retrospective reviews of patient medical records may identify some previously undetected (or detected but unreported) ADRs. However, this information may be difficult to evaluate and may not be helpful in determining if the patient was cared for appropriately.

ADR Detection Programs (Active)—Detection and reporting of ADRs is increased when pharmacists take an active role. An active ADR detection program encourages nurses, physicians, and other health care personnel to notify (orally, electronically, or in writing) the pharmacy of suspected ADRs for subsequent investigation and reporting by a pharmacist. Other active detection methods include targeting specific patients or specific medications for monitoring.

ADR Detection (Targeting Patients)—Although ADRs can occur in any patient, the following "target" patients can be selected for close observation:

- Patients who have experienced an ADR
- Patients who receive stat doses of medications that are often used for managing ADRs (e.g., parenteral diphenhydramine, epinephrine, aminophylline, corticosteroids, phenytoin, vitamin K, diazepam, phenobarbital, topical steroids, and sodium polystyrene sulfonate)
- Patients who have stat serum drug concentrations ordered
- Patients with serum drug concentrations above the therapeutic range
- Patients who receive only one or two doses of a medication that is usually administered on a regular schedule for a long period
- Patients who have an abrupt dosage reduction or discontinuation of long-term maintenance medications (e.g., antihypertensives)
- Patients with impaired renal function (e.g., serum creatinine above a specified level or a noticeable change in serum creatinine) or impaired liver function
- Patients older than a specified age
- Pediatric patients or patients younger than a specified age

- Patients under a specified weight
- Patients taking more than a specified number of medications
- Patients whose condition worsens after a dose is increased or a new medication is administered

ADR Detection (Targeting Medications)—Monitoring of patients receiving selected target medications can also improve ADR detection. Although any medication may cause an adverse reaction, targeted medications can include the following:

- Medications frequently associated with ADRs (e.g., analgesics, antibiotics, anti-inflammatory agents, anticoagulants, cardiovascular agents, diuretics, antineoplastics, antihyperglycemic agents, and central nervous system agents)
- Diagnostic imaging and nuclear medicine preparations
- Respiratory therapy medications
- Recently released medications (e.g., medications approved by the FDA during the preceding 3 years)

ADR Detection (Electronic Monitoring)—An electronic monitoring program can facilitate detection and evaluation of ADRs and can be used to identify trends. For example, a computer can identify stat or one-time doses of medications used to treat ADRs and compile a report in a format that can be used by the pharmacy to investigate and record the reasons for the doses. In addition, electronic data mining of medical records information can identify patients whose diagnostic and treatment codes indicate a drug reaction.

ADR Detection (Other Methods)—Other methods to improve detection of ADRs include the following:

- Informing physicians and nurses of target patients, target medications, and symptoms of common ADRs
- Questioning nurses about target patients and target medications
- Reviewing nurses' notes for evidence of ADRs
- Rounding with physicians
- Attending nursing "end-of-shift reports" and listening for clues to possible ADRs
- Providing incentives for detecting and reporting (e.g., recognition, awards, or monetary rewards)
- Interviewing patients who claim that their condition or symptoms are medication related
- Reviewing records of clinical trials of investigational medications for possible ADRs
- Reviewing incident reports to identify potential medication-related incidents (e.g., patient falls due to vertigo associated with hypnotic therapy)

ADR Response

If an ADR is detected early (i.e., before serious consequences develop), the medication can be stopped or the dosage reduced and appropriate care provided. Appropriate patient care includes the following:

- Taking the patient's vital signs before and after administering a new medication
- Ensuring that emergency medications and antidotes used to treat ADRs are readily available (e.g., parenteral diphenhydramine, epinephrine, and corticosteroids)
- Notifying the prescriber or the attending physician immediately if an ADR is suspected
- Discontinuing the medication if the reaction poses a risk to the patient
- Substituting a less toxic medication
- Providing the patient with written notice stating the medication or type of medication responsible for the reaction and precautions to prevent or minimize further reactions (*see* Example 4-28)

ADR Reports

ADRs should be reported immediately by persons who have the greatest knowledge of the reaction (usually a physician, nurse, or pharmacist). The reporter may or may not be the person who first observed the reaction. The reaction should be reported to the prescriber. If the prescribing practitioner is not available, the reaction should be reported to the attending physician or house officer. The person who reports the reaction should record a description of the reaction, action taken, and outcome in the patient's medical record.

Written Reports—In addition to the initial, immediate report to the prescriber (which is usually oral), ADRs should be reported to the pharmacy in writing. Some pharmacies simply ask to be notified of a suspected reaction, name and location of the patient, and name of the person reporting. Pharmacy personnel then assist the reporter or observer in completing an ADR report. Information reported to the pharmacy should include the following:

- Patient's name
- Patient's medical and medication history (including all medications administered to the patient)
- Description of the suspected ADR (including the name of the medication suspected of causing the reaction)
- Timed sequence of the event (including date and time of the reaction)
- Relevant laboratory tests or diagnostic findings
- Comments relating to the severity of the reaction
- Any remedial treatment required
- Outcome of the event and patient prognosis

In addition to the above, written reports of ADRs often include the following:

- Patient's age, sex, and race
- Name and title of the person making the report
- A notation that the reaction is *suspected* if a medication is not clearly the cause

ADR report forms should provide areas to be completed by the observer or reporter, pharmacist reviewer, prescriber, physician responsible for the patient, and reviewing committee. (*See* Example 4-27.)

Improving Reporting—To improve ADR reporting, ADR monitoring and reporting procedures should be included in orientation and ongoing education programs for pharmacists, nurses, physicians, and others who are in a position to detect and report ADRs. At a minimum, ADR education should include the following:

- The organization's ADR definition
- Detecting and reporting procedures for ADRs
- Care for the patient
- Review by the pharmacy and medical staff

Other methods to improve ADR reporting include the following:

- Ensuring that ADR report forms are available at nursing units and other areas where medications are used (e.g., diagnostic, procedural, and ambulatory areas) and in the pharmacy
- Ensuring that personnel know when and how to complete ADR report forms (e.g., by describing the forms in detail during ADR educational programs)
- Offering rewards for reporting ADRs, installing an ADR telephone recorder and/or hotline, and posting ADR-related posters and reminders at nursing stations and other appropriate areas

ADR Review and Evaluation

ADRs should be reviewed and evaluated by the prescriber and/or the physician responsible for the patient, a pharmacist, and the medical staff. They are described below.

ADR Review by the Prescriber and/or the Physician Responsible for the Patient—The prescriber and/or physician responsible for the patient should review and evaluate the reported reaction and comment in the appropriate area of the report form. Physician comments should include the following:

- The physician's assessment of the reported reaction (e.g., likely or unlikely to be associated with a medication)
- Treatment ordered, if any
- An assessment of the patient's condition

ADR Review by a Pharmacist—A pharmacist should review all ADR reports and record comments in the pharmacist section of the report form. Pharmacist comments should include the following:

- A review of the literature and the package insert for the suspected medication
- A note if the reaction has been previously reported (e.g., in the literature or package insert)
- A statement on the likelihood of the medication being responsible for the reaction
- A recommendation related to reporting the reaction to the FDA or the manufacturer

If recurrences appear likely and pose a significant risk to patients, the pharmacist should notify the medical staff and nursing service immediately.

ADR Review and Assessment by the Medical Staff—The pharmacy should submit ADR reports to the medical staff (usually through the P&T Committee) at least quarterly. Some medical staffs prefer that pharmacists screen ADR reports and withhold reports of reactions that are (in the pharmacy's opinion) insignificant (anticipated and unanticipated) or unlikely to be due to a medication. However, many organizations assess all ADRs (including minor ADRs and common side effects). The rationale for assessing all ADRs is that many of them can be prevented and preventing them minimizes patient discomfort. Organizations should consider assessing all ADRs and common side effects but place the highest priority on significant ADRs.

At a minimum, all serious ADRs (e.g., potentially life-threatening or harmful or contributed to death or disability) should be intensively assessed (e.g., studying the process, determining the cause, and conducting a root cause analysis). The ADR assessment should determine the severity of the reaction (*see* Ranking ADRs) and determine whether:

- The reaction was due to a medication (*see* ADR Probability Estimates)
- The ADR was listed in the package insert
- The ADR was reported in the literature
- The ADR was predictable
- The ADR could have been prevented (*see* ADR Preventability Assessments)
- The administration of another medication would have been more appropriate
- The dosage of the medication was appropriate
- Appropriate care was provided (e.g., appropriateness of the response to the ADR and the choice of medications for treatment)
- The care was effective
- Documentation in the patient's medical record was appropriate
- The patient was informed (or is to be informed) of potential reactions to the medication (or similar medications) and precautions to take

The ADR should be reported to the FDA and manufacturer. To ensure prompt reporting, some organizations permit the pharmacist and prescriber to determine if the ADR should be reported to the FDA and manufacturer prior to P&T review. The communication with the FDA and manufacturer is reported later to the P&T Committee.

Medical Staff Action on ADR Reports—The medical staff (through the P&T Committee) should take action to reduce the incidence and severity of ADRs. Examples of effective action include the following:

- Education that promotes appropriate dosing, administration, monitoring (e.g., serum drug concentrations), and early detection of symptoms of toxicity or adverse reaction
- Restricting use of the medication
- Administering test doses, identifying high-risk patients, and reducing the dose of medications associated with ADRs
- Requiring another physician to agree that the medication is indicated (e.g., a countersignature on a medication order)
- Ensuring that medications needed to treat ADRs are readily available in emergency stocks
- Including the medication in the medication use improvement program or targeting the medication for close monitoring

ADR Probability Estimates

Careful evaluation of ADR reports may prevent incrimination of a useful medication. There are several methods for estimating the probability of ADRs. The Naranjo algorithm, a well-known method, is described in Table 21-1.

ADR Severity Ranking

Ranking ADRs by severity can be helpful in evaluating patterns and trends. A simple 0–5 scale for ranking ADRs follows:

0—The reaction required little or no treatment, no change in therapy, did not require significant reduction in dosage or discontinuation of the medication, and did not cause harm or extend the stay in the facility.

1—The reaction caused no harm to the patient but required a significant reduction in dosage, or discontinuation of the medication, and required treatment or caused an extension of stay in the facility.

2—The reaction contributed to or resulted in temporary harm to the patient and required initial or prolonged hospitalization.

3—The reaction contributed to or resulted in permanent patient harm or disability.

4—The reaction required intervention necessary to sustain life.

5—The reaction contributed to or resulted in the patient's death.

ADR Preventability Assessment

Although many ADRs are unexpected and unavoidable, some may be preventable. The questions in Table 21-2 may be helpful in assessing the preventability of ADRs. If the answer is "Yes" to any question, the reaction may have been preventable or avoidable.

ADR Report Summaries

Summarizing reported ADRs by medication, description of reaction, classification, severity, preventability, and action taken can be helpful in identifying trends (e.g., medications most often associated with ADRs and the numbers and severity of specific reactions). Examples 4-32 and 4-33 are forms for summarizing ADRs.

ADR Rate Calculations and Comparisons

Although it is difficult to compare ADR rates across organizations (because of variability in ADR definitions, types of patients, and types of medications used), a comparison of rates over time within one organization can be valuable. Rates are often expressed as a percentage of total admissions and may reflect one or more of the following:

- Reported (including suspected) reactions
- Confirmed reactions
- Serious reactions
- Reactions involving selected medications (i.e., those responsible for the highest percentages of confirmed reactions in the organization such as morphine and cytotoxic agents)

Some organizations measure the success of their ADR reporting program by the number of ADRs detected and reported. However, numbers alone are not reliable indicators of quality. Furthermore, there are no "national," "standard," or "acceptable" ADR rates against which an organization can compare its ADR rate. Comparison of ADR rates between organizations is meaningless because there are too many variables (e.g., organization size, type, patient mix, and employee culture; and types of medications used, frequency of use, and ADR definition). For example, some organizations may have a high census of patients who are hypersensitive to medications; other organizations may have a high use of medications that are associated frequently with ADRs. Furthermore, high rates can mean that many ADRs occurred—or that the organization has an excellent process for detecting and reporting ADRs; low rates can mean that only a few ADRs occurred—or that ADRs were not detected and reported. An organization's rate may be significantly higher or lower than rates reported by other organizations.

As there are no standard ADR rates, an organization should establish its own benchmark rate. This can best be done after a 1- or 2-year trend analysis (i.e., an evaluation of the type and seriousness of the ADRs). The rate in an organization should reflect the organization's patient characteristics, types of medications used, and the organization's definition of reactions that must be reported.

An analysis of changes in rates should consider variables that can influence the number of occurrences and distort the ADR rate. They might include changes in patient mix, changes in services offered, numbers of new medications used, numbers of medications in clinical trials, and different emphases on reporting. Example 4-33 can be used to compare ADR rates and the numbers and types of ADRs. An organization should periodically review its ADR program to ensure effective detection and reliable reporting (e.g., by determining if low rates are due to failure to report ADRs).

ADR Reports to the FDA

The FDA requires extensive drug testing (premarketing trials) prior to granting marketing approval. Because these tests are conducted frequently on young, healthy individuals for a short period of time, the nature, severity, and frequency of ADRs may not be evident during premarketing trials.

ADR Postmarketing Reports—In contrast to premarketing trials, postmarketing use of a medication may involve millions of patients of all ages and states of health. The FDA relies on postmarketing reports from manufacturers and health care professionals to increase its database on ADRs. Well-documented ADR reports lead to the addition of previously unreported or unnoted ADRs to the package insert, publicity to health care professionals (e.g., on the FDA's Web site) (*see* Appendix), and, if necessary, recall of dangerous medications. Manufacturers, who are required to report adverse reactions, provide most postmarketing reports. Health care professionals, including pharmacists, physicians, and nurses, may submit reports voluntarily.

MedWatch Program—The FDA has established MedWatch for voluntary reporting by health professionals of serious adverse events (including ADRs) and product problems.[1] See the ADR Definitions section in this chapter for the FDA's definition of an ADR.

The FDA encourages health care professionals to report their adverse experiences with the following:

- Medications (drugs or biologicals)
- Medical devices (including in vitro diagnostics)
- Combination products (medication and medical devices)
- Special nutritional products (dietary supplements, medical foods, and infant formulas)
- Other products regulated by FDA

Health care professionals are also encouraged to report their quality, performance, or safety concerns related to products. Examples of product problems include, but are not limited to, the following:

- Suspected contamination
- Suspected counterfeit product
- Questionable stability
- Defective components
- Therapeutic failures
- Product confusion (caused by name, labeling, design, or packaging)
- Suspected super potent or subpotent medication
- Labeling problems caused by printing errors/omissions

The FDA encourages reports even if it is uncertain that the product caused the event and not all details are known.

MedWatch Confidentiality—The FDA holds the patient's identity in strict confidence. The FDA will share the reporter's identity with the manufacturer unless requested otherwise. Reporters can indicate on the report form that their identities are not to be released to the manufacturer. The FDA will not disclose the reporter's identity in response to a request from the public.

MedWatch Voluntary Reporting of Adverse Events to the FDA—Written reports of serious ADRs and other serious events should be made to the FDA MedWatch program on FDA Form 3500. (*See* Example 4-29.) Reports can be mailed, faxed, telephoned, or submitted online to the FDA. (*See* Appendix.) If ADRs are also reported to the manufacturer, this fact should be noted on FDA Form 3500 so that duplicate reports can be identified.

MedWatch Mandatory Reporting of Suspected Device-Related Deaths and Serious Injuries to the FDA—Risk managers and other personnel within user facilities (e.g., hospitals and nursing homes) are legally required to report suspected medical device-related deaths to both the FDA and the manufacturer, if known, and serious injuries to the manufacturer or to the FDA, if the manufacturer is unknown. Reports of suspected device-related deaths and serious injuries must be made in writing on FDA Form 3500A. (*See* Example 4-31.)

Pharmacies that provide or support infusion devices for patients must be aware of their proper use and how to detect problems. Where it is probable that a manufacturer's defect or problem has caused or contributed to death or serious illness or injury, the facility must report the information to the manufacturer within 10 days and must annually inform the FDA of all such reports that have been sent. If the manufacturer is unknown, the reports must be made directly to the FDA. Further information is available at the MedWatch Web site. (*See* Appendix.)

MedWatch Information Resource—You can obtain up-to-date MedWatch information (including FDA Forms 3500 and 3500A) from the MedWatch Web site. (*See* Appendix.)

Vaccine Adverse Events Reporting System (VAERS)

The FDA requires persons who administer selected vaccines to report specified adverse events. Adverse events that must be reported under the Vaccine Adverse Events Reporting System (VAERS) are those related to administration of diphtheria, tetanus, pertussis, polio, measles, mumps, rubella, hepatitis B, hemophilus influenzae, varicella, rotavirus, pneumococcal, hepatitis A, and influenza vaccines.[4] A complete list of the vaccines is available on the VAERS Web site. (*See* Appendix.) The VAERS also accepts all reports of suspected adverse events, in all age groups, after the administration of any U.S. licensed vaccine.

Adverse events and product problems that occur with vaccines should not be reported to the MedWatch program or on the MedWatch form but should be sent to the VAERS. (*See* Appendix.) Form VAERS-1 is used to report these events. (*See* Example 4-30.)

VAERS Information Resource—Up-to-date VAERS information (including Form VAERS-1) is available on the VAERS Web site and MedWatch Web site. You can also contact VAERS by telephone. (*See* Appendix.)

Vaccine Information Statements—The Public Health Service (PHS) Centers for Disease Control and Prevention (CDC) requires organizations to provide relevant information to any adult to whom the vaccine is to be administered and to the legal representative of any child to whom the vaccine is to be administered. Your organization may develop its own information materials or obtain them from the PHS or vaccine manufacturers. Information materials developed by the organization must meet PHS requirements. The CDC provides Vaccine Information Statements (VIS) on its Web site. (*See* Chapter 8 and Appendix.)

ADR Publishing

ADRs are often published in the literature before they are published by the FDA or are incorporated into the package insert. Furthermore, many ADRs never appear in FDA material. To ensure widespread dissemination of ADR information, pharmacists and other health care professionals should report serious, unusual, and unexpected reactions to the pharmacy literature.

Table 21-1. Naranjo Algorithm for Estimating the Probability of Adverse Drug Reactions

Drug	Yes	No	Not Known	Score
1. Are there previous *conclusive* reports on this reaction?	+1	0	0	
2. Did the adverse event appear after the suspected drug was administered?	+2	-1	0	
3. Did the adverse reaction improve when the drug was discontinued or a *specific* antagonist was administered?	+1	0	0	
4. Did the adverse reaction reappear when the drug was readministered?	+2	-1	0	
5. Are there alternative causes (other than the drug) that could on their own have caused the reaction?	-1	+2	0	
6. Did the reaction reappear when a placebo was given?	-1	+1	0	
7. Was the drug detected in the blood (or other fluids) in concentrations known to be toxic?	+1	0	0	
8. Was the reaction more severe when the dose was increased, or less severe when the dose was decreased?	+1	0	0	
9. Did the patient have a similar reaction to the same or similar drugs in *any* previous exposure?	+1	0	0	
10. Was the adverse event confirmed by any objective evidence?	+1	0	0	
			TOTAL SCORE	

$\geq$ 9 = Definite 5–8 = Probable 1–4 = Possible $\leq$ 0 = Doubtful

Source: Naranjo CA, Busto U, Sellers EM, et al. A method for estimating the probability of adverse drug reactions. *Clin Pharmacol Ther.* 1981; 30:239–45.

Table 21-2. Assessing the Preventability of Adverse Drug Reactions

1.	Yes____	No____	Was the medication(s) involved ***not*** appropriate for the patient's condition?
2.	Yes____	No____	Was the dose, route, or frequency of administration ***not*** appropriate for the patient's age, weight, lab tests, or disease state?
3.	Yes____	No____	Was required therapeutic drug monitoring or other necessary laboratory test(s) ***not*** performed or ***not*** performed frequently enough?
4.	Yes____	No____	Did the patient have a history of allergy or previous reaction to the medication?
5.	Yes____	No____	Was a known interaction the suspected cause of the reaction?
6.	Yes____	No____	Was the serum drug concentration above the therapeutic range documented?
7.	Yes____	No____	Was noncompliance associated with the reaction (for outpatient only)?
8.	Yes____	No____	Was a medication error associated with the reaction?

Source: Adapted from Almut G. Winterstein et al. Identifying clinically significant preventable adverse drug events through a hospital's database of adverse drug reaction reports. *Am J Health-Syst Pharm.* 2002; 59:1742–9.

CHAPTER 22

Centers for Medicare and Medicaid Services (CMS) Surveys

Organizations that are not accredited by The Joint Commission, the Healthcare Facilities Accreditation Program (HFAP) of the American Osteopathic Association (AOA), or the National Integrated Accreditation for Healthcare Organizations (NIAHO^{SM}) program of Det Norske Veritas (DNV) Healthcare Incorporated must meet federal Conditions of Participation of the Centers for Medicare and Medicaid Services (CMS) to be certified to participate in the federal Medicare program.[1] This chapter provides information and suggestions for meeting each medication-related Condition of Participation (CoP).

> ***Note:*** CMS CoPs and related information are found in the Federal Register at the CMS Web site. (*See* Appendix.)

CMS Conditions of Participation and Standards

Each CoP consists of one or more standards that define the requirements for compliance. Organizations do not need to comply with all standards to comply with a CoP. However, they must comply with all CoPs to be certified. Certification of a facility's compliance with each CoP is accomplished through observations, interviews, and document/record reviews.

> ***Note:*** CMS *certifies*; The Joint Commission, HFAP, and NIAHO *accredit*. Either CMS certification or Joint Commission, HFAP, or NIAHO accreditation qualifies the organization to participate in the Medicare program. (*See* Chapter 1.)

The standards take into consideration that health care organizations and departments within organizations are subject to state and federal laws and undergo substantial state inspection through licensure programs (hospital, pharmacy, fire and safety, health department, etc.). Therefore, CMS standards encourage practices in accordance with generally recognized principles and avoid conflict with state and federal laws, state licensure requirements, and Joint Commission, HFAP, and NIAHO standards.

Although CMS CoPs and standards are uniform throughout the country, interpretation and stringency of application vary considerably from state to state. However, if the pharmacy meets state board of pharmacy rules and regulations and practices are generally in accordance with accreditation (i.e., The Joint Commission, HFAP, NIAHO) standards, it should be compliant with CMS CoPs in most states.

CMS Interpretive Guidelines

Each CoP contains general requirements and expectations. In most cases, interpretive guidelines immediately follow each CoP. The guidelines contain additional information and in many instances state what is required to demonstrate compliance with the CoPs.

CMS Survey Procedures—In most cases, survey procedures follow the interpretive guidelines for each CoP. Survey procedures give surveyors information on how to conduct that portion of the survey and how to measure compliance with a CoP and its standards. When preparing for a survey, the pharmacy should review the interpretive guidelines and survey procedures to determine the surveyors' expectations.

CMS Surveys

Regular CMS surveys are conducted periodically (e.g., annually) and are unannounced. Surveys are usually conducted Monday through Friday during normal (daytime) working hours. Surveyors may conduct portions of the survey outside normal working hours and will modify the survey agenda to fit staffs' schedules and patients' activities.

CMS Validation Surveys—CMS selects a small percentage (usually about 5%) of Joint Commission, HFAP, and NIAHO accredited organizations to undergo validation surveys. Validation surveys are conducted to ensure that accreditation surveys are equivalent to CMS surveys and CoPs are met. A validation survey is usually conducted shortly after a Joint Commission, HFAP, or NIAHO survey.

CMS Surveyors

CMS surveys are conducted by a state agency (often the state health department) under contract to CMS. The size and composition of survey teams and the length of surveys vary from state to state. The survey is conducted under the leadership of a team coordinator. Each survey team includes at least one registered nurse with survey experience as well as other surveyors (e.g., physician, administrator, pharmacist, and laboratory technologist) who have the expertise needed to determine whether an organization is in compliance.

Note: A typical survey team for a full survey of a mid-sized organization would include two to four surveyors who would be onsite at the facility for 3 or more days.

CMS Survey Documents

The following documents are often requested on the first morning of most surveys:

- A current list of inpatients, including patients' names, room numbers, diagnosis(es), admission date, age, attending physician, and other significant information
- A list of department heads, their locations, and telephone numbers
- A copy of the facility's organizational chart
- Names and addresses of all off-site locations operating under the same provider number
- The organization's infection control plan
- A list of employees
- Medical staff bylaws and rules and regulations
- Policy and procedure manuals
- A list of contracted services
- A copy of the organization's floor plan, including location of patient care and treatment areas

Note: Whenever possible, surveyors will review the records of patients who are in the facility during the survey (i.e., open records). Open records allow surveyors to conduct a patient-focused survey and enable surveyors to validate information obtained through record reviews with observations and patient and staff interviews. Surveyors will select patients who represent a cross-section of the patient population and the services provided.

Note: Some surveyors base the sample size of patient records on the organization's average daily census (ADC). The sample size is at least 10% of the ADC but not less than 30 inpatient records. In hospitals with an ADC of fewer than 20 patients, the sample size should not be fewer than 20 inpatient records. The sample will include at least one patient selected from each patient care area (e.g., emergency department, ICU, OB, pediatrics, medical/surgical, and specialty units).

CMS Conditions and Standards Compliance

The following information is adapted from pharmacy CoPs that were in effect in 2009. Also included are pharmacy-related CoPs (e.g., nursing services—preparation and administration of drugs), standards, and interpretive guidelines that specifically apply to pharmacy (e.g., Quality Assessment and Performance Improvement, Physical Environment, Infection Control, and Nuclear Medicine). Conditions, standards, and interpretive guidelines are subject to change. The pharmacy should obtain a current edition of the CoPs prior to the survey.

Numbers with upper-case letters are data tag numbers (i.e., A-0490 is the tag number for the condition for pharmaceutical services). Each condition and standard has a unique tag number. Numbers without letters in the suffix are conditions (i.e., §482.25 is the condition of participation for pharmaceutical services). Numbers with lower-case letters in the suffix are standards; for example, §482.25(a) and §482.25(a)(1) are standards for condition §482.25. Authors' comments are in italics and reflect their suggestions and experiences or provide clarification.

A-0490

§482.25 Condition of Participation: Pharmaceutical Services

The hospital must have pharmaceutical services that meet the needs of the patients. The institution must have a pharmacy directed by a registered pharmacist or a drug storage area under competent supervision. The medical staff is responsible for developing policies and procedures that minimize drug errors. This function may be delegated to the hospital's organized pharmaceutical service.

Authors' Comment: *Although the standards stress the need for pharmaceutical services, they do not require an organized pharmacy supervised on a day-to-day basis by a registered pharmacist. CMS continues to allow a drug storage area in lieu of a pharmacy, because that is the only way pharmacy services can be furnished in some small organizations. CMS does not believe that prescriptive federal regulations should be imposed on organizations that can meet this requirement in other ways that are consistent with federal and state laws and patient needs.*

Authors' Comment: *If the organization does not have an organized pharmacy service, surveyors look for medical staff policies and procedures that address the management of pharmaceuticals.*

Interpretive Guidelines §482.25

Provision of pharmaceutical services must meet the needs of the patients' therapeutic goal by promoting a safe medication use process that ensures optimal selection of medications, dose, dosage form, frequency, route, and duration of therapy and that substantially reduces or eliminates adverse drug events and duplication of treatment.

The hospital's pharmacy must be directed by a registered pharmacist. If a drug storage area is used instead of a pharmacy at any location providing pharmacy services that storage area must be under competent supervision in accordance with state and federal laws.

Pharmaceutical services would include:

- The procuring, manufacturing, compounding, packaging, dispensing, ordering, distributing, disposition, use, and administering of all medications, biologicals, chemicals, and the use of medication-related devices.
- Provision of medication-related information to hospital health care professionals and patients necessary to optimize therapeutic outcomes.
- Provision of pharmaceutical care. Pharmaceutical care is defined as the direct, responsible provision of medication-related care for the purpose of achieving definite outcomes that improve a patient's quality of life while minimizing patient risk.

Functions of pharmaceutical care are the following:

- Collection and organization of patient-specific information
- Determination of the presence of medication-therapy problems both potential and actual
- Summary of the patient's medication-related health care needs
- Identification and specification of pharmacotherapeutic goals
- Development of a pharmacotherapeutic regimen
- Implementation of a monitoring plan in collaboration with the patient, if applicable, and other health care professionals
- Monitoring the effects of the pharmacotherapeutic regimen
- Redesigning the regimen and monitoring plan as indicated

Medication errors are a substantial source of morbidity and mortality in the hospitalized setting. Therefore, the development of policies and procedures to minimize medication errors should be based on accepted professional principles; external alerts and proactive review of facility reported and reviewed adverse drug events. It is important to flag new types of mistakes and continually improve and refine things, based on what went wrong.

The hospital's medical staff must develop policies and procedures to minimize drug errors, but may delegate this function to the hospital's organized pharmaceutical service.

Policies and procedures to minimize drug errors should include:

- High-alert medications—dosing limits, administration guidelines, packaging, labeling, and storage
- Limiting the variety of medication-related devices and equipment. For example, limit the use of general-purpose infusion pumps to one type
- Availability of up-to-date medication information
- Availability of pharmacy expertise—pharmacist available on-call when pharmacy does not operate 24 hours a day
- Standardization of prescribing and communication practices to include:
    - Avoidance of dangerous abbreviations
    - All elements of the order—dose, strength, units (metric), route, frequency, and rate
    - Alert systems for look-like and sound-alike drug names
    - Use of facility-approved pre-printed order sheets whenever possible
- That orders to "resume previous orders" are prohibited

- A voluntary, non-punitive, reporting system to monitor and report adverse drug events (including medication errors and adverse drug reactions)
- The preparation, distribution, administration, and proper disposal of hazardous medications
- Drug recalls
- That patient-specific information is readily accessible to all individuals involved in provision of pharmaceutical care. The patient information must be sufficient to properly order, prepare, dispense, administer, and monitor medications as appropriate
- Identification of when weight-based dosing for pediatric populations is required
- Requirements for review and revision based on facility-generated reports of adverse drug events and Quality Assessment/Performance Improvement (QAPI) activities

Authors' Comment: *See CoP §482.21 in this chapter.*

The hospital should have policies and procedures to actively identify potential and actual adverse drug events. Proactive identification could include direct observation of medication administration, review of patient's clinical records, identification of patient signals that would warrant immediate review of patient's medication therapy, and implementation of medication use evaluation studies.

The hospital should have a means to incorporate external alerts and/or recommendations from national associations and governmental agencies for review and facility policy and procedure revision consideration. National associations could include Institute for Safe Medications Practice, National Coordinating Council for Medication Error Reporting and Prevention, and Joint Commission *Sentinel Event Alerts*. Governmental agencies may include Food and Drug Administration (FDA), MedWatch Program, and Agency for Health Care Research and Quality.

The hospital's pharmacy services must be integrated into its hospital-wide QAPI program.

Authors' Comment: *It is critical to demonstrate to surveyors that the facility has procedures in place that promote the safe use of medications and reduce the potential for adverse medication events. Throughout the survey, surveyors look for written policies that establish safeguards for the use of medications and evidence of compliance with those policies.*

Survey Procedures §482.25

- Interview the chief pharmacist or the individual delegated to fulfill the chief pharmacist's functions. Determine that either the medical staff has developed policies and procedures regarding the management of pharmaceuticals or that this function is fulfilled by the pharmacy service.
- Verify that the purpose of pharmaceutical policies and procedures is to minimize drug errors. Review the pharmaceutical policies and procedures, the hospital's formulary, and, if there is a Pharmacy and Therapeutics (P&T) Committee, the minutes of the committee meetings.
- Does a multidisciplinary committee composed of representatives from nursing, pharmacy, administration, and medicine develop policies and procedures?
- Are there policies and procedures to minimize drug errors?
- Are policies and procedures reviewed and amended based on:
  - Facility-generated reports of adverse drug events
  - Facility QAPI activities pertaining to pharmaceutical care
  - Evaluation of external alerts and/or recommendations from national associations
  - Evaluation of literature for new technologies or successful practices that have demonstrated enhanced medication safety in other organizations
- Is the staff familiar with the medication-related policies and procedures?
- Is there a method to periodically review and evaluate the actual implementation of pharmaceutical policies and procedures by staff?
- Upon review of patient clinical record, are issues with regard to provision of pharmaceutical services identified? Is the facility aware of the issues? Was there a failure to implement a policy and procedure?
- Are pharmacists an integral component of pharmaceutical care?
- Verify that the hospital's pharmacy services are integrated into its hospital-wide QAPI program.

A-0491

§482.25(a) Standard: Pharmacy Management and Administration

The pharmacy or drug storage area must be administered in accordance with accepted professional principles.

Authors' Comment: *Surveyors review policies and procedures and records of medication receipt and dispensing and examine medication storage areas to ensure that practices conform to state law and professional standards. Surveyors specifically look for evidence of inspections of medication storage areas as well as an established medication recall procedure.*

Interpretive Guidelines §482.25(a)

The hospital may utilize a unit-dose system, individual prescription, floor stock system, or a combination of these systems, properly stored.

Pharmaceutical services must be administered in accordance with accepted professional principles. Accepted professional principles include compliance with applicable federal and state laws, regulations, and guidelines governing pharmaceutical services as well as standards or recommendations promoted by nationally recognized professional organizations. Agencies and organizations could include FDA, National Institute of Health (NIH), American Society of Health-System Pharmacists (ASHP), etc.

A fundamental purpose of pharmaceutical services is to ensure the safe and appropriate use of medications and medication-related devices. The pharmacy director, with input from appropriate hospital staff and committees, develops, implements, and periodically reviews and revises policies and procedures governing provision of pharmaceutical services.

Methods that a hospital may use to maintain professional principles include:

- Policies and procedures have been developed and are being followed
- Drugs and biologicals are stored in accordance with manufacturer's directions and state and federal requirements
- Employees provide pharmaceutical services within their scope of license and education
- Pharmacy records have sufficient detail to follow the flow of pharmaceuticals from their entry into the hospital through dispensation/administration
- Maintaining controls over drugs and medications, including the floor stock and those of the pharmacy or drug room
- Maintaining pharmacy and accounting records pertaining to the requisitioning and dispensing of drugs and pharmaceutical supplies
- Ensuring that drugs are being dispensed only by a licensed pharmacist
- Only pharmacists or pharmacy-supervised personnel compound, label, and dispense drugs or biologicals

Survey Procedures §482.25(a)

- Are the policies and procedures consistent with accepted professional principles?
- Determine that professional principles are maintained by verifying that:
  - Policies and procedures have been developed and are being followed
  - Drugs and biologicals are stored in accordance with manufacturers directions and state and federal requirements
  - Records have sufficient detail to follow the flow of control from entry through dispensation
  - Employees provide pharmaceutical services within their scope of license and education
- Does the hospital have a means to incorporate external alerts and/or recommendations from national associations and governmental agencies for review and facility policy and procedure revision consideration?
- Are policies developed to promote consistent application of pharmaceutical services and care throughout the hospital?
- Is the pharmacy director periodically monitoring implementation of policies and procedures?
- Are policies and procedures reviewed and revised as warranted?
- Are services provided in a manner consistent with accepted professional principles?
- Is the pharmacy responsible for the procurement, distribution, and control of all medication products used in the hospital (including medication-related devices) for inpatient and outpatient care?

A-0492

§482.25(a)(1) A full-time, part-time, or consulting pharmacist must be responsible for developing, supervising, and coordinating all the activities of the pharmacy services.

Authors' Comment: *A designated individual must be responsible for the day-to-day operation of the pharmacy. That person does not have to be on the premises; however, surveyors look for evidence (e.g., schedules and time logs) of regularly scheduled visits. Surveyors also review job descriptions or written agreements to ensure that this pharmacist's responsibilities are clearly defined and include development, supervision, and coordination of all pharmacy services.*

Interpretive Guidelines §482.25(a)(1)

Direction of pharmaceutical services may not require continuous on-premise supervision at the hospital's single pharmacy or at any pharmacy location but may be accomplished through regularly scheduled visits and/or telemedicine in accordance with federal and state law and regulation and accepted professional principles.

A single pharmacist must be responsible for the overall administration of the pharmacy service and must be responsible for developing, supervising, and coordinating all the activities of the hospital-wide pharmacy service.

The job description or the written agreement for the responsibilities of the pharmacist should be clearly defined and include development, supervision, and coordination of all the activities of pharmacy services.

A professional, competent, legally qualified pharmacist must manage the pharmacy. The director of pharmacy service must be thoroughly knowledgeable about hospital pharmacy practice and management.

Pharmacists and pharmacy technicians must perform their duties within the scope of their license and education.

The pharmacy director should be actively involved in those committees responsible for establishing medication-related policies and procedures.

Survey Procedures §482.25(a)(1)

- Determine whether the pharmacist is a full-time or part-time employee or employed on a consultative basis.
- Review the implementation of the chief pharmacist's responsibilities by:
  - Reviewing written status reports
  - Reviewing minutes of meetings (if any) with facility staff regarding pharmaceutical services
  - Reviewing schedules, time logs, etc.
  - Reviewing the job description or the written agreement to see that the responsibilities of the pharmacist are clearly defined and include development supervision and coordination of all the activities of pharmacy services
  - Determining whether the pharmacy director routinely evaluates the performance and competency of pharmacy personnel. Do performance evaluations include high-risk activities such as the compounding of hazardous medications, pharmacy-based prescriptive activities (e.g., aminoglycoside protocols), and pharmaceutical care for high-risk patients (pediatric, ICU, geriatric etc.)?
  - Determine whether the pharmacy director is actively involved in those committees responsible for establishing medication-related policies and procedures

A-0493

§482.25(a)(2) The pharmaceutical service must have an adequate number of personnel to ensure quality pharmaceutical services, including emergency services.

Authors' Comment: *CMS does not establish minimum staffing levels for pharmaceutical services. Surveyors expect pharmacy staff to be adequate in terms of training, education, and licensure as well as number. Pharmaceutical services must be available at all times, even when a pharmacist is not present. Policies and procedures must address the provision of pharmaceutical services in the absence of a pharmacist.*

Interpretive Guidelines §482.25(a)(2)

There must be sufficient personnel to respond to the pharmaceutical needs of the patient population being served.

The pharmaceutical services staff must be sufficient in types, numbers, and training to provide quality services, including 24 hour, 7-day emergency coverage, or there is an arrangement for emergency services, as determined by the needs of the patients and as specified by the medical staff.

The number of pharmacists and/or the number of hours of services provided by pharmacists at the hospital, or at each location of the hospital that provides pharmaceutical services, must meet and be in accordance with the needs of its patients and accepted professional principles (as previously defined) and reflect the scope and complexity of the hospital's pharmaceutical services.

There must be sufficient numbers and types of personnel to provide accurate and timely medication delivery, ensure accurate and safe medication administration, and provide appropriate clinical services as well as the participation in continuous quality improvement programs that meet the needs of the patient population being served.

Survey Procedures §482.25(a)(2)

- Determine that the pharmaceutical services staff is sufficient in number and training to provide quality services, including 24 hour, 7-day emergency coverage, or there is an arrangement for emergency services, as determined by the needs of the patients and as specified by the medical staff.
- Determine if there are sufficient personnel to provide accurate and timely medication delivery, ensure accurate and safe medication administration, and provide appropriate clinical services as well as the participation in continuous quality improvement programs that meet the needs of the patient population being served.

A-0494

§482.25(a)(3) Current and accurate records must be kept of the receipt and disposition of all scheduled drugs.

Authors' Comment: *A complete audit trail for all controlled substances from receipt to disposition is required. Surveyors spot-check records of medication use and inventory to ensure that medications are accounted for; they also interview pharmacy staff to determine their knowledge of policies on handling controlled substances.*

Authors' Comment: *Surveyors expect the organization to have policies and procedures in place to minimize diversion of Schedule I, II, III, IV, and V medications.*

Authors' Comment: *Wastage and destruction of controlled substances must be witnessed and properly documented in accordance with state and federal regulations and the organization's policy. Organizations should be particularly attentive to documentation of waste and destruction of controlled substances patches, patient controlled analgesia (PCA), epidurals, and other controlled substances infusions.*

Interpretive Guidelines §482.25(a)(3)

Components of a record system to maintain current and accurate records of the receipt and disposition of scheduled drugs would include:

- Accountability procedures to ensure control of the distribution, use, and disposition of all scheduled drugs.
- Records of the receipt and disposition of all scheduled drugs must be current and must be accurate.
- Records trace the movement of scheduled drugs throughout the service.
- The pharmacist is responsible for determining that all drug records are in order and that an account of all scheduled drugs is maintained and reconciled.
- The record system, delineated in policies and procedures, tracks movement of all scheduled drugs from the point of entry into the hospital to the point of departure either through administration to the patient, destruction, or return to the manufacturer. This system provides documentation on scheduled drugs in a readily retrievable manner to facilitate reconciliation of the receipt and disposition of all scheduled drugs.
- All drug records are in order and an account of all scheduled drugs is maintained, and any discrepancies in count are reconciled promptly.
- The hospital system is capable of readily identifying loss or diversion of all controlled substances in such a manner as to minimize the time frame between the actual loss or diversion to the time of detection and determination of the extent of loss or diversion.
- Facility policies and procedures should minimize scheduled drug diversion.

Survey Procedures §482.25(a)(3)

- Determine if there is a record system in place that provides information on controlled substances in a readily retrievable manner.
- Review the records to determine that they trace the movement of scheduled drugs throughout the service.
- Determine if there is a system, delineated in policies and procedures, that tracks movement of all scheduled drugs from the point of entry into the hospital to the point of departure either through administration to the patient, destruction, or return to the manufacturer. Determine if this system provides documentation on scheduled drugs in a readily retrievable manner to facilitate reconciliation of the receipt and disposition of all scheduled drugs.
- Determine if the pharmacist is responsible for determining that all drug records are in order and that an account of all scheduled drugs is maintained and periodically reconciled.
- Is the hospital system capable of readily identifying loss or diversion of all controlled substances in such a manner as to minimize the time frame between the actual losses or diversion to the time of detection and determination of the extent of loss or diversion?
- Determine if facility policy and procedures minimize scheduled drug diversion.

A-0500

§482.25(b) Standard: Delivery of Services

In order to provide patient safety, drugs and biologicals must be controlled and distributed in accordance with applicable standards of practice, consistent with federal and state law.

Authors' Comment: *Surveyors interview pharmacy staff and the organization's staff, observe dispensing procedures, and review pharmacy records to verify that this standard is met.*

Authors' Comment: *Some surveyors state that unit-dose medication distribution systems help to minimize the potential for medication errors and provide a more efficient process to provide patient care.*

Interpretive Guidelines §482.25(b)

Drugs and biologicals must be controlled and distributed in accordance with applicable federal and state laws and regulations and in accordance with applicable standards of practice. Applicable standards of practice include compliance with all federal and state laws, regulations, and guidelines as well as standards and recommendations promoted by nationally recognized professional organizations that apply to pharmaceutical care and the control and distribution of drugs and biologicals.

The procedures established to prevent unauthorized usage and distribution must provide for an accounting of the receipt and disposition of drugs subject to the Comprehensive Drug Abuse Prevention and Control Act of 1970.

The pharmacist, in consultation with appropriate hospital staff and committees, is to develop and implement guidelines, protocols, policies, and procedures for the provision of pharmaceutical services that ensure patient safety through the appropriate control and distribution of medications, medication-related devices, and biologicals.

For high-risk medications and high-risk patients (pediatric, geriatric or patients with renal or hepatic impairment), there should be systems in place to minimize adverse drug events. Such systems could include, but not be limited to, checklists, dose limits, pre-printed orders, special packaging, special labeling, double-checks, and written guidelines. "**High risk medications**" are those medications involved in a high percentage of medication errors and/or sentinel events and medications that carry a higher risk for abuse, errors, or other adverse outcomes. Lists of high-risk or high-alert drugs are available from such organizations as the Institute for Safe Medication Practices (ISMP) and the United States Pharmacopeia (USP). Examples of high-risk drugs may include investigational drugs, controlled medications, medications not on the approved FDA list, medications with a narrow therapeutic range, psychotherapeutic medications and look-alike/sound-alike medications, and those new to the market or new to the hospital.

All medication orders (except in emergency situations) should be reviewed for appropriateness by a pharmacist before the first dose is dispensed.

Review of medication orders should include:

- Therapeutic appropriateness of a patient's medication regimen
- Therapeutic duplication in the patient's medication regimen
- Appropriateness of the drug, dose, frequency, route, and method of administration
- Real or potential medication–medication, medication–food, medication–laboratory test, and medication–disease interactions

- Real or potential allergies or sensitivities
- Variation from organizational criteria for use
- Other contraindications

The effects of medication(s) on patients are monitored to assure medication therapy is appropriate and minimizes the occurrence of adverse events. That monitoring process includes:

- Clinical and laboratory data to evaluate the efficacy of medication therapy to anticipate or evaluate toxicity and adverse effects
- Physical signs and clinical symptoms relevant to the patient's medication therapy
- Assessing the patient's own perceptions about side effects, and, when appropriate, perceived efficacy

Sterile products should be prepared and labeled in a suitable environment by appropriately trained and qualified personnel.

The pharmacy should participate in hospital decisions about emergency medication kits. The supply and provision of emergency medications stored in the kits must be consistent with standards of practice and appropriate for a specified age group or disease treatment as well as consistent with applicable federal and state laws.

The pharmacy should be involved in the evaluation, use, and monitoring of drug delivery systems, administration devices, and automated drug-dispensing machines. The evaluation and monitoring should include the potential for medication errors.

There must be a process to report serious adverse drug reactions to the FDA in accordance with the MedWatch program.

There is a policy that addresses the use of medications brought into the hospital by patients or their families.

There is a process and policy to ensure that investigational medications are safety controlled and administered. Procedures for the use of investigational medications include the following: A written process for reviewing, approving, supervising, and monitoring investigational medications specifying that when pharmacy services are provided, the pharmacy controls the storage, dispensing, labeling, and distribution of the investigational medication.

Medications dispensed by the hospital are retrieved when recalled or discontinued by the manufacturer or the Food and Drug Administration (FDA) for safety reasons.

The hospital pharmacy must ensure that medication orders are accurate and that medications are administered as ordered. The pharmacy should have a system to reconcile medications that are not administered, that remain in the patient's medication drawer, slot, etc., when the pharmacy inventories patient medications or restocks patient medications. The pharmacy should determine the reason the medications were not used. For example, did the patient refuse the medication, was there a clinical or treatment reason the medication was not used, or was the medication not used due to an error?

Survey Procedures §482.25(b)

- Are there limits on the number of possible concentrations for a medication, particularly high-alert drugs like morphine and heparin?
- Is access to concentrated solutions (e.g., potassium chloride, sodium chloride solutions greater than 0.9%) restricted?
- Are questions regarding the order resolved with the prescriber and a written notation of these discussions documented in the patient's medical record or pharmacy copy of the prescriber's order?
- Identify and assess the quality assurance procedures for the preparation of sterile products.
- Is appropriate monitoring of medication therapy being conducted?
- Is the pharmacy involved in the evaluation, use, and monitoring of drug delivery systems, administration devices, and automated drug dispensing machines? The evaluation and monitoring should include the potential for medication errors.
- Is there a process to report serious adverse drug reactions to the federal MedWatch program?

Authors' Comment: *See Chapter 21—Adverse Drug Reactions.*

- Review the procedures established to prevent unauthorized usage and distribution. These procedures must provide for an accounting of the receipt and disposition of drugs subject to the Comprehensive Drug Abuse Prevention and Control Act of 1970.
- Are medication storage areas periodically inspected to make sure medications are properly stored?
- Does the hospital retrieve and remove medications available for patient use when the hospital has been informed of a drug recall? Does the recall include notification of patients who have been impacted and those who would order, dispense, or administer the medication?

A-0501

§482.25(b)(1) All compounding, packaging, and dispensing of drugs and biologicals must be under the supervision of a pharmacist and be performed consistent with state and federal laws.

Interpretive Guidelines §482.25(b)(1)

All compounding, packaging, and dispensing of drugs and biologicals must be conducted by a registered pharmacist or under the supervision of a registered pharmacist and be performed consistent with state and federal laws.

Medications must be prepared safely. Safe preparation procedures could include:

- Only the pharmacy compounds or admixes all sterile medications, intravenous admixtures, or other drugs except in emergencies or when not feasible (for example, when the product's stability is short).
- Whenever medications are prepared, staff use safety materials and equipment while preparing hazardous medications.
- Wherever medications are prepared, staff use techniques to assure accuracy in medication preparation.
- Whenever medications are prepared, staff use appropriate techniques to avoid contamination during medication preparation, which include but are not limited to the following:
  - Using clean or sterile technique as appropriate
  - Maintaining clean, uncluttered, and functionally separate areas for product preparation to minimize the possibility of contamination
  - Using a laminar airflow hood or other appropriate environment while preparing any intravenous (IV) admixture in the pharmacy, any sterile product made from non-sterile ingredients, or any sterile product that will not be used within 24 hours
  - Visually inspecting the integrity of the medications

Medications should be dispensed in a manner that is safe and meets the needs of the patient:

- Quantities of medications are dispensed, which minimize diversion and potential adverse events while meeting the needs of the patient.
- Medications are dispensed in a timely manner. The hospital must have a system that ensures that medication orders get to the pharmacy and medications get back to patients promptly.
- Whenever possible, medications are dispensed in the most ready-to-administer form available from the manufacturer or, if feasible, in unit doses that have been repackaged by the pharmacy.
- The hospital consistently uses the same dose packaging system, or, if a different system is used, provides education about the use of the dose packaging system.
- All concerns, issues, or questions are clarified with the individual prescriber before dispensing.

Authors' Comment: *Some surveyors look for evidence that the pharmacy is compliant with requirements of USP Chapter <797>.*

Authors' Comment: *See Chapter 19—Overview of the United States Pharmacopeia chapter <797>: Pharmaceutical compounding—Sterile Preparations.*

Survey Procedures §482.25(b)(1)

- Determine that only pharmacists or pharmacy supervised personnel compound, label, and dispense drugs or biologicals in accordance with state and federal laws and regulations and as accepted national principles by:
  - Reviewing policies and procedures
  - Interviewing pharmacy and hospital staff to determine how drugs and biologicals are prepared and dispensed
  - Observing on-site dispensing and compounding operations (if applicable)
  - Reviewing records of drugs and biologicals removed from the pharmacy by non-pharmacy personnel
  - Inspecting drug storage areas
- Verify through interviews of pharmacy and hospital staff, observation of on-site dispensing operations, inspection and review of hospital records that compounding, dispensing, and packaging of drugs and biologicals are performed under the supervision of a pharmacist, in accordance with applicable laws and in a manner to promote patient safety.

A-0502

§482.25(b)(2)(i) All drugs and biologicals must be kept in a secure area, and locked when appropriate.

Interpretive Guidelines §482.25(b)(2)(i)

A secure area means that drugs and biologicals are stored in a manner to prevent unmonitored access by unauthorized individuals. Drugs and biologicals must not be stored in areas that are readily accessible to unauthorized persons. For example, if medications are kept in a private office or other area where patients and visitors are not allowed without the supervision or presence of a health care professional (e.g., ambulatory infusion), they are considered secure. Areas restricted to authorized personnel only would generally be considered "secure areas." If there is evidence of tampering or diversion, or if medication security otherwise becomes a problem, the hospital is expected to evaluate its current medication control policies and procedures, and implement the necessary systems and processes to ensure that the problem is corrected and that patient health and safety are maintained. (71 FR 68689)

All controlled substances must be locked. Hospitals are permitted flexibility in the storage of non-controlled drugs and biologicals when delivering care to patients and in the safeguarding of drugs and biologicals to prevent tampering or diversion. An area in which staff are actively providing care to patients or preparing to receive patients (i.e., setting up for procedures before the arrival of a patient) would generally be considered a secure area. When a patient care area is not staffed, **both** controlled and non-controlled substances are expected to be locked.

Generally labor and delivery suites and critical care units are staffed and actively providing patient care around the clock, and, therefore, considered secure. However, hospital policies and procedures are expected to ensure that these areas are secure, with entry and exit limited to appropriate staff, patients, and visitors.

The operating room suite is considered secure when the suite is staffed and staff are actively providing patient care. When the suite is not in use (e.g., weekends, holidays, and after hours), it would not be considered secure. A hospital may choose to lock the entire suite, lock non-mobile carts containing drugs and biologicals, place mobile carts in a locked room, or otherwise lock drugs and biologicals in a secure area. If an individual operating room is not in use, the hospital is expected to lock non-mobile carts and ensure mobile carts are in a locked room. (71 FR 68689)

This regulation gives hospitals the flexibility to integrate patient self-administration of non-controlled drugs and biologicals into their practices as appropriate. When a hospital allows a patient to self-administer selected drugs and biologicals, the hospital authorizes the patient to have access to these medications. This regulation is consistent with the current practice of giving patients access at the bedside to urgently needed medications, such as nitroglycerine tablets and inhalers. It supports the current practice of placing selected nonprescription medications at the bedside for the patient's use, such as lotions and creams, and rewetting eye drops. Hospitals are expected to address patient self-administration of non-controlled drugs and biologicals in their policies and procedures. This regulation supports hospital development, in collaboration with the medical staff and the nursing and pharmacy departments, of formal patient medication self-administration programs for select populations of patients, including hospital policies and procedures necessary to ensure patient safety and security of medications. The policies and procedures are expected to include measures to ensure the security of bedside drugs and biologicals. They are also expected to address both the competence of the patient to self-administer drugs and biologicals as well as patient education regarding self-administration of drugs and biologicals. (71 FR 68689)

Due to their mobility, mobile nursing medication carts, anesthesia carts, epidural carts, and other medication carts containing drugs or biologicals (hereafter, all referred to as "carts") must be locked in a secure area when not in use. Hospital policies and procedures are expected to address the security and monitoring of carts, locked or unlocked, containing drugs and biologicals in all patient care areas to ensure their safe storage and to ensure patient safety. (71 FR 68689)

Medication automated distribution units with security features, such as logon and password or biometric identification, are considered to be locked, since they can only be accessed by authorized personnel who are permitted access to the medications. Such units must be stored in a secure area.

> ***Authors' Comment:*** *Organizations must have a written policy that defines "secure area." The policy should include a statement defining automated dispensing cabinets as secure areas.*

Survey Procedures §482.25(b)(2)(i)

- Review hospital policies and procedures governing the security of drugs and biologicals to determine whether they provide for securing and locking as appropriate.
- Review hospital policies and procedures governing patient self-administration of drugs and biologicals.

- Observe whether medications in various areas of the hospital are stored in a secure area, and locked when appropriate.
- Determine that security features in automated medication distributions units are implemented and actively maintained, e.g., that access authorizations are regularly updated to reflect changes in personnel, assignments, etc.
- Interview staff to determine whether policies and procedures to restrict access to authorized personnel are implemented and effective.
- Interview patients and staff to determine whether policies and procedures regarding patient self-administration of drugs and biologicals are implemented and effective.

A-0503

§482.25(b)(2)(ii) Drugs listed in Schedules II, III, IV, and V of the Comprehensive Drug Abuse Prevention and Control Act of 1970 must be kept locked within a secure area.

Interpretive Guidelines §482.25(b)(2)(ii)

All schedule II, III, IV, and V drugs must be kept locked within a secure area. A secure area means the drugs and biologicals are stored in a manner to prevent unmonitored access by unauthorized individuals. Medication automated distribution units with logon and password/biometric identification are considered to be locked, since they can only be accessed by authorized personnel who are permitted access to Schedule II–V medications.

Mobile nursing medication carts, anesthesia carts, epidural carts, and other medication carts containing Schedule II, III, IV, and V drugs must be locked within a secure area.

Survey Procedures §482.25(b)(2)(ii)

- Determine whether there is a hospital policy and procedure that requires Schedule II, III, IV, and V drugs to be kept in a locked storage area.
- Observe in various parts of the hospital whether Schedule II, III, IV, and V drugs are locked and stored in a secure area.
- Determine whether security features in automated medication distribution units are implemented and actively maintained, e.g., that access authorizations are regularly updated to reflect changes in personnel, assignments, etc.
- Interview staff to determine whether policies and procedures to restrict access to authorized personnel are implemented and effective.

A-0504

§482.25(b)(2)(iii) Only authorized personnel may have access to locked areas.

Interpretive Guidelines §482.25(b)(2)(iii)

The hospital must assure that only authorized personnel may have access to locked areas where drugs and biologicals are stored.

A hospital has the flexibility to define which personnel have access to locked areas, based on the hospital's needs as well as state and local law. For example, a hospital could include within its definition of "authorized personnel" ancillary support personnel, such as engineering, housekeeping staff, orderlies, and security personnel as necessary to perform their assigned duties. The hospital's policies and procedures must specifically address how "authorized personnel" are defined for purposes of this section. It is not necessary for the policy to name specific authorized individuals, but the policy should be clear in describing the categories of personnel who have authorized access as well as whether there are different levels of access authorized in different areas of the hospital, or at different times of day, or for different classes of drugs and biologicals, etc.

The hospital's policies and procedures must also address how it prevents unauthorized personnel from gaining access to locked areas where drugs and biologicals are stored. Whenever unauthorized personnel have access, or could gain access, to those locked areas, the hospital is not in compliance with this requirement and is expected to re-evaluate and tighten its security measures.

Survey Procedures §482.25(b)(2)(iii)

- Determine whether there is a hospital policy and procedure defining authorized personnel who are permitted access to locked areas where drugs and biologicals are stored.

- Determine whether there is a hospital policy and procedure for limiting access to locked storage areas to authorized personnel only.
- Observe whether or not access to locked storage areas is limited to personnel authorized by the hospital's policy.

Authors' Comment: *Surveyors look for a policy addressing the safeguarding, transferring, and availability of keys (or codes to electronic locks) to the locked storage area, particularly where a pharmacist is not on duty full time.*

A-0505

§482.25(b)(3) Outdated, mislabeled, or otherwise unusable drugs and biologicals must not be available for patient use.

Interpretive Guidelines §482.25(b)(3)

The hospital must have a pharmacy labeling, inspection, and inventory management system that ensures that outdated, mislabeled, or otherwise unusable drugs and biologicals are not available for patient use.

Survey Procedures §482.25(b)(3)

- Spot-check the labels of individual drug containers to verify that they conform to state laws and/or contain the following minimal information:
  - Each patient's individual drug container bears his/her full name, the prescriber's name, and strength and quantity of the drug dispensed. Appropriate accessory and cautionary statements are included as well as the expiration date.
  - Each floor stock container bears the name and strength of the drug, lot and control number or equivalent, and expiration date.
- If the unit-dose system is utilized, verify that each single unit-dose package bears the name and strength of the drug, lot and control number equivalent, and expiration date.
- Inspect patient-specific and floor stock medications to identify expired, mislabeled, or unusable medications.

A-0506

§482.25(b)(4) When a pharmacist is not available, drugs and biologicals must be removed from the pharmacy or storage area only by personnel designated in the policies of the medical staff and pharmaceutical service, in accordance with federal and state law.

Authors' Comment: *Designated individuals should be identified by name and qualifications in your pharmacy's policies and procedures, and the amount of medications(s) sufficient for immediate therapeutic needs that may be removed should be specified. Surveyors examine records of medications removed from the pharmacy by non-pharmacy personnel to verify compliance.*

Interpretive Guidelines §482.25(b)(4)

Routine after-hours access to the pharmacy by non-pharmacists for access to medication should be minimized and eliminated as much as possible. The use of well-designed night cabinets, after-hours medication carts, and other methods may preclude the need for a non-pharmacist to enter the pharmacy. Policies and procedures should be consistent with federal and state law.

If an urgent or emergent patient need occurs, the hospital must be able to provide medications to the patients in its facility.

The hospital must have a process for providing medications to meet patient needs when the pharmacy is closed.

When non-pharmacist health care professionals are allowed by law and regulation to obtain medications after the pharmacy is closed, the following safeguards are applied:

- Access is limited to a set of medications that has been approved by the hospital. These medications can be stored in a night cabinet, automated storage and distribution device, or a limited section of the pharmacy.
- Only trained, designated prescribers and nurses are permitted access to medications.
- Quality control procedures (such as an independent second check by another individual or a secondary verification built into the system, such as bar coding) are in place to prevent medication retrieval errors.

- The hospital arranges for a qualified pharmacist to be available either on-call or at another location (e.g., at another organization that has 24-hour pharmacy service) to answer questions or provide medications beyond those accessible to non-pharmacy staff.
- This process is evaluated on an on-going basis to determine the medications accessed routinely and the causes of accessing the pharmacy after hours.
- Changes are implemented as appropriate to reduce the amount of times non-pharmacist health care professionals are obtaining medications after the pharmacy is closed.

Survey Procedures §482.25(b)(4)

- Determine through pharmacy records that when the pharmacist is not available, drugs are removed from the pharmacy (drug storage area) only by a designated individual (in accordance with state law if applicable) and only in amounts sufficient for immediate therapeutic needs.
- Review policies and procedures to determine who is designated to remove drugs and biologicals from the pharmacy or storage area and the amount a non-pharmacist may remove in the absence of a pharmacist. The individual(s) designated should be identified by name and qualifications.
- Determine that a system is in place that accurately documents the removal of medications (type and quantity) from either the pharmacy or the after-hours supply.
- Determine that the pharmacist reviews all medication removal activity and correlates the removal with current medication orders in the patient medication profile.
- Determine if the pharmacist routinely reviews the contents of the after-hours supply to determine if it is adequate to meet the after-hours needs of the hospital.

A-0507

§482.25(b)(5) Drugs and biologicals not specifically prescribed as to time or number of doses must automatically be stopped after a reasonable time that is predetermined by the medical staff.

Authors' Comment: *CMS considers the extended use of any medication a risk to patient safety and thus requires the medical staff to set a reasonable time limit for all medications.*

Authors' Comment: *Surveyors look for automatic stop order policies and examine medication administration records to determine whether these policies are followed. Some surveyors suggest the following statement in an automatic stop order policy: "All orders for medications not specifically included in this policy shall be discontinued after (a specific number) days."*

Authors' Comment: *Some states mandate automatic stop orders for specific medications and types of agents.*

Interpretive Guidelines §482.25(b)(5)

In accordance with accepted standards of practice, the medical staff, in coordination and consultation with the pharmacy service, determines and establishes the reasonable time to automatically stop orders for drugs and biologicals not specifically prescribed as to time or number of doses. The hospital must implement, monitor, and enforce this automatic stop system.

Survey Procedures §482.25(b)(5)

- Review policies and procedures to determine that there is a protocol established by the medical staff to discontinue and review patients' medical records to determine compliance with stop-order policy.

A-0508

§482.25(b)(6) Drug administration errors, adverse drug reactions, and incompatibilities must be immediately reported to the attending physician and, if appropriate, to the hospital-wide quality assurance program.

Interpretive Guidelines §482.25(b)(6)

Drug administration errors, adverse drug reactions, and drug incompatibility must be immediately reported to the patient's attending physician, or when appropriate the covering physician. When the covering physician is notified due to the attending physician not being available, the patient's attending physician must be notified as soon as he/she is available. Additionally in accordance with the regulation and 482.21, the hospital must report drug administrative errors, adverse drug reactions, and drug incompatibilities to its hospital-wide QAPI program.

Reduction of medication errors and adverse reactions can be achieved by effective reporting systems that proactively identify causative factors and are used to implement corrective actions to reduce or prevent recurrences. To facilitate reporting, the facility should adopt a medication error and adverse drug reaction (ADR) definition that is broad enough in scope to capture "near misses" and suspected ADRs as well as actual medication errors and ADRs.

An example is the use of the National Coordinating Council Medication Error Reporting and Prevention definition of a medication error.

> "Any preventable event that may cause or lead to inappropriate medication use or patient harm while the medication is in the control of the health care professional, patient, or consumer. Such events may be related to professional practice, health care products, procedures, and systems, including prescribing; order communication; product labeling, packaging, and nomenclature; compounding; dispensing; distribution; administration; education; monitoring; and use."

When compared to the traditional definition of a medication error (right patient, right drug, right route, right time, right dose), all errors secondary to any aspect of medication utilization (including purchasing, ordering, dispensing, administrative, preparation, compounding, etc.) would be reported versus only those that occurred in the administration phase of medication utilization.

In addition to broad scope definitions, the facility must also proactively identify medication errors and adverse drug reactions. Reliance solely on incident reporting fails to identify the majority of adverse drug events. Proactive identification includes observation of medications passes; concurrent and retrospective review of patients' clinical records; ADR surveillance team; and implementation of medication usage evaluations for high-alert drugs and identification of indicator drugs or "patient signals" that, when ordered, or noted automatically generate a drug regimen review for a potential adverse drug event.

The facility must have a method by which to measure the effectiveness of their reporting system so as to identify whether or not their system(s) is identifying as many medication errors and adverse drug reactions that would be expected for the size and scope of services provided by their hospital. Such methods could include use of established benchmarks or studies on reporting rates published in peer-reviewed journals.

To improve incident reporting, the facility should adopt a non-punitive system with the focus on the system and not the involved health care professionals.

> ***Authors' Comment:*** *See Chapter 20—Medication Safety Improvement and Chapter 21—Adverse Drug Reactions.*

Survey Procedures §482.25(b)(6)

- Determine that the hospital has an effective procedure that ensures drug administration errors, adverse drug reactions, and drug incompatibilities are immediately reported to the attending physician.
- Review records of medication errors and adverse drug reactions to determine that they are reported immediately in accordance with written procedures, and that medications administered and/or drug reactions are promptly recorded in the patient's medical record.
- Is the facility's definition of an adverse drug reaction and medication error based on established benchmarks or studies on report rates published in peer-review journals? Is it identifying as many medication errors and adverse drug reactions as would be expected for the size and scope of services provided by the hospital?
- If upon review of patient's clinical records, a suspected ADR or medication error is identified, determine if it was reported immediately to the attending or on-call physician, in accordance with written procedures and that it was promptly recorded in the patient's medical record.
- Review QAPI activities for medication errors and adverse reaction reports to determine, if upon analyses of the reports, that potential corrective actions are identified and implemented, if appropriate.
- Determine if the number of medication errors and adverse drug reactions reported is consistent with the size and scope of services provided by the hospital.
- Interview facility staff (nursing, pharmacy, and medicine) to ascertain awareness of the facility's policy on reporting and documentation of medication errors and adverse drug reactions.

A-0509

§482.25(b)(7) Abuses and losses of controlled substances must be reported, in accordance with applicable federal and state laws, to the individual responsible for the pharmaceutical service and to the chief executive officer, as appropriate.

Authors' Comment: *Some surveyors review reports of abuses and losses to determine what action was taken to correct the situation.*

Survey Procedures §482.25(b)(7)

- Interview the pharmacists or pharmacy employees to determine their understanding of the controlled drug policies.
- Conduct a spot check of drug use and other inventory records to ensure that drugs are properly accounted for.
- Review reports of pharmaceutical services to determine if there are reported problems with controlled drugs and what actions have been taken to correct the situation.
- Interview the pharmacy director, pharmacist, and pharmacy employees to determine their understanding of the controlled drug policies. Is there a policy and procedure for handling controlled drug discrepancies?
- Review reports of pharmaceutical services to determine if there are reported problems with controlled drugs and what actions have been taken to correct the situation.
- Determine if controlled drug losses were reported to appropriate authorities in accordance with state and federal laws.

A-0510

§482.25(b)(8) Information relating to drug interactions and information on drug therapy, side effects, toxicology, dosage, indications for use, and routes of administration must be available to the professional staff.

Authors' Comment: *Surveyors determine whether staff development programs on medication therapy and new medications are offered and check references to be sure that they are current. Surveyors also expect a pharmacist to be readily available (e.g., by telephone) to discuss medication therapy with practitioners and assist in selection of medications and identification of adverse drug reactions.*

Interpretive Guidelines §482.25(b)(8)

The facility has immediately available sufficient texts and other resources on drug therapy. The pharmacist also should be readily available by telephone or other means to discuss drug therapy, interactions, side effects, dosage etc., with practitioners to assist in drug selection and with nursing personnel to assist in the identification of drug-induced problems.

Survey Procedures §482.25(b)(8)

- Examine the sources of drug information available at the nursing station and/or drug storage area and determine if they are current.
- Determine whether staff development programs on drug therapy are available to facility staff to cover such topics as new drugs added to the formulary, how to resolve drug therapy problems, and other general information as the need arises.

A-0511

§482.25(b)(9) A formulary system must be established by the medical staff to assure quality pharmaceuticals at reasonable costs.

Authors' Comment: *To meet this requirement, the formulary system should provide a mechanism for evaluating and selecting products and entities that are most useful and cost effective. A formulary (i.e., a compilation of medications approved for use in the organization) should be developed and continuously revised. Although CMS no longer requires a P&T Committee, the requirement that the medical staff establish a formulary system is best fulfilled by a P&T Committee.*

Authors' Comment: *See Chapter 13— Pharmacy and Therapeutics Activities.*

Interpretive Guidelines §482.25(b)(9)

The medical staff must establish a formulary system. The formulary lists medications for dispensing or administration that the hospital maintains or that are readily available. In accordance with accepted standards of practice, the medical staff, in consultation with the pharmacy service, should develop written criteria for determining what medications are available for dispensing or administration. At a minimum, the criteria include the indication for use, effectiveness, risks (including propensity for medication errors, abuse potential, and sentinel events), and costs.

Processes and mechanisms should be established to monitor patient responses to a newly added medication before the medication is made available for dispensing or administration within the hospital.

Medications designated as available for dispensing or administration are reviewed periodically based on emerging safety and efficacy information.

The hospital should have processes to approve and procure medications that are not on the hospital's medication list.

The hospital should have processes to address medication shortages and outages, including the following:

- Communicating with appropriate prescribers and staff
- Developing approved substitution protocols
- Educating appropriate licensed independent practitioners (LIPs), appropriate health care professionals, and staff about these protocols
- Obtaining medications in the event of a disaster

Survey Procedures §482.25(b)(9)

- Interview the pharmacist to determine that the medical staff has established a formulary that lists drugs that actually are available in the hospital.
- Interview the pharmacy director to determine that there is a process for creation and periodic review of a formulary system.
- Determine that the formulary lists drugs that are available.

A-0404

§482.23(c) Standard: Preparation and Administration of Drugs

§482.23(c) Drugs and biologicals must be prepared and administered in accordance with federal and state laws, the orders of the practitioner or practitioners responsible for the patient's care as specified under §482.12(c), and accepted standards of practice.

Interpretive Guidelines §482.23(c)

Drugs and biologicals must be prepared and administered in accordance with federal and state laws.

Drugs and biologicals must be prepared and administered in accordance with the orders of the practitioner(s) responsible for the patient's care as specified under §482.12(c).

Drugs and biologicals must be prepared and administered in accordance with accepted standards of practice.

Accepted standards of practice include maintaining compliance with applicable federal and state laws, regulations (including all the hospital Conditions of Participation [CoPs] such as Pharmacy, Medical Records, Patients' Rights, QAPI), and guidelines governing drug and biological use in hospitals as well as any standards and recommendations promoted by nationally recognized professional organizations.

Survey Procedures §482.23(c)

- Select patients from the patient sample. Review their medication orders, medication administration records, and appropriate medication documentation in the medical record. Observe the preparation and administration of medications to those patients.
- Are medications prepared and administered in accordance with federal and state laws, other hospital CoPs, accepted national standards of practice, manufacturers' directions, and hospital policy?

A-0405

§482.23(c)(1) All drugs and biologicals must be administered by, or under supervision of, nursing or other personnel in accordance with federal and state

laws and regulations, including applicable licensing requirements, and in accordance with the approved medical staff policies and procedures.

Survey Procedures §482.23(c)(1)

Verify that there is an effective method for the administration of drugs. Use the following indicators for assessing drug administration:

- Verify that there are policies and procedures approved by the medical staff covering who is authorized to administer medications, and that the policies are followed.
- Review a sample of medication administration records to see that they conform with the practitioner's order, that the order is current, and that drug and dosage are correct and administered as ordered.
- Observe the preparation of drugs and their administration to patients in order to verify that procedures are being followed. Are patients addressed by name and/or identiband checked? Does the nurse remain with the patient until medication is taken? Are drugs administered within 30 minutes of the scheduled time for administration?
- Verify that nursing or other personnel authorized by medical staff policy to administer drugs have completed appropriate training courses or are licensed or authorized to do so by state law and function under supervision as necessary.
- Check the QAPI activities to see if the administration of drugs is regularly monitored. The monitoring should include reports of medication irregularities or errors, their nature, frequency, and the corrective action taken.
- Interview supervisory nursing personnel to determine how supervision is provided. Also interview personnel who administer medication to verify that the supervision is, in fact, provided.
- Are personnel other than nursing personnel administering drugs or biologicals? If yes, determine if those personnel are administering drugs or biologicals in accordance with federal and state laws and regulations. Use the above procedures to determine compliance.

Authors' Comment: *The CMS surveyor procedures suggest that an indicator for assessing appropriate administration of drugs should include administration within 30 minutes of the scheduled time.*

A-0406

§482.23(c)(2) With the exception of influenza and pneumococcal polysaccharide vaccines, which may be administered per physician-approved hospital policy after an assessment of contraindications, orders for drugs and biologicals must be documented and signed by a practitioner who is authorized to write orders by hospital policy and in accordance with state law, and who is responsible for the care of the patient as specified under §482.12(c).

Authors' Comment: *See CoP §482.23(c)(2)(i) and CoP §482.23(c)(2)(ii) in this chapter.*

Interpretive Guidelines §482.23(c)(2)

All orders for drugs and biologicals, with the exception of influenza and pneumococcal polysaccharide vaccines, must be documented and signed by a practitioner who is authorized by hospital policy, and in accordance with state law, to write orders and who is responsible for the care of the patient as specified under §482.12(c). In accordance with §482.12(c)(1), practitioners who are authorized to provide care for Medicare patients include:

- A doctor of medicine or osteopathy
- A doctor of dental surgery or dental medicine
- A doctor of podiatric medicine, but only with respect to functions which he or she is legally authorized by the state to perform
- A doctor of optometry who is legally authorized to practice optometry by the state
- A chiropractor who is licensed by the state or legally authorized to perform the services of a chiropractor, but only with respect to treatment by means of manual manipulation of the spine to correct a subluxation demonstrated by x-ray to exist
- A clinical psychologist as defined in §410.71, but only with respect to clinical psychologist services as defined in §410.71 and only to the extent permitted by law

Consistent with delegation agreements, collaborative practice agreements, hospital policy, and the requirement of state law, nurse practitioners, and physician assistants responsible for the care of specific patients are also permitted to order drugs and biologicals.

Influenza and pneumococcal polysaccharide vaccines may be administered per physician-approved hospital policy after an assessment of contraindications.

In accordance with standard practice, elements that must be present in orders for all drugs and biologicals to ensure safe preparation and administration include:

- Name of patient (present on order sheet or prescription)
- Age and weight of patient, when applicable
- Date and time of the order
- Drug name
- Exact strength or concentration, when applicable
- Dose, frequency, and route
- Quantity and/or duration, when applicable
- Specific instructions for use, when applicable
- Name of prescriber

Hospitals are encouraged to promote a culture in which it is not only acceptable, but also strongly encouraged, for staff to bring to the attention of the prescribing practitioner questions or concerns they have regarding orders. Any questions about orders for drugs or biologicals are expected to be resolved prior to the preparation, dispensing, or administration of the medication.

Survey Procedures §482.23(c)(2)

- Review the hospital's policy for drugs and biological orders. Does it require that orders be in writing and signed by a practitioner who is authorized by hospital policy and in accordance with state law, to write orders and who is responsible for the care of the patient?
- Review a sample of open and closed patient medical records. Although the regulation applies to both inpatient and outpatient medical records, the sample should be weighted to include more inpatient records.
- Determine whether all orders for drugs and biologicals, with the exception of influenza and pneumococcal polysaccharide vaccines, are written in the patient's medical record and signed by a practitioner who is authorized to write orders by hospital policy and in accordance with state law, and who is responsible for the care of the patient.
- Determine whether all orders for drugs and biologicals contain the required elements.
- Verify that the prescribing practitioner has reviewed and authenticated the orders in accordance with medical staff policy and/or applicable state laws.

A-0407

§482.23(c)(2)(i) If verbal orders are used, they are to be used infrequently.

> ***Authors' Comment:*** *CMS requires all verbal orders to be authenticated (countersigned) based on federal and state laws. However, if there is no state law that designates a specific time frame for authentication of verbal orders, federal law 482.24(c)(1)(iii) requires authentication within 48 hours.*

Interpretive Guidelines §482.23(c)(2)(i)

Verbal orders, if used, must be used infrequently. This means that the use of verbal orders must not be a common practice. Verbal orders pose an increased risk of miscommunication that could contribute to a medication or other error, resulting in a patient adverse event. Verbal orders should be used only to meet the care needs of the patient when it is impossible or impractical for the ordering practitioner to write the order or enter it into a computer (in the case of a hospital with an electronic prescribing system) without delaying treatment. Verbal orders are not to be used for the convenience of the ordering practitioner. (71 FR 68679)

Hospitals are expected to develop appropriate policies and procedures that govern the use of verbal orders and minimize their use, such as:

- Describe limitations or prohibitions on the use of verbal orders
- Provide a mechanism to ensure validity/authenticity of the practitioner issuing a verbal order
- List the elements required for inclusion in the verbal order process
- Describe situations in which verbal orders may be used
- Define the types of personnel who may issue and receive verbal orders
- Establish protocols for clear and effective communication, verification, and authentication of verbal orders

The content of verbal orders must be clearly communicated. CMS expects nationally accepted read-back verification practice to be implemented for every verbal order. (71 FR 68680) Verbal orders should be recorded directly into an order sheet in the patient's medical record or entered into the computerized order entry system, if the hospital employs one. As required by §482.24(b), all verbal orders must be promptly documented in the patient's medical record and signed by the individual receiving the order.

Survey Procedures §482.23(c)(2)(i)

- Are there policies and procedures in place to minimize the use of verbal orders?
- Interview direct care staff to determine whether actual practice is consistent with verbal order policies and procedures.
- Review both open and closed patient medical records for the use of verbal orders.
- Were the policies and procedures for the use of verbal orders followed?
- Does the number of verbal orders found in the sampled records suggest routine use, which the regulations do not permit? The number of verbal orders is not in itself evidence of noncompliance, but should result in more focused analysis. For example:
    - Is there a pattern to the use of verbal orders? Some patterns might make sense—e.g., for orders entered between midnight and 7 a.m., it might be impossible for the prescribing practitioner to write/computer-enter the order. On the other hand, if one patient care unit has a high proportion of verbal orders while another does not, this might be a flag for inconsistent implementation of the hospital's policies and procedures for verbal orders.
    - Are verbal orders used frequently for certain types of situations; if so, is it reasonable to assume that it is impossible or impractical for the prescribing practitioners to write/enter the orders in such situations?
    - Do certain practitioners use verbal orders frequently? From the limited number of records sampled, it may be difficult to detect trends related to specific practitioners. But if a surveyor finds such evidence, further investigation is warranted to determine if it is evidence of noncompliance.

A-0408

§482.23(c)(2)(ii) When verbal orders are used, they must only be accepted by persons who are authorized to do so by hospital policy and procedures consistent with federal and state law.

> ***Authors' Comment:*** *CMS standards allow acceptance of telephone and verbal orders by registered nurses, licensed practical nurses, pharmacists, respiratory care personnel, and others, provided they are permitted to do so by state and federal law and medical staff policies and procedures.*

Interpretive Guidelines §482.23(c)(2)(ii)

A verbal order for drugs and biologicals may only be accepted by a practitioner who is permitted by federal and state law and hospital policy to accept verbal orders. Consistent with the requirements of §482.24(b), the practitioner must promptly document the verbal order in the medical record.

Survey Procedures §482.23(c)(2)(ii)

- Determine whether the hospital has policies and procedures governing who is authorized to accept verbal orders.
- Determine whether the hospital's polices and procedures for acceptance of verbal orders are consistent with federal and state law.
- Review open and closed patient medical records containing verbal orders for drugs and biologicals. Determine whether the orders are documented by authorized hospital personnel, consistent with federal and state law.
- Interview several direct care staff to determine if they are permitted to take verbal orders for drugs and biologicals, and determine whether such staff have been authorized to do so in accordance with hospital policy.

A-0409

§482.23(c)(3) Blood transfusions and intravenous medications must be administered in accordance with state law

and approved medical staff policies and procedures. If blood transfusions and intravenous medications are administered by personnel other than doctors of medicine or osteopathy, the personnel must have special training for this duty.

Survey Procedures §482.23(c)(3)

- Review the transfusions and intravenous medications practices:
  - Does the hospital have special training for administering blood transfusions and intravenous medications?
  - Are blood transfusions and IVs administered in accordance with state law and approved hospital policies and procedures?
  - Are blood transfusions and IVs administered by personnel who are trained and working within their scope of practice in accordance with state law and hospital policies?
  - Review transfusion records. Determine the identity of practitioners who administered the blood. Do they have documented special training?
  - Review a sample of medical records to determine that only doctors of medicine or osteopathy or specially trained personnel perform this duty. If the nursing service trains personnel for IV administration, look at the content of the in-service course. It should include:
    - Fluid and electrolyte balance
    - Blood components
    - Venipuncture techniques, demonstrations and supervised practice

A-0410

§482.23(c)(4) There must be a hospital procedure for reporting transfusion reactions, adverse drug reactions, and errors in administration of drugs.

Survey Procedures §482.23(c)(4)

- Request the hospital procedure for reporting adverse drug reactions, errors, and transfusion reactions. Review the incident reports or other documentation that the procedure is being implemented and regularly monitored through hospital's QAPI program.

A-0263

§482.21 Condition of Participation: Quality Assessment and Performance Improvement

The hospital must develop, implement, and maintain an effective, ongoing, hospital-wide, data-driven quality assessment and performance improvement program. The hospital's governing body must ensure that the program reflects the complexity of the hospital's organization and services; involves all hospital departments and services (including those services furnished under contract or arrangement); and focuses on indicators related to improved health outcomes and the prevention and reduction of medical errors. The hospital must maintain and demonstrate evidence of its QAPI program for review by CMS.

> ***Authors' Comment:*** *Although similar in their intent, CMS QAPI standards are not as detailed as The Joint Commission's performance improvement (PI) standards. However, a program that is generally in compliance with Joint Commission PI standards should also meet CMS QAPI requirements.*
>
> ***Authors' Comment:*** *The organization evaluates all organized services related to patient care, including services (e.g., pharmacy) furnished by a contractor.*

A-0286

§482.21(c)(2) Performance improvement activities must track medical errors and adverse patient events.

A-0287

§482.21(c)(2) continued

[Performance improvement activities must track medical errors and adverse patient events,] and analyze their causes, and

A-0288

§482.21(c)(2) continued

[Performance improvement activities must track medical errors and adverse patient events, analyze their causes, and] implement preventive actions and mechanisms that include feedback and learning throughout the hospital.

Authors' Comment: *The organization takes and documents appropriate remedial action to address deficiencies found through the QAPI program in regards to medication errors and adverse drug reactions.*

Authors' Comment: *Documentation should describe the action taken and the extent to which the problem is resolved or patient care is improved. Surveyors will look at staff meeting minutes, memoranda, and other records to see if problems are addressed and corrected.*

A-0700

§482.41 Condition of Participation: Physical Environment

The hospital must be constructed, arranged, and maintained to ensure the safety of the patient, and to provide facilities for diagnosis and treatment and for special hospital services appropriate to the needs of the community.

A-0701

§482.41(a) Standard: Buildings

The condition of the physical plant and the overall hospital environment must be developed and maintained in such a manner that the safety and well being of patients are assured.

Interpretive Guidelines §482.41(a)

Assuring the safety and well-being of patients would include developing and implementing appropriate emergency preparedness plans and capabilities. The hospital must develop and implement a comprehensive plan to ensure that the safety and well-being of patients are assured during emergency situations. The hospital must coordinate with federal, state, and local emergency preparedness and health authorities to identify likely risks for their area (e.g., natural disasters; bioterrorism threats; disruption of utilities such as water, sewer, and electrical communications; and fuel: nuclear accidents, industrial accidents, and other likely mass casualties) and to develop appropriate responses that will assure the safety and well-being of patients. The following issues should be considered when developing the comprehensive emergency plan(s):

- Pharmaceuticals, food, other supplies, and equipment that may be needed during emergency/disaster situations
- Qualifications and training needed by personnel, including health care staff, security staff, and maintenance staff, to implement and carry out emergency procedures

A-0724

§482.41(c)(2) Facilities, supplies, and equipment must be maintained to ensure an acceptable level of safety and quality.

Interpretive Guidelines §482.41(c)(2)

Equipment must be maintained to ensure an acceptable level of safety and quality.

Equipment includes both facility equipment (e.g., elevators, generators, air handlers, medical gas systems, air compressors, and vacuum systems) and medical equipment (e.g., biomedical equipment, radiological equipment, patient beds, stretchers, IV infusion equipment, ventilators, and laboratory equipment).

A-0726

§482.41(c)(4) There must be proper ventilation, light, and temperature controls in pharmaceutical, food preparation, and other appropriate areas.

Interpretive Guidelines §482.41(c)(4)

There must be proper ventilation in at least the following areas:

- Areas using ethylene oxide, nitrous oxide, guteraldehydes, xylene, pentamidine, and other potentially hazardous substances
- Locations where oxygen is transferred from one container to another
- Isolation rooms and reverse isolation rooms (both must be in compliance with federal and state laws, regulations, and guidelines such as the Occupational Safety and Health Administration [OSHA], the Centers for Disease Control and Prevention [CDC], NIH, etc.)
- Pharmaceutical preparation areas (e.g., hoods and cabinets)
- Laboratory locations

There must be adequate lighting in all the patient care areas as well as food and medication preparation areas.

The hospital must ensure that an appropriate number of refrigerators and or heating devices are provided and ensure that food and pharmaceuticals are stored properly and in accordance with nationally accepted guidelines (food) and manufacturer's recommendations (pharmaceuticals).

Survey Procedures §482.41(c)(4)

- Verify that all food and medication preparation areas are well lighted.
- Verify that pharmaceuticals are stored at temperatures recommended by the product manufacturer.

A-0747

§482.42 Condition of Participation: Infection Control

The hospital must provide a sanitary environment to avoid sources and transmission of infections and communicable diseases. There must be an active program for the prevention, control, and investigation of infections and communicable diseases.

> ***Authors' Comment:*** *The pharmacy must participate in the organization-wide program for the prevention, control, and investigation of infections and communicable diseases.*

A-1026

§482.53 Condition of Participation: Nuclear Medicine

If the hospital provides nuclear medicine services, those services must meet the needs of the patients in accordance with acceptable standards of practice.

A-1036

§482.53(b)(1) In-house preparation of radiopharmaceuticals is by, or under, the direct supervision of an appropriately trained registered pharmacist or doctor of medicine or osteopathy.

> ***Authors' Comment:*** *The pharmacy must be aware of the hospital's process for procuring radiopharmaceuticals, including the nuclear pharmacy used to provide the service if contracted. Radiopharmaceuticals should be supplied to the hospital in unit-dose format.*

CHAPTER 23

Healthcare Facilities Accreditation Program (HFAP) Surveys

The Healthcare Facilities Accreditation Program (HFAP) of the American Osteopathic Association (AOA) is a recognized alternative to certification by the Centers for Medicare & Medicaid Services (CMS) and accreditation by The Joint Commission or the National Integrated Accreditation for Healthcare Organizations (NIAHO) program of Det Norske Veritas (DNV) Healthcare. HFAP is recognized nationally by the federal government, some state governments, insurance carriers, the National Committee for Quality Assurance (NCQA), the Accreditation Council for Graduate Medical Education (ACGME), and managed care organizations. HFAP accreditation is not limited to osteopathic hospitals, and some health care organizations are accredited by both HFAP and The Joint Commission.[1]

HFAP Requirements

The HFAP requirements were revised in August 2008 and are published in the 2009 HFAP *Accreditation Requirements for Healthcare Facilities* manual.[2] The requirements address all departments and functions, including pharmacy and medication use. Several new pharmacy standards have been added and others revised.[1] Organizations should access the HFAP Web site for the most current HFAP standards and revisions. (*See* Appendix.)

Some HFAP standards are more prescriptive than other accreditation standards and Centers for Medicare and Medicaid Services (CMS) standards. Therefore, compliance with other accreditation standards or CMS standards is not necessarily sufficient to meet HFAP standards and vice versa.

HFAP Surveys

Any health care organization may request an accreditation survey to determine its level of compliance with HFAP requirements. Surveyors review key systems, assess compliance with all standards, and determine how well the organization provides care, treatment, and services.

HFAP accreditation surveys are unannounced. Surveys are usually performed by three surveyors consisting of a physician, who heads the team, a hospital administrator, and a registered nurse. Larger organizations may require additional surveyors and/or additional days. The composition of the survey team is dependent on the size and scope of care of the health care organization to be surveyed. A typical survey takes approximately 3 days.

HFAP Accreditation

If HFAP determines an organization is compliant with its requirements, it awards the organization the status of "Accredited." The length of accreditation is 3 years. HFAP provides hospitals with a written report of any areas of noncompliance after completion of the survey. This report clearly identifies any issues of non-compliance with CMS Conditions of Participation (CoPs) and standards as well as HFAP standards. Organizations are required to demonstrate corrective actions of all deficiencies prior to the awarding of accreditation. Note that HFAP, The Joint Commission, and NIAHO accredit health care organizations; Medicare certifies. HFAP accreditation, Joint Commission accreditation, NIAHO accreditation, or Medicare certification qualifies an organization to participate in the Medicare program. (*See* Chapters 1 and 24.)

HFAP Standards and Elements Organization

The HFAP *Accreditation Requirements for Healthcare Facilities* manual is organized by department, service, or function. Each chapter includes standards and elements that link directly with CMS CoPs or other regulations. Chapter 25, Pharmacy Services and Medication Use, consists of standards 25.00.00 through 25.03.06. In the HFAP *Accreditation Requirements for Healthcare Facilities* manual, all CMS standards are italicized for easy identification. Most standards have an explanation that gives specific information concerning the intent of the standard. All standards are arranged in four columns as described in Table 23-1.

HFAP Standards and Elements for Pharmacy Services/Medication Use

Many of the HFAP standards and elements requirements quote the CMS CoPs, CMS Standards, and CMS Interpretative Guidelines. (*See* Chapter 22.) The information contained in other chapters of this book may be helpful in complying with HFAP standards.

This chapter lists HFAP standards and elements from Chapter 25 (Pharmacy Services/Medication Use) of HFAP's standards manual. CMS CoPs and CMS Standards are quoted and the appropriate CMS number (beginning with 482) follows each standard/element that is a CoP or Standard. The quotations that follow are taken from the Federal Register and may differ slightly from the HFAP standards. The authors have paraphrased HFAP standards and elements, except those that are direct restatements of CMS.

The authors' comments, experiences, and suggestions that follow many of the HFAP standards are in italics. They are based on the authors' personal experiences, reports from surveyed organizations, and surveyors' statements. Some reflect legal requirements, previous HFAP standards, or commonly accepted standards of practice. Others note variations in interpretations or provide clarification (e.g., additional explanation, scoring procedure).

Pharmacies should obtain a copy of current HFAP requirements prior to the survey. For additional information and compliance guidelines, they should review the actual standards/elements as well as the relevant explanations and scoring procedures. Other chapters in the *Accreditation Requirements for Healthcare Facilities* may also contain requirements for pharmacy services.

HFAP uses several terms for medications (e.g., drugs, biologicals, items, products, and preparations). The authors have paraphrased the HFAP standards and elements and usually use the term "medications," which should be considered interchangeable with the other terms used by HFAP.

25.00.00 Pharmaceutical Services

The hospital must have pharmaceutical services that meet the needs of the patients. The institution must have a pharmacy directed by a registered pharmacist or a drug storage area under competent supervision. The medical staff is responsible for developing policies and procedures that minimize drug errors. This function may be delegated to the hospital's organized pharmaceutical service. §482.25

The pharmacy or drug storage area must be administered in accordance with accepted professional principles. §482.25(a)

The pharmacy or drug storage area must meet all legal requirements.

The medical staff must develop policies and procedures to minimize drug errors. These must address the following:

- High-alert medications, dosing limits, administering guidelines, and guidelines for packaging, labeling, and storing high-alert or high-risk medications
- Placing limits on the variety of medication-related devices and equipment
- Ensuring that current medication information is available
- Ensuring that pharmacy expertise is available when the pharmacy is not staffed 24 hours a day, 7 days a week
- Standardizing prescribing and communicating practices to include the following:
    - Avoiding dangerous abbreviations
    - Stating that a complete medication order includes the dose, strength, units, route of administration, and rate of administration
    - Providing a system for alerting staff to medications with look-alike and sound-alike names
    - Using pre-printed order sheets, approved by the organization, whenever possible
- Prohibiting the use of the expression "resume previous orders"
- Providing a voluntary, nonpunitive system for monitoring and reporting medication errors, adverse drug reactions, and other adverse drug events
- Ensuring that hazardous medications are prepared, distributed, administered, and disposed of properly
- Handling medication recalls and external alerts
- Ensuring that patient-specific information is readily available to all individuals who provide pharmaceutical care
- Identifying when weight-based dosing for pediatric patients is required

- Stating when review and revision are required based on the organization's reports of adverse drug events and Quality Assessment/Performance Improvement (QAPI) activities
- Providing a pharmacy leader who plays an active role on the administrative leadership team. This leader should report to the Chief Executive Officer or Chief Operating Officer and have a title consistent with others reporting at the same organizational level.

Authors' Comments, Experiences, and Suggestions

The explanation for 25.00.00 notes that competent supervision for a medication storage area must be in accordance with state and federal law.

The pharmacy leader may report to the CNO if on the same organizational level as the CFO or the COO.

25.00.01 Licensure

The pharmacy (including each separate pharmacy location) must be currently licensed to meet state requirements, and the licenses must be prominently displayed if required.

Authors' Comments, Experiences, and Suggestions

The explanation for 25.00.01 states that the pharmacy must be licensed as a retail pharmacy if the facility provides outpatient dispensing and is required by the state.

25.00.02 Permits and Certifications

Other required permits and certificates must be current and, if required, be prominently displayed within the pharmacy area.

Authors' Comments, Experiences, and Suggestions

The explanation for 25.00.02 states that examples of permits and certificates include the Drug Enforcement Administration registration, state-controlled substances permit, tax free alcohol permit, and a permit to be a preceptor for pharmacist interns.

25.00.03 Scope of Service

Pharmaceutical services must reflect the organization's scope of services.

Authors' Comments, Experiences, and Suggestions

The scoring procedure for 25.00.03 states the organization's statement of service identifies the needs of the patients served and pharmaceutical services are adequate to meet those needs.

25.00.04 Management

A full-time, part-time, or consulting pharmacist must be responsible for developing, supervising, and coordinating all the activities of the pharmacy services. §482.25(a)(1)

Authors' Comments, Experiences, and Suggestions

The explanation for 25.00.04 states that a single pharmacist is responsible for the administration of pharmacy services. The job description for this individual clearly states that job responsibilities include the development, supervision, and coordination of all pharmaceutical services activities.

25.00.05 Staffing

The pharmaceutical service must have an adequate number of personnel to ensure quality pharmaceutical services, including emergency services. §482.25(a)(2)

Authors' Comments, Experiences, and Suggestions

The explanation for 25.00.05 states that staff for pharmaceutical services is sufficient in types, numbers, and training to meet the needs of patients served by the organization.

25.00.06 Scheduled Drugs

Current and accurate records must be kept of the receipt and disposition of all scheduled drugs. §482.25(a)(3)

A complete and accurate record system for the receipt and distribution of scheduled medications must include the following components:

- Procedures that ensure the accountability and control for distributing, using, and disposing of all scheduled medications
- Current and accurate records of the receipt and distribution of all scheduled medications
- Records that trace how scheduled medications move throughout the organization
- A means to ensure that a pharmacist is responsible for keeping orderly medication records and that accounts of all scheduled medications are maintained and reconciled
- A record system, described in policies and procedures, that tracks how scheduled medications move from their point of entry (e.g., receipt) through administration to a patient or their return to the manufacturer (Documentation relating to scheduled medications is readily retrievable in order to facilitate reconciliation of their receipt and disposition.)
- Records for scheduled medications that are in order (An account of all scheduled medications must be maintained, and if discrepancies in the count of such medications is discovered, they are reconciled promptly.)
- A means for the organization to readily identify any loss or diversion of scheduled medications (The time between the actual loss or diversion to the time the loss or diversion is detected and the extent of the loss or diversion determined must be minimized.)
- Policies and procedures that minimize the diversion of scheduled medications

Authors' Comments, Experiences, and Suggestions

The term "scheduled drugs," as used in this standard, refers to controlled substances.

The explanation for 25.00.06 requires the maintenance of a perpetual inventory of scheduled drugs.

25.00.07 Space Requirements

Pharmacy space must be adequate so that medications can be stored securely.

Authors' Comments, Experiences, and Suggestions

The explanation and scoring procedure for 25.00.07 state that space must permit orderly storage of medications and there must be separate double-locked storage for Schedule II controlled substances.

25.01.01 Medication Control and Distribution

In order to provide patient safety, drugs and biologicals must be controlled and distributed in accordance with applicable standards of practice, consistent with federal and state law. §482.25(b)

Authors' Comments, Experiences, and Suggestions

The explanation for 25.01.01 states that examples of high-alert medications include those medications involved in a high percentage of medication errors and/or critical events and medications that carry a higher risk for abuse, errors, or other adverse outcomes. Additional high-alert medications are identified as those listed by the Institute for Safe Medication Practices and the United States Pharmacopeia, which include investigational medications, controlled medications, medications that are not FDA approved, medications with a narrow therapeutic range, psychotherapeutic medications, medications with look-alike/sound-alike names, and medications that are new to the organization. The scoring procedure requires limited concentrations of morphine and heparin solutions and limited access to concentrated potassium chloride and potassium phosphate solutions and sodium chloride solutions with a concentration greater than 0.9%.

The explanation for 25.01.01 requires a pharmacist to review each medication order prior to the medication being dispensed, except in the case of an emergency. The pharmacy should be involved in the development of a process to ensure that patients are monitored after medications are administered to minimize the likelihood of adverse events.

This standard requires that sterile preparations be prepared and labeled in an appropriate environment and by qualified, trained personnel.

The pharmacy is expected to participate in the organization's process for managing emergency medications and the evaluation of medication delivery systems, including automated dispensing cabinets.

The scoring procedure for 25.01.01 indicates that medication storage areas are to be inspected periodically. The explanation for 25.01.05 states that monthly inspections are required.

25.01.02 Supervision of Pharmacy Activities

All compounding, packaging, and dispensing of drugs and biologicals must be under the supervision of a pharmacist and performed consistent with state and federal laws. §482.25(b)(1)

Authors' Comments, Experiences, and Suggestions

The explanation for 25.01.02 lists several safe medication preparation procedures that must be followed. These should be read carefully.

The explanation for 25.01.02 states that the work of all non-pharmacists must be verified by a pharmacist prior to leaving the pharmacy/drug room. A pharmacist must review all medication orders prior to delivery of the medication to the patient care area.

25.01.03 Security of Medications

Consistent with state and federal requirements, in the pharmacy and throughout the organization:

All drugs and biologicals must be kept in a secure area, and locked when appropriate. §482.25 (b)(2)(i)

Drugs listed in Schedules II, III, IV, and V of the comprehensive Drug Abuse Prevention and Control Act of 1970 must be kept locked within a secure area. §482.25(b)(2)(ii)

Only authorized personnel may have access to locked areas. §482.25(b)(2)(iii)

Authors' Comments, Experiences, and Suggestions

The explanation for 25.01.03 requires that all controlled substances must be locked within a secure area. Schedule II, III, IV, and V drugs must be locked (e.g., locked storage cabinet, locked cart) within a secure area, regardless of whether the area is staffed. Schedule II, III, IV, and V drugs cannot be stored on a shelf or unlocked cabinet/container within a locked area (e.g., surgical suite, special procedure area).

Organizations have the flexibility to determine the most effective method to safeguard non-controlled medications and biologicals when they are not stored in a locked area. Medications in the pharmacy and throughout the organization must be stored in a secure area and locked when appropriate, as required by laws or regulations.

The explanation and scoring procedure for 25.01.03 emphasize the need for security. Unauthorized individuals must not have access to medications. Keys and access codes must be safeguarded. Carts containing medications (e.g., nursing carts and anesthesia carts) must be locked or stored in a locked room or secure location.

Medications are considered to be secure when unauthorized individuals cannot obtain access to them. Individuals who are not legally permitted access to medications must be monitored. They cannot have keys to medication storage areas or carts containing medications. An area would generally be considered secure when staff are actively providing patient care or preparing to receive patients.

The explanation for 25.01.03 requires organizational policies to specifically address:

- *Storage, security, and monitoring of non-controlled medications and biologicals in all patient care areas*
- *Safeguards in place to prevent tampering and minimize diversion of medications*
- *Identification of "secure" areas*
- *Identification of authorized personnel who have access to locked and secured areas and the degree of supervision needed in carrying out their routine duties and responsibilities (e.g., housekeeping, maintenance)*
- *Security of bedside medications*
- *Assurance of patient competence to self-administer their medications*

When the surgical suite is closed or not in use, the organization must lock the entire suite. Within the suite, all non-controlled medications and biologicals must be locked in a secure area, locked in non-mobile carts, or stored in mobile carts within a locked room.

Bedside medications must be secured to prevent tampering and access by unauthorized individuals.

25.01.04 Pharmacy Security

The pharmacy has locking entities (i.e., it must be capable of being locked).

Authors' Comments, Experiences, and Suggestions

The explanation and scoring procedure for 25.01.04 states that the pharmacy must be locked when staff are not present. Access codes, security codes, and keys must be strictly controlled and secured.

25.01.05 Inventory Management System

Outdated, mislabeled, or otherwise unusable drugs and biologicals must not be available for patient use. §482.25(b)(3)

The director of pharmacy must ensure that all medication inventories are reviewed, medications are sequestered if necessary and logged, and recalled and/or unusable medications are destroyed or returned.

Authors' Comments, Experiences, and Suggestions

The explanation and scoring procedure for 25.01.05 states that medications, including those in crash carts, must be inspected at least monthly for products that are about to expire. Recalled medications and expired medications are pulled from stock and sequestered separately to prevent them from inadvertently being used.

Medications for patients must include the patient's full name as well as the prescriber's name. Additional requirements are listed.

Expired Schedules II through V medications must be sequestered separately from non-scheduled medications.

25.01.06 Pharmacy Access

When a pharmacist is not available, drugs and biologicals must be removed from the pharmacy or storage area only by personnel designated in the policies of the medical staff and pharmaceutical services, in accordance with federal and state law. §482.25(b)(4)

Authors' Comments, Experiences, and Suggestions

The explanation for 25.01.06 requires that after-hours access to the pharmacy by non-pharmacists be minimized and eliminated to the extent possible. It permits non-pharmacists (e.g., registered nurses and physicians) to have access to the pharmacy after-hours if strict conditions are met. (Some state laws do not permit after-hours access to the pharmacy.) Access must be strictly controlled and limited to medications that have been approved by the organization. Access must be limited to trained, designated prescribers and nurses. A pharmacist must review and evaluate the removals and make changes to reduce the frequency of access. Additional requirements are listed.

25.01.07 Automatic Stop Medication Orders

Drugs and biologicals not specifically prescribed as to time or number of doses must automatically be stopped after a reasonable time that is predetermined by the medical staff. §482.25(b)(5)

The medical staff must set time frames for automatically stopping orders for medications, and those orders are automatically stopped as required.

Authors' Comments, Experiences, and Suggestions

The explanation for 25.01.07 lists medications that are usually included in an automatic stop order policy. The practitioner must be notified before automatically stopping the order. Surveyors look for documented evidence that the policy is followed.

25.01.08 Drug Reactions and Administration Errors and Incompatibilities

Drug administration errors, adverse drug reactions, and incompatibilities must be immediately reported to the attending physician and, if appropriate, to the hospital-wide quality assurance program. §482.25(b)(6)

Authors' Comments, Experiences, and Suggestions

HFAP adds "performance improvement program" to §482.25(b)(6).

There must be a hospital procedure for reporting transfusion reactions, adverse drug reactions, and errors in administration of drugs. §482.23(c)(4)

Authors' Comments, Experiences, and Suggestions

The explanation for 25.01.08 states that errors must include "near misses." Adverse drug reactions (ADRs) must be classified by probability, severity, mechanism, and dosing location. The National Coordinating Council Medication Error Reporting and Prevention (NCC MERP) definition of a medication error is satisfactory to HFAP. Organizations must report all medication errors, drug reactions, and drug incompatibilities through their Quality Assessment/Performance Improvement and Risk Management programs.

25.01.09 Reporting of Controlled Drug Loss and/or Abuse

Abuses and losses of controlled substances must be reported, in accordance with applicable federal and state laws, to the individual responsible for the pharmaceutical service and to the chief executive officer, as appropriate. §482.25(b)(7)

Authors' Comments, Experiences, and Suggestions

The explanation and scoring procedure for 25.01.09 states that the organization must be able to detect, track, and appropriately report abuses and losses.

25.01.10 Informational Resources

Information relating to drug interactions and information of drug therapy, side effects, toxicology, dosage, indications for use, and routes of administration must be available to the professional staff. §482.25(b)(8)

Authors' Comments, Experiences, and Suggestions

The explanation and scoring procedure for 25.01.10 indicates that the state pharmacy practice act, toxicology reference (including the regional poison control center telephone number), and pharmacy texts must be available. There must be an on-call pharmacist available for consultation.

25.01.11 Formulary System

A formulary system must be established by the medical staff to assure quality pharmaceuticals at reasonable costs. §482.25(b)(9)

Authors' Comments, Experiences, and Suggestions

The explanation and scoring procedure for 25.01.11 states that a formulary must be available in clinical areas. The formulary must be reviewed at least annually, and surveyors are instructed to verify the date that the medical staff approved it. There must be written criteria for selecting medications included in the formulary.

25.01.12 Non-Formulary Medications

There must be provisions for ordering medications that are not listed in the organization's formulary.

Authors' Comments, Experiences, and Suggestions

The explanation and scoring procedure for 25.01.12 states that there must be methods for changing or amending the formulary.

25.01.13 Integrity of Medication

Medications must be stored at the proper temperatures, and records of medication refrigerator and freezer temperatures must be maintained.

Authors' Comments, Experiences, and Suggestions

The explanation and scoring procedure for 25.01.13 states that daily temperature logs are required for all medication refrigerators, freezers, and warmers. Surveyors are instructed to verify that daily logs are maintained. Thermometers must be accurate, and their accuracy must be verified against a known standard (e.g., a reference thermometer) semiannually. Medications must be stored within the manufacturer's guidelines.

25.01.14 Consultations/Resource Availability

The pharmacy must ensure that those who prescribe and administer medications as well as patients and families are provided with pharmaceutical consultation as appropriate.

Authors' Comments, Experiences, and Suggestions

The explanation for 25.01.14 states that a pharmacist must serve on the medical staff committee that discusses medication therapy (e.g., a P&T Committee). A pharmacist must provide inservice education programs for nursing staff.

25.01.15 Medication Protocols

There must be a review and revision of standing, routine, or protocol orders at least annually. (Signed, master copies of these orders are kept in the pharmacy.)

Authors' Comments, Experiences, and Suggestions

Protocol orders are individualized for each patient. The order is dated, timed, and signed by the ordering prescriber. All protocol orders are approved by the medical staff and reviewed annually thereafter.

HFAP uses the terms standing, routine, and protocol orders interchangeably.

25.01.16 Home Medications

There must be policies and procedures that provide standards for the use of medications that patients bring into the organization.

Authors' Comments, Experiences, and Suggestions

The explanation for 25.01.16 states that a pharmacist or physician must positively identify patients' home medications that are to be administered to patients. The manufacturer's lot number must be included in the identification.

25.01.17 Labeling

Labels of medications intended for the use of specific patients must include the patient's full name, the name of the prescriber, the name of the medication, strength, quantity, expiration or beyond-use date, and accessory or cautionary statements as appropriate for the medication.

Authors' Comments, Experiences, and Suggestions

The explanation for 25.01.17 states that labeling of repackaged medications must meet state and federal requirements. There must be a way to track the manufacturer's lot number. The manufacturer's lot number must be on medications dispensed to outpatients.

25.01.18 Standardization of Labeling

Medications must be labeled, packaged, and stored in a standardized manner throughout the organization.

Authors' Comments, Experiences, and Suggestions

The intention of this requirement is to reduce adverse events. Surveyors look for evidence of compliance with this standard throughout the organization.

25.01.19 High-Alert Medications

The organization's actions to ensure the safe use of high-alert or high-risk medications must include identifying such medications that are present in the organization, identifying new high-alert or high-risk medications as they are introduced into the organization, establishing protocols for their safe use and making the protocols available to staff who must use the medications, auditing compliance with the protocols, and using a multidisciplinary team to review the safeguards in place for these medications.

Authors' Comments, Experiences, and Suggestions

The explanation for 25.01.19 states that examples of high-alert medications are intravenous adrenergic agonists and antagonists, chemotherapeutic agents, anticoagulants and antithrombotics, concentrated parenteral electrolytes, general anesthetics, neuromuscular blockers, insulin and oral hypoglycemics, narcotics, and opiates. Compare this list with 25.01.01.

25.01.20 Dispensing Methods

Whenever possible, the pharmacy must dispense medications in unit-dose, unit-of-use, or ready-to-administer forms. Medications so dispensed must be labeled with the medication name, strength, manufacturer, expiration or beyond-use date, and lot number in machine-readable code. No more than a 24-hour supply is to be provided to patient care areas at any one time. The medication distribution system must be monitored so that performance relating to medication distribution can be improved.

Authors' Comments, Experiences, and Suggestions

The explanation for 25.01.20 states that medications purchased in bulk must be repackaged into unit-dose aliquots.

25.01.21 Preparation of Intravenous Drugs and Fluids

To prevent contamination, the pharmacy must compound sterile preparations (including intravenous medications and fluids) according to pharmacy practice standards and state/federal regulations. The methods used must reduce the potential for contamination by bacteria and drug incompatibilities.

Authors' Comments, Experiences, and Suggestions

The explanation and scoring procedure for 25.01.21 states that the beyond-use date of a reconstituted or admixed preparation must be prominently displayed on the label. Horizontal and vertical laminar airflow hoods must be used for their intended purposes. Spill kits, spill procedures, and personal protective equipment must be immediately available if cytotoxic medications are prepared.

25.01.22 Sample Drugs

The pharmacy must control the use of medication samples in accordance with state/federal laws.

Authors' Comments, Experiences, and Suggestions

The explanation for 25.01.22 states that there must be full accountability for the storage, distribution, and use of medication samples and a log must be maintained. Medication samples must be stored securely and labeled according to the organization's written policy. Medication samples must be included in the medication recall procedure.

25.01.23 Patient Medication Profile

There must be a medication profile maintained for each inpatient and outpatient who receives medications. The profile must include information that will assure that medications are administered safely and accurately.

Authors' Comments, Experiences, and Suggestions

The explanation for 25.01.23 states that data to be entered into a patient medication profile includes diet orders, history of prescribed medications, nonprescribed medications, over-the-counter medications, home remedies, and street drugs. Additional requirements are listed.

25.01.24 Profile Review

A pharmacist must review patient profiles daily and whenever a medication order is changed. The review must occur before dispensing the medication or providing the medication for administration (unless the delay would be medically unacceptable). Profile reviews must include potential drug–drug and food–drug interactions as well as interferences and incompatibilities. There must be documentation of the reviews in the patient's record. Pharmacists who review patient profiles must maintain documentation of their interventions. The organization must audit compliance with the patient profile review requirements and use the findings to improve medication safety.

Authors' Comments, Experiences, and Suggestions

The scoring procedure for 25.01.24 states that policies must define when a delay would be medically acceptable.

25.01.25 Drug Administration

The organization must have mechanisms in place to ensure that medications are safely, accurately, and effectively administered.

Authors' Comments, Experiences, and Suggestions

The explanation for 25.01.25 says that this is self explanatory. The scoring procedure says that surveyors are to compare physicians' orders against medication administration records for safety and accuracy.

25.01.26 Label Medications and Solutions on the Sterile Field

The organization must develop and implement policies for labeling medications and solutions used on and off the sterile field in perioperative settings. Policies must include at least the following:

- Required labeling of medications and solutions, regardless of container type, used throughout the procedure
- Process for labeling look-alike and sound-alike medications and solutions
- Process used to verify and confirm each medication and solution label against the label on the original container

A label is required even if only one solution is involved in the procedure.

Two staff members must verbally and visually confirm each medication and solution with the respective label. At least one of the staff must be a licensed individual participating in the procedure.

Original medication and solution containers must be retained until the procedure is completed in case they are needed for reference.

Authors, Comments, Experiences, and Suggestions

All types of containers, including cups, basins, syringes, and specimen cups, must be labeled.

25.01.27 Investigational Drugs

The organization must have policies that address administration of the following:

- Medications for indications that are not approved by the FDA
- Experimental medications
- Investigational medications when one or more of the primary investigators are members of the organization's medical staff
- Investigational medications brought by patients into the organization that have been prescribed by practitioners who are not members of the organization's medical staff

Authors' Comments, Experiences, and Suggestions

The explanation for 25.01.27 lists seven concepts that must be addressed in investigational drug policies. The scoring procedure for 25.01.27 requires surveyors to verify that each of the seven concepts is addressed.

25.01.28 Documentation

The effects of therapy (including medication therapy) must be noted in patient medical records. The record must include the following:

- Accurate documentation of all doses administered
- The effects of the medications or products
- Progress notes of prescribing practitioners and medical consultants
- Nursing staff notes relating to the effects of prn dosing and dosing for clinical outcomes
- Record of clinical outcomes
- Record of laboratory, imaging, cardiogram, and other objective testing to determine therapeutic effects

Authors' Comments, Experiences, and Suggestions

The scoring procedure for 25.01.28 requires that medical records provide documented evidence that all medication doses were administered.

25.01.29 Anti-Thrombotic Therapy

The organization must have policies and procedures that ensure safe and effective antithrombotic (i.e., anticoagulation) therapy is provided by dedicated, antithrombotic services.

Authors' Comments, Experiences, and Suggestions

The explanation and scoring procedure for 25.01.29 states that policies and procedures must define staff training requirements, dose scheduling and tracking mechanisms, patient education materials, and mechanisms for training.

25.02.01 Preparation and Administration of Drugs

Drugs and biologicals must be prepared and administered in accordance with federal and state laws, the orders of the practitioner or practitioners responsible for the patient's care as specified under §482.12(c), and accepted standards of practice. §482.23(c)

Authors' Comments, Experiences, and Suggestions

The explanation for 25.02.01 states that policies must identify the categories of personnel who can administer various kinds of medications. Organizations may require competency testing of these personnel. Personnel are not permitted to administer medications outside their scope of practice or area of competence.

25.02.02 Preparation and Administration of Drugs

All drugs and biologicals must be administered by, or under the supervision of nursing or other personnel in accordance with federal and state laws and regulations, including applicable licensing requirements and in accordance with the approved medical staff policies and procedures. §482.23(c)(1)

The organization's medical staff and P&T Committee must approve medication preparation and administration policies that address, at a minimum, the following:

- Review of medication orders and patient profiles by a pharmacist, documenting the review, and any exceptions to the requirements for review by a pharmacist
- The pharmacist's role in the organization's medication use process
- On-call availability of a pharmacist when a full-time pharmacist is not available in the organization. The policy must ensure that a pharmacist can be contacted by telephone or can be accessed at a location that provides 24-hour pharmacy services
- Verification of an order by the dispensing pharmacist if the medication is not stocked in the patient care area
- Verification of orders by staff who administer medications
- How to ensure positive identification of patients before administering medications
- Accurate recording of the medication name, route of administration, dose administered, and time(s) of administration (The record must show that the medication was administered to the correct patient.)
- How to provide a bedside supply of medications for patients authorized to self-administer medications
- How to teach patients and/or their families about medications
- How to identify and respond to medication variances

Authors' Comments, Experiences, and Suggestions

Bedside medication storage must be consistent with 25.01.03 in regards to the security of medications.

The scoring procedure for 25.02.02 requires surveyors to observe the preparation and administration of medications to verify that procedures are followed. Patients are to be positively identified (e.g., addressed by name and their wristband checked). Medications must be identifiable up to the point of administration.

Though not specified in the CMS standards or Interpretive Guidelines, the CMS Surveyor Procedures suggest that an indicator for assessing administration of drugs should include administration within 30 minutes of the scheduled time.

25.02.03 Drug Orders

With the exception of influenza and pneumococcal polysaccharide vaccines, which may be administered per physician-approved hospital policy after an assessment for contraindications, orders for drugs and biologicals must be documented and signed by a practitioner who is authorized to write orders by hospital policy and in accordance with state law, and who is responsible for the care of the patient as specified under §482.12(c). §482.23(c)(2)

I. If verbal orders are used, they are to be used infrequently. §482.23(c)(2)(i)

II. When verbal orders are used, they must be accepted only by persons who are authorized to do so by hospital policy and procedures consistent with federal and state law. §482.23(c)(2)(ii)

III. All orders, including verbal orders, must be dated, timed, and authenticated promptly by the ordering practitioner. §482.24(c)(1)(i)

IV. For the 5-year period following January 26, 2007, all orders, including verbal orders, must be dated, timed, and authenticated by the ordering practitioner or another practitioner who is responsible for the care of the patient as specified under §482.12(c) and authorized to write orders by hospital policy in accordance with state law. §482.24(c)(1)(ii)

V. All verbal orders must be authenticated based upon federal and state law. If there is no state law that designates a specific time frame for the authentication of verbal orders, verbal orders must be authenticated within 48 hours. §482.24(c)(1)(iii)

If permitted by state and local regulations, electronically transmitted orders (e.g., FAX orders) may be treated as an original document and considered to be an original order.

Telephone orders are a type of verbal orders. All requirements for verbal orders apply to telephone orders.

The organization discourages the use of verbal orders when the ordering practitioner is physically present, except in emergency situations. Verbal orders should be limited to situations when it is impractical for an ordering practitioner to write or electronically transmit the order.

All verbal orders must be:

- Used infrequently
- Dated, timed, and signed (authenticated) promptly by the ordering practitioner
- Read back immediately (after transcription) to the ordering practitioner to verify the accuracy of the order received
- Not permitted for orders relating to chemotherapy
- Not permitted for other high-risk medications as defined by the organization

The organization must have policies/rules and regulations that address the following:

- Any limitations or prohibitions on verbal orders
- A method to ensure the validity and authenticity of prescribers
- The elements that must be included in a complete verbal order
- A description of the situations in which verbal orders are permitted
- A list of individuals who have been authorized to accept verbal orders
- Guidelines that ensure verbal orders are communicated clearly and effectively

Services must be provided in accordance with the orders of practitioners who the medical staff has authorized to order the services. Orders of these practitioners must be incorporated in the patient's record.

Authors' Comments, Experiences, and Suggestions

The explanation and scoring procedure for 25.02.03 list a number of requirements relating to ordering medications. Some of the requirements address electronically transmitted orders, verbal and telephone orders, who may receive orders, authentication of orders, who can order medications, questioning prescribers and clarifying orders, reading back verbal orders, and co-signing orders. These must be read carefully to ensure compliance with all requirements.

25.02.04 Administration of Blood Products and IV Medications

Blood transfusions and intravenous medications must be administered in accordance with state law and approved medical staff policies and procedures. If blood transfusions and intravenous medications are administered by personnel other than doctors of medicine or osteopathy, the personnel must have special training for this duty. §482.23(c)(3)

Authors' Comments, Experiences, and Suggestions

The scoring procedure for 25.02.04 states that surveyors must verify that personnel are trained and working within their scope of practice.

25.02.05 Medication Preparation Environment

The environment for preparing medications must foster attention to detail and the accurate filling and dispensing of medication orders. Policies and procedures must provide for nursing and pharmacy environments and guidelines that foster medication preparation safety. They must include a means for ongoing monitoring for compliance with the guidelines.

Authors' Comments, Experiences, and Suggestions

The scoring procedure for 25.02.05 states that surveyors must inspect medication preparation areas to ensure they are clean, well lighted, and free of clutter, distractions, and noise.

25.02.06 Monitoring of Appropriateness

The organization must use multiple mechanisms to document the monitoring of patients who receive medications.

Authors' Comments, Experiences, and Suggestions

The explanation for 25.02.06 states that this is self-explanatory.

25.02.07 Medication Reconciliation

There must be an organization-wide process to reconcile medications across the continuum of care. The process must address the reconciliation of medications at key intervals such as:

- On admission, prepare a complete list of medications the patient takes at home
- The patient or family member validates the list when possible
- Any variance is reconciled when the pre-admission list is compared to admitting orders
- A complete, current list of each patient's medications is available to prescribers when writing medication orders
- When patients are transferred or discharged, a complete list of medications is provided to the next care provider
- When patients are discharged, a complete list of medications is provided to the patient

25.03.01 Performance Improvement

There must be an organization-wide Quality Assessment/Performance Improvement program that includes the findings from adverse drug responses. The program must monitor the desired outcomes of medication use.

Authors' Comments, Experiences, and Suggestions

The explanation for 25.03.01 indicates that priority should be given to high-volume, high-risk, or problem-prone areas. It requires the organization to prepare an annual Medication Use Review Plan (e.g., Drug Utilization Effectiveness [DUE] plan).

25.03.02 Data Collection and Monitoring

Medication use monitoring must assess the appropriateness of prescribing, preparing and dispensing, administering, and outcomes of medication use.

Authors' Comments, Experiences, and Suggestions

The explanation for 25.03.02 indicates that all four processes (e.g., prescribing, preparing or dispensing, administering, outcomes) must be reviewed.

25.03.03 Medication Use Review

The organization's medication use review program must monitor medications used in all principal populations that the organization serves.

Authors' Comments, Experiences, and Suggestions

The explanation for 25.03.03 states that populations should be age specific (e.g., pediatric to geriatric) and cover inpatient, outpatient, and emergency care patients.

The organization should publish and distribute an antibiogram at least once a year.

25.03.04 Data Reporting

The organization must ensure that medication use review findings are reported to the appropriate medical staff committee and/or departments. The findings must be considered by the organization's Quality Assessment/Performance Improvement (QAPI) program and used to make improvements in the organization's service areas. Reports must be shared with other disciplines so they may be used in their QAPI activities.

25.03.05 Annual Report on Medication Use

The organization must document improvement due to medication use review in an annual summary.

Authors' Comments, Experiences, and Suggestions

The scoring procedure for 25.03.05 notes that reviews may not always result in improvements and that this is legitimate.

25.03.06 Performance Improvement in Medication Use

The organization must use the information from its review of medication processes and outcomes to continuously improve the safety of administering medications to patients. To improve its processes, the organization must consider implementing technological advances that are available. If the organization is not able to implement technological advances, the organization must implement alternatives that will resolve medication safety issues and reduce adverse events associated with medication use.

Authors' Comments, Experiences, and Suggestions

The scoring procedure for 25.03.06 instructs surveyors to determine if the organization has considered new technologies; if new technologies are not feasible, surveyors should determine if the organization implemented alternative strategies.

Table 23-1. Arrangement of HFAP Standards/Elements

Standard/Element	Explanation	Scoring Procedure	Score
HFAP incorporates Medicare Conditions of Participation (CoPs) in each chapter. As appropriate, CMS Standards and relevant CMS Interpretative Guidelines are also included. HFAP requirements also include non-Medicare quality standards, which provide focus and continuity to the survey process.	CMS Interpretative Guidelines are often quoted as a source of reference. Specific HFAP explanations of the requirements are also included.	HFAP incorporates Medicare regulations. Therefore, the CMS Survey Procedures are reflected in this column. Also includes specific scoring guidelines for HFAP surveyors.	Most HFAP standards are scored on a scale of 1 to 4. A score of 1 usually reflects full compliance (or an equivalent). A score of 4 usually reflects noncompliance (or an equivalent). Any score greater than 1 reflects varying levels of noncompliance and will result in the need for the facility to submit a corrective action plan.

CHAPTER 24

National Integrated Accreditation for Healthcare Organizations (NIAHO^{SM}) Surveys

The National Integrated Accreditation for Healthcare Organizations (NIAHO^{SM}) surveys of Det Norske Veritas (DNV) Healthcare is a recognized alternative to certification by the Centers for Medicare & Medicaid Services (CMS) and accreditation by the Healthcare Facilities Accreditation Program (HFAP) of the American Osteopathic Association or The Joint Commission. CMS first recognized DNV with "deemed status" (*see* Chapter 22) in September 2008.[1]

NIAHO Requirements

The NIAHO requirements were established in 2008. The requirements address all departments and functions, including pharmacy and medication use. Organizations should access the DNV Web site for the most current NIAHO standards and revisions. (*See* Appendix.)

Some NIAHO standards are more prescriptive than other accreditation standards and CMS standards. Therefore, compliance with other accreditation standards or CMS standards is not necessarily sufficient to meet NIAHO standards and vice versa.

NIAHO Surveys

Organizations may request an accreditation survey to determine their level of compliance with NIAHO requirements. Surveyors review key systems, assess compliance with standards, and determine how well the organization provides care, treatment, and services.

NIAHO accreditation surveys are unannounced. Surveys are usually performed by three surveyors consisting of a clinical surveyor (a physician or nurse with hospital experience) who is primarily responsible for the patient care units, a physical environment surveyor who is primarily responsible for Life Safety Code® issues and related areas such as biomedical engineering, and a generalist surveyor who is primarily responsible for quality management, medication management, medical staff, human resources, laboratory, and radiology. Larger organizations may require additional surveyors. One of the surveyors is designated as the Team Leader or Lead Surveyor. The composition of the survey team is dependent on the size and scope of care of the organization to be surveyed, the complexity of the services, location of all components (e.g., offsite clinics), and whether the organization has a history of serious deficiencies or complaints.[2]

Although accreditation is granted for 3 years, organizations accredited by NIAHO have annual surveys and must maintain compliance and/or progress toward compliance to continue their accreditation. In addition to compliance with NIAHO standards, DNV incorporates international quality standards that are developed through consensus committees of the International Organization for Standardization (ISO). (*See* Appendix.) Organizations must become ISO 9001 compliant within three years of the inital NIAHO accreditation. The ISO 9001 standards guide an organization through a Quality Management System of continual improvement.[3] Table 24-1 shows the arrangement of NIAHO standards and requirements.

Findings that are not compliant with standards are called nonconformities. There are three types of nonconformities[2]:

- NC-1 Condition Level—A requirement that is completely or substantially out of compliance with the standard.
- NC-1—A requirement that has not been addressed (intent), a practice differs from the defined system (implementation), or the system is not effective (effectiveness).
- NC-2—A lapse of either discipline or control during the implementation of a system/procedural requirement, which does not indicate a system breakdown or raise doubt that the services will meet requirements. Overall system is defined, implemented, and effective.

NIAHO provides organizations with a written report of any nonconformity after completion of the survey. All nonconformities require documentation of corrective action within 60 days of the survey report. An NC-1 Condition Level finding requires a follow-up survey.

The influence of the ISO quality standards is apparent in NIAHO documents and surveys. Document control is a key component of the ISO standards. Policies and procedures, job descriptions, standing orders, and other documents must be written using the organization's template, be up to date, reflect the version number, and accurately reflect practices.

An internal audit by an interdisciplinary group is a key component of the ISO standards. Pharmacy personnel may be expected to participate in a review of other departments, and the pharmacy and medication management system will be audited by personnel from outside the department.

NIAHO Accreditation

If NIAHO determines an organization is compliant with its requirements, it awards the organization the status of "accredited." The length of accreditation is 3 years. Organizations are required to demonstrate corrective actions of all nonconformities prior to the awarding of accreditation. Note that NIAHO, The Joint Commission, and HFAP accredit health care organizations; Medicare certifies. NIAHO accreditation, Joint Commission accreditation, HFAP accreditation, or Medicare certification qualifies an organization to participate in the Medicare program. (*See* Chapters 1 and 22.)

NIAHO Standards and Organization

The NIAHO *Accreditation Requirements for Healthcare Facilities, Interpretive Guidances and Surveyor Guidance* manual[1] is organized by department, service, or function. The standards are based on CMS Conditions of Participation (CoP), Life Safety Code®, International Organization for Standardization (ISO) quality standards, and standards of practice of national professional organizations. The Medication Management (MM) section contains standards MM.1 through MM.7. Some standards contain additional standard requirements.

NIAHO Standards and Standard Requirements for Medication Management

Many of the NIAHO standards and standard requirements (SRs) quote the CMS CoPs,[4] CMS Standards, and CMS Interpretative Guidelines. The information in other chapters of this book may be helpful in complying with NIAHO standards. (*See* Chapters 4, 6, and 22.)

NIAHO standards and SRs for the Medication Management (MM) section are listed below. CMS CoPs and CMS Standards are quoted or paraphrased, and the appropriate CMS number follows each standard or standard requirement (i.e., §482.23 for Nursing Services, §482.24 for Medical Record Services, and §482.25 for Pharmaceutical Services). The authors have summarized and paraphrased NIAHO interpretive guidelines and surveyor guidance, except those that are direct restatements of CMS.

The authors' comments, experiences, and suggestions that follow many of the NIAHO standards are in italics. They are based on the authors' personal experiences, reports from surveyed organizations, and surveyors' statements. Some reflect legal requirements or commonly accepted standards of practice. Others note variations in interpretations or provide clarification (e.g., additional explanation).

Pharmacies should obtain a copy of current NIAHO requirements prior to the survey. For additional information and compliance guidelines, they should review the actual standards and standard requirements as well as the relevant explanations. Other chapters in the *Accreditation Requirements for Healthcare Facilities, Interpretive Guidelines and Surveyor Guidance* may also contain requirements for pharmacy services.

MM.1 Management Practices

SR.1 The organization shall have a pharmacy service that meets the needs of the patients. §482.25 Medications will be administered in accordance with accepted professional principles. §482.23(c)(1) The pharmacy service will be directed by a full-time, part-time, or consulting registered pharmacist responsible for developing, supervising, and coordinating all the activities of the pharmacy services. §482.25(a)(1) The pharmacy service must have an adequate number of qualified personnel to ensure effective medication management services, including emergency services. §482.25(a)(2)

Summary of Interpretive Guidelines and Surveyor Guidance for MM.1, SR.1

Direction of pharmaceutical services may not require continuous on-premise supervision at the hospital's single pharmacy or at any pharmacy location, but may be accomplished through regularly scheduled visits and/or telemedicine in accordance with federal and state law and regulations and accepted professional principles. [Interpretive Guidelines of §482.25(a)(1)]

The pharmaceutical services staff must be sufficient in types, numbers, and training to provide quality services, including twenty four (24) hour, seven (7) day emergency coverage. In the alternative, there must be an arrangement for emergency services, as determined by the needs of the patients and as specified by the medical staff and within the scope and complexities of services provided. §482.25(a)(2)

A pharmacist must be available on-call for pharmacies that are not open 24 hours a day, 7 days a week.

Licenses, permits, contracts, job descriptions, and other documents must be current and available for review.

The director of pharmacy must be actively involved in committees responsible for establishing medication-related policies and procedures (e.g., Pharmacy and Therapeutics, Infection Control, Safety).

Policies and procedures address [Interpretive Guidelines of §482.25]:

- Access to patient-specific information to properly order, prepare, dispense, administer, and monitor medications
- Availability of current medication information
- High-alert medication practices, including dosing limits, packaging, labeling, storage, administration guidelines, and an alert system for look-alike and sound-alike medications
- Preparation, distribution, administration, and proper disposal of hazardous agents
- Medications brought into the hospital by patients and their families
- Investigational medications
- Drug recalls
- Routine inspection of all drug storage and preparation areas
- Labeling of medications
- Avoidance of dangerous abbreviations
- Guidelines and criteria for selection from a menu of medication options addressing similar indications for use (e.g., analgesics)
- Use of pre-printed order sheets whenever possible
- Prohibiting orders such as "resume previous orders"
- Require that protocols and standing orders have an order from a licensed independent practitioner (LIP)
- Require that multiple page orders have a physician signature, date, and time on each page
- Identification of when weight-based dosing for pediatric populations is required
- Limiting the variety of medication-related devices and equipment
- Implementation of a voluntary, non-punitive, reporting system to monitor and report medication errors and adverse drug reactions
- Proactive review and analysis of external alerts, internal practice variances, and adverse drug events

SR.2 All medications shall be administered by or under the supervision of nursing or other qualified personnel in accordance with applicable federal and state laws. All drugs and biologicals shall be administered only upon the orders of the practitioner responsible for the care of the patient in accordance with approved medical staff policies and procedures and accepted standards of practice. §482.23(c)

Authors' Comments, Experiences, and Suggestions

Personnel who administer medications must do so only within their scope of practice.

Though the interpretive guidelines specify action for non-controlled medications and biologicals, policies addressing controlled medications must also be developed and implemented.

Though not specified in the CMS standards or Interpretive Guidelines, the CMS surveyor procedures suggest that an indicator for assessing appropriate administration of medications should include administration within 30 minutes of the scheduled time.

Summary of Interpretive Guidelines and Surveyor Guidance for MM.1, SR.2

The hospital must maintain medical staff-approved policies and procedures that identify who is authorized to administer medications; that nursing and other personnel (if other than nursing) administering medications are appropriately training or licensed, function under supervision as required; and that the policies are followed and are in accordance with federal and state laws.

The medication ordering process must include reconciliation of medication orders with the medication administration records (MARs) and pharmacy dispensing records.

Administration of medications must include a process to ensure correct patient identification, how medications are administered, how the clinical staff ensures that oral medications are taken, and what actions are taken when medications are not given on time.

Policies for patient self-administration of medications include:

- Authorization for the patient to have access to the self-administered medication(s)
- Security of non-controlled drugs and biologicals
- Safe medication practices
- Determination of competence
- Patient education

SR.3 All compounding, packaging, and dispensing of medication shall be under the supervision of a pharmacist. §482.25(b)(1)

Authors' Comments, Experiences, and Suggestions

The pharmacy must provide or mix all IVs except in an emergency or for medications with short stability.

Summary of Interpretive Guidelines and Surveyor Guidance for MM.1, SR.3

Medications must be prepared and administered in accordance with federal and state laws, accepted national standards of practice, manufacturer's directions, and hospital policy.

Unit-dose labels must include the name and strength of the drug, lot number, and an expiration date.

Patient-specific medication labels must include the patient and prescriber full name, quantity and strength of the medication, expiration date, and appropriate cautionary statements.

Sterile products must be prepared and labeled in a suitable environment.

SR.4 All drugs and biologicals must be controlled, secured, and distributed in accordance with applicable standards of practice and consistent with federal and state law at all times. §482.25(b)(2)(i)

SR.4a Drugs listed as Schedule II, III, IV, and V of the Comprehensive Drug Abuse Prevention and Control Act of 1970 must be kept locked within a secure area. §482.25(b)(2)(ii)

SR.4b Only personnel authorized by the pharmacy service shall have access to locked areas. §482.25(b)(2)(iii)

Authors' Comments, Experiences, and Suggestions

Medication access must be limited to the scope of practice of the individual.

Access to medications must be denied when an individual leaves the employ of the organization or transfers to a position where he or she should not have access.

Summary of Interpretive Guidelines and Surveyor Guidance for MM.1, SR.4

Drugs and biologicals are stored in accordance with manufacturer's directions and state and federal requirements; §482.25(a)

Authors' Comments, Experiences, and Suggestions

Thermometers in medication refrigerators, freezers, and warmers must be calibrated and temperatures logged.

Hospital policies and procedures must define which personnel are authorized to have access to locked areas based on their own needs as well as state law.

Non-controlled drugs and biologicals must be stored in a secure area in a manner that prevents tampering and diversion. A medication is considered secure if unauthorized individuals are prevented from obtaining access.

A secure area is one in which staff are actively providing patient care or preparing to receive patients with procedures to ensure limited entry and exit to appropriate staff, patients, and visitors.

- This includes critical care areas or labor and delivery suites, which actively provide patient care around the clock and the operating room when staffed and providing care.

- All non-controlled substances must be locked when a patient care area is not staffed.
- The operating room suite is considered secure when the suite is staffed and staff are actively providing patient care. When the suite is not in use (e.g., weekends, holidays, and after hours), it would not be considered secure. A hospital may choose to lock the entire suite, lock non-mobile carts containing drugs and biologicals, place mobile carts in a locked room, or otherwise lock drugs and biologicals in a secure area. If an individual operating room is not in use, the hospital is expected to lock non-mobile carts, and ensure mobile carts are in a locked room. [Interpretive Guidelines of §482.25(b)(2)(i)]

All medications listed in Schedule II, III, IV, and V of the Comprehensive Drug Abuse Prevention and Control Act of 1970 must be kept and locked in secured container and/or room. In the event these drugs are stored in a container that is readily portable, it must be stored in a locked room, monitored location, or secured location that will ensure their security when not in use.

Policies and procedures address the security and monitoring of carts or emergency boxes (locked or unlocked) containing drugs and biologicals in all patient care areas to ensure their safe storage, availability in emergency situations, and patient safety.

SR.5 Outdated, mislabeled, or otherwise unusable medications shall not be available for patient use. §482.25(b)(3)

Summary of Interpretive Guidelines and Surveyor Guidance for MM.1, SR.5

The hospital must have a pharmacy labeling, inspection, and inventory management system that ensures that outdated, mislabeled, or otherwise unusable medications are not available for patient use.

SR.6 Medications prescribed without specific duration or number of doses shall automatically be stopped after a reasonable time that has been predetermined by the medical staff. §482.25(b)(5)

Authors' Comments, Experiences, and Suggestions

An automatic stop order policy is required.

SR.7 Staff other than doctors of medicine or osteopathy who administer blood transfusions and intravenous medications shall have special training. §482.23(c)(3)

Authors' Comments, Experiences, and Suggestions

Pharmacy must provide oversight to validate nursing and other clinical staff training concerning infusion therapy. The hospital (but not necessarily the pharmacy) must ensure that the training addresses scope of practice and competence is documented.

Summary of Interpretive Guidelines and Surveyor Guidance for MM.1, SR.7

Education concerning infusion therapy must include fluid and electrolyte balance, blood components, and venipuncture technique, including return demonstration and supervised practice.

The hospital must have a defined process for addressing blood transfusion reactions and the procedure to be followed when this occurs.

MM.2 Formulary

The medical staff or pharmaceutical oversight group shall select a list of medications to be available within the organization. The list shall be available to all appropriate staff at all times. §482.25(b)(9)

Authors' Comments, Experiences, and Suggestions

A current copy of the formulary should be available in all areas where medication orders are written and where medications are stored, dispensed, or administered.

Summary of Interpretive Guidelines and Surveyor Guidance for MM.2

In accordance with accepted standards of practice, the medical staff, in consultation with the pharmacy service, should develop written criteria for determining what medications are available for dispensing or administration. At a minimum, the criteria include the indication for use, effectiveness, risks (including propensity for medication errors, abuse potential, and sentinel events), and costs.

The formulary must list medications for dispensing or administration that the hospital maintains or that are readily available.

The formulary may be maintained either electronically on the hospital's information management system or in a hardcopy form. The hospital must have an effective means of notifying the hospital staff and medical staff when changes are made to the formulary.

The hospital must have a process in place that addresses medication-related issues to include:

- Communicating with appropriate prescribers and staff
- Developing approved substitution protocols
- Educating appropriate LIPs, appropriate health care professionals, and staff about these protocols
- Obtaining medications in the event of a disaster

The hospital must have a medical staff-approved policy and procedure in place to address the process for requests for medications to be added to the formulary before the medications are available for dispensing and administration.

The hospital must have processes to approve and procure medications that are not on the hospital's formulary.

MM.3 Scheduled Drugs

SR.1 Current and accurate records must be kept of the receipt and disposition of all scheduled drugs, and in compliance with all federal and state documentation requirements. §482.25(a)(3)

Authors' Comments, Experiences, and Suggestions

In this standard, "scheduled drugs" refers to controlled substances.

Summary of Interpretive Guidelines and Surveyor Guidance for MM.3, SR.1

The hospital must maintain a record system to maintain current and accurate records of the receipt and disposition of all scheduled drugs that is in compliance with all federal and state documentation requirements.

The record system must address the following:

- Accountability procedures to ensure control of the distribution, use, and disposition
- Current and accurate receipt and disposition
- Ability to trace the process for moving scheduled drugs throughout the service from the point of entry into the hospital to the point of departure either through administration to the patient, destruction, or return to the manufacturer
- Identify the pharmacist responsible for determining that all drug records are in order and that an account of all scheduled drugs is maintained and reconciled
- Accounting of all scheduled drugs and any discrepancies in count are reconciled promptly
- Readily retrievable records

A pharmacist must be responsible for determining that all drug records are in order and that an account of all scheduled drugs is maintained and periodically reconciled.

Authors' Comments, Experiences, and Suggestions

Wastage of controlled substances must be documented and reconciled.

SR.2 Abuses and losses of controlled substances must be reported, in accordance with applicable federal and state laws, to the individual responsible for the pharmaceutical service and to the chief executive officer, as appropriate. §482.25(b)(7)

Authors' Comments, Experiences, and Suggestions

The tracking system must be robust enough to identify losses or diversion within a reasonably tight time frame.

MM.4 Medication Orders

All medication orders shall:

SR.1 Include the name of the drug, the dosage and frequency of administration, and the route of administration. [Interpretive Guidelines of §482.23(b)]

Summary of Interpretive Guidelines and Surveyor Guidance for MM.4, SR.1

Elements that are to be included in any medication order (including all written and verbal/telephone orders):

- Name of patient
- Age and weight of patient, when appropriate
- Date and time of the order
- Drug name
- Dosage form (e.g., tablets, capsules, inhalants)
- Exact strength or concentration
- Dose, frequency, and route
- Quantity and/or duration
- Indication for use when appropriate
- Specific instructions for use
- Name of prescriber

SR.2 Be in writing and signed, including date and time, by the practitioner(s) responsible for the care of the patient as specified under 42 CFR§482.12(c) and authorized to write such orders by hospital policy and in accordance with state law. §482.23(c)(2)

SR.2a Influenza and polysaccharide vaccines may be administered in accordance with a policy approved by the medical staff after an individual assessment for contraindications.

Authors' Comments, Experiences, and Suggestions

All orders must be timed.

Summary of Interpretive Guidelines and Surveyor Guidance for MM.4, SR.2

If a hospital uses other written protocols or standing orders for drugs or biologicals that have been reviewed and approved by the medical staff, initiation of such protocols or standing orders requires an order from a practitioner responsible for the patient's care.

SR.3 Telephone or verbal orders are to be used infrequently and when used must be accepted only by personnel authorized by the medical staff and in accordance with federal and state law. §482.23(c)(2)(i)

Authors' Comments, Experiences, and Suggestions

Both active and closed records may be used during the survey.

SR.4 Verbal orders must be signed or initialed by the prescribing practitioner and must be authenticated in accordance with federal and state law. If there is not state law that designates a specific time frame for the authentication of verbal orders, the orders must be authenticated within 48 hours. §482.24(c)(1)(iii)

Summary of Interpretive Guidelines and Surveyor Guidance for MM.4, SR.4

The entire verbal or telephone order must be written down and then repeated back to the prescriber and be signed by the individual receiving the order. Verbal orders must be documented in the patient's medical record and be reviewed, authenticated, and timed by the prescriber as soon as possible.

Authors' Comments, Experiences, and Suggestions

Verbal and telephone orders must be authenticated (i.e., timed) within the required time frame.

Policies and procedures must include:

- Limitations or prohibitions on use of verbal or telephone orders
- A mechanism to ensure validity and authenticity of the prescriber
- The elements required for inclusion in a complete verbal or telephone order
- List of situations in which verbal or telephone orders may be used
- A list defining the individuals who may send and receive verbal/telephone orders
- Guidelines for clear and effective communication of verbal or telephone orders

Authors' Comments, Experiences, and Suggestions

The pharmacy should have a current signature log of all authorized prescribers.

MM.5 Review of Medication Orders

A licensed pharmacist must review all medication orders prior to administration of the first dose to a patient. If these individuals are not available at that time, the following shall occur: [Interpretive Guidelines of §482.25(b)]

SR.1 The practitioner caring for the patient must determine the urgency of administration. [Interpretive Guidelines of §482.25(b)]

Summary of Interpretive Guidelines and Surveyor Guidance for MM.5, SR.1

All medication orders (except in emergency situations) must be reviewed for appropriateness by a pharmacist or doctor of medicine or osteopathy before the first dose is dispensed.

Review of medication orders must include:

- Therapeutic appropriateness of a patient's medication regimen
- Therapeutic duplication in the patient's medication regimen
- Appropriateness of the drug, dose, frequency, route, and method of administration
- Real or potential medication–medication, medication–food, medication–laboratory test, and medication–disease interactions
- Real or potential allergies or sensitivities
- Variation from organizational criteria for use
- Other contraindications

The hospital must arrange for a qualified pharmacist to be available either on-call or at another location (e.g. at another organization that has 24-hour pharmacist availability) to answer questions or provide medications beyond those accessible to non-pharmacy staff.

Quality control procedures (such as an independent second check by another individual or a secondary verification built into the system, such as bar coding) must be in place to prevent medication retrieval errors.

The effects of medication(s) on patients must be monitored to assure medication therapy is appropriate and minimizes the occurrence of adverse events. The monitoring process must include:

- Clinical and laboratory data to evaluate the efficacy of medication therapy to anticipate or evaluate toxicity and adverse effects
- Physical signs and clinical symptoms relevant to the patient's medication therapy
- Assessing the patient's own perceptions about side effects, and, when appropriate, perceived efficacy

SR.2 When a pharmacist is not available medications shall be retrieved from the pharmacy or storage area (including automated dispensing) only by licensed staff designated by the pharmacy service and approved by the medical staff, in accordance with principles of patient safety and federal and state law. §482.25(b)(4)

Authors' Comments, Experiences, and Suggestions

Some states specifically prohibit after-hours access into the pharmacy by nursing and other non-pharmacy personnel.

Summary of Interpretive Guidelines and Surveyor Guidance for MM.5, SR.2

Medications used for after-hours access may be stored in a night cabinet, automated distribution cabinet, or a limited section of the pharmacy.

> ***Note:*** Routine after-hours access to the pharmacy by non-pharmacists for access to medication should be minimized and eliminated as much as possible. The use of well-designed night cabinets, after-hours medication carts, and other methods may preclude the need for a non-pharmacist to enter the pharmacy. Policies and procedures should be consistent with federal and state law.

If medications may be retrieved from the pharmacy or storage area by non-pharmacy personnel, it may only be by licensed staff designated by the pharmacy service and approved by the medical staff, in accordance with principles of patient safety and federal and state law;

SR.3 The licensed individual that obtains the medication shall have an orientation to the storage area for the medication.

Authors' Comments, Experiences, and Suggestions

The orientation for individuals who obtain medications must be documented and available for surveyors.

SR.4 All high-risk medications in this area shall be segregated and unavailable.

Authors' Comments, Experiences, and Suggestions

The organization must identify and define in writing a list of those medications that are high-risk.

SR.5 There shall be a documented protocol requiring that this licensed individual have access to appropriate information to process the order in a formal manner. Information shall include: [Interpretive Guidelines of §482.25(b)(4)]

SR.5a potential drug–drug interactions

SR.5b potential allergies or cross sensitivities

SR.5c proper dose ranges

SR.5d proper indications for administration

SR.6 This licensed individual shall leave a duplicate dose with a copy of the order or comparable method for verification by a licensed pharmacist upon arrival in the organization.

SR.7 The removal of the medication must be documented, tracked, and trended and the results analyzed to determine need for additional pharmacy staff or medication storage resources and appropriateness of any pharmacy after-hour practices, as appropriate. [Interpretive Guidelines of §482.25(b)(4)]

Authors' Comments, Experiences, and Suggestions

Tracking after-hours medication needs should be included in the department's quality improvement activities.

Summary of Interpretive Guidelines and Surveyor Guidance for MM.5, SR.7

This process must be continually evaluated to determine the medications accessed routinely and the causes of accessing the pharmacy after hours. Action should be taken to reduce the number of times non-pharmacist health care professionals obtain medications after the pharmacy is closed.

MM.6 Oversight Group

SR.1 The medical staff is responsible for developing policies and procedures that minimize drug errors. §482.25 The medical staff may delegate this responsibility to an organized pharmacy oversight group.

Summary of Interpretive Guidelines and Surveyor Guidance for MM.6, SR.1

Medical staff-approved policies and procedures must include:

- Methods to minimize medication errors
- Identification and assessment of adverse drug reactions
- Identification and assessment of drug incompatibilities

SR.2 There shall be procedures for reporting transfusion reactions, adverse drug reactions, and errors in prescribing, preparing, and administering of drugs, in the aggregate, for trending and analysis. §482.23(c)(4)

Authors' Comments, Experiences, and Suggestions

All staff involved in the medication use process must be aware of and participate in the medication error and adverse drug reaction reporting system.

Summary of Interpretive Guidelines and Surveyor Guidance for MM.6, SR.2

Medication errors, adverse drug reactions, and drug incompatibilities must immediately be reported to the attending physician. The hospital should define the time frame for this process.

The hospital policies must define medication errors and adverse drug events. The source of the definition should be included in the policy.

The medication error and adverse drug reaction reports must be trended, analyzed, and evaluated.

SR.3 Drug preparation, administration, and prescribing errors, adverse drug reactions, and incompatibilities shall be immediately reported to the attending physician and to the organization-wide quality management program. §482.25(b)(6)

Summary of Interpretive Guidelines and Surveyor Guidance for MM.6, SR.3

The hospital must have a means for aggregating this information and related data to be trended and analyzed and continually evaluated in order to identify and implement corrective/preventive action.

Authors' Comments, Experiences, and Suggestions

Be prepared to demonstrate examples of corrective actions that have been implemented.

MM.7 Available Information

Information relating to drug interactions and information on drug therapy, side effects, toxicology, dosage, indications for use, and routes of administration shall be available to the professional staff. §482.25(b)(8)

Table 24-1. Arrangement of NIAHO Standards/Elements

Standard/Standard Requirement	Interpretive Guidelines	Surveyor Guidance
NIAHO incorporates Medicare Conditions of Participation (CoPs) in each chapter. As appropriate, CMS Standards and relevant CMS Interpretative Guidelines are also included.	CMS Interpretative Guidelines are often quoted as a source of reference.	NIAHO incorporates Medicare regulations. Therefore, the CMS Survey Procedures are reflected in the surveyor guidance.
NIAHO requirements also include non-Medicare quality standards, which provide focus and continuity to the survey process.	Specific NIAHO explanations of the requirements are also included.	

EXAMPLE 3-1

SUGGESTED ACTIVITY FREQUENCY CHART

Minimum Frequency:

S = Each Shift	M = Monthly	Y = Yearly	ON = Ongoing
D = Daily	Q = Quarterly	2Y = Every 2 Years	AR = As Required
W = Weekly	6M = Every 6 Months	3Y = Every 3 Years	

ACTIVITY	S	D	W	M	Q	6M	Y	2Y	3Y	ON	AR
Licensure verification							X				
Job description updating							X				
Performance evaluations							X				
Competence assessments							1				1
Staff orientation											X
Pharmacy staff meetings			2	2							
In-service programs for pharmacy				X							
In-service programs for nursing					X						
In-service programs for medical staff						X					
Formulary approval							X				
Formulary additions/deletions (updating)					X						
Emergency medication inspections	3	3		3							
Controlled substances inventories							4	4			
Refrigerator/Freezer/Warmer temperature checks		X									
Refrigerator inspections				X							
Medication area inspections				X							
P&T committee meetings				5	5						
Policy and procedure review & revision							X				
Policy and procedure approval							X				
Laminar Airflow Workbench cleaning	X										
Pre-filter cleaning or changing					X	X					
Primary Engineering Control Certification						X					
Non-Viable Environmental Monitoring for Buffer and Ante Area						X					
Viable Environmental Monitoring for Buffer and Ante Area						X					
Performance Improvement activity										X	
Medication use improvement activity										X	

1: Before or soon after hiring, before performing new tasks, and yearly.
2: Monthly staff meetings are the suggested minimum. Weekly meetings may be more appropriate.
3: Monthly inspections by pharmacy. Inspections, at least daily, by those who use the drugs.
4: DEA requires a biennial inventory. Some states require annual inventories. Time of year varies.
5: Quarterly is the minimum frequency. Some hospitals may need more frequent meetings (e.g., monthly).

EXAMPLE 4-1

CONFIDENTIALITY OF PATIENT INFORMATION AGREEMENT

I, ____, understand that patients have a need and right to confidentiality.

I also understand that:

- Discussions relating to patients must be out of the hearing range of staff, visitors, other patients, and individuals who do not have a need or reason to know the information.
- Medication orders, pharmacy patient profiles, labels, meeting minutes, and other patient-related documents (i.e., those that contain patients' names or identifying numbers, or information related to patients' status, treatment, diagnosis, and medications) must be securely stored and access restricted to those who have a legitimate need or reason to know and use the information therein.
- Disposal of patient-related documents must guarantee confidentiality. Patient-related documents must not be placed in regular trash for disposal.
- E-mail and other electronic communication pose a particular risk of inadvertent dissemination inside and outside the facility. Care must be taken to protect e-mail communications.
- Patient-related information must not be released to the news media or unauthorized individuals, firms, and agencies. Requests for information must be forwarded to the facility's administration.

I hereby affirm that I will protect the confidentiality of patient-related information.

___________________________________ ______________________________

Signature Date

EXAMPLE 4-2

Please complete the form, provide supportive references, and return to the Director of Pharmacy. Copies of the request and references will be distributed to the Committee. The Committee meets on a monthly basis. You will be asked to attend the meeting and present the request. The Committee will vote on the change in inventory after review of all information is completed. Please print legibly.

FORMULARY ADDITION REQUEST FORM

DRUG REQUESTED:

Generic Name ______________________________

FDA Approval Status ______________________________

Black Box Warning ______________________________

FDA REMS Required ______________________________

DESCRIPTION:

FDA Approved Indication(s) ______________________________

Request for other than FDA-approved indications ______________________________

____

Is there a drug similar to this currently on formulary? Yes No If so, which? __________

If yes, are you proposing this drug as a replacement? Yes No If so, which? __________

CLINICAL TRIALS (brief overview with copies of studies): ______________________________

____

____

____

____

RISKS (including propensity for medications errors, look-alike/sound-alike mistakes, abuse potential and/or Sentinel Events): __________

____

ADVERSE EFFECTS: ______________________________

____

DOSAGE & ADMINISTRATION (cite reference): ______________________________

____

____

____

____

COST ANALYSIS (brief overview with copies of studies): ______________________________

____

EXAMPLE 4-2 (continued)

FACTORS:

What do you believe are the relevant factors in requesting this drug as opposed to using drugs available already? (*circle all that apply)*

1) The drug is FDA approved for the proposed indication where the others are not.

2) The drug is more clinically efficacious.

3) The drug has an improved side effect profile.

4) The drug is more convenient.

5) The drug costs less.

6) The drug is more cost effective.

7) Other: ____

____

AVAILABILITY:

How should the drug be offered?

1) Available to all providers.

2) Restricted to a service.

3) Restricted to an individual.

4) Restricted to a treatment protocol.

ANTICIPATED USAGE:

1) It is a continuous use product.

2) It is a seasonal product. During what months is it used? ______________________

3) How much of the drug should be on hand? ______________________

CONFLICT OF INTEREST DISLOSURE:

Has the requester received any grants, current or pending, to support research on this or any product associated with the company manufacturing, repackaging, marketing, or distributing this drug?

Yes No

Has any member of the requester's service/section received any grants, current or pending, to support research on this or any product associated with the company manufacturing, repackaging, marketing, or distributing of this drug?

Yes No

Has the requester, any member of his/her family, or any organization in which the requester serves as an officer, director, trustee, general partner, employee, or consultant received gifts of training, transportation, or honoraria, or manufacturing, repackaging, marketing, or distributing this drug?

Yes No

SIGNATURE OF REQUESTER: ______________________ PRINTED: ______________________ DATE: __________

PHONE #: ______________________ E-MAIL ADDRESS: ______________________

SIGNATURE OF SERVICE/SECTION CHIEF: ______________________

EXAMPLE 4-3

NONFORMULARY MEDICATION REQUEST FORM

Completion of this form does **NOT** constitute a request for addition of this medication to the formulary. Proposals for addition to the formulary must be made on a Request for Formulary Addition form, which is available from the pharmacy.

PATIENT NAME________________________________ **PATIENT NUMBER**____________________

LOCATION________________________________ **DATE**____________________

A separate request must be completed for each patient for whom the following medication is prescribed.

MEDICATION REQUESTED

GENERIC NAME ____

INDICATION FOR USE ____

DOSAGE FORM ____________________________ **ROUTE**____________________________

DOSE PRESCRIBED ____________________________ **FREQUENCY**____________________________

BLACK BOX WARNINGS ____

EXPECTED DURATION OF THERAPY WITH THIS MEDICATION (the pharmacy will obtain an initial supply sufficient to treat this patient for the expected duration of therapy)

____

REASON FOR USING THIS MEDICATION RATHER THAN ONE LISTED IN THE FORMULARY

__No equivalent formulary medication available

__Patient failed therapy with alternative medications

__Patient had adverse effect from alternative medications

__ Alternative medications unacceptable

__ Other ____________________________

____

I understand that the above medication has not been accepted by the medical staff for use in this facility and is not listed in the formulary. I further understand that since this medication must be obtained from outside the facility, its procurement might be delayed. If the expected delay will exceed four hours, I will be so notified.

I anticipate a recurring need for this medication. Yes ______ No _______

____ Date ____________________

Signature of requesting practitioner

____ E-mail: ____________________

Print Name

Phone #: ____________________

PHARMACY USE ONLY

COST OF NONFORMULARY MEDICATION ____

ALTERNATIVE MEDICATION SUGGESTED BY PHARMACY ________________________________

SUGGESTED BY (PHARMACIST)____________________________ **DATE/TIME** ____________________

OUTCOME/COMMENTS____

____

____

EXAMPLE 4-4

NONFORMULARY MEDICATION SUMMARY

DATE	MEDICATION	PRESCRIBER	REASON	DATE PRESENTED TO P&T COMMITTEE

EXAMPLE 4-5

NOTIFICATION OF SHORTAGE AND OUTAGE

DATE OF NOTIFICATION	UNAVAILABLE MEDICATION	CURRENT INVENTORY STATUS	PHARMACY AND THERAPEUTIC COMMITTEE NOTIFIED	COMMUNICATION SENT TO PRESCRIBERS AND STAFF (SEE ATTACHED)	RESOLUTION DATE	STATUS

EXAMPLE 4-6

REFRIGERATOR/FREEZER/WARMER MONTHLY TEMPERATURE LOG

Place an "X" in a box to the right to indicate the type of use.

	Medication: 36 to 46°F, 2 to 8°C
	Freezer: -13 to 14°F, -25 to -10°C
	Warmer

UNIT: ______________________ **MONTH:** ______________________

LOCATION/ROOM#: ______________________ **YEAR:** ______________________

Note corrective action if temperature is not within the acceptable range (e.g., adjust temperature, replace thermometer, or call Facilities Management [date/time]). Notify pharmacy if out of range.

DATE	TEMP	NAME	ACTION TAKEN	CLEAN DATE
1				
2				
3				
4				
5				
6				
7				
8				
9				
10				
11				
12				
13				
14				
15				
16				
17				
18				
19				
20				
21				
22				
23				
24				
25				
26				
27				
28				
29				
30				
31				

COMMENTS: ______________________

EXAMPLE 4-7

MONTHLY MEDICATION REFRIGERATOR TEMPERATURE LOG

DEPARTMENT ______________________ LOCATION ______________________ MONTH ________ YEAR ________

TEMPERATURES WILL BE LOGGED ON THE DAYS THE DEPARTMENT IS OPEN FOR BUSINESS

F°	1	2	3	4	5	6	7	8	9	10	11	12	13	14	15	16	17	18	19	20	21	22	23	24	25	26	27	28	29	30	31
49°																															
48°																															
47°																															
46°																															
45°																															
44°																															
43°																															
42°																															
41°																															
40°																															
39°																															
38°																															
37°																															
36°																															
35°																															
34°																															
33°																															

Temperature Range: Refrigerator = 36 to 46 degrees Fahrenheit (note: shaded areas = out of range temperatures)

Note: If not within acceptable range, call the Pharmacy and Facilities Management. Note time the call is made. Corrective action must be noted (e.g., turned temperature down, replaced thermometer, etc.)

DATE	❑ PHARMACY NOTIFIED	❑ MAINTENANCE NOTIFIED, if applicable	CORRECTIVE ACTION/COMMENTS

EXAMPLE 4-8

MONTHLY MEDICATION FREEZER TEMPERATURE LOG

DEPARTMENT ________________________ LOCATION ________________________ MONTH ________ YEAR ________

TEMPERATURES WILL BE LOGGED ON THE DAYS THE DEPARTMENT IS OPEN FOR BUSINESS

	1	2	3	4	5	6	7	8	9	10	11	12	13	14	15	16	17	18	19	20	21	22	23	24	25	26	27	28	29	30	31
20°																															
18°																															
16°																															
14°																															
12°																															
10°																															
8°																															
6°																															
4°																															
2°																															
0°																															
-2°																															
-4°																															
-8°																															
-10°																															
-13°																															
-14°																															
-16°																															

Temperature Range: Freezer = -13 to 14 degrees Fahrenheit (note: shaded areas = out of range temperatures)

Note: If not within acceptable range, call the Pharmacy and Facilities Management. Note time the call is made. Corrective action must be noted (e.g., turned temperature down, replaced thermometer, etc.)

DATE	❑ PHARMACY NOTIFIED	❑ MAINTENANCE NOTIFIED, if applicable	CORRECTIVE ACTION/COMMENTS

EXAMPLE 4-9

CONTROLLED SUBSTANCES INVENTORY COVER PAGE

Name of Registrant: ______________________________

Address: ______________________________

City: ____________________ **State:** _____ **Zip code:** ______

DEA Registration Number: ____________________________

Date of Inventory: ______________________________

Inventory taken at Opening of business

Close of business

Actual Time Completed: ____________________________

____

Signature of Person Taking Inventory

____

Signature of Pharmacist In Charge

Note: Do not send this completed inventory to the DEA. Retain this inventory at the above address for at least two years.

EXAMPLE 4-10

CONTROLLED SUBSTANCES BIENNIAL INVENTORY RECORD

Check Only One of the Following: Schedule II___ Schedules III, IV, and V___

DRUG	DOSAGE FORM	STRENGTH	UNIT SIZE	NUMBER OF COMMERCIAL UNITS	MANUFACTURER	ACTUAL COUNT

EXAMPLE 4-11

OMB Approval No. 1117 - 0007	U. S. Department of Justice / Drug Enforcement Administration **REGISTRANTS INVENTORY OF DRUGS SURRENDERED**	PACKAGE NO.

The following schedule is an inventory of controlled substances which is hereby surrendered to you for proper disposition.

FROM: *(Include Name, Street, City, State and ZIP Code in space provided below.)*

Signature of applicant or authorized agent
Registrant's DEA Number
Registrant's Telephone Number

NOTE: CERTIFIED MAIL (Return Receipt Requested) IS REQUIRED FOR SHIPMENTS OF DRUGS VIA U.S. POSTAL SERVICE. See instructions on reverse (page 2) of form.

	NAME OF DRUG OR PREPARATION Registrants will fill in Columns 1,2,3, and 4 ONLY.	Number of Containers	CONTENTS *(Number of grams, tablets, ounces or other units per container)*	Controlled Substance Content, *(Each Unit)*	**FOR DEA USE ONLY** DISPOSITION	QUANTITY GMS.	QUANTITY MGS.
	1	*2*	*3*	*4*	*5*	*6*	*7*
1							
2							
3							
4							
5							
6							
7							
8							
9							
10							
11							
12							
13							
14							
15							
16							

FORM DEA-41 (9-01) Previous edition dated **6-86** is usable. *See instructions on reverse (page 2) of form.*

EXAMPLE 4-11 (continued)

DEA-41 (6/1986) Pg. 2

NAME OF DRUG OR PREPARATION Registrants will fill in Columns 1,2,3, and 4 ONLY.	Number of Containers	CONTENTS (*Number of grams, tablets, ounces or other units per container*)	Controlled Substance Content, (*Each Unit*)	FOR DEA USE ONLY DISPOSITION	QUANTITY GMS.	 MGS.
1	2	3	4	5	6	7
17						
18						
19						
20						
21						
22						
23						
24						

The controlled substances surrendered in accordance with Title 21 of the Code of Federal Regulations, Section 1307.21, have been received in _______packages purporting to contain the drugs listed on this inventory and have been: ** (1) Forwarded tape-sealed without opening; (2) Destroyed as indicated and the remainder forwarded tape-sealed after verifying contents; (3) Forwarded tape-sealed after verifying contents.

DATE ______________________ DESTROYED BY: ______________________

** *Strike out lines not applicable.*

WITNESSED BY: ______________________

INSTRUCTIONS

1. List the name of the drug in column 1, the number of containers in column 2, the size of each container in column 3, and in column 4 the controlled substance content of each unit described in column 3; e.g., morphine sulfate tabs., 3 pkgs., 100 tabs., 1/4 gr. (16 mg.) or morphine sulfate tabs., 1 pkg., 83 tabs., 1/2 gr. (32mg.), etc.

2. All packages included on a single line should be identical in name, content and controlled substance strength.

3. Prepare this form in quadruplicate. Mail two (2) copies of this form to the Special Agent in Charge, under separate cover. Enclose one additional copy in the shipment with the drugs. Retain one copy for your records. One copy will be returned to you as a receipt. No further receipt will be furnished to you unless specifically requested. Any further inquiries concerning these drugs should be addressed to the DEA District Office which serves your area.

4. There is no provision for payment for drugs surrendered. This is merely a service rendered to registrants enabling them to clear their stocks and records of unwanted items.

5. Drugs should be shipped tape-sealed via prepaid express or certified mail (**return receipt requested**) to Special Agent in Charge, Drug Enforcement Administration, of the DEA District Office which serves your area.

PRIVACY ACT INFORMATION

AUTHORITY: Section 307 of the Controlled Substances Act of 1970 (PL 91-513).
PURPOSE: To document the surrender of controlled substances which have been forwarded by registrants to DEA for disposal.
ROUTINE USES: This form is required by Federal Regulations for the surrender of unwanted Controlled Substances. Disclosures of information from this system are made to the following categories of users for the purposes stated.
A. Other Federal law enforcement and regulatory agencies for law enforcement and regulatory purposes.
B. State and local law enforcement and regulatory agencies for law enforcement and regulatory purposes.
EFFECT: Failure to document the surrender of unwanted Controlled Substances may result in prosecution for violation of the Controlled Substances Act.

Under the Paperwork Reduction Act, a person is not required to respond to a collection of information unless it displays a currently valid OMB control number. Public reporting burden for this collection of information is estimated to average 30 minutes per response, including the time for reviewing instructions, searching existing data sources, gathering and maintaining the data needed, and completing and reviewing the collection of information. Send comments regarding this burden estimate or any other aspect of this collection of information, including suggestions for reducing this burden, to the Drug Enforcement Administration, FOI and Records Management Section, Washington, D.C. 20537; and to the Office of Management and Budget, Paperwork Reduction Project no. 1117-0007, Washington, D.C. 20503.

EXAMPLE 4-12

DEA's Diversion Control Program - DEA Form 106 - Theft or Loss of Controlled Substances 11/3/09 2:14 AM

U.S. DEPARTMENT OF JUSTICE
DRUG ENFORCEMENT ADMINISTRATION

OFFICE OF DIVERSION CONTROL

HOME | PRIVACY POLICY | CONTACT US | WHAT'S NEW | HOT ITEMS | SITEMAP | SEARCH

DIVERSION PROGRAMS

APPLICATIONS & ON-LINE FORMS
ARCOS
CHEMICALS
CONTROLLED SUBSTANCE SCHEDULES
CSOS
IMPORT AND EXPORT
NFLIS
QUOTAS
REGISTRATION SUPPORT
REPORTS REQUIRED BY 21 CFR

RESOURCES

CAREER OPPORTUNITIES
DEA MAILING ADDRESSES
DRUGS/CHEMICALS OF CONCERN
e-COMMERCE INITIATIVES
FEDERAL REGISTER NOTICES
MEETINGS & EVENTS
OFFICES & DIRECTORIES
PROGRAM DESCRIPTION
PUBLICATIONS
QUESTIONS & ANSWERS
REGULATIONS & CODIFIED CSA
SIGNIFICANT GUIDANCE DOCUMENTS

LINKS

FEDERAL AGENCIES & RELATED
INDUSTRY RELATED
PUBLIC INTEREST

REGISTRATION VALIDATION

CASES AGAINST DOCTORS

Reports Required by 21 CFR > **Theft or Loss of Controlled Substances**

Theft or Loss of Controlled Substances

DEA Form 106

IMPORTANT NOTICE: Only those persons registered with and authorized by DEA to handle controlled substances may utilize/submit this form.

The Report of Theft or Loss of Controlled Substances (DEA Form 106) is available through the on-line application system.

DEA announces that on Tuesday, October 28, 2008, an updated electronic version of the DEA form 106 will be available through the Diversion website. This newer version requires the registrant to include the National Drug Code (NDC) which will help to accurately track controlled substances reported as stolen or lost.

The attached letter will be posted on the Diversion website advising all DEA registrants of this change in reporting requirements. DEA will notify any registrant that submits a paper copy of the obsolete DEA form 106 after October 28, 2008, to discontinue using this form. DEA advises registrants wishing to obtain an electronic copy of the new DEA form 106 go to DEA's website and select the icon "DEA Form 106 Online, Report Theft or Loss of Controlled Substances."

Although the paper version is still available, DEA encourages registrants to use the updated electronic version. A registrant can still receive a paper copy of the updated form by writing to DEA Headquarters, Attn: Registration/ODR, P.O. Box 2639, Springfield, VA 22152.

- DEA Form 106 On-line -
  Data will be entered through a **secure connection** to the on-line application system. **Your web browser must support 128-bit encryption.**
  - See Federal Register Notice - Reports by Registrants of Theft or Significant Loss of Controlled Substances for more information.
- Letter detailing change in reporting requirements

Privacy Act Information for DEA Form 106

Authority: Section 301 of the Controlled Substances of 1970 (PL-513).

Purpose: Report theft or loss of Controlled Substances.

Routine Uses: The Controlled Substances Act authorizes the production of special reports required for statistical and analytical purposes. Disclosures of information from this system are made to the following categories of users for the purposes stated:

A. Other Federal law enforcement and regulatory agencies for law enforcement and regulatory purposes.
B. State and local law enforcement and regulatory agencies for law enforcement and regulatory purposes.

Effect: Failure to report theft or loss of controlled substances may result in penalties under Section 402 and 403 of the Controlled Substances Act.

EXAMPLE 4-12 (continued)

DEA's Diversion Control Program - DEA Form 106 - Theft or Loss of Controlled Substances 11/3/09 2:14 AM

Regulations.gov

Controlled Substance Ordering System (CSOS) www.DEAecom.gov

GOOD MEDICINE, BAD BEHAVIOR: Drug Diversion in America

To view PDF documents

Get Adobe Reader

External links included in this website should not be construed as an official endorsement of the views contained therein.

Under the Paperwork Reduction Act, a person is not required to respond to a collection of information unless it displays a currently valid OMB control number. Public reporting burden for this collection of information is estimated to average 30 minutes per response, including the time for reviewing instructions, searching existing data sources, gathering and maintaining the data needed, and completing and reviewing the collection of information. Send comments regarding this burden estimate or any other aspect of this collection of information, including suggestions for reducing this burden, to the Records Management Section, Drug Enforcement Administration, Washington, D.C. 20537; and to the Office of Management and Budget, Washington, D.C. 20503.

HOME **CONTACT US** **SEARCH** **BACK TO TOP**

EXAMPLE 4-13

MEDICATION SAMPLE RECEIVING AND DISPENSING LOG

MEDICATION / STRENGTH ______________________

DATE	PATIENT NAME	ADDITIONAL HOSPITAL ID	PRESCRIBER	MFGR / LOT #	EXP. DATE	AMOUNT Rec(+) / Disp (-)	BALANCE

EXAMPLE 4-14

MEDICATION PREPACKAGING LOG

Instructions: Complete all necessary information. Label must have medication name, strength, dosage form, manufacturer's name, pharmacy lot# and beyond-use date. Beyond-use date = 1 year from date packaged unless the manufacturer's expiration date is less than this or packaging material stability data indicates it is less than 1 year.

LABEL	DATE PACKAGED	MANUFACTURER'S			AMOUNT PER UNIT	NUMBER UNITS PACKAGED	PACKAGED BY	CHECKED BY RPh
		NAME	LOT NO.	EXP. DATE				

EXAMPLE 4-15

MEDICATION AREA INSPECTION

Location ______________________________ **Month / Year** ____________

	YES	NO	N/A	REMARKS
MEDICATION PREPARATION AREA				
Medication prep area is clean, neat and well organized.				
IV preparation area is clean, uncluttered and functionally separate				
PATIENT AND STOCK MEDICATIONS				
Only authorized medications are present. (There is no excess stock, unauthorized storage areas or unidentified patient medications.)				
All medications are locked.				
Tops of automated dispensing cabinets and med carts are free of medications.				
Medications to be returned to pharmacy are in the authorized location.				
All medications are within their expiration or beyond-use date. (Check bulk supplies, refrigerator, etc.)				
Check of two patient records and medications (automated dispensing cabinets, med drawer, MAR, Kardex, chart) matched.				
Check of two MARs show nursing reconciliation documentation.				
Check of automated dispensing cabinets for two items reveal correct count and within expiration date.				
Internal and external bulk stock is separated.				
CONTROLLED SUBSTANCES				
Automated dispensing cabinets and manual systems are free of discrepancies.				
REFRIGERATOR				
Refrigerator temperature is between 36°F and 46°F. Note temperature:				
Freezer temperature is between -13°F and 14°F. Note temperature: Note freezer drugs:				
Refrigerators/Freezers containing vaccines are monitored constantly or check twice a day.				
Refrigerator is clean.				
Freezer is free from frost.				
Refrigerator and freezer logs are complete for every day this month.				
Only drugs are stored in the refrigerator and freezer. (No food, lab reagents or specimens are allowed.)				
Floor-stock insulins are in the appropriate bin.				
MISCELLANEOUS				
Single dose vials are destroyed after one entry.				
Multiple-dose vials are dated with the beyond-use date of within 28 days (or shorted date if appropriate).				
The current Formulary is present and can be located by a nurse.				
Only current (with 2 years) reference books are present.				
Saline syringes are appropriately stored.				
The necessary changes have been made since the last inspection. Note:				

CORRECTIVE ACTIONS FOR ANY "NO"

____

____

____

______________________________ ______________________________

Pharmacy signature / Date **Care Unit signature / Date**

EXAMPLE 4-16

MEDICATION AREA INSPECTION - CLINICS

Location ______________________________ **Month / Year** ____________

	YES	NO	N/A	REMARKS
STOCK MEDICATIONS				
Only authorized medications are present. (There is no excess stock, unauthorized storage areas or unidentified patient medications.)				
All medications are locked.				
Medications in treatment rooms are locked.				
Medications to be returned to pharmacy are in the authorized location.				
All medications are within their expiration or beyond-use date. (Check bulk supplies, refrigerator, etc.)				
Internal and external bulk stock is separated.				
MEDICATION PREPARATION AREA				
Medication prep area is clean, neat and well organized.				
IV preparation area is clean, uncluttered and functionally separate				
SAMPLE MEDICATIONS				
Sample cabinet/room is locked and accessible only to licensed individuals in the practice.				
Log is complete (check two items).				
Samples present reflect appropriate medications for type of practice.				
No controlled substances are present.				
All medications are within their expiration date.				
CONTROLLED SUBSTANCES				
Controlled substance records are complete. (Check count for two items.)				
Wastage is appropriately documented.				
REFRIGERATOR				
Refrigerator temperature is between 36°F and 46°F. Note temperature:				
Freezer temperature is between -13°F and 14°F. Note temperature: Note freezer drugs:				
Refrigerators/Freezers containing vaccines are monitored constantly or check twice a day.				
Refrigerator is clean.				
Freezer is free from frost.				
High/low thermometer is properly reset.				
Refrigerator and freezer logs are complete for every day this month.				
Only drugs are stored in the refrigerator and freezer. (No food, lab reagents or specimens are allowed.)				
MISCELLANEOUS				
Single dose vials are destroyed after one entry.				
Multiple-dose vials are dated with beyond-use date within 28 days (or shorted date if appropriate).				
Saline syringes are appropriately stored.				
The necessary changes have been made since the last inspection. Note:				

CORRECTIVE ACTIONS FOR ANY "NO"

____

____

____

____

______________________________ ______________________________

Pharmacy signature / Date Clinic signature / Date

EXAMPLE 4-17

INSPECTION ASSIGNMENT GRID

Year___________

Area	Assigned To	Jan	Feb	Mar	Apr	May	Jun	Jul	Aug	Sep	Oct	Nov	Dec

EXAMPLE 4-18

EMERGENCY SUPPLIES AND TACKLE BOX INSPECTION RECORD UNIT: ________________ Month/Year: ______________

Type of Cart (check one): Adult ______ Pediatric _____ Neonatal _____ Hyperthermia _____

Complete each day. Mark CLOSED if department is not open. File completed log in manager's office.

CART/BOX #	1	2	3	4	5	6	7	8	9	10	11	12	13	14	15	16	17	18	19	20	21	22	23	24	25	26	27	28	29	30	31
NEW # Circle date received																															
Verify lock and #																															
Defib – plugged																															
Defib - battery																															
Broselow tape (most current)																															
CPR backboard																															
Defib pads in date																															
Box of medium gloves																															
Box of fluid shield masks																															
Oxygen – min 500 psi																															
Secure sharps box																															
Oral airway																															
Checked by (initials) Initials and signature log on reverse																															

EXAMPLE 4-19

PATIENT'S PERSONAL MEDICATIONS STORAGE RECORD

If the medications are not to be used during the patient's stay in the facility, they should be given to the patient's family. If these medications must be retained in the facility, they shall be inventoried, packaged, sealed, and labeled with the patient's name, and stored until returned to the patient at the time of discharge (provided such action is approved by the practitioner responsible for the patient).

PATIENT NAME____________________________________ **LOCATION**________________________

PATIENT NUMBER ____________________ **DATE**________________

ADMITTING PHYSICIAN _____________________________________

RX NUMBER	MEDICATION	QUANITY	NOTES

MEDICATIONS IDENTIFIED AND COUNTED BY ____________________________________

PATIENT SIGNATURE ____

EXAMPLE 4-20

RECEIPT AND DISPOSAL OF PATIENTS' PERSONAL MEDICATIONS

PATIENT ________________________ **PATIENT NUMBER/HOPSITAL ID** ______________ **LOCATION** __________

ADDRESS ____

ATTENDING PHYSICIAN________________________ **DATE**______________

FORM COMPLETED BY________________________

PRESCRIPTION NUMBER	MEDICATION NAME	QUANITY	RECEIVED BY (Signature)	DATE OF DISPOSAL	DISPOSAL METHOD	RETURNED OR DESTROYED BY (Signature)	NOTES

Patient's personal medications shall be stored securely and the appropriate information recorded above. Medications shall be returned to the patient, patient's family, or other authorized person upon discharge unless otherwise directed by a physician. Medications that are not returned shall be retained for 30 days after discharge. Medications on hand 30 days after discharge shall be destroyed.

Disposal Method: 1 = Returned to Patient 2 = Returned to Family 3 = Returned to Other Authorized Person 4 = Not Returned (Physician's Directive) 5 = Not Returned 6 = Destroyed

I acknowledge receipt of the above medications (with exceptions noted) ________________________ Date Returned ______________

Signature of Person to Whom Medications Were Returned

EXAMPLE 4-21

INTERVENTION LOG

MONITORING PERIOD ______________________________ **PAGE** _____ **OF** _____

A. REASON CODES: 1. Medication 2. Dose/Strength 3. Route 4. Change Frequency/Rate 5. Allergy 6. Interaction 7. Diagnosis/Contraindication 8. Incomplete Order 9. Duplicate Order 10. Nonformulary Medication 11. Restricted Medication

B. RECOMMENDATION CODES: 1. Change Medication 2. Change Dose/Strength 3. Change Route 4. Change Frequency/Rate 5. Discontinue Medication

DATE	PATIENT NAME/NUMBER	PRESCRIBER	REASON FOR INTERVENTION	PHARMACIST RECOMMENDATION	ACCEPTED Y/N	OUTCOME/COMMENT

EXAMPLE 4-22

PHARMACY COMPETENCE CHECKLIST

After-Hours Medication Retrieval

Name: ______________________________ Title: ________________

Method of Evaluation

☐ Actual Event ☐ Post-Event Discussion ☐ Demonstration

Actual Event:	Reviewer evaluates individual during actual patient care
Post-Event Discussion:	Reviewer debriefs individual after an actual patient care event
Demonstration:	Individual demonstrates knowledge, skill, and judgement to reviewer

Criteria	**Competence Components** *(check all that apply)*			**Demonstrated Correctly**
	Knowledge	**Skill**	**Judgement**	*Reviewers Initials*
Demonstrates ability to identify and locate the following items and areas: • Primary retrieval area • Tablets/capsules • Oral liquids • Injectables/parenterals • Topicals • Ophthalmics/otics • Refrigerated medications • Outdated medications • Crash cart medications • Controlled substances				
Demonstrates ability to prepare IV products in an aseptic manner and use the following correctly: • Prepares only for immediate use • Incompatibility/stability charts and tables • Completed sterile preparation competency				
Knows pharmacy hours of operation: • Weekdays • Weekends • Holidays				

EXAMPLE 4-22 (continued)

Can locate necessary phone numbers if after-hours assistance is needed: • Pharmacist on-call				
Understands and can state the importance of after-hours medication stock security: • Access to after-hours medication stock • Keys/security codes				
Understands regulations and policies relating to: • Required elements of medication order review • Re-labeling medications • Physician dispensing (in emergency room) • Handling patients' personal medications • Medication error report form • ADR report form				
Completes all necessary documentation before removing medications from the after-hours medication stock: • After-hours medication retrieval log				
Understands and documents the required checks (i.e., verifies) medications per pharmacy policy: • Each medication removed is checked by another authorized individual for: • Correct medication • Correct dose • Correct dosage form • Patient allergies				
Understands and demonstrates how to use the formulary properly: • Hospital formulary • Non-formulary request • Therapeutic interchange lists				

Reviewer: ______________________________ Date: _________________

EXAMPLE 4-23

INDIVIDUALS WHO CAN REMOVE MEDICATIONS FROM AFTER-HOURS STOCK

When medications are not available after-hours, the following persons may remove them from the after-hours stock. The amount removed should be sufficient to meet immediate therapeutic needs and should not exceed the amount needed to last until a pharmacist is available.

The person who removes a medication shall enter the following information in the After-Hours Log:

- Name of the patient (first and last name), second patient identifier, and room number
- Name of medication
- Medication strength
- Dosage form removed (tablet, capsule, suspension, ampules, injections, etc)
- Dose prescribed (1 three times a day, 2 at bedtime, 50 mg every four hours, etc)
- Amount removed
- Name of prescribing physician
- Time and date of removal
- Signature and title of person making removal

NAME (Please print or type)	TITLE	SIGNATURE	DATE ORIENTATION COMPLETED

EXAMPLE 4-24

AFTER-HOURS MEDICATIONS RETRIEVAL LOG

DATE	TIME	PATIENT NAME/ PATIENT ID# /ROOM #	DRUG, STRENGTH, AND FORM	DOSE ORDERED	AMOUNT	REMOVED BY	WITNESS	Pharmacist Review Initial, Date & Time	CODE

INDICATE THE REASON FOR THE REMOVAL IN THE CODE COLUMN

CODE: 1 NEW ORDER 2 MISSED DOSE 3 WASTED DOSE 4 NOT IN FLOOR STOCK 5 ORDER NOT RECEIVED IN PHARMACY

ALL AFTER HOURS REMOVALS MUST BE REVIEWED AND SIGNED BY A PHARMACIST

EXAMPLE 4-25

RECALLED MEDICATION AND DEVICE RECORD

MEDICATION(S) OR DEVICE______________________________ **RECALL DATE**______________________

AREAS INSPECTED	DATE INSP.	NUMBER FOUND	BY	NOTES

EXAMPLE 4-26

MEDICATION ERROR REPORT

PATIENT NAME / IDENTIFICATION NUMBER________________ **LOCATION** ________________
AGE OR DOB____ **SEX** _____ **PHYSICIAN** ________________________________
MEDICATIONS INVOLVED

____
____
____

DESCRIPTION OF ERROR

____
____
____

DATE AND TIME OF ERROR ________________________________
DATE AND TIME PHYSICIAN NOTIFIED (and how notified)

____

PHYSICIAN'S INSTRUCTIONS ________________________________
____
____

ACTION TAKEN ____
____
____

SEVERITY OF ERROR

Category	***Result***
No Error	
Category A	Circumstances or events that have the capacity to cause error.
Error, No Harm	
Category B	An error occurred but the medication did not reach the patient. (An "error of omission" does reach the patient)
Category C	An error occurred that reached the patient but did not cause patient harm.
Category D	An error occurred that reached the patient and required monitoring to confirm that it resulted in no harm to the patient and/or required intervention to preclude harm.
Error, Harm	
Category E	An error occurred that may have contributed to or resulted in temporary harm to the patient and required intervention.
Category F	An error occurred that may have contributed to or resulted in temporary harm to the patient and required initial or prolonged hospitalization.
Category G	An error occurred that may have contributed to or resulted in permanent patient harm.
Category H	An error occurred that required intervention necessary to sustain life.
Error, Death	
Category I	An error occurred that may have contributed to or resulted in the patient's death.

TYPE OF ERROR

__ Prescribing error
__ Omission error
__ Wrong time error
__ Unauthorized medication error
__ Improper dose error
__ Wrong dosage-form error
__ Wrong medication-preparation error
__ Wrong administration-technique error
__ Deteriorated medication error
__ Monitoring error
__ Compliance error
__ Other medication error

EXAMPLE 4-26 (continued)

CAUSE(S) OF ERROR

Failed Communication	Poor handwriting Inaccurate transcription of orders Medications with similar names Inappropriate use of zeroes and decimal points Use of metric and apothecary systems Use of inappropriate abbreviations Ambiguous or incomplete orders Other ______________________
Poor Medication Distribution Practices	Unlabeled and mislabeled medications Improper storage practices Unlimited access to medications and pharmacy Improper use of dispensing equipment Other ______________________
Dose Miscalculations	Failure to stock standardized concentrations and commercially pre-mixed products Other ______________________
Problems Related to Medication and Medication Devices	Labeling and packaging problems Device design issues Other ______________________
Incorrect Administration of Medication	Failure to check or improper patient identification Wrong route administration Other ______________________
Lack of Patient Education	Patients not involved Patients do not understand their medications Other ______________________
Other Causes	

HOW ERROR COULD HAVE BEEN PREVENTED ______________________________________

____

____

____

____

PERSON(S) HAVING KNOWLEDGE OF THE ERROR ______________________________

____

____

PERSON COMPLETING THIS FORM ______________________________________

THIS REPORT SHALL *NOT* BE PLACED IN THE PATIENT'S MEDICAL RECORD.

EXAMPLE 4-27

ADVERSE DRUG REACTION REPORT

REPORT (check one): ________ Concurrent ________ Retrospective
METHOD OF IDENTIFICATION (check all that apply): _____ Orders _____ADR card _____ MUE _____ MAR
_____ Radiology _____ Quality Management _____ Other: ______________

PATIENT NAME: ______________________ **MR #:**____________ **ROOM #** ________

AGE OR DOB_______ **SEX** _____ **WT. (kg)** ________ **HT.**_______ **ADMIT DATE:** __________ **DISCHARGE DATE:** __________

ATTENDING PHYSICIAN: ______________________ **MEDICAL SERVICE**: ______________

REASON FOR ADMIT/DIAGNOSES: ______________________

SECONDARY DIAGNOSES: ______________________

MEDICAL HISTORY: ______________________

ALLERGIES - on admission: ______________________ **added during stay:** ______________________

DATE OF REACTION:______________________ **TIME OF REACTION:** ______________________

ORDERING PHYSICIAN AWARE OF ADR? _____ **YES** _____ **NO (IF NO, DATE NOTIFIED)**______________________

DESCRIPTION OF REACTION:______________________

RELEVANT LABS: ______________________

____

TREATMENT (check all that apply): ______ No treatment ______ Discontinue suspect medication(s) ______ Adjust dose, route, frequency

______ Treatment w/ medications (list): ______________________

______ Switch to alternative agent (list): ______________________

______ Other medical treatment (list): ______________________

OUTCOME: ______ Resolved without sequelae ______ Resolving ______ Ongoing

______ Permanent disability/damage ______ Death ______ Unknown

INCREASED LENGTH OF STAY? _____ YES _____ NO

DRUG REGIMEN AT REACTION TIME (use generic names):

Medication/Dose/Route/Schedule	Date Started	Date Stopped	Time of Last Dose	Manufacturer

SUSPECTED DRUG(S): 1.______________________ 2. ______________________
(use generic names)
3.______________________ 4. ______________________

EXAMPLE 4-27 (continued)

ASSESSMENT OF ADR:

1. **REACTION TYPE** (check one):

_______ A = Exaggerated pharmacological action (exaggerated, but otherwise normal pharmacological action of a drug given in the usual therapeutic doses)

_______ B = Unpredicted/unexpected reaction (not to be expected from the known pharmacological actions of a drug given in usual therapeutic doses)

2. **REACTION SEVERITY** (check one):

________1 = Severe (life threatening, death, permanent injury)

________2 = Moderate (medical treatment, prolongs hospitalization)

________3 = Minor (no medical treatment)

3. **AVOIDABLE/PREVENTABLE:**

_____ YES _____ NO Suspected drug(s) were inappropriate for patient's condition?
_____ YES _____ NO Dose, route, frequency were inappropriate for age, weight, lab tests, and disease state?
_____ YES _____ NO Necessary monitoring/lab tests were not performed?
_____ YES _____ NO Patient had a history of allergy to the drug(s)?
_____ YES _____ NO Drug interaction was involved in the reaction?
_____ YES _____ NO Toxic serum drug level was documented?
_____ YES _____ NO Patient was not compliant with drug therapy?

3. **PROBABILITY** (complete the Naranjo Algorithm below by answering the questions and giving the corresponding pertinent score):

DRUG:	YES	NO	DK/NA	SCORE
1. Are there previous conclusive reports on this reaction?	+1	0	0	_____
2. Did the adverse event appear after the suspected drug was administered?	+2	-1	0	_____
3. Did the adverse reaction improve when the drug was discontinued or a specific antagonist was administered?	+1	0	0	_____
4. Did the adverse reaction reappear when the drug was readministered?	+2	-1	0	_____
5. Are there alternative causes (other than the drug) that could on their own have caused the reaction?	-1	+2	0	_____
6. Did the reaction reappear when a placebo was given?	-1	+1	0	_____
7. Was the drug detected in the blood (or other fluids) in concentrations known to be toxic?	+1	0	0	_____
8. Was the reaction more severe when the dose was increased or less severe when the dose was decreased?	+1	0	0	_____
9. Did patient have a similar reaction to the same or similar drugs in any previous exposure?	+1	0	0	_____
10. Was the adverse event confirmed by any objective evidence?	+1	0	0	_____
(Taken from Naranjo CA, et al. Clin Pharmacol Ther 1981;30:239-45)	TOTAL SCORE			_____

Check one: > or = 9 DEFINITE ______ 1 - 4 POSSIBLE _______
5 - 8 PROBABLE _______ < OR = 0 DOUBTFUL _______

REPORT BY:______________________________ TITLE____________ DATE____________

FOR ADMINISTRATIVE USE ONLY: REVIEWED BY:______________________________

DATE:______________ REPORT TO: ______P&T Committee ______FDA

EXAMPLE 4-28

NOTICE OF DRUG REACTION FORM

Date ___________

Dear ________________________________:

You had a reaction to ____________________________when you were a patient in this facility. The signs and symptoms of your reaction included:

____

____

____

____

____

____

____

____

____

____

____

____

____

____

____

Other medications are similar to the medication that caused your reaction. You may have a reaction to these medications as well. Your physician or pharmacist can advise you of the appropriate precautions to take.

You should show this letter to physicians or dentists who treat you, pharmacists who fill your prescriptions, and to persons who admit you to this or other medical facilities so they can note the reaction in your medical record.

Sincerely,

EXAMPLE 4-29

U.S. Department of Health and Human Services

MEDWATCH

The FDA Safety Information and Adverse Event Reporting Program

For VOLUNTARY reporting of adverse events, product problems and product use errors

Page 1 of ____

Form Approved: OMB No. 0910-0291, Expires: 12/31/2011
See OMB statement on reverse.

FDA USE ONLY

Triage unit sequence #

PLEASE TYPE OR USE BLACK INK

A. PATIENT INFORMATION

1. **Patient Identifier** — In confidence
2. **Age at Time of Event or Date of Birth:**
3. **Sex** — ☐ Female ☐ Male
4. **Weight** — ____ lb or ____ kg

B. ADVERSE EVENT, PRODUCT PROBLEM OR ERROR

Check all that apply:

1. ☐ **Adverse Event** ☐ **Product Problem** *(e.g., defects/malfunctions)*
☐ **Product Use Error** ☐ **Problem with Different Manufacturer of Same Medicine**

2. **Outcomes Attributed to Adverse Event** *(Check all that apply)*

☐ Death: ____ *(mm/dd/yyyy)* ☐ Disability or Permanent Damage
☐ Life-threatening ☐ Congenital Anomaly/Birth Defect
☐ Hospitalization - initial or prolonged ☐ Other Serious (Important Medical Events)
☐ Required Intervention to Prevent Permanent Impairment/Damage (Devices)

3. **Date of Event** *(mm/dd/yyyy)*
4. **Date of this Report** *(mm/dd/yyyy)*
5. **Describe Event, Problem or Product Use Error**
6. **Relevant Tests/Laboratory Data, Including Dates**
7. **Other Relevant History, Including Preexisting Medical Conditions** *(e.g., allergies, race, pregnancy, smoking and alcohol use, liver/kidney problems, etc.)*

C. PRODUCT AVAILABILITY

Product Available for Evaluation? *(Do not send product to FDA)*

☐ Yes ☐ No ☐ Returned to Manufacturer on: ____ *(mm/dd/yyyy)*

D. SUSPECT PRODUCT(S)

1. **Name, Strength, Manufacturer** *(from product label)*

#1 Name:
Strength:
Manufacturer:

#2 Name:
Strength:
Manufacturer:

2. **Dose or Amount** / **Frequency** / **Route**

	Dose or Amount	Frequency	Route
#1			
#2			

3. **Dates of Use** *(If unknown, give duration) from/to (or best estimate)*
#1
#2

4. **Diagnosis or Reason for Use** *(Indication)*
#1
#2

5. **Event Abated After Use Stopped or Dose Reduced?**
#1 ☐ Yes ☐ No ☐ Doesn't Apply
#2 ☐ Yes ☐ No ☐ Doesn't Apply

6. **Lot #**
#1
#2

7. **Expiration Date**
#1
#2

8. **Event Reappeared After Reintroduction?**
#1 ☐ Yes ☐ No ☐ Doesn't Apply
#2 ☐ Yes ☐ No ☐ Doesn't Apply

9. **NDC # or Unique ID**

E. SUSPECT MEDICAL DEVICE

1. **Brand Name**
2. **Common Device Name**
3. **Manufacturer Name, City and State**
4. **Model #** — **Lot #**
Catalog # — **Expiration Date** *(mm/dd/yyyy)*
Serial # — **Other #**
5. **Operator of Device**
☐ Health Professional
☐ Lay User/Patient
☐ Other:
6. **If Implanted, Give Date** *(mm/dd/yyyy)*
7. **If Explanted, Give Date** *(mm/dd/yyyy)*
8. **Is this a Single-use Device that was Reprocessed and Reused on a Patient?**
☐ Yes ☐ No
9. **If Yes to Item No. 8, Enter Name and Address of Reprocessor**

F. OTHER (CONCOMITANT) MEDICAL PRODUCTS

Product names and therapy dates *(exclude treatment of event)*

G. REPORTER *(See confidentiality section on back)*

1. **Name and Address**
Name:
Address:
City: State: ZIP:

Phone # **E-mail**

2. **Health Professional?** ☐ Yes ☐ No
3. **Occupation**
4. **Also Reported to:**
☐ Manufacturer
☐ User Facility
☐ Distributor/Importer
5. **If you do NOT want your identity disclosed to the manufacturer, place an "X" in this box:** ☐

FORM FDA 3500 (1/09) Submission of a report does not constitute an admission that medical personnel or the product caused or contributed to the event.

EXAMPLE 4-29 (continued)

ADVICE ABOUT VOLUNTARY REPORTING

Detailed instructions available at: http://www.fda.gov/medwatch/report/consumer/instruct.htm

Report adverse events, product problems or product use errors with:

- Medications *(drugs or biologics)*
- Medical devices *(including in-vitro diagnostics)*
- Combination products *(medication & medical devices)*
- Human cells, tissues, and cellular and tissue-based products
- Special nutritional products *(dietary supplements, medical foods, infant formulas)*
- Cosmetics

Report product problems - quality, performance or safety concerns such as:

- Suspected counterfeit product
- Suspected contamination
- Questionable stability
- Defective components
- Poor packaging or labeling
- Therapeutic failures (product didn't work)

-Fold Here-

Report SERIOUS adverse events. An event is serious when the patient outcome is:

- Death
- Life-threatening
- Hospitalization - initial or prolonged
- Disability or permanent damage
- Congenital anomaly/birth defect
- Required intervention to prevent permanent impairment or damage (devices)
- Other serious (important medical events)

Report even if:

- You're not certain the product caused the event
- You don't have all the details

How to report:

- Just fill in the sections that apply to your report
- Use section D for all products except medical devices
- Attach additional pages if needed
- Use a separate form for each patient
- Report either to FDA or the manufacturer *(or both)*

Other methods of reporting:

- 1-800-FDA-0178 - To FAX report
- 1-800-FDA-1088 - To report by phone
- www.fda.gov/medwatch/report.htm - To report online

If your report involves a serious adverse event with a device and it occurred in a facility outside a doctor's office, that facility may be legally required to report to FDA and/or the manufacturer. Please notify the person in that facility who would handle such reporting.

-Fold Here-

If your report involves a serious adverse event with a vaccine, call 1-800-822-7967 to report.

Confidentiality: The patient's identity is held in strict confidence by FDA and protected to the fullest extent of the law. FDA will not disclose the reporter's identity in response to a request from the public, pursuant to the Freedom of Information Act. The reporter's identity, including the identity of a self-reporter, may be shared with the manufacturer unless requested otherwise.

The public reporting burden for this collection of information has been estimated to average 36 minutes per response, including the time for reviewing instructions, searching existing data sources, gathering and maintaining the data needed, and completing and reviewing the collection of information. Send comments regarding this burden estimate or any other aspect of this collection of information, including suggestions for reducing this burden to:

Department of Health and Human Services
Food and Drug Administration
Office of Chief Information Officer (HFA-710)
5600 Fishers Lane
Rockville, MD 20857

Please DO NOT RETURN this form to this address.

OMB statement:
"An agency may not conduct or sponsor, and a person is not required to respond to, a collection of information unless it displays a currently valid OMB control number."

U.S. DEPARTMENT OF HEALTH AND HUMAN SERVICES
Food and Drug Administration

FORM FDA 3500 (1/09) (Back) **Please Use Address Provided Below -- Fold in Thirds, Tape and Mail**

DEPARTMENT OF HEALTH & HUMAN SERVICES

Public Health Service
Food and Drug Administration
Rockville, MD 20857

Official Business
Penalty for Private Use $300

NO POSTAGE NECESSARY IF MAILED IN THE UNITED STATES OR APO/FPO

BUSINESS REPLY MAIL
FIRST CLASS MAIL PERMIT NO. 946 ROCKVILLE MD

POSTAGE WILL BE PAID BY FOOD AND DRUG ADMINISTRATION

MEDWATCH
The FDA Safety Information and Adverse Event Reporting Program
Food and Drug Administration
5600 Fishers Lane
Rockville, MD 20852-9787

EXAMPLE 4-30

WEBSITE: www.vaers.hhs.gov E-MAIL: info@vaers.org FAX: 1-877-721-0366

VAERS

VACCINE ADVERSE EVENT REPORTING SYSTEM

24 Hour Toll-Free Information 1-800-822-7967
P.O. Box 1100, Rockville, MD 20849-1100
PATIENT IDENTITY KEPT CONFIDENTIAL

For CDC/FDA Use Only
VAERS Number ______
Date Received ______

Patient Name:	Vaccine administered by (Name):	Form completed by (Name):
Last First M.I.	Responsible Physician ______	Relation to Patient ☐ Vaccine Provider ☐ Patient/Parent ☐ Manufacturer ☐ Other
Address	Facility Name/Address	Address *(if different from patient or provider)*
City State Zip	City State Zip	City State Zip
Telephone no. (____) ______	Telephone no. (____) ______	Telephone no. (____) ______

1. State	2. County where administered	3. Date of birth __/__/__ mm dd yy	4. Patient age	5. Sex ☐ M ☐ F	6. Date form completed __/__/__ mm dd yy

7. Describe adverse events(s) (symptoms, signs, time course) and treatment, if any

8. Check all appropriate:
- ☐ Patient died (date __/__/__ mm dd yy)
- ☐ Life threatening illness
- ☐ Required emergency room/doctor visit
- ☐ Required hospitalization (________days)
- ☐ Resulted in prolongation of hospitalization
- ☐ Resulted in permanent disability
- ☐ None of the above

9. Patient recovered ☐ YES ☐ NO ☐ UNKNOWN

10. Date of vaccination __/__/__ mm dd yy Time ______ AM PM

11. Adverse event onset __/__/__ mm dd yy Time ______ AM PM

12. Relevant diagnostic tests/laboratory data

13. Enter all vaccines given on date listed in no. 10

	Vaccine (type)	Manufacturer	Lot number	Route/Site	No. Previous Doses
a.					
b.					
c.					
d.					

14. Any other vaccinations within 4 weeks prior to the date listed in no. 10

	Vaccine (type)	Manufacturer	Lot number	Route/Site	No. Previous doses	Date given
a.						
b.						

15. Vaccinated at:
☐ Private doctor's office/hospital ☐ Military clinic/hospital
☐ Public health clinic/hospital ☐ Other/unknown

16. Vaccine purchased with:
☐ Private funds ☐ Military funds
☐ Public funds ☐ Other/unknown

17. Other medications

18. Illness at time of vaccination (specify)

19. Pre-existing physician-diagnosed allergies, birth defects, medical conditions (specify)

20. Have you reported this adverse event previously? ☐ No ☐ To health department ☐ To doctor ☐ To manufacturer

Only for children 5 and under

22. Birth weight ______ lb. ______ oz.

23. No. of brothers and sisters

21. Adverse event following prior vaccination (check all applicable, specify)

	Adverse Event	Onset Age	Type Vaccine	Dose no. in series
☐ In patient				
☐ In brother or sister				

Only for reports submitted by manufacturer/immunization project

24. Mfr./imm. proj. report no.

25. Date received by mfr./imm.proj.

26. 15 day report? ☐ Yes ☐ No

27. Report type ☐ Initial ☐ Follow-Up

Health care providers and manufacturers are required by law (42 USC 300aa-25) to report reactions to vaccines listed in the Table of Reportable Events Following Immunization. Reports for reactions to other vaccines are voluntary except when required as a condition of immunization grant awards.

Form VAERS-1(FDA)

EXAMPLE 4-30 (continued)

"Fold in thirds, tape & mail — DO NOT STAPLE FORM"

NO POSTAGE NECESSARY IF MAILED IN THE UNITED STATES OR APO/FPO

BUSINESS REPLY MAIL

FIRST-CLASS MAIL PERMIT NO. 1895 ROCKVILLE, MD

POSTAGE WILL BE PAID BY ADDRESSEE

VAERS

VAERS
P.O. Box 1100
Rockville MD 20849-1100

DIRECTIONS FOR COMPLETING FORM

(Additional pages may be attached if more space is needed.)

GENERAL

- Use a separate form for each patient. Complete the form to the best of your abilities. Items 3, 4, 7, 8, 10, 11, and 13 are considered essential and should be completed whenever possible. Parents/Guardians may need to consult the facility where the vaccine was administered for some of the information (such as manufacturer, lot number or laboratory data.)
- Refer to the Reportable Events Table (RET) for events mandated for reporting by law. Reporting for other serious events felt to be related but not on the RET is encouraged.
- Health care providers other than the vaccine administrator (VA) treating a patient for a suspected adverse event should notify the VA and provide the information about the adverse event to allow the VA to complete the form to meet the VA's legal responsibility.
- These data will be used to increase understanding of adverse events following vaccination and will become part of CDC Privacy Act System 09-20-0136, "Epidemiologic Studies and Surveillance of Disease Problems". Information identifying the person who received the vaccine or that person's legal representative will not be made available to the public, but may be available to the vaccinee or legal representative.
- Postage will be paid by addressee. Forms may be photocopied (must be front & back on same sheet).

SPECIFIC INSTRUCTIONS

Form Completed By: To be used by parents/guardians, vaccine manufacturers/distributors, vaccine administrators, and/or the person completing the form on behalf of the patient or the health professional who administered the vaccine.

Item 7: Describe the suspected adverse event. Such things as temperature, local and general signs and symptoms, time course, duration of symptoms, diagnosis, treatment and recovery should be noted.

Item 9: Check "YES" if the patient's health condition is the same as it was prior to the vaccine, "NO" if the patient has not returned to the pre-vaccination state of health, or "UNKNOWN" if the patient's condition is not known.

Item 10: and 11: Give dates and times as specifically as you can remember. If you do not know the exact time, please indicate "AM" or "PM" when possible if this information is known. If more than one adverse event, give the onset date and time for the most serious event.

Item 12: Include "negative" or "normal" results of any relevant tests performed as well as abnormal findings.

Item 13: List ONLY those vaccines given on the day listed in Item 10.

Item 14: List any other vaccines that the patient received within 4 weeks prior to the date listed in Item 10.

Item 16: This section refers to how the person who gave the vaccine purchased it, not to the patient's insurance.

Item 17: List any prescription or non-prescription medications the patient was taking when the vaccine(s) was given.

Item 18: List any short term illnesses the patient had on the date the vaccine(s) was given (i.e., cold, flu, ear infection).

Item 19: List any pre-existing physician-diagnosed allergies, birth defects, medical conditions (including developmental and/or neurologic disorders) for the patient.

Item 21: List any suspected adverse events the patient, or the patient's brothers or sisters, may have had to previous vaccinations. If more than one brother or sister, or if the patient has reacted to more than one prior vaccine, use additional pages to explain completely. For the onset age of a patient, provide the age in months if less than two years old.

Item 26: This space is for manufacturers' use only.

EXAMPLE 4-31

Form Approved: OMB No. 09 10-029 1, Expires 12/31/11
See OMB statement on reverse.

U.S. Department of Health and Human Services
Food and Drug Administration

MEDWATCH

FORM FDA 3500A (1/09)

For use by user-facilities, importers, distributors and manufacturers for MANDATORY reporting

Page 1 of 15

Mfr Report #

UF/Importer Report #

FDA Use Only

PLEASE TYPE OR USE BLACK INK

A. PATIENT INFORMATION

1. **Patient Identifier** — In confidence
2. **Age at Time of Event:** or ____ **Date of Birth:**
3. **Sex** ☐ Female ☐ Male
4. **Weight** ____ lbs or ____ kgs

B. ADVERSE EVENT OR PRODUCT PROBLEM

1. ☐ **Adverse Event** and/or ☐ **Product Problem** *(e.g., defects/malfunctions)*
2. **Outcomes Attributed to Adverse Event** *(Check all that apply)*
   - ☐ Death: ____ *(mm/dd/yyyy)*
   - ☐ Life-threatening
   - ☐ Hospitalization - initial or prolonged
   - ☐ Required Intervention to Prevent Permanent Impairment/Damage (Devices)
   - ☐ Disability or Permanent Damage
   - ☐ Congenital Anomaly/Birth Defect
   - ☐ Other Serious (Important Medical Events)
3. **Date of Event** *(mm/dd/yyyy)*
4. **Date of This Report** *(mm/dd/yyyy)*
5. **Describe Event or Problem**
6. **Relevant Tests/Laboratory Data, Including Dates**
7. **Other Relevant History, Including Preexisting Medical Conditions** *(e.g., allergies, race, pregnancy, smoking and alcohol use, hepatic/renal dysfunction, etc.)*

Submission of a report does not constitute an admission that medical personnel, user facility, importer, distributor, manufacturer or product caused or contributed to the event.

C. SUSPECT PRODUCT(S)

1. **Name** *(Give labeled strength & mfr/labeler)*
   #1
   #2
2. **Dose, Frequency & Route Used**
   #1
   #2
3. **Therapy Dates** *(If unknown, give duration) from/to (or best estimate)*
   #1
   #2
4. **Diagnosis for Use** *(Indication)*
   #1
   #2
5. **Event Abated After Use Stopped or Dose Reduced?**
   #1 ☐ Yes ☐ No ☐ Doesn't Apply
   #2 ☐ Yes ☐ No ☐ Doesn't Apply
6. **Lot #**
   #1
   #2
7. **Exp. Date**
   #1
   #2
8. **Event Reappeared After Reintroduction?**
   #1 ☐ Yes ☐ No ☐ Doesn't Apply
   #2 ☐ Yes ☐ No ☐ Doesn't Apply
9. **NDC# or Unique ID**
10. **Concomitant Medical Products and Therapy Dates** *(Exclude treatment of event)*

D. SUSPECT MEDICAL DEVICE

1. **Brand Name**
2. **Common Device Name**
3. **Manufacturer Name, City and State**
4. **Model #** — **Lot #**
   Catalog # — **Expiration Date** *(mm/dd/yyyy)*
   Serial # — **Other #**
5. **Operator of Device**
   ☐ Health Professional
   ☐ Lay User/Patient
   ☐ Other:
6. **If Implanted, Give Date** *(mm/dd/yyyy)*
7. **If Explanted, Give Date** *(mm/dd/yyyy)*
8. **Is this a Single-use Device that was Reprocessed and Reused on a Patient?**
   ☐ Yes ☐ No
9. **If Yes to Item No. 8, Enter Name and Address of Reprocessor**
10. **Device Available for Evaluation?** *(Do not send to FDA)*
    ☐ Yes ☐ No ☐ Returned to Manufacturer on: ____ *(mm/dd/yyyy)*
11. **Concomitant Medical Products and Therapy Dates** *(Exclude treatment of event)*

E. INITIAL REPORTER

1. **Name and Address** — **Phone #**
2. **Health Professional?** ☐ Yes ☐ No
3. **Occupation**
4. **Initial Reporter Also Sent Report to FDA** ☐ Yes ☐ No ☐ Unk.

EXAMPLE 4-31 (continued)

FDA USE ONLY

MEDWATCH

FORM FDA 3500A (1/09) *(continued)* Page 2 of 15

F. FOR USE BY USER FACILITY/IMPORTER *(Devices Only)*

1. **Check One**
   - ☐ User Facility ☐ Importer
2. **UF/Importer Report Number**
3. **User Facility or Importer Name/Address**
4. **Contact Person**
5. **Phone Number**
6. **Date User Facility or Importer Became Aware of Event** *(mm/dd/yyyy)*
7. **Type of Report**
   - ☐ Initial
   - ☐ Follow-up # ____
8. **Date of This Report** *(mm/dd/yyyy)*
9. **Approximate Age of Device**
10. **Event Problem Codes** *(Refer to coding manual)*
    - Patient Code ☐ - ☐ - ☐
    - Device Code ☐ - ☐ - ☐
11. **Report Sent to FDA?**
    - ☐ Yes ____ *(mm/dd/yyyy)*
    - ☐ No
12. **Location Where Event Occurred**
    - ☐ Hospital
    - ☐ Home
    - ☐ Nursing Home
    - ☐ Outpatient Treatment Facility
    - ☐ Outpatient Diagnostic Facility
    - ☐ Ambulatory Surgical Facility
    - ☐ Other: ____ *(Specify)*
13. **Report Sent to Manufacturer?**
    - ☐ Yes ____ *(mm/dd/yyyy)*
    - ☐ No
14. **Manufacturer Name/Address**

G. ALL MANUFACTURERS

1. **Contact Office - Name/Address** *(and Manufacturing Site for Devices)*
2. **Phone Number**
3. **Report Source** *(Check all that apply)*
   - ☐ Foreign
   - ☐ Study
   - ☐ Literature
   - ☐ Consumer
   - ☐ Health Professional
   - ☐ User Facility
   - ☐ Company Representative
   - ☐ Distributor
   - ☐ Other:
4. **Date Received by Manufacturer** *(mm/dd/yyyy)*
5. (A)NDA # ____
   - IND # ____
   - STN # ____
   - PMA/ 510(k) # ____
   - Combination Product ☐ Yes
   - Pre-1938 ☐ Yes
   - OTC Product ☐ Yes
6. **If IND, Give Protocol #**
7. **Type of Report** *(Check all that apply)*
   - ☐ 5-day ☐ 30-day
   - ☐ 7-day ☐ Periodic
   - ☐ 10-day ☐ Initial
   - ☐ 15-day ☐ Follow-up # ____
8. **Adverse Event Term(s)**
9. **Manufacturer Report Number**

H. DEVICE MANUFACTURERS ONLY

1. **Type of Reportable Event**
   - ☐ Death
   - ☐ Serious Injury
   - ☐ Malfunction
   - ☐ Other: ____
2. **If Follow-up, What Type?**
   - ☐ Correction
   - ☐ Additional Information
   - ☐ Response to FDA Request
   - ☐ Device Evaluation
3. **Device Evaluated by Manufacturer?**
   - ☐ Not Returned to Manufacturer
   - ☐ Yes ☐ Evaluation Summary Attached
   - ☐ No *(Attach page to explain why not)* or provide code: ____
4. **Device Manufacture Date** *(mm/yyyy)*
5. **Labeled for Single Use?**
   - ☐ Yes ☐ No
6. **Evaluation Codes** *(Refer to coding manual)*
   - Method ☐ - ☐ - ☐ - ☐
   - Results ☐ - ☐ - ☐ - ☐
   - Conclusions ☐ - ☐ - ☐ - ☐
7. **If Remedial Action Initiated, Check Type**
   - ☐ Recall ☐ Notification
   - ☐ Repair ☐ Inspection
   - ☐ Replace ☐ Patient Monitoring
   - ☐ Relabeling ☐ Modification/ Adjustment
   - ☐ Other: ____
8. **Usage of Device**
   - ☐ Initial Use of Device
   - ☐ Reuse
   - ☐ Unknown
9. **If action reported to FDA under 21 USC 360i(f), list correction/ removal reporting number:**

10. ☐ **Additional Manufacturer Narrative** and / or 11. ☐ **Corrected Data**

The public reporting burden for this collection of information has been estimated to average 66 minutes per response, including the time for reviewing instructions, searching existing data sources, gathering and maintaining the data needed, and completing and reviewing the collection of information. Send comments regarding this burden estimate or any other aspect of this collection of information, including suggestions for reducing this burden to:

Department of Health and Human Services
Food and Drug Administration
Office of Chief Information Officer (HFA-710)
5600 Fishers Lane
Rockville, MD 20857

Please DO NOT RETURN this form to this address.

OMB Statement:
"An agency may not conduct or sponsor, and a person is not required to respond to, a collection of information unless it displays a currently valid OMB control number."

EXAMPLE 4-32

ADVERSE DRUG REACTION SUMMARY

YEAR ________ PAGE ____ OF ____

Drug	Date	Reaction	Probability	Severity	Preventability	Action	Recorded	FDA Report

Probability: (**Def**)inite, (**Pro**)bable, (**Pos**)sible, (**Dou**)btful

Severity: **0 1 2 3 4 5**

Preventability (**Y**)es or (**N**)o

Action Taken: Describe action(s) taken

Recorded: Reaction recorded on patient's medical record (**Y**)es or (**N**)o

FDA Report: Report sent to FDA (**Y**)es or (**N**)o, and date sent

EXAMPLE 4-33

ADVERSE DRUG REACTION RATES

YEAR ______________________ **PAGE** _____ **OF** _____

	Jan	Feb	Mar	Apr	May	Jun	Jul	Aug	Sep	Oct	Nov	Dec	Total
Total Admissions													
Total Suspected Reactions Reported													
Rate per 100 Admissions													
Total Reactions Confirmed													
Rate per 100 Admissions													
Total Serious Reactions													
Rate per 100 Admissions													

MONTHLY ADVERSE DRUG REACTION SUMMARY

Enter Type of Reaction and Number of Reactions for Each Drug per Month

Drug	Reaction	Jan	Feb	Mar	Apr	May	Jun	Jul	Aug	Sep	Oct	Nov	Dec	Total

EXAMPLE 6-1

Request for Review of an Alternative Approach to a National Patient Safety Goal (NPSG) Requirement

Organization name		**HCO #**
□ **Individual organization** □ **Multiple org or system**	Multiple organizations and systems must attach a separate sheet listing all of the organizations and HCO numbers for which the RFR is being requested.	
City, State, Zip		
Contact Name (for questions about this request)		
Contact E-mail		
Contact Phone		
Alternative for NPSG Requirement: Submit only one alternative per form. Indicate accreditation program and requirement (ex: Hospital "Two Identifiers")		

Instructions for filling out the form
Please follow these instructions closely in order to facilitate the review process and to allow more efficient and timely judgment to be rendered on your organization's proposed alternative. If information is missing or judged to be unacceptable, the form will be returned for completion prior to further processing of the request.

□ Submit a separate form for each proposed alternative.

□ Your description—which should be explicit and comprehensive—needs to include the following:
□ the NPSG in question;
□ your organization's current practice and how it departs from the NPSG requirement;
□ the rationale and benefits of the proposed alternative;
□ why your organization's current practice is equivalent in achieving the NPSG requirement; and
□ why your organization's approach should be accepted.

□ Provide one or both of the following, whichever best illustrates your approach:
□ a matrix of; and/or
□ a crosswalk between
the NPSG and your organization's proposed alternative approach.

□ For each alternative request, the organization must submit a comprehensive literature search that includes:
□ support for the proposed alternative process; and
□ arguments against the proposed alternative and/or any risks and barriers to implementation.
This should not be a list of references; it should include abstracted excerpts cited from the literature that show support, risks and barriers.

Submitting the form
Forms should be submitted to your account representative. If you do not know your account representative, call (630) 792-3007. **To facilitate the review process, transmit the form electronically.** To do this, go to File, Save As, and save the form to a file in your computer system. Fill out the form using the keyboard, and send it via e-mail as an attachment. If possible, try to send any additional pages or materials in electronic format. Forms and additional materials can also be faxed or mailed; however, this may delay the review process.

E-mail: npsg@jointcommission.org
Fax: (630) 792-4522
Mail: One Renaissance Blvd., Oakbrook Terrace, IL 60181

Timeframe for response
The timeframe to receive a response varies, depending on the alternative and the Sentinel Event Advisory Group members' agreement on whether the alternative meets the intention of the requirement for which it is to replace. The timeframe may also be extended for additional research, to gather expert opinion, or for debate about the alternative. The detailed instructions on this page are intended to help expedite the review of your RFR. Please contact your account representative for the current status of any outstanding RFRs.

EXAMPLE 6-1 (continued)

HCO#________________________

Alternative for NPSG Requirement:____

- □ **Submit only <u>one</u> alternative per form.**
- □ **Indicate accreditation program <u>and</u> requirement. (Ex: Hospital "Two Identifiers")**
- □ **Additional pages may be attached if needed.**

1. **Describe:** **a) the proposed alternative (which may be your organization's current practice);**
   b) how it departs from the NPSG requirement; and
   c) why it is equivalent in achieving the NPSG.

2. **Describe why this approach was selected instead of the recommended NPSG approach.**

3. **Explain the rationale of the alternative approach.**

4. **Explain the benefits of the alternative approach.**

5. **Explain why the alternative approach should be accepted.**

6. **Identify references in the literature that:**
   a) support the efficacy of this approach; and
   b) argue against the approach and/or describe any potential risks or barriers.

7. **Describe how you are monitoring or will monitor the effectiveness of this approach.**

8. **Attach a matrix and/or a crosswalk between the NPSG and your alternative approach.**

For Joint Commission Use

Acceptability of the approach described above as an alternative to the NPSG Requirement:

_____ Acceptable

_____ Acceptable with the following modification(s):

_____ Not acceptable because of the following reason(s):

EXAMPLE 7-1

ORIENTATION RECORD

EMPLOYEE ______________________________

THE FACILITY

Review of Facility Organization . . . . ________

Administration	________	Nursing	________
Medical Staff	________	Department Heads	________
Pharmacy	________		

Facility Policies and Procedures . . . . ________

Patient's Rights and Confidentiality of Patient Information	________
E-mail	________
Patient Safety Program	________
Employee Health Examination Policy	________
Cultural Diversity and Sensitivity	________
Emergency Management Plan	________
Fire Plan	________

Tour of Facility (to include at least the areas listed below) . . . . ________

Surgery	________	Emergency Department	________
Eating Areas	________	Central Supply	________
Lounges	________	Restrooms	________
Patient Care Areas	________	Fire Extinguishers	________
Fire Alarms	________		

THE PHARMACY

Pharmacy Hours. . . . . ________

Weekday	________	Holiday	________
Weekend	________	Breaks (meals, rest)	________

After-Hours Services. . . . . ________

Personnel Information . . . . ________

Work Schedule	________	Lockers	________
Pay Rate	________	Absenteeism	________
Overtime	________	Tardiness	________
Timecards	________	Holidays	________
Benefits	________	Vacation	________
Insurance	________	Sick Leave	________
Smoking	________	Personal Phone Calls	________
Dress Code	________	Pay Rate Changes	________

Review of Job Description . . . . ________

Employee is enrolled in Benefit Program . . . . ________

Payroll Documents Are Complete. . . . . ________

PHARMACY PERSONNEL

Introduction to the Pharmacy Staff . . . . ________

Director of Pharmacy	________	Pharmacists	________
Support Staff	________	Part-Time Staff	________

PHARMACY AREAS

Pharmacy Responsibility for the Following Areas . . . . ________

Main Pharmacy	________	Office Area	________
Sterile Preparation	________	Storage	________
Emergency Drugs	________	Refrigerators	________
Outdated Drugs	________	Other Areas	________

EXAMPLE 7-1 (continued)

PHARMACY SERVICES

Brief Description of Basic Pharmacy Services . . . . ________

Dispensing	________	Sterile Preparations	________
Emergency Drugs	________	Inventory Control	________
Formulary	________	Drug Therapy Monitoring	________
Drug Information	________	Education Programs	________
Pharmacokinetics	________	FDA REMS	________

SECURITY

Basic Security Requirements . . . . ________

Controlled Substances ________
Other Drugs ________
Pharmacy Areas ________
Confidential Materials ________

MEDICATION SAFETY

Basic Medication Safety Requirements . . . . ________

Medication Error Reports ________
Adverse Drug Reaction Reports ________

CONTINUING EDUCATION

Scope of Continuing Education . . . . ________

Initial Orientation ________
Subsequent Training ________
Responsibility of Professional Staff to Conduct Educational Programs (Make presentations) ________
Attendance at Meetings and/or In-service Education Programs ________
Medical/Nursing In-service Education Provided by Pharmacy ________
Records/Documentation of Attendance (number of meetings or hours required per year) ________

PHARMACY POLICIES AND PROCEDURES

Pharmacy Policy and Procedure Manual . . . . ________

(Read the following policies or sections now—others later)
Personnel ________
Infection Control ________
Safety ________
Medication Recalls ________
Hazardous Materials (handling) ________
Incident Reports ________
Responsibilities and Duties in a Medical Emergency ("Code") ________

EMPLOYEE ACKNOWLEDGMENT

I have completed the above orientation and am aware of my responsibilities and duties. I understand that pharmacy and facility policies are established to promote quality patient care and to ensure the health and safety of patients and staff.

I further understand that there are potential occupational health and safety risks associated with my duties. I have read and fully understand the pharmacy policies and procedures relating to infection control, safety, and handling of hazardous materials and agree to comply with these policies and procedures as well as all other applicable policies and procedures of the facility.

Completed ______________________ ______________________
Employee Signature Date

Certified ______________________ ______________________
Supervisor Date

EXAMPLE 7-2

EDUCATION PROGRAM AND MEETING RECORD

FACILITY_________________________________ **DATE(S)** ___________________________________

LENGTH (HOURS/MINUTES)__________________ **TIME(S)** ___________________________________

FOR: Medical Staff _______ Nursing _________ Pharmacy ________ Other ___________________

SUMMARY OF PROGRAM AND/OR MEETING TOPIC

Attach Handouts and Meeting Materials

SPEAKER, CHAIRPERSON, AND/OR INSTRUCTORS

CONTINUING EDUCATION CREDIT ________

ATTENDEES

NAME AND TITLE OR DEPARTMENT	NAME AND TITLE OR DEPARTMENT

Use reverse side and/or attach additional information, if necessary.

For the Pharmacy ____________________________ Date________________________________

EXAMPLE 7-3

PHARMACY EDUCATION AND TRAINING PROGRAM RECORD

NAME OF PROGRAM: ______________________________

OBJECTIVE(S): ______________________________

____

RELATIONSHIP TO JOB PERFORMANCE: ______________________________

DATE(S) OF PROGRAM: ____________________ **LENGTH OF PROGRAM:** __________

NAME OF PRESENTER: ____________________ **SPONSOR:** ____________________

METHOD OF PRESENTATION: ______________________________

GROUP ATTENDING (CHECK ALL THAT APPLY): __ **PHARMACISTS** __ **TECHNICIANS** __ **SUPPORT STAFF**

THOSE IN ATTENDANCE:

NAME	EMPLOYEE ID #

EXAMPLE 7-4

CONTINUING EDUCATION RECORD

SOURCE CODES:

In-service (pharmacy)................ 1
In-service (medical staff)............ 2
In-service (other department)........ 3
Home Study...4
Journal Articles 5
Seminars, Conferences, etc. (outside facility) 6

NAME ______________________________ **POSITION** ______________________________

DATE	SUBJECT/TITLE	SOURCE CODE	NUMBER OF CREDITS*

* Contact Hours or CEUs if applicable

EXAMPLE 7-5

Competence Assessment Test for Pediatric and Adolescent Patients

Name: ________________________________ **Date:** ____________

Use the following case report to answer questions 1 through 5.

D.M. is a 3-year-old, 23 pound male brought to the outpatient pediatric clinic this morning. His mother indicates that he developed a cold with nasal congestion, fever, and cough 3 days ago. In the last 24 hours, D.M. has become increasingly irritable with episodes of crying and pulling on his right ear and was unable to sleep last night. His mother has been administering acetaminophen for his fever.

Upon examination of D.M.'s right ear, he begins crying loudly and resists examination. The tympanic membrane is bulging and opaque with some inflammation. Nasal congestion and rhinorrhea are also present. D.M.'s temperature is 101°F. There are also crusted erythematous lesions on his face and neck. His mother says the areas have been present about a week and that D.M. constantly scratches them. D.M. has no known allergies.

D.M.'s physician diagnoses acute otitis media and atopic dermatitis and prescribes the following medications:

Augmentin ES-600 90 mg (amoxicillin component)/kg/day PO given in divided doses every 12 hours for 10 days

Antipyrine/benzocaine otic drops 2 to 4 drops in right ear every 2 hours prn ear pain

Hydrocortisone 0.5% cream bid to rash on face and neck

1. How many milligrams of amoxicillin clavulanate (amoxicillin component rounded to the nearest 10 milligrams) are needed for one dose?

2. Augmentin ES-600 is available in a 600 mg (amoxicillin component) per 5 mL suspension. How many milliliters are needed for one dose?

__ 3. Which of the following medications is appropriate for treating fever in this patient?
   a. ibuprofen
   b. acetaminophen
   c. aspirin
   d. a and b
   e. b and c

__ 4. D.M.'s physician orders acetaminophen 160 mg PO every 4 to 6 hours as needed for fever or pain. Which of the following dosage forms of acetaminophen would be appropriate for this patient's age group?
   a. chewable tablets
   b. oral liquid
   c. capsules
   d. rectal suppository
   e. a, b, and d

EXAMPLE 7-5 (continued)

__ 5. The physician gives instructions to D.M.'s mother to apply the hydrocortisone cream sparingly and as directed to the areas of dermatitis. Explain why this precaution is necessary.

Use the following case report to answer questions 6 through 10.
C.L. is an 8-year-old , 55 pound male brought to the emergency room after suffering a seizure at school. During the seizure he lost consciousness and fell, hitting his head on a desk. He had a second seizure while being transported to the hospital. He has a history of attention deficit hyperactivity disorder (ADHD), depression, and headaches. There is a family history of depression. His current medications include methylphenidate, imipramine, and ibuprofen. C.L. is admitted for observation and evaluation of his seizure.

__ 6. C.L. is unable to swallow solid oral dosage forms such as tablets and capsules. Which of the following formulations of methylphenidate may be safely administered by crushing and mixing with food or beverages?
a. Ritalin tablets
b. Ritalin SR tablets
c. Concerta tablets
d. Metadate ER tablets
e. a and c

7. The attending physician wishes C.L. to continue his home medications. C.L.'s depression was stabilized with imipramine 3 mg/kg/day administered in divided doses three times a day. How many milligrams of imipramine are needed for one dose?

__ 8. C.L.'s physician wishes to begin anticonvulsant therapy with carbamazepine. Which of the following methods of drug dosing in pediatric patients is the <u>least</u> dependable?
a. dosage calculations based on Young's Rule
b. dosages based on pharmacokinetic data
c. dosages based on body surface area
d. dosing information found in pediatric dosage publications

__ 9. C.L.'s physician orders carbamazepine 100 mg PO bid. Which of the following formulations are appropriate for this patient?
a. 100 mg chewable tablets
b. 100 mg/5 mL suspension
c. 200 mg tablets divided in half
d. a and b
e. a, b, and c

10. If C.L. remains on carbamazepine therapy long term, explain why it may be necessary to adjust the dose as he ages through childhood and adolescence.

EXAMPLE 7-5 (continued)

Use the following case report to answer questions 11 through 18.
G.B. is a 6-year-old (height 45 inches, weight 42 pounds) female diagnosed with acute lymphocytic leukemia (ALL). She is currently entering the third week of remission induction therapy. Current medications include

Allopurinol 78 mg bid
Prednisone 30 mg PO daily
Docusate 50 mg PO daily

IV fluids with sodium bicarbonate have been started for adequate hydration and alkalinization of the urine. G.B.'s oncologist orders the following antineoplastic agents:

Vincristine 1.5 mg/m^2 IV times one dose today
Daunorubicin 25 mg/m^2 IV times one dose today

11. How many milligrams of vincristine are needed for today's dose?

12. How many milligrams of daunorubicin are needed for today's dose?

__ 13. Which of the following IV delivery systems are appropriate for this patient's age group?
a. IV push
b. syringe pumps
c. IV infusion pumps
d. b and c
e. a, b, and c

__ 14. Which of the following are important factors to consider when preparing and administering medications to pediatric patients?
a. selection of correct syringe size
b. fluid volume
c. accuracy of dilutions
d. a and c
e. a, b, and c

15. What are the implications for pediatric patients associate with medication retention in administration devices?

16. What special precaution is required when dispensing vincristine?

17. Allopurinol is available as 100 mg tablets, 300 mg tablets, and 500 mg injection (lyophilized powder for reconstitution). What methods may be used to administer the dose needed for this patient?

__ 18. Which of the following precautions can minimize the potential for drug-related problems in pediatric patients?
a. including the dose per weight on medication orders
b. dispensing oral liquid medications in unit-dose oral syringes
c. ordering oral liquid medications by volume
d. a and b
e. a, b, and c

EXAMPLE 7-5 (continued)

Use the following case report to answer questions 19 through 20.
J.P. is a 14-year-old, 90 lb female who has been admitted to the intensive care unit following a motor vehicle accident. Her physician has ordered a dopamine drip to be administered at a rate of 5 mcg/kg/min.

19. At what rate (mL/hr) should a dopamine infusion of 200 mg in 250 ml be infused?

20. List three medications that are potentially lethal in adolescent patients if prepared or administered inappropriately.

Competence certified by: ______________________________ **Date:** ______________

EXAMPLE 7-5 (continued)

Pediatric and Adolescent Patients
Answer Key

1. 470 mg
2. 3.9 mL
3. d. Aspirin would not be an appropriate choice because the patient has a viral illness (i.e., a cold). Salicylate use in children during viral illnesses is associated with Reye's syndrome.
4. e
5. Systemic absorption of medications through the skin is increased in young children compared to adults and may result in adverse effects.
6. a. Ritalin SR, Concerta, and Metadate ER are extended release formulations that must not be crushed or chewed.
7. 25 mg
8. a
9. d
10. It may be necessary to adjust the dose of carbamazepine because biological functions such as metabolism change and mature throughout childhood and adolescence.
11. 1.2 mg
12. 19.5 mg
13. e
14. e
15. The patient may be underdosed due to a significant amount of the medication retained in the administration device. Medication delivery to the patient may also be delayed.
16. Vincristine is required to be dispensed in a labeled overwrap with the statement "Do not remove covering until the moment of injection. Fatal if given intrathecally. For IV use only."
17. Allopurinol may be administered intravenously using the IV formulation or as an extemporaneous oral suspension compounded using allopurinol tablets.
18. d
19. 15 mL/hr
20. Examples include potassium chloride, atropine, lidocaine, digoxin, opiates, local anesthetics, barbiturates, epinephrine, and phenytoin.

EXAMPLE 7-6

Competence Assessment Skills Checklist for Pediatric and Adolescent Patients

Name: ______________________________ **Date:** ____________

KNOWLEDGE AND SKILLS	YES	NO
Explains the differences in drug absorption, distribution, metabolism, and elimination for pediatric and adolescent patients compared to adult patients. Describes how these processes mature.		
Explains how disease processes impact medication therapy.		
Lists medications that are potentially lethal in pediatric and adolescent patients if prepared or administered inappropriately. Describes precautions to prevent errors. Does not store adult-only concentrations and multiple-dose vials containing lethal amounts of medications in pediatric and adolescent patient care areas.		
Explains why younger children have an increased potential for ADRs. Identifies potential sources of ADRs and implements precautions to reduce the incidence and severity of ADRs.		
Accurately prepares extemporaneous formulations and dilutions of commercially available products. Uses appropriate procedures.		
Calculates drug dosages using information in the product information and pediatric dosage publications (when available). Uses body surface area rather than dosing rules when calculating doses for pediatric patients.		
Uses appropriate medication formulations, dosage forms, and routes and methods of administration for pediatric and adolescent patients. Explains how medications may be retained in administration devices and the implications for the patient. Makes recommendations to prevent retention.		
Explains the potential for fluid overload from IV administration. Makes recommendations to prevent fluid overload.		
Demonstrates knowledge of the following IV delivery systems: IV push, IV piggyback, IV infusion, and syringe pumps.		

EXAMPLE 7-6 (continued)

KNOWLEDGE AND SKILLS	YES	NO
Takes necessary steps to prevent drug-drug, food-drug, drug-laboratory test, and drug-disease interactions and monitors for evidence of ADRs, overdosage, and other drug-related problems in pediatric and adolescent patients.		
Monitors medication therapy and makes recommendations to manage medication-related problems, ensuring positive therapeutic outcomes for pediatric and adolescent patients.		

Competence certified by: ___________________________ Date: ______________

EXAMPLE 7-7

JOB DESCRIPTION, COMPETENCE ASSESSMENT SUMMARY, AND PERFORMANCE EVALUATION

Type of Evaluation □ New Employee Evaluation □ Annual Evaluation □ Self-assessment

Employee Name: **Date:**

Job Title/Position: Staff Pharmacist

Job Summary: Staff pharmacists fill orders for medications, monitor patient medication therapies, and provide drug information. Staff pharmacists supervise and direct support personnel. In the absence of the pharmacy manager, a staff pharmacist may be required to assume the essential responsibilities and perform the duties of the pharmacy manager.

Reports To: Director of Pharmacy **Supervises:** All pharmacy support personnel

Education: Graduate of an ACPE- accredited School of Pharmacy with a Pharmacy degree.

Licenses: Currently licensed to practice pharmacy in the state of

Experience: Health system experience preferred, but not required.

Work Schedule: Minimum of 40 hours per week, but hours may be long and irregular; includes evenings, weekends, and holidays as necessary.

Physical Requirements: Repetitive use of hands and fingers (e.g., preparing IV admixtures, use of a computer keyboard). May require lifting and carrying light loads (up to 40 lb.), including boxes, equipment, unit dose-cassettes, and IV solutions and stooping or kneeling (e.g., to pick up items from the floor, to remove and replace items on lower shelves, and to file documents in lower file drawers). Sitting, walking, or standing for long periods of time (4–8 hours) is often necessary. Must be able to physically operate the equipment used for the job.

Critical Demands: Ability to work independently with minimal direct supervision. Ability to work cooperatively with health-system and pharmacy staff. Ability to handle frequent interruptions and adapt to changes in workload and work schedule. Ability to set priorities, make critical decisions, and respond quickly to emergency requests. Ability to exercise sound professional judgment. Ability to communicate effectively (orally and in writing). Ability to meet the pharmaceutical care needs of neonatal, pediatric, adolescent, adult, geriatric, psychiatric, oncology, obstetric, rehabilitation, and skilled-nursing patients.

Occupational Hazards: Potential for exposure to infectious patients or materials. Potential for exposure to hazardous and toxic substances (including chemotherapy, cytotoxic drugs, and cleaning solutions). Potential for sticks or cuts by needles and other sharp items. Potential for musculoskeletal injuries if proper lifting and carrying techniques are not used.

EXAMPLE 7-7 (continued)

I. Principal Duties/Responsibilities
Scoring Guide: 2 = Meets Standards 0 = Does Not Meet Standards

Performance Criteria/Standards	Rating	Comments
A. Prepares and dispenses medication orders per physician request according to established policies, procedures, and protocols.		
1. Interprets medication orders (verbal and written) and transcribes to computerized patient medication profiles accurately. Maintains accurate, complete patient medication profiles.		
2. Prepares and dispenses medications, including sterile, chemotherapy, and parenteral nutrition preparations safely and accurately using appropriate techniques.		
3. Issues controlled substances to patient care areas and maintains records as required by law.		
B. Ensures safe, appropriate, cost-effective medication therapies for patients according to established policies, procedures, and protocols.		
1. Monitors medication therapy regimens for contraindications, drug-drug interactions, drug-food interactions, drug-laboratory test interactions, allergies, appropriateness of drug and dose, and therapeutic duplications.		
2. Assists with pharmacokinetics consult service and drug dosing per organizational protocol.		
3. Reviews/interprets culture and susceptibility data for antibiotic appropriateness and recommends changes, as needed.		
4. Reads, extracts, and interprets information in patient charts accurately.		
5. Detects and reports suspected adverse drug reactions and medication errors accurately and in a timely manner.		
6. Sustains the formulary by minimizing nonformulary procurements, utilizing therapeutic substitution protocols, and promoting rational medication therapy selection.		
7. Provides clinical consultation and clarification to practitioners. Recommends evidence-based medication therapy regimens and monitoring plans. Suggests appropriate, cost-effective therapeutic alternatives to medical staff, as needed.		
8. Provides accurate, adequate, and timely drug information to the professional staff.		
9. Provides drug information to patients and their families.		
10. Documents all clinical activities and interventions accurately and completely.		
11. Participates in the quality improvement and medication use review activities of the department. Collects data; conducts quality monitors and inspections; and maintains logs, records, and other documentation as assigned.		
12. Participates in the development and presentation of orientation, education, and training programs to the pharmacy, medical, nursing, and other staffs.		

EXAMPLE 7-7 (continued)

C. Contributes to the quality and effective operation of the department.		
1. Supervises and directs pharmacy support personnel. Verifies the daily activities of pharmacy technicians. Participates in the performance appraisal of pharmacy support personnel.		
2. Works independently with minimal supervision. Organizes and prioritizes work assignments. Ensures pharmacy services are provided in a timely manner.		
3. Completes and documents inspections of all assigned medication storage areas at least monthly. Identifies and replaces outdated and unusable medications.		
4. Answers the telephone, identifying self and department. Directs calls to appropriate personnel. Answers requests at the window.		
5. Keeps pharmacy areas and equipment clean, neat, and well-organized.		
6. Performs essential duties of the pharmacy director in his/her absence.		
D. Maintains competence required for current job title/position.		
1. Maintains current pharmacist licensure.		
2. Attends pharmacy staff meetings.		
3. Attends orientation, education, and training programs. Reviews literature and other materials pertinent to the practice of pharmacy.		
4. Completes all competence/skills assessment requirements (see attached competence assessment/skills list).		
E. Performs other duties as assigned by supervisor.		
TOTAL POINTS (maximum available points = 52)		

EXAMPLE 7-7 (continued)

II. Departmental Standards Scoring Guide: 2 = Meets Standards 0 = Does Not Meet Standards

Performance Criteria/Standards	**Rating**	**Comments**
1. Is punctual and dependable; reports to work as scheduled. Fulfills on-call obligations per prearranged schedule. Absenteeism and tardiness are within policy guidelines.		
2. Maintains a neat, professional, well-groomed appearance. Observes pharmacy dress code. Wears identification badge at all times.		
3. Performs work within specified time frames. Adapts positively to frequent interruptions and changes in workload and/or work schedule.		
4. Provides courteous, cooperative, and timely service to patients, visitors, and staff. Demonstrates good oral and written communication.		
5. Works cooperatively with all staff. Voices concerns and suggestions to appropriate persons in a positive manner.		
6. Demonstrates sound professional judgment consistent with clinical/academic background.		
7. Maintains strict confidentiality of patient, visitor, and employee information. Complies with the HIPAA Privacy Rule standards.		
8. Fosters a team environment by providing orientation and training to new team members. Assists coworkers in tasks, as time permits.		
9. Adheres to health system and departmental policies and procedures. Complies with all requirements related to risk management, safety, medication use safety, security, fire safety, and infection control. Complies with all applicable federal, state, and local laws, rules, and regulations.		
TOTAL POINTS (maximum available points = 18)		

III. Organizational Standards Scoring Guide: 2 = Meets Standards 0 = Does Not Meet Standards

Performance Criteria/Standards	**Rating**	**Comments**
1. Performance demonstrates efforts to improve patient satisfaction, lower costs, and improve quality.		
2. Understands and meets customers' needs and expectations. The patient and family members always come first.		
3. Demonstrates the ability to address problems in a group setting using tools and techniques for identification and resolution of problems.		
4. Demonstrates the values and behaviors of the organization.		
TOTAL POINTS (maximum available points = 8)		

EXAMPLE 7-7 (continued)

IV. Goals and Accomplishments **Scoring Guide:** 4 = Goals met *and* special accomplishments achieved
2 = Goals met
0 = Did not achieve set goals

A. Describe status of goals set at previous evaluation.

____
____
____

B. Describe special accomplishments achieved since previous evaluation.

____
____
____

TOTAL POINTS (maximum available points = 4)

V. Scoring

PERFORMANCE CRITERIA/STANDARDS	TOTAL POINTS AVAILABLE	EMPLOYEE SCORE
Principal Duties/Responsibilities	52	
Departmental Standards	18	
Organizational Standards	8	
Goals and Accomplishments	4	
TOTAL SCORE	**82**	

SCORING GUIDELINES:

____points Exceptional performance
____points Exceeds standards
____points Consistently meets standards
____points Improvement required*
____points Does not meet standards*
*Requires action plan

EXAMPLE 7-7 (continued)

ACTION TAKEN:
1. None at this time _____
2. Extended probation _____days.
3. Corrective action _____

Type: ______________________________

Action: ______________________________

____

____

PERFORMANCE GOALS AND OBJECTIVES:
Provide assessment of own needs for growth and development. Develop a plan to meet educational and professional growth within the next 12 months.

____

____

____

COMMENTS:
A. Supervisor's Comments:

____

____

____

B. Employee's Comments:

____

____

____

______________________________ ______________
Employee's Signature **Date**

______________________________ ______________
Supervisor's Signature **Date**

EXAMPLE 7-7 (continued)

PHARMACY DEPARTMENT
Competence Checklist for Staff Pharmacist

Employee Name: ______________________________

Knowledge/Skills	Date	Method of Assessment	Name of Evaluator	Rating
Initial Skills				
Confidentiality and Patient Rights				
Safety[1]				
Medication Use Safety[1]				
Fire Safety[1]				
Security[1]				
Hazardous Materials[1]				
Emergency Management[1]				
Infection Control[1]				
Compounded Sterile Preparations and Laminar Airflow Workbenchs				
Chemotherapy Preparation and Biological Safety Cabinets				
Pharmaceutical Care Needs of Neonatal and Infant Patients				
Pharmaceutical Care Needs of Pediatric and Adolescent Patients				
Pharmaceutical Care Needs of Adult Patients				
Pharmaceutical Care Needs of Geriatric Patients				
Pharmaceutical Care Needs of Obstetric Patients				
Pharmaceutical Care Needs of Oncology Patients				
Pharmaceutical Care Needs of Psychiatric Patients				
Pharmaceutical Care Needs of Skilled-Nursing Patients				
Adult Enteral Nutrition				
Adult Parenteral Nutrition				
Renal Dosing				
Medication Therapy Monitoring				
Antibiotic Therapy Monitoring				
Emergency Drug Therapy				
Pain Management				

EXAMPLE 7-7 (continued)

Competence Checklist for Staff Pharmacist (continued)

Pharmacokinetics				
Patient Counseling				
Adverse Drug Reaction Reporting				
Medication Area Inspections				
Information Management				
Prepackaging Medications				
Controlled Substances				
Equipment	**Date**	**Method of Assessment**	**Name of Evaluator**	**Rating**
Automated Compounding Equipment				
Automated Distribution Equipment				
Bar Code Scanning Equipment				
Medication Prepackaging Equipment				
Pharmacy Balance				
Fax Machine				
Telephone				
Pharmacy Computer				
Computer Printer				
Word Processing Software				
Spreadsheet Software				
Database Software				
Graphics/Presentation Software				
E-mail				
Calculator				

[1] Periodic review and documentation of this competence is suggested by The Joint Commission.

Method of Assessment				**Method of Rating**	
O	Direct Observation	**P**	Peer Review	**C**	Performs competently
V	Verbal Response	**Q**	QA Findings	**A**	Performs with assistance*
S	Skill Demonstration	**C**	Continuing Education	**N**	Does not perform competently*
T	Testing				

* Requires Action Plan

EXAMPLE 7-7 (continued)

Competence Checklist for Staff Pharmacist (continued)

PHARMACIST LICENSURE VALIDATION:

License Number: ____________________ Expiration Date: ____________________

Date of Validation: ____________________

______________________________ ______________________________
Employee's Signature **Date**

______________________________ ______________________________
Supervisor's Signature **Date**

(Attach to Employee's Performance Evaluation.)

EXAMPLE 7-7 (continued)

ACTION PLAN TO CORRECT DEFICIENCIES IDENTIFIED IN JOB-SPECIFIC PERFORMANCE EVALUATION

Employee Name: ______________________ **Title:** ______________________

Employee has not met the following performance standards/criteria/competencies:
1.
2.
3.

Retraining in the following areas will occur within the specified time frame:
1.
2.
3.

Re-evaluation of deficiencies will occur _____________________.

Additional Comments:

________________________ ____________________
Employee's Signature **Date**

________________________ ____________________
Supervisor's Signature **Date**
(Retain with Performance Evaluation in employee's departmental personnel file.)

EXAMPLE 9-1

LAMINAR AIRFLOW WORKBENCH CLEANING RECORD

Workbench Location/Number: ______________ Month __________ Year ________

Cleaning Agent: Sterile Water for Irrigation
Disinfecting Agent: Sterile 70% Isopropyl Alcohol

Place initials in appropriate box when hood is cleaned

DATE	DAY SHIFT	EVENING SHIFT	NIGHT SHIFT
1			
2			
3			
4			
5			
6			
7			
8			
9			
10			
11			
12			
13			
14			
15			
16			
17			
18			
19			
20			
21			
22			
23			
24			
25			
26			
27			
28			
29			
30			
31			

Pre-Filter Changed **Date:**____________________

EXAMPLE 11-1

POLICY AND PROCEDURE FOR NONFORMULARY MEDICATION REQUESTS

Page number _______ of ______
Policy number _______________

DEPARTMENT: Pharmacy

SUBJECT: Nonformulary Medication Requests

ISSUED BY: Pharmacy and Therapeutics Committee

REVIEWED: ______________________ Director of Pharmacy ______________ Date

APPROVED: ______________________ For the Medical Staff ______________ Date

PURPOSE

The purpose of this policy and procedure is to provide for the procurement of medications that are not in the facility's formulary.

BACKGROUND

The formulary lists medications that have been approved by the medical staff for use in this facility. Prescribers must use formulary medications when possible.

POLICY

Nonformulary medications shall be used in this facility only after the prescriber has determined that a formulary medication is not appropriate. However, a prescriber shall NOT use a medication that the medical staff has specifically prohibited from use in this facility.

PROCEDURE

Nonformulary Medication Request Form—A request for a nonformulary medication shall be made on a Nonformulary Medication Request form (available at nursing units and from the pharmacy). A separate request form shall be completed for each nonformulary medication ordered. The completed form(s) shall be forwarded to the pharmacy.

Review by a Pharmacist—A pharmacist shall review the request. If, in the opinion of the pharmacist, there is an appropriate alternative medication on the formulary, the pharmacist shall inform the prescriber of the alternative. The pharmacist shall indicate the following on the request form: the suggested alternative(s) and the action taken by the pharmacy to obtain the medication.

Procurement of a Nonformulary Medication—If an alternative medication is not acceptable, the pharmacy shall obtain the nonformulary medication from another facility, community pharmacy, or other approved source. The pharmacy shall obtain a supply of the medication sufficient to meet the anticipated needs of the patient for whom it is ordered. If the nonformulary medication cannot be obtained within 4 hours, the pharmacy shall notify the prescriber and nursing service.

Requests for Addition to the Formulary—Completion of a Nonformulary Medication Request form does not constitute a request for addition of the medication to the formulary. A request may be made on a Request for Formulary Addition form, which is available from the pharmacy.

EXAMPLE 12-1

VERIFICATION OF LICENSURE/REGISTRATION/CERTIFICATION FOR PHARMACY PERSONNEL

The primary source (agency issuing license/registration/certification) verified that the individual's license, registration or certification numbers listed below are current, valid, do not have any disciplinary action pending, and authorized to practice pharmacy as of the date noted below. Copy of original verification is available in each individual's human resource record.

NAME	PHARMACIST OR TECHNICIAN	PRIMARY SOURCE	EXPIRATION DATE	DATE VERIFIED	VERIFIED BY	NOTES

EXAMPLE 12-2

Power of Attorney for DEA Form 222 and Electronic Orders

(Name of registrant) ______________________________

(Address of registrant) ______________________________

____

(DEA registration number) ______________________________

I, ______________________ (name of person granting power), the undersigned, who am authorized to sign the current application for registration of the above-named registrant under the Controlled Substances Act or Controlled Substances Import and Export Act, have made, constituted, and appointed, and by these presents, do make, constitute, and appoint ______________________ (name of attorney-in-fact), my true and lawful attorney for me in my name, place, and stead, to execute applications for Forms 222 and to sign orders for Schedule I and II controlled substances, whether these orders be on Form 222 or electronic, in accordance with 21 U.S.C. 828 and Part 1305 of Title 21 of the Code of Federal Regulations. I hereby ratify and confirm all that said attorney must lawfully do or cause to be done by virtue hereof.

_________________________(Signature of person granting power)

I, _________________________ (name of attorney-in-fact), hereby affirm that I am the person named herein as attorney-in-fact and that the signature affixed hereto is my signature.

_________________________(Signature of attorney-in-fact)

Witnesses:

1. _________________________ (Signature of witness)

2. _________________________ (Signature of witness)

Signed and dated on _________________________ (current date).

Notice of Revocation – to be completed only when Power of Attorney is revoked

The foregoing power of attorney is hereby revoked by the undersigned, who is authorized to sign the current application for registration of the above-named registrant under the Controlled Substances Act or the Controlled Substances Import and Export Act. Written notice of this revocation has been given to the attorney-in-fact _________ this same day.

_________________________ (Signature of person revoking power)

Witnesses:

1. _________________________ (Signature of witness)

2. _________________________ (Signature of witness)

Signed and dated on _________________________ (current date).

EXAMPLE 12-3

MEDICAL STAFF INFORMATION RECORD

The organization is required to maintain information relating to the medical staff (including a means of identifying the signatures of practitioners and their Drug Enforcement Administration [DEA] numbers).

Please provide the following information and return this form to the pharmacy.

NAME____

ADDRESS____

____

____

____

____

SERVICE/DEPARTMENT ______________________________

TELEPHONE **Office** ______________________________

Mobile ______________________________

Fax ______________________________

E-MAIL ADDRESS ______________________________

STATE LICENSE NUMBER ______________________________

DEA NUMBER ______________________________
(Or hospital assigned number)

CONTROLLED SUBSTANCE LICENSE (STATE OR OTHER) ____________________

APPROVED SCHEDULES PRESCRIBERS MAY PRESCRIBE
(Circle all that apply)

2 2N 3 3N 4 5

SAMPLE SIGNATURE ______________________________
(For signing medication orders)

EXAMPLE 13-1

Example of Pharmacy and Therapeutics Committee Minutes

Date of Meeting

TOPIC	FINDINGS / DISCUSSION	RECOMMENDATIONS / ACTION
Call to Order	The meeting was called to order at *TIME* by *PHYSICIAN*, Chairman. A quorum was present.	
Attendance	The attendance list was signed by those attending and is attached to these minutes.	
Minutes of Last Meeting	The minutes of the MONTH meeting were approved as distributed.	
Medical Executive Committee action	The Medical Executive Committee approved the following action items from the last P&T Meeting: • *LIST*	
Formulary		
Additions	The committee approves the indications for use of the medications.	
Deletions		
Changes		
Emerging safety data	The FDA released a Black Box warning for the following formulary agents: *LIST*. The Committee voted to:	
FDA REMS Program		
Annual Review	The 201X Formulary was approved.	
Nonformulary medications		
Policies and Procedures		
Floor stock		
Emergency medications		
Investigational medications		
Annual Review	The Committee approved the current policies and procedures regarding medication management, including high-alert, look-alike/sound-alike, and hazardous medications.	
Medication Safety		
Medication errors	The *QUARTER* medication error summary was presented to the Committee.	

EXAMPLE 13-1 (continued)

ADRs	*NUMBER* ADRs were reported in *QUARTER*. A preventability assessment was performed on each. The pharmacy was directed to send *SPECIFICS* to the FDA.	
Joint Commission Sentinel Event Alert		
ISMP Medication Safety Alert!		
Marketplace		
Recalls		
Shortages		
Medication Use		
MUEs		
Protocols		
Review of preprinted orders		
Antibiogram		
Pharmacist interventions		
Other Performance Improvement activities		
Evaluation of Drug Cost information		
Items requiring further approval	The following items approved during this meeting will be forwarded to the Medical Executive Committee for final action: • *LIST*	
Next meeting	The next meeting will be held on *DATE* at *TIME* in *LOCATION*.	
Adjournment	The meeting was adjourned at *TIME*.	

PHYSICIAN Chairman

PHARMACIST Secretary

EXAMPLE 20-1

HIGH-ALERT MEDICATIONS AND PRECAUTIONS

The following medication examples pose a high risk for serious errors:

- Concentrated Electrolytes:
  - Potassium chloride
  - Potassium phosphate
  - Sodium chloride greater that 0.9%
  - Magnesium sulfate
  - Calcium chloride
  - Calcium gluconate
- Insulin
- Opiates and narcotics
- Anticoagulants (e.g., warfarin, heparin, low molecular weight heparin)
- Antineoplastic medications
- Neonatal and pediatric medications
- Epidural medications
- Patient controlled analgesia medications
- Neuromuscular blocking agents
- Medications with look-alike/sound-alike names

Precautions

- Persons who administer high-alert medications must:
  - Verify the medication name and strength
  - Prepare the amount of medication to be administered
  - Compare and confirm the medication name, strength, and amount to administer with the patient's record
  - Ensure that the amount to administer does not exceed the maximum amount permitted for administration
  - Contact a pharmacist if the amount to administer exceeds the maximum permitted
  - Have a second qualified individual verify the medication name, strength, and amount to administer
  - Have a second qualified individual check the calculations used in determining the amount to administer
  - Document the double-check in the patient's record

- Staff must contact the pharmacy/pharmacist on-call if there are any questions about the medication or calculating the amount to administer.

Contact Information

Agency for Healthcare Research and Quality (AHRQ)

Office of Communications and Knowledge Transfer
540 Gaither Road
Suite 2000
Rockville, MD 20850
Telephone: 301-427-1364
Web site: www.ahrq.gov

American National Standards Institute (ANSI)

1819 L Street, NW, 6th Floor
Washington, DC 20036
Telephone: 202-293-8020
Fax: 202-293-9287
Web site: www.ansi.org

American Osteopathic Association (AOA)

142 East Ontario Street
Chicago, IL 60611
Telephone: 312-202-8000 or 800-621-1773
Fax: 312-202-8200
Web site: www.osteopathic.org/index.cfm?PageID=con_consumermain
Web site: www.do-online.org

American Pain Society

4700 West Lake Avenue
Glenview, IL 60025
Telephone: 847-375-4715
Fax: 866-574-2654, 847-375-6479
Web site: www.ampainsoc.org

American Society of Health-System Pharmacists (ASHP)

7272 Wisconsin Avenue
Bethesda, MD 20814
Telephone: 301-657-3000
Customer Service: 866-279-0681
Web site: www.ashp.org

Association of periOperative Registered Nurses (AORN)

2170 South Parker Road
Suite 400
Denver, CO 80231
Telephone: 303-755-6304 or 800-755-2676
Fax: 303-750-3212
Web site: www.aorn.org

Centers for Disease Control and Prevention (CDC)

1600 Clifton Road
Atlanta, GA 30333
Telephone: 800-CDC-INFO (800-232-4636)
Web site: www.cdc.gov
Web site for Hand Hygiene Guidelines: www.cdc.gov/handhygiene

Centers for Medicare and Medicaid Services (CMS)

7500 Security Boulevard
Baltimore, MD 21244
Telephone: 800-633-4227
Web site: www.cms.hhs.gov
Web site for Conditions of Participation (CoPs) and related information: www.cms.hhs.gov/manuals/Downloads/som107ap_a_ hospitals.pdf.

Code of Federal Regulations

Web site: www.gpoaccess.gov/CFR/

DNV Healthcare U.S. (National Integrated Accreditation for Healthcare Organizations, NIAHO)

463 Ohio Pike
Suite 203
Cincinnati, OH 45255
Telephone: 513-947-8343
Fax: 513-927-1250
Web site: www.dnv.com/focus/hospital_accreditation/index.asp

Drug Enforcement Administration (DEA)

Mailstop: AES
8701 Morrissette Drive
Springfield, VA 22152
Telephone: 202-307-1000
Web site: www.dea.gov

ECRI Institute

5200 Butler Pike
Plymouth Meeting, PA 19462
610-825-6000
Web site: www.ecri.org

Food and Drug Administration (FDA)

10903 New Hampshire Avenue
Silver Spring, MD 20993
Telephone: 888-INFO-FDA (888-463-6332)
Web site: www.fda.gov

Hand Hygiene Resource Center (HHRC)

Hospital of Saint Raphael
1450 Chapel Street
New Haven, CT 06511
Telephone: 203-789-3000
Web site: www.handhygiene.org

Healthcare Facilities Accreditation Program (HFAP)

American Osteopathic Association
142 East Ontario Street
Chicago, IL 60611
Telephone: 312-202-8258
Web site: www.hfap.org

Hospital Pharmacy

Thomas Land Publishers, Inc.
255 Jefferson Road
St. Louis, MO 63199
800-633-4931
Web site: www.thomasland.com

Immunization Action Coalition

1573 Selby Avenue
Suite 234
St. Paul, MN 55104
Telephone: 651-647-9009
Fax: 651-647-9131
Web site: www.immunize.org

Institute for Safe Medication Practices (ISMP)

200 Lakeside Drive
Suite 200
Horsham, PA 19044
Telephone: 215-947-7797
Fax: 215-914-1492
Web site: www.ismp.org

International Organization for Standardization (ISO)

1, ch de la Voie-Creuse
Casa postale 56
CH-1211 Geneva 20
Switzerland
Telephone: (+41-22)-749-01-11
Fax: (+41-22)-733-34-30
Web site: www.iso.org

The Joint Commission

One Renaissance Boulevard
Oakbrook Terrace, IL 60181
Telephone: 630-792-5000
Fax: 630-792-5005
Customer Service: 630-792-5800
Standards Interpretation: 630-792-5900
Web site: www.jointcommission.org
ORYX® Information: 630-792-5085
ORYX e-mail: oryx@jointcommission.org
Quality Check® Web site: www.qualitycheck.org/consumer/searchQCR.aspx

Joint Commission Resources (JCR)

Telephone (Customer Service): 877-223-6866
Web-site: www.jcrinc.com

Massachusetts Coalition for the Prevention of Medical Errors

5 New England Executive Park
Burlington, MA 01803
Telephone: 781-272-8000
Fax: 781-272-0605
Web site: www.macoalition.org

MedWatch

The FDA Safety Information and Adverse Event Reporting Program
Food and Drug Administration
5600 Fishers Lane
Rockville, MD 20852-9787
Telephone: 800-FDA-1088 (800-332-1088)

Fax: 800-FDA-0178 (800-332-0178)
Web site: www.fda.gov/medwatch

National Association of Boards of Pharmacy (NABP)

1600 Feehanville Drive
Mount Prospect, IL 60056
Telephone: 847-391-4406
Fax: 847-391-4502
Web site: www.nabp.net

National Coordinating Council for Medication Error Reporting and Prevention (NCCMERP)

Web site: www.nccmerp.org

National Institute for Occupational Safety and Health (NIOSH)

395 E Street, SW
Suite 9200
Patriots Plaza Building
Washington, DC 20201
Telephone: 800-35-NIOSH (4674)
Fax: 513-533-8347
Web site: www.cdc.gov/niosh

National Quality Forum (NQF)

601 13th Street, NW
Suite 500 North
Washington, DC 20005
Telephone: 202-783-1300
Fax: 202-783-3434
Web site: www.qualityforum.org

Occupational Safety and Health Administration (OSHA)

U.S. Department of Labor
200 Constitution Avenue, NW
Washington, DC 20210
Telephone: 800-321-OSHA (6742)
Website: www.osha.gov
Web site for Hazard Communication information: ww.osha.gov/dsg/hazcom

Quantros, Inc.

690 North McCarthy Boulevard
Suite 200
Milpitas, CA 95035
Telephone: 408-957-3300
Fax: 408-957-3320
Web site: www.quantros.com

United States Pharmacopeia (USP)

12601 Twinbrook Parkway
Rockville, MD 20852-1790
Telephone: 800-227-8772 or 301-881-0666
Web site: www.usp.org

Vaccine Adverse Event Reporting System (VAERS)

PO Box 1100
Rockville, MD 20849-1100
Telephone: 800-822-7967
Fax: 877-721-0366
Web site: www.vaers.hhs.gov

World Health Organization (WHO)

Avenue Appia 20
1211 Geneva 27
Switzerland
Telephone: (+-41-22)-791-21-11
Fax: (+-41-22)-791-3111
Web site: www.who.int

References and Resources

Chapter 1

1. The Joint Commission. About us. Available at www.jointcommission.org/AboutUS. Accessed March 6, 2010.
2. The Joint Commission. *Comprehensive Accreditation Manual for Hospitals: The Official Handbook.* Oakbrook Terrace, IL: The Joint Commission; 2010.

Chapter 2

1. The Joint Commission. *Comprehensive Accreditation Manual for Hospitals: The Official Handbook.* Oakbrook Terrace, IL: The Joint Commission; 2010.

Chapter 3

[NO REFERENCES]

Chapter 4

1. The Joint Commission. *Comprehensive Accreditation Manual for Hospitals: The Official Handbook*, Oakbrook Terrace, IL: The Joint Commission, 2010.
2. Centers for Medicare and Medicaid Services, Department of Health and Human Services. *State Operations Manual Appendix A–Survey Protocol, Regulations and Interpretive Guidelines for Hospitals*, Rev 47 (06-05-09). Washington, DC: Government Printing Office; 2008. Available at www.cms.hhs.gov/manuals/downloads/som107ap_a_hospitals.pdf. Accessed March 6, 2010.
3. National Institute for Occupational Safety and Health [NIOSH]. NIOSH alert: preventing occupational exposure to antineoplastic and other hazardous drugs in health care settings. Available at www.cdc.gov/niosh/docs/2004-165/. Accessed March 6, 2010.
4. Centers for Disease Control and Prevention. Guidelines for maintaining and managing the vaccine cold chain. *MMWR*. 2003;52(42):1023–5. Available at: www.cdc.gov/mmwr/preview/mmwrhtml/mm5242a6.htm. Accessed March 6, 2010.
5. The Joint Commission. FAQs for 2009 Patient Safety Goal 02.02.01, Do not use abbreviations. Available at www.jointcommission.org/AccreditationPrograms/Hospitals/Standards/09_FAQs/NPSG/Communication/NPSG.02.02.01/Do+not+use+abbreviations.htm. Accessed March 6, 2010.
6. The Joint Commission. FAQs for 2009 Patient Safety Goal 02.01.01, Read back orders. Available at www.jointcommission.org/AccreditationPrograms/Hospitals/Standards/09_FAQs/NPSG/Communication/NPSG.02.01.01/Read+Back+Orders.htm. Accessed March 6, 2010.
7. The Joint Commission. Standard MM 4.10, EP 1 in the emergency department – interim action suspended effective immediately. *Joint Commission Perspectives*. 2007;27(7):3.
8. The Joint Commission. Interim action for Standard MM 4.10, Element of Performance 1, for critical access hospitals and hospitals. *Joint Commission Perspectives*. 2007;27(1):9.
9. The Joint Commission. Clarifying information for MM.4.10 and oral contrast media. *Joint Commission Perspectives*. 2005;25(6):9.
10. American College of Radiology [ACR]. ACR practice guideline for the use of intravascular contrast media, 2007 (Resolution 38). Available at www.acr.org/SecondaryMainMenuCategories/quality_safety/guidelines/dx/iv_contrast.aspx. Accessed March 6, 2010.
11. Macaulay TE, et al. Pharmacists' role in facilitating evidence-based prescribing for unlabeled use of medications. *Am J Health-Syst Pharm*. 2009;66:1735–39.
12. The United States Pharmacopeial Convention [USPC]. General Chapter <797>: Pharmaceutical compounding - sterile preparations. In: *The United States Pharmacopeia*, 32nd rev. ed., and the *National Formulary*, 27th ed. Rockville, MD: USPC; 2009.
13. Callahan RJ, et al. Procedure guideline for the use of radiopharmaceuticals 4.0. *J Nuc Med Tech*. 2007;35(4):272–5.

14. Code of Federal Regulations, Title 42: Public Health, Chapter IV – Centers for Medicare and Medicaid Services, Department of Health and Human Services, Part 482 - Conditions of Participation for Hospitals, §482.12 *Governing Body*. Available at www.law.justia.com/us/cfr/title42/42-3.0.1.5.21.2.199.2.html. Accessed March 6, 2010.

Chapter 5

[NO REFERENCES]

Chapter 6

1. The Joint Commission. *Comprehensive Accreditation Manual for Hospitals: The Official Handbook*. Oakbrook Terrace, IL: The Joint Commission; 2010:NPSG-1.
2. The Joint Commission. 2010 National Patient Safety Goals. *Joint Commission Perspectives*. 2009;29 (10):1, 20–31.
3. The Joint Commission. Request for review of an alternative approach to a National Patient Safety Goal requirement. Available at www.jointcommission.org/PatientSafety/NationalPatientSafetyGoals/npsg_rfr.htm. Accessed March 6, 2010.
4. The Joint Commission. *Comprehensive Accreditation Manual for Hospitals: The Official Handbook*. Oakbrook Terrace, IL: The Joint Commission; 2010.
5. The Joint Commission. Standards FAQs. Available at www.jointcommission.org/Standards/FAQs. Accessed March 6, 2010.
6. Rich DS. More on the requirements of the medication-related national patient safety goals for 2003-2004. *Hosp Pharm*. 2003;38:977–81.
7. Siegel JD, et al. Management of multidrug-resistant organisms in healthcare settings, 2006. Centers for Disease Control and Prevention. 2006. Available at www.cdc.gov/ncidod/dhqp/pdf/ar/MDROGuideline2006.pdf. Accessed March 6, 2010.
8. Delitt TH, et al. Infectious Diseases Society of America and the Society for Healthcare Epidemiology of America guidelines for developing an institutional program to enhance antimicrobial stewardship. *Clin Infect Dis*. 2007;44:159–77.
9. 5 Million Lives Campaign. Getting Started Kit: *Prevent Surgical Site Infections How-to Guide*. Cambridge, MA: Institute for Healthcare Improvement; 2008. Available at www.ihi.org/IHI/Programs/Campaign/SSI.htm. Accessed March 6, 2010.
10. The Joint Commission and Centers for Medicare and Medicaid Services. *Specifications Manual for National Hospital Quality Measures*. Available at www.jointcommission.org/PerformanceMeasurement/Performance Measurement. Accessed March 6, 2010.
11. The Joint Commission. Using medication reconciliation to prevent errors. *Sentinel Event Alert*, Issue 35, Jan. 25, 2006. Available at www.jointcommission.org/SentinelEvents/SentinelEventAlert/sea_35.htm. Accessed March 6, 2010.

Chapter 7

1. The Joint Commission. *Comprehensive Accreditation Manual for Hospitals: The Official Handbook*. Oakbrook Terrace, IL: The Joint Commission; 2010.

Chapter 8

1. The Joint Commission. *Comprehensive Accreditation Manual for Hospitals: The Official Handbook*. Oakbrook Terrace, IL: The Joint Commission; 2010.
2. American Society of Health-System Pharmacists. *AHFS MedMaster Medication Information* [database]. Bethesda, MD: American Society of Health-System Pharmacists; 2010.
3. Murdaugh LB. *Competence Assessment Tools for Health-System Pharmacies*. 4th ed. Bethesda, MD: American Society of Health-System Pharmacists; 2008.

Chapter 9

1. The Joint Commission. *Comprehensive Accreditation Manual for Hospitals: The Official Handbook*. Oakbrook Terrace, IL: The Joint Commission; 2010.
2. Centers for Disease Control and Prevention. Guideline for hand hygiene in health-care settings. *MMWR*. 2002;51:31–4. Available at www.cdc.gov/handhygiene/. Accessed March 6, 2010.
3. The United States Pharmacopeial Convention [USPC]. General Chapter <797>: Pharmaceutical compounding - sterile preparations. In: *The United States Pharmacopeia*, 32nd rev. ed., and the *National Formulary*, 27th ed. Rockville, MD: USPC; 2009.

4. Centers for Disease Control and Prevention. Guideline for isolation precautions: preventing transmission of infectious agents in healthcare settings 2007. Available at www.cdc.gov/ncidod/dhqp/pdf/guidelines/Isolation2007.pdf. Accessed March 6, 2010.

5. The Joint Commission. Measuring hand hygiene adherence: Overcoming the challenges. Available at www.jointcommission.org/NR/rdonlyres/68B9CB2F-789F-49DB-9E3F-2FB387666BCC/0/hh%20monograph.pdf. Accessed March 6, 2010.

6. Occupational Safety and Health Administration. Bloodborne pathogens, 29 CFR – 1910.1030. Available at: www.osha.gov/pls/oshaweb/owadisp.show_document?p_table=STANDARDS&p_id=10051. Accessed March 6, 2010.

7. The United States Pharmacopeial Convention [USPC]. General Chapter USP <51>: Antimicrobial effectiveness testing. In: *The United States Pharmacopeia*, 32th rev. ed., and the *National Formulary*, 27th ed. Rockville, MD: USPC; 2009.

8. The United States Pharmacopeial Convention [USPC]. General Chapter USP <1>: Injections. In: *The United States Pharmacopeia*, 32th rev. ed., and the *National Formulary*, 27th ed. Rockville, MD: USPC; 2009.

Chapter 10

1. The Joint Commission. Standards FAQs. Available at www.jointcommission.org/Standards/FAQs. Accessed March 6, 2010.

2. National Institute for Occupational Safety and Health [NIOSH]. NIOSH alert: preventing occupational exposure to anti-neoplastic and other hazardous drugs in health care settings. Available at www.cdc.gov/niosh/docs/2004-165. Accessed March 6, 2010.

3. The United States Pharmacopeial Convention [USPC]. General Chapter <797>: Pharmaceutical compounding - sterile preparations. In: *The United States Pharmacopeia*, 32nd rev ed., and the *National Formulary*, 27th ed. Rockville, MD: USPC; 2009.

4. Centers for Disease Control and Prevention. Guidelines for maintaining and managing the vaccine cold chain. *MMWR*. 2003;52(42):1023-5. Available at www.cdc.gov/mmwr/preview/mmwrhtml/mm5242a6.htm. Accessed March 6, 2010.

5. National Center for Immunization and Respiratory Diseases. Vaccine storage and handling toolkit: Temperature monitoring. Available at www2a.cdc.gov/vaccines/ed/shtoolkit/pages/temp_monitoring.htm. Accessed March 6, 2010.

Chapter 11

1. Centers for Medicare and Medicaid Services, Department of Health and Human Services. *State Operations Manual Appendix A–Survey Protocol, Regulations and Interpretive Guidelines for Hospitals*, Rev 47 (06-05-09). Washington, DC: Government Printing Office; 2008. Available at www.cms.hhs.gov/manuals/downloads/som107ap_a_hospitals.pdf. Accessed March 6, 2010.

Chapter 12

1. Drug Enforcement Administration [DEA]. *Pharmacist's Manual.* Washington, DC: DEA; March 2001. Available at www.deadiversion.usdoj.gov/pubs/manuals/pharm2/index.htm. Accessed March 6, 2010.

Chapter 13

1. American Society of Health-System Pharmacists [ASHP]. ASHP statement on the pharmacy and therapeutics committee and the formulary system. *Am J Health-Syst Pharm.* 2008;65:2384–6. Available at www.ashp.org/DocLibrary/BestPractices/FormStPTCommFormSyst.aspx. Accessed March 6, 2010.

2. American Society of Health-System Pharmacists [ASHP]. ASHP guidelines on the pharmacy and therapeutics committee and the formulary system. *Am J Health-Syst Pharm.* 2008;65:1272–83. Available at www.ashp.org/DocLibrary/BestPractices/FormGdlPTCommFormSyst.aspx. Accessed March 6, 2010.

Chapter 14

1. Kane MT. The assessment of professional competence. *Eval Health Prof.* 992;15(2):163–82.

2. Murdaugh LB. *Competence Assessment Tools for Health-System Pharmacies*. 4th ed. Bethesda, MD: American Society of Health-System Pharmacists; 2008.

Chapter 15

1. The Joint Commission. *Comprehensive Accreditation Manual for Hospitals: The Official Handbook.* Oakbrook Terrace, IL: The Joint Commission; 2010.

2. Vinson BE. Evaluating and improving an organization's medication use system. In: *Medication Use: A Sys-*

tems Approach to Reducing Errors. 2nd ed. Oakbrook Terrace, IL: Joint Commission Resources; 2008. p. 57–90.

3. National Quality Forum. Serious reportable events. Available at www.qualityforum.org/projects/completed/sre/fact-sheet.asp. Accessed March 6, 2010.

4. Santell JP and Kienle PC. Preventing medication errors. In: *Medication Use: A Systems Approach to Reducing Errors*. 2nd ed. Oakbrook Terrace, IL: Joint Commission Resources; 2008. p. 29–48.

Chapter 16

1. The Joint Commission. Facts about ORYX®. Available at www.jointcommission.org/AccreditationPrograms/Hospitals/ORYX/oryx_facts.htm. Accessed March 6, 2010.

2. The Joint Commission. Performance measurement and the ORYX® initiative. In: *Comprehensive Accreditation Manual for Hospitals: The Official Handbook*. Oakbrook Terrace, IL: The Joint Commission; 2010.

3. US Department of Health and Human Services. Hospital Compare. www.hospitalcompare.hhs.gov. Accessed March 6, 2010.

4. The Joint Commission. Quality Check®. Available at www.quality check.org. Accessed March 6, 2010.

5. Hospital Quality Alliance. Measure comparison (Inpatient Hospital Quality Measures). Available at www.qualitynet.org/dcs/ContentServer?cid=1138900297065&pagename=QnetPublic%2FPage%2FQnetTier3&c=Page. Accessed March 6, 2010.

Chapter 17

1. Occupational Safety and Health Administration. Hazard communication standard. Available at www.osha.gov/dsg/hazcom/standards.html. Accessed March 6, 2010.

2. Occupational Safety and Health Administration. Hospital eTool pharmacy module. Available at www.osha.gov/SLTC/etools/hospital/pharmacy/pharmacy.html#HazardCommunicationStandard. Accessed March 6, 2010.

3. Occupational Safety and Health Administration. Some common drugs considered to be hazardous. Available at www.osha.gov/dts/osta/otm/otm_vi/otm_vi_2.html#app_vi:2_1. Accessed March 6, 2010.

4. National Institute for Occupational Safety and Health. Drugs considered hazardous. Available at www.cdc.gov/niosh/docs/2004-165/2004-165d.html#o. Accessed March 6, 2010.

5. Murdaugh LB. *Competence Assessment Tools for Health-System Pharmacies*. 4th ed. Bethesda, MD: American Society of Health-System Pharmacists; 2008.

Chapter 18

1. National Institute for Occupational Safety and Health [NIOSH]. NIOSH alert: preventing occupational exposures to antineoplastic and other hazardous drugs in health care settings. Available at www.cdc.gov/niosh/docs/2004-165. Accessed March 6, 2010.

2. American Society of Health-System Pharmacists [ASHP]. ASHP guidelines on handling hazardous drugs. *Am J Health-Syst Pharm*. 2006; 63:1172–93. Available at www.ashp.org/DocLibrary/BestPractices/PrepGdlHazDrugs.aspx. Accessed March 6, 2010.

3. The United States Pharmacopeial Convention [USPC]. General Chapter <797>: Pharmaceutical compounding - sterile preparations. In: *The United States Pharmacopeia*, 32nd rev ed., and the *National Formulary*, 27th ed. Rockville, MD: USPC; 2009.

4. National Institute for Occupational Safety and Health. Drugs considered hazardous. Available at www.cdc.gov/niosh/docs/2004-165/2004-165d.html#o. Accessed March 6, 2010.

5. National Institute for Occupational Safety and Health [NIOSH]. NIOSH medical surveillance for health care workers exposed to hazardous drugs. Available at www.cdc.gov/niosh/docs/wp_solutions/2007-117. Accessed March 6, 2010.

Chapter 19

1. The United States Pharmacopeial Convention [USPC]. General Chapter <797>: Pharmaceutical compounding - sterile preparations. In: *The United States Pharmacopeia*, 32nd rev. ed., and the *National Formulary*, 27th ed. Rockville, MD: USPC; 2009.

2. Trissel LA. *Handbook on Injectable Drugs*. 15th ed. Bethesda, MD: American Society of Health-System Pharmacists; 2009.

3. American Society of Health-System Pharmacists. *Basics of Aseptic Compounding Technique Video*

Training Program. Bethesda, MD: American Society of Health-System Pharmacists; 2006.

4. Davis K and Sparks J. *Getting Started in Aseptic Compounding Video Training Program.* Bethesda, MD: American Society of Health-System Pharmacists; 2008

5. Power L and Jorgenson J. *Safe Handling of Hazardous Drugs Video Training Program.* Bethesda, MD: American Society of Health-System Pharmacists; 2006.

6. Kienle PC. *Compounding Sterile Preparations: ASHP's Video Guide to Chapter <797> and Companion Guide.* Bethesda, MD: American Society of Health-System Pharmacists; 2009.

7. Murdaugh LB. *Competence Assessment Tools for Health-System Pharmacies.* 4th ed. Bethesda, MD: American Society of Health-System Pharmacists; 2008.

8. Controlled Environment Testing Association [CETA]. *CETA CAG-001-2005, Applications Guide for the Use of Compounding Isolators in Compounding Sterile Preparations in Healthcare Facilities (revised December 8, 2008).* Raleigh, NC: CETA; 2008. Available at www.cetainternational.org/reference/Applications GuideBarrierIsolator-CAG-001-2005.pdf. Accessed March 6, 2010.

9. Controlled Environment Testing Association [CETA]. *CETA CAG-002-2005 Compounding Isolator Testing Guide (revised December 8, 2008).* Raleigh, NC: CETA; 2008. Available at www.cetainternational.org/reference/CETACompoundingIsolatorTestingGuide 2006.pdf. Accessed March 6, 2010.

10. Controlled Environment Testing Association [CETA]. *CETA CAG-003-2006 Certification Guide for Sterile Compounding Facilities (revised December 8, 2008).* Raleigh, NC: CETA; 2008. Available at www.cetainternational.org/reference/CETAAseptic CompoundingCertificationGuide.pdf. Accessed March 6, 2010.

11. Controlled Environment Testing Association [CETA]. *CETA CAG-004-2007 Application Guide for the Use of Surface Decontaminants in Biosafety Cabinets, January 30, 2007.* Raleigh, NC: CETA; 2007. Available at www.cetainternational.org/reference/CAG00 42007i.pdf. Accessed March 6, 2010.

12. Controlled Environment Testing Association [CETA]. *CETA CAG-005-2007 Servicing Hazardous Drug Compounding Primary Engineering Controls.* Raleigh, NC: CETA; 2007. Available at www.ceta international.org/reference/CAG005-v15.pdf. Accessed March 6, 2010.

13. Bing CM. *Extended Stability for Parenteral Drugs.* 4th ed. Bethesda, MD: American Society of Health-System Pharmacists; 2009.

Chapter 20

1. National Coordinating Council for Medication Error Reporting and Prevention Web site. Available at www.nccmerp.org. Accessed March 6, 2010.

2. The Joint Commission. *Comprehensive Accreditation Manual for Hospitals: The Official Handbook.* Oakbrook Terrace, IL: The Joint Commission; 2010.

3. American Society of Health-System Pharmacists [ASHP]. ASHP guidelines on preventing medication errors in hospitals. *Am J Health-Syst Pharm.* 1993;50:305–14. Available at www.ashp.org/Doc Library/BestPractices/MedMisGdlHosp.aspx. Accessed March 6, 2010.

4. Cohen MR, ed. *Medication Errors.* 2nd ed. Washington, DC: American Pharmacists Association; 2007.

5. Institute for Safe Medication Practices. Guidance on the interdisciplinary safe use of automated dispensing cabinets. Available at www.ismp.org/Tools/guidelines/ADC_Guidelines_Final.pdf. Accessed March 6, 2010.

6. Trissel LA. *Handbook on Injectable Drugs.* 15th ed. Bethesda, MD: American Society of Health-System Pharmacists; 2009.

7. Institute for Safe Medication Practices. ISMP's list of high-alert medications, 2008. Available at www.ismp.org/Tools/highalertmedications.pdf. Accessed March 6, 2010.

Chapter 21

1. Food and Drug Administration [FDA]. MedWatch: The FDA Safety Information and Adverse Event Reporting Program. Available at www.fda.gov/medwatch. Accessed March 6, 2010.

2. American Society of Health-System Pharmacists [ASHP]. ASHP guidelines on adverse drug reaction monitoring and reporting. *Am J Health-Syst Pharm.* 1995;52:417–9. Available at www.ashp.org/Doc Library/BestPractices/MedMisGdlADR.aspx. Accessed March 6, 2010.

3. The Joint Commission. *Comprehensive Accreditation Manual for Hospitals: The Official Handbook.* Oakbrook Terrace, IL: The Joint Commission; 2010.

4. Centers for Disease Control and Prevention and Food and Drug Administration. Vaccine Adverse Event Reporting System. Available at www.vaers.hhs.gov. Accessed March 6, 2010.

Chapter 22

1. Centers for Medicare and Medicaid Services, Department of Health and Human Services. *State Operations Manual Appendix A–Survey Protocol, Regulations and Interpretive Guidelines for Hospitals*, Rev 47 (06-05-09). Washington, DC: Government Printing Office; 2008. Available at www.cms.hhs.gov/manuals/downloads/som107ap_a_hospitals.pdf. Accessed March 6, 2010.

Chapter 23

1. Healthcare Facilities Accreditation Program. Available at www.hfap.org. Accessed March 6, 2010.
2. American Osteopathic Association. *Accreditation Requirements for Healthcare Facilities.* Chicago: American Osteopathic Association; 2008.

Chapter 24

1. DNV Healthcare. *National Integrated Accreditation for Healthcare Organizations (NIAHO^{SM}) Accreditation Requirements, Interpretive Guidelines and Surveyor Guidance, Rev 8.0, September 19, 2009.* Cincinnati, OH: DNV Healthcare; 2009.
2. DNV Healthcare. *NIAHO^{SM} Accreditation Program Accreditation Process, Revision 12, effective September 18, 2009.* Cincinnati, OH: DNV Healthcare; 2009.
3. Arter DB and Russell JP. *ISO Lesson Guide 2008.* 3rd ed. Milwaukee, WI: American Society for Quality; 2009.
4. Code of Federal Regulations, Title 42: Public Health, Chapter IV – Centers for Medicare and Medicaid Services, Department of Health and Human Services, Part 482 - Conditions of Participation for Hospitals, §482.12 *Governing Body*. Available at www.law.justia.com/us/cfr/title42/42-3.0.1.5.21.2.199.2.html. Accessed March 6, 2010.

Index

A

B

C

I

N

O

P

Q

R

S

T